Betsy A. Travis

The Book of

POTTERY AND PORCELAIN

VOLUME II

SPANISH: GLAZED EARTHENWARE BOWL. TERUEL.   CHELSEA: DISH PAINTED IN THE STYLE OF KAKIEMON

16th Century?   Metropolitan Museum of Art. See Plate 105.   Dia. 9½ Inches   Coll. of Dr. & Mrs. Bellamy Gardner

The Book of
Pottery and Porcelain

BY

WARREN E. COX

3000 illustrations. Pictures selected by the author. Lay-outs by A. M. Lounsbery

VOLUME II

CROWN PUBLISHERS

NEW YORK

Sixth Printing, January, 1947

PRINTED IN THE UNITED STATES OF AMERICA
BY THE AMERICAN BOOK-STRATFORD PRESS, INC., NEW YORK

CONTENTS OF VOLUME TWO

CHAPTER   PAGE

XX   THE CH'ING DYNASTY (continued)   559

XXI   EUROPEAN "SOFT PASTE" AND PORCELAIN   625

XXII   THE EUROPEAN DISCOVERY OF PORCELAIN   641

XXIII   18TH CENTURY EUROPEAN PORCELAIN CONTIN-
UED: FRANCE, ITALY, SPAIN, PORTUGAL, SWIT-
ZERLAND, RUSSIA, NETHERLANDS, BELGIUM,
DENMARK, SWEDEN   682

XXIV   ENGLISH "SOFT PASTE" AND "BONE CHINA"   742

XXV   EUROPEAN 18TH CENTURY POTTERY   781

XXVI   THE POTTERIES AND STONEWARE OF ENGLAND
AND WALES   864

XXVII   AMERICAN INDIAN POTTERIES   924

XXVIII   AMERICAN COLONIAL TO 19TH CENTURY WARES   979

XXIX   CONTEMPORARY CERAMICS   1009

XXX   CONTEMPORARY AMERICAN CERAMICS   1048

THE MARKS OF POTTERIES AND PORCELAINS   1079

INDEX TO THE TWO VOLUMES   1151

LIST OF COLOR PLATES

Spanish: Glazed Earthenware Bowl. Teruel   *Frontispiece*

Chelsea: Dish Painted in the Style of Kakiemon   *Frontispiece*

Sèvres: Louis XV Rose Pompadour Soupière and Pair of
    Elephant Vases with Chinoiserie Painted by Dodin   *Facing Page* 686

Chelsea: Chinese Group after Boucher   *Facing Page* 750

CHAPTER XX

THE CH'ING DYNASTY (Continued)

BISCUIT OR UNGLAZED WARE

"Fan ts'u" in Chinese means "turned porcelain" and suggests that bisque ware was turned inside out, which is a lovely and amusing conception borne out frequently by just a touch of glaze on some inner part to carry out the illusion. Most pieces so made were signed by artists, which is a rare occurrence indeed in these so commercial times. The objects consist of lions, figures of Buddhist Arhats, or those who have achieved Nirvana, etc. All the pieces were very small and they are quite rare.

TING YAO OF THE CH'ING DYNASTY

The imitations of Sung Dynasty Ting yao continued and some quite good examples were made. The body used was opaque and earthy looking and the glaze was much like the early type being creamy and crackled. The ware was used to make objects for the writer's table and simple small vases, bowls and the like. One shape often seen is of a bottle with a hydra twisting about the neck in relief. Of course these pieces were fired at the high temperatures prevalent and cannot be confused with the Sung wares.

CLAIR DE LUNE

Even more expensive and rarer than the peach bloom wares is the clair de lune which is of equal quality and made in the same forms with a few added. This glaze, as the name indicates, is of the palest possible blue just off white and it is made of very refined cobalt perfectly handled. Less good specimens are deeper and later ones always are. All that has been said about the potting and marks of the peach bloom applies here.

FIG. 799. Clair de Lune K'ang Hsi writer's coupe with the six character mark delicately pencilled under the bottom. Dia. 4". The Michael Friedsam Coll. Metropolitan Mus. of Art.

OTHER BLUE WARES

From this palest blue we find shades all the way to "ta ch'ing" or dark blue and variations of lavender blue and slate blue. These are heavier wares and not so sought after but pleasant.

559

Celadon and Other Iron Glazes

Among the many continuations of celadon glazes we can distinguish three entirely different types:

1.—First, at Ching-tê Chêng a pale and very clear glaze was developed which rivaled the clair de lune and it was used on small vases and objects

FIG. 800. Pale "celadon" vase with incised decoration and bisque handles of the K'ang Hsi period (1662–1722 A.D.). Ht. 9". Metropolitan Mus. of Art.

of the same shapes as the peach bloom ones although vases of the "chrysanthemum shape" like that illustrated seem to dominate. These may be a trifle less well made and heavier than the other two classes but they are nevertheless very perfect and do command high prices.

2.—Second, also at Ching-tê Chêng larger vases were made of a fairly thinly potted ware very true and perfect and usually having all-over incised decoration under a rather yellowish green celadon glaze thinly applied and not crackled. The handles were often left in biscuit and sometimes colored brown or black. They are usually given the double ring and some mark in underglaze blue under the bottom where the glaze is typical K'ang Hsi pitted white.

3.—The factories at Lung-ch'üan continued and turned out a ware exactly like that which they had made all during the Ming period and on back into the Sung. It is interesting to note that Père d'Entrecolles wrote in 1722, "I was shown this year for the first time a kind of porcelain which is now in fashion; its color verges on olive and they call it long tsiven." Bushell says (*op. cit.*, p. 214), "Long tsiven is a rendering of Lung-ch'üan, the district celebrated for celadons in the Sung and Ming periods. In another place d'Entrecolles describes the making of celadons in the Sung style with intent to deceive." Many other kilns were also engaged in the making of celadon wares and particularly Chü-chou, the capital of Chekiang province and just northeast of Lung-ch'üan. Some new styles of decoration were used such as the application of slip as on the vase illustrated and the greater use of the mold as shown in the square example with sides and top secured by the glaze. The perfection of technique, shown in the small tea-pot which has a tapered chimney built in it to provide a better draft for the lamp below and to heat the tea more quickly, is something to note, but the exact old styles also continued without change.

To make this point entirely clear I illustrate a temple vase which belongs to Mr. Lem Sec Tsang and which innumerable collectors have passed upon as being Ming and not one single one has even suspected as being later although several have said it could be "Yüan or Ming," and yet which bears

FIG. 801. Ch'u chou candlestick of white porcelain covered with a pale transparent green glaze irregularly crackled. Probably late Ming to K'ang Hsi period c. 17th cent. Ht. 8". Lem Sec Tsang Coll. Warren E. Cox Coll.

FIG. 802. Ch'u-chou "celadon" vase of gray ware covered with a transparent green glaze full of bubbles and showing irregular crackle. Ht. 8". The Lem Sec Tsang–Warren E. Cox Coll.

FIG. 803. K'ang Hsi Ch'u-chou vase as heavily potted as many Ming ones but having a slip relief decoration over which is a more transparent and less green glaze than is seen on the usual Ming specimen. Ht. 11¼". Warren E. Cox Coll.

the date of the year 1671 a good ten years into the K'ang Hsi period. The body, the potting and every detail of this piece corresponds perfectly with similar ones of the Ming period. The glaze is applied somewhat thinly and is, therefore, less green than some specimens but these potteries always varied in this respect and whether this would be a characteristic of later ones I am not prepared to say. The translation of the inscription on this piece by Mr. Han of the Metropolitan Museum of Art and corrected by Sir Percival David is as follows: "The faithful person, Hsü Ming-jui, who is a native of Chu-kou town, Ch'ing-yüan Hsien, Chekiang, offers a pair of vases in great cheer in the main hall in front of the Three Precious Ones in the White Cloud Temple, Nanking. In giving these vases he asks for the peace and luck of his family, for satisfaction of his business, and for the prosperity of his descendant." It is then dated, "On the lucky day of the middle month of Summer in the year hsin-hai, that is the 10th year of K'ang Hsi," which is 1671.

When, then, did the Chü-chou kilns cease to work? Judging by the fact that we have also excellent copies or continuations of the wares but which have all the characteristics of modern pieces I should say that they continued at least up to this last war.

GREY, BUFF AND BROWN IRON WARES

During the K'ang Hsi period a large number of crackled wares ranging from light grey to brown and almost black were made. Similar ones were also made uncrackled. The best known are called "tzu chin" (lustrous brown),

562   POTTERY AND PORCELAIN

FIG. 804. K'ang Hsi Ch'u chou vase of greyish white porcelain. Glaze is typical transparent grey-green and strongly crack-led. Ht. 20". Lem Sec Tsang–Warren E. Cox Coll. See below enlarge-ment of neck with writing.

FIG. 805. Unique tea-pot of Ch'u-chou yao made in four pieces, a lamp with support for circular wick on saucer, a reticulated stand, the pot itself and a cover. A most ingeni-ous device in the pot causes the tea to heat quicker. By means of a bent hollow cone the heat is conducted up through the center of the pot. Late Ming or K'ang Hsi period. I have never seen anything else like it. Warren E. Cox Coll.

but these are also termed, "dead leaf" brown, "cafe-au-lait," "brown gold," "chocolate brown," "old gold brown" and "wu chin" or black gold, etc. The cafe-au-lait is used not only for single colored pieces but as a background for panel decoration much as was powder blue. Hobson tells us that this ware is called "Batavian" because it was largely imported by the Dutch who had an entrepôt in Batavia, Java. The panel decoration is most often in famille rose colors of the late K'ang Hsi or later periods. It occurs on the outside of bowls and also is combined with silver decoration.

Sometimes these glazes were shaded and mottled, coffee brown to olive or perhaps brown mottled with black and other effects. There are also examples of the lighter tones over engraved or relief decorations.

Mirror Black

Mirror black was called "wu chin" or "black gold" and was made by mixing the cobaltiferous ore of manganese with the iron of coffee brown with the result that a glaze was made which was black with brownish or bluish reflections. It is spoken of as related to the Chien yao of Sung times but actually there is no connection whatsoever. An interesting point is that reports have it that the dark blue, the celadon, the lustrous brown and the mirror black glazes were applied with numerous coatings. It was said that some-

Fig. 806. White porcelain vase with white crackled glaze covered with a transparent brown enamel. K'ang Hsi. Ht. 4½". Metropolitan Mus. of Art.

times as many as nine were used, six by blowing and three more by painting with the brush.

Fig. 807. K'ang Hsi mirror black bottle of dull surface. Ht. 16½". Metropolitan Mus. of Art.

Fig. 808. K'ang Hsi. One of pair of unique triple gourd shaped vases with *wu chin* or "black gold" treatment of the bottom sections, greenish white center sections decorated with iron red, gold and yellow green, and the top treated in blue glaze with gold decoration. Ht. 18". Bequest of Mary Clark Thompson. Metropolitan Mus. of Art.

Another black of dull quality and usually crackled was said to go back to the K'ang Hsi period but I have never seen one which could be so attributed and I believe it was actually later. On the black, gilt designs were painted much as they were on the powder blue and these designs are usually almost worn out by handling. Frequently they are more or less crudely retouched. D'Entrecolles also mentions reserved panels in brown and painted in black designs but we have none of these, if they were made, though there do exist rare examples of enamel decorated medallions reserved in black.

Fig. 809. K'ang Hsi vase with deep turquoise blue glaze and very fine "fish roe" crackle. Ht. 4¾". Ex D. Abbes Coll.

Fig. 810. Imperial yellow K'ang Hsi writer's bottle made almost identically in the same form as peach bloom ones. Dia. 3¾". Metropolitan Mus. of Art.

Fig. 811. Orange yellow K'ang Hsi vase. Transparent and somewhat mottled glaze. Ht. 13½". Altman Coll. Metropolitan Mus. of Art.

YELLOW WARES

"Nanking yellow" was simply a thin coating of a glaze very similar to the brown ones and it is always brownish. "Imperial yellow" is quite different for it was made of a medium fired lead-silicate not so hard as the others. This appears darker over the biscuit and lighter when applied over a white glaze. Sometimes light engraving is traced under it and when the piece was for Imperial use the design was of dragons and pearls. This color is the clearest and strongest but there were many others such as primrose, canary, lemon and mustard, although they are all variations of the same thing. D'Entrecolles says these yellows were produced by the use of iron but we must agree with Mr. Hobson that it was probably antimony which gave the colors with perhaps a trace of iron. By the end of the K'ang Hsi period nearly every color had been obtained and mastered.

TURQUOISE AND LEAF GREEN

Turquoise was obtained with copper and had been a favorite color since Ming days. It has also been continuously produced up to the present. The K'ang Hsi wares have a fine grained white body but we must add that some of the later examples also have the same characteristics. The glaze was called "fei ts'ui" or "kingfisher blue," "chi ts'ui" and "k'ung ch'iao lü" or "peacock green." It is almost always crackled, and this crackle is usually small an of the "fish roe" type that is almost round in appearance. It always stands out more on the greener—or that is the thicker glazed—examples. At times there were engraved examples but these are likely to be later. Some of the pieces have the K'ang Hsi mark and the wares seem to vary from the finest porcelain to almost pottery-like bodies though all are vitreous. The greens are called "leaf green," "cucumber green," "yellow leaf green," "snake skin green," etc. The latter called by the Chinese "shê p'i lü" is quite iridescent and transparent. The *T'ao lu* says this is one of the four famous glazes made under Ts'ang's regime.

APPLE GREEN

Apple green is not a glaze but an enamel applied over a greyish or brownish crackled white glaze. This green is transparent and, just as was explained in our section treating sang de boeuf, it was given greater brilliancy because of the white ground beneath it. It varies from a light to dark emerald color, is highly lustrous and iridescent and where the enamel has been broken internally by the crackle it has shining flakes called by the French "ailes de mouches" or "fly's wings" which is just exactly what they look like. These are not blemishes but were thought by collectors to indicate authenticity, but they are natural to the enamel and glaze and have been perfectly reproduced in modern fakes.

FIG. 812. "Emerald green" bottle of the "apple green" type. Late Ming or early K'ang Hsi. 17⅝". Metropolitan Mus. of Art.

FIG. 813. K'ang Hsi "apple green" jar of a form similar to the Sung Kuan and Ko type but softer and more rounded. White porcelain covered with strongly crackled white glaze over which a transparent enamel has been fired at lower temperature. Ht. 9". Metropolitan Mus. of Art.

Apple green treatment was given chiefly to small vases and cups and as the prices were always high the ware has been made continuously to the present. To one who has handled the K'ang Hsi wares it is not difficult to distinguish between the originals and later examples, however, the ware was always heavy and it is difficult indeed to distinguish pieces which have been made during the period intended as grey crackled wares and enameled over with the green at a later time. Ch'ien Lung apple greens, Hobson says, "Will be recognized by the characteristic finish of the base (wedge shaped rather than straight sided), and it will be noticed that the enamel in these pieces commonly covers the raw edge of the base rim, giving it a brown appearance."

Other green enamels were also used and some are as dark as the color of a ripe cucumber while collectors have labeled others "Camellia-leaf, myrtle, spinach and sage green," but these again are most likely to occur at later times. In Kiangsu at "Kashan" they used the same sort of green over a pottery base. The treatments were also sometimes not over another glaze but applied direct and either crackled or not.

It should also be noted that crackle had been so mastered generally that the potters could make it occur just where wanted and some vases even had bands of different sized crackles about their bodies. However, never was it possible to reproduce one of the ancient crackles perfectly because too many elements were involved. D'Entrecolles says that the Chinese used "sui yu" or "crackle glaze" mixed with the other glaze and says it was made of pebbles. The *T'ao lu* says it was from the rock of San-pao-p'eng. Scherzer obtained samples of this rock in 1882 and Vogt proved that it was not, as was supposed, steatite but pegmatite, as it contains no magnesium. Scherzer also tells us that the two layers were given to produce the finer, or as the French say "truité" crackle and that four were applied to make the larger crackle. Hobson says that the "sui yu" was light grey but was not noticeable when mixed with the colored glazes. He also says that they colored the crazing purposely with red ochre, ink, tea, etc., while the ware was still warm and before the cracks had completely closed. This may be true but the reader should not gain the impression that the cracks at a given temperature were any more open just after the vase had been taken from the kiln than at any subsequent time and frequently the cracks were colored naturally due to substances in the body such as iron, or due to the use of liquids in the vessels, such as tea which during years might penetrate even a fairly dense body. Hobson also points out that in some cases the color went beyond the crackle and has "given the glaze a clouded appearance." He also says that the buff or oatmeal crackles are sometimes combined with underglaze blue and enameled colors and that when the enameled colors are used with this combination they are generally laid on pads of white slip locally applied. He adds, "The intentional crackle is quite distinct from the accidental crazing or faint crackling which develops on most of the medium fired glazes, such as aubergine and turquoise." But this is getting a bit too complex. Who is to know whether the old potter meant to have crackle or just obtained it and let it go at that?

In truth Hobson seems somewhat confused in his own mind concerning crackle; he says, "All pottery shrinks in the kiln and to ensure an even surface it is necessary that the body and the glaze should contract to the same extent. If the glaze contracts more than the body it will split up into a network of cracks." We must say that this is only half right for cracks will be produced also if the glaze contracts *less* than the body. This may cause the rumpled or "orange skin" effect and also a crackle.

Again Mr. Hobson says, "In the end they discovered several methods.

One was to heat the ware as much as possible in the sun whilst it was drying and then plunge it into pure water. A crackle was produced by this means after firing." In "Chinese Pottery and Porcelain," (p. 197, vol. 2) he says, "Another method is mentioned in the K'ang Hsi *Encyclopaedia*, viz. to heat the unglazed ware as much as possible in the sun, then plunge it into pure water. By this means a crackle was produced on the ware after firing." Of course this is ridiculous to anyone who understands the nature of crackle and either the source must have been all out of line or the translation was incorrect. Hannover comes a step nearer the truth in his "Pottery & Porce-

Left: Figure of Shou Lao of the usual porcelain painted in enamels and with bisque face and hands, the latter added after firing. At times these figures were made nearly a yard high. Ht. 19". Salting Bequest. Victoria and Albert Mus.

Taoist deity *Chen Wu* or *Hsüan T'ien* in the usual enamel on biscuit colors with the hands and face left in biscuit. Ht. 17". Michael Friedsam Coll. Metropolitan Mus. of Art.

Right: Figure of Kuan Yin of the K'ang Hsi period with enamel decoration. The faces and hands of such figures are frequently in bisque and, as in this case, the hands were made separately and added after firing. Ht. c. 19". Metropolitan Mus. of Art.

K'ANG HSI PORCELAIN FIGURES WITH ENAMEL DECORATION

PLATE 160

Middle K'ang Hsi "beaker shaped" vase with design perhaps showing Korean influence of flying cranes and lambrequin borders of "brocade design," Ht. 18". Bequest of Edward C. Converse. Metropolitan Mus. of Art.

(c)

(b)

(a)

Rare and beautiful K'ang Hsi famille noire with alternating yellow and black ground panels. Ht. 21". Metropolitan Mus. of Art.

(a) K'ang Hsi "club shaped vase" with stylized elongated neck. About 1700 A.D. Ht. 28½". Metropolitan Mus. of Art.
(b) One of the finest "temple vases" of the K'ang Hsi period known. This vase has a bright green enamel ground against which the aubergine branches, white blossoms and black and white birds seem to breathe the very essence of Spring. Ht. 29½". Altman Coll. Metropolitan Mus. of Art.
(c) K'ang Hsi "temple vase" of the middle part dating about 1700 A.D. The colors are the usual famille verte enamels with iron red. Ht. 29½". Metropolitan Mus. of Art.

PLATE 161

K'ANG HSI ENAMEL DECORATED PORCELAIN VASES

lain of the Far East," when he says, "Another Chinese source gives, for instance, as serving the same purpose, the method of heating in the sun and rapid cooling in cold water of the unfired, glazed vessels." However, what one did in the way of heating and quickly cooling "the unfired, glazed vessels," would have no effect at all. What can be easily demonstrated is that AFTER *a piece is fired with its glaze and is still in a state of tension between body and glaze, the crackle can be* ACCENTED *(not actually produced in the case where the glaze and body expand and contract to the same degree) by heating and sudden cooling.* This gives it a jolt which makes more crackle where some already existed but it will not make crackle on an uncracked piece. As for the myths concerning "pure water" and such operations "before" firing, they could only be passed on by those who had never fired a crackled pot in their lives.

The pegmatite might bring about crackle as would any other substances which would act simply to change the coefficient of expansion either of the glaze or the body so that they were made unequal. In fact the difficulty generally speaking is to match a body and glaze so that they will *not* cause crackle when it is not wanted. But the Chinese became very proficient in handling it, by Ming times.

POLYCHROME PORCELAINS

Besides the single colored wares there were many which combined several of the glazes. The "hu p'i" or "tiger-skin" ware was splashed and spotted with aubergine, yellow and green and as the glazes were thinner and the spots more sharply defined than such splashed effects in T'ang wares the effect was less pleasant. This ware is also called "spinach and egg" somewhat derisively but collectors often have a piece or two.

FIG. 814. K'ang Hsi rhyton after a T'ang model. "Egg and spinach" effect in green, yellow and white. The horns are brown. Length 5″. Metropolitan Mus. of Art.
FIG. 815. K'ang Hsi bowl and plate of "egg and spinach" glazes of yellow, green and aubergine on white. Dias. 7″ and 8″. Warren E. Cox Coll.
FIG. 816. K'ang Hsi black enamel on biscuit cat with green glass eyes. Length 5¼″. The Michael Friedsam Coll.

The "yao pien" or transmutation glaze of red (probably with blue streaks) was made by accident and destroyed as of no worth after an attempt to make red soufflé, d'Entrecolles tells us. He describes them simply as looking like a sort of agate.

High fired mixed colors were also made on small figures and ornaments in colors of celadon, red and blue. These were probably from Kwangtung in imitation of the real Ming ones. At any rate they do not come from Ching-tê Chêng.

"San ts'ai" or enameled wares were made with medium fired glazes of yellow, green, turquoise, aubergine and purple blue. Bowls with engraved designs may have the designs washed over with one color and the background

FIG. 817. K'ang Hsi water jar with yellow body and top handle and spout in leaf green. Length 6". Bequest of Mary Clark Thompson. Metropolitan Mus. of Art.

FIG. 818. K'ang Hsi enamel on biscuit figure of *Li Po* or *Li Peh* the famous poet leaning on his wine jar. Length 6". Courtesy of Walter Blumenthal.

with another. "Brinjal bowls" are a variety of this with simply engraved sprays of flowers rather crudely filled in in green, white or yellow on an aubergine or "brinjal" ground. The same type was also made with green grounds. Raised outlines were no longer used but the same colors were employed on shapes that would keep them apart as we see on the peach shaped

FIG. 819. K'ang Hsi enamel on biscuit iridescent black horse made with transparent green over brownish black, pale aubergine, yellow and green, also with touches on the base rim, crop, etc., of muddy dark iron red. Ht. 7". Metropolitan Mus. of Art.

FIG. 820. K'ang Hsi enamel on biscuit porcelain lion in yellow green, pale aubergine, white and yellow with a rider on his back in European costume. Ht. 6". Metropolitan Mus. of Art.

wine pots. The bowls have meaningless seals called incorrectly, "shop marks" or "hall marks." A better class is the Imperial sort of dish or rice bowl with five clawed dragons engraved in them and colored yellow on green, green on aubergine, or aubergine on yellow but these again are hard to date and most that one sees are of Ch'ien Lung or later times.

A group of little animals, birds, deities and humans on rocks, in boats or in grottos are colored with green and aubergine but also with vermilion added, only traces of which can still be found. The good Père tells us that these were first fired in the biscuit and then daubed and refired in the less hot parts of the kiln. They are late K'ang Hsi, of course, or later as he wrote about them in the last year of the reign. Of them Hobson says, "They are apt to be confused with the enamels of the muffle kiln which were also used in washes on the biscuit body; but the latter, in spite of a superficial similarity, are in reality much more fusible and soft." There are also differences in color: The yellow is browner and darker, the aubergine is a little more red and the greens do not include the pale apple green color. A black was developed and made with a transparent glaze over a dull brown-black. A dirty white was also added in time.

"SUR BISCUITE" OR ENAMEL ON BISCUIT WARE

FIG. 821. Fine famille noire beaker with the usual white, green, yellow and aubergine enamels. Ht. 18¼". Metropolitan Mus. of Art.

The term "famille verte" means simply "green family" of wares and may be applied to all the enamel wares except those of the very end of the reign when rose enamels were introduced and we designate them as "famille rose." Under the "famille verte" name we have subdivisions depending on the color of the ground used; "famille noir" for black, "famille jaune" for yellow, etc. Also under the famille verte classification we have the "sur biscuite" and the more ordinary on glaze types, the first having been derived from the "san ts'ai" or "three color" type and the second from the "wu ts'ai" or "five color" type, of the Ming period, but the enamels used for all are very much alike. The K'ang Hsi enamels are different from the Ming in the following characteristics:

1.—The yellow is lighter and clearer.

2.—There are new shades of green including the "apple green."

3.—The iron red is lighter and more coral-color. (But not so light as the original Sung color, being applied more heavily.)

4.—The violet-blue was only very occasionally used in Ming times but it now replaces the turquoise-green.

Hobson says that the connoisseur looks to this blue especially in appraising a piece and, "If the blue is bright and clear, the piece will be highly valued." All very well it is to have a good blue color but there are after all the considerations of proportion, of line, the trueness of potting, the drawing of the design and its adaptation to the vase form among many other things to be considered. He says that around the blue there was at first a "curious oily stain which is lustrous like the track of oil on water," and that it was later overcome but that collectors are not disturbed by it and consider it a mark of genuineness. I do not know to what he refers unless it might be the slight touching of some transparent white glaze over the blue as it was applied over the black simply to produce greater gloss and depth of color. If this is so, we must sadly add that it is no mark of authenticity whatsoever for it was done on perfectly modern pieces as well.

The technique was a simple one. The usual famille verte sur biscuite vase was first fired in biscuit state. Upon the mat surface the design is drawn completely in brown-black manganese. Some colors are painted within outlines and others are washed right over the detail which shows through them. The full range of colors was not always used and green, yellow and aubergine form the usual combination. The white is a very slightly greenish tinged and lustrous glaze, the lustre being compared to a snail's track. The black is dull brown-black but becomes true black when the white is applied over it. Only rarely is the coral red used and still more rarely the violet-blue. Sometimes these are applied over a patch of porcelain glaze.

The amphora is like Ming ones but the neck has grown heavier and cer-

FIG. 822. Famille jaune square vase of the K'ang Hsi period with decoration in green, aubergine, etc. Ht. about 19½". Boston Mus. of Fine Arts.

FIG. 823. Typical *famille jaune* square vase decorated with the enamels of the day and iron red. Ht. 19". Altman Coll. Metropolitan Mus. of Art.

FIG. 824. K'ang Hsi *famille jaune* "temple vase" or "amphora" having a clearer than usual yellow ground fairly evenly applied and enamel colors painted direct on the biscuit. Ht. 27". Altman Coll. Metropolitan Mus. of Art.

FIG. 825. Rectangular *famille jaune* K'ang Hsi vase with handles imitating twigs and later called "crabstock" by the English. Ht. 21". Altman Coll. Metropolitan Mus. of Art.

tainly less beautiful than the Ch'ü Chou one shown in the celadon section under the Ming Dynasty. The tapering square vase is a new style and varies considerably in the form of the shoulders, the neck, etc. Beakers and club shapes are also frequent but it is obvious that shape meant less to these potters than the decoration and here we have almost as static an idea of shape as we found when the Athenians became so intent upon their painting.

In point of rarity and therefore also of value the yellow ground ones stood first, the black second and the green third. White ground vessels were, of course, done over the glaze as in Ming times. Many of the figures and particularly the larger ones such as that from the Victoria and Albert Museum were predominantly yellow. This question of color of ground as related to price probably never occurred to the Chinese and certainly they never wrote anything about it. It is merely one of those arbitrary whims of western collectors and certainly the finest specimen I know, the beautiful vase illustrated from the Altman Collection with birds and hawthorn blossoms, has a pale green ground that is as fresh as the earliest sprouts. No illustration can give the slightest impression of the glorious spring-like quality of this design filled with bursting blossoms and crazy birds filled with the ecstasy of the season.

It seems unnecessary in this day to mention that such wares are certainly not Ming, but recently a foremost German authority quoted that beautifully illustrated but totally unauthoritative work "Chinese Porcelain & Hard Stones" by Edgar Gorer and J. F. Blacker, published in 1911 by Bernard Quaritch of London in which Ming attributions are given wholesale.

Naturally such an expensive ware would be copied and it was by the Japanese and Chinese since K'ang Hsi days. Some such specimens are surprisingly correct in details and colors. The glazes are easily artifically worn Thus the collector has to be very careful indeed. Mr. Hobson has made some notes which I pass on for what they are worth. He says that in the finer pieces the black is not allowed to appear in too solid masses but is broken and graded to vary the surface. I believe this was merely due to the difficulty of getting an even black ground. During Ch'ien Lung's time, he says, the black was not allowed in such large areas and diapering came into style. However we have seen diapering in the Wan Li period and before so this is no new invention. In fact after the Yung Chêng period there was a reversion to the old Ming taste and this may have been a result of such a trend. He also says, which is quite true, that the black in later copies was sometimes mixed with the enamel which gives a dull and mat surface while in others the over transparent enamel is laid on too much and gives a sticky appearance.

More dangerous fakes are made by building vases up on old bases or by stripping some or grinding off the surface of some worthless but correct vase of the period and redecorating it.

The designers had difficulties with these wares simply because the whole ground had to be covered with enamel as we can see in the uneven grounds and the return to diapering. The painting in of such a ground is tedious and clumsy and, being conscious of this, the artists would naturally fill in as much detail as he could, particularly to avoid large and mussy areas of ground color.

Another difficulty was that of painting up to two sides of a line. The most spirited drawing with fine brush work and all the life a master might give it, would be ruined by such an after treatment. The filling in was simply a tedious and stupid method and naturally here and there the enamel would go over the line on one side of it or the other thus killing all its life and vigor. Is it not amazing that the Chinese people after making the joyful and alive paintings on pottery that they did in the Sung times could possibly sink so low as to return to kindergarten technique of outline filling?

So tedious and uninspiring was this whole medium of expression that weariness shows up in the fact that the backs of most of the round vases are not considered. Most of them contain no thoughtout design whatsoever and one sees only scraggly tips of branches approaching each other haphazardly. Certainly the greatest collection, if turned with the backs out, would show a sorry spectacle. Here we find the clearest sign of decadence; that of putting up a good front and not finishing off the job properly. It would be difficult to find an example in which a Sung artist had done this.

When one studies these wares with an open mind unbiased by their cost in the auction market and with an eye only for artistic merit one can see that they are bombastic attempts toward grandeur made by artists who were mere copyists at best and not very good ones at that.

FAMILLE VERTE DECORATION ON THE GLAZE

With the same enamels decorations were carried on much as in Ming days on the glazed wares. D'Entrecolles tells us that this glaze had less of the softening element of lime and fern ashes in it than that intended for the blue

FIG. 826. K'ang Hsi porcelain plate with a picture of the "Three Heroes," Chang Liang, Han Sin and Ch'ên P'ing, founders of the Han dynasty. Dia. 7¼". Metropolitan Mus. of Art.

FIG. 827. K'ang Hsi famille verte porcelain plate with the very best of swift and virile painting. Dia. 8⅛". Fuller Coll. Seattle Art Mus.

FIG. 828. Late K'ang Hsi porcelain plate with uneven white ground and decorated with palest iron red flowers, three greens, a gray-brown and purplish blue. Dia. 9½". Michael Friedsam Coll. Metropolitan Mus. of Art.

and white wares. This harder and higher fired glaze is stronger, more opaque and slightly cream. The second firing for the enamels is said to have harmed the softer blue and white type glaze and this is probably the reason that we see only seldom the underglaze color used with enamels. In fact the only ones I have seen were direct copies of Ming examples. The blue usually used in K'ang Hsi times with enamels was the newly developed

FIG. 829. Two rather better than average famille verte K'ang Hsi vases and one of the same period of the very rare type of relief bisque examples. It was thought by some collectors that these were intended for enamel coloring later but the careful touching in of the pupils of the eyes would not then have been necessary. Hts. 34″, 31″ and 28¾″. Fuller Coll. Seattle Art Mus.

FIG. 830. K'ang Hsi "temple" vase. Decorated with famille verte colors on a white ground. Ht. about 30″. Ross Coll. Boston Mus. of Fine Arts.

violet-blue enamel which is nowhere nearly so beautiful as the underglaze color.

It will be recognized at once that this painting of enamels on a glazed ground is a natural method of painting not beset by all the hampering tech-

FIG. 831. Middle K'ang Hsi cup or earlier. Ming shape, a simple design fairly well drawn, in famille verte enamels. 4″. Bequest of E. C. Converse.

FIG. 832. Late K'ang Hsi lantern of thin porcelain decorated with famille verte enamels and iron red. 13″. Metropolitan Mus. of Art.

FIG. 833. Late K'ang Hsi famille verte enamels on glaze jar with three greens, clear iron red, muddy yellow and underglazed blue on the horizontal lines. Ht. 12″. Bequest of Mary Clark Thompson, Metropolitan Mus. of Art.

nical difficulties which had to be overcome with the on-biscuit technique. The ground did not have to be filled in and it was also a pleasant and smooth surface on which to paint. The method used, however, was an outcome of the old system of manufacturing. The outlining was done in red or brown by several artists who specialized in various things. These outlines were then filled in either carefully or carelessly. Space-fear was not so pressing and we see some freedom, and once in a while a fine piece of composition.

FIG. 834. Late K'ang Hsi tea-pot of white porcelain decorated with famille verte enamels in the style of rather overcrowded flowers which is more often associated with the following periods of famille rose. Length 8". Bequest of Mary Clark Thompson. Metropolitan Mus. of Art.

FIG. 835. K'ang Hsi plate with low relief design and underglaze blue and brown rim edge, redecorated in Holland with colored enamels. Dia. 8". Bequest of Maria P. James. Metropolitan Mus. of Art.

Père d'Entrecolles however says, "Sometimes the painting is intentionally reserved for the second firing; at other times they only use the second firing to conceal defects in the porcelain, applying the colors to faulty places. This

FIG. 836. Possibly early K'ang Hsi gallipot with deep iron red ground over white glaze allowed to show in the clouds and yellow, blue and green enamels. Ht. 7". Bequest of Mary Clark Thompson. Metropolitan Mus. of Art.

FIG. 837. Early K'ang Hsi double wine or tea pot of heavily potted white ware with underglaze blue, iron red and green enamel decoration. Ht. 6". Ex Avery Coll. Metropolitan Mus. of Art.

FIG. 838. Early K'ang Hsi wine ewer heavily potted with white glaze and decoration in iron red and famille verte enamels. This shows a continuance of the Near Eastern shapes. Ht. 8". Metropolitan Mus. of Art.

porcelain, which is loaded with colors, is not to the taste of a good many people. As a rule one can feel the inequalities on the surface, whether due to the clumsiness of the workmen, to the exigencies of light and shade, or to the desire to conceal defects in the body of the ware." Of course he was reflecting Chinese taste.

Among the export famille verte wares there are many pieces which have decoration in places which were obviously the location of a flaw of some sort, and this again tended to make the style overornate and crowded. Again the enamels were pale in color and had to be "heaped and piled" as the old Ming potters had put it to get a sufficient depth.

GENERAL DATING

There is no point and little possibility in dividing these wares into actual years but we can generally allocate them as Early, Middle or Late K'ang Hsi.

Early K'ang Hsi (1672–1680)—Like Ming wares, enamels applied in broad washes, designs simple and direct, iron red still fairly dark and blue enamel and gilding are little used.

FIG. 839. Middle K'ang Hsi plate of rare type. "Brocade pattern" of famille verte colors. The rim is finished with a cafe au lait edge. Dia. 10½". Metropolitan Mus. of Art.—FIG. 840. K'ang Hsi early plate showing simple almost Minglike floral treatment. Dia. 8". Bequest of Maria P. James. Metropolitan Mus. of Art.

FIG. 841 below. Middle K'ang Hsi box for perfumed herbs. "Brocade pattern" in famille verte enamels including blue. Length 14". Gift of Robert E. Tod. Metropolitan Mus. of Art.

FIG. 842. Early K'ang Hsi vase showing bold and vigorous drawing. Ht. 22". Warren E. Cox Coll.—FIG. 843. A typical late K'ang Hsi vase with flowers drawn in a style only a little more vigorous than those which appear on many famille rose pieces. There is no rose on this piece, the blue is pinkish or lavender in tone and the glaze very thin and dry. Ht. 21". Warren E. Cox Coll.

Middle K'ang Hsi (1680 to 1700 or 1710)—Best quality, large vases with brocade patterns on grounds with reserve medallions, full designed plates with many figures, directly and well drawn birds and flowers, vases with coral red used partly or in the whole for ground, and vases with large figures of ladies.

Late K'ang Hsi (1700 or 1710 to 1722)—Delicate drawing, lightening and effeminacy throughout, like famille rose but in famille verte colors, egg shell "birthday plates," which were supposed to have been made for the birthday of the emperor in 1713 are typical, egg shell lanterns, etc.

Toward the very end of the reign two new colors were devised, a *muddy, mauve-pink* (1710–1720) followed by other opaque colors and *"arsenical white"* which was also opaque. These were the beginning of the famille rose colors.

Even over the glaze the grounds were sometimes filled in with enamel probably to cover up defects. Again enamels might be used over colored grounds such as in the "lang yao green glazed bowl in the British Museum" mentioned by Hobson as probably a faulty specimen and therefore decorated. I submit the suggestion that it was probably a good red to begin with but the second firing turned it unexpectedly green. (See discussion of Sang de Boeuf.) There are also powder blues with enamel decoration, grey crackled grounds and "Nanking yellow" but all are tricky stunts and not harmonious.

FIG. 844. K'ang Hsi bottle of white glaze decorated with gold only. Ht. 17". Bequest of E. C. Converse. Metropolitan Mus. of Art.

FIG. 845. Late K'ang Hsi reticulated porcelain basket decorated in two greens and purple, blue and pale yellow enamels and iron red. Length 4½". Bequest of Mary Clark Thompson. Metropolitan Mus. of Art.

FIG. 846. One of a pair of baluster ornaments acquired in India. They are definitely of K'ang Hsi famille verte ware and were said to have been imported during the days of the Monguls and were probably made to order. Ht. 5¾". Fuller Coll. Seattle Art Mus.

FIG. 847. Middle K'ang Hsi gallipot with covers. White glaze and pale, uneven red decoration. Ht. 9". Bequest of Mary Strong Shattuck. Metropolitan Mus. of Art.

CHINESE IMARI WARE

We have described the Kakiemon ware and the more ornate "Old Imari" ware made in Arita in Hizen province, Japan, and probably influenced by the Dutch traders. This in a sense grew out of Chinese wares but it became so popular that the Chinese at Ching-tê Chêng copied it back as it were. The Chinese ware is better than the Japanese being thinner and clearer of color. The red is coral in the Chinese examples while it is more dull and like Indian red on the Japanese. The black is greenish on the Chinese examples and brownish on the Japanese ones.

RED AND BLUE WARE

Another ware had red and gold over glaze and blue underglaze design. It was an export ware and of poor quality.

During this enlightened reign we could have expected great things but the blight of commercialism, mass production and foreign influence was too great.

FIG. 848. K'ang Hsi Imari style vase of white porcelain decorated with dark underglaze blue, gold, green and iron red. Ht. 10". Metropolitan Mus. of Art.

FIG. 849. Late K'ang Hsi jar in the style of Japanese Imari ware decorated with pale underglaze blue, deep iron red and gold. Ht. 6". Metropolitan Mus. of Art.

FIG. 850. K'ang Hsi bowl decorated in Holland with iron red, green, purplish blue, a too bright yellow, dark brown and gold. Dia. 5½". Metropolitan Mus. of Art.—FIG. 851. Late K'ang Hsi bowl decorated in underglaze blue, iron red and green enamel. The blossoms on the outside are in slight relief. The inside lambrequins are distinctly European in design. Dia. 7½". Metropolitan Mus. of Art.

FIG. 852. Large K'ang Hsi plate with the arms of the city of Louvain. Dia. 17". Metropolitan Mus. of Art.

FIG. 853. Late K'ang Hsi plate in the Imari style. Dia. 10". Metropolitan Mus. of Art.

FIG. 854. K'ang Hsi plate showing strong Near Eastern influence. Dia. 8". Metropolitan Mus. of Art.

THE YUNG CHENG REIGN
(1723–1735)

Neither national history nor religion have much bearing upon art from this time forward. Commerce alone counts, and money became the prime incen-

Yung Chêng bottle of white porcelain with creamy light green glaze and brown dressing on the body where exposed at the foot-rim. The six character mark is in underglaze blue. Ht. 6". T. C. Lee–Warren E. Cox Coll.

Beautiful Yung Chêng celadon bowl of white porcelain, the foot dressed with brown, and having a thick, rich, soft green glaze full of bubbles and crackled with brown. It also has the "brown mouth." Dia. about 7". Mrs. Warren E. Cox.

Right: Rare egg-shell apple green jar with finely crackled white glaze over which a transparent green enamel has been applied. The mark is K'ang Hsi in a blue slightly more purple in tint than it would be if of the period. Yung Chêng. Ht. 8¾". Perry Moore–Warren E. Cox Coll.

Yun Chêng reproduction of a Kuan type oblong dish with greyish body coated with a fat bluish-grey glaze with large crackles. Length 8½". C. T. Loo & Co.

Kuan type jardiniere with dragon handles of greyish porcelain covered with a fat greyish glaze. Yun Chêng period. Length 6". C. T. Loo & Co.

YUNG CHÊNG PORCELAINS
PLATE 162

tive, with a consequent decline in the integrity and quality of the art.

The fourth son of K'ang Hsi was a strong and hard ruler who put to death his own brothers but the good of the country burned in his heart. The *T'ao lu* says that he at once made a good appointment of Nien Hsi-yao as supervisor of the factories and in 1728 T'ang Ying was appointed assistant director of Ching-tê Chêng. Thus we hear of T'ang yao and Nien yao of the period though attributions are difficult to ascertain.

Above: Beautiful Yung Chêng soft paste bottle thinly and sensitively potted and having a "secret design" incised all over with a clear, transparent glaze having a helically twisted crackle. Ht. 12¾". Altman Coll. Metropolitan Mus. of Art.

Below: Yung Chêng vase of a light starch blue incorrectly often called "clair de lune" which should be much lighter. Ht. 8½". T. C. Lee—Warren E. Cox Coll.

Yung Chêng tea-dust glazed vase of beautiful shape. The body is dark brown and the mark in relief under the bottom. Ht. 7". T. C. Lee—Warren E. Cox Coll.

Yung Chêng vase in the style of and with the mark of Ch'êng Hua but somewhat heavier and more glossy in glaze. Ht. 10½". Warren E. Cox Coll.

YUNG CHÊNG VASES
PLATE 163

A list of the wares made at Ching-tê Chêng was made by Hsieh Min, governor of the Kiangsi province from 1729 to 1734. It has been translated by Bushell in his "Oriental Ceramic Art" and repeated in about the same form in Hobson's "The Later Ceramic Wares of China." As this list is referred to by collectors the world over, it is important enough to give in detail following.

FIG. 855. Pair of plates with famille verte design. The mark is in underglaze blue of the six character Cheng Hua type although it is of late K'ang Hsi period. Dia. 8⅛". Guy Mayer Coll.

FIG. 856. Pair of plates with Ho ho birds in deep underglaze blue in center yellow medallions, bands of white glaze and pencilled underglaze blue cloud whorls at rim. The back has three blue birds in apple green ground and the six character K'ang Hsi mark in usual double ring. Dia. 7⅞". Guy Mayer Coll.

1.—Glazes of the Ta Kuan (Imperial) ware on an "iron body" including "yüeh pai" (moon white), "fên ch'ing" (pale blue or green) and "ta lü" (deep green).

2.—Ko yao glaze on an "iron body," including millet colour (mi sê) and fên ch'ing.

3.—Ju glaze without crackle on a "copper" body: the glaze colours copied from a cat's food basin of the Sung dynasty, and a dish for washing brushes moulded with a human face.

4.—Ju glaze with fish-roe crackle on a "copper" body.

5.—White Ting glaze. Only fên Ting was copied, and not the t'u Ting.

6.—Chün glazes. Nine varieties are given, of which five were copied from old palace pieces and four from newly acquired specimens.

7.—Reproductions of the chi hung red of the Hsüan Tê period: including the fresh red (hsien hung) and the ruby red (pao shih hung).

8.—Reproductions of the deep violet-blue (chi ch'ing) of the Hsüan Tê period. This glaze is deep and reddish, and has orange-peel marks and palm eyes.

9.—Reproductions of the glazes of the Imperial factory: including eel yellow, snake-skin green and spotted yellow.

10.—Lung-ch'üan glazes: including pale and dark shades.

11.—Tung-ch'ing glazes: including pale and dark shades.

12.—Reproductions of the Sung millet-coloured (mi sê) glaze: copied in form and colour from fragments dug up at Hsiang Hu.

13.—Sung pale green (fên ch'ing): copied from wares found at the same time as the last.

14.—Reproductions of "oil green" (yu lü) glaze: "copied from an old transmutation (yao pien) ware like green jade (pi yü) with brilliant colour broken by variegated passages and of antique elegance."

15.—The Chün glaze of the muffle kiln (lu chün): "the colour is between that of the Kuangtung wares and the Yi-hsing applied glaze (kua yu); and in the ornamental markings (hua wên) and the transmutation tints of the flowing glaze it surpasses them."

16.—Ou's glazes, with red and blue markings.

17.—Blue mottled (ch'ing tien) glazes: copied from old Kuang yao.

18.—Moon white (yüeh pai) glazes. "The colour somewhat resembles the Ta Kuan glaze, but the body of the ware is white. The glaze is without crackle, and there are two shades—pale and dark."

19.—Reproductions of the ruby red (pao shao) of the Hsüan Tê: the decoration consisting of (1) three fishes, (2) three fruits, (3) three fungi, or (4) the five Blessings. . . . Hobson adds this note:—"Symbolized by five bats. The Blessings are: longevity, riches, peace and serenity, love of virtue and an end crowning the life."

20.—Reproductions of the Lung-ch'üan glaze with ruby red decoration of the kind just described. "This is a new style of the reigning dynasty."

21.—Turquoise (fei ts'ui) glazes. Copying three sorts: (1) pure turquoise, (2) blue flecked, and (3) gold flecked (chin tien).

22.—Soufflé red (ch'ui hung) glaze.

23.—Soufflé blue (ch'ui ch'ing) glaze.

24.—Reproductions of *Yung Lo* porcelain: eggshell *(t'o t'ai)* pure white with engraved *(chui)* or embossed *(kung)* designs.

25.—Copies of *Wan Li* and *Chêng Tê* enamelled *(wu ts'ai)* porcelain.

26.—Copies of *Ch'êng Hua* enamelled *(wu ts'ai)* porcelain.

27.—Porcelain with ornament in *Hsüan Tê* style in a yellow ground.

28.—*Cloisonné* blue *(fa ch'ing)* glaze. "This glaze is the result of recent attempts to match this colour (i.e. the deep blue of the *cloisonné* enamels). As compared with the deep and reddish *chi ch'ing*, it is darker and more vividly blue *(ts'ui)*, and it has no orange-peel or palm-eye markings."

29.—Reproductions of European wares with lifelike designs carved and engraved. "Sets of the five sacrificial utensils, dishes, plates, vases and boxes and the like are also decorated with coloured pictures in European style."

30.—Reproduction of wares with incised green decoration in a yellow glaze *chiao huang).*

31.—Reproductions of yellow glazed wares: including plain monochromes and those with incised ornament.

32.—Reproductions of purple brown *(tzŭ)* glazed wares: including plain monochromes and those with incised ornament.

33.—Porcelain with engraved ornament: including all kinds of glazes.

34.—Porcelain with embossed *(tui)* ornament: including all kinds of glazes.

35.—Painted red *(mo hung)*: copying old specimens.

36.—Red decoration *(ts'ai hung)*: copying old specimens. Note by Hobson:—"The *ts'ai hung* has the design painted in iron-red on a white ground."

37.—Porcelain in yellow after the European style.

38.—Porcelain in purple brown *(tzŭ)* after the European style.

39.—Silvered *(mo yin)* porcelain.

40.—Porcelain painted in ink *(shui mo).*

41.—Reproductions of the pure white *(t'ien pai)* porcelain of the *Hsüan Tê* period: including a variety of wares thick and thin, large and small.

42.—Reproductions of *Chia Ching* wares with blue designs.

43.—Reproductions of *Ch'êng Hua* pale painted *(tan miao)* blue designs.

44.—Millet coloured *(mi se)* glazes. "Differing from the Sung millet coloured." In two shades, light and dark.

45.—Porcelain with red in the glaze *(yü li hung)*: including (1) painted designs exclusively in red, (2) the combination of blue foliage with red flowers.

46.—Reproductions of lustrous brown *(tzŭ chin)* glaze: including two varieties, brown and yellow.

47.—Porcelain with yellow glaze *(chiao huang)* decorated in enamel colours *(wu ts'ai)*. "This is the result of recent experiments."

48.—Reproductions of green-glazed porcelain: including that with plain ground and engraved ornament.

49.—Wares with foreign colours *(yang ts'ai)*. "In the new copies of the Western style of painting in enamels *(fa-lang)* the landscapes and figure scenes, the flowering plants and birds are without exception of supernatural beauty and finish."

50.—Porcelain with embossed ornament *(kung hua)*: including all kinds of glazes.

51.—Porcelain with European *(hsi yang)* red colour.

52.—Reproductions of *(wu chin)* mirror black glazes: including those with black ground and white designs and those with black ground and gilding.

53.—Porcelain with European green colour.

54.—European *wu chin* (mirror black) wares.

55.—Gilt *(mo chin)* porcelain: copying the Japanese.

56.—Porcelain with gilt designs *(miao chin)*: copying the Japanese.

57.—Porcelain with silver designs *(miao yin)*: copying the Japanese.

58.—Large jars *(ta kang)* with Imperial factory glazes. "Dimensions: diameter at mouth, 3′ 4″ or 5″ to 4′; height, 1′ 7″ or 8″ to 2′. Glaze colours: (1) eel yellow, (2) cucumber green, and (3) mottled green and yellow *(huang lü tien)."*

Certain conclusions are obvious from a perusal of Hsieh Min's list:—First and most evident is a desire to retreat from the contemporary decadent designs and practices and return to the old traditions. Sick art often like the captive octopus sets out to devour itself. There is commendable revulsion of feeling against what is bad but, with the old spirit lacking, the reproduction is still revealing of the decadence in the heart of the people. The wares of Lung-ch'üan, Ch'ü-chou, Ting Chou and Chün Chou (now called Fu Chou) were attempted but they could not come alive again. The bodies of the reproductions are perfect and cold, hard and white. The potters sensed this and tried to dress the foot-rims with ferruginous clay but this would not look the same or *be* the same, of course. Second, the Ming wares were closer in imitation because the bodies were similar white porcelain. The K'ang Hsi wares were continued rather than copied but with differences and with even more perfection.

Third, we see another revolt against the overcrowded design which had

FIG. 857. Ko type pentagonal bottle with greenish grey glaze and the usual broad crackle of black. Ht. 8″. Guy Mayer Coll.

FIG. 858. Yung Chêng cherry red porcelain bottle of glossy but somewhat pitted glaze of even red more lightly mottled than streaked as in the sang-de-boeuf ones of the former reign. Ht. 12½″. Metropolitan Mus. of Art.

FIG. 859. Pale "celadon" glazed vase with paler glaze inside and brown lip rim. The glaze, not crackled is very glossy. Yung Chêng period. Ht. 12″. Metropolitan Mus. of Art.

FIG. 860. Yung Chêng, Ko type bottle with brownish grey glaze and large black and brown crackle. Ht. 17½″. Ex T. C. Lee–Warren E. Cox Coll.

FIG. 861. "Mazarine blue," vase of the Yung Chêng period. Ht. 15″. Metropolitan Mus. of Art.

FIG. 862. Large Yung-chêng vase of what is known as "orange peel" surface on a glaze of pale celadon green mottled with a dull strawberry color. Ht. 14½″. Altman Coll. Metropolitan Mus. of Art.

FIG. 863. Yung Chêng vase with clear green celadon glaze similar to the finest Lung chuan type but more even. Ht. 14¼″. T. C. Lee–Warren E. Cox Coll.

FIG. 864. Corinthian purple vase with greenish white glaze onto which was blown manganese in a technique like that of the powder blue wares. Yung Chêng. Ht. 6¾″. Perry Moore–Warren E. Cox Coll.

FIG. 865. Yung Chêng sage green plate with arabic inscription seemingly on an etched ground in low relief. Dia. 7″. Metropolitan Mus. of Art.

FIG. 866. Bottle with "Kuan yao" glaze of pale blue-green crackled irregularly with brown on a white porcelain body but with the foot-rim dressed with brown-black. Ht. 21″. Warren E. Cox Coll.

grown in greater and greater trade demands. The Chinese themselves seemed to prefer monochromes. Crackle was mastered in technique. Flambé of copper red streaked with blue or grey or purple was richly made although the actual fact was that tendencies had always been apparent in the sang de boeuf to streak in this way and what really happened was that rather than strive to

FIG. 867. Yung Chêng vase decorated with underglaze blue and peachbloom pink. A good sturdy shape and beautiful design. Ht. 14¼″. Seattle Art Mus. Fuller Coll.
FIG. 868. Yung Chêng black glazed vase with gold decoration. Ht. 19″. Formerly Garland Coll.
FIG. 869. Yung Chêng bottle in the wrongly called "Mazarine blue" which has a more porous and duller glaze than usually seen on K'ang Hsi pieces of the same color. Ht. 8½″. Metropolitan Mus. of Art.
FIG. 870. Blue and white vase of the period showing a typical softened "Mingish" shape and over ornate dragon design. The dragon has iron red added over the blue. (1723–1735). Metropolitan Mus. of Art.

overcome the effect the potters decided it was easier to make use of it. Tea-dust of olive and brownish-green finely speckled and smooth, but a sort of super refined Sixth Dynasty glaze with less appeal for many, was developed.

There were also glazes made to imitate the poor European imitations of Chinese glazes. Blue and white was made frequently without shading to imitate the Ming ones but with a dull blue. The fashion for these was past and no care was taken in their manufacture. The imitations of Chia Ching dark violet Mohammedan blue and also of the Ch'êng Hua light tracery in blue were good enough to fool those who had not seen the real thing. The peculiar Ming foot was meticulously copied and every effort seemed to have been made to deceive. "Soft paste" blue and white was very well copied. And the wares with underglaze blue and enamels of yellow or red were not neglected.

The various underglaze reds were so well copied that collectors are still doubtful about many of the existing stem cups with red fishes on them and other red wares. Most that we see are, of course, of this period, if they have any age at all. The use of ruby red under a celadon glaze was supposed to have been invented at this time but, as we have seen, actually goes back much

Left: Yung Chêng very pale celadon vase with underglaze red mottled with green (like peach-bloom glaze). Note that this shape has slightly more rounded shoulders than the K'ang Hsi peach-bloom vases, the rings on the neck are higher. Ht. 8″. Metropolitan Mus. of Art.
Center: Yung Chêng large vase of a shape typical of the period. It is pale celadon decorated with gray, blue, brown, green, iron red and gold. Ht. 17″. Metropolitan Mus. of Art.
Right: Yung Chêng gallipot with low relief design of dragons in pale greenish white and ground of waves in underglaze red. Ht. 13″. Bequest of Mrs. H. O. Havemeyer. Metropolitan Mus. of Art.

Bowl decorated "in underglaze copper red and enamels." Dia. 6½″. Bequest of Edward G. Kennedy. Metropolitan Mus. of Art.

Yung Chêng porcelain cup of the type known as *Ku Yüeh Hsüan.* Dia. about 3″. Freer Gallery of Art, Washington.

Right: "Wine pot" (hu) or "sêng-mao-hu" (monk's cap jug) which originated in the Yung Lo reign and were often made in red and celadon in the Hsüan-tê reign *(see text).* Ht. 6″. Smaller than the Ming ones. Bequest of Mrs. H. O. Havemeyer. Metropolitan Mus. of Art.

One of pair of stem cups for wine. Ming type and decorated similarly but of the Yung Cheng period (1722–. 1735). Ht. 3″. Metropolitan Mus. of Art.

A large fish bowl of the Yung-chêng period decorated with *famille rose* enamels and having a black ground. Inside is a broad and lively treatment of lotus and gold fish which must be very effective when waterplants and real fish are added. Ht. 15¼″. Altman Coll. Metropolitan Mus. of Art.

One of pair of eggshell porcelain lanterns with vivid famille verte enamel decoration. The stands are modern. Bequest of Edward C. Kennedy. Metropolitan Mus. of Art.

YUNG CHÊNG DECORATED WARES

PLATE 164

earlier. Variations grew out of this ware to include underglaze red and blue on white slip with a celadon ground or a lavender blue ground. These colors were all rather unpleasant together but the French liked them and even mounted specimens with ormolu mounts.

FIG. 871. Bowl of Ku-yüeh-hsüan type of semi-eggshell delicately painted with a poppy design on the outside and fruits inside, in polychrome. The mark is Yung Chêng as is the period. Dia. about 3". Guy Mayer Coll.

FIG. 872. Wine pot and jar of the Yung Chêng period and decorated with underglaze blue and red. The pieces are fitted nicely together to form what appears to be a gourd wine pot. It is thought that hot water was placed in the lower jar to keep the wine warm. Ht. 7½". Metropolitan Mus. of Art.

In enameled wares the new opaque colors almost at once became popular and we have the full flowering of the famille rose decorations, ornate to begin with and growing ever more so. On the other hand copies were made of the Ch'êng Hua underglaze blue and pale transparent enameled ware. T'ang Ying explains in his twenty illustrations of the processes of porcelain manufacture, that "yang ts'ai" or "foreign coloring" was used and adds that the

FIG. 873. Yung Chêng plate with greenish white ground, flowers in uneven iron red and gold, deep blue enamel, three greens and no rose. Dia. 14". Gift of W. B. Osgood Field. Metropolitan Mus. of Art.

FIG. 874. Yung Chêng "marriage plate." The border is in iron red and gold, the rest is in famille rose colors, the rose being pale in color and the blue also pale. Dia. 8". "Eggshell potting." Metropolitan Mus. of Art.

FIG. 875. Yung Chêng plate with famille rose enamel decoration including a pale rose. Dia. 13". Metropolitan Mus. of Art. Gift of W. B. Osgood Field.

colors were the same as those for enameling on metal, "fo lang yao," which was a term used to speak of cloisonné and painted enamels such as were applied near Canton. These were, according to Hobson, believed by the Chinese to have come from Ku li (Calicut) and might possibly have been French enamels imported through that port. Hippisley probably correctly

FIG. 876. Yung Chêng
Ko type cup with gray
glaze and dark gray
crackle. It seems to be
of gray ware and to have
about a ¼″ wide foot rim.
Ht. 1¾″. Metropolitan
Mus. of Art.

FIG. 877. Yung Chêng plate
c. 1725 of the so called "Jesuit
ware" painted in iron red and
gold with "the baptism of
Christ." Dia. 8½″. Metropolitan Mus. of Art.

FIG. 878. Yung Chêng Tê-
hua, Fukien cup rather heavily potted and pure white.
The glaze is more glassy than
in Ming examples and less
full of bubbles than in the
Ch'ien Lung ones. Ht. 3″.
Metropolitan Mus. of Art.

suggests that pictures by Jesuit artists such as Ghérardini and Belleville were
also sources of design.

The arsenious white continued and also a rose-pink made from precipitate
of gold or "purple of Cassius" and this latter was developed into many
shades of ruby, carmine and light rose called by the Chinese "yen chih hung"
or rouge red. Most enamels were more opaque than the K'ang Hsi ones and
many new colors were brought about by mixing. This was not so easy as it
sounds for the chemical reactions of one color upon another cannot always
be foreseen: Iron red was mixed with a flux to make "tsao hung" or "jujube-
red" as it is called and the brown-black mixed with a flux made "European
black."

The wares painted at Ching-tê Chêng were delicate and effeminate but
with some taste and allowed a fair amount of the pure white to show. This
white is more glossy than the K'ang Hsi and very perfect. However, other
wares were made and shipped as "blancs" to Canton where they could be
decorated in closer touch with the foreign buyers. These were of course a
step down, and it was here that the designs took on more of the characteristics
of cloisonné and were made more and more ornate to give the customer more
for his money in competition with other wares. "Seven border" plates on
which you can count the borders were made with center medallions of flower
baskets, Chinese interiors with ladies and children (a subject the Chinese
love), dishes of fruit, bird and flower subjects such as pheasants and rocks,
cocks and peonies, and quail in millet, etc. Sometimes these borders were
broken with inserted medallions to add further richness. Some of these
plates had decoration in overglaze blue, or black and gold, or at times in
ruby pink or gold alone. Many of them have the solid ruby color on the
backs and are known in Europe as "ruby backed porcelain." Another
large group has the plain ruby ground broken by medallions of white
containing varicolored decorations, and these are not only small objects
and plates but great garniture sets.

These were painted in and about Canton and some are even so signed.
One in the B.M. is signed Pai-shih and has the inscription "ling nan hui che"
which means "Canton picture."

T'ang Ying is supposed also to have invented the use of silver for grounds and for painting, but Père d'Entrecolles referred to it as early as 1722.

One favorite trick that the Yung Chêng artists employed was to start the design on the back of a plate, bring it on over to the front, and sometimes around to the back again as though it were wrapped about the piece.

It can be said that these painters did render natural objects with simple mastery and that their flowers are beautiful if they were only not so crowded. Of course they were nowhere nearly so alive as were those of the Sung period even though all the colors were employed now and the Sung ones were in brown or black. Yung Chêng flowers are like those drawn for the scientists of a natural history museum with all the parts correct but no living, growing unity; they are painstaking rather than swift and alive.

THE CH'IEN LUNG PERIOD (1736–1796)

A fourth son again ascended the throne and there seemed luck in this for he was one of the most enlightened monarchs of history. Master not only of

FIG. 879. Ch'ien Lung vase called "clair de lune" by the museum but actually of a pale celadon color. Ht. 6". Bequest of Mary Clark Thompson. Metropolitan Mus. of Art.

FIG. 880. Rare Ching Period "Celadon" and Blue Jar. Possibly a mortuary jar for the characters on the shoulder read, "Precious grasses in the mountain shall have no seeds, Peach blossoms in a cave have their own spring," and the four large characters read, "never," "mountain," "get old or die," "green." The seal reads, "Mr. Wu Chang, Fairy Kiln near Soo Chou."

FIG. 881. Ch'ien Lung camellia green bottle with fine crackle of the sort called "fish roe." It has a black lip rim. Ht. 15". Metropolitan Mus. of Art.

the arts of peace but also of war, his empire included Chinese Turkestan and Tibet while he exerted some power over India. Burma, Siam and Annam also became tributaries.

The technician T'ang Ying succeeded Nein Hsi-yao at Huai-an Fu as director of the factories. In 1739 he was transferred to Kui-kiang but before he took his post he wrote notes covering his work. The *T'ao-lu* eulogizes him as the all time master of porcelain and claims that "The Imperial wares attained their greatest perfection at this time," but actually his inventions consisted chiefly of new additions to the already too broad palette of the "foreign colors" and further copies of the old glazes which were in some cases even more meticulous than those of Yung Chêng times. One popular stunt

Left: Cherry red flambé jar with only the faintest streaks of blue toward the top. Glazed under the foot with transparent yellow brown and at lip with greenish white. Ht. about 16″. Courtesy of Mrs. David Zipkin. Ex Warren E. Cox Coll.

Right: Ch'ien Lung vase with olive green tea dust glaze of a greener and more even and thinner texture than that seen on Sung examples. The inside has an irregularly crackled greenish white glaze. Ht. 14″. H. O. Havemeyer Bequest. Metropolitan Mus. of Art.

Left: Impressive turquoise blue vase with low relief decoration under a brilliant transparent glaze. Ch'ien Lung period. Ht. 24″. Altman Coll. Metropolitan Mus. of Art.

Ch'ien Lung porcelain *ku* or beaker cup made at Ching-tê Chên after an ancient Shang period bronze type. It is of white porcelain with a rich turquoise glaze, crackled. Ht. 11″. Gift of Mrs. Dora Delano Forbes. Mus. of Fine Arts, Boston.

Ch'ien Lung turquoise blue or "peacock blue" bottle with delicately incised design under the glaze. The potting is thin and true. Ht. 10½″. Metropolitan Mus. of Art.

Right: Deep cobalt blue vase with rich glaze. Ch'ien Lung seal mark and of the period. Ht. 7½″. Perry Moore–Warren E. Cox Coll.

Ko type 18th cent. vase with greenish gray glaze and dark gray crackle. It is very much like the real Ko yao (See Sung section) but more glossy. Ht. 7½″. Metropolitan Mus. of Art.

Left: Peacock blue vase with the usual fine "fish roe" crackle. Ch'ien Lung period. Ht. 8½″. Perry Moore–Warren E. Cox Coll.

CH'IEN LUNG SINGLE COLOR PORCELAINS

PLATE 165

of bad taste was the attempt to copy ancient bronzes and jades by casting direct from specimens and making glazes to more or less imitate the textures.

CH'IEN LUNG GLAZES

The sang de boeuf reds were, according to Hobson, conspicuously wanting in control of glaze and streaked with grey or blue and purple much as were the flambé types. This seems highly doubtful to me for in one breath we say that these craftsmen were over careful in detail and in the next we declare them careless. Why suddenly at the end of the K'ang Hsi reign at just the time when the great technician was put in charge of the factories should the potters suddenly become careless in the handling of this one ware? All of the K'ang Hsi sang de boeuf pieces were certainly not perfectly controlled as to glaze, as we have said, and now I am certain that some of the Ch'ien Lung ones were quite perfectly made. How to make a clear distinction between the wares of the two periods in a case like this where style of design cannot be considered is impossible to answer. Yet to the old collectors of K'ang Hsi sang de boeuf vases, who were millionaires and, by their very natures, precisionists at heart, it would have been almost a personal insult to say that one of their treasures might have been made after 1736 instead of just before 1722. Those 14 years might mean the difference between $200 and $20,000 literally, while the same generation thought nothing of slapping a whole classification such as the "three color" K'ang Hsi wares back a hundred years into Ming. Actually there was an increasing decadence but it was a general and gradual one and the trend was not toward loss of meticulous care in Ch'ien Lung times but quite the opposite; too much embroidered care exerted on subjects of too little taste. Carelessness did creep in but certainly not invariably.

FIG. 882. Ch'ien Lung olive green vase with gray crackle and dark brown foot. It is more glassy than the Ch'u-chou examples of the Ming and K'ang Hsi periods. Ht. 7″. Bequest of Mary Clark Thompson. Metropolitan Mus. of Art.

FIG. 883. Ko type Ch'ien Lung vase of pale "celadon" green with a black crackle in a bubbly but glassy glaze. Ht. 6½″. Metropolitan Mus. of Art.

FIG. 884. Ch'ien Lung "mirror black" bottle with rough glaze and pasty white inside. The body is grayish. Ht. 8″. Isaac D. Fletcher Bequest. Metropolitan Mus. of Art.

FIG. 885. Ch'ien Lung iron rust glazed vase. Ht. 7″. Metropolitan Mus. of Art.

While we are on this subject I should like to point out to the reader that ever since Ming days we have repeatedly described the paste as being smooth and dense and the glaze high-fired, perfect and white. Of course, it is true that both improved in this 100-year span just as they improved in the 275-year span of the Ming Dynasty, but to say that some of the finest and most delicate Ming wares are not just as pure and well potted as the finest of the 18th century ones is ridiculous. To say that all Ming paste has minute pits in it is false as it is to say that pits never occur in later pastes. Actually when we get down to facts there is little or no real *proof* that such a vase is K'ang Hsi and such an one Ch'ien Lung, or that such a piece is Yung Chêng and such an one Ming. It is not always the easiest thing in the world for a collector to be sure that some odd specimen was made before or after the 450-year stretch from Sung to Yung Chêng days, though this is, of course, easier. We can only go on the rather vague and often badly translated Chinese written descriptions, on the comparatively few drawings which were

FIG. 886. Ch'ien Lung vase with soft rose colored glaze which is glossy and unlike *sang de pigeon* ones of similar shape. Ht. 11″. Ex T. C. Lee–Warren E. Cox Coll. Now Mrs. Clark Getts Coll.

FIG. 887. Bottle vase with glaze of Kuan type of pale blue-green with hardly perceptible helically twisted crackle. White porcelain but with foot dressed in black. Ht. 22½″. Warren E. Cox Coll.

FIG. 888. Ch'ien Lung bottle of a shape never earlier than Yung Cheng covered with an iron rust glaze to emulate that of the Honan temmokus of the Sung period. Ht. 13″. Bequest of H. O. Havemeyer. Metropolitan Mus. of Art.

none too perfect either in color or scale and on the putting of two and two together. Therefore, we must be just as careful not to become too pedantic as we are not to become too loose in our judgments.

Liver red and sang de pigeon or "crimson" mat glazes filled with small pores and even in texture were more popular than in K'ang Hsi times for many thousands must have been made judging by the number still available. The series of almost identical vases illustrated show how difficult it is to judge between Yung Chêng and late 19th century pieces unless they are marked and comparisons can be made.

Iron rust glaze of dark brown with metallic flakes in it, "ch'a yeh mo" or tea-dust, an ocherous brown or bronze green dusted with tea-green and

A large garniture set of famille rose vases with reserve medallions painted with landscapes set on a black ground ornamented with green leaves and rose enamel flowers. Type often called Yung Chêng but that was a short period and most of them are more likely Ch'ien Lung as these are marked in the museum. Hts. 24″ and 19″. Metropolitan Mus. of Art.

CH'IEN LUNG FAMILLE ROSE GARNITURE SET

PLATE 166

such glazes were frequent. All the range of green from the yellowish tones of the "camellia green" to those of turquoise blue and peacock were continued as were also the grey crackled wares after Ko yao. Sage tints and also "robin's egg blue" both plain and soufflé continued. It is said that the turquoise ones of the later period had a more reddish body which was sometimes rough because iron was mixed with it to help develop the color, but this is again a mere rule of thumb and highly doubtful.

Large bottle of pale "celadon" color with rose and yellow peaches, two greens, white and pink blossoms, etc. Ht. 18". Ch'ien Lung period. Bequest of Isaac D. Fletcher. Metropolitan Mus. of Art.

Yung Chêng large jar with greenish white ground and famille rose enamel decoration freely and well painted. The handles are coral or iron red. Ht. 19". Metropolitan Mus. of Art.

Ch'ien Lung bottle of a shape which originated in the Yung Chêng period with greenish white ground and decorated in famille rose colors and black. Ht. 10". Metropolitan Mus. of Art.

Ch'ien Lung bowl of the "Chinese Lowestoft" type rather heavily potted with famille rose colors, iron red and gold, the whole rather deep in color. The rim is unglazed at the top of the cover. Dia. 11". Metropolitan Mus. of Art.

Center: Ch'ing dynasty, Ch'ien Lung porcelain vase with famille rose colors. Ht. 9¾". Freer Gallery of Art, Washington.
Right: Cafe au lait vase and cover with reserved medallions. Ht. 18". Bequest of Mary Clark Thompson. Metropolitan Mus. of Art.

CH'IEN LUNG FAMILLE ROSE ENAMEL DECORATED VASES

PLATE 167

ENAMEL MONOCHROMES

The "mei kuei" or rose pink which T'ang Ying writes about was an enamel color such as that used for decorations and also for the backs of the "ruby backed plates." It now was applied with a rumpled surface like an orange peel and is sometimes clouded with deeper tones making a sort of famille rose flambé. The ware is usually thin and small cabinet vases are in the majority.

Other enamel monochromes are: lemon yellow which is opaque and rough, mustard yellow which is crackled, cloisonné blue, amaranth blue, "jujube-red" which is a thickly fluxed iron red, opaque turquoise green and finally an enamel black called "lac black." Of course all of the K'ang Hsi enamels and glazes too were continued.

FAMILLE ROSE WARES AND OTHERS

Among other enamel stunts we find the imitation bronzes made with imitations of inlay and also various copies of cloisonné, green jade, Peking lacquer, grained wood, millefiore glass, etc. The *T'ao shuo* says, "Among all the works of art in carved gold, embossed silver, chiselled stone, lacquer, mother of pearl, bamboo and wood, gourd and shell, there is not one that is not now produced in porcelain, a perfect copy of the original piece." Of course this outrages one of the first principles of good art namely that one should express the medium in which the work is done.

At this time most of the "lac burgauté," which was also made in K'ang

FIG. 889. Ch'ien Lung blue and white jar of a shape often seen in Yung Chêng soft paste. Note the relief floral decoration. Ht. 11½". Metropolitan Mus. of Art.

FIG. 890. K'ang Hsi white porcelain vase with black lacquer (cold color) inlayed with mother of pearl. Ht. 8". Metropolitan Mus of Art.

FIG. 891. Ch'ien Lung porcelain vase decorated with carved cinnabar lacquer applied cold, of course. From *Chinese Lacquer* by Ed. F. Strange. Ht. 13½".

FIG. 892. Porcelain vase in lac burgautée of green and reddish-purple on black lacquer ground. Ch'ien Lung. Ht. 12¾". From *Chinese Lacquer*.

Hsi and even Ming times, was made. This is porcelain covered with black lacquer inlayed with mother of pearl. Even in Chou times this unhappy combination of lacquer on a pottery body was employed but there was more excuse for it before glaze was developed.

The Ch'ien Lung blue and white is supposed to be far inferior to that of the K'ang Hsi reign and this is true of the ever declining export wares but in some instances there is fine drawing and good color. The blue came from the mountains of Chekiang now. Much of it has a reddish tinge and

FIG. 893. One of a pair of beautiful tile panels measuring 33″ by 14″ and painted in famille rose enamels. Ch'ien Lung or later. Ex Warren E. Cox Coll.

FIG. 894. Pilgrim bottle of heavy porcelain with greenish glaze and deep blue underglaze decoration in the feeling of Chêng Tê examples. Ht. 9⅜″. Warren E. Cox Coll.

FIG. 895. "Celadon" with underglaze red and blue design of pomegranates and "hands of Buddha." The glaze is glossy but rich, the ware is white but the foot rim, which is rounded, is dressed with brown. Ht. 6¾″. Ch'ien Lung period. Ex Warren E. Cox Coll.

all of it is softer looking than the earlier sort. Large services were made with identical designs on many pieces. When the blue was not covered with the glaze it fired black and we see specimens from time to time of this mat ware with dry black, whether intended as finished or not we do not know.

The soft paste was made in large quantities and had a better general quality probably because of the cost of the material. One sort had very definite brush strokes and was called "onion sprout ware."

Underglaze red with the combinations of celadon, etc., were carried on from the Yung Chêng reign. The only way to distinguish the one from the other is by general feel and style.

The *T'ao shuo* says in reference to the designs on enameled wares that, "out of every ten designs you will get four of foreign colors, three taken from

Left to Right: Ewer of fine white porcelain having a glossy glaze and "mille fleur" medallions in a slightly reddish blue. Ht. 10¼". Ch'ien Lung. Metropolitan Mus. of Art.

Ch'ien Lung porcelain vase with pale celadon glaze and decoration in dull blue with raised white edges similar to some of the Ming "Three color" jars in technique. Ht. 15". T. C. Lee—Warren E. Cox Coll.

Soft paste vase of the Ch'ien Lung period showing a soft "orange-peel" type glaze and slightly more reddish blue color. Ht. 15". Metropolitan Mus. of Art.

Ch'ien Lung blue and white porcelain vase with soft rich glaze and deep color. Ht. 16". Metropolitan Mus. of Art.

CH'IEN LUNG UNDERGLAZE BLUE DECORATION

PLATE 168

nature, two copies of antiques and one from silk brocade or embroidery." The nature subjects were landscapes, flowering plants, birds and trees, "mille fleurs" or thousand flowers, the "hundred deer," the "hundred birds" and combinations of pines and willows, etc. The brocade patterns use many borders as in earlier times.

The European influence is seen on every hand and the use of careful shading to produce a round or three dimensional effect is frequent.

One rather pleasant texture is obtained in incising the surface of the ground all over with feathery scrolls, etc., and covering them with enamel colors such as turquoise, pink, yellow, green, lavender or grey. Some of these are monochromes and some have reserved medallions unincised and uncolored in which paintings are made of flowers, etc. "Peking bowls" were made at Ching-tê Chêng like the others and sent to Peking to the palace or for sale. These were continued in subsequent reigns and the best of them are of Tao Kuang times (1821–1850).

Fig. 897. "Mille-fleurs vase" of the Ch'ien Lung period with reserve medallions in famille rose enamels. Ht. 31". Metropolitan Mus. of Art.
Fig. 898. The character Fu means bat and also happiness. This Ch'ien Lung gourd vase has "a thousand bats" in iron red against a gold ground while the scarf tied about it is in yellow and blue enamel. The seal mark is in overglaze blue. Ht. 8½". Warren E. Cox Coll.
Fig. 899. Famille rose type Ch'ien Lung vase with rose enamel and gilding. Ht. about 16".
Fig. 900. Famille rose Ch'ien Lung vase with well styled design more dynamic than usual in this period. Ht. 17⅜". Fuller Coll. Seattle Art Mus.

Left: Octagonal porcelain dish with greenish white ground, deep rose flowers, deep blue enamel, brown, gold and white enamel, etc. Ht. 14". Metropolitan Mus. of Art.

Right: Armorial plate with the arms of Antoni van Leeuwenhock. Dia. 8". Metropolitan Mus. of Art.

Left: Ch'ien Lung plate commemorating the signing of peace at Aix la Chapelle (1748), in iron red and gold,—a little pale pink, green blue, etc. The patterns afforded by the book shelves, pictures and the hats hung on the walls have amusingly been taken account of. Dia. 8". Metropolitan Mus. of Art.

Right: Marriage plate with arms of two Dortrecht families, Beaumont and Backus and a design from the title page of an 18th cent. wedding song in black with flesh tones and a gold border. Dia. 8". Metropolitan Mus. of Art.

Plate with reticulated rim and decoration in pale famille rose colors. Ch'ien Lung period. Dia. 10½". Metropolitan Mus. of Art.

Portrait plate in famille rose colors of Antoni van Leeuwenhock, the Dutch microscopist. Dia. 8". Metropolitan Mus. of Art.

CH'IEN LUNG PLATES

PLATE 169

Another type is covered with a faintly greenish white which appears shrivelled and chilled and slightly lustrous.

Instead of incising under the iron red color similar designs of scrolls or foliage are painted in gold on top of it, and the same technique was used for a black ground, bronze-green and celadons. Gold also replaced brown on the edges of plates. "Foreign black" was applied like an enamel in famille rose design and also as a ground color with enameled scrolls in it looking like a sort of inlay. The old famille verte black was used in a special way in which a close floral scrollwork is reserved in white on the black ground and the whole covered with a transparent green.

"KU-YÜEH PORCELAIN"

At Peking were Imperial glass factories under the supervision of an artist whose name was Hu. As the component parts of the character Hu, if separated, read ku yüeh meaning ancient moon, naturally enough Hu adopted the studio name of Ku Yüeh Hsüan meaning Ancient Moon Pavilion. This glass was made in the Yung Chêng as well as the Ch'ien Lung reigns and the Emperor once expressed his admiration for the painting in enamels on it and wished that the same effect could be produced upon porcelain, whereupon T'ang Ying set out to make porcelain that looked like the glass and also did his best to copy the Ku-yüeh style of decoration consisting of floral designs and landscapes with figures, at times in foreign taste, very delicately painted and with an unusual amount of light and shade while being at the same time in the softest of colors. The glass was translucent and the porcelain gave a semblance of the material in its milky texture and glassy finish. The porcelain was known as "fang ku yüeh hsüan" or "imitation of Ku-yüeh-hsüan" and was greatly prized. Bushell ("Chinese Art" vol. ii, fig. 74.) shows a yellow glazed snuff bottle with the actual mark "Ku yueh hsuan chih." The glass itself is rare and Hobson refers to one example in the Hippisley Collection and another in the Ezekial Collection which is described as typical. The designs are, to quote him, "Landscapes with dark brown rocks, flowering plants exquisitely drawn and coloured to Nature, and white robed figures," which he goes on to say should be characteristic of the porcelain. He shows what he is sure is a real example ("Later Ceramic Wares of China," Fig. 1 Pl. 26) and which has a stanza of verse on it with seals of the artist and under the foot the mark of Ch'ien Lung period in mauve enamel. This is a small bottle 3⅗" high with a flowering begonia, iris and hovering insect well painted on it. Actually the modeling which we are led to believe characteristic in strong light and shade is entirely missing. Perhaps this piece in the Sir Percival David Collection is actually the ware and perhaps not. Certainly the other pieces that are shown in the same book are very distant cousins.

At the Boston Museum of Fine Arts there is a vase about 9" tall which is thought to be at least of the style but probably not one of T'ang Ying's actual pieces. Yamanaka & Co. sold one reportedly to Mrs. Christian R. Holmes for some $60,000 and were offering it recently for $25,000. This example certainly has the modeling in light and shade and the greatest delicacy of painting and it is probably entirely correct so far as I can see. On the

KU-YÜEH PORCELAIN

PLATE 170

Possibly a real "Ku-yüeh Hsüan" porcelain reportedly sold to the late Mrs. C. R. Homes for $60,000 and now offered by Yamanaka & Co. for $25,000. Note the modeling of the faces and delicate flower painting. Also the poem supposedly a characteristic. Ht. 6". Yamanaka & Co.

other hand the style carried on into the 19th century and perfectly modern copies are made today which sell for only a few dollars. The meticulous skill in detail of painting is not wanting either even on these modern examples though they are likely to show some carelessness in such details as the even spacing of the borders, if examined carefully. Certain of these modern pieces

FIG. 901. Bottle (tan p'ing) said to be in Ku Yüeh style. Poem reads, "With morning light the lovely moon has gone: But every year we know that spring comes on." Usual square Ch'ien Lung four character mark appears on bottom in pale blue enamel. Ht. 5½". Sir Percival David Coll.

FIG. 902. Vase of the "Ku-yüeh-hsüan type," but certainly not a real one. Note careful shading of flowers, the poem on shoulder and very white, soft looking ground. Ht. c. 9". Mus. of Fine Arts, Boston.

were sold quite unsuspectingly by reputable dealers when they first appeared on the market and others have been sold with intent to deceive.

This was not the only departure from the standard porcelain for there were others and we also find such combinations as the Ku-yüeh painting on ordinary porcelain or on a peculiarly ivory white ware of fine quality. The glassy porcelain also occurs with delicate underglaze blue decoration and that very delicate sort which is first incised and then rubbed with a little blue so that only a faint tracery is perceived under the glaze. Other wares are seen in the snuff bottles which came into use during the 18th century and some of these were probably not made at Ching-tê Chêng at all.

CARVED AND MODELED WARES

Modeled figures or partly modeled and partly molded figures decorated with famille rose enamels are fairly common. Carving and reticulation were carried to a technical extreme and there are vases hung on porcelain chains, with freely moving belts or necks made so that they can turn and yet cannot be removed from the body. One of the most amazing I have seen consisted of three vases in a stand made to embrace them and yet allow free turning. The bases which were hidden in the bottom of the stand had been made like cogwheels which engaged so that when one vase was turned the others also moved. How this was fired it would be difficult to conceive for there was no

Tea pot heavily potted, of glossy white with relief flowers in iron red, gold and famille rose. 6" long. Metropolitan Mus. of Art.

Lantern of white porcelain with famille rose decoration. Ht. 14". Metropolitan Mus. of Art.

Ch'ing-tê Chên porcelaneous vase with brown glaze molded meticulously after ancient shape of Shang bronze "ku." 18th cent. Ht. 9¾". Mus. of Fine Arts, Boston.

Ch'ien Lung bottle with tea-dust glaze and plums modeled in round and colored, pink, white, green and turquoise. Ht. 8¾". Fuller Coll. Seattle Art Mus.

Porcelain box and cover in famille rose decoration. Length 8".

Left to Right: Boy with mille-fleurs decoration on his robe, in famille rose of light int. Ht. 14". Metropolitan Mus. of Art.

Pair of famille rose birds. Ht. c. 10". C. T. Loo & Co.

Reticulated vase with solid container inside decorated in famille rose colors of white, blue, yellow, rose, green, etc., enamels. Ht. 10½". Ex Avery Coll. Metropolitan Mus. of Art.

CH'IEN LUNG CARVED AND MODELED WARES

PLATE 171

way of getting inside to cut the parts free after firing. Very thin and often pierced lanterns on stands were a general output but bring high prices, if finely detailed.

One of the influences of metal work in the countries of Syria and Persia was the technique known in "Gombroon ware" of the Near East and the "devil's work" of the Far East. As early as the 12th century the Western Asian countries made reticulated ware the design of which was filled in with glaze. Such spaces had to be small or the glaze would melt out of them, and in China the ware was copied and called "rice grain" or "grain de riz" in French. The Japanese call it poetically "hotaradu" or "fire-fly" ware. This was also made with the soft paste of China, and at times supplemented with underglaze blue painting. It probably did not occur there until the 18th century and is typical of Ch'ien Lung work.

"Lace-work ware" was deeply incised, closely drawn floral scrolls covered with a glaze of faint celadon green tone. The result is a sort of overdoing of the incising of the Yung Lo bowls, etc.

"Mandarin porcelain" was so named because the figures on it were supposed to be in mandarin dress and the idea was to deceive the purchaser into believing that the ware was made for Imperial use. Actually no self-respecting Chinese would tolerate such a ware in his house. It was often covered with flowers and even figures stuck on in the round and overlayed with enamels in the worst possible taste with juxtaposition of pinks and reds plus gilding,

FIG. 904. Man with large head and small hands with enamels used to decorate robe. Holes for introduction of human hair for beard are found in figures back even in Ming days. Ht. 14¾". Metropolitan Mus. of Art.

FIG. 905. Figure of a woman in usual porcelain with enamel decorations. Ht. 15¼". Metropolitan Mus. of Art.

FIG. 906. Figure of Shou-lao after K'ang Hsi style but with famille rose enamel decoration which makes it Ch'ien Lung. Ht. 14". Metropolitan Mus. of Art.

etc. It is interesting to note similarities in expression between these decadent wares and those of Canosa. It took China a long time to arrive but when she did she not only added the extraneous junk but colored it to boot.

THE 19TH CENTURY

CHIA CH'ING (1796–1820), TAO KUANG (1821–1850), HSIEN FÊNG (1851–1861), T'UNG CHIH (1862–1873), KUANG HSÜ (1875–1908)

As I have said, history now had little effect upon the very sick art of ceramics. The Manchus were soft, and revolt and discontent were everywhere. A foreign war took place between 1840 and 1842 ending in the ceding of Hongkong to the British. In 1850 a band of semi-Christian fanatics brought about the T'ai P'ing Rebellion which lasted until 1865, with the result that legations were established in Peking. Many more ports were opened to foreign trade and the whole Far East was taught the real meaning of Western Civilization in detail.

FIG. 907. "Mandarin style" vase with iron red, black and gold ground and relief flowers and figures in gold, blue, turquoise, pale green, rose and plum colored enamels. Worst taste of a well nigh tasteless period. Ht. 17". Metropolitan Mus. of Art.

CHIA CH'ING PORCELAIN (1796–1820)

In the Chia Ch'ing reign the potters tried to hold at least to Ch'ien Lung standards but were unable to do so. The wares were cruder and less well made.

TAO KUANG PORCELAIN (1821–1850)

By the Tao Kuang reign the wares show a marked degeneration. The body is chalky and coarse grained and the glaze though oily and bubbly has that muslin-like texture like the coarser Japanese wares. Peking medallion bowls are still of fairly good quality. A thin and very lustrous greenish wash was used to depict water in the landscapes. A ware with lightly incised Imperial dragons and covered with this same light greenish wash over which are enamel decorations is of this period though it has been contended that it might be earlier. It usually bears K'ang Hsi marks. Some other wares show a weak attempt to revive Yung Chêng styles and stunts.

HSIEN FÊNG (1851–1861) AND T'UNG CHIH (1862–1873)

In 1853 the T'ai P'ing Rebellion caused the burning down and wreckage of the kilns at Ching-tê Chêng and they were not rebuilt until 1864. Copies of sang de boeuf, apple green, peach bloom and famille noire wares are fairly good but not dangerous to any collector who had ever seen the real thing. Scherzer in 1882 was of the opinion that they might fool an unsuspecting collector but we have learned much since that time. He also speaks of one family named Ho which made sang de boeuf wares with coarse stoneware body and rather

Tao Kuang vase with turquoise ground and pale famille rose decoration. Ht. 12″. Metropolitan Mus. of Art.

Tao Kuang vase with underglaze blue and red on white ground and with brown biscuit bands. Ht. 6″. Metropolitan Mus. of Art.

Tao Kuang vase with underglaze blue decoration, underglaze red touches and white glaze. Dark bands are biscuit left unglazed and dressed with dark brown. Ht. 6½″. Metropolitan Mus. of Art.

Hsien Fêng pale "celadon" plate with rounded foot dressed with brown slip and four character underglaze mark not centered and poorly written as usual with such late pieces. Dia. 5″.

Left: Chia Ch'ing vase with yellow ground and iron red handles. Decoration in robin's-egg blue, and other famille rose colors of light tones. Inside is finished with blue. Ht. 12″. Metropolitan Mus. of Art.
Right: Yellow ground vase with enamel decoration from Peking, of Kuang Hsü period and mark. Ht. 13″. Ex Warren E. Cox Coll.

CHIA CH'ING, TAO KUANG, HSIEN FÊNG, AND KUANG HSÜ PORCELAIN

PLATE 172

too thick and uneven glaze and he calls this ware "kun houng" and says that no effort was made to control the glaze at the foot-rim. This may be the source of Hobson's statement but I have already gone into this and stated that even in K'ang Hsi times pieces were made with the glaze flowing over the foot-rim while later examples do also occur on which the glaze is stopped. Actually this is a generality and not an absolute rule at all. The

Jar of well modeled Chinese mandarin made in modern Shanghai factory. Courtesy of The Fan Co.

Pair of modern white porcelain figures with greyish body clay, probably made at Ching-tê Chêng. Ht. 15½". George Jensen, Inc.

Left: Mirror black vase of 19th cent., poorly made, glaze unrefined, having many raised specks in it and being roughly finished off at foot-rim. Glassy greenish white glaze faintly crackled inside. Ht. 11". Metropolitan Mus. of Art.

Right: Small "kuei kung" or "devil's work" dish with "ling lung" or pierced work in white porcelain which is more delicately handled than the best of Ming or later periods. Made in Ching-tê Chêng, 20th cent. Dia. 3⅛". Mrs. Charles William Ensign.

MODERN CHINESE PORCELAIN

PLATE 173

only way to judge between these later wares and the original ones is by that very hard to define element of quality. The later wares were made of less well refined clay, therefore the bodies are not so smooth to the touch nor the scratch of a fingernail. The potting was also less well done from start to finish. This is about all that can be said.

KUANG HSÜ AND MODERN (1875–1908)

Again the quality became steadily worse. Only recently, just before the war, some few pieces did come on the market which were of egg-shell thickness and made with incised dragon decorations and Yung Lo marks in the bottoms. At the same time certain all-over enameled decorations were applied on a similar very thin ware. They sold for fairly high prices ranging between $5 and $25 in this country, that is for modern wares, because they were well made. Also "devil's work" pieces were exceedingly well made, not in copy of the old but with original designs. Again the modeling shown in the pair of white figures illustrated and the jar in the form of a head is pleasing although the pair is so very much like two shown by a prominent dealer here, marked Ch'ien Lung and priced at $800, that they are probably direct copies.

OTHER CH'ING WARES
"INDIA CHINA," "LOWESTOFT," "JESUIT PORCELAIN," ETC.

Though lacking in any particular artistic merit some other wares have intrigued some collectors because of their historical interest. The various trading companies had made what are called "Company Porcelain" pieces. This ware in general is known as "East India Porcelain" not because it was ever made in India but because it came through the East India companies of the Dutch and English. Jacquemart thought that it came from Japan

FIG. 908. Imposing example of Canton decoration probably inspired by some Portuguese merchant for medallions show Spanish dancers. Scenes are almost monochrome being salmon buff with touches of color here and there. Ht. c. 15". The Fan Co.

FIG. 909. 19th-cent. Canton vases with carefully copied illustrations from a fairy tale book painted in western manner. Hts. c. 8". The Fan Co.

and the English characteristically, thinking it good and commendable as a product, adopted it, and their writers for some unknown reason attributed it to a little factory in Lowestoft which had never attained any distinction and never made any real "hard paste" porcelain. The ware was made in China and much of it right at Ching-tê Chêng from where it was sent to places about Canton to be decorated in the merchant's taste. Hannover thinks the ware too poor to have been made at the chief center but I think he forgets how many factories were operating there and how poor were some of the wares made by some of them during this decline. That other factories also might have made blanks is undeniable for the quality varies greatly in its poor way.

Porcelain plate decorated with enamels in so-called "Sino-Lowestoft" manner and dated 1756. Metropolitan Mus. of Art.

"Chinese-Lowestoft" plate with Crucifixion in enamel colors and gold, made at Ching-tê Chêng and possibly decorated near Canton. Dia. 8¾". (c. 1750). Metropolitan Mus. of Art.

Plates having famille rose decoration of sort known for years as "Lowestoft" but made in China, probably for the French market as the borders show that taste. Dia. c. 10". John Gibbons Coll.

"CHINESE LOWESTOFT" OF THE 18TH CENTURY

PLATE 174

The decorations may be classed as follows:
1.—Ornamental borders only, outlined in brown and with gold, or with red and gold, or again with this combination and sprays of green added.
2.—Small scattered flowers in green and red.
3.—Large scattered flowers in underglaze blue of poor quality.
4.—Chinese landscapes in same medium.
5.—Same in iron red and gold.
6.—Same with little vases of flowers in black and gold.
7.—Customers' monograms in various colors.
8.—Large pieces with scenes from some historical painting or engraving and

Fig. 910. Chinese, so-called "Lowestoft" examples. Plate is of "Jesuit" type and platter "armorial." Plate dates c. 1750 and other pieces late 18th cent. Wm. H. Plummer & Co.

frequently with some added comical Chinese interpretation. These are usually punch bowls.

The Jesuit porcelain, the decoration of which was inspired by priests living in China, is a little better in quality and some is said to have been as early as Ming but I have never seen a convincing piece of this period. Père d'Entrecolles speaks of a piece as a rarity and we are therefore led to believe it was not made at Ching-tê Chêng during this time. The subjects comprise the crucifixion and other biblical subjects in black and gold. The same sort of porcelain was made with mythological subjects and some are frankly erotic.

Armorial wares were simply the same sort of porcelain with family shields, arms, etc., the designs of which were sent over and often misinterpreted by the Chinese artists. Monkhouse mentions one service in which the names of the colors were carefully copied but with the colors changed around so that the blue was labeled red, etc. The main interest lies in the fact that these wares can be dated closely. Thus the transition colors are placed about 1720 by examples in the B.M. Again we find that between 1711 and 1720 the "Chinese Imari" style was used. Those in the Yung Chêng reign show the pencilled underglaze blue. From Ch'ien Lung times the designs are more

FIG. 911. "Lowestoft" Chinese porcelain montieth-handled jardinière of late 18th-cent. showing neo-classic influence. Philip Suval, Inc.

FIG. 912. "Sino-Lowestoft" porcelain bowl in soft enamel colors of sort possibly used to celebrate sailing of a certain ship and certainly not used on the ship itself. Dia. 10⅜". (Late 18th cent.). Metropolitan Mus. of Art.

FIG. 913. Interesting tureen and stand of Chinese late 18th-cent. "armorial ware" showing also Japanese influence and rather crude enameling which commerce imposed. Wm. H. Plummer & Co.

FIG. 914. Plate from well-known "Murhall Service," having coat of arms, crest and picture of castle. Ships to right are shown leaving for China and on left leaving China for home port, Plymouth, probably. Colors naturalistic. Made in South China near Canton, of type incorrectly known as "Lowestoft." John Gibbons Coll.

and more Europeanized until about the middle of the 18th century we find Meissen floral sprays and later the little swags of flowers such as were used on Bow and Bristol, and again the French corn flower sprays. But all this gets out of our field. It got so complicated that the terrible "willow pattern" sentimentally concocted from Chinese originals was sent back to China to copy. Such is the effrontery of merchants!

There are many curiosities such as a pair of figures painted in enamels and made to represent Louis XIV and his queen. There were imitations of Delft ware, French faïence, and other things made for sale in Turkey, Siam, India and Persia.

TÊ-HUA, FUKIEN PORCELAIN

The Ming ware from Tê-hua has already been described and we have pointed out that during K'ang Hsi times the ware became whiter perhaps influenced by the white wares of Ching-tê Chêng. During the 17th and 18th centuries much of this ware was brought to Europe from Amoy and attempts were made to copy it in St. Cloud, Mennecy, Meissen and early Bow and Chelsea wares. None of these need bother the collector from the viewpoint of being mistaken for the original.

As for definitely dating Fukien porcelain our problem is somewhat more difficult. The Ming ones are heavily potted, with glaze melting into body, have a warm slightly rosy tinted glaze and the glaze is soft and melting; not glassy at all. I have never seen a fire crack in the bottom of one of these finest specimens.

The K'ang Hsi type, which may also extend back into late Ming times, seems somewhat higher fired, has fire cracks in the inside of the bottom, is made with thinner potting (probably in an effort to get away from the difficulties of fire cracks), has a pure white body and white glaze without warmth and the modeling is still very good but somewhat more detailed. D'Entrecolles wrote that in 1712 some of the Ching-tê Chêng potters went over to Tê-hua so that they could be nearer the Amoy port but that their ventures failed. Though the pure white ware had been made before, it is likely that from this date we get the much thinner glazed and harder looking ware.

We find in the *Li t'a k'an k'ao ku ou pien,* published in 1877 the following according to the Hobson translation, probably originally by Bushell, "When the glaze is white like jade, glossy and lustrous, rich and thick, with reddish tinge, and the biscuit heavy, the ware is of first quality . . . enameled specimens are second rate." Note that this does not specifically state that all such pieces are Ming. It also seems to indicate that the poorer type that is sometimes enameled is contemporary. However, I think we can assume that the enameled technique must have originated in Ching-tê Chêng, that, just as it was used in Meissen, the enamel was applied to cover up faults and that all such pieces are probably after 1712 or in late K'ang Hsi times.

In Yung Chêng times I think the general idea of reproducing antique pieces must have been responsible for a new technique which consisted of making the bodies somewhat heavier again but not so heavy as the Ming ones, allowing the body to stay white but covering it with a more glassy and warm colored glaze full of minute bubbles. Such a ware ran through Ch'ien Lung's reign and probably also later but sometime toward the end of the 18th century a reversion to the white ware in a cheaper and more pasty form was under way. The figures in the Yung Chêng and Ch'ien Lung glaze, which

Fine small white porcelain figures with cream glaze more glassy, filled with bubbles and less closely tied with body than in Ming ones. Ht. 5″. Warren E. Cox Coll.

Figure of Pu-tai a Buddhist priest of the Five Dynasties said to be an incarnation of Mi-lo-fu. Hands were made separately and stuck in by the glaze. Glaze is glassy and full of minute bubbles. 7″. Metropolitan Mus. of Art.

Right: 18th-cent. figure of slightly greenish white. Foot c. 3/16″ thick and evenly glazed inside. Ht. 7½″. Metropolitan Mus. of Art.

CH'IEN LUNG, TÊ-HUA, FUKIEN PROVINCE FIGURES

PLATE 175

Left: Vase with delicately incised design of conventional petals above and below globular part. Into incising has been rubbed light blue under glaze. Has impressed Ch'ien Lung mark. Ht. 8". Warren E. Cox Coll.

Ornament consisting of pierced oval dish on which is modeled a fish. Biscuit pure white and glaze cream with warm colored crackle and high gloss, an exceedingly delicate and refined example, length 8". From T. C. Lee–Warren E. Cox Coll.

A fine example of *"blanc de chine"* obviously derived from bronze form but much added to by ornate low relief design which may have been carved direct and not simply cast in mold. Ht. 14½". Altman Coll. Metropolitan Mus. of Art.

18th-cent. vase with moulded design. Ht. 9". Metropolitan Mus. of Art.

Vase moulded with relief design, form being inspired by bronze model. Ht. 9". Bequest of Mrs. H. O. Havemeyer. Metropolitan Mus. of Art.

CH'IEN LUNG "BLANC DE CHINE" WARES MADE BY CHING-TÊ CHÊNG POTTERS

PLATE 176

Fig. 915. Ch'ien Lung greenish white porcelain bell with incised design and the 8 triagrams around rim in pure white slip. Ht. 6". Metropolitan Mus. of Art.

Fig. 916. Fukien Tê Hua figure of Kwan Yin with child. Ch'ien Lung. Ht. 10". Warren E. Cox Coll.

Fig. 917. Kwangtung gallipot of porous buff stoneware covered with opaque oyster-white crackled glaze showing pale green spots. Type still called "Ming" by trade though they date more often as late as Ch'ien Lung period (1736–1796). Ht. 11". Warren E. Cox Coll.

cannot be distinguished one from the other, are all sweeter and more effeminate in feeling.

Modern examples appear either cold, dead white or very glassy and sticky if of a warm color. The warm color is yellowish rather than rosy in tinge. The ware is coarse and gritty and there are almost always flaws due to careless workmanship.

The subjects of Tê-hua figures are the usual deities of both Buddhistic and Taoist faiths, lions for joss-sticks, imitations in form of rhinocerous horn cups, ewers and cups for tea and also for wine, furnishings of the writer's table, some rare European shapes (for these potters did not give in so readily to foreign trade suggestions), and finally, according to a Jesuit missionary who wrote in 1604, caricatures of Europeans particularly as the actors from Macao portrayed the Portuguese. The Chinese hated such things as, "the wearing of short garments which seemed ridiculous, praying on beads by men in the temples with swords girded on them and kneeling on one knee, their quarrels with one another and combats, women going with men in company, and the like." Hobson tells of the natives making shrines such as Buddha should have occupied and placing Europeans in them and also of placing Europeans on kylins as though they were Arhats. Some of these are real attempts at portraiture or caricature.

On some of the Kwan-yin figures and those of other deities traces can be found of gilding over a black ground or traces of an ungilded red and black lacquer. This would indicate that they were of the K'ang Hsi or later times, of course.

Once in a while others turn up with sketchy floral ornaments in green and red, done in Europe to give the impression that they were so decorated in China. While still others fell entirely to the itching brushes of the "Hausmaler" who put European decoration all over them.

Any that may have well authenticated Ming enamels on them were probably taken in the same way to Ching-tê Chêng and touched up, but actually authenticated specimens of Ming enamel I have not seen.

Marks are not of the period but of the individual artist's seal. They are usually impressed in the biscuit before glazing on the backs of the figures and later ones are often slanting. They can seldom be read. The earliest figures have no marks. A few artists are known such as Ho Chao-tsung and Lai-kuan but their work has not been so classified as to be recognizable in unsigned pieces. Ming marks are always an indication that the piece is late.

Even the latest of these figures and vessels can rival the finest modeling ever done in Europe and the only factory that can rival them at all is the Royal Copenhagen one in Denmark. It is remarkable that since about 1550 or perhaps earlier a continuous industry has existed in Tê-hua and with so little change. Only in China would this be possible.

OTHER CH'ING POTTERIES AND PORCELAINS

Although pottery and some less well known porcelain formed a large amount of the trade from every port of China, little is known about it. The English, being a tea-drinking nation, paid some attention to the Yi-hsing stonewares as did also certain potters of the continent such as Ary de Milde of Holland, Böttger of Germany, as well as Dwight, Elers, Astbury and Wedgwood of England. In order to have a framework upon which to allocate what information we have, I have prepared the following chart giving first the *province,* then the *port or ports,* then the probable *sources* and finally the *descriptions* of the wares. This includes some of the late Ming as well as the 17th and 18th century wares.

I need not go into a general criticism of what happened in China for the last three centuries. We have seen the heart and soul go out of ceramics. We have witnessed the endeavors to supplant these real qualities first by absolute perfection, secondly by an attempt to return to the antique and thirdly by a wealth of detail in the K'ang Hsi, Yung Chêng and Ch'ien Lung reigns respectively. To the small mind of the perfectionist a work of art full of human appeal and close to the soul of the artist is less beautiful than a precise and machine-made or machine-aided thing. Few great men are perfect and no perfect man was ever great. Few great works of art are perfect and no perfect work of art can ever be great.

Antique objects can never be reproduced. We study the antique things because we want to learn how men thought and we wish to benefit by the good things of the past and avoid the errors the conclusions of which are already known to be unhappy. If we learn how to work in the best ways that the old artists worked, we can turn out things of our own in those ways avoiding their mistakes. It is beginning at the wrong end, however, to do as they tried to do in the Yung Chêng reign

CHART OF CH'ING POTTERY AND PORCELAIN SOURCES

PROVINCE	PORTS	SOURCES	DESCRIPTIONS
Kwangtung	Pakhoi	Yamchow	Quoted from Maritime Customs Reports, 1892–1901, p. 422. "The ware comprises vases, incense-pots, bowls, teapots, plates, etc., or any domestic article in two shades of terra-cotta—light and dark—ornamented with appropriate figures and characters in Chinese style. . . . The glazed surface is produced by rubbing with wax and polishing with wood and pumice stone after baking." (This would seem an exceedingly primitive method for the 19th century but the unevenness of creative developments must be considered.)
Kwangtung	Canton Delta about a dozen ports	Many small factories	Buff pottery or stoneware with frequent brown and yellow and more seldom turquoise, blue and aubergine glazes with only partial covering of jars, incense burners, figures, etc., usually of grotesque feeling.
		Shekwan near Fatshan	(See Ming section for descriptions but note that most specimens are not of this early date.) Chün type, etc.
			General Canton wares characteristics are:—Hard fired stoneware. Bodies:—dark brown, buff and light greyish yellow. Glazes:—blue streaked with grey green or white over a substratum of olive brown, or green with grey and blue mottling, or brown. Seals:—*Ko Ming-hsiang* and *Ko Yüan-hsiang* placed their seals on some and probably lived in the 18th century.
			Other types are:— Bodies:—porcelaneous, white but burns dark brown where exposed. Glazes:—"Celadon" of a watery olive crackled type quite transparent and dark, thick flambé of dull surface. (This is often erroneously called Ming.)
Kwangtung	Swatow & Chaochowfu	Funkai—has beds of kaolin and other common clays.	Hobson says these wares are described as "pottery of every description, from common earthenware to finely finished articles with coloured glazes or enamels . . . including immense stoneware jars holding 100 to 150 liters." Also a coarse porcelain.—This may be one source of the jars found in the Philippines, Malay archipelago, etc.
Fukien	Amoy & Chüanchowfu	Shih-ma & Tung-an Hsien	Common porcelain dishes, bowls, etc., of much of the "archaic-looking blue and white and coloured ware." Often found in India and the Eastern archipelago.
		Tê-hua	White wares. (See "Fukien" porcelain of both *Ming* and *Ching* periods.) Also commonly known as *blanc de chine*.

CHART OF CH'ING POTTERY AND PORCELAIN SOURCES—*Continued*

PROVINCE	PORTS	SOURCES	DESCRIPTIONS
Chekiang	Ningpo	Not known	Simply reported in the Consular Reports as "china ware, fine."
Kiangsu	Nanking	Ching-tê Chêng	See main descriptions of *Ming* and *Ching* wares. This was the most important center of the Imperial Kilns.
	Shanghai	Southern Kiangsu (Kashan)	Buff pottery bowls, incense burners, etc., with opaque, finely crackled camellia-leaf green glaze.
		Yi-hsing	See description of wares of red and brown stoneware largely unglazed but sometimes imitating *Chün yao* and later sometimes enameled.
Anhwei	Wuhu	Ching-tê Chêng	See above.
Hunan	Changsha	Not known	Described as shipping "fine porcelain" down the *Yangtze* river.
Shantung	Kiaochow Weihaiwei Chefoo	Poshan decayed slate clay	Tz'u Chou type wares of various types, etc. (See Sung section.) Hobson says further, "A government factory for glazed pottery was started there at the end of the last century." It produced "vases of all shapes and dimensions, jars, flower-stands, flower-pots, etc., in two colours—a bluish grey and tea colour—perfect in form and glazing and looking like porcelain."
		Yenchowfu Tz'u Chou in Chihli	Similar to Poshan wares. See Sung section. Being so far south probably many were exported through these *Shantung* ports.
Chihli	Peking & Tiensin	Liulichu	Near Peking, exists today and makes copies of Tz'u Chou wares, etc. Also tiles with aubergine, green and brown glazes. Also vases with turquoise and aubergine iridescent glazes.
		Tz'u Chou	Stoneware of heavy but refined texture, and very fine taste, of cream color incised or decorated with brown or black painting. (See Sung section.)—These same wares are being made today.
Shansi	Those of Chihli & of Shantung	Machuang near T'ai-yüan Fu	Buff stoneware ornaments, figures and vases with moulded designs with part glazes of green turquoise and aubergine.
			This type are also made in many of the interior provinces and many are shipped from *Kwangtung* and *Fukien* ports.
Shensi	Shantung ports	Yo Chou	Imitations of Tz'u Chou wares and also greyish white with sketchy designs in blue.

Multiplication of details in art is much like the man who talks too much in life, neither are convincing.

There is much historical interest shown in the 18th century but this must not be confused with art, or human appeals. There are those who know so much about a work of art that they cannot enjoy it. Such people look at a thing and immediately pigeonhole it saying, "It is so and so and so and so," and then turn quickly away as though to say, "Now that little task is done, let us see what else I can find to tell about." This is the kind of person that knows the names of all the flowers and birds but couldn't draw or paint one to save his neck. Such people never really look at anything.

Thus we reach a time of ever increasing byways and pitfalls for those who do not keep to the center of the road of honest enjoyment. Most pitfalls catch those who do not really enjoy art but want to give the impression that they do. No advice as to how to make love is necessary to the one who sincerely loves and no advice as to how to enjoy beauty is necessary to him who enjoys it.

In our aesthetic approach which admits all human appeals and does not attempt to distill them down to an unnatural essence called ART we avoid the latter in the belief that such metaphysical distillation is bound to produce artificial results as different from the real understanding of what man calls beauty as distilled perfume is different from the original fragrance of the flower. Each well known group of pottery or porcelain has its appeal to some people or it would not have become well known, but in China through the ages we find more appeals than elsewhere; appeals to the most sophisticated of cultured taste as well as to the newly rich merchants; appeals to the poet dreamers as well as to the show off swelled heads. We have not found every appeal in China, as for instance it was in Japan that the nature loving people loved asymmetry, but in China there is rich ground into which to delve and it is for that reason that artists the world over for centuries have gone there to study.

CHINESE MARKS

As early as the Shang Yin and Chou cultures (1766?–1122? B.C.) and (1122?–249 B.C.) the Chinese cast characters in their bronzes and it is natural to expect that in the Han potteries made partly to imitate bronzes we might expect to find the same thing but this is not so, probably because the pottery vessels were not considered precious enough to warrant such inscriptions. Occasionally we see examples of Han pottery bearing marks which were in the mold and appear on the bases but these are usually to be looked upon as fraudulent and, if the object happens to be an animal or figure, though it may be perfectly correct in every other way and actually of the period, it will usually be found that the base bearing the mark has been tampered with or attached so as to look as though it had been broken off and replaced, that is, it is really new and has been cleverly made to imitate the original base in every detail but with the mark added.

Other early inscriptions are sometimes carved into the already fired pottery. One can tell this only by close examination under a glass which will disclose small bubbles in the clay cut open here and there leaving a sharp edge quite unlike the bubbles which may have reached the surface while it was being fired. The actual carved edge even of soft pottery after firing is also sharper than would be carying in the soft clay before firing. But one has to be very careful and all such early pieces are suspect to say the least.

During the Six Dynasties and T'ang times no marks were used to indi- cate the reigns and very few occur that in any way help to date a piece. How- ever some Yüeh yao had marks which Brankston used in his establishments of dates of the wares from the Chiu-yen sites. These are not reign marks but names of persons, such as that of the famous poet found on the frog, etc., and such marks as that meaning "five" on the bottom of the "Kian temmoku" vase in my collection which may be late T'ang or early Sung.

By the Sung Dynasty we rarely find actual reign marks such as that on the small Tz'u Chou type vase formerly in my collection and now in the Metropolitan Museum of Art and again on Lung ch'üan celadons and Yüeh wares. (See Sir Percival David pieces and sherd found by Plumer under those sections.) We also note the numerals 1 to 10 incised before firing on the bottoms of one type of Chün yao pieces. These are as given below:

1.—	一	i	6.—	六	liu
2.—	二	erh	7.—	七	ch'i
3.—	三	san	8.—	八	pa
4.—	四	ssǔ	9.—	九	chiu
5.—	五	wu	10.—	十	shih

These numerals refer only to the size of the vessels and in no way even prove authenticity for we learned that they were copied by imitations of the original Chün ware.

Yuan marks are also few and far between but in *The Early Ceramic Wares of China* by A. L. Hetherington there is shown on Plate 44 a heavily potted dish with hexagonal foliated sides which have warped and with three small and ill proportioned little legs. On the bottom is a felicity symbol of two fish and an inscription which is translated, "A product of the Ling Ho factory: made by Chiang Ch'i in the first year of Chih Chêng (*i.e.*, A.D. 1341), example copy number 109," in a poor underglaze red. Concerning it Mr. Hetherington gives the following arguments:

1.—Chemical analysis proves it to contain phosphate and this would indicate a pre-Manchu origin for, "this substance has not been found by Professor Collie in Manchu wares except those made at Kuangtung with which this specimen has no analogies."

2.—It is chemically similar to certain Korean and Northern Chinese wares.

3.—If it were of Ming origin why should they have used the name of a Mongol emperor and the least worthy at that? For it will be remembered that this last Yüan emperor was a pretty poor sort and not to be glorified by his own people let alone a conquering people.

4.—A Chinese emigrant to Korea would hardly have used the *nien hao* or honorific title of a bygone Mongol.

5.—It is not likely that it might be a fake by some Japanese for the piece is so roughly fired and potted and the red of so uneven and poor a color that this would not be likely. Also one would not expect a faker to use the name of so obscure a kiln and so out of the way a nien hao.

He gives various other reasons including the fact that red was highly developed by the time of the Hsüan Tê reign (1426–1435) but he neglects to point out that this was at Ching-tê Chêng and not in every obscure little factory in the country. Moreover each of his reasons has possible answers which the reader can think of himself and must weigh. Thus we are confronted with the three following possibilities:

1.—The piece is a Yüan specimen as marked.

2.—The piece is a Ming copy.

3.—The piece is an out and out modern fake.

I am inclined to agree entirely with Mr. Hetherington but I go through all this reasoning to show the reader how one should think about marks, and to make clear that they are at best one small contributing piece of evidence.

Ming Dynasty marks may be divided about as follows: 1.—Reign marks, 2.—Date marks, 3.—Hall marks (referring to the hall, study or pavilion), 4.—Potter's marks, 5.—Marks of praise or commendation and finally 6.—Marks of dedication, good wishes, etc.

Mr. A. L. Hetherington has made a very ingenious chart which is in universal use for determining the cyclical date marks. First it must be understood that the Chinese have a unit of sixty years and each year is named by two characters representing one of the *ten stems* with one of the *twelve branches*. The full explanation of the system with tables is given in W. F. Mayer's "Chinese Reader's Manual" (page 381). All we wish to be able to do is to quickly translate the cyclical dates which we may see, into our own system of dating. This can be done by means of the chart (see marks section).

"The first horizontal line of characters represent the ten stems. One of these stems will be found in combination with one of the branches in every cyclical date mark. If the eye is carried down vertically from the stem which has been detected in the inscription until it recognizes the branch character, the year can be read off at once." As an instance Mr. Hobson in "The Wares of the Ming Dynasty" shows the mark of a bowl (Pl. 15, fig. 2.) with the character 癸 (kuei) on it. This is found in the upper right hand corner, and the second character is 丑 (ch'ou) which is found in the sixth square below it indicating the 50th year.

Now the commencing of the cycles are: Beginning with the Han period 236, 176, 116, 56, A.D. 4, 64, 124, 184, 244, 304, 364, 424, 484, 544, 604, 664, 724, 784, 844, 904, 964, 1024, 1084, 1144, 1204, 1264, 1324, 1384, 1444, 1504, 1564 and 1624, etc. Therefore our cyclical years would not be of much use were it not for the fact that the title of the emperor is also given on this bowl namely Hsüan Tê (1426–1435). Taking 1324, the beginning of one cycle, and adding 50 years we find that the bowl was made in the year of 1373 which is too early. The next date would be 1384 plus 50 which equals 1433 which falls in the time of the reign and must be the right one. In some marks only the cyclical one is mentioned and we then have to guess the proper cycle by technical and stylistic means.

Only very rarely, as I have said, do the pre-Ming inscriptions include a nien hao or title name, therefore we do not need to give the individual names of the pre-Ming rulers here. Occasionally there are date marks incised in the paste or rarely in underglaze decoration.

The Ming period marks came generally into use because of the factory methods and the growing financial importance of the ceramic industry. They were stamped, incised before firing or painted, the latter being in underglaze blue as a rule though rarely in overglaze iron red or other colors. Usually they were in script and not in seal characters although the script is sometimes framed with a single or double box border. They are, of course, read from top to bottom beginning at the right and working to the left as in all Chinese writing. It is interesting to note in this connection that Sir Percival David in discussing the marks on certain Chü-chou celadons of the Yüan period told me that the Mongols read from top to bottom beginning at the left and working right and thus we may deduct that inscriptions that read around a vase to the right are Mongolian and those which read around to the left are Chinese.

The complete reign mark has six characters and these read for instance beginning with one on the upper right:

4.— 德	tê (Tê)	1.— 大	ta (great)
5.— 年	nien (title)	2.— 明	ming (Ming) (dynasty)
6.— 製	chih (made)	3.— 宣	hsüan (Hsüan)

or:—"Made in the Great Ming Hsüan Tê reign."

Sometimes the marks are reduced to four characters by eliminating the first two. At times again the last character chih is replaced by tsao but both have the same meaning. The marks also occur enclosed in a double ring and we find occasional examples having the rings alone. Much stress is laid upon the quality of the calligraphy by the Chinese and after one has seen the real examples of fine marks the difference is often perceptible even to the untrained eye between fake marks and real ones but we must hastily add that splitting hairs on this subject is bad, for excellent and undoubted pieces exist which are badly marked and some modern fakes of the worst sort have really beautiful marks.

Complete tables will be found in the *Chinese Reader's Manual* (by Mayers) but we will content ourselves with the nien hao of each of the Ming Emperors (see marks section).

Hall marks include the words "t'ang" 堂 (hall), or "chai" 齋 (study), or "t'ing" 亭 (pavilion) and they are open to a variety of meanings indicating a certain room in which there may be an inscription perhaps bearing upon some outstanding event in family history, a title, an ancestral hall, etc., and the mark may refer to the name of the studio or building of the potter or dealer who ordered the wares, etc. There are few hall marks in the Ming dynasty but one occurs fairly often in the late Ming wares of many kinds. It is "yu t'ang chia ch'i" meaning "beautiful vessel of (or for) the Jade Hall," and may be simply a complimentary statement or may have some definite reference to some certain hall. We do not know.

Sometimes the marks will definitely indicate that a piece is spurious. Such is the "Shên tê t'ang" meaning "Shên Tê Hall" which is found on pieces imitating Wan Li blue and white and enameled wares well made with radiating lines in the bases and defects in the glazes.

Potter's names rarely appear on porcelain but are found on potteries although not enough have been brought to light to determine any specific dates or locations. We have already mentioned a few and it may be noted that Ming-yüan signed with a seal while Hui Mêng-ch'ên used script at Yi-hsing.

Pleasant good wishes are sometimes expressed such as "wan fu yu t'ung," "may infinite happiness embrace all your affairs," or "ch'ang ming fu kuei," "long life, riches and honors," or some reference to well known quotations such as "tan kuei," "red cassia." The saying was "To pluck the cassia in the moon," meaning to obtain a high place in the State Examinations.

Some of the marks recurring on Chia Ching porcelain and Wan Li porcelain are given as follows, by R. L. Hobson:

1.—"Fu kuei chia ch'i"—"Fine vessel for rich and honorable."
2.—"T'ien hsia t'ai p'ing"—"Great peace throughout the Empire."
3.—"Lu wei ch'ing kao"—"Rank and emolument without corruption." This is typical of some which have a moralizing tone about them.

There are also symbols which are used for marks such as the peach and stork for longevity, the bat for happiness, the hare which helps the toad to pound the elixir of life in the moon in Taoist lore. Some of these are Ming though most of them are later.

All Ch'ing marks are placed on the bottoms underneath, except those occasional potter's, artist's or calligrapher's seals included in the decoration, none of which have as yet been identified. Unlike the Ming marks, they appear both in "k'ai shu" script and in "chuan shu" or angular seal characters and may be in enamel colors, iron red or even gilt as well as the underglaze blue. This was brought about because most of the time of making the piece was put into the decoration which was done after glazing. If the blue mark was put on first it was not sure but that the piece might turn out badly or the artist might do something not so successful or the glaze might have faults and it would be wished that the mark was not on it. Sometimes the Ch'ien Lung mark is in red on a turquoise background. They are usually all enclosed in a double ring or a square frame. Mr. Hobson points out that the enameled wares in the style of Ku Yüeh Hsüan have the marks in heavy relief enamel, usually blue, and that these wares are always of some importance. We must hastily add that such wares have the marks in lavender and the Yamanaka one is in grey enamel. Also the cheap reproductions on egg-shell porcelain carry the blue marks. All these are similar to the Ming marks and are read in the same way.

We find some more unexplained new marks during Ch'ing times such as the one which looks like a G and which seems to have a western origin as there is no Chinese character which is similar.

An exception to the above rule is the use of the names "Chieng Ming-kao" and "Ch'en Kuo-chih" which are found on biscuit porcelain of early 18th century and occasional seal signatures on Tê-hua, Yi-hsing and Fat-shan pieces.

Another curious mark found on export blue and white ware of the K'ang Hsi period represents "shou" or "longevity" written in a fanciful form which is appropriately called the spider mark.

As we have noted, there was an edict against using the Emperor's name on porcelain in the K'ang Hsi reign because of the danger that the object might be broken thus desecrating its use. Whether for this reason or not we do not know but it is likely that both the habit of marking the piece with a double ring alone, or of using a symbol such as those below was brought about. However, the Ming examples exist and the Emperor's edict was not of long standing so we cannot hold fast to this rule. The Eight Buddhist Emblems, Eight Precious Things, swastika in a lozenge, the cloud or fungus scroll, "fu," artemisia leaf, etc., are typical. Even the dragon and the lion are painted on the bottoms of snuff-bottles and small cabinet pieces. Thus many of the decorative or artistic elements were used for marks as well.

Finally this must be made clear: Do not trust marks save as *one* of many factors which must be considered in making an attribution. Learn to look first at the body clay, then the way the foot is made, then the way the glaze is applied, then what sort of glaze it is, then the crackle if there is any, then feel the weight of the piece and note its general potting, then note the decoration, its color, its way of application, etc., and then look at the mark in the way we have described above and, if *all* elements are correct, you may be fairly sure, while, if one or two are not correct, get an expert's opinion before buying. Two experts are better than one. Three are better than two. And your own eye and intelligent understanding plus experience are best of all.

CHAPTER XXI

EUROPEAN "SOFT PASTE" & PORCELAIN

WE HAVE shown how the art of *Lustre* originated in the Near East, was carried by the Arabs to Spain and thence spread to Italy where it died because it could not be used for the naturalistic painting there in vogue. We have traced *Enamel* decoration also from the ancient Near East as it spread east to China and west, as it also came back from China to the Near East in return and thence to Europe. We have seen how *Modeled* decoration after Rome increased in Europe and also in China, and how it spread north in Europe in preference to the painted or enameled wares. This was the situation at the beginning of the 18th century while at the same time the Europeans yearned to make porcelain, that great ware called "China" after the country of its origin.

Porcelain or *"China"* was a medium of great creation particularly during the Ming period in China but the technique came too late to Europe for the production of any really great works of art. The decadence of industrialism, commercialism and their attendant ills had already set in long before the technique was mastered. A quaintness here, a touch of humor there, a titillating bit of sex appeal or a pompous sort of strutting, though mere crumbs from the table of the gods have to help satisfy our everlasting hunger for beauty or appeals in any form and this is all the 18th century has to offer.

MEDICI "PORCELAIN"

One of the first, if not the very first, attempts to make porcelain in Europe was made in Venice, that great center of world trade, to which Chinese examples had been brought. This city was a glass making center as well and it was naturally thought that the translucence of porcelain was due to a content of glass. In 1470 Father Ulielmo da Bologna made a present of a small vase of "porcelain" made by the alchemist Maestro Antonio, and wrote a letter about it. The next record is of a payment in 1508 for seven bowls of "porcellana contrafacta" or imitation porcelain which shows that it was perfectly understood that they were not making real porcelain. Bernardo Buontalenti, sculptor, architect, painter and potter, under the patronage of the Grand Duke Cosimo I of the Medici, developed this imitation porcelain at the Medici factory and it was called "Medici porcelain."

Marks used on it are fairly well known and consist of a dome of the cathedral of Florence under which there is an F which may stand for either "Firenze" or "Franciscus." Another is the arms of the Medici with or without the letters "FMMDE II OR FMMED II" standing for "Franciscus Maria Medicis Magnus Dux Etruriae Secundus," on six palle or round spots. Only

three dated specimens are known: The earliest a square flask having on the front the arms of Philip II with the chain of the Golden Fleece, flanked by ribbons on each of which is "1581." This piece is at Sèvres. An undated similar piece is also there. Another dated piece is a medallion of white porcelaneous ware with the portrait of the Grand Duke Francesco in low relief surrounded by the inscription "Franc. Med. Mag. Dux Etruriae II 1586." The making of the ware continued through the reigns of Ferdinando I and Cosimo II although sometime during the latter's time the kiln was moved to Pisa.

The body of this ware is translucent but lighter in weight than porcelain and the glaze is imperfect. From a manuscript found in the Magliabechian Library in Florence we find that it is composed of 24 parts sand, 16 of glass, 10 parts of powdered rock crystal, 8 parts of soda and 12 parts of the white earth of Faenza, to which was added in the proportion of 12 parts to 3 of the kaolinic clay of Vincenza. The piece was covered with a lead glaze containing tin. Most of the pieces are coated and then decorated with blue or blue and manganese, though the jug in the Adolphe de Rothschild Col. is polychrome. Designs are of simple symmetrical sprays of flowers or at times asymmetrical arrangements. At times grotesques were used. Some show distinct influence of middle Ming wares. Some have relief decoration and the one in the Spitzer Col. is composed of two baroque masks above which are three spouts. The

FIG. 918. Dish of "Medici porcelain," actually soft paste, of course, decorated with grotesques and depicting Death of King Saul. Mark shown below, but letters on the palle do not show very well (See text). Metropolitan Mus. of Art.

shapes are what Hannover calls, "Venetian Oriental" and include double flasks, square bottles, pilgrim bottles, while dishes have flat rims parallel to the flat bottoms. Less than 40 pieces are known all told. Naturally forgeries are plentiful. Also they resemble some of the worst of the Chinese wares. One museum in Germany had a Chinese dish not only labeled Medici ware but also published it in color.

FRENCH SOFT-PASTE

At Rouen, famous for its pottery for some time, was discovered a material similar to Medici ware but made about 100 years later. A privilege was granted Edme and Louis Poterat in 1673. A few odd pieces of blue and

Ewer (Brocca) with blue on white ground of "Medici porcelain" with mark of a dome in blue, F in black, and mitre and sword in black. Ht. 8″. Gift of J. Pierpont Morgan. Metropolitan Mus. of Art.

"MEDICI PORCELAIN" EWER (BROCCA), VENICE

PLATE 177

white ware of very poor quality and opaque consistency are marked AP but how this stands for either Edme or Louis we do not know.

At St. Cloud, we are told by Dr. Martin Lister, a soft ware was made by Pierre Chicaneau in 1677 and by 1698 a factory was well under way. When Pierre died his widow married Henri Trou and he and his son bettered the factory. Marks are first *St.C.*, which is rare, then in 1696 the mark was a

FIG. 919. Saucer in style of and possibly from Poterat kiln, Rouen, which Hannover places c. 1675. Museum simply calls it "St. Cloud (1712–1760)." Metropolitan Mus. of Art.

FIG. 920. Soft paste vase made at Rouen (1673–1687) resembling Medici ware but much later, of course. Ht. 17½". Metropolitan Mus. of Art.

sun alluding to *"Le Roi Soleil"* and in either 1712, 1722 or 1724 (depending upon which authority you believe) it was again changed to SC with a cross above and a T below. The first marks are in underglaze blue and the last in blue, red or incised. The factory failed in about 1766.

The objects made were small and often decorated with enamels. Some large pieces are in turquoise pale celadon and warm white or yellowish white. All are highly translucent and always greenish by transmitted light rather than amber tinged as are the Fukien wares which they resemble in general appearance. In decoration there was some influence by Berain and Rouen faïence but chiefly it was Chinese. An underglaze blue at times harsh and again greyed was used plus turquoise, iron red, yellow and gold leaf afterwards fired.

Not much faking of this ware was done but Samson has made some copies and Hannover tells of 19th century Tournai plates decorated in blue and gold and marked falsely with the STC in muffle colors. Also some wares from the Rue de la Ville-l'Eveque (Faubourg St. Honoré, Paris) and some from Lille and Chantilly are similar.

The Lille factory was founded by Barthélemy Dorez and his nephew Pierre Pelissier for the making of both faïence and porcelaneous ware, about 1716 but they copied the St. Cloud things and only a few are definitely established by an L above a cross while there are some doubtful examples marked BF perhaps meaning Barthélemy-François.

Chantilly had a factory in 1725 founded by Louis-Henri de Bourbon, Duc de Condé, under the management of Sicaire Cirou. The first ware was pure white because of tin in the glaze but later a lead glaze was used and a warm

Left: St. Cloud cachepot of relief soft paste seeming more opaque than usual. Ht. 7¼". Metropolitan Mus. of Art.
Center: Cup of St. Cloud with underglaze blue decoration and relief ribbing. Ht. 3" Metropolitan Mus. of Art.
Right: Cachepot from Chantilly factory decorated in natural colors. 18th cent. Ht. 7⅞". Metropolitan Mus. of Art.

Left: Mennecy-Villeroy snuff-box with delicate polychrome decoration on yellowish body similar to that of St. Cloud but not so pure. Early 18th cent. Length 2¾".
Center: Chantilly cup and saucer in polychrome decoration which is cross between Kakiemon and naturalistic styles. 18th cent. Dia. 4¾".
Right: Chantilly cup and cover with enamel decorated relief floral sprays. 18th cent. Ht. 3½". Metropolitan Mus. of Art.

FRENCH 18th CENTURY "SOFT PASTE"

Plate 178

18th cent. cane handle possibly from St. Cloud, decorated with enamel blue and yellow-orange vases with orange flowers. Length 5¼″. Metropolitan Mus. of Art.

Right: Cane handle possibly St. Cloud. Decorated in enamel colors with red and green dominating. Early 18th cent. Length 3″. Metropolitan Mus. of Art.

Bowl with cover and tray in dirty white, pitted glaze (1700–1750). Dia. of tray 7⅞″. Metropolitan Mus. of Art.

St. Cloud (1712–62) cup and saucer moulded in design probably of Japanese origin. Dia. 4¾″. Metropolitan Mus. of Art.

Cups called "French 18th cent." but typical of relief scale pattern of St. Cloud and probably made there. Ht. 2¾″. Metropolitan Mus. of Art.

Small patch boxes made at St. Cloud in early 18th cent., one of Chinese god of plenty and other a lamb. About 3″ long. Walter Blumenthal.

ST. CLOUD "SOFT PASTE"

PLATE 179

toned translucent body obtained. Some designs were from Kakiemon. There is a theory that the change in glaze took place because of the competition with Mennecy and Vincennes and, providing this is true, the white ware would date from 1725 to about 1735 or 1740, and the warm ware would date from this time to the close of the factory in 1789 due to the French Revolution. The designs also changed from the Kakiemon type to other oriental

Left: Jars dating c. 1730–40 decorated with bright enamels in Kakiemon style. Ht. 5⅝″. Metropolitan Mus. of Art.
Right: Basket work rimmed plate with flower decoration in natural colors. Type may have been inspiration of "Flora Danica service" of Copenhagen factory later.

Blue and white plate, with typical basket work rim. Metropolitan Mus. of Art.

Cup and saucer decorated in slightly blurred underglaze blue. (1725–1773). Dia. 4½″.

CHANTILLY "SOFT PASTE"

Plate 180

patterns and "Indian Flowers," which were really Chinese in character but thought to be Indian because the India Companies brought wares so decorated. This was a simple following of the trend of Meissen toward more and more naturalistic flowers, birds, insects, etc. Toward the end copies were made of the Sèvres wares with colored grounds and flowers were made for the ornamentation of clocks, wall sconces, etc. Very rarely figures of birds and humans were made.

The underglaze blue is softer than that of St. Cloud but was not very popular. Rare but not very valuable plates have flowers which look something like comets (see illustration). Green "camaïeu" painting was done also over the glaze.

By 1780 Sèvres had completely overshadowed Chantilly and the latter declined to poor potting and painting. After the revolution an Englishman named Potter tried to revive the work and there were half a dozen other attempts but they all failed. Samson has made some close copies but otherwise there was little imitation and less stealing of the marks, which were a hunting horn sometimes later obliterated and changed to the monograms of the Kings of France.

Mennecy-Villeroy had a factory started by François Barbin of the Rue de Charonne, Paris, where wares were made which are unknown today. In 1748 he moved to Mennecy under the patronage of Louis-François de Neufville, Sieur de Villeroy. Between 1753 and 1762 Barbin took his son into partnership. After the elder Barbin's retirement Joseph Jullieh and Symphorien Jacques managed, but later in 1773 they went to the factory at Bourg-la-Reine which was patronized by the Comte d'Eu.

Fig. 921. "Mennecy-Villeroy" jar and cover. Metropolitan Mus. of Art.
Fig. 922. Soft paste, Mennecy, 18th-cent. jars probably copied from Fukien, Tê-hua examples. Strangely enough such copies bring many times prices of far superior Chinese originals. Ht. 6¼″. Metropolitan Mus. of Art.
Fig. 923. Mennecy pot-pourri of white glazed ware. Late 18th cent. Metropolitan Mus. of Art.

Most of the work of these places imitates that of Vincennes and Sèvres or that of St. Cloud despite the fact that the paste is yellowish and soapy looking and quite different from that of either. Here we see that even in the early days of the 18th century creative spirit had become so atrophied that factory copied factory and there was no slightest respect for the rights of personal design or desire to cultivate it. One small bright idea was dragged from place to place until it was worn to pieces.

Distinguishing characteristics of Mennecy-Villeroy wares are a purple-red frequently employed in shell borders and the thick enamel-like application of the colors, blue, green, red and yellow, particularly the red. The usual small articles were made including knife handles, walking stick knobs, boxes, cups, etc. Grotesque figures comprised most of the large articles.

In 1751 biscuit porcelain was made at Vincennes and promptly copied at Mennecy in the form of portrait medallions and busts, but the ware never approached the whiteness and softness of Sèvres.

Long after Böttger had made real hard porcelain and its secret had been stolen by other German-speaking centers the French continued to make soft paste although it is much less serviceable. It chips easily, is likely to crack in hot water and was difficult to handle in the kiln because it was inclined to wilt and become uneven. Perhaps the color did appeal, for it is less cold than hard paste, but there was certainly no reason to build an aura of false values about it. I suspect that the clever French shopkeepers had to do with this much as they have sold the Americans and English more recently on the great values of their post impressionist paintings. In any event many collectors pay high prices for these inferior wares from Europe while some, like Hobson, criticize the Americans for paying high prices for the actually superior soft paste wares of China.

German Soft Paste

In Berlin two brothers named Schackert applied to Frederick the Great for the right to set up a factory at Basdorff. They were only glass cutters and knew nothing about the work. We know of only two pieces although this was 1751. One is a jug in Hamburg and the other a piece in Berlin but they are nothing but milky glass.

Also in 1751 Wilhelm Kaspar Wegely was given permission to open in Berlin and encouraged by a free site and exemption from customs duties on materials. A certain unprincipled Herr Benckengraff aided him with men and materials from the Höchst factory. Then in 1756 the "Seven Years War" brought Frederick to Meissen and Wegely thought he would surely benefit but the monarch was so impressed by what he found there that he promptly sold out Wegely's place and put his army contractor Schimmelmann in charge. This gentleman soon entered the Danish service while Wegely, broken hearted and now deprived of his royal patronage, closed up in 1757.

The ware he made was neither a true soft paste nor like that of Meissen, being more chalky and less transparent, for it contained less felspar and quartz, but of course all of these wares both in France and Germany differed one from another. Many of Wegely's wares were undecorated and when they were, the colors were inclined to chip off. Even cold lacquer colors were used. One stunt was to apply flowers, birds and boys to a base with white ground, in the round, and then to color them. There were also uncolored figures, strongly colored ones, services with Watteau scenes and polychrome flower decorations in which purple dominated. These were copied from Höchst. The underglaze blue was poor but the gilding of good quality.

The mark was an underglaze blue, incised or impressed W made in four strokes to which were added numerals which were probably factory marks to indicate certain formulas, etc. By making the outside strokes of the W short, a nice similarity to the crossed swords of Meissen was obtained.

As the other German factories were true hard-porcelain manufacturers, we will come to them after the description of the discovery of porcelain by Böttger. In Thuringia, however, there were several other primitive attempts.

THURINGIAN WARES

Due to the natural resources, wood for fuel and other materials, the "Waldfabriken" or "forest factories" of Thuringerwald came into being to supply the local people. There were a few "arcanists" who were alchemists claiming to know the secrets of porcelain manufacture. But also books such as "Die Kunst das ächte Porzellain zu verfertigen" by Franz Joseph Weber, 1798, told "The art of making true porcelain" for all to read.

FIG. 924. Hard paste Volkstedt tea-caddy decorated in enamel colors and gilt (c. 1770). Metropolitan Mus. of Art.

The wares, at first very crude and uneven in color, became better as the designs became worse, due to growing commercial progress. The figures are often amusing and avoid the rococo pretentiousness of the big factories.

Volkstedt, southwest of Leipzig and Dresden and near Rudolstadt, was founded by a theologian, George Heinrich Macheleid. "Soft porcelain" was first made and in 1760 when experiments had succeeded with hard porcelain, permission was given to establish a factory by the Prince of Schwartzburg-Rudolstadt. In 1767 this privilege was transferred to Christian Nonne who managed for 33 years. The factory still exists so far as we know.

The marks were first two pitchforks which luckily could be drawn quite similar to the crossed swords of Meissen and in 1787 the Elector of Saxony complained so that a single pitchfork was used. In 1799 the factory was sold to W. Greiner and C. Holzapfel and the mark was changed to R standing for Rudolstadt. In the eighteen nineties the factory was split into three firms: Eckert & Cie., Karl Ens and Alteste Volkstedter Porzellan Fabrik, the last of which made a reputation for the making of fine fakes and forgeries.

The "soft porcelain" comprises chiefly small handleless cups decorated in the style of famille rose of China. The hard porcelain is slightly transparent, cold, grey and has a spotted glaze often covered for this reason with flowers, landscapes and figures. Much rococo twisting and writhing was also resorted to. The specialty of the factory was small painted or modeled portraits with fixed rococo frames and genre subjects and landscapes of the Dutch style along with maps of an ornamental character. This idea was at least more consistent than the painting of pictures on cases and pots although the results were hardly impressive art.

Kloster Veilsdorf, northeast of Frankfort, unlike the other places of the district, came into being at the desire of a prince, Friedrich Wilhelm Eugen of Hildburghausen, who hired the arcanist Johann Hermann Meyer in about 1765 or a little earlier and it turned out better wares at the then usual penalty of running always at a loss.

The most characteristic decoration was of large freely painted flowers on thread-like stems in a predominant reddish-violet, a purple and yel-

Fig. 925. Kloster Veilsdorf, German cup and saucer of 1762–1770. Metropolitan Mus. of Art.

low, an iron red and two coppery greens. They also occur in purple only. Other designs are Boucher children painted in yellow, flowered trellises, green borders with a guarry-pattern in violet and edged with small rococo scrolls, chinoiseries after Herold of Meissen, figure subjects after Watteau and Teniers, etc. The shapes are fairly simple, going into neo-classic urns toward the end of the century with the French influence. The figures are not marked and are easily confused with those of Fulda but of no great excellence. One "Venus" in the Thüringer museum at Eisnach shows a fairly firm teat, an attractive umbilicus on a rounded paunch and nice legs not too much draped and seemingly inclined to spread. Of this our good Hannover says, "a seated Venus (?) with outstretched hand," (I hadn't even noticed that she had a hand!) "somewhat remarkable for its breadth and boldness of style." I go into detail because I want to bring out the fact that these factories all over Europe did not in this time lose the opportunity to include sex appeal for which there was an admitted desire so long as it was paraded under the name of "classic art." Other figures included a "Venus lying down with Cupid," a "Cupid having enchained two women," and a walking stick handle of a "charming female half figure." Of course the usual figures of the Italian comedies, many gods and goddesses and genre groups were made.

The mark was CV or C or V written separately and the V elongated could also luckily be made to look like the Meissen swords. Sometimes the latter were simply forged. Hannover says, "In 1782 for instance a whole case of porcelain from this factory was confiscated at the New Year fair at Leipzig, on the ground that its contents bore the mark of the electoral crossed swords."

At Gotha, northeast of Frankfort and north of Kloster Veilsdorf, was opened a small factory by Wilhelm Theodor von Rothberg in 1757 probably under court protection. Christian Schultz, Johann Georg Gabel and Johann Adam Brehm, three important artists were hired and the factory was taken over by them in 1782. In 1803 it was owned by Prince Augustus of Gotha and later sold to Gebrüder Simson. Schultz was a flower painter, Brehm was both a painter and modeler and Gabel was a pupil of the older Tischbein. At one time 38 artists were hired and even in 1803 there were 13 still at work.

As a result of this ownership the wares were as excellent as could be expected for this time and place. They were the best decorated in Thuringia. The first ware had a brownish or greyish glaze like earthenware but this was soon improved to a light, translucent paste with a creamy-yellowish glaze. The earliest wares are strongly rococo but changed to the prevailing Louis XVI style. Figures were sometimes painted in natural colors and sometimes were monochrome in blue, red or yellow. A specialty was the painting of flowers in gold or in gold and silver. In 1790 the pastoral scenes were changed to landscapes with very romantic nay almost heartbreaking ruins painted in iron red, or in brown over brown and in grisaille. There were also antique heads in the same treatments and with gold frames. At length Greek red figure vases were copied after the book by Hamilton. A marble-like biscuit was developed for figures and busts of which Hannover says, "It copied models from elsewhere with the ingenuousness of the period."

The first mark was R in underglaze blue or rarely impressed, standing for Rothberg, the founder, and of course not unlike that for Rudolstadt of Volkstedt. About 1790 it changed to R.g. or R-G. In 1805 it was changed to *GOTHA* or G and the Gotha was always in italics and in black and iron red, while the G is in underglaze blue, black, iron red or yellow. Wares with a hen on a mound with the word Gotha and the mark Porzellan Manufaktur Gotha are 19th century or later.

Wallendorf, the estate in Coburg-Sallfeld, southeast of Gotha, had a factory opened by Johann Wolfgang Hammann who with the help of some arcanists had made porcelain at Katshütte. He was joined by his two cousins Johann Gottfried Greiner and Gotthelf Greiner sometimes called the father of Thuringer potters.

The ware was light and translucent but always greyish or yellowish and the blue was blackish while the other colors were dull. The specialty was in blue, brown or black glazes with reserved medallions in polychrome. The same stages of rococo, then chinoiseries (which were carried into the 19th century in blue and white), then polychrome flowers and birds and then in the 1780's painting in purple and in the 1790's in dark brown, grey and black of landscapes with ruins, were followed Pipe bowls were a specialty and "Turkish cups" without handles were copied from Meissen. The figures were clumsy and uninspired.

The W could, of course, again be made to resemble the crossed swords and the matter was protested from Saxony. Truly we are sinking lower and lower as the weight of the pennies grows greater and greater and the story takes on the aspects of a Greek tragedy. So low into the mire of indecency had porcelain sunk that it could never shake off the weight of deception and fraud to take wing and soar to the heights of stirring beauty. There can be beauty in hate and bloodshed. There can be beauty of a kind in oppression and even in cruelty. But there can never be beauty in snivelling and picayune stealing and the grovelling deceit with which money had inoculated the soul of man.

Gera was founded by Johann Gottlob Ehwaldt and Johann Gottleib Gottbrecht in 1779 and was at once bought by the two Greiner brothers and Wilhelm and Johann Andreas, an assistant director at Volkstedt and for a while it was a sort of branch of that place but in 1782 gained its independence. Hannover puts it very well when he says, "In one way it was capable of everything, in another of nothing, inasmuch as its material was very poor." Wood grained ware was a specialty with what appeared to be an engraving in red nailed on it. People marveled at this wonderful achievement. Other specialties were keepsakes, loving-cups, saucers, vases, pots and pitchers with landscapes having ruins all in natural colors. The modeling was weak and consisted of copies from Meissen but one group of "Indians" in the Grassi Museum is wonderful in concept and execution. This group would probably fetch a good price on 57th Street in one of the decorators' establishments which specialize in Victorian interiors.

The G resembled the Gotha mark and that of Gotskowsky. Later Gera was used and underlined. It is usually in red. Of course it was difficult to make the G look like crossed swords but this was overcome around 1780 by marking the blue and white wares with crossed swords with or without a dot. The only way to distinguish this ware from Meissen is its very poor quality.

Gotthelf Greiner was thought to be the father of Thuringerwald porcelain because what he did not accomplish in quality he did in quantity. He started a factory at Limbach and another in the neighboring town of Grossbreitenbach. He leased the Ilmenau factory. His five sons inherited all this and added Kloster Veilsdorf. Greiner was also associated with Hammann in 1764 at Wallendorf.

Limbach made only a "useful porcelain" chiefly blue and white. The early ware is similar to that of Gotha, is slightly yellowish and not so highly glazed. By Empire times it became fine and white. To the usual landscapes were added copies of Meissen chrysanthemum design taken from the Japanese and in the Biedermeier period portraits with natural colors and much gold. In the early times the factory made interesting figures with strange proportions, either too tall or too short and with exaggerated movement. Many were genre, others were gods and goddesses and a crucifixion copied from Meissen was often repeated. The colors are pleasant on the figures and the seemingly original naïveté is attractive.

The first mark was LB or two crossed L's with a star below slightly resembling the Meissen Marcolini mark. The LB is in purple, iron-red or black and the L's in underglaze blue and occur chiefly on the blue and white wares. After trouble about the marks a clover was adopted in 1797 for all the Greiner factories.

At Ilmenau, Christian Zacharias Gräbner in 1777 established a factory and after some financial difficulties absconded in 1782. The Prince of Weimar then directed it. Gräbner came back and ran away again and then in 1784 Franz Josef Weber was put in charge until 1786 when Gotthelf Greiner leased the place. He later turned it over to Nonne and Roesch who ran it until 1871 when it was taken over by a limited company.

The mark was a small "i" in underglaze blue and only a few pieces are known, and those are of poor quality. In the Empire and Biedermeier periods it was better but had a light tint of green or blue. The factory is chiefly known by imitations of the Wedgwood "jasper ware," of poor quality and uneven blue grounds. This same ware was also made with a suggestion of a glaze. The frames of pictures were always white and glossy. The usual subjects were treated and the "Venus Kallipygos" is also, as Hannover says, "rather broadly treated."

On the back of some of these picture panels is the name Sneff in italics incised. Greiner used two crossed Roman I's for the obvious reason until forced to use the cloverleaf. N & R stood for Nonne and Roesch.

Grossbreitenbach was established by Kammerjunker Major Anton Friederich Wilhelm Ernst von Hopfgarten in 1777–1779 and sold in 1782 to Greiner, and its wares, though of the blue and white type, cannot be distinguished from those of Limbach which had the same mark. This place is just east of Ilmenau, south of Leipzig.

Rauenstein was started by no less than three Greiners and all not related to Gotthelf so far as we know. It began in 1783. Their names were Johann, Johann Friederich and Christian Daniel Sigmund. About all that is known for certain is that in 1787 it produced a common blue and white ware and about 1800 there were some 120 workmen including polychrome painters employed. The wares were even poorer copies of the other factories than theirs were of Meissen, and the figures without any interest.

The mark should be known to be avoided and is an R with or without a star below it in underglaze blue or overglaze red. It is like the Gotha R for Rotberg but smaller. It is difficult to tell it from the R for Rudolstadt used at Volkstedt in the first part of the 19th century. There were also a pair of crossed hoes with the letters R-n. If half the inventiveness had been used in the designs of these places that they employed in faking the Meissen mark, they might have turned out something worth while.

Ansbach was founded by Margrave Charles Alexander and directed by Johann Friederich Kändler, cousin to the famous Kändler at Meissen, in 1758. The specialty was gods and goddesses with big noses, comedians with half closed and seemingly swollen eyes, coffee pots with female masks under the spouts and purple landscapes painted in medallions in gold decked out with ribbons.

The mark was a Prussian eagle with A under it, the arms of the town and also a fake of the Meissen mark.

Passau was founded by Nikolaus Paul from Cassel and later went to Karl Hagen and is now called Dressel Kistler & Co. It did nothing of virtue in the early days and made dangerous forgeries with marks of Ludwigsburg and Höchst, though these places were hardly beyond reproach themselves.

A kiln at Würzburg started in 1775 by Johann Caspar Geyger is thought to have made gay little plain white figures or painted ones on uniform white pedestals. The mark was a bishop's mitre.

In Mannheim in 1767 Laurentius Russinger, a former modeler from Höchst

FIG. 926. Würzburg tea and coffee service which is exceedingly rare. Note interesting use of a lattice band not unlike in feeling the so-called "Mosaik" ones of Höchst but different in detail, and also the floral festoons. A. Beckhardt Coll. c. 1775–80.

made an ordinary blue and white and a polychrome decorated ware marked PZ. It had also a peculiar scroll pattern in green.

In Ottweiler in 1763, Prince William Henry of Nassau-Saarbrücken with the aid of the arcanist Dominique Pellevé made wares with the usual flowers and also mythological scenes or scenes of gallantry after Boucher and Wilson. One white figure of a boy has the mark NS with an added W and the date 1766.

In Kelsterbach, 1758, the output was chiefly of well modeled figures after Bustelli and these were probably done by Antonius Seefried in part at least, who it is fairly sure must have worked at Nymphenburg. They seem to have open mouths and raised eyebrows and a brilliant white glaze. A few were polychrome. The mark is HD standing for Hessen-Darmstadt surmounted with a crown, impressed or painted in underglaze blue. It also occurs in purple without the crown and in italics. Little useful porcelain was made.

At Fulda between Frankfort and Gotha we finally come to more interesting work.

FIG. 927. Interesting pipe bowl from Kelsterbach by Vogelmann, 1763–65. Mounted with silver and jewels. A. Beckhardt Coll.

The quality of paste and the workmanship and painting are all excellent. The factory was started in 1765 by Prince-Bishop Heinrich von Bibra and called "Furstlich Füldaische feine Porzellan-Fabrik," and run by the same

Nikolaus Paul who worked for Wegely and also at Passau and Cassel under the directorship of Abraham Ripp. It ended in 1780.

Most of the ordinary wares were decorated with flowers in polychrome, red, or a strong purple. The usual landscapes and portraits were also made, and the later influence of Boucher, etc., carried through, but all were done in good taste and well painted. Landscapes in grey resting on gold scrolls and silhouette portraits set in tooled gold frames on cups seemed a favorite treatment. The wares are among the most expensive of these times in Germany though they are not rare.

The figures of the usual Italian comedy and amatory groups as well as religious figures are all full of natural grace. A 10-inch Madonna Immaculata standing on a globe on a baroque pedestal is well known. The figures resemble those of Karl Gottlieb Lück of Frankenthal though a little less alive.

The mark was an F until 1780 when a double F in italics sometimes with a crown and sometimes with a small cross on top was used or a simple cross like a plus sign, the arms of the city. It should be noted that this cross is never pulled together to resemble in any way the Meissen mark.

Cassel, like many of these places had had an old faïence factory for years but the porcelain factory was started in 1766 also by Nikolaus Paul just a year after he had started the Fulda factory. It was not until 1769 that real porcelain was made successfully, as it was advertised, "Complete colored and blue-and-white, reeded and smooth coffee and tea services at low prices." The useful wares are mostly blue and white and of poor quality, and the figures stodgy. Some are of a white chalky look and some greyish. The mark was the Hessian rampant lion or HC standing for Hessen-Cassel. Barber also gives a running animal that looks like a dog perhaps but this is not surely authenticated, and should not be accepted.

Thus we survey the preliminary wares and those country wares which were not true porcelains. Of course many of them were made long after the actual discovery of porcelain but I thought it best to place them all together. The reader has probably gathered that I think them of no artistic importance and of very little appeal in any sense. There used to be collectors who paid fair prices for some of them but time has proven them of little account.

CHAPTER XXII

THE EUROPEAN DISCOVERY
OF PORCELAIN

BRIEF HISTORICAL OUTLINE OF THE 18TH CENTURY

THE 18th century divides itself roughly into three sections; the Opening (1700–1715), the Middle (1715–1775) and the Close (1775–1800), with fifteen years, sixty, then twenty-five, respectively.

The *Opening* (1700–1715) was the time of Louis XIV (1643–1715), Queen Anne (1702–1714) and Joseph I (1705–1711) in France, England and Germany. The War of the Spanish Succession resulted in a succession of defeats of the French by the English, and the Peace of Utrecht (1713) gave large territorial additions to England. Prussia was made a kingdom under Frederick I in 1701.

In furniture it was the "Walnut Period" from about 1660 to 1720 and the Baroque style was breaking all precedents of proportion and classic tradition but the exaggeration was so great that people soon tired of it and began to tone it down to the more sentimental age of Rococo. Jean Antoine Watteau (1684–1721) was a favorite painter with his gay shepherds and shepherdesses, fêtes champêtres, rustic dances, etc.

Ever since the 16th century in Italy the Princes and Popes had been making collections of antique sculpture, and artists had been copying them. Also a strangely mixed conception of Chinese art had occurred, intriguing but entirely misunderstood.

The *Middle Period* (1715–1775) was the time of Louis XV (1727–1760) of George I (1714–1727) and George II (1727–1760) in England and of the North Countries there were Charles VI (1711–1740), Maria Theresa (1740–1780) and Frederick II (1740–1786). A troublous time in truth! The following dates give a very rough idea of what was taking place:

1720—Financial panic, bursting of the "South Sea Bubble" in England and the collapse of John Law's Mississippi scheme in France. (Penny gathering had become a craze in truth.)

1740—War of the Austrian Succession, England and Austria against France. Frederick II invades Silesia.

1748—Treaty of Aix-la-Chapelle.

1754—Continuous war between England and France in India, America and Europe.

1756—"The Seven Years War" France and Austria against England and
     Frederick the Great.
1770—Rise of Du Barry and fall of Choiseul.

The Marquise de Pompadour (1721–1764) had great influence on art and
politics at least between 1745 and 1764. François Boucher (1703–1770) was
a dispenser of sweetness and light with his pastoral, genre and historical subjects. His women, girls and nudes were famous.

In 1748, through the making of an underground aqueduct, it was found
that the ruins of Pompeii were accessible. In 1763 intensive excavations
were begun and much interest was stirred in both Pompeii and Herculaneum.
Thus the artistic ground was ready for the results of the Napoleonic conquests
which brought about an entirely new style during the Empire.

The *Close* of the century (1775–1800) was represented by Louis XVI
(1774–1792), the First Republic (1792–1795), Directory (1795–1799) and
finally the Consulate (1799–1804)—France was busy! In England George
III (1760–1820) was doing little or nothing but imitating the French in
culture. The spinning "mule" was invented in 1779, the weaving machine
in 1785 and Nelson annihilated the French fleet at the Battle of the Nile
in 1798. There was continuous social discontent partly due to the inventions
which threw men out of work, and to the costs of the wars. Frederick II
was the great personality of the northern countries. Napoleon invaded Italy
in 1796, Egypt in 1798 and then continued his campaigns of victory in Italy
and Germany about 1800. He loved show and was interested in antiques.
He changed the face of art as much as he changed the map of Europe and
neither were for the better.

Jacques Louis David (1748–1825) won the Grand Prix de Rome in 1775
and stayed there until 1780. He was made a court painter under Louis XVI,
was associated with Robespierre, voted for the death of his king and so was
made court painter by Napoleon. He was a pupil of Boucher and Vien but
changed and became the leader of the classic revival.

MEISSEN AND THE DISCOVERY OF PORCELAIN

France was satisfied with "soft-paste" and Holland with faïence or "Delft,"
but neither were very durable being given to chipping and easy cracking
through quick changes of temperature. However, Holland had a good im-
port business in hard porcelain wares from the East and did not want to
lose that through any home manufacture of similar wares. England never
did have a native pottery of any importance even in the last half of the 17th
century. True, John Dwight, the Elers brothers and others imitated Rhenish
stoneware and Chinese "buccaro" ware, but although Dwight tried to make
a porcelain he never succeeded in making anything but a white stoneware.
Perhaps all these men knew too much about ceramics to become inventors
of porcelain for often a man who knows it all does not see beyond what he
thinks is reason. It was not a potter who discovered porcelain for Europe
but an alchemist.

Johann Friederich Böttger

Junckel, the inventor of ruby glass, had made a white milky glass, but nothing nearer, while Ehrenfried Walther Tschirnhausen can be credited with establishing the idea that porcelain could be made from different earths. He was a physicist who was searching for a means of creating an industry based upon his native soil.

To Böttger goes the real credit. He, Johann Friederich Böttger, was born at Schleiz in Thuringia in 1682 and was apprenticed to an apothecary when he was only 16. He was fascinated with the strange reactions of various chemicals and dreamed of finding the "philosopher's stone," and of the transmutation of metals. One who fooled with the "natural laws" was not particularly popular in those days but this did not deter the King of Prussia from attempting to capture the man when he heard rumors about his supposed ability to make gold. Böttger fled to Saxony where he was captured by the King of Poland and Elector of Saxony, August the Strong. Here he was kept prisoner, given working expenses and assistants including Tschirnhausen and told to make gold or else. . . . This caused considerable activity on Böttger's part as can be imagined and with some enormous burning glasses which Tschirnhausen had invented many substances were melted. The Elector grew impatient and Böttger tried several times to run away but was recaptured. Things were pretty black when his suggestion was finally accepted that he endeavor to start an industry of faïence making from which taxes could be squeezed first and then go back to the gold making later.

A factory was established at Dresden for this faïence making but Tschirnhausen and Böttger with enthusiasm set out to make porcelain. Luckily all of the melting experiments with the glasses had actually taught them a good deal, and in 1708 the first "red porcelain," very much like the ancient "buccaro" ware, and also like that made at Yi-hsing in China, and so appreciated by tea-drinkers, was made of "Nuremberg red earth," which contains iron oxide and a mixture of the local clay from the Plauenscher Grund near Dresden. This ware was very fusible and so hard that it was found that it could be cut with the wheel after firing. The Portuguese had been making a fine thing of the importing of Yi-hsing ware and, if the same thing could be made in Saxony the revenue would help to reinstate the impoverished country, start new wars and accomplish all manner of great things.

But at Dresden there were no throwers, moulders, modelers and in fact no one who knew anything at all about pottery. Therefore Peter Eggebrecht, a thrower, was brought from Berlin, Johann Jakob Irminger, a goldsmith, and other assistants were employed. We have found that as a rule pottery suffers when it is patterned after metal work. The handles are likely to be too thin, the forms too tenuous and applied decoration seems always necessary. But this conservative goldsmith did better things.

It would be expected that Böttger would now settle down to work with the new medium but he seems to have been a restless soul. Tschirnhausen and he had already noticed that white earth which remains white after firing is precisely that which is the most difficult to fuse. Thus they turned to the search for another substance which would act as a flux, which would be easily fusible and transparent after firing. Chalk, alabaster, marble and other siliceous minerals were tried from far and near. Yet right in Colditz a clay almost like kaolin was at hand.

There is no documentary evidence even as to the year of discovery for all was kept a dark and mysterious secret, but probably in late 1708 or early 1709 it was made. We hope that it was before October 1708 for it was then that old Tschirnhausen died and it would have been nice to have had him witness the results of all their struggles. However, it was not until March of 1709 that the king was informed. Böttger foolishly asked the king to appoint a committee to report upon the practical importance of his invention and of course the committee was unenthusiastic as might be expected, but the king on January 23d, 1710, nevertheless issued a royal patent for the erection of a factory in the castle of Albrechtsburg high on a hill overlooking Meissen. From 1710 to 1713 only the red ware was made and it cannot be said that the making of porcelain was fully solved until 1715.

MEISSEN RED STONEWARE

Though stonewares are treated separately in this book it will aid the coherence of this section to keep all of the Meissen endeavors together. The color of this first ware produced was of red-brown to black and a dull, muddy yellow. It resembled the Bizen yaki of Japan and the terra sigillata of Rome and was not unlike the prehistoric wares save that it was harder. The 6 chief types are: 1.—even red, 2.—red with black surface, 3.—marbled ware, 4.—a different and lightly fired black glazed ware treated with gilding and lacquer colors, 5.—a polished surface ware having appliqués of mat branches in Chinese style and 6.—the yellow ware.

Methods of decoration and design included: 1.—casts particularly of Yi-hsing teapots, 2.—casts from Chinese soapstone and porcelain figures particularly such as were made at Tê-hua, Fukien, 3.—enamel decoration on teapots (all of these were before Johann Jakob Irminger's time but after he was employed the following processes came into being), 4.—molded and cut decoration after Turkish brass work, particularly ewers, 5.—wares labeled "classic" with appliqués, and 6.—"Laub and Bandelwerk" or cut with the wheel in foliate scrolls or "Muscheln" faceted decorations of the whole surface, which were Böttger's favorites.

Hannover says, "Grinding, polishing and cutting were for the most part executed in the 'Schleif und Poliermühle' at Dresden; the resources of this institution, however, did not suffice for dealing with the whole of his production. In the year 1712 there were at Dresden six, in Meissen three, in Bohemia ten glasscutters at work on the red stoneware, while goldsmiths and jewelers in Munich, Augsburg and presumably elsewhere were engaged in mounting it." Then he comes to an interesting sidelight on Böttger himself, "The fact was that Böttger had, as time went on, become so possessed with the idea that his beloved ware was a sort of precious stone, that he had the finest specimens mounted in precious metals overlaid with enamels, and set with turquoises and garnets after the manner of the Renaissance period."

There were also polished or partly polished pieces from Roman sculpture or from Bernini, or again from ivory carvings. Then reliefs from medals were made and rarely modeled pieces such as a dashing statuette of August the Strong, a crucifix in Gotha and figures from the Italian Comedies.

Böttger was kept prisoner and every means of keeping the secret was resorted to, yet it leaked and one of the traitors was Samuel Kempe who went to Berlin where he failed to make good but did encourage Friederich von Görne to set up a factory near the town of Plaue-an-der-Havel. When Böttger in 1715 sent an assistant to spy on the owner of this place, David Pennwitz, he received the report that they were making fairly good red stoneware, and it is supposed that they continued until 1730 when the place failed. Strangely the pieces traced to this factory, though they were less well made, brought just as high prices as did Böttger's own at the Lanna and Gasser sales, adding insult to injury.

Kempe, having failed at Berlin, went on to Bayreuth where a factory turned out very lightly fired and porous ware covered with a glaze of brown, black and rarely yellow, with delicate chinoiseries on it in gold and silver both unfired.

Böttger White Ware

Böttger himself didn't mind stealing ideas and credit as is proven by tea-pots copied from the Chinese by Arij de Milde and copied from him by Böttger including his mark of an animal in an oval with the name above. Arij de Milde was born at Delft in 1634 and never could have made these high-fired examples.

Criss-crossed lines and numerals, particularly 13 and 7 with letters also appear on these wares. Any which have the crossed swords are later. Graesse, the director of the Porcelain Collection at Dresden, was entirely mixed up and included many actual Chinese pieces as those of Böttger, even going so far in his book as to include several Chinese marks as those of Meissen. The fact that Edwin Atlee Barber passes them on in his books should be a warning.

The real wares are much harder than any of the contemporary attempts to copy them, and cannot be scratched with a steel blade or file. The danger-ous copies are those from Kamenz, Saxony, of about 40 years ago. Still others were originally plain and have been cut or decorated later, particularly with coats of arms. There are also cheap Bohemian wares of black with lacquer designs. The Johanneum Sale showed prices of real Böttger examples ranging from 20,000 to 40,000 marks, while in the Grasser Sale similar examples brought only a few hundred and now they would bring less.

An eye witness tells us that in 1710 the porcelain made by Böttger was "indistinguishable from 'Indian' ware." Yet only in 1713 did white ware come on the market at the Easter Leipzig Fair. He had used "Schnorrsche Erde" named after the owner of the estate on which it was found near Erzegebirge, had discarded it for a clay found near Dresden until 1717 and then returned to it and continued ever after. For the fusible element he used alabaster only and never seems to have found out about feldspar or quartz.

The last ingredient has never been used at Meissen and this accounts for the strength of the ware for quartz makes a brittle and easily chipped porcelain.

By 1713 they had a stock of overglaze colors and an artist named Funke was working there. Underglaze blue was the king's favorite color as is proved by his large collection of Chinese blue and white pieces intended for the "Japanese Palace," but Böttger never mastered this and only later did his best workman, David Köhler make it. Never did Meissen equal the Chinese color.

The porcelain was not very translucent and had a creamy yellowish tinge. The glaze is thick, even and pure. Very rarely are pieces found which were made before Böttger discovered the glaze. Enamels are yellow, blue, green, pink and less pure iron-red, grey-green and violet. They were all used together but monochromes do occur, always to be regarded as later. A "mother-of-pearl" was very rarely used as a ground color instead of in the design. Gold and silver were strangely enough fired onto the porcelain even when he could not accomplish it on the stoneware and there are cups with metal all over either the inside or outside. There are also examples of burnished gold designs on mat ground and of relief gold.

This white ware was made in similar forms to the red ware. Even at an early date outer walls were reticulated as in Chinese "devil's work." Very early pieces were also impressed with bookbinder's stamps in the paste before firing. There were also the so-called "Callot figures" in the baroque taste and after the artist of that name.

The great genius and inventor of European porcelain had burned himself out by 1719 and in that year he finally worked and drank himself into his grave on March 13th.

HEROLD PERIOD

The factory was in financial straits. Two of the "arcanists" sold their secrets to du Paquier in Vienna. These were Stölzel and Hunger. However, through the strange irony of the powers that seem to control this universe, or just chance, Johann Gregor Herold was trained by du Paquier and in 1720 the Royal Commission at Dresden found him technically better equipped even than Böttger had been, and he obtained the directorship. His colors were higher fired and he added a brilliant iron-red, a purple, two kinds of

FIG. 928. Meissen bowl, Herold period, with gold Chinese figures. 1720–1725. Dia. 6". Metropolitan Mus. of Art.

FIG. 929. Meissen tea-pot, Herold period, c. 1725. Decorated with gold chinoiseries. Ht. 4¼". Metropolitan Mus. of Art.

FIG. 930. Meissen cup and saucer with gold chinoiseries of Herold type but marked with crossed swords in underglaze blue, which came into being in 1726. Dia. 5⅛". Metropolitan Mus. of Art.

Sugar-bowl c. 1720 to 1725. Gold decorations of chinoiseries. Length 6″. Metropolitan Mus. of Art.

Right: Jar and cover of type known as "Augustus Rex vases" having Japanese decoration and dating c. 1725–1730. Ht. 16½″. Metropolitan Mus. of Art.

Tea-pot c. 1724 with grotesque figures in style of Callot, marked M P M in underglaze blue. Ht. 4¼″. Metropolitan Mus. of Art.

Left: Tea-caddy decorated with views of sea, figures and flowers in insets in rich enamels framed with gold lambrequins. Crossed swords mark in underglaze blue, 19 impressed and 52 in gold. Date between 1725–1750. Ht. 4⅛″. Metropolitan Mus. of Art.

HEROLD PERIOD MEISSEN PORCELAIN

PLATE 181

green, a yellow and a light and dark blue. He also made a fine, thin porcelain which has never been surpassed in Europe.

Before Herold the factory continued the same wares described above probably under Funke and some pieces with silver lacquer, black and iron-red showing figures in medallions with the flesh in the last color, also pieces with designs from Watteau poorly painted and nowhere nearly so good as the later ones after the same painter. The Chinese gave over slowly to the baroque style and thus we place Herold's chinoiserie designs earlier than 1727 when his sketch book showed he was taking interest in the later style. It was just during this early period that August the Strong was also making further plans for his "Japanese Palace." It was about this time that the Kakiemon designs after the Japanese artist of that name became popular,

Turkish woman with hamper by Kändler. c. 1745. Ht. 6¼". Metropolitan Mus. of Art.

Sugar bowl with *"Mosaik"* or scale rococo reserves and landscape with figures. Marked with crossed swords in blue and 43 in violet. c. 1760-70. Ht. c. 3¾". Metropolitan Mus. of Art.

"Augustus Rex" vase and cover with raspberry colored ground and *chinoiserie* in enamels. Ht. 20". (c. 1730). Metropolitan Mus. of Art.

Figure described by museum simply as "Meissen 1730-80" but possibly by Friedrich Elias Meyer for it is like his things in rather affected pose and soft treatment. c. 1755. Ht. 11½". Metropolitan Mus. of Art.

MEISSEN WARES c. 1730–1770

PLATE 182

and the "red dragon service" and "yellow tiger service" date 1728 by Zimmerman and 1738 by Berling. Hannover has a good thought that the difficulty with the underglaze blue saved us the trite Imari style for years.

The perfect technique led to simple shapes and open designs for spots did not have to be covered with painting or modeling.

A group of vases made for the king only are marked AR for Augustus Rex in underglaze blue and are very rare. These show an attempt to do the

Dish, between 1725 and 1740, marked with crossed swords in blue. "Oriental design" with its *strohblumen* has evidently been used to cover worst pitting much of which could not be covered. Metropolitan Mus. of Art.

Tea-pot with design after Kakiemon but having baroque handle and spout. Between 1725 and 1750. Metropolitan Mus. of Art.

Above: Piece with baroque ornamentation and landscapes in polychrome enamels, c. 1730–1735. Ht. 8¼". Metropolitan Mus. of Art.

Below: These pieces, c. 1735 show typical *"Laub-und Bandelwerk"* baroque frames to landscapes. Cup and saucer have light blue ground color. Cup ht. 3⅛". Saucer 5⅛" dia. Metropolitan Mus. of Art.

MEISSEN WARES

PLATE 183

Chinese vases as translated by the Japanese and at once we see flamboyance of curve, exaggeration of color or other features which take them out of the class even of the Ch'ien Lung wares. The ways of the copyist are ever the same.

Likewise, the stunt of drawing without perspective came into use in the Meissen factory. Often the Chinese artist sacrificed the tricks of perspective for the making of a better design more suited to a flat or curved surface. This is not to say that the Chinese did not understand perspective for they often drew dragons or tree branches perfectly curving forwards or backwards from a plane and the aërial perspective of mountains behind mountains and of twisting streams was beautifully handled. Nevertheless the trite European critic likes to say that the Chinese did not understand perspective. Johann Gottlob Schlimpert and C. F. Herold, the brother of Johann Gregor Herold, seem to have been chiefly responsible for making pictures framed with baroque frames. The chinoiseries had had their run and European landscapes took their place. These were generally lifted from Watteau, Wouverman, Rugendas, etc. There were also water scenes difficult to explain from an inland country but due to pure copying. Many of these were in monochrome purple, iron-red or black, probably due to the influence of the engravings from which the artists worked.

Medallions were marked on colored grounds and then painted in as were the Chinese powder blue wares. Attempts were also made to color the porcelain all the way through, but these are exceedingly rare, as in truth also are the colored ground wares for many of them are also marked AR. These colors were laid on with the brush and none can be considered glazes. Only one minor glaze was finally developed and that was a brown similar to what the Chinese call "dead leaf brown," and it was used as in the East in conjunction with blue and white.

FIG. 931. Tea-caddy with canary yellow ground and "Kakiemon" type design. Ht. 4⅜". Metropolitan Mus. of Art.   FIG. 932. Tea-pot, cup and saucer with rose or mauve ground. Saucer has enamel painting directly on colored ground. Metropolitan Mus. of Art.

FIG. 933. Cup and saucer with metal mounts. Magenta ground with white medallions and Chinese floral designs in bright enamels, Meissen, c. 1735. Ht. 4⅞″. Dia. 6¾″. Metropolitan Mus. of Art.

This new underglaze blue was never good but some fairly close copies of Chinese wares were made. Some blue and white bears the AR mark but much was of common household variety and decorated with the "Zweibelmuster" or "Onion pattern" and the "Strohblumen" or "Strewn blossoms" or a thin Japanese plum blossom pattern. The latter was adopted by Royal Copenhagen and slightly modified. This porcelain has the crossed sword mark from 1726 and usually some letter probably indicating the artist. Blue was also combined rather unsuccessfully with iron-red.

Plastic wares resulted from the appointment of Gottlob Kirchner in 1727 who did some large vases of grotesque character in the style of J. Stella, and also some clock cases, wall fountains, etc., until 1729, when he was discharged. Later he was taken back after Ludwig Lück, an ivory carver, was also discharged for his lazy and disorderly ways, but did not last long and failed in the making of some large animal figures for the "Japanese Palace."

THE KÄNDLER PERIOD

Johann Joachim Kändler was appointed in 1731 and was a very different character for he started great activity at once. He continued with the factory until his death in 1775 and just about covers our middle 18th century period, adding considerably to it. The great animals were accomplished with Kirchner doing a rhinoceros after a Dürer woodcut, an elephant, a bear, a fox, a lioness and a leopard. After he left for Berlin, where he spent the rest of his life, Kändler completed a number more, making some of them life size, but the whole lot are very crude and full of flaws and fire cracks. Kirchner also completed a statuette of August the Strong and one of the Apostle Peter before his final departure.

Kändler wrote in one of his reports that, "There is not a single properly made handle in the whole factory," and he set out to make new shapes for

Left: Hard paste figures representing Autumn and Winter decorated with brilliant polychrome, moulded by Friedrich Elias Meyer c. 1755. Hts. 10⅛″ and 10¼″. Metropolitan Mus. of Art.
Right: Mark in underglaze blue. Decorated in yellow underdress with polychrome sprays of flowers, pale coat lined with gray and white fur and hat in buff. Ht. 7⅛″. Metropolitan Mus. of Art.

Left: Chinaman in white hard paste porcelain with enamel colors made during Kändler period, possibly George Fritzsche, c. 1735–40. Ht. 3½″. Metropolitan Mus. of Art.
Right: Lithophane from Guido Reni's "Magdalene," German 19th cent., probably Meissen. Metropolitan Mus. of Art.

MEISSEN FIGURES

PLATE 184

all the knobs, feet, spouts, etc. He also made the "Sulkowsky service" (1735–1738) and the Brühl "Swan service" (1737–1741) executed for the Saxon Minister, Count Heinrich Brühl, who until his fall in 1763 had charge of the Meissen factory. These services were inspired by silver services and suffered all the involved and busy illnesses of these.

Johann Freirich Eberlein was at the factory between 1735 and 1749 and did some good modeling including figures of the "Three Graces" and "Four Seasons." Other pieces of his are the Atlanta and Meleager, Acis and Galatea, a sweetmeat stand for the Swan service, a drunken Silenus, etc.

There were still others who gave some character to the factory including Friederich Elias Meyer and Peter Reinicke.

Kändler made several figures two or three feet high and the age seemed on the whole to express lack of understanding of scale. He had said, "You can make anything you please in porcelain; if it is too big, it can be made in two pieces." No one has ever said just how large or small a piece of porcelain should be, aside from the technical difficulties of firing, etc., yet in each of us an invisible scale tells us what to expect. When this expectation is upset by surprise, there is always a loss of aesthetic appeal. Somehow we expect large sculpture to be of stone or bronze and it is a shock to find it in breakable porcelain. But Kändler evidently saw the error of his ways and turned to smaller figures.

In the 18th century "Schauessen" were used, that is, table decorations of sugar or wax figures arranged with scenes of rocks, trees, palaces, temples, pyramids, etc., either on the dining table or on a table to one side for the amusement and wonder of the guests. Now they carried into porcelain. Hundreds of these things were concocted and many of the figures we see today belonged to them but probably not the little ones with bocages, etc., for they are not made to be looked at from all sides. It is easy to see how people might get into the habit of keeping certain choice pieces on permanent display and particularly if they were of porcelain which could be easily washed off when necessary. In this way Kändler came to create a new art, that of representing the people of the day in the dress of the period. Thus from a caterer's art we derive all the little genre porcelains made at Meissen and elsewhere. These were not at once taken from real life but from the opera or such romantic scenes as lovers kissing, dancing couples and the famous "crinoline groups," Columbine and Scaramouche and more lovers. Before all this the figures were from classic sources.

Kändler used taste in keeping the colors pure and simple. The flesh parts are hardly tinted at all while the dresses are of plain color or sometimes with small all-over designs of "Indian flowers." The whole effect is not to make them too naturalistic and the sentimentality of the rococo from France does not come until later. Yet I cannot help but feel that the prices such toys have brought are out of all proportion to their intrinsic merit. Hannover tells us that some were sold for up to around $10,000 and that there are many fakes as a result.

It was natural to set candles near these "Schauessen" and so it was that some of the figures were made as candle holders themselves with ormolu mounts and leafy arbors to hold candle sockets.

A well known group of figures are the "Saxon Miners" (1735–1740) with a representation of August the Strong in a miner's costume among them. There were also foreign figures such as Turks, Poles, Negroes, etc. Kändler did not like the Royal Orchestra in Dresden so he made the well known "Monkey Band" as a dig. He also made small figures with boxes near them

Left: Cup and saucer attr. to Marcolini period (1774–1814) by museum. Kakiemon style but overcrowded. Plate dia. 5″. Metropolitan Mus. of Art.
Right: Cup and saucer, cup having two medallions in white on red-violet ground, filled with "German flowers" in natural colors. Both have blue crossed swords, and cup an impressed 74, saucer 117. Ht. 2¾″, dia. 5¼″. Metropolitan Mus. of Art.

Left: Tureen and tray c. 1760–90 with landscape and marine views. Tray 12½″ long. Metropolitan Mus. of Art.

Right: Tray and teacup with ribbon and flower design and marked with crossed swords and dot in blue. c. 1760–70. Tray 10″ long. Metropolitan Mus. of Art.

MEISSEN WARES

PLATE 185

and finally copying the Chinese more or less, he made a number of birds and animals.

Here is the meeting and marriage of the two techniques of *sculpture* and *painting* and never are the two entirely separated again in the art of porcelain.

Many horrible vases with pierced walls and carefully modeled flowers and insects painted in pastoral colors on them and even worse "Schneeball" and "guelder-rose" jars were made, having small white flowers all over them in snowballs with cupids added, relief portraits, etc. Thus we find that Kändler's taste was both good and atrocious at the same time, and now added to his own bad taste comes the influence of the rococo with all the faults of the baroque and many added weaknesses.

So perfectly adapted was the medium to his new expression that it was thought by some that the rococo style actually originated at Meissen, but it came from France. After about 1750 the oriental influence is about gone as are also the "Indian flowers." The wares are now less massive and lighter in weight and design. European flowers were copied from such books as those by Preisler and Schmidhammer with stiff drawing and color incorrect. Shadows were introduced in what was known as "Saxe ombré." These date about 1742.

About 1750 both birds and flowers improve for they were painted from real ones and from Buffon's *Natural History,* a better book. These were known as "German flowers." Scattered small flowers were continued.

After Herold's time the frames were omitted from landscapes painted on vases and at most a rococo scroll was used at the bottom. Frames were also removed from the birds and flowers and the design became more free and open. Children after Boucher were also popular and after about 1760 the factory was obviously feeling the competition of Sèvres.

As the lighter colors were more easily fusible and not suitable for ground colors a "mosaic" pattern was devised which was really a sort of scale pattern, usually seen in green, purple or blue and sometimes was confined to the edges as on the sugar bowl illustrated. When so used it was bound by delicate scrolls. This was about the last spark of invention, as was even recognized at the factory, for men were sent out to steal ideas from Sèvres, Höchst, Frankenthal, Munich, Paris and Vienna. As these places were largely run by men who had stolen their ideas from Meissen, there was little to be gained. A new school of art was started but was ineffective. Kändler continued but was thought old fashioned. He made some busts of children and more horribly pompous and involved vases.

Acier followed Kändler and then the "bourgeois-sentimental" style of Greuze, Chardin and Moreau le Jeune with such groups as "The Happy Parents," "The Broken Foot Bridge," "The Broken Eggs," and "Children with Mottoes." The work was photographic in detail even to the imitation of the lace of a dress and entirely lacking in spirit of any sort. Others such as Zeizig, called Schenau, Carl Schonheit, etc., posed as artists for a short while. Friederich Elias Meyer at least tried to do nudes but they were chiefly known for their small heads and affected poses.

Marcolini or Neo-Classical Period

Competition was now strong from the Thuringian factories, the large European ones and such places as that of Wedgwood. Kändler died in 1775 leaving the management of the factory to Count Camillo Marcolini from 1774.

People were sick to death of the restlessness of the baroque and rococo. As early as 1766 we have record of a style referred to as "à la Grecque" and "Hetrurische Kante" or "Etruscan borders" and now by 1780 we see the surfaces gilded all over with reserved medallions simply framed enclosing stiff painting. All is now static and in "good taste."

In 1782 the much envied "bleu-de-roi" of Sèvres was accomplished and called "Gutbrennblau." An underglaze green was also found. Miniature painters worked "en grisaille" (in grey) or with flowery natural colors. Illustrations were copied from books and the works of Canaletto, Hogarth and Berchem were copied. Marcolini had the Magdalen of Correggio reproduced from the Dresden gallery on a large oval plaque. Thus naturalism went hand in hand with neo-classicism by 1800. They could do anything but they really did nothing.

Fig. 934. Meissen teapot having "*Mosaik*" decoration about shoulder and top. Ht. 3⅝". Mark, crossed swords in blue. c. 1765. Metropolitan Mus. of Art.

Fig. 935. Plates with *Alt Osier* pattern (wickerwork) on rims and *chinoiserie* flowers and birds. c. 1735. Dia. 13½". Metropolitan Mus. of Art.

Fig. 936. Dresden or Meissen Marcolini period "monteith" decorated with "German flowers" in natural colors. Mark is crossed swords and star (c. 1785). Used for cooling glasses. Length 11". John Gibbons Coll.

Fig. 937. Meissen coffee-pot decorated with rococo frame and marine view on either side in puce, yellow, green, black, red and blue enamels. Marks are crossed swords in blue and 20 in gold. c. 1740–45. Ht. 9½". Metropolitan Mus. of Art.

Then they turned to repeating their own old styles and the flowers were crude and poorly colored while oriental subjects were reproduced but in simplified and insipid form. There was, as Hannover so well puts it, "an unparalleled fumbling about in all directions and periods." They tried to copy Wedgwood but the figures are hard in feeling and the paste too white and unpleasant. Actually the situation was not unlike the one which we ourselves went through between the first and second world war and, therefore, needs no more description.

The factory closed in 1810. It was revived but when Marcolini died in 1814 it was in debt for 400,000 thalers. In 1828 it tried "lithophanes" or plaques molded on the reverse in intaglio so that when light passed through them the pictures appeared in relief. These were also made in Berlin and some were used for sconce shades or lamp shades. In 1831 casts were made from molded glass. Lithography was brought into use and transfer printing was done. H. G. Kühn was the director from 1833 and his modeler, Ernst August Leuteritz, made a psuedo-rococo mode out of all feeling of the times and with it the wares sank lower and lower.

We have often repeated that the Meissen marks mean nothing, for they were so extensively copied everywhere in Germany, elsewhere in Europe and even in England. However, they are included as one should know what they were. It is enough to have forgotten the Meissen marks, as it has been said, "It is enough to have forgotten one's Latin."

The factory gave the worst failures to the workmen and sold the "Mittlegut" wares to "Pfuscher," "Hausmaler," "Wilde Maler," and "Chamberlans," at reduced prices and with the mark of the factory already on them. These gentlemen then decorated them as seemed best. In 1740 it was decided that such wares should not be sold except with a little decoration on them but this did not bother the outside painters for they built around this decoration. In 1760 a system of lines was cut into the mark and it may be taken as certain that any mark with a stroke through the swords where they meet was not decorated at the factory. This cancellation was not used on figures.

The mark when accompanied by a T is simply that stolen by Thieme, a factory which is still working under the name of Sächsische Porzellanfabrik Carl Thieme and making forgeries. The proprietor is or was C. Kitsch and the place is near Dresden at a town called Potschappel. The wares are also faked by Samson in the Rue Béranger, Paris, or were up to this last war. The only obvious distinguishing characteristic is a slightly weaker color than that of the originals. Samson, of course, attempted to fake everything and was usually fairly successful at it.

VIENNA PORCELAIN

The factory in Vienna was established in 1718 by Claudius Innocentius du Paquier with the help of Christoph Conrad Hunger the same enameler and gilder who started at Meissen, and then turned up at Vienna, Venice, Stockholm and finally at St. Petersburg, one of the peddlers of secrets from place to place, and Samuel Stölzel another arcanist. Herold too was there, as we have said, and in 1720 Stölzel and Herold went to Meissen, and Hunger to Venice.

The oldest piece of Vienna known is a two handled cup of Meissen shape and material, for Stölzel even took the precaution to bring along some of the "Schnorrische Erde" when he came. It is marked "Gott allein die Ehr'und sonst keinem meh—3 May—1719," ("To God alone and to none other be the honor—3 May—1719"). A finger vase of Delft shape is marked "Vienna 12 July 1721" and decorated in underglaze blue which seems to have been mastered before it was at Meissen.

Vienna, like Meissen, Plaue and Bayreuth, made a red stoneware decorated in silver and gold as well as white porcelain so decorated. Hannover makes four divisions of the early wares:

1.—Polychrome chinoiseries like Herold's with flowers and birds similar to Japanese Imari, about 1725, but without Böttger's mother-of-pearl and with spaces filled with trellises.

Hard paste porcelain dish in style of Jacob Helchis (c. 1740) decorated in black and gold. Dia. 16⅛". Metropolitan Mus. of Art.

Left: Group of white porcelain enamelled in colors, c. 1765-70. Ht. 8¼". Metropolitan Mus. of Art.

Right: Chocolate pot c. 1780-1800, showing Empire influence. Ht. 9½". Metropolitan Mus. of Art.

Cup of du Paquier period (c. 1720-1730). Hard paste with decoration in enamel colors. Ht. 3⅛". Metropolitan Mus. of Art.

Cup and saucer of Sorgenthal type but given dating of 1823-26 by museum. Metropolitan Mus. of Art.

Cup and saucer, c. 1750-60 of type painted in (Schwarzlot) black and gold. Dia. 5". Ht. 3". Metropolitan Mus. of Art.

VIENNA PORCELAIN

PLATE 186

2.—Polychrome "Laub and Bandelwerk" or leafy scrolls with flowers, fruits, canopies, figures in landscapes in panels and cartouches, about 1730 to 1740.
3.—The black with gold decoration of the same sort of the same years.
4.—German naturalistic flower decorated pieces also of the same period.

Also the beginnings of the mythological, battle, genre scenes, and scenes with putti, etc., are rare but existent.

Much Vienna ware was decorated by outside painters like Bottengruber who was in the city between 1730 and 1736, Wolfsburg and Preussler. At the palace of the Count Dubsky there was a porcelain room such as was thought quite the thing in those days and walls, fireplace, furniture and all are made of porcelain. This seemed to be du Paquier's chief job.

Among the artists was Joseph Philipp Danhofer (1737) later of Bayreuth, Höchst and Ludwigsburg. Jakobus Helchis came from Trieste and did a few pieces decorated with fighting animals, etc., but chiefly in the black and gold style he did drawings of putti in all manner of scenes. He also did some "en camaieu" things in violet and also some "Schwarzlot" at first grey and later a rich black with red for the flesh parts of figures. About the only plastic work done at Vienna was the "panther handle." The most characteristic part of the style was the love of trellises, acanthus-palmettes, the scale pattern and lozenges as in the style of Baumgartner and Eissler, mixed with Japanese flowers or "German flowers," or "Indian flowers," and a strong tendency to overdecorate.

Du Paquier sold the factory in 1744 and it was placed under Mayerhofer who perhaps aided the factory by the discovery of a new kaolin deposit in Hungary in 1749. New artists worked in rococo taste. Christian Daniel Busch came from Meissen but went on to Nymphenburg. Johann Gottfried Klinger also came from Meissen but remained 30 years. Johann Sigmund Fischer was another famous painter and the modeler Johann Josef Niedermayer came from the Vienna Academy and remained between 1747 and 1784. Ludwig Lück drifted in for one year and then went to Fürstenberg and on to Copenhagen.

EARLY PART OF "SECOND PERIOD" AT VIENNA

During the first four or five years or between 1744 and about 1750 there were figures and landscapes painted in purple or grey with gilt rococo frames as well as naturalistic flowers, birds, animals, etc., after Meissen. Relief patterns also were used in the "Ozier" or "Brandenstein" manner. There remained also many of the du Paquier designs, of course, including "Schwarzlot" and Imari styles. European chinoiseries also continued until around 1780 when they had been replaced by lacquer designs in slight relief in gold on red or black ground. Baroque scrolls lost ground and the black was used for slight borders and landscapes.

Philip Ernst Schindler who did the finest figure painting about 1750 to 1760 made scenes of galanterie after Watteau, peasant scenes after Teniers and cavalry skirmishes in the style of Rugendas. The factory began to feel the weight of Meissen in competition which was going strong up to 1756 when the war started. Lück did a few figures and Niedermayer's can be recognized by their academic feeling, almost dancing movement and gentle smiles.

The earliest figures copied Meissen coloring as well as modeling but the later ones developed their own coloring dominated by brown, red and pale violet, light copper green, black, yellow and gold but always light in character and meticulous in execution. Characteristic is the lack of any base (1), a formal frieze of pendant tongue motives in gold on small bases (2), and a simple wave band of acanthus leaves about a small base (3).

In 1764 the manager was Josef Wolf and in 1770, von Kestler. In 1766 Meissen sent a scout to steal the new neo-classic designs which had begun about 1760. This sincerest form of flattery seemed to be most graciously extended in the whole European development of porcelain.

The tie between the Austrian and French courts through Marie Antoinette brought about strong influences from Sèvres as can be seen in the coquettish shapes, effeminate colors and such specialties as the bleu-de-roi over which was painted a gold network to lighten the depth of solid color, the "chiné" pattern and the "nach Taffet Art" (like taffeta effects).

In 1784 the factory was offered for sale and no purchaser found but a real manager was found in Konrad von Sorgenthal. The chief artist of this time was Anton Grassi who worked from 1778 and replaced Niedermayer in 1784. He was a pupil of Wilhelm Beyer who had been 8 years in Rome and was later a modeler at Ludwigsburg and later was made Court Sculptor, but his style by 1807 when he died was typically neo-classic, Empire.

Between about 1780 and 1785 he made figures with rococo feeling and polychrome glazes. Then Vienna like other factories tried to copy Wedgwood's jasper ware, largely in casts from French originals after Boucher, Bachelier and Pigalle, but the biscuit was somewhat yellowish. This was a transition type and soon Grassi, ever alert, made groups of his own such as "The Greeting" (1785) with a bit more life than his glazed pieces. Almost at once the neo-classic influence was seen in his "Judgment of Paris." Contemporary were his portrait busts and those of his pupil Elias Hütter.

Empire Period at Vienna (1791–1864)

Sorgenthal made a mistake which cost much in taste and prestige by appointing Josef Leithner in 1791. He made "Leithner blue" a copy of bleu-de-roi and various iridescent glazes running from mauve to copper red and finally an imitation bronze glaze. It was the custom to cover entirely the porcelain and also to try to make it look like other materials. Laurenz Herr imitated onyx cameos while Moritz Michael Daffinger did miniatures. Kothgasser could make very perfect borders in relief gold.

Sorgenthal died in 1805 and Grassi in 1807. Niedermayer, the son of the modeler, took charge but resigned in 1827 and in 1864 the Austrian Parliament shut the factory down. The blight of commerce had once again triumphed. A powerful royalty had cultivated porcelain, a luxury-loving aristocracy had sustained it, though with degraded taste, and now the masses had no interest. The murderous competition in appealing to the masses had

raised the cry for cheaper and ever cheaper products. Nothing could stop
the landslide to the present day depths of artistic degradation.

Under du Paquier in Vienna, as under Böttger in Meissen, there were no
marks. Braun gives 15 odd examples, perhaps artists' marks, but they are
unique. In 1744–1749, the "Bindenschild" mark, a shield with round fesse,
the arms of the house of Austria, was used in iron-red, purple, black or impressed. In 1749 to about 1770 it was large, slanting and with thick strokes
of underglaze blue. From 1770 to 1810 it was the same but symmetrically
rounded and smaller. Then until the 1820's it was elongated and became
triangular and about 1827 it was impressed and more regular. During the
last few years the blue marks were imitated on wares of inferior sort to be
sold to England. In 1783 impressed year marks were introduced, those before 1800 being only the last two numerals and those after, the last three.
Impressed letters were only factory marks but painted numerals were artists'
marks.

A Latin A meant "Ausschuss" on rejected wares. X was cut in undecorated
wares.

Even before the last war the taste was such that du Paquier's period wares
did not bring as much as the Sorgenthal stupid Empire things.

BERLIN PORCELAIN

We have described the abortive attempts of Wilhelm Kaspar Wegely to
start a porcelain factory in Berlin and of the closing of his factory in 1757.
It had never made anything but a sort of soft porcelain and now in 1763
the king bought up the place for 225,000 reichsthalers from an "industrial
magnate," Johann Ernst Gotzkowsky who had started in without a cent. His
published autobiography is not to be taken seriously.

The manager put in charge was Johann Georg Grieninger from 1761 to
his death in 1798. The artistic director was Ernst Heinrich Reichardt who
had been working under Wegely. He, however, died in 1764 and was followed by Theodor Gotthilf Manitius and under his management we find the
figure painter Johann Balthasar Borrmann and the modeler Friedrich Elias
Meyer, who was at Meissen (1748–1761), and Isaak Jakob Clauce who had
been head painter under Wegely. Two other new artists from Meissen were
Klipfel and Boehme and this background plus the beneficent help of King
Frederick II assured success.

At first the paste was yellowish-grey but in 1765 a new body was presumably brought from the newly conquered province of Silesia, from Ströbel
near Zobten and by 1770 this had added whiteness when mixed with the
original clay. About 1771 kaolin was found in Brachwitz near Halle and
later more at Sennewitz and Morl and these additions made the ware cold,
bluish-white.

The Gotzkowsky "porcelain" is rare but grey and speckled and of little
account. Some seemed to have been marked with an underglaze G. At
Meissen a special pattern was made for this man before he took over the
Berlin factory and it is called "Gotzkowsky erhabene Blumen." At Berlin
the same pattern was called "Floramuster" while other designs were simply

Parts of set in natural colors. Probably after 1771 as they are hard paste. Pot and cover c. 3½" high. Metropolitan Mus. of Art.

Plate dated by museum c. 1765–70 and having well painted naturalistic flowers and pierced rim. Dia. 9⅝". Metropolitan Mus. of Art.

Hard paste milk-jug with flowers in natural colors and bands of green and pink with gilt trim. (1761–1786). Metropolitan Mus. of Art.

Part of tea and coffee service dated by museum between 1761 and 1830 but not likely to have been made before 1770 or later. Platter c. 10½" long. Metropolitan Mus. of Art.

BERLIN PORCELAIN
PLATE 187

pirated, such as the "Osier" and "Brandenstein." One new idea was the "Reliefzierat mit Spalier" (relief decoration with trellis) as used on the service for the Neues Palais at Potsdam. This is a really lovely pattern of interesting texture and color, being in gold on iron-red and with flowers in various colors. Some have thought it better than anything at Meissen. Another was the "Antikzierat" from about 1767 with blue "Mosaik" and gilt sprays with flowers in natural colors. Others were "new smooth" (1769), "vase shape with reeding" (1776), "smooth royal" (1780–81) and "smooth English" of the same year, and then the "smooth with beads" (1782). Most of these have some relief and much gold, with "German flowers" but no "Indian flowers" or chinoiseries. Purplish-red was also used for landscapes, figures, birds, etc.

It was noticeable that one single color would be predominant in the background such as green, iron-red, yellow, purple or gold. Painting en camaïeu was also done with two colors such as red and gold or pink and

Parts of a set of Berlin porcelain dating about 1763–1800 probably about 1780, with monogram in floral technique. Platter about 13″ long. Metropolitan Mus. of Art.

"Royal Berlin" tureen and stand of late 19th cent. with natural fruits and flowers like many earlier examples, and continuance of rococo feeling. Wm. H. Plummer & Co.

BERLIN PORCELAIN

PLATE 188

grey. The painting all tended toward drawing more and more and engravings were the source of much material. The underglaze blue was only used for common wares with "Muschel" (shell) patterns or "Zwiebelmuster" (the onion pattern) already used at Meissen and later to go with modification to Copenhagen.

As usual Watteau, Teniers and Boucher with the latter's children rendered in monochrome as well as natural colors, were the chief sources. Frederick the Great was not pleased with the imaginary batfle scenes of Rugendas and so had some real scenes depicted. Exact naturalism was imposed by this particular monarch and the painters could not add or subtract figures from original paintings which they were set to copy. J. E. Nilson, Lessing, Chodowiecki and Piranesi were also followed in their engravings.

About 1765 the factory copied Sèvres wares and in the following year Frederick decided he would like to throw copies of Sèvres on the French market. Naturally this endeavor met with no success and a few large vases with poor underglaze, blue grounds and flower decoration in medallions only are left. The English influence with large jars having royal portraits in a wreath, etc., was felt slightly. And, of course, in the 1790's Wedgwood things were copied and then silhouettes by Ditmar, floral monograms and then relief portraits on gilt or monochrome grounds became popular.

The useful wares are not particularly worse than those of other factories of the period but the figures are certainly not good. Friedrich Elias Meyer's figures with too small heads continued, but his brother Wilhelm Christian Meyer joined the factory in 1766 having completed some monumental sculptures and the trend turned toward monumental forms not suited to porcelain. The young brother was the better of the two and he made many "allegorical children," "Muses," etc., and most of his things are more French than German in style. He had much to do with a large central table decoration given by Frederick to Catherine II to seal the alliance of Hubertsburg. This was completed in 1772 and shows Catherine enthroned under a canopy with attendants in biscuit and other figures paying homage rendered in polychrome. A grand affair!

Between 1785 and 1789 Johann George Müller made a whole series of tiresome allegorical figures without expression and in light colors. Some fairly good copies were made of Meissen birds and those of Pedrozzi.

Johann Carl Friederich Riese made naturalistic figures during the neoclassic times and collaborated with the architect Genelli in making table decorations.

During Gotzkowsky's time G was used in underglaze blue, brown and gold, those in blue are probably painted later for some 10,000 such pieces remained when he left the factory.

Berlin was never a very popular ware and never commanded high prices; therefore, it is less copied.

From 1763 to 1786 during the life of Frederick the Great a sceptre of various sizes was used in underglaze blue; 1763 to 1765 it is short like a clove; 1765 to 1770 it is long and slender with a distinct knob, grip, cross stroke and three-pointed finial with a letter sometimes below it; in the 1770's it is short again with cross stroke about middle; in 1780's it is thin with thickening of stem above and below cross stroke and fork at one end; from 1835 the K.P.M. is used; in 1844 to 1847 an eagle with same letters and in 1870 the sceptre with variations was used again with intent to deceive. The K.P.M. is also like the 1723 mark of Meissen but the ware is entirely different.

HÖCHST WARES

That I am not alone in my feeling about these 18th century wares is proven by the following from Emil Hannover, "Generally speaking, a breach of faith leads to no good. And yet it was through a breach of contract and disloyalty in many other forms that it was made possible in the 18th century for the art of porcelain to blossom for the service and delight of mankind, in practically every spot where it awakened the interest of some art-loving prince. For wherever it gained a footing it was due to the betrayal of the secret of porcelain production. Again and again this secret was revealed by workmen deserting from Meissen, and soon there were so many

FIG. 938. Hard paste Höchst jug c. 1770 to 1775, Louis Viktor Gerverot decorated after an engraving which represents "October" by Johann Esaias Nilson. Metropolitan Mus. of Art.

FIG. 939. Höchst "Woman with hen" and "Egg seller" made about 1750 before the French influence of rococo was felt. Ht. 6¼". A. Beckhardt Coll.

FIG. 940. Hard paste condiment jar with figure symbolizing "Summer." Ex Collection of Adolf Beckhardt. Metropolitan Mus. of Art.

initiated that—at any rate among the circle of the arcanists—it was no longer a secret at all." Perhaps the art did blossom but it was truly a malodorous flower which filled the air with stagnation of thought and the death of all inspired originality, alert observation and exploration of the beautiful and appealing, which is the business of the true artist.

This time it was Adam Friedrich von Löwenfinck who brought the Meissen secret to two merchants, Johann Christoph Göltz and Johann Felician Clarus, who applied in 1746 to the Elector of Mainz for the opening of a place in Höchst. Löwenfinck had left an unpleasant trail behind him also at Fulda but a 50-year grant was given and even permission to use the wheel from the electoral arms, but in 1749 he had to resign and Johann Benckgraff took his place only to depart hastily for Fürstenberg in 1753, while Löwenfinck trotted on to Strasburg.

Up to 1760 the factory made as much faïence as porcelain. In 1765 Göltz was forced to hold up payments to the workers and the factory came under the management of Johann Heinrich Masz. In 1765 it was reorganized as the "Churfürstlich-Maynzische privilegierte Porzellaine-Fabrique." The last elector, Friedrich Karl Joseph, took an interest and had to take the whole company in 1778 or shortly after, because the other stockholders had exploited it. The financial condition became worse and worse until 1796 when it was closed, with liabilities three times its assets. Some of its models were sent to Damm, near Aschaffenburg, for the making of "Steingut."

Practically all Höchst designs and models came direct from Meissen. One helmet cup with sturdy base and involved handle suggests a Delft form. The ware was at first grey but later became white. The only invention in color is an unpleasant red-purple approaching carmine and this was often used in monochrome landscapes.

FIG. 941. Höchst set of five vases with painting in purple. The gourd vases are interesting and new but involved. Made about 1755. A. Beckhardt Coll.

FIG. 942. Two figures from Höchst dating about 1750 or the second period showing the faïence appearance which is typical. A. Beckhardt Coll.

Dr. Hans C. Krüger and E. W. Braun divide the figures into four periods:

1746–1749—To the resignation of Löwenfinck they are short and clumsy with large hands with crude movement. They are from the Italian Comedies, religious subjects, peasants, signed Zeschinger. All are on domed white bases with stumps supporting them. They look more like faïence than porcelain.

1749–1754—Similar to first but improvement in some figures of gods, groups of lovers, seasons, a fortune teller, etc., done by Simon Feilner and Job

Zeschinger. There are also some Italian comedy figures with square baroque bases which are so wooden that Krüger thinks they were from the carvings of Simon Troger.

1754–1767—Strong similarity to Frankenthal perhaps through Johann Friederich Lück who probably spent some time at Höchst before going to Frankenthal in 1758. Figures still stiff under direction of Laurentius Russinger as late as 1760 when the "Freemasons group" was made. A little later some "Kissing groups" and candlesticks were made after compositions by Pater and are fairly graceful and light in color, not too much of the ware being covered with enamel.

1767–1779—Johann Peter Melchior came after Russinger left to open a factory at Pfalz-Zweibrücken and brought fame though he was only 25 when he started at Höchst. In 1769 Grieninger tried to get hold of him at Berlin as did also Sèvres and Frankenthal. In Höchst he was Court Sculptor.

He did not go to Paris but was influenced by Flaconet and Claud Michel ("Clodion"); however, his child figures are entirely his own and are gay, lively and usually up to some prank. His "Venuses" have the rounded look and false modesty of the styles of the age. An excessively sweet pink seemed a favorite color. He was no great artist but a good craftsman and did about 300 pieces. Perhaps the nearest to great things he did were the portraits of Goethe and of the poet's family. From this association he turned his hand to writing and made a stupid and unreadable work on the theory of art.

In 1746–1770 the mark was the electoral wheel with or without the hat above it, impressed or painted in overglaze black, brown, purple, iron-red and gold. About 1770 it was only in underglaze blue. Legend has it that the gold was used only for the superior pieces but it was also on many poor examples. This is seldom a mark on the bisque figures. A letter G over the wheel may have stood for Göltz. Many letters are used including HM which dealers like to say stands for Melchior but does not as he signed only a few pieces and then with his full name. I.Z. stands for Zeschinger and A.L. for Löwenfinck.

Fürstenberg Wares

Fürstenberg is slightly southwest of Berlin and Plaue. The factory was in a castle above the Weser on the outskirts of the Sollinger Wald in the worst possible place for such a plant, but the whim of Duke Charles I of Brunswick placed it there and filled it with ne'er-do-well adventurers. In 1753 Benckgraff arrived with Johann Zeschinger, the painter, and Simon Feilner, the modeler, and soon the factory began to make porcelain.

FIG. 943. Höchst tea-caddy with scene of Mongolfier's Balloon in natural colors and gold. Made about 1785. Ht. 5". A. Beckhardt Coll.

FIG. 944. Cup and saucer which the museum attributes to "Furstenberg, 1750–95" but as the factory was not making porcelain until after 1753 is hardly correct. Actually the pieces are likely to date between 1770 and 1780. Plate dia. 5". Metropolitan Mus. of Art.

Benckgraff died and Feilner helped manage while he turned out some fairly original figures of miners, Greek gods, comedy figures, etc., having expressive little faces quite different from the doll-like faces on most other figures of the time.

Zeschinger produced a better palette and the other painters divided themselves into specialties much as was reported done in the K'ang Hsi period in China but on a less extensive scale.

The oldest known piece is a plate dated 1758 which has a monochrome purple picture of two lovers in a garden with the borders decorated with alternating rococo panels and perforated trellises. Even as late as 1767 the factory lacked a yellow, a brown and an underglaze blue that would not run. Up to 1770 the paste was impure, yellowish and inclined to warp, while the glaze was greyish and full of specks.

The Seven Years War brought about the close of the factory in 1762 until peace was concluded. The Meissen and Berlin "Reliefzieraten" were copied but a more involved form was developed probably with the hope of hiding the glaze imperfections. The only ground painting was done with a sea-green and the underglaze blue. The designs were about like those of other factories of the period and much monochrome was used because they were taken from engravings so that the artists did not know what colors to use, and also some colors were missing. However landscapes were done in polychrome as well as iron-red, purple or sepia following Weinrotter, Waterloo, Watteau, Eisen, Leprince, Milson and Pillement though the chinoiseries of the latter are rare.

At length the ultimate has been achieved! We have witnessed the prostitution of ceramic art by painters ever since Greek days but here at length the painters made actual pictures of porcelain to hang on walls; not tiles, not plaques but pictures complete with ornate rococo gold frames also of porcelain. Art with a capital A was achieved by the great C. G. Albert with his chickens, turkeys and other birds and George Heinrich Holtzmann painted pastorals while others did portraits of gods and goddesses with great pomposity, bad colors and the worst of taste. They all date about 1767 or 1768 and Scherer thinks they were done as samples of skill in the days of adversity to help the artists to obtain work in the faïence kiln at Brunswick. This may or may not be true.

From about 1760 the plastic work seems to have been abandoned, except for a few figures by Feilner of about 1766, probably because of the difficulties in handling the paste. In 1770, however, Trabert, the director, died and was replaced by Kaulitz and Johann Ernst Kohl who improved the clay and revived the art. The new artists were Johann Christian Rombrich, Anton Carl Luplau (who later in 1776 left to become the master modeler at the Royal Porcelain Factory at Copenhagen), Carl Gottlieb Schubert (until 1804), P. Hendler and the Frenchman Desoches (until 1744). First there were putti in the Meissen manner but less lively and then birds and animals from Meissen models and ivories. Luplau did Greek figures, some things after Feilner and some original things such as "Flohsucherin" (woman looking for a flea). Desoches followed Chardin and Greuze as in the "Family at the Coffee-table." Schubert copied some "Seasons" from ivory ones by Permoser, "artisans" from Höchst, "street-vendors" and such from Berlin and a Leda from a bronze model. Hendler was just about as original.

As early as the 1760's biscuit portrait plaques and busts were made. The plaques had usually white, blue or gilt frames attached and bear the factory mark and often the name of the person represented, scratched in the paste. Both Desoches and Rombrich did these and seemingly from life. Another type represents Greek poets, statesmen, and philosophers in the Wedgwood manner, white on light blue, the frames of laurel leaves inscribed in gold with the name of the person represented. These are by Schubert and copied from the gems and cameos in the ducal Kunstkammer in Brunswick.

Busts of all sizes up to life were made again from life and this might have led to an original art but the ground was barren and the spark died out.

The "Transition Period of Painting" took place in 1770 and lasted until about 1785 and the biscuit and glaze was improved, the shapes simpler and the painting so much improved that it reached about the best for that day and age. However, this was not for long as the Neo-Classicism killed the larger spaces which had brought freedom to the painting by flutings like those on the "Apulian vases" of Italy

FIG. 945. Furstenberg porcelain of about 1785 to 1790 with an antique head in grey showing the neo-classic trend of the times. Metropolitan Mus. of Art.

and covering of the ground with colors. Painting sunk to silhouettes, antique portraits en grisaille and figures after Angelica Kauffmann or little elegaic landscapes enclosed in medallions. Wedgwood shapes were copied and about the only invention was the making of garniture sets of five or seven vases ranging from small at the ends to highest in the center. Many of these vases bear inscriptions commemorating persons or certain days, for this was a period when memories were carefully kept alive and such things were regarded with sweet smiles of sadness.

Another type had "Arabian vases" resting on "Arabesque scrolls" painted on them with precision and centered in large areas of white with garland borders. Of course these were no more Arabian than the gypsies were Egyptian but this was a day of strange beliefs.

In 1795 the factory came under the management of Gerverot who remained until 1814. He had had a checkered career, born in Luneville, worked at Sèvres, then Niderviller, whence he stole a copy of all the recipes of the factory, and then to Ludwigsburg, Höchst, Frankenthal, Weesp (Holland), Schrezheim, Loosdrecht (Holland), Wedgwood, Cologne and several other places. He had a thorough system of pillage and naturally had learned a lot; almost everything, in fact, except the fundamentals of real art enjoyment or art practice, which cannot be stolen. His period parallels that of Sorgenthal at Vienna and rested upon the same misconceptions through leaning on Sèvres and Wedgwood. The best known painter was Heinrich Christian Brüning who worked diligently. Even the biscuit busts became tight, stiff and meaningless.

The factory mark F is used right up to today often on old models in order to deceive. The medallions had an F in gold on the backs and the busts had a running horse impressed and a blue F on the pedestals.

Nymphenburg Wares

The Elector Max III. Joseph of Bavaria provided a site at Neudeck-ob-der-Au in 1747 under the supervision of Franz Ignaz Niedermayer from Munich. Three workmen were hired away from Vienna and a fourth from the same place, Joseph Jakob Ringler, came as arcanist in 1753. The factory was state property under the management of Count Sigmund von Haimhausen and shortly Ringler decamped for Ludwigsburg. However, his own secrets were stolen by a "Chymikus," J. P. Rupert Härtl so all was well and in 1761 the factory was moved to Nymphenburg, northwest of Munich, where it became famous. In 1765 it had 200 workmen but during the famine of 1770 to 1771 there were only 30. When Max III. Joseph died in 1777 the Bavarian Electorate came to Karl Theodor of the Palatinate who already owned Frankenthal and it was not until his successor in 1799, Max IV. Joseph came into power that the factory was revived. It gained in 1800 when Frankenthal was closed and continued until 1862 as a state institution. It suffered the same Neo-Classic fate as the other factories and in 1822 an architect named Gärtner became head and proceeded to provide classical forms. In 1862 it was turned over to private hands and the usual revival of the old forms was tried with little effect.

Among the useful wares were "Rechauds" or food warmers which seemed to have been a specialty. These date about 1760 and preserve the rococo feeling. An early jar made between 1755 and 1760 in the National Museum, Stockholm, is treated like the Niderviller faïence that is painted to imitate grained wood on which is tacked a piece of paper bearing an engraving in red. It has the first mark of the factory, a hexagram. Another piece has cupids in gray on a purple ground and with etched gold borders. Still another type made about 1765 is a heavy and hard ware painted meticulously with naturalistic flowers and butterflies, but with crude colors.

A series of jugs or coffee-pots are decorated with park views, German flowers, country scenes, birds in landscapes, etc., in gold with brown details, gold and purple and other combinations. The influences were, of course, the same J. E. Nilson, Teniers, etc. All such medallions had rococo frames at first which gradually narrowed and disappeared because they involved too much labor.

BUSTELLI PERIOD

Another type was covered with imitation striped textile patterns, one of which was called chiné (chintz). But all the wares were overshadowed by the figure work due to an "unknown Italian," as Nagler calls him, who worked there between 1754 and 1763. This "unknown Italian" was Franz Anton Bustelli (or, as he was formerly known, Bastelli), and though he ranks with the famous Kändler and actually had better taste in proportions, etc., nothing whatsoever is known of his early life before he came to Nymphenburg in 1754.

At Neudeck between 1747 and 1749 the master modeler was Johann Theophil Schreiber who was an assembler rather than a modeler and after 1749 it was Johann Georg Härtl. They created little ladies and gentlemen in rococo costumes and stiff poses, with expressionless faces but stylized and elongated and with a certain toss of the head. These are on low irregular stands while those of Bustelli have regular oval or polygonal or rococo scroll bases showing his immediate tendency to design which would not leave an unmeaning detail, if it was possible to improve it. Bustelli's color was improved and sparingly used. He gradually developed his bases into rising rococo scrolls from flat ones and these were brought up so high as to act as supports and at the same time as counterpoise for the departure from the vertical of the figures, which was an invention of a kind. His figures become more and more vital and overflowing with life. Those from the Italian Comedies dance and turn their heads with the most capricious and Latin characteristics and truly they show by contrast how heavy is the Teuton conception of such things, but the genre subjects are as alive, and the street vendors, flower girls, fishmongers, cheese-sellers and Chinese figures are all personalities into which he has breathed life. His children are especially humorous and the putti very naughty and gay.

There is in his work an exaggerated turn or drop of the head to one side and an accompanying shrug of the shoulder which is over-coy. It is seen in most of the figures and the busts of laughing children which are so well

FIG. 946. Nymph-
enberg porcelain
stein with pewter
cover and base and
typical polychrome
monogram in flowers.
Late 18th cent. J.
Gibbons Coll.

FIG. 947. Nymph-
enberg horseman of
about 1760 and prob-
ably by Bustelli as
can be told by the
small head and exag-
gerated pose. The
colors are natural-
istic. A. Beckhardt
Coll.

known. There is also a sentimental languishing at times, as in the Mater
Dolorosa, but at other times he seems to rise above his day and make fun
of the sweet gentlemen and so charming ladies kissing the tips of their
fingers, flirting behind fans and reading love letters with a bashful smile.

FIG. 948. Nymphen-
burg hard paste figures
of chinoiserie type.
White paste with trans-
parent glaze. Ht. 4″
and 4½″. Designed
by Bustelli. Metro-
politan Mus. of Art.

Certainly his humor comes beautifully to light in the groups of two lovers.
These were done about 1760 and the bases have risen into backgrounds.
"The Impetuous Suitor" is fairly crawling forward on his knees as he im-
portunes his terribly shocked and outrageously insulted lady for the ancient
favor (she nevertheless has raised her skirt well above her knee in the
anxiety of the moment) and she pushes him away with one hand while she
raises the other in a gesture of astonishment and opens her mouth noise-
lessly, while cupid, hanging to the branch of a tree with one hand and caress-
ing his chest with the other, looks on. In "The Love among the Ruins" we
see a more casual approach as the figures recline against rococo scrolls as
large as they are and the lady seems properly reluctantly willing, while on
the coping adjacent to a broken stone tower sits a bored goat looking off
into the distance, and the lady's dog barks through jealousy in the foreground. Bustelli did dogs well as we see in the "Lady Attacked by a Dog"

FIG. 949. A figure of the "Dottore" by the Furstenberg factory decorated in black and flesh with touches of red, blue and yellow.
FIG. 950. A small Bustelli bust of a coy young lady, Nymphenburg (c. 1760) after one by Kandler of the same year.
FIG. 951. Nymphenburg figure of the comedy character "Pantaloon" colored in red, black, gold and flesh.

and how well he rendered her startled turn as the dog snaps and tears her dress. He seemed to have difficulty in tying more than two figures together in movement and did only a few with a number of figures such as the "Hunting Group."

In 1763 Bustelli died and his place was taken by Dominikus Jakob Auliczek who had had a long academical training as a sculptor. He had studied architecture in Rome under Gaetano Chiaveri, who built the Catholic church at Dresden. His works show that he knew anatomy and the other academic essentials very well but had absolutely no feeling for the medium of porcelain. His "Shepherd and Shepherdess with Bird and Cage" is poor as compared with Bustelli's things. The shepherdess has plunked herself down in a most uncomfortable and unnatural

FIG. 952. Late Nymphenburg coffee-pot of the neo-classic influence long after Bustelli. Metropolitan Mus. of Art.

pose and seems to be looking beyond the bird in a dream state and this is rather typical of the lack of feeling in all his things. His large "Hercules and Omphale," "Mars and Vulcan," etc., are simply small editions of the works of

Bernini. His animal combats are after engravings by Ridinger, dry, unpleasant. Even so, many terra cotta casts were made of them in the 19th century.

Auliczek was pensioned off in 1797 and succeeded by J. P. Melchior who had exhausted his powers at Höchst before leaving. He made some portrait medallions and busts. Nymphenburg ended in the cold and uninteresting biscuit technique as did the other factories. Nothing about the colors was exceptional except the black. Many of Bustelli's things are left white but have a pleasant greyish or greenish tint accented in the hollows where the glaze runs thick.

Frankenthal, Kelsterbach and Ansbach copied Bustelli's works unsuccessfully and they are still being made so far as we know in the old factory. In 1792 much Nymphenburg porcelain was sold white and decorated outside the factory. Some of these outside painters were discovered by Hofmann who deciphered the marks.

FIG. 953. About 20 to 30 years ago the porcelain works at Nymphenburg started work again making an excellent porcelain. These well painted jars with white reserved medallions in yellow ground and natural colored flowers are typical. Ht. 17½″. Warren E. Cox Coll.

Between 1753 and 1760 the mark was a *hexagram or six pointed star* with chemical or alchemical letters and numerals outside the points of the two intersecting triangles in underglaze blue, while the factory was at the old site of Neureck, also in paste impressed a *small shield* with oblique lozenges, the Bavarian "Rautenschild" at first sharp and after a few years blunted with design slanting from upper right hand corner to lower left.

In 1761 the same shield was used and occasionally a larger shield, while in 1763 the smaller one was resumed. Around 1800 the shield became carelessly drawn in a shape rather like a turtle shell. In 1810 to 1815 the old original shield was used but contrary to heraldic usage, slanting from the upper left corner to lower right. In about 1850 the five pointed star above a shield was impressed with a stamp.

There are many exceptions to these general rules: 1.—A St. Andrew's cross may replace the shield; 2.—An oval with lozenges may replace the shield; 3.—The hexagram may be used later by Auliczek; 4.—A series of "Turchenkopgen" (Turkish cups) to be sent to the Near East was marked with two crossed staves made to resemble the Meissen mark in various forms.

Many letters and signs are also used but have not been deciphered. The most usual is an intwined AC for Adam Clair, a pupil of Melchior's about 1799.

FRANKENTHAL WARES

Paul Hannong, the faïence maker of Strasburg, had with the help of Löwenfinck just begun to make porcelain in 1754 when Vincennes, later to be Sèvres, was given the monopoly for France. He was a resident of Alsace which was now in France and now out and found himself in a difficult position. He tried to sell his secret to the French government but was not successful and so finally went to the Elector Palatine, Carl Theodor, and was given the privilege to open a factory in 1755 at Frankenthal, though he had wanted to go to Mannheim.

The son, Charles Hannong, was superintendent and meanwhile the father returned to Strasburg to continue his faïence business, while supplying his son with materials, workmen and models. In 1757 the son died and was succeeded by another son, Joseph Adam Hannong, who finally bought the factory from his father in 1759 and, after the father's death in 1860, carried on both factories. The faïence factory was a success but the porcelain one could not be made to pay and finally he had to sell out to the Elector Carl Theodor who put it under a complicated management under Adam Bergdoll.

In 1770 Simon Feilner of Höchst and Für-stenberg was an assistant in charge of modeling. Bergdoll was ousted by Feilner who stayed on until about 1794 or 1795 when the French occupied Frankenthal and leased the factory to Peter van Recum. Then the French left and it reverted to the electoral administration until 1797 when it became French again and was leased to the heir of Peter van Recum, a relative named Johann Nepomuk van Recum, but it was not successful and in 1800 it was abolished and some of the workmen were transferred to Nymphenburg.

Thus the place lasted only half a century and under ever-changing management. The first master modeler was Johann Wilhelm Lanz who was under Joseph Adam Hannong in most of the first electoral period. He had no specialty but copied the usual subjects and technique from Meissen. His color was bold, not always in good taste and not well applied.

FIG. 954. Dancer from Frankenthal c. 1760, possibly by J. W. Lanz. White hard paste with overglaze enamel colors. Ht. 5½". Metropolitan Mus. of Art.

Johann Friedrich Lück was contemporary and took Lanz' place in 1761 when he departed, keeping it until 1764 and then going on to Meissen and Höchst. His work is stiff and over-ornate but well colored. His best known Frankenthal groups are "The Pair of Dancers," "The Five Senses," "The Princess and Her Retinue" and some arbor groups with pairs of lovers

Joseph Adam Hannong was an arcanist but may have tried his hand at art with "The Woman Playing a Hurdy-gurdy" signed "J.A. Hannong 1761" which looks exactly like Lück's work in biscuit. Perhaps the style was so quickly contagious or perhaps it was just one more of those things.

The Carl Theodor Period (1762–1794–5) changed the figures to those with antique draperies or none at all. In 1762 Konrad Link was master modeler having studied at Vienna and Berlin and practiced at Mannheim. After he left Frankenthal in 1766 he returned to Mannheim but continued to furnish the factory with models and drawings. He did "The Nine Muses," "Twelve Months," "The Seasons," "The Elements," relief portraits of Carl Theodor and his consort, "The Graces" and the usual gods, allegorical figures, etc., one of the finest of which is "Meleager and Atlanta," simple and lovely in pose. His figures have expressive eyes and he seems to have liked to do them looking at each other. His use of drapery for support and to give movement is well handled.

Karl Gottlieb Lück took his place and is supposed to have been a relative of both Johann Freirich and also the ivory carver Johann Christoph Ludwig Lück who was employed at Meissen, Vienna and Copenhagen. His style was made up of that of Johann Freirich's and of Konrad Link's with a leaning toward the former, than whom he seemed to have more humor and a lighter touch with more vitality. He was a good colorist. He preferred to do things from actual life, though his "Europa and the Bull" and "Pluto and Diana at the Altar" are fairly good. Such groups as "The Birthday of the Child," "The Dismissed Servant Maid," "The Good Mother," and "The Naughty Children," are his forte and, in fact, this story telling sort of art was typical of the period. He also did conventional Chinese groups, pastoral groups and hunting groups as well as a cavalry engagement, all of which are lacking in form and life. He died in 1775.

FIG. 955. Frankenthal salt cellar with pastoral scenes and floral spray simply said to be 18th cent. by the museum but bearing the mark CT in blue, standing for Carl Theodor, which would make it between 1762 and 1770. Length 2½". Metropolitan Mus. of Art.

Adam Bauer, who took his place was not much of an artist though he had been the Court Sculptor at Württemberg. His figures were academic but often with heads too large which gives them a dwarf-like look.

Johann Peter Melchior took his place in 1779 with a dry technique and some of the old models from Höchst and Frankenthal. He also did some of the little children figures, portrait medallions, etc.

Adam Clair and his pupil, Landolin Ohmacht, carried on the medallions and biscuit busts in the same style.

The earliest pieces have P.H. for Paul Hannong and are according to Polaczek made in Strasburg between 1751 and 1754 before Hannong set up his factory in Frankenthal. They are rouge boxes in the form of a fragment of fluted column, a round tureen with German roses in polychrome and a set of vases with "Mosaik" and large panels showing theatrical scenes after Watteau, etc., including "Chinese style" and wicker patterns.

Just a little later the style became florid and "Indian flowers" were used in two shades of purple. A great centerpiece of rococo scrolls and lattice upon which are many detachable figures, dates 1760. An even more ornate chandelier after a Konrad Link model was made about 1765 for the Residential Palace at Karlsruhe and is mentioned by Hannover as being, "probably, as regards structure, the finest of all 18th century chandeliers." If this is so, we must conclude that his ideas of structure and ours are at variance. Nothing much was actually invented unless it be the rhomboidal platters with rounded corners which seem to be a specialty. There was much ordinary figure painting, the best known artists being Winterstein, Magnus and Osterspey. Another specialty was the painting of exotic birds.

Between 1770 and 1780 the factory of Carl Theodor tried to copy Sèvres and adopted a spotted pattern known as "oeil-de-perdrix" and a textile pattern with gold stripes and polychrome flowers along with other textile

FIG. 956. Frankenthal, German porcelain group with polychrome decoration and mark in underglaze blue. (1787). Ht. 7¼". Metropolitan Mus. of Art.
FIG. 957. Pieces from a set dating about 1770 and made at Frankenthal during the John Hannong period. Ht. of coffee pot 9". Metropolitan Mus. of Art.

patterns. They also did grained wood like Niederviller faïence and Nymphenburg porcelain and with the same sort of engraving in red. How worn out even so simple and cheap a trick does get in this century!

Feilner is said to have invented an underglaze black, a "bleu-de-roi" and a sky blue. We also hear that in 1769 Berthevin sold the secret of transferring prints in colors to the factory but no known pieces exist. The technique of the body of Frankenthal was brought from Passau and is as a rule soft white resembling French soft paste, and even at times yellowish. In 1774 a kaolin deposit was found but it was rather poor and from that date the ware is grey and often blistered on the surface. The factory was lucky in that work stopped before it came to the final period of the decline.

The first mark is a "Rautenschild" like that of Nymphenburg but painted in underglaze blue rather than impressed. Rarely is there an impressed P.H. for Paul Hannong. Later the same was used without the shield and the initials were sometimes impressed several times on a piece. An F (for Frankenthal) often is also used. The *lion rampant* in underglaze blue for the Palatinate was introduced while Paul Hannong was still in charge before 1760 and Joseph Adam Hannong added his initials JAH from 1759 to 1762. In 1762 CT for Carl Theodor was used, surmounted with the electoral cap and also in underglaze blue. Between 1762 and 1770 we find below this AB for Adam Bergdoll. After 1770 abbreviated dates such as 71 or 77 were impressed or painted. In 1795 the electoral initials ceased because of the French taking of the factory and there are very rare pieces with P V R in underglaze blue. In 1797 V R in underglaze blue stood for van Recum the heir. There are also the usual painter's and modeler's marks.

Before the first World War figures brought between 20 and 200 pounds in London but now they are nowhere nearly so much liked. The factory did not come to the point of copying its own old wares.

LUDWIGSBURG WARES

Ludwigsburg is just north of Stuttgart and with it we come to the last of the "important" factories of Germany which sprouted around Meissen like "suckers" about a willow stump, and this was much like the others. Charles Eugene, Duke of Württemberg, was a spendthrift and as luxury loving as most of the princes of the time. Of course he had to have a porcelain factory to add to his magnificence. His was a long reign from 1737 to 1793 and in 1758 he simply took over a small place that had been running a few years in Ludwigsburg near Stuttgart. He placed in charge of it Joseph Jacob Ringler who had previously worked at Vienna and Neudeck, and in this he was either wise or lucky for Ringler stuck for 40 years in spite of the troubles at the factory.

As was usual, the factory had been started without thought as to proper location and there was no fuel or kaolin in the surrounding country so the latter had to be brought from Hafnerzell, near Passau, far to the east. It was said that the richest of the merchants could not pay what the porcelain cost so the factory was attached to the faïence factory from about 1763 to help defray the expenses. In 1766 the ducal residence was transferred to the same City of Ludwigsburg and demands kept 154 workers busy; but in 1775 the residence was moved again to Stuttgart and a decline set in, the number of employees dropping to 81 in 1776. The Duke Charles took a journey to Sèvres and Wedgwood and was enthused, but when he died in 1793 the factory declined still more. Elector Frederick tried to revive it by bringing in some French workmen from Sèvres but in 1824 the undertaking was liquidated.

The porcelain is actually inferior to that of the other German factories, being grey and unevenly glazed, but it was cohesive and very delicate details could be modeled in it. Also large pieces could be made.

The art director Johann Gottfried Trothe (1758–1762) as well as Gottlieb Friedrich Riedel, who came to the factory in 1759 from Frankenthal, and Johann Göz, who was the first assembler "repairer" or "Oberpoussierer" as they were called, were all of the rococo school. Riedel left behind him engravings, sketches and models which were used by many factories. Göz was the leading figure modeler and is probably more or less responsible for the "Apollo Candlestick," in white porcelain at the Altertümersammlung in Stuttgart, as well as the companion piece, the "Diana Candlestick," and other figures (see Hans Christ on Ludwigsburg). Frankenthal is the undoubted influence due to Riedel who had been born in Dresden, worked at Meissen (1743–56), Höchst (1757–59) and then at Frankenthal before coming to Ludwigsburg. In 1779 he made engravings in Augsburg. He died in 1784. He and Göz both are probably responsible for the little dancing group of two men crowning a lady, and others of the same stiff and fussy sort. The ones with regularly shaped pedestals are possibly correctly attributed to Göz or Johann Jacob Louis who took his place.

Louis worked at the factory between 1762 and 1772 and, to the delight of collectors, marked his work, with an L. He did a parrot, and the birds as well as animals which are often fighting. He also did a fairly good "Turk with Horse" and possibly some Chinese figures which Hannover says remind him of Bustelli but he makes it clear, it should be noticed, that he is not contributing to the false legend which Balet built up concerning a mythical "Pustelli" supposed to have been a famous artist at Ludwigsburg. There was no such person.

Hans Christ in his book claims that these Chinese figures were actually done by Domenico Ferretti but Hannover says, "apparently without adequate reason." Ferretti had come to Stuttgart to work on the residency before he went to work in the porcelain factory in 1764. He brought a classical influence which soon became predominant as elsewhere. Most of his things were simply small scale adaptations of his work in stone and the heads are sometimes very small to give them a monumental look.

More than Ferretti, Christian Wilhelm Beyer brought classicism. He had been a painter and architect in Rome before deciding to become a sculptor. He went to Württemberg in 1759. There are two collections of his etchings in Vienna, one done in 1779 and the other in 1784 which give us a fine idea of his style. He was influenced by Wincklemann in Rome and by Natoire of the French Academy there. It is interesting to see how strongly contrasted are his alive and sexual Dionysiac Graeco-Roman divinities and his rather stupid Olympian ones. In such subjects as "The Satyr Kissing a Bacchante or others with his male and female figures embracing and crushing grapes he finds life and lust, while in his "Mourning Artemisia," "Venus," as well as his allegories such as "Veritas" and "Libertas" he becomes so banal that we can hardly believe the same artist did them.

In his "Musical Solos" (if in truth they are his), which is a series well known, he gets a pensive, coquettish feeling which is more tolerable in the female than in the male figures.

In 1767 he left for Vienna where he assisted in decorating with sculpture the court at Schönbrunn.

There were other sculptors of whom we know very little. Joseph Weinmüller was certainly there and did some work but has only been credited on doubtful grounds with a "Hercules Fighting the Nemean Lion." Pierre

François Lejeune has been credited by Balet with the above mentioned "Musical Solos," etc., instead of Beyer and this is not difficult to believe, for I cannot very well conceive of the same man doing such widely different things, technically speaking, as the bacchanalian figures and the almost silly "Player on the French Horn" in Stuttgart, who looks as though he were about to weep. But these arguments are of little interest to us and we need only note that another authority, Schnorr von Carolsfeld, denies him any part at all in modeling at Ludwigsburg.

FIG. 958. Ludwigsburg figure of a street sweeper by Beyer (1762–1767) decorated with enamel colors. Ht. 5⅛". Metropolitan Mus. of Art.
FIG. 959. Ludwigsburg late 18th cent. group representing Summer, one of a series of the seasons, decorated with pale lilac, blue, apple-green, yellow, red and black and flesh colors. Ht. 8¾". Metropolitan Mus. of Art.

All at least agree that Johann Heinrich Schmidt was the "repairer" at the factory from 1774 and did two white urns supported by three figures and a pair of memorial columns with a couple placing a wreath on them.

Later in the years 1790 to 1795 two more academic sculptors, Philip Jacob Scheffauer and Johann Heinrich Dannecker worked in biscuit. The latter did children groups representing, originally enough for that day at least, the "Seasons" and a boresome "Ariadne on the Panther."

It is very likely that part of the trend toward the biscuit was brought about by disgust on the part of the public for the garish and unpleasant color applied in the immediately preceding years. At Ludwigsburg the best period was between 1760 and 1770. Beyer's color was pleasant; his draperies were often a subdued violet or lilac or soft pink. During his time strong color was also used but it was dull and the nude parts were only delicately tinged. Later the color becomes cruder and darker, the nude's cheeks, knees, ears and other prominent parts are reddened and the figures at this time are below the average of the other factories in quality.

The enthusiasm shown in the figures was lacking for the "ordinary wares" which are dirty, grey and full of flaws while also being altogether too ordinary in design. One stunt was a relief scale surface over which strewn flowers were painted without regard to the surface. The "Osier" or wicker pattern was taken freely from other factories. The cohesive quality of the clay made possible some vases based on molded projecting supports.

Due to so many flaws, more decoration was dabbed on to hide them than good taste could stand. The flowers and birds are often also too large for the pieces and design sprawls all over the vessels in confusion and lack of organization. Again it bunches up tightly in a hard knot of flowers that look as strangled as a bouquet of wild flowers in the hand of a six-year-old child. The birds are probably from Riedel; certainly not from nature. The flowers are after Friedrich Kirschner. The usual Boucher, Watteau and Rugendas samples were made and landscapes with ruins were supported on rococo scrolls. With these noble themes we are often startled to find a bug or butterfly resting on the edge of the plate and so carefully painted as to make nearsighted ladies exclaim. In other words just everything was mastered including nature itself.

The mark is two C's placed back to back and intersecting, referring to Duke Charles, and surmounted, therefore, by a crown at times. Hannover says that some writers regard the crown as a mark of quality but that it is not. This mark was in underglaze blue but very rarely in red. An antler is sometimes with the C's or by a single L or three of them. Another L refers to Duke Ludwig. FR was used for King Fredrick (Fredrick Rex), surmounted by a royal

FIG. 960. Cup and saucer said to be from Ludwigsberg between 1758 and 1824. These pieces are of course strongly Japanese in style. Dia. of plate 5″. Metropolitan Mus. of Art.

crown and in red, gold or impressed. Also LOUISBOURG was painted in red. From 1816 to 1824 the monogram WR crowned for Wilhelm Rex was usually in gold.

CHAPTER XXIII

18TH CENTURY EUROPEAN PORCELAIN CONTINUED: FRANCE, ITALY, SPAIN, PORTUGAL, SWITZERLAND, RUSSIA, NETHERLANDS, BELGIUM, DENMARK, SWEDEN

FRANCE

VINCENNES & SÈVRES

RETURNING to France where no Böttger was captured and "soft paste" continued for years we find that just west of Frankenthal, Mannheim and Ludwigsburg the cities of Lille, St. Amand, Valenciennes and Strasburg were

slow to steal the secret of hard porcelain. True, the potters were conscious of the fact that they must learn to compete with the northern and eastern factories, but it was slow to come. However, when the Dubois brothers, who had worked at St. Cloud and Chantilly, came to Orry de Fulvy, brother of the Comptroller General and financial advisor for France, it was not difficult to get the patronage in 1738 of Louis XV, and a riding-school at Vincennes was put at their disposal. Here they experimented and used up all the money granted plus 10,000 more livres and produced nothing. Later a workman named François Gravant in 1745 produced a semblance of porcelain, and a syndicate was formed with 90,000 livres and later 250,000 livres capital and was granted a 20-year privilege. Even so the king was again and again obliged to contribute to the organization's maintenance.

About 1750 the factory had about 100 hands or 10 throwers, 11 molders, 7 "makers of handles and spouts," 10 modelers, 10 painters and some 46 girls

FIG. 961. Soft paste vase made at Vincennes about 1750. Ht. 7½". Metropolitan Mus. of Art.

682

under the heading of "fleurs" who possibly made the flowers copied from Meissen and made for decoration of vases, chandeliers, clocks, etc. and which were also popular when mounted on wire stems with metal leaves to serve as bouquets in vases. These flowers date from 1748 and in that year Madame de Pompadour bought 270 livres worth, while the king and queen paid 4,200 livres for flowers alone. In 1749 the crown princess, wishing to prove to her father, the King of Saxony, that the Vincennes factory compared with Meissen, sent him a blanc de chine vase with figures on either side mounted in ormolu and containing a large bouquet of flowers, some 480 in number. Of total sales that year of 44,600 the flowers brought 36,000 livres.

FIG. 962. Vincennes cachepot of about 1750 with scenes in pale enamel colors, handles decorated in purple, and gold bands. Ht. 4". Metropolitan Mus. of Art.

Probably at the instigation of the art loving Madame de Pompadour the king reorganized the factory and placed it under the technical leadership of Jean Hellot, Director of the Academy of Sciences. The artistic leaders were Duplessis, goldsmith to the court, and Bachelier and Hults who created the real "porcelaine de France."

With the usual unfortunate influence of the metal crafts, Duplessis made some ornate and involved forms one of which was called "vase vaisseau à mat" and somewhat resembles a boat, while another vase had elephant heads on either side with the trunks turned up into candle holders. These terrible things are very costly and considered rare and beautiful by some collectors.

Other examples of the period are white wares with relief blossom design made by workmen from St. Cloud and painted pieces after the Meissen wares after Kakiemon, with "Indian flowers," etc. made by workmen from Chantilly. Perhaps the earliest piece known dates about 1750 and has "Indian flowers" and insects about the edge with the center treated much like the "yellow tiger" design of Meissen. Even at this early period the gilding was laid thickly and burnished with a hob-nail "au clou," finely chased and engraved. A charming effect was obtained by even spacing of dots graduating from large to small and more closely spaced towards the center or the reverse. Such plates usually have a simple center medallion and border. There were dress fabrics similarly treated which one may recall having seen in pictures of the costumes towards the end of the century.

A strong blue was used for painting "children among clouds" and flowers. A purple was also used for these, for landscapes and for ornaments and birds. The polychrome effects were too brilliant to be pleasant. The birds look like imaginary pheasants and the figures, which were painted by artists recruited from the fan painters, remind one of the less good examples of this kindred art. Perhaps to get away from this unpleasant style, Viellard painted figures with the flesh parts natural and the drapes in monochrome shading.

Perforated wares and relief wares similar to the "Gotzkowsky erhabene Blumen" were tried. Then there were blue grounds with gold spots or reserved white stars, the use of large scattered corn-flowers and a "seme" or strewing of the same flowers.

Hellot with his assistants Gravant, Gerin, Caillat, Massue and Taunay obtained a large range of colors which united perfectly with the glaze of the soft porcelain. Hellot made the rule that all discoveries belonged to the factory and in 1753 he collected all the results and published them in a book still kept by the factory. A cup at the Sèvres Museum is signed by Taunay and dated 1748. It has sample strokes of many colors. Hellot invented the famous "bleu-de-roi" (royal blue) in 1749 superseding the "grosbleu." The turquoise blue was invented in 1752 and this is certainly one of the most beautiful of the Sèvres colors.

FIG. 964. Sèvres covered bowl which is decorated by Xrowet, 1767. Ht. 3⅞". Metropolitan Mus. of Art.

FIG. 963. Soft paste Sèvres ewer of 1756 with sprays of flowers in enamel colors on white ground, edges gilt, silver mountings. Ht. 6⅝". Metropolitan Mus. of Art.

The death of Orry de Fulvy led to a reorganization in 1751 and the king took a fourth of the capital in 1753 amounting to some 800,000 livres, allowed the factory to use the name "*Manufacture Royale de Porcelaine de France*," and to mark the wares with two intertwined Ls which had, however, already been used for a few years unofficially. The factory was moved to Sèvres, half way between Paris and Versailles near the Palace of Bellevue which Madame de Pompadour had built three years before and where she received the king in her much talked of winter garden of porcelain flowers. The new building cost about a million livres and in 1756 the factory was solemnly inaugurated.

In 1757 the painter Xrowet or Xhrouet invented the pink ground, it is said, but Hellot must have had something to do with it for after his death in 1766 it disappears forever. This is the color which the English miscall "rose Dubarry" though the pieces decorated with it were made at a time when that little lady was still quite unknown. The French correctly call it "rose Pompadour." It is a color of great purity and opacity, neither bluish nor yellowish. A similar color had been invented in China in the K'ang Hsi reign (1662–1722) but of quite different consistency, and, to tell the truth, deeper, richer and more pleasant.

A yellow called "jaune jonquille" is rare. Then there was also a delicate violet, deep green, light apple green among others which are even more seldom seen than the early colors.

Fig. 965. Cup and saucer with *bleu-de-roi* ground with birds in gold in reserved medallions, Vincennes about 1753. Plate dia. 6". Metropolitan Mus. of Art.

The paste was made of sand from Fontainebleau, sea-salt, saltpetre, soda, alum and plaster-of-Paris or alabaster which were mixed together and fired at least 50 hours to yield a white frit which was pounded to a fine powder and mixed with marl from Argenteuil and then kneaded in a mill for weeks at a time, so it is said. It was then dried in troughs, crushed between rollers and sifted before being saturated with pure water and brought to the texture for use.

The glaze was no less complicated and from the same sand from Fontainebleau, litharge, soda, flint and potash also first mixed and smelted and then ground for use.

The soft paste was first fired as biscuit unglazed and then glazed by "arrosement" or spraying, rather than dipping, in order to make it adhere better to the biscuit, a little

Fig. 966. Oval dish of soft paste either Vincennes or Sèvres of 1756 or earlier. The flowers are in natural colors with the base and rim gilt. Length 10¼". Metropolitan Mus. of Art.

vinegar first having been added to the glaze. The ware was then fired again before it was ready for decoration. The decoration took another firing and, if gold was used, that had to be fired yet again. Each firing was at a lower temperature than the preceding, of course. The colors became so fused with the glaze that they are as smooth as the unpainted parts and seemingly no thicker.

The dotted pattern was developed further into the famous "oeil-de-perdrix" consisting of tiny circles or double circles dotted in green or blue and reserved in white on a monochrome or dotted ground. Another pattern in gold was called "caillouté" or pebble pattern and looks somewhat like grease spots floating on broth. Scales, marbling, network and such were used over the blue to soften its too intense effect.

The biscuit turned out to be such a beautiful material that it could not help but appeal yet the intent was to compete with Meissen so it was not used at first. A sculptor named Blondeau did the first groups which were hunting scenes after Oudry. Fournier in 1747, very likely the same who started the Copenhagen factory, is thought to have modeled a "Naiad" and a "River Goddess," a late copy of which is in the Louvre. Chavagnac and Grollier mention only 19 colored figures. A little girl with bird cage is said to be after Boucher but must be quite a bit after. In fact Boucher is said to have worked at the factory, not as a sculptor but in making sketches, supervising, etc. Such groups as "Le jaloux" by an otherwise unknown artist named Vandrevolle or van de Voorst are very perfectly in the Boucher feeling.

In 1754 Madame de Pompadour, though she had the same figures in enamel, bought eight Boucher biscuit figures of children modeled by Blondeau and this may have given the impetus, for biscuit immediately became popular. Bachelier requested many sketches from Boucher and the sculptor Fernex carried them out, as did also Suzanne. One cannot distinguish the work of these two one from the other. They are not marked with the names of the artists but simply "après Boucher" and the best known are "La laitière, La merchande de crême, Les mangeurs raisins, La leçon de musique, Le mouton chéri," etc. All of which are rustic but elegant, naïf yet blasé, child-like, yet full of a pretty sophistication typical of the painter at his best.

Even in Vincennes we find a neo-classic taste as can be seen in the group of four young Tritons and the companion group of young Bacchus with his retinue playing with a panther, in the Victoria and Albert Museum. These are by Louis Felix de la Rue. A far greater sculptor, Etienne Falconet, became regularly associated with the factory in 1757 after having supplied some models to Vincennes. One of these is the statuette of Madame de Pompadour as the "Goddess of Friendship" of which only three known examples exist, one in a private collection in France, one in Sèvres and one in the Pierpont Morgan Collection.

After the factory moved it was under the management of Boileau. In 1756 the expenses were 1,200,000 livres while sales were only 300,000. The whole staff got along on payments on account. In 1759 the king took the factory over and a host of artists were hired. The scope of our book is such that these cannot be listed and we refer the reader to "Pottery and Porcelain. European Porcelain" by Emil Hannover, pages 283 to 295. A few deductions from this list are offered by the above authority which we give briefly:

1.   The list of flower painters is about twice that of the figure painters.
2.   Bird painters are few, as are also landscape painters.
3.   A large part of the output was in the form of services, either large dinner

SEVRES: LOUIS XV ROSE POMPADOUR SOUPIÈRE AND PAIR OF ELEPHANT VASES WITH CHINOISERIE
PAINTED BY DODIN.

Vases: Ht. 12¼ inches   c. 1760   Soupiere: Width 11¾ inches   Dated 1757   Coll. of Mrs. Henry Walters

FIG. 967. Bowl and tray (1777 ?) of Sèvres ware. Length 7¾". Metropolitan Mus. of Art.

FIG. 968. Sèvres covered bowl and tray by Aloncle (the bird painter) (1776). Length of tray 9". Metropolitan Mus. of Art.

FIG. 969. Sèvres tureen and tray with relief ornamentation gilded and the flowers and fruits in natural colors. (1777). Length of tray 24". Metropolitan Mus. of Art.

services, tête-a-tête or solitaire; and whole services were frequently given by the king as presents. Thus the Danish king was given in 1768–69 a service of some 377 pieces valued at some 32,918 livres. "Even the Emperor of China, who might be thought well able to provide himself with fine porcelain, repeatedly received large consignments of gifts from Sèvres," says Hannover. I wonder what he did with them and if they were not possibly a sort of hint for return favors.

In 1759 there were the critical moments of French finances and the king, followed by others, sent his silver and gold services to be melted at the mint, replacing them by porcelain. At exhibitions each year Madame de Pompadour frequently spent 80,000 to 100,000 livres on porcelain and this was a strong suggestion to the other ladies of the court. Catherine of Russia ordered a 744-piece service at some 328,000 livres which seems enough, but single pieces sold for as high as 40,000 reichsmarks in Frankfort while a pair of wine coolers brought 100,000.

All this made possible a technique between 1760 and 1780 which in some ways has never been equalled.

Etienne Falconet was at first influenced by Boucher and even in 1757 when he was appointed this persisted. "Les enfants Falconet" differ little from "les enfants Boucher,"—and "La lanterne magique" and "Le tourniquet" are actually after Boucher compositions along with other groups. Others such as the dairymaid at Sèvres are suggestive of Defernex. But in 1757 he made the famous "bather" in marble and in 1759 in biscuit. This was soon copied by other factories and is even made today. About this same time he made the marble "Amour" for the Hotel d'Evreux in Paris for Madame de Pompadour. That he was as appreciative of the qualities of the biscuit as of the other materials is shown by his adoption of it for his monumental works such as "Pygmalion" of the Salon of 1763, and the serious busts of Louis XV. Soon, however, his fame had outgrown this work and he was employed by Catherine II of Russia to make the monument to Peter the Great at St. Petersburg.

Bachelier then became manager of the sculpture and Pigalle was ordered to carry out some of his things among the most famous of which are the "L'amour et l'amitié" and the statue of Mercury from Frederick the Great's palace of Sansouci at Potsdam (1770). Antiques were now copied. When the Dauphin married Marie Antoinette in 1770 the factory wanted to make a present and decided to create a centerpiece of the *whole Palace Royal at Rheims with the statue of Louis XV* for a table decoration and on this foolish task Pigalle, Allegrain and Mouchy spent nearly 10 years. But Bachelier had even greater ideas of grandeur: The tapestry output of Gobelins and Beauvais had spread knowledge of the famous paintings of France. Why then should not Sèvres make all the worthy sculpture of France both antique and contemporary and, why, forsooth, should it not go a step further and make figures from the paintings and tapestries themselves? Nothing was impossible! Alors! And so the "History of Don Quixote" was made after Charles Antoine Coypel (1771) and the "Conversation Espagnole" of Carle Vanloo (1772), etc. It doesn't take much critical sense to realize what such transpositions would involve and we can only add that expectations were fulfilled.

La Du Barry, in pursuit of the Pompadour tradition, took interest in the factory and it in turn flattered her by rendering her as a "Spanish Singer" and making for her services with the initial D in gold and B in flowers. Pajou did a rather alive and charming bust of her in 1771.

THE FIRST TRUE PORCELAIN AT SÈVRES

Paul Hannong had tried to sell the secret of hard porcelain in 1753 but had failed perhaps because he could show the French no kaolin deposits on their soil. In 1760 a deposit was found at Alençon but the porcelain made from it was grey and coarse. Comte de Brances-Lauraguais made some experiments in 1764 with little result other than a few plates in psuedo-Chinese style which are signed LB and a couple of casts from medals and a portrait medallion of the Comte de Caylus signed "Nini." Then in 1768 the chemist Macquer found the wonderful deposits in Yrieix near Limoges and made a little figure of a child, now in the Sèvres Museum. Yet it was not until 1772 that production was actually under way at Sèvres and even then the hard paste was secondary to soft paste.

In this year the director Boileau died and was replaced by Parent who hired Louis-Simon Boizot, a pupil of Slotz and winner of the Prix de Rome. He was no genius but was able to carry out the work of such men as Clodion, Falconet, Bouchardon, Pigalle, Cafferi and Pajou and form a sort of representative style. At first he worked in soft paste but in 1775 he turned to "pate dure" and made such things as "L'Autel Royal" and the "Allegory of the Wedding of Louis XVI and Marie Antoinette" or "Le triomphe de Bacchus" as well as his pet theme of a woman and child, done as subjects mytho-

FIG. 970. Bisque hard paste figure, one of a series reduced from statues. This is the Baron De Montesquieu after Clodion. Sèvres 1783. Ht. 13¾". Metropolitan Mus. of Art.

FIG. 971. Sèvres (1779) porcelain pitcher with lilac ground covered with gilt dots in the center of white spots surrounded by blue dots, and medallions in pink, blue and lilac. The rims and some details are gilt. Ht. 4½". Metropolitan Mus. of Art.

logical, allegorical, from the theatre or from real life. His assistants followed him so well that their work can hardly be distinguished from his. Le Riche was one of these but he also did some original things such as "La nourrice," "Le déjeuner," "La toilette," etc., which are influenced by the scènes de moeurs of Moreau le jeune.

FIG. 972. Sèvres cup and saucer 1781 decorated by Commelin. Dia. 2⅛". Metropolitan Mus. of Art.

The hard paste things lose much of the charm that belonged to the soft paste. The new material was dead white, bluish and slightly glistening rather than warm and softly dull. It was on the other hand less liable to distortion in firing and could be more easily washed. Imitations of both the German wares and of Wedgwood were made and it was a boast that the latter particularly were perfect. Now that the factory had this medium it seemed that it had nothing to do with it for the blight had already taken hold.

Some oddities are interesting. There is a cup and saucer by Lamprecht with goats and sheep drawn in black. Fallot made a cup with pheasants and other birds in silver and gold evidently after Japanese lacquer effects. A plate of 1790 and marked G.I. has a black glaze with chinoiseries in gold. Brown tortoise-shell was made with iron and manganese which with the addition of cobalt blue became "green tortoise-shell" and which became a passion with some British collectors.

Then in 1780 Cotteau invented the "jewelled Sèvres" which was costly. This involved the fusing on of drops of enamel which to the not too observing eye might faintly resemble rubies, emeralds, sapphires, pearls and other gems. Later small glass jewels were stuck on so insecurely that they came off, if not handled with care.

Plaques of porcelain for insets for furniture and pictures of porcelain to hang on the wall were approved by Marie Antoinette. Some as large as two feet square have hunting scenes by Asselin after Oudry.

In 1778 Parent was succeeded by Regnier and in 1780 by d'Angivilliers, formerly Director des Batiments. He believed in the Classics and ordered to be made some copies of "Etruscan" vases supplied by Denon. An outstanding monument to his taste and discipline is the "Vase Medicis" standing 2 meters high, with blue ground, biscuit reliefs by Boizot and ormolu mountings by Thomire, finished in 1783. It is said that for two of these a bill of 108,000 livres was sent.

Another of his brilliant ideas resulted in the making of small figures after the statues of great men. He was also a loyal royalist and demonstrated it by having Pajou in 1781, at the birth of the Dauphin, make a "Venus rising from the sea," bringing a Dauphin to France. This is a really beautiful piece. But the jobs became more and more difficult and Boizot fell down badly in 1785 when, at the birth of the Duke of Normandy, he was given the task of representing "The French monarchy, on the stem of which the Genius of Fertility plants the third shoot."

Marie Antoinette is said to have had one service in which each plate took two months of solid work and cost nearly 500 livres. The "arabesque service" was designed by the architect Masson after motives from the Loggia of Raphael and there were others of great grandeur.

Boizot held a fairly good quality in the modeling as can be traced by the "Toilet of Venus" (1783), "The Birth of Bacchus" (1784), "The Rape of Prosperine" (1787), "The Childhood of Silenus" (1788) and "The Muses" of the same year. But wealthy people were already leaving Paris. In 1789 the hands revolted because they could not get their wages. Late in 1790 a

FIG. 973. Bisque figures mounted in ormolu which the museum calls Sèvres 1780–90 but which could not be much earlier than the later date and have a distinct Empire feeling. Ht. of central figure 13½". Metropolitan Mus. of Art.

syndicate made an offer for the factory but the king could not bring himself to let it go. In 1791 in May, the National Assembly declared that the factory of Gobelins and of Sèvres were both on the Civil List of the king, and were not to be treated like the other "biens nationaux."

After the Revolution there was, of course, a chaotic period but in May of 1800 Brongniart took the post of manager and held it for 47 years. During the Revolution the old artists had fled fearing that their work under d'Angivilliers might bring them under suspicion. Many had signed works designed for the glorification of the royal house and had seen such things smashed to pieces in 1793 by order of the men of the factories' own staff in the short space of four hours. Only a few such works were spared such as a bust of Frederick the Great by Boizot for the reason that he had been not only a king but also a philosopher and a friend of Voltaire, some busts of Diderot, Rousseau, Brutus and Socrates.

During the years 1790 to 1795 the wares are only of historical interest. Fasces, Phrygian caps and the tricolored ribbon were the chief motives and some of the old stock designs were used but poorly. The factory, you see, was of no use at all to the masses.

DIRECTOIRE PERIOD

The man of the Directorate was not averse to the old time luxury and the factory supplied grandiose things which were, however, not always paid for and so the financial difficulties became acute. Auction sales and lotteries were held and large amounts of undecorated pieces were sold off. Thus most of the pieces of the period which are seen now were decorated outside the factory and hundreds are of quite recent decoration even though they bear every resemblance to the real thing.

One of the first steps that Brongniart took was to stop the production of soft paste in 1804. That he was vitally interested is proven by his book, "Traite des arts ceramiques," (1844), but his was entirely a scientific mind and the taste continued lower and lower. He made the same mistake that

FIG. 974. Cup and saucer of Sèvres 1807. Metropolitan Mus. of Art.

FIG. 975. Sèvres biscuit bust of Louis XVI. Ht. 10¼". Made in 1820. Metropolitan Mus. of Art.

FIG. 976. Sèvres bust of Marie Antoinette, in biscuit. Ht. 12". 1821. Metropolitan Mus. of Art.

Sorgenthal had made at Vienna and turned loose a group of historical painters who had not the slightest idea of decorative beauty. Over the stiff, mechanical empire shapes they worked with dull colors and too bright gold. They were busy for the Revolution had emptied all the palaces of porcelain and at the same time the trend was toward grandeur and pomposity. It was an urge to hurry but a demand for much detail; a bad combination which led to shortcuts and trickery.

Many outside influences were not digested. The "Egyptian service" (1808) had a blue ground with hieroglyphics in gold and pictures by Sweebach drawn from Napoleon's expedition to the Nile. The "Olympian service" was another, and a "Medici vase" had 150 figures in the foreground and 2,000 in the background while a "Vase Etrusque" had a frieze of the solemn conqueror's procession into Paris with the stolen Italian works of art. The little plaquets for furniture were not grand enough so whole table tops were used to glorify some great personage.

MARKS

1753—L's entwined, up to Revolution.

Starting with 1753 the alphabet was used for year marks and in 1778 when it had been used up, double letters were used in the intervals between the L's. The following table is given for ready reference:

A—1753	J—1762	R—1770	AA—1778	II—1786
B—1754	K—1763	S—1771	BB—1779	JJ—1787
C—1755	L—1764	T—1772[1]	CC—1780[2]	KK—1788
D—1756	M—1765	U—1773	DD—1781	LL—1789
E—1757	N—1766	V—1774	EE—1782	MM—1790
F—1758	O—1767	X—1775	FF—1783	NN—1791
G—1759	P—1768	Y—1776	GG—1784	OO—1792
H—1760	Q—1769	Z—1777	HH—1785	PP—until 17th
I—1761				of July 1793.

Hard porcelain between 1769 and 1793 has as a rule a crown above the two L's.

1793—17th of July until 1800 RF meaning Republique Francaise either used
        separately or in a monogram and with the word Sèvres or seve beneath.

1801 to 1816—There were the following year marks:

T9 (Year IX	of the Republic) 1801	9	1809
X (" X	" " ") 1802	10	1810
II (" XI	" " ") 1803	oz (onze)	1811
(" XII	" " ") 1804	dz (douze)	1812
(" XIII	" " ") 1805	tz (treize)	1813
(" XIV	" " ") 1806	qz (quatorze)	1814
7 1807		qn (quinze)	1815
8 1808		sz (seize)	1816
		ds (dix-sept)	1817

To these were added:

1801–1802 "Sèvres" in gold or color

1803–1804 (8 May)—"M N[le] Sèvres" in red, meaning (Manufacture Nationale de Sèvres)

1804–1809 "M. Imp[le] de Sèvres" in red

1810–1814 A crowned eagle in red surrounded by the words "Manufacture Imperiale Sèvres"
        (The three last were printed with a stamp)

1815—Two L's again printed in blue (under Louis XVIII)

The marks before 1800 were usually in blue and generally over the glaze (except in the early Vincennes ones which were *gros bleu* in decoration) or on hard paste. These are under the glaze, if in blue, but also in red and other colors over the glaze.

Sèvres biscuit has no factory mark until after 1860, but sometimes has marks denoting the moulder. Pieces with marks are modern.

Naturally there were as many fakes here at this important factory as at

Meissen. The chances of reward were so great that they have existed from the very beginning. It was against the law to use either color or gold in France for the long period of protection and any piece which shows either must, therefore, have been done with intent to deceive, if it did not come from the factory direct. Let us list a few statements:

1. Some hard porcelain bears the marks of the soft porcelain period, often marked A, going the whole hog.

2. The mark of a well known flower painter may appear on a piece bearing figures.

3. Any piece covered entirely with enamel and mounted with ormolu should be mistrusted. Many fake table tops were sold to tourists in the Rue de Rivoli.

4. At St. Amand-les-Eaux, Bettignies and his descendants made a material resembling the soft paste of Sèvres between 1815 and 1877.

5. Modern forgeries never have the color blended with the glaze as in the real Sèvres pate tendre.

6. The gold is etched "au clou" on the old pieces while modern ones are treated with thinner gold and agates are used giving a smoother, thinner effect.

7. At Minton, England, French artists were hired about 1860 to imitate the wares but they were clearly marked of that factory. However, such marks have been tampered with.

8. At Coalport in Shropshire imitations were made of the bleu-de-roi, turquoise and rose Pompadour and the Sèvres mark was nicely copied.

9. Thomas Martin Randall, at Madeley near Coalport, made an artificial porcelain between 1830 and 1840 which was covered with a turquoise ground like Sèvres. He also bought undecorated pieces, dressed them up and sold them through a dealer named Baldock in London.

10. Both Derby and Worcester made successful copies.

11. Most of the French factories made copies with bodies usually heavier and less white.

12. Fischer and Herend of Hungary made successful copies.

13. Genuine Sèvres pieces often have a small glazed hole (note the "glazed") in the foot-rim for hanging them up. When this is missing there is reason for doubt but its presence is no sure guarantee.

14. If the green is chrome of warm yellowish tone and lacking that slight iridescence generally on copper green, the piece was not decorated in the 18th century as this color came into being only in 1804.

15. If gilding has been fired too often in processes of faking and redecoration, it sinks into the glaze and loses brilliance.

16. Little black specks often occur on the white after repeated firings.

17. The turquoise on late pieces is usually greenish and the pink is too muddy, transparent or off color.

18. Naturally jewelled pieces with year marks prior to 1780 are fakes.

19. All biscuit with the Sèvres marks are fakes or made during the latter half of the 19th century.

20. Biscuit figures which have been glazed show black specks under the glaze according to Chavagnac and Grollier. There are "barely a score" of

known figures in glazed Sèvres porcelain, so one is not likely to find one on 2nd or 3rd Avenue, New York.

21.   The hard porcelain was not so much copied in France but inferior wares have often their marks removed so that they can be palmed off on the unsuspecting purchaser.

FIG. 977. Tournai plate with flowers in natural colors, soft paste said by the museum to be between 1750 and 1755. Dia. 8¾″. Metropolitan Mus. of Art.

FIG. 978. Tournai, cup and saucer of soft paste with enamels of brown, green and rose with edges gilt. On the cup is the fox and the lion from the Fables of La Motte. On the saucer are two mules from the Fables of La Fontaine. Metropolitan Mus. of Art.

FIG. 979. Tournai milk jug with underglaze design in blue. This piece is of such faulty soft paste that it is likely to date between 1756 and 1762. (Note the greyish blotches near the bottom and pitting.) Ht. 5½″. Metropolitan Mus. of Art.
FIG. 980. Valenciennes plate with polychrome decoration. Note the poor quality of the paste showing pitting, etc. Metropolitan Mus. of Art.
FIG. 981. Late example of La Seynie 1774–1799. Metropolitan Mus. of Art.

SMALLER FRENCH FACTORIES

It will be seen immediately upon reflection that no such free-for-all among the small factories as occurred in Germany could possibly take place in France, for in this country there was an all powerful central government and that government had given its protection to the *Vincennes Sèvres* factories. Two movements defied this condition: First, there was a revival in the second half of the 18th century of soft porcelain, which was naturally dominated by the artistic dictates of *Sèvres* and at the same time had a hard fight for existence, commercially speaking, in competition with the royal factory and its privileges. Second, after hard porcelain had been discovered, the secret, with help from Germany, spread like wild fire throughout the country and a tremendous number of little factories was started almost over night, only to run afoul of the same difficulties with the parent factory just as soon as they became of troublesome size. These conditions determined the fact that the small French factories all slavishly copied Sèvres but never in any way rivalled this center in technique, as those in Germany in some instances rivalled or surpassed, in certain details, Meissen.

TABLE OF SMALLER FACTORIES OF FRANCE

Name	Marks	Period of activity	Description of wares, artists, etc.
Sceaux in the Department of Seine.	SX	Founded by *Jacques Chapelle* under patronage of *Duchesse de Maine* later under *Duc de Penthièvre* managed by *Julien Jacques Richard Glot.*	Soft porcelain and *faïence.* Only in 1784 given full freedom to make porcelain. Had to edge its wares with pink and not gold, forced by *Sèvres.*
	anchor as also on the faïence.		Paste like *Mennecy.*
			Small articles, pomade-pots, mustard-pots, salt-cellars, covered bowls, etc.
			Polychrome birds, flowers, etc., like their own *faïence* and *Vincennes.* Also small comet-like flowers like Chantilly.
Tournai in the 18th century it was French.	1750–1781 Tower with gate, and windows and battlements from arms of town in color or gold.	*Francois-Joseph Peternick.* Factory declined in 1799 at his death.	See Netherlands section under *faïence.*
			Style resembles *Meissen* and *Derby* as well as *Sèvres.*
			Made a typical French soft porcelain so good that it could be used to counterfeit *Sèvres.*
Tournai	1756 to end also 2 crossed swords like those of Saxony the 4 angles having crosses in gold or underglaze blue on ordinary wares.	Head painter was *Ghislain-Joseph Mayer.*	1750–56 paste greyish and faulty polychrome flowers after *Meissen* and birds *"sur terrasse"* in pink or in four colors:—blue, yellow, green and brownish grey.
			1756–1762 paste yellowish and colors more numerous and paler, with flowers like *Strasburg faïence,* also in pink; also *chinoiseries* and birds.
			1762–1781 prime of factory— warm tone like *Sèvres* all colors and designs with also touches of gold, also gold alone, bright birds were favorites by *Henri-Joseph Duvivier* (1763–1771), also landscapes with ruins in pink, children after Boucher in pink and a *bleu-de-roi* was made. About 1735 painting in *grisaille* in medallions on yellow, green, blue or red ground.

TABLE OF SMALLER FACTORIES OF FRANCE—*Continued*

Name	Marks	Period of activity	Description of wares, artists, etc.
		A. J. Mayer.	Also "décor bois" like the other wood imitations with engravings. Also blue and white, which was late and distinguished by division of edge with radially placed curved lines in relief.
	Stork given at the Hague which were decorated there.		The Hague factory made hard porcelain but bought blanks of soft paste from Tournai to decorate.
Orleans	O with crown over it.	1753 M. Gerré	Faïence and soft paste—from 1768 hard porcelain.
	Also heraldic label with C under it on soft paste.		Soft paste decorated in blue like Chantilly rarely in polychrome like Vincennes.
	Fleur-de-lys on hard paste.		Pretty without distinction.

Note:—*Chavagnac* and *Grollier* have furnished proof that the label was one of the marks used by the second *Vincennes* factory on its hard porcelain.

Name	Marks	Period of activity	Description of wares, artists, etc.
Crepy-en-Valois	D.C.P. ?	1762–	Children figures in glassy paste ? (Sèvres Museum).
Étiolles Seine-et-Oise	"Étiolles 1770 Pellevé"		Reeded jug with poorly painted flowers, also reeded cup, with greenish tone. (British Museum.) Also a coffee-pot and cup with pale polychrome flowers and landscape in purple (B.M.) This last is of hard porcelain.
	"Étiolles"		
	MP (Monier & Pellevé)		
Arras	AA in monogram.	1770– I. F. Boussemaert from Lille.	Soft porcelain like Chantilly, St. Cloud or Tournai.
	AR in monogram or separately.	Four maiden ladies took over factory in 1771. Their name was Delemer.	Chiefly blue and white, seldom polychrome—(see two plates with pale flowers at Sèvres).
Saint-Amand-les-Eaux (Nord)	J.F. in a double monogram flanked by SA, same as on faïence.	1771–1778, Jean-Baptiste-Joseph Fauquez. 1778 passed to the family of Bettignies and up to present.	One plate at Sèvres with greyish glaze painted in purple with castles by a river and a narrow border.
	Imitated Sèvres marks.		19th century imitations of Sèvres pâte tendre.
	S.A. to 1830.		In 1851 Salvetat wrote "The ground colors are in every way comparable to those which have won for Sèvres so great a reputation." But Hannover does not agree.
Strasburg	H in underglaze blue for Chas. period.	Chas. Hannong died in 1760, his son Joseph Adam Hannong returned to the faïence factory in Strasburg in 1762 but did not make porcelain until 1774.	Had secret as early as 1721 but tried to sell it and failed and opened in Frankenthal, discontinued making porcelain in 1754. Only a few trial-pieces.
	? Ph in monogram.		

TABLE OF SMALLER FACTORIES OF FRANCE—*Continued*

Name	Marks	Period of activity	Description of wares, artists, etc.
	H usually also with various letters and numbers incised in underglaze blue or with a dot above the first stroke of the letter. JH His *Frankenthal* porcelain was marked I.A.H.		For *Paul Hannong* see *Frankenthal,* some might have been made at *Strasburg,* we are not sure. Useful porcelain ordinary and strangely imperfect in technique, thick, coarse and faulty like faïence. The known pieces seem to be mere trials. Figures, a flute player (*Kunstgewerbemuseum, Strasburg*), children *(Hamburg),* a flute-playing faun. (Also *Hamburg* in glaze and the Victoria & Albert in biscuit), etc.—these are better and with well harmonized colors.
Niderviller	JLB monogram BLe or BN monogram CN or with or without coronet. CFL monogram all in underglaze blue, also Niderviller Nider Nid N	1754–1765—hard porcelain *Baron Jean-Louis Beyerle* 1774 to *Comte de Custine.* (*Claude) Francois Lanfrey Mgr.*	Faïence reorganized for hard porcelain figures in polychrome and biscuit by *Charles Sauvage Lemire—Virgin and Child* 1784 (*Sèvres*), Bacchante in biscuit (V. & A.), Polychrome Bacchante (*Musée de Cluny*) etc., also children in biscuit. See also section on *Luneville* and *Cyfflé.* Useful porcelain with flowers, the usual landscapes similar to those of *Sceaux faïence,* etc. The underglaze blue was inclined to run and resembled the soft paste of *St. Cloud.* *Porringer* with Louis XVI designs in iron red, blue and gold. Marbled grounds, reliefs in white in biscuit and landscapes in black only. (V. & A. Mus. and *Sèvres.*)
Lille	Crowned dauphin. The earlier pieces have (à Lille). On the back of a saucer in *Sèvres: "Cuit au charbon de terre. Fait à Lille en Flandre,* 1785" "Fired with coal. Made at Lille in Flanders, 1785"	c. 1784 hard porcelain *Leperre Durot* under patronage of the *Dauphin,* existed to 1917.	Scattered cornflowers *"(décor barbeau)"* in blue, polychrome flowers poorly painted, landscapes insipid in polychrome and purple landscapes like many others. Also still-life objects such as a hare hung up and pastoral subjects. All poor and spiritless.
Valenciennes	LV or FLV may stand for either Vanier or Valenciennes	c 1771– *Jean-Baptiste Fauquez* the owner also of the factory at *St. Amand-les-Eaux.* *Michel Vanier.*	No interest to collectors. Polychrome resembles Lille and inferior Paris wares. Mostly monochrome—black, violet or iron red, sometimes starred and dotted with gold, some have alternating blue and violet flowers ornamentally arranged.

TABLE OF SMALLER FACTORIES OF FRANCE—*Continued*

Name	Marks	Period of activity	Description of wares, artists, etc.
Caen	Caen, written, painted or printed in red overglaze.	c 1800–	White porcelain to be decorated in Paris after *Sèvres*. Coffee-pot with rare and difficult canary yellow with frieze of conventional ornament reserved in green, purple and gold *(Sèvres)*. Also cruder milk-jug, bowl and cup with small square landscapes in black suspended by thin green festoons and garlands in gold. (V. & A.)
Limoges	CD apart or interlaced. Used even after Louis XVI owned the factory. Earliest mark G. R. et Cie.	1771 First of 40 factories at *Saint Yrieix* section by *Grellet, Massié* and *Fourniera.* 1777 Patronage of the *Comte d'Artois* 1784 Purchased by Louis XVI, in few years returned to private ownership	Porcelain of slightly yellowish hue with flowers in dull colors, also the strewn corn-flowers. Cup and saucer with roughly painted pair of peasants dancing *(Sèvres)*. Porringer with Graces holding Cupid on their shoulders in delicate brown monochrome. *(Sèvres.)*
La Seynie	LS singly or as a monogram.	1774 Founded by some gentleman of high rank but unknown.	Chiefly white porcelain to Paris for decoration.
Tours	A. Tours 1772 on only two cases also 1782 Cupid figure.	1776–1783	Only two biscuit vases known *(Sèvres)*. And a biscuit figure which represents Cupid as a child.
Boissette near Melun south of Paris.	B shakily written with or without 2 dots.	1778 *Duke of Orleans* *Vermonet père et fils*	Chiefly decorated with polychrome flowers in the style of *Meissen* but poorly done. Also occasionally with ornamental flowers and an infrequent landscape.
Bordeaux	W Two V's joined so as to make a W similar to Berlin of Wegely and Wallendorf but the ware is quite French. AV monogram in circle the upper part of which was enclosed in a semi-circle with the inscription "Bordeaux."	1781 *Pierre Verneuilh* and a relative 1787–1790 under *Vanier* and *Alluaud*	Not remarkable but table wares of fine quality in both paste and the decoration. *Semé* patterns not only of corn flowers but also of pansies and yellow daisies, also bouquets in polychrome. Particularized in festoons of foliage in Louis XVI style. A stone-cutter in biscuit *(Sèvres)*. Cup with rebus design *"elle à bon coeur"* (V. & A. Mus.)
Marseilles	R or JR monogram or rarely JRG (Joseph Gaspard Robert).	c 1776 Joseph Robert	Was *faïence* factory. No particular sense of material, the faïence and porcelain being decorated much alike. Greyish, uneven glaze, polychrome flowers like *faïence* ones, flowers in a strong dark blue. (Dish at *Sèvres*).

Around Paris at the close of the 18th century were innumerable private factories under the patronage of many princely or distinguished dabblers who were interested in aping the king and his interest in *Sèvres*. They are of no particular interest because the height of their ambitions seemed to be to ape also the wares of that place. We will list, however, a few taken in the order of their founding:

Vincennes in same château as the old home of soft paste.	HL or h et L. and LP crowned or uncrowned as decorative initials.	1767– *Pierre Antoine Hannong* and *Joseph Adam Hannong* were given permission to open a factory for *faïence* and porcelain. *de Laborde Mgr.* 1774 Sold to *Séguin* under patronage of *Louis-Philippe Duc de Chartres* then called "Manufacture royale."	Quite rough flowers and the initials LP in monogram in blue on a service made in 1779 (V. & A.). (*Sèvres* and others.) Custard-cup with finer garlands and decorative monogram in green and gold over a purple line. (*Kunstindustrimuseum, Copenhagen*)
	ducal heraldic label		

Fig. 982. Paris, Rue de La Courtille chocolate pot of about 1773–1784 showing usual refinement but lack of invention in design. Ht. 8¼". Metropolitan Mus. of Art.

Rue Faubourg Saint-Denis or sometimes called by the north section: *Rue Faubourg Saint-Lazare* or again *Fabrique du Comte d'Artois*	h and two crossed clay pipes with or without h in intersection. CP with or without coronet. Schoelscher in full or S	1779 *Pierre Antoine Hannong* Patron was *Louis XVI's* brother *Charles-Philippe Comte d'Arois* and later *Charles X* also patron of *Limoges* 1782 *Bourdon des Planches* who constructed the first kiln for firing with coal. After Revolution Schoelscher Mgr.	*Bleu-de-roi* and gold service now owned almost completé by Dr. Clarholm of *Karlstad, Sweden,* bears *Schoelscher's* name in full. Many copies without individuality. Nicely painted flowers and various ornaments in polychrome.

FIG. 983. Covered cup from *Clingnancourt* or *Fabrique de Monsieur* 1775-1790, Paris. Ht. 3¾". Metropolitan Mus. of Art.

FIG. 984. Angoulême, Paris porcelain (Guerhard & Dihl) early 19th cent. Ht. 3½". Metropolitan Mus. of Art.

FIG. 985. Paris, *Rue de Bondy* (1780) decorated with floral designs in black. It is hard paste and the mark is Dihl & Guerhard stencilled at length in red. Length 9½". Metropolitan Mus. of Art.

FIG. 986. Paris chocolate-pot decorated with landscape and marine views in sepia on white, hard paste. c. 1750 to 1800. Ht. 10¾". Metropolitan Mus. of Art.

La Courtille or *Rue Fontaine-au-Roy* or *Manufacture de Porcelaine*	Crossed torches. Crossed arrows points downward also DP Initials of artists	1771– *Jean-Baptiste Locré* 1774– Russinger from Höchst ? 1830 end.	No surprises, shapes pseudo-antique, decorated with flowers, landscapes, animals and ornaments in *Louis XVI* style. Dainty and elegant in make, with white paste, clean glaze

Allemande and modelers. and tooled or chased gilding.

A large vase with ornaments in violet and green partly on an orange-yellow ground. (*Sèvres*)

FIG. 987. Cup and saucer marked *P. L. Dagoty à Paris* in red. They are of hard porcelain and date about 1802 when the "Etruscan style" was popular. The designs are in red and white on black ground. Dia. of saucer 5″. Metropolitan Mus. of Art.

FIG. 988. Paris, Rue Thiroux gilt hard paste porcelain cup and saucer of the delicate usual effeminate style, 1778–1799. Saucer dia. 5¼″. Metropolitan Mus. of Art.

FIG. 989. Vieux Paris (DeGotte) coffee pot of about 1810–20. The ground is cobalt blue known as "Roi-du Bleu" with rich gilding. Ht. 11″. John Gibbons Coll.

FIG. 990. Pair of early 19th cent. "Empire" vases of French porcelain such as have been made ever since and are very popular even now in the decorative trade, particularly, if the gold is rubbed down a bit to make it possible to sell them as antique. Metropolitan Mus. of Art.

Cup with purplish red roses suspended by ribbons in same color is dated 1772 and marked DP without torch or arrow mark. (Sèvres)

Figures in biscuit by trees with sometimes applied leaves.

Factory	Mark	Date / Patron	Description
Clignancourt or Fabrique de Monsieur	Windmill stylized to 1775 then— LSX monogram with or without coronet plus sometimes a crowned B occasionally enclosed in 2 L's after Sèvres. Also M	1771– Pierre Deruelle Patron was Louis-Stanislas-Xavier, Comte de Provence brother of the king and later Louis XVIII 1790– Deruelle transferred it to his son Moitte 1798 last mentioned	Strewn cornflowers the serrated blue petals of which were here rendered in red and gold. Decoration in gold alone, see Kettle with spirit lamp (V. & A.). Ewers and wash basins with flowers, landscapes in monochrome. Lamprech, who later worked at Sèvres, painted in brownish-yellow monochrome. Biscuit statuette of the Farnese Hercules.
Rue de la Roquette	Crossed arrows with points upward only to be designated when accompanied by letters, often an S.	1774– Vincent Dubois 1790– last mention	Breakfast service with landscape vignettes in medallions suspended in delicate ornament (V. & A.). Biscuit less fine and rougher than that of La Courtille and that is rougher than that of Sèvres.
Rue de Charonne on same street as the above.		1795 Darte Brothers	Colored landscape with richly gilt borders (V. & A.) bleu-de-roi with gilt and cameo portraits of Caligula and of Vespasian plates.
Rue du Petit Carousel	PCG also "Manufacture (du) Petit Carousel à Paris" or "Petit Carousel à Paris"	1775 no patron	Respectable level. Polychrome butterflies between ornaments in gold (see ewer and basin (Sèvres). Grisaille. Much gold in slight Louis XVI style.
Rue Thiroux de Porcellaine de la Reine	MA or A crowned	1776– Andre-Marie Leboeuf patron: Marie Antoinette	Copied Sèvres too well and had difficulties when it started gilding and using color. There was practically no blue and white, the only kind supposed to have been allowed. Technique good but taste often questionable, very feminine with small semé cornflowers and daisies, also yellow roses on a pale pink ground, also "horrible" poppies, as Hannover says. (Sèvres) The paste has a soft tone resembling soft paste which it also copied. Strong also in exotic birds, ornamental friezes and white ware with simple lacework border in gold.

Rue de Bondy or *Manufacture d'Angoulême* later *Rue du Temple* and later *Boulevard St. Martin*	GA with or without a coronet and other symbols after the Revolution, the marks of the owners and finally just **Dihl**	1781 *Louis-Antoine de Bourbon, Duc d'Angoulême* and later Charles X founded by *Dihl* 1785 took as partner *Guerhard.*	Copies of *Sèvres* which brought trouble at once. 1806 a medal was awarded to the exhibition. *Bleu-de-roi* and gold on usual shapes, also monochrome or marbled grounds, cornflowers strewn as usual, flowers in gold, large naturalistic flowers. It had one invention which was scattered ears of corn in gold.
Rue Popincourt	Nast used his name in full for his mark.	1782– *Johann Nepomuc Hermann Nast* 1784 He re-established himself. 1817–1835 His sons	Nast's first little factory in which he was his own thrower, moulder, painter and fireman, burnt down twice. Influenced by *Sèvres* and *Wedgwood* — made plastic clocks in biscuit, richly gilt, daintily decorated glazed porcelain. Had a *Wedgwood* pale blue and lavender ground. Also made cups and saucers, etc., with cornflowers in blue, which are not rare. Three sorry plates spoken of by Hannover with the style of German transfer pictures (such as a lovely lady holding a dear little lamb [B.M.]) belong to son's period.
Petite Rue Saint-Gilles	Dagoty also Honoré also both together also "Manufacture de Madame Duchesse d'Angoulême or "Dagoty— Manufacture de S.M. l'Impératrice"	1785 ?*Dagoty* or ?—*Honoré* Whoever opened it, there was a partnership in 1810 dissolved in 1812.	Vases in relief in *Wedgwood* style. Colored grounds were much used, including terra cotta and olive-green. A few figures were done in biscuit. The decorations were landscapes, flowers and *grisaille* painting. Hannover says:—"All is lacking in any distinctive individuality, sober and neutral, but treated with neatness and accuracy."
Rue Amelot or *Rue Pont-aux-Choux*		1786 Patron *Duke of Orleans*	Its patron was its only distinction. Did invent the use of scattered roses stiffly drawn and the same in little medallions on dotted or *semé* ground.
Rue de Crussol or *Manufacture du Prince de Galles*	Potter or "potter à pari"	1789 *Charles Potter* an Englishman	Said to have had the great distinction of being the first man in Paris to practice the method of transfer printing on porcelain. Also an ordinary ware of the times with genre and portraits *en grisaille,* polychrome ornaments, cornflowers, butterflies, insects, etc.

ITALIAN PORCELAIN

VENETIAN WARES
1720–1740

The old Renaissance center of the world, Venice, which had been the first in the discovery of "soft porcelain" through the urge to imitate the real porcelain of the Far East was not long in acquiring the secret of Böttger and, in point of fact, it has been said to be the third factory in all Europe.

FIG. 991. Venetian cup and saucer from the Cozzi factory, of soft paste with pastel colors, c. 1765–1775. Dia. 4⅜". Metropolitan Mus. of Art.

FIG. 992. Venetian covered dish in soft paste with pastel colors. Ht. 3½". Metropolitan Mus. of Art.

There were two goldsmiths, Francesco Vezzi and Giuseppe Vezzi who bought patents of nobility in 1716 and they, together with two other gentlemen of nobility, having first provided the services of Christoph Conrad Hunger established the "Casa Eccelma Vezzi" near San Niccolò in Venice

FIG. 993. Venetian soft paste cup and saucer of about 1765 to 1812 with figures in the costumes of the period. Dia. 4⅞". Metropolitan Mus. of Art.

FIG. 994. Soft paste Venetian cups of about 1720–40 decorated in yellow, red, green and blue. Ht. 3¼". Metropolitan Mus. of Art.

in 1720. This Hunger is the same who wandered later to Meissen again, then to Stockholm and finally to Copenhagen—one of the untrustworthy disseminators of other people's secrets who was always ready to sell his information to the highest bidder, and when he came to Venice, he had not only the information but also the means of bringing "Schnorr'sche Erde" from Saxony and many of the stock designs of Herold and early Vienna porcelain. He had also the secret of Böttger's mother-of-pearl glaze, though his own was slightly warmer in hue and more glassy. The Venetian porcelain is much like that of Meissen, the pink lustre is not so even and the other colors are paler and lighter, but sometimes it takes a keen and practiced eye to tell the difference. Hannover says that Venetian baroque designs in gold in the style of Herold are, as a rule, outlined with iron-red. This is a distinction I have not seen commented upon by other authorities, but Hannover is a trustworthy and cautious observer.

MARKS HELP IN ATTRIBUTIONS

From about 1720 to 1725, they did not mark their wares. Therefore, unmarked porcelain which resembles early Vienna, or is decorated with leafy scroll work, the "Laub-un Bandelwerk" of Germany, with Chinese or European figures or harbor scenes in the style of Herold, or which are in the shapes of Böttger are likely to belong to this period and place.

In 1740 Francesco Vezzi died and it is supposed that the factory soon went out of existence. It is during this time, then from 1725 to 1740 that we should place all pieces marked with the name of Venice, or with abbreviations of it, or simply the initial V.

DEVELOPMENT IN SECOND PERIOD
1725–1740

After Hunger took his departure the factory was less influenced by Meissen. We see a new playful development of fantastic shapes far from reasonable or structural but at least relieving us from the monotony which

FIG. 995. Vase said by the museum to be "Venice, 1765–1812" but which is actually from the Cozzi factory in Venice and dates about 1770. Ht. 7½". Metropolitan Mus. of Art.
FIG. 996. Tea pot simply called "Italian 18th cent." by the museum but which may likely be from the Vezzi factory about 1725–1740. Ht. 5". Metropolitan Mus. of Art.
FIG. 997. Urn with flowers said by the museum to be from Venice, 18th cent. The neo-classic forms would indicate the latter part of the century. Ht. 13¼" over all. Metropolitan Mus. of Art.

prevailed among the copyists of other countries. The designs were not always conventional either as we can see in a cup of about 1725–30 or a little later, now in Dresden, with its design of a monster man's head and two hands filling a window and smoking a pipe amidst scrolls, and flanked by a parrot on one side and a monkey on the other plus two fantastic figures, a basket of flowers, etc. Composition too became loose, very thin and uncertainly drawn, reminiscent of late Near Eastern influences from metal, as may be seen in a cup and saucer at Dresden with decoration in iron-red only.

CAPO DI MONTE	VILLA REALE, PORTICI	NAPLES
1743–1759	1771–1773	1773–1821

King Charles III of Naples and his consort, a daughter of Augustus II of Saxony, were passionately fond of porcelain and in 1740, he, with the help of a Belgian chemist, Livio Ottavio Schepers, and a painter and cameo cutter, Giovanni Caselli, determined to start a factory in the palace of Capo di Monte on a hill just outside of Naples. The inscription over the doorway, which can still be read, states that the factory was opened in 1743 and remained in operation until 1759 when Charles III left Naples to become the King of Spain, taking with him some forty of the best workmen. In 1771 Ferdinand IV revived the works and transferred them to Villa Reale in Portici and again in 1773 they were transferred to Naples where they remained until 1821 when a great many of their old models were transferred to the Ginori factory at Doccia. In its first period the factory had made both soft paste and true porcelain but from 1773 it added also porcelain biscuit in large quantities. During the time from 1806 to 1815 when the factory was under Joseph and Murat this seems to have been its only output.

The palace in Naples has the only real collection of Capo di Monte. Hannover claims there are less than one hundred pieces of this ware north of the Alps in France, Germany or England. However, based upon his recollections of a visit about 50 years ago, a study of the pieces in the northern museums and a carefully edited catalogue of the Naples show in 1877 where there were 2000 pieces shown, he gives the following descriptions of the wares of the two period:

THE FIRST PERIOD OF CAPO DI MONTE

The soft paste was glassy, yellowish, greenish, bluish or livid in tone and was used for smaller pieces, as we would expect, being only different from that of the more northerly factories in the inclusion of such motives as dolphins, shells, periwinkles, coral and other designs taken from the sea. Among the earliest are a small number with no painted decoration, but the majority are "decorated in the Oriental style, viewed from the same angle as in the factories north of the Alps." This phase was displaced by the natural flowers, birds, landscapes and figures as elsewhere. Mythological figures and particularly those which are in some way associated with the sea, are the rule and *they are represented in relief and also colored.* We do not know who invented this style which was a natural result of the meeting of the old relief urge instigated by the copying of metal work and the color urge natural to the Italian soul. Hannover suggests Giuseppe Gricci but also mentions other distinguished modelers, Antonio Falcone, and Giuseppe Verdone and the painters Giovanni Fischer and Luigi Restile who executed the principle work of the period consisting of a "camera di porcelana" which was in the palace in Portici and later in 1865 taken to the palace of Capo di Monte, and which is entirely covered with porcelain panels having high relief colored rococo scroll work and primitive chinoiseries in the style of Boucher, some

FIG. 998. Typical Capo di Monte cup and with a mythological subject. Metropolitan Mus. of Art.

FIG. 999. Capo di Monte plate dating about 1750 to 1760 with relief decoration painted in enamel colors and gilt. It is soft paste, of course.

FIG. 1000. Capo di Monte coffee-pot of 1750 to 1760 showing the "Flaying of Marsya," on one side and Silenus with Bacchantes and Satyrs on the other. Metropolitan Mus. of Art.

FIG. 1002. Group of Venus and Cupid from Capo di Monte about 1759 to 1780. Metropolitan Mus. of Art.

FIG. 1001. Snuff-box possibly of *Capo di Monte*, porcelaneous ware with white ground, colored sea shells. Inside of box gilt. 1749–1759? Ht. 2″. Hispanic Society of America.

sconces, a chandelier and some furniture including a console which is now at Sèvres. Though the use of relief and colored figures was typical of the period there is strangely little figure modeling in the round and the few examples consist of the "to be expected" ones from the Italian comedy such as Colombines, Pulcinellas, etc., a few mythological groups such as Apollo and Daphne, Venus and Cupid, etc., some Biblical subjects and some genre subjects in costumes of the day. A rather typical figure is of an effeminate youth dressed in yellow and with a hen under his arm, in the Victoria and Albert Museum. The figures are all painted in polychrome, though sometimes sparingly. The painting on the porcelain of useful shapes was done in polychrome and in such monochromes as crimson, bluish-violet and black, "encre à la plume" or in pen and ink style.

THE SECOND OR SECOND AND THIRD PERIODS OF CAPO DI MONTE AT PORTICI AND NAPLES 1771–1821

Hannover deduces from the marks RF and FRF which were supposed to have been used at the factory only between 1771 and 1773, when it was at Portici, that it had already begun to use hard porcelain as well as soft, for they are found as often on the one as on the other. There was also more figure modeling in the second period, comprising allegorical ones, *putti*, and figures in the dress of the period as well as colossal groups.

The neo-classic influence put an end to the relief modeling. Upon plain surfaces were painted natural flowers, sea shells, fish and so forth taken

FIG. 1003. Capo di Monte late 18th cent. porcelain vase. Ht. 7½". Metropolitan Mus. of Art.

FIG. 1004. Naples tea pot of about 1780 in shape and style much like some English examples except for the handle and the leopard on the cover. Length 9¼". Metropolitan Mus. of Art.

from books, exotic flowers, peasants in natural costumes and views of the town, views of Vesuvius, etc. The latter became more dominant after the move of the factory to Naples. At the Hamburg Museum is a dish with a fish after a work by an English naturalist, Catsby.

Neo-Classic Influences

With Pompeii and Herculaneum close by, we are not surprised to hear that the neo-classic movement became strong in the development of shapes and of surface decorations. A good example is a jug closely following the form of an oenochoe in the British Museum. The surface decorations consisted not only of figures but also of designs. A whole service of this kind was sent to George III of England by the King of the Two Sicilies in 1787. These were painted in natural polychrome and carefully shaded to give rounded modeling. A typical ware is decorated only in black and gold on a grey ground "a chiaroscuro."

Figures of Capo di Monte at Naples

The figures are chiefly colored. A few are in soft paste but most in hard. The best were from models by the Viennese, Tagliolini, who came to the factory in 1781 and became its chief support when later the style turned to biscuit. His principal works are Olympian figures in biscuit and in painted porcelain at the Museo Civico at Bologna. Hannover says that about the group can be arranged a whole Olympus in biscuit, the larger part of the figures from the Iliad and many Greek philosophers and Roman emperors plus numerous figures from the every day life of Naples and its environs (see Victoria & Albert Museum). The latter are often in a biscuit of a dirty yellowish tone.

Another skillful worker was Giuseppe Giordano who was called "Peppe" but he was even more dependent upon antique models than was Tagliolini and often merely copied them as exactly as he could.

Little real Capo di Monte ever comes onto the market though one can see many hundreds of fakes in shops along 59th Street and Lexington Avenue in New York and in London, Paris and most large cities of Europe. The tourist is almost sure to bring back spurious pieces from Italy marked with a crowned N which may have been made in France or Germany as well as in Italy. In early ceramic handbooks we were told that we could distinguish the real specimens because they were painted with a stippled technique similar to that of the miniature painters but the forgers also read the books.

Doccia Wares
1735 or 1737

Second in age, if not importance among the Italian factories is that of Doccia near Florence, which was founded by the Marchese Carlo Ginori who was so thoroughgoing that he actually sent an expedition in a ship to the East to collect samples of the materials used in Chinese porcelain, and is thought, by some authorities, to have sent to Vienna for Carl Wandhelein to act as chemist. The early wares are painted with quasi-Chinese flowers with peculiar "trunk-like" stamens either in polychrome or iron-red.

When Carlo Ginori died in 1757, his son Lorenzo extended and improved the kilns so that they could at any rate make colossal figures and vases, if not better ones.

The factory has remained in the Ginori family right down to modern times and makes it a business to reproduce all kinds of wares from old moulds. As early as 1821 Doccia acquired the old models from the famous Neapolitan factory of the Capo di Monte porcelain when it ceased to be made in that factory, and for the past thirty or forty years it has copied them en masse, unscrupulously adding the original mark. Italian majolica of

FIG. 1005. Three plates from either Venice or Doccia and dating between 1760 and 1800. Lengths about 11″. Metropolitan Mus. of Art.

FIG. 1006. Figure probably from Doccia of about 1740 to 1770. Ht. about 6½″. Metropolitan Mus. of Art.

Faenza, Urbino, Castel Durante and Gubbio, Medici porcelain together with its mark, and other wares have been grist for this disreputable mill which, even in its more respectable days of the 18th century, never achieved any independence of style, though its modern wares are promising.

In some of the early wares considerable uncertainty naturally exists and they may be confused with those of Nove which used also a six pointed star for a mark as did Doccia at times.

FIG. 1007. Doccia, cup and saucer with design of oriental feeling in enamels and gold. Dia. 5″. Metropolitan Mus. of Art.

FIG. 1008. Nove, (c. 1760–65) cup and saucer with yellow ground and medallions in violet, (outlined in violet) and red, orange and green. Dia. 4½″. Metropolitan Mus. of Art.

NOVE WARES
1752 OR 1761

Giovanni Battista Antonibon and his son Pasquale founded a factory at Nove, near Bassano, for the making of faïence. In 1752 Pasquale persuaded

Sigismund Fischer to leave the factory at Meissen but nothing seems to have come from the attempt that we know. In 1761 Antonibon had two kilns in operation for the making of porcelain in the French style. The following year he took his son Giovanni Battista into the business and in 1781, Signor Parolini. In the period between 1802 and 1825 the firm was in the hands of some interests we do not know about but it reverted to the Antonibon family at the end of this time and they made porcelain until 1835. After this date it was discontinued and only faïence and earthenware were made.

The faïence was always good and during the 18th century ranks with the best in both appeal and technique. Only soft porcelain has been discovered bearing the Nove mark. Flowers seem to be the chief decoration and are in polychrome, green and gold, or purple. A few large pieces such as jardinières and teapots moulded with relief ornament are painted with figures, grotesque, mythological or historical. There are also birds and landscapes. A well known and finely executed piece is the teapot in the Hamburg Museum decorated with relief, moulded ornament of rococo type and painted figure panels. There are others of this typical sort, all dating from about 1765 to 1770. After 1770 the classical trend set in and a good example is the cylindrical cup with "bat wing" handle, *bleu-de-roi* ground and panels in reserve painted with the "Toilet of Venus, the Judgment of Paris, and the Death of Meleager" which is in the Franks Collection in the British Museum. The factory tried various experiments including the wood graining stunt. An interesting though perhaps doubtful example is a porringer in the Sèvres Museum decorated on the outside with a landscape with ruins in purple and on the inside with a Virgin and Child and three angels and with the following inscription around the rim: *"Scudella fabricata con la polvere delle S. Mura di Santa Casa di Loreto"*—"Porringer made of dust from the holy walls of the Holy House at Loreto." This is an exceptional piece in that it is the only one of hard porcelain from the Nove factory known. It bears the mark but there is naturally some doubt about it. Figures were also made but they are very rare and most of them found are doubtful specimens.

CONTRADA DI SAN GIOBBE
1765

At Contrada di San Giobbe in 1765, Geminiano Cozzi founded a factory, obtaining his clay from Tretto in the Venetian territory.

The earliest known specimen is a coffee-pot dated 1765 of greyish porcelain with pale bouquets of flowers, a handle and spout still bearing rococo influences and a cover which is without a knob. It is in the British Museum. Another dated 1766 and in the Musée des Arts Décoratifs, Paris, has flowers in relief on a gold ground. There is also a set of five potpourri vases with relief heads and garlands and painted flowers after Meissen and a porringer in the V. & A. Museum with stand in the same style having a character also like several cups in the Sèvres Museum treated with polychrome fruit and flowers, scale patterns *("Mosaik")* in red, green or purple, etc. Various cups in Hamburg, and Limoges show that the chinoiseries of Herold were also copied as were designs from Sèvres, Chelsea and Derby. There are no wares in underglaze blue. The gold was of fine quality and treated with great precision. Iron-red was used alone or with it at times.

The inclination of soft porcelain makers, due to the inconveniences of their wares and the danger of handling them for washing, was to make ornamental rather than useful things and figures, especially in plain white. An Oriental figure of this sort at Stockholm and a soldier talking to a woman which is of grey glassy porcelain in Sèvres are examples of the early types. In Hamburg there is a "Pieta" which is said to date about 1780. This is full of the sentimental and theatrical spirit of the day.

VINOVO (NEAR TURIN)

1776–1820

Near Turin at Vinovo, Giovanni Vittorio Brodel, beginning in 1765, made many vain attempts to manufacture porcelain but it was not until 1776 when he was joined in partnership by Pierre Antoine Hannong of Strasburg that a factory was started in the royal palace and called "La reale manifattura di Vinovo," but he found it quite as difficult as had others to get along with Hannong and retired from the business in 1778 and the business was sold in 1780.

The new proprietor was a famous chemist, Dr. Vittorio Amadeo Gioanetti and under him the factory made some technical advancement but he died in 1815 and in 1820 it had to be closed.

Only one specimen is known from the Brodel-Hannong period and that is an oblong tray with handles missing in the British Museum, painted with small and poorly done scattered flowers in polychrome and marred by large kiln flaws. It is dated 1776. In the same museum there are several later pieces, including a white cup and saucer decorated in gold with the arms of the King of Sardinia and a "Virgin" or Eve kneeling on the globe with a serpent in plain white. Other pieces at Turin and elsewhere include portraits, flowers, etc., in polychrome and gold, in purple alone, in gold alone and, in fact, all of the technique and much of the style of the smaller French factories, though it has a yellowish tone and thick and faulty glaze which makes it look like soft porcelain, though Brongniart claims it is hard.

ROME

1790–1831

Rome was the last founded of the 18th-century Italian factories and as its founder was Giovanni Volpato, the engraver, it is natural that it is known only for figures copied from the antique and from Canova. A little later Wedgwood was copied. Examples may be found at Gisselfeld in Denmark, at Hamburg, in the Traugott Collection at Stockholm and elsewhere. The Hamburg Museum has two figures of Centaurs with Cupids on their backs which are excellent and, in fact some of these figures are as good as were done in the age.

ESTE

There was also a small factory at Este between Padua and Ferrara which produced a greyish green glaze like thin "celadon" and some white figures probably by Jean-Pierre Varion who formed a partnership with Girolamo Franchini in 1780 to form the factory. Varion had formerly worked at Nove.

TREVISO

In the little town of Treviso in the Venetian territory, there was also some soft porcelain made in Venetian style and decorated with landscapes in large medallions. These date about 1799 to 1800 when the factory was owned by the brothers Giuseppe and Andrea Fontebasso. The mark is "Treviso G.A.F.F." (Giuseppe-Andrea Fratelli Fontebasso) or simply the two letters F.F.

Thus from the half promise of something new or at least different in Italy which seemed to be indicated by the background of all the potteries which had been made there in earlier days, we find that in actuality the blight of the 18th-century factory methods and copyist principles was too strong and there is not much to distinguish Italian wares from those of the other countries.

SPAIN

"LA CHINA" OR BUEN RETIRO

Charles III left Naples in 1759, taking with him the best workmen from Capo di Monte, as well as porcelain earth and other materials, and, having ascended the throne of Spain, set up a factory called "La China" but known better as Buen Retiro because it was situated in a palace of that name near Madrid.

We learn authentically that the construction of this factory cost 11,500,000 reales and that its annual expenses were something like 3,000,000. There was no source of revenue; it was merely a court plaything but the demands were not, as one might imagine, small. Not to be outdone by Portici, two rooms were ordered and probably carried out by Giuseppe Gricci, one being dated 1763 and so signed, in all the mussy grandeur of the rococo style, with chinoiseries, mirrors, masks, cupids, etc. Other jobs of whole ceilings and massive works are said to have been in palaces in Escorial, La Granja, Aranjuez and elsewhere. In the Royal Palace at Madrid was a clock crowned by biscuit figures and four vases 6 feet high holding bouquets of porcelain flowers. They date from 1802 when Sureda, director of the factory, went to Sèvres to get ideas. At about 1800 the cult of Wedgwood was also taken seriously. Then in 1808, during the French invasion, it was turned into a fortress.

"LA MONCLOA" OR "FLORIDA"

In 1817, Ferdinand VII started a new factory called "La Moncloa" or "Florida" and it continued until 1849 but did nothing of note. In fact, aside

FIG. 1009. Candelabrum made at *Buen Retiro* with pastel shades of natural polychrome on white. It has the typical blue *fleur-de-lis* mark. Late 18th cent. The ormolu mounts are contemporary. Ht. 18″. Hispanic Society of America.

FIG. 1010. Figure called simply "Spanish 18th cent." by the museum but undoubtedly from Buen Retiro about 1765. It is decorated with soft tones of pink, mauve and green. Ht. 7¼″. Metropolitan Mus. of Art.

FIG. 1011. Porcelain vase of *Buen Retiro*. The colors are purple and green grapes with gold handles. Second half of 18th cent. Ht. about 8″. Hispanic Society of America.

FIG. 1012. Buen Retiro porcelain of 1759 to 1808 decorated in soft colors. Metropolitan Mus. of Art.

from the rooms there seems to be little to be said about the earlier work of the factory, though the prices that pieces from it command are high. The Capo di Monte association helped in boosting its prestige, and, in fact, so close is the technique that it is often quite impossible to distinguish between them. This was made even more difficult in that the fleur-de-lys mark was also used.

Group representing Summer and Autumn made at *Buen Retiro* during the 18th cent. with colors of blue, stippled flesh tones and gilt. Ht. 6¾". Hispanic Society of America.

Right: Jar and cover made at the Royal Porcelain Factory of *Buen Retiro* with white ground, decorations in lilac and touches of gilt. The mark is a blue *fleur-de-lis*. Late 18th cent. Ht. 13¾". Hispanic Society of America.

BUEN RETIRO SOFT PASTE OF THE 18TH CENTURY

PLATE 189

The wares were hard paste, soft paste and biscuit. In general the Buen Retiro wares are thought to be whiter than those of Capo di Monte but yellowish exceptions do occur.

In the earlier days the factory was strongest in the modeling of figures, less successful in applied relief decoration and even weaker in purely painted technique, though there are some exceptions. A truly lovely and charming "Venus and Cupid" of yellowish white porcelain is in the Schlossmuseum in Berlin and the children such as the polychrome figures of a little boy drinking water and a little girl braiding her hair in the *Sèvres* collection, and the Bacchanalian children groups all show the happy influence of Gricci and are as good as anything the Capo di Monte factory ever turned out. The useful wares are, however, mediocre.

La Moncloa
1817

The second period of Buen Retiro came too late for us to expect anything of artistic merit from it. It was started at La Moncloa, as we have said above, in 1817 and the cylindrical cups, plain trays of uninteresting shapes and such, decorated in all-over enamels, marbled and agate grounds with reserves for undecorative painting of a poor character and much gilding, make them like all the rest of the period.

Alcora
1764

The Count of Aranda had started a faïence factory at Alcora about 1750. The factory turned out almost every kind of ware; three kinds of "Spanish porcelain," "frita" (soft porcelain), "English pipeclay porcelain," "blue pipeclay porcelain," "marbled pipeclay porcelain," "buccaro" (Chinese stoneware type), "Strasburg ware" (faïence), etc., etc.

There was no style established because of constantly shifting managements. There are breakfast services now in the style of Sèvres and now following Wedgwood. The pipeclay was used for a ware similar to Leeds pottery. It was made in large quantities and much of it is erroneously called Leeds. Likewise much actual Alcora porcelain is probably erroneously identified.

Most Alcora porcelain is greenish-grey in tint, commonplace in shape and meagerly decorated. Bleu-de-roi grounds and gold, polychrome flowers, ornamental friezes sometimes broken by medallions with miniature painted heads, landscapes and such form the idiom which marked the time and not the place.

PORTUGAL

Vista Alegre
1790

About 1790 Pinto Basto started a porcelain factory near Oporto at a place called Vista Alegre and there are a few specimens in museums.

LISBON

The only pieces known from the Lisbon factory are portrait "cameos" in Wedgwood style but on a brown or grey ground and are marked *"Lisboa Arsenal Real do exercito Joao de Figueiredo fecit."* There are a pair in Sèvres and another in the British Museum dated respectively 1783 and 1792.

SWITZERLAND

ZURICH OR SCHOREN (ITS ACTUAL LOCATION)
1763

The factory which was founded at Schoren near Bendlikon but spoken of as "Zurich" near which it also is, started as a faïence factory, made soft porcelain usually painted in blue or red or polychrome and later learned the secret of hard porcelain. It was founded by a group including Salomon Gessner, the painter-poet and had Adam Spengler of Schaffhausen as technical chief and Valentin Sonnenschein, the modeler and sculptor as part owner and practical assistant.

FIG. 1013. Jug of hard paste porcelain from Zurich, dated "1759–1799" by the museum but the factory started in 1763 and made soft paste at first. It should date 1770 to 1780. Ht. 3″. Metropolitan Mus. of Art.

FIG. 1014. Zurich cup and saucer with flowers in natural colors. They are hard paste of 1770–1780, not 1759–1799 as stated by the museum. Dia. of saucer 5⅛″. Metropolitan Mus. of Art.

Of the soft paste there is little except a teapot in the British Museum and some pieces in the Swiss Museums, a jug in the Victoria & Albert Museum and a few pieces at Sèvres.

The kaolin for the hard porcelain was obtained from *Lorraine* and even in its best period it is yellowish or greenish-grey and rather dirty in shade with many firing flaws. Gold was sparingly used if at all. The designs are of Swiss landscapes, birds and flowers and very infrequently figures. There were also imitations of Meissen *"Zwiebelmuster"* and other simple designs in underglaze blue. The subjects from nature were in polychrome or *en camaïeu*, at times also in two color combinations and these latter nearly always seem to have been executed by good painters.

The figures are bourgeois or rustic types done in an amateurish but fresh style with perhaps a bit of the spirit of Gessner. The painted ones are in a light and sometimes dingy color scheme which is not always happy. Much of the work, particularly the painting, is delicate in execution.

NYON

It is interesting to see that, though the porcelain of Zurich is quite German in character, that of Nyon is so French that it gave rise to the false legend that the factory was set up by workmen who were driven from Sèvres during the revolution.

Actually the factory was founded by two Germans, Ferdinand Müller of Frankenthal and his son-in-law, Jean-Jacques or Jacob Dortu from Berlin and after 1777 Marieberg in Sweden. Its porcelain was entirely imitative.

In 1786 the partnership was dissolved and until 1813 Dortu was the sole director and in 1813 it gave up porcelain and went into faïence copies of "Etruscan" vases and Wedgwood wares.

FIG. 1015. Nyon cup and saucer with typical festoons and a silhouette, 1785–1790. Saucer 4¾" dia. Metropolitan Mus. of Art.

Most of the wares are of the useful type and the hard porcelain is cold and white. The decorations are in underglaze blue and polychrome and then later garlands, ribbons, trophies, love emblems and ornaments of the Louis XVI style together with strewn flowers, or rather geometrically arranged flowers, and such, in blue, red and gold and copying, the other French schemes, which were in themselves nothing to boast of.

RUSSIA

ST. PETERSBURG

In Russia the story is much the same; a ruler with ambitions, who was in this case Peter the Great. He had the desire to create national industries for the good of his land rather than to have a plaything for the purposes of showing how great he was.

In 1717 an emissary to Amsterdam entered into a contract with an Italian, Carlo Antonio Bonaveri to have him teach four Russians the secrets of porcelain in a year but nothing came of it. In the same year the Ambassador to Berlin persuaded Peter Eggebrecht to leave Dresden and set up a factory in St. Petersburg. He did go in 1718 but evidently stayed only a few years and returned without any recorded success. It was 25 years before porcelain was first produced at St. Petersburg. But bad fortune was not even yet overcome for with the first production we again run afoul of that major faker and charlatan Christoph Conrad Hunger who had been from Meissen to Venice, thence to Vienna, thence back to Meissen, and then to Stockholm where he was met by the Russian Baron N. A. Korff who was on a diplomatic mission for the Empress Elizabeth and arranged to send Hunger to St. Petersburg after payment of a 1,000 specie dollars and the guarantee of 1,000 rubles a year with the title of "Director of the Porcelain Factory of Her Imperial Majesty."

A factory was erected at Neva nearby and in 1745 Hunger was still mak-ing unsuccessful attempts to do something. In 1748 he had made six im-perfect little cups in all and then was dismissed, having cost the Russian government the tidy sum of 15,000 rubles or thereabouts.

Vinogradov was put in charge and after a short while did succeed in mak-ing small pieces of porcelain of fairly good quality but was fired from the factory for drinking too much in 1751, and Johann Schlatter the Director of the Russian Mint took his place. Later the "arcanist" Johann Gottfried Müller was appointed for technical supervision.

The early production was naturally Meissen in style up to 1753 and con-sisted chiefly of little cups and saucers, small jugs and particularly snuff boxes which were used as presents from the court and frequently made in the shape of envelopes with red seals and the names of the recipients on them. Statuettes were tried, but the first are childlike models of a cow and a "dog Foo" of Chinese type. Then came Oriental racial types also crudely modeled.

The useful porcelain was usually decorated in monochrome purple, green, black or with gold alone or combined with the others. The "Gold China-men" decoration after Herold of Meissen was copied and became popular but gave way to scenes from daily life, landscapes and animals, and the palette was increased.

THE SECOND PERIOD—CATHERINE II
1762–1796

In 1762, when Catherine II ascended the throne, it marked a new period and in 1763 she visited the factory and there was an immediate and radical change of staff there. In her usual way, she took a lieutenant of the horse guards, Alexander Tchepotiev, and put him in charge with a Viennese, Joseph Regens-burg as "arcanist" and Karlovsky from Meissen as master-modeler, adding a little later the French modeler J. S. Rachette. By 1780 most of the staff were Russians but by that time the factory style had been set as so nearly that of Sèvres that again it is difficult to tell them apart except for the marks. However, the Russian factory also made a commercial ware which was yel-lowish or greyish, crude and mediocre. *The only other way to distinguish the finer Russian ware from that of Sèvres is when it carries a picture from Russian towns, a picture of the Empress or an allegory concerning her or something of the sort.* The flowers were, strangely, on the other hand like those of early Copenhagen but can be distinguished because the Russian plates are edged with brown which was never done in the Danish factory. In general, the rest of the wares follow the neo-classical trend and toward the end of the century the same struggle was made to create huge services and colossal pieces. One of the services known as "Les Arabesques" consisted of about 1,000 pieces and cost 25,000 rubles, and had a table decoration to go with it consisting of six allegorical groups as well as a centerpiece which was a statue of the Empress on a pedestal flanked by "Justice" and "Charity." Figures copied the antique or Falconet or Clodion and the colored ones gave way to biscuit as elsewhere.

PAUL I PERIOD
1796–1801

Paul I was keenly interested in the factory but it was now the time of the Empire period which suited the Russian porcelain no more than it did any other and we see the naturalistic pictures, the covering of all surfaces with enamel and gold and the total loss of any national characteristics.

OTHER RUSSIAN FACTORIES

There developed many other Russian factories and on the accession of Catherine II there were 12 faïence and porcelain factories of which 7 were for porcelain only, by 1800 there were nearly 20, in 1813 there were 30, and in 1817 some 45 and most of these were around Gschely, which section was rich in kaolin.

THE GARDNER FACTORY

It was in this general location in the town of Verbilki that an Englishman, named Gardner founded one of the largest factories in 1758. About 1780 it was moved to Tver near Moscow.

POPOFF & GULIN

Two other factories marked their wares with full names or monograms in Russian characters, that of Popoff which was in the village of Gorbunovo (1806–1872) and that of the brothers Gulin or Gulina at Friasino. They are, of course, all Empire in style.

KORZEC

In Korzec, which was in the government of Volhynia, in 1780 or thereabouts, Prince Czartoryski founded a factory. From about 1803 it was placed under the management of Merault, a painter from Sèvres. The mark was either "Korzec" or a triangular drawn eye, and the style again typically Empire.

MEZER

Of about the same period and turning out much the same sort of thing was the factory of Mezer at Baranovka which mostly stamped its wares with the name of the place with or without the name of the maker.

In summing up the Russian factories we must conclude that they learned the secrets of porcelain too late and thus became decadent almost before they began. They added nothing new to the so-called art except the envelope shaped snuff boxes, which are not good taste at best, and the making of imitation Easter eggs painted with Biblical and other paintings in the worst possible taste.

THE NETHERLANDS

As we have already said, Holland was not particularly interested in Böttger's invention for in that country faïence had been developed to the most excellent possible technique and the porcelain demands could readily be filled by importation from the Orient. There is little of distinction about the Dutch 18th-century porcelain except a pleasant bourgeois character.

WEESP, 1764, OUDE LOOSDRECHT, 1771
OUDE AMSTEL, 1784, NIEUWER AMSTEL, 1799–1810

Count (or Baron) Gronsfeldt-Diepenbrock established the first hard porcelain factory in the plant of a bankrupt faïence factory at Amsterdam and transferred it to Weesp in the same neighborhood. It was a propitious moment, for the Seven Years' War had thrown many of the German workers out of occupation and they were easily persuaded to come and work. It is reported that the output was so good technically that Gronsfeldt actually made advances to Sèvres for an amalgamation, but the answer given was that the French factory preferred to go on with the soft porcelain until the materials could be found on their own territory, and nothing came of the suggestion. But, if the factory had opened under the best of circumstances, these were not to continue; the German hands soon wished to return home and, added to the labor difficulties, there came sales troubles even greater, for just at this time the country was flooded with cheap Japanese porcelain. Financial sickness, the common complaint of the 18th-century porcelain factories in all countries, brought about the purchase of the factory by a Calvinist preacher named Mol.

FIG. 1016. Dish of Dutch hard paste (1775–1786) with trellis work in gilt, baskets of flowers in colors, etc., and circles in bright blue. Dia. 9½″. Metropolitan Mus. of Art.

OUDE LOOSDRECHT, 1771–1784

Mol moved the factory at once in 1771 to Oude Loosdrecht which lies between Utrecht and Amsterdam.

OUDE AMSTEL, 1784–1799

Mol died in 1782, and in, 1784 the factory belonged to a limited company which moved it again to Oude Amstel and appointed a German named F. Däuber as manager.

NIEUWER AMSTEL, 1799–1810

The company underwent changes in 1799 and was then known as G. Dommer & Co. which transferred the wandering factory still again to Nieuwer Amstel where it lasted only until 1810 and finally closed down for good.

In spite of all of this moving the productions are so alike and so continuous in their development that, were it not for changes in marks, they could not be surely distinguished one from another.

WEESP WARES

Between 1765 and 1770 roughly, a white porcelain was made ornamented with floral festoons, sprays or other motifs in relief. Perforated baskets were made and delicately picked out in blue. There were also rococo relief decorated wares very sparingly decorated with landscapes in cartouches or with birds or scattered flowers. Then there were also such pieces as the breakfast services with Watteau scenes and scenes from the Italian comedies, and other pieces such as tureens with large bouquets of flowers and a cut lemon or bird finial for the cover. In all of these the paste is white and the glaze even, while the colors are well fused, but perhaps a little lacking in brilliance for some tastes, though I find them very pleasant.

OUDE LOOSDRECHT

The quality seems to improve under Mol and there seems to me to creep in more of the Dutch characteristics as seen in certain elongation and, let us say, opening up of the tighter German forms. A good example of this may be seen in the perforated vase from a service which is in the Nederlandsch Museum and which is decorated with painted swans. In this the foot and the perforated neck are, as it were, stretched upward and the handles have become slender, though not losing in seeming strength, and are set further away from the sides. Such pieces could be neither German nor French and show that they were made after many of the Germans had returned home and before the French workers were brought in.

On the other hand a breakfast service in the Gemeente Museum painted with figures in landscapes in dark brown has nothing new to offer. Some pieces of the period have cupids in red camaïeu or monochrome decorations in purple. Others have gold borders and blue floral festoons around the edges. There were also polychrome landscapes, not by any means all Dutch in characteristics, birds, flowers and very rarely copies of the Japanese competitive wares but with a certain difference in the curves and scrolls used, making them wobbly and not improving even upon these lowly wares.

Some busts were made of biscuit and placed on fluted and often green-striped pedestals, and a vague beginning of the neo-classical feeling from France was taking form.

OUDE AMSTEL

With the change of location surprisingly the factory lost none of its technical excellence, which seems perfect except for the slight running of the blue at times, but it becomes somehow stiffer and dryer, and the originality of form has been lost. French models seem to have been copied and the work takes on the look of Sèvres.

The last days see the usual decline which we have learned to expect with the opening of the 19th century.

THE HAGUE
1775

The Viennese, Anton Leichner (Linker or Lyncker), founded at The Hague in 1775 a factory which, though it lasted only about ten years, turned out some fairly respectable works. He had a miniature painter who was well known at the time, Leonardus Temminck, who had been a pupil of Benjamin Bolomey, who in turn had studied in Paris under Boucher and this explains why we see the "Boucher children" painted in purple with such good understanding, and spirit.

FIG. 1017. Porcelain plate from The Hague about 1775–1786. Dia. 10¾". Metropolitan Mus. of Art.

FIG. 1018. Tureen with overglazed blue mark of stork with branch in beak, that of "The Hague" but the shape is a Tournai one and the body may even have been made there. The decoration is in natural colors except the flowers which are in underglaze blue with gilt scrolls. The ware is soft paste dating about 1785. Length 12". Leon van Biene.

The neo-classical blight is seen almost at once in the sober and stupid shapes, and figures were not attempted at all but the painting seemed to cover every possibility of the day. There were polychrome flowers, which were thinner and dryer than those of Meissen, landscapes with and without figures, birds on plates with bleu-de-roi shell edging around them, and much en camaïeu and grisaille painting, the latter used especially for antique profile heads in medallions with pale pink ground, a pleasant individual contrast and perhaps the best of the work turned out by the factory.

Occasionally this factory decorated white wares made elsewhere and particularly soft porcelain which it did not make at all itself. We have spoken of this connection with Tournai. The probable reason lies in the excellence of the Hague painting, as is pointed out, perhaps a bit too enthusiastically, but nevertheless with much truth, in the argument by H. E. van Gelder in his catalogue. How-ever, we cannot conclude that the other factories sent their wares to be decorated and then returned to them for sale, because we find in the Gemeente Museum a pastille-burner and a sugar-bowl on which an attempt has obviously been made to cancel the original mark A (which van Gelder explains is the Ansbach mark and further claims that he believes he has found a confirmation in the archives of a relationship between the two places) by painting over it in overglaze blue The Hague stork. If there was a

FIG. 1019. Dutch tea-pot of the 18th cent. and probably from The Hague. Decorated with a green band of foliage with purple foliated design. Ht. 5″. Metropolitan Mus. of Art.

relationship, it would not seem to have been a friendly one. These pieces are the stranger because, though hard paste, they are decorated like the soft paste of Tournai. Perhaps we had better conclude simply that once in a while the factory might have bought a few undecorated examples and allowed the workers to amuse themselves dressing them up as experiments.

BELGIUM

MANUFACTURE DE MONTPLAISIR, 1784–1791

The country that is now Belgium was even later in starting porcelain making. The first hard porcelain factory was the Manufacture de Montplaisir which was started in 1784 by J. S. Vaume near Schaerbeek. It remained in existence only seven years and made simply decorated porcelain of the period style such as landscapes in the manner of India ink drawings, small evenly scattered or arranged flowers or monochrome landscapes particularly in green. It also tried the "décor bois" or wood grain stunt and specialized in scattered sprigs in combination with friezes or festoons of leaves and flowers.

ETERBEEK

Near Brussels, at Eterbeek a factory was started in 1775 by Chretien Kühne of Saxony. It made useful ware decorated with all the expected methods of the day and is said to have closed down in 1803.

DENMARK

Denmark can take justifiable pride in its ceramic history, for it is the home of the world famous Royal Copenhagen factory.

There is a little confusion concerning the first porcelain made in Denmark for it was the custom to refer to porcelain as "Delfs porcelain" inferring Delfsware which was faïence. However, we know that in 1737 Christoph Conrad Hunger approached the government and was luckily or wisely turned down. In 1752 and 1757 the ivory carver from Germany Christoph Ludwig Lück and his son Karl Gottlieb Lück were granted subsidies as were also Jürgen Gülding in 1753, and Johann Gottlieb Melhorn in 1754. The latter had attained distinction as a blue and white painter at Meissen. In 1755 Niels Birch found kaolin on the island of Bornholm. Melhorn had to quit his factory and go to Kastrup but there too he failed and we know of nothing from either place.

Fournier, a Frenchman, produced soft paste at Blaataarn about 1760 to 1765. He had worked at Vincennes and Chantilly as a modeler yet there is only one insignificant work attributed to him at Copenhagen, a medallion of Frederik V. of Denmark. Otherwise the wares are of common useful type with one service having a wicker patterned border with four reserves

Fig. 1020. Fournier Period (1760–1766) soft-paste service design presented to King Charles XV of Sweden by the Countess Dannemand. Marked F 5 in gold. 1760–1765. National Mus., Stockholm.

Fig. 1021. One of a pair of rococo vases with a medallion showing a shield supported by cupids and having a crown and F 5 in gold. The flowers are in natural colors. 1760–1765. Count Moltke Coll. in Bregentved.

in light rococo feeling of flowers. The edge is in rudimentary petal form which seemed to be a favorite treatment. The painting was done by Jürgen Gülding, Joseph Brecheisen, George Christian Sciptius and others with a decidedly French style. The material is yellowish and with a soapy feel, having little brilliance not unlike Chantilly. There was a Meissen influence

GROUP. FLORA AND MINERVA
Height 11⅝ inches.

Left to Right: One of a pair of vases painted with portraits of Queen Juliane Marie and the Crown Prince Frederik. c. 1785. Ht. 15". Rosenborg Castle. Vase of gold and white with garland in natural colors. The playful treatment of cupids arranging the garlands shows at least a spark of invention. c. 1788. The Rosenborg Castle.
Typical of the gods made in European factories is this group of Flora and Minerva having the three line and personal mark of Jacob Schmidt, (1778–1807). Ht. 11 4/5". Dansk Folke Mus., Copenhagen.
Biscuit group with incised mark A HALD 1797. Dansk Folke Mus., Copenhagen.

COPENHAGEN PORCELAIN OF THE LATE 18TH CENTURY

PLATE 190

in the use of "mosaik." The thickness varies and it seems experimental. The colors have little depth and the only red tone is a characteristic pale pink. Otherwise there was a powerful copper green, and a very soft yellow sometimes hardly visible.

C7 stood for Christian VII on one piece. The usual mark is F5 for Frederik V. A month before his death Frederik V gave an order that the factory cease (1765).

J. G. Richter, a painter from Strasburg, and Frantz Heinrich Müller, were given Fournier's secrets and Müller started in 1771 to experiment and finally made a poor piece of real porcelain, with yellowish glaze and underglaze blue decoration. He was granted 1,000 rigsdalers in 1772 to start a factory and went in 1773 to Bornholm which helped him to get better results.

In 1774 he was trying to sell stock when Queen Dowager Juliane Marie took an interest and a company was formed with a capital of 19,000 rigsdalers with Holm, and the historian, Suhm, in charge. A privilege was granted on March 13, 1775 conferring a monopoly for 50 years and the post office in Købmagergade became the factory.

The mark was decided as "three wave-shaped lines representing the three streams of Denmark, namely, "The Sound and the Great and Little Belts." Hannover makes the point that the fact that it was adopted in 1775 does not exclude the possibility that Müller had been using it before.

The mark alone shows that Müller had an underglaze blue but this was, at first, greyish or even blackish. Probably the kaolin brought from GrødbyAa improved the paste. The sand came from Robertsdal and the felspar from near Nexø. Also the chalk from Faxe and fluorspar from Gislöf in Sweden helped the glaze. Later kaolin was brought from Limoges and felspar from Arendal in Norway while the chalk of the island of Møen was preferred to that of Faxe.

BORNHOLM PERIOD (1773–1776)

During the Bornholm period from 1773 to the beginning of 1776, the ware was bluish-grey with a tendency to "wreathing" which caused worry to Müller when C. F. G. Clar of Rendsburg applied for a privilege for himself, and he forthwith got help from workers from Saxony and Furstenberg. He even took a trip under a false name to Germany in the hope of getting some secrets. After this Johann Georg von Langen came bringing secrets from Furstenberg where he had been, and also from Höchst, through Benckgraff's notes. He urged the employment of Luplau.

This Anton Carl Luplau in 1795 applied to the governors to give him equal rank with Müller and in a report by Gronland we pick the few follow-ing statements as representative of the state of affairs: "It was not until Luplau brought with him a tried method that Müller learned that quartz is a principal ingredient." "Apart from alterations introduced by Justitsraad Müller, and to which I expressly attribute the ill-success of our factory, it is the paste of Luplau, his glaze and his kiln, that we are using at the moment." In the same year Luplau wrote a book, afterward edited by his son, giving "all the secrets of a true porcelain factory."

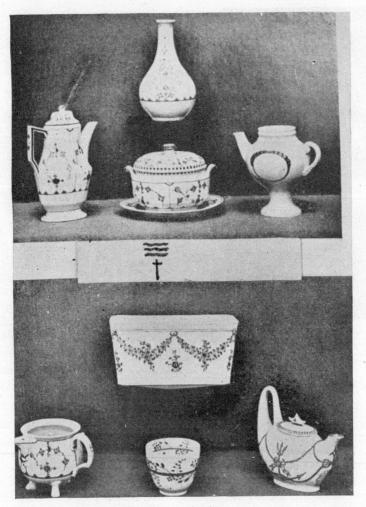

FIG. 1022. The upper group is said by Hayden to be of the "Bornholm period."
The cup with three feet lower left is marked with the three lines and cross in
blue under the handle. The tea-pot is the only one known with three blue lines
under the handle. Mus. of the Royal Copenhagen Porcelain Factory.

In the meantime the factory was having the usual financial difficulties
all kilns seemed subject to and in 1779, through the instigation of Juliane
Marie, under the influence of her Cabinet Secretary, Holm, the king gave
his consent to the acceptance of the factory, for the bright idea had occurred to the members of the board that it would be a good thing to make
the gift. The factory was then called *Den Kongelige Danske Porcelains
Fabrik.* This is the factory, popularly known as Royal Copenhagen, that
became famous the world over for its fine wares.

In 1780 the first sales room was opened. Many new artists were brought in,

FIG. 1023. Dowager-Queen Juliane
Marie bust signed "Luplau fec: 1781."
At Rosenborg Castle.

FIG. 1024. Ewer and cover painted in aubergine
(manganese) and certainly from a German model.
Ht. 9½". c. 1779. Kunstindustri Mus., Bergen.

mainly German, but a sufficient number of Danes were there to give the
work a flavor of its own.

In 1776 a rule was made not to paint the porcelain with colors other
than underglaze blue and at about this time was made the ware with festoons
of flowers in blue on a grey porcelain. In 1778 iron-red was resumed sometimes on flowers in slight relief. At the same time a purple was added and
yet the underglaze blue was the chief medium, though not yet mastered. In
1779 the purple became dominant along with a good copper green. By 1780
the iron-red is predominant with purple a close second while polychrome
flowers in rococo panels in slight relief and accented with pale copper green
or gold are also made. This sort of shadow treatment seems probably original. The flowers were simple and broad but with a stiff, quaint style not
without appeal. Soon, however, the rococo was replaced by the neo-classic
trends of the day.

It was in 1780 that a new and whiter as well as more translucent porcelain
was produced and most of the neo-classical shapes were done. By 1781
most of the old paste seems to have been used up and at the same time the
painting of flowers is brighter and better, undoubtedly due to the German
artists. One hand bell of the period is decorated in "mosaik" surrounding

FIG. 1025. Of the period between 1780 and 1796 a service painted with fruits in natural colors. Coll. of Her Majesty the Queen of Denmark.

harvest scenes in somewhat inky tones of polychrome almost exactly like those of the Berlin factory. But the Danish influence made the Germans do flowers that looked soft and fresh, like those of northern summers. The gilding was also moderate and in good taste. The usual purple and natural colored landscapes with, of course, romantic ruins, "altars of love," "altars of friendship," and "memorial columns," and the silhouettes, cupids in grey and in natural colors, etc., had their turn as elsewhere. A specialty was ini-

FIG. 1026. Front and top of casket which is mounted in gold and set with rubies, richly gilt and painted in natural colors. The royal crown appears on the front and the key is designed with the monogram of Christian VIII. c. 1781. Length 7¾". J. Pierpont Morgan Coll.

tials in flowers. And the northern people took the sweet-to-cloying sentimentality of the French seriously to their hearts and made it even more
sentimental.

Søren Preuss was responsible for many of the flowers and Luplau himself
for the cupids that are handles on the covers. In 1782 they introduced "flower
vases with cupids in black"
(painted of course) and in 1783
black pastoral scenes and "India
ink painting with cupids in
clouds." The iron-red was a
favorite with Ondrup.

Another decoration is called
"Quodlibets" meaning "what you
please" and consists of all manner of objects thrown together
and painted in various shades of
grey or natural colors. In 1788
there were cupid-surmounted
vases with portraits in brown of
Raphael, Durer, Leonardo, etc.

Fig. 1027. Tray with landscape in deep green
and wreaths in manganese with the borders gilt by
Elias Mever. It was given by Frederik VI to Pastor
Mandal of Sørum, Norway, 1790. Kunstindustri
Mus., Copenhagen.

Breakfast sets were made for
two to twelve people and these latter were usually 51 pieces. The famous
"Müller service" made for the founder was of 46 pieces and 32 still exist. It
was made in 1784 by all of the artists in the factory supervised by Camradt,
and is a sampler with each piece differently treated. Some pieces are even
decorated differently on either side. For example one teapot is pink on one
side and white on the other. The
bleu-de-roi border holds the set together though even this border is
varied, so far as the gold design on
it is concerned. Three silhouette
portraits of Müller's sons with their
initials and ages are on one tea-
caddy and Charles A. Been also
pointed out portraits of Müller
himself and his second wife. There
was a rule in the factory that artists should not sign their work and
unfortunately this was adhered to
even in this service. Ondrup did
surreptitiously write his name in

Fig. 1028. Tray dated 1783 and painted with
"Quodlibet" or "attrap" decoration. Coll. of Hr.
Nörgaard, Sölyst, Denmark.

tiny letters in hidden places like the inside of a foot-rim, but we know his style
already from the constant use of iron-red in inharmonious combinations. Camradt did cupids en grisaille and portraits of the royal family. Lehmann did
polychrome flowers and "shadow pictures." Elias Meyer did landscapes, polychrome birds, "antique heads," and "quodlibet."

The decline began to take place and in 1785 mirror frames, toilet services, caskets, brush handles, etc., and cups with "kommik" paintings were so successful that they were often repeated. By 1786 flutes and dress buttons were added, plus pipe bowls with dates and inscriptions and breakfast services decorated by Meyer and Poggendahl. In 1787 came the first "Ovidian paintings" by Camradt and in 1788 large potpourri vases with figure handles, rams' heads, garlands and fluted or reeded pedestals.

The Flora Danica Service of world fame was commenced in 1789 or 1790 with botanical paintings by Johann Christoph Bayer, from Nuremberg, who had been at the factory since 1776. Tradition has it that the intention was to present this service to Catherine II of Russia but she died before it was completed. The first decorator of the factory was Holm, who had laid out the gardens at Sorø and Copenhagen. He had just published his large and beautiful work dealing with Danish fungi and had the idea of using the plates to decorate a dinner service. Each piece had on the back a reference to the learned work and the Latin name of the plant. Yet, unlike the Palissy wares, these decorations, though accurate, were also beautiful. The colors were more brilliant than the printed plates of the book and the painting was graceful as the flowers themselves and without scientific stiffness. Here suddenly in the miasma of deceit and larceny of the penny grubbing 18th century, nay at its most odorous and marshy depths, two men, a

FIG. 1029. Vase with cupids in natural colors and gilt decoration. Ht. 18". Dansk Folke Mus., Copenhagen.

manager and an artist have turned back to first sources; back to nature and regardless of the baroque or the rococo, the empire or directoire styles, have set out to take things from nature and arrange them so as to be beautiful and give delight. To arrange them on what principles?

Well, here again we are confronted by the age old argument as to what constitutes art. Man has, through the ages tried to take the simple things around him and arrange them so as to suggest his feelings for them. He has tried to change nature just a little to please him the better. He has also taken a delight in placing things within certain bounds and making them fit those bounds properly. He carved a bear on the handle of a knife so that anyone would recognize it as a bear and yet, if the design was drawn on paper anyone could also see that it was the handle for a knife. He also unconsciously put something of himself into it, for he carved it differently than his brother would, or than any other man would. Whole tribes carved their bears differently from other tribes yet often nearly enough alike to be recognizable as from their tribe and no other. This was just as the language of one tribe might differ from all others and be understandable only to the members of that one tribe, and this marvelously enough despite the fact that each member of the tribe talked differently from every other member.

All this simple and sincere way of things had been lost to the 18th century for 1.—the artists were not close to nature, 2.—the artists were trying to

Plates, tureen and cruet stand of the Flora Danica service made for Catherine II of Russia. Rosenborg P
Copenhagen.

PIECES FROM THE FLORA DANICA SERVICE

PLATE 191

make things look more expensive and grand and did not keep within the bounds, 3.—artists were so pushed for time in the everlasting competition that they could not take the time to think out anything of their own and had to keep their brushes working without an idea behind them, 4.—as several generations had been taught simply to steal the ideas of each other, the whole thing dried up and there was nothing to steal.

But here in Copenhagen two men saw a gleam of light. On what principles could old Bayer arrange his flowers? He had no traditional tea-ceremony. He had no time to sit and watch each flower grow, blossom and die so as to try to catch the very spirit of the flower. He had never, like the Chinese, watched the bamboo day after day in summer rain, in hot sun, in a fall storm when birds could hold to it only a few seconds before being torn away by the wind. He had probably never thought of painting a flower in its surrounding atmosphere and under the conditions of its life, of painting it in his own way and as an expression of his own mood. He could only see it cold and alone, detached from all the world and laid out dead on a porcelain plate.

He, with the help of other artists who did the borders and general work, had turned out 1,000 pieces by 1792 in a little over 2 years, or about 40 a month or 10 a week. By 1794 he had totaled 1,335 including some big pieces valued at 10,400 rigsdaler. In 1797 there were 2,528 pieces and 180 still to be made. Then the court gave the order that it should be even greater so as to seat 100 guests. In 1802 it was still uncompleted and the court ordered work to stop. But work of real charm had been accomplished and

FIG. 1030. Two Sea Horses painted in brown and other colors and marked with three blue lines. c. 1800. National Mus., Stockholm.

FIG. 1031. Antique and modern plates with fluted rims and "Muschel" pattern. Note deeper blue but heavier drawing on modern plate. George Jensen, Inc.

FIG. 1032. Empire feeling threw its blight upon this factory as upon others of Europe. Bowl at top was made in memory of brave Danes who fell at Battle of Copenhagen, dated April 2nd, 1801. Cups show "The King's Square, Copenhagen," and "Kronborg Castle" showing the Sound. Dansk Folke Mus., Copenhagen.

it may be that this return to first principles made by Holm and Bayer was responsible for the beautiful and natural charm of the present day Copenhagen work.

However, there is no doubt but that this undertaking, which was slow in being paid for, caused financial difficulties, which lasted until 1807 when the English bombarded Copenhagen and all production stopped. Between 1790 and 1800 there were "belt-plaques" and "ice-bells," plaques for furniture called "piano plaques," butter dishes in the form of apples, some square salvers, dishes with covers like a bunch of asparagus, scent bottles in the form of infants in swaddling-clothes (the appropriateness depending on the point of view I suppose), pipe-bowls in the shape of vases, tobacco-boxes in the shape of dogs' heads and such table decorations as sea-nymphs, mermen and sea-horses designed to stand on a mirror. The usual Wedgwood, "Egyptian" and "Etruscan" things were made.

The blue and white ware consisted chiefly of the "Muschel" pattern, the bouquet of flowers, the "onion" pattern or "Zwiebelmuster" of Meissen and a "Chinese" design from the same source. The blue and white of clear paste is later and that of good blue, later yet. The latest is too harsh and aggressive. The "Muschel" pattern became increasingly misunderstood and corrupted and in all late pieces the drawing gets more and more stiff with cautiousness yet somehow at the same time careless and heavy in composition.

After 1800 the purple continues but less pure and strong in color. Gold and white became increasingly popular because of the "good taste" of the day. Hannover states, and I think we should believe him, that collectors have placed a too high value on the plastic works of the old factory. Perhaps this is due to the modern fame, for at no time did the place have a modeler of note on its staff. We hear of J. J. Smidt and Andreas Hald whose marks appear on widely different things, and were possibly simply retouchers.

There have not been many forgeries except the baskets of flowers like those of the Flora Danica service which Samson copied, and carefully marked with the wave mark. Also a "restorer" in Dresden bought the bottoms of undecorated boxes with wave marks on them and made lids of Saxon porcelain, covering the whole with decoration so as to disguise the fact that the wares were different.

SWEDEN

MARIEBERG

In Sweden Ehrenreich applied for a privilege in 1758. In the same or following year the Marieberg property at Kungsholmen, Stockholm, was purchased from Baron C. F. Scheffer "for the establishment of a true porcelain factory," but after the place had burned down and been reerected Ehrenreich decided to give up porcelain and make faïence. There is only one insignificant piece to represent his experiments.

Possibly from France and copied at Marieberg are some pieces which Strole in the Rorstrand Museum has said were made by Ehrenreich's successor, Pierre Berthevin (1766–1769) which are soft-paste candlesticks and pastilleburners with decorations of freely modeled flowers applied. There are also animals such as a goat, a cat and a dog, but all of these are probably French and not Marieberg at all.

From Mennecy came the design for the custard cups with single handle and cover and decorated with flowers. Some of these cannot be distinguished except for the mark.

Strole classes the early wares as follows:
1. Earliest: Custard cups, miniature vases with dolphin handles and small modeled figures in highly translucent, greenish-yellow and faulty paste of soft type, marked MB incised which he says meant "Marieberg-Berthevin" while Hannover says it meant "Marie Berg."
2. Chalky white soft paste marked MB in color. (Possibly Sten's.)
3. True porcelain thinly glazed and probably of the last of the period of Henrik Sten (1769–1778).

The second period was a transitional period and probably started about 1770 when the modeler Fleurot was called in followed by Huret and Jacques or Jacob Dortie or Dortu, Frenchmen of no particular renown but workmen who may have helped the general technique.

It is definitely established that the F which sometimes occurs on figures

FIG. 1033. Woman with chickens painted in overglaze natural colors and, black and gold on belt and pendant ornaments. Mark M incised. Kunstindustri Mus., Copenhagen.
FIG. 1034. Statue of a Hero having the incised mark: I HOLM 1780 and three blue lines. Ht. 12¼". National Mus., Stockholm.
FIG. 1035. Not entered in books but probably dating c. 1786 to 1796 this dancing pair in contemporary costumes are in soft colors and gold.

and custard cups has nothing to do with Fleurot, and, as Huret is mentioned specifically in old documents of the factory as having "occasioned the flint porcelain" it is not likely that he especially concerned himself with hard porcelain. Sten did begin to experiment with hard porcelain on his own account. Hannover does not think it impossible that he might be responsible for the second or chalky type of ware. The third type may have been brought about by the man called Jacques Dortie by Strole and Jacob Dortu by Hannover, who identifies him as Müller's assistant at Nyon "for" as he says, "shortly after his engagement in 1777, the state of affairs at the factory is thus descr'bed: 'Old Franzen attends the faïence, Sten to the flint porcelain and Dortie the true porcelain.' If this line of thought is correct the third class must belong to the year 1777 and 1778 for Dortu only worked at the factory at that time. Dortu seems to have taken the secret with him when he left,

FIG. 1036. Large vases in white porcelain dating between 1780–1796. Ht. 48". Frederiksborg Castle.

for otherwise had the factory gone on making it until 1782 when it was transferred to Rorstrand or to 1788 when it was closed down, that porcelain could not have been such a rarity as it now is. It was probably superseded by the second type again. Some dated pieces would tend to confirm this.

These are cups decorated in gold and black with festoons and the arms of the family of Baron Liljencrants, dated 1781 and are of semi-porcelain; a tea-caddy and coffee-pot painted in purple, red and green, and in purple and gold respectively are dated the same year and are of the same material."

Thus according to Hannover's well thought out logic we conclude that:
1. Under Berthevin (1766–1769) we have the greenish-yellow soft paste after Mennecy models.
2. Under Henrik Sten (1769–1788) we have the chalky white semi-porcelain save for a brief period of 1777 and 1778 when the hard porcelain was made and then lost or discarded.

There are no hard porcelain custard cups probably because the material was not suitable for the thin walls. There are rare trays or platters with handles at each end and painted with landscapes in purple or with polychrome flowers and green edging. There are also perforated baskets with modeled and painted flowers, some ink stands and tête-à-tête sets with modeled flowers or a torch and quiver on a pedestal. These are seldom marked.

The semi-porcelain is of a limey character white as chalk and uneven like faïence. It is slightly and irregularly translucent, light in weight and without resonance. The glaze is often cracked. It is seldom decorated. The custard cups are usually molded in slight relief with helical lines and have handles with rococo feeling. The decorations are polychrome, purple, blue or green bunches of flowers on either side and smaller ones on the covers. The colors of the flowers are sometimes combined with gold, and black is rare but not unknown. When gold is used it is sparingly touched in and the knobs and edges are also gilded.

There are no landscapes in natural colors but only small ones in iron red, reddish purple and copper green. These are in quatrefoil medallions or round ones suspended from festoons in relief and framed with leaf garlands. All were in good taste but there is no real life or vigor.

The plastic work was small in quantity and surprisingly small in number of models. They are chiefly figures from life such as a poultry-maid, a vintner, a bag-piper, a dancing boy or girl, some figures from the Italian comedy and a few mythological ones. The children are graceful but lifeless. A shepherd trying to kiss a shepherdess is full of action but poorly modeled. Most of them are unpainted.

There is utmost confusion about the marks. The chief one is three small crowns sometimes decoratively drawn, sometimes just indicated with four little strokes and at times just three little dots in underglaze blue are used with or without the crowns. At times a little fleur-de-lis from the House of Vasa was used. The mark is most frequently in iron red or underglaze blue but it occurs also in black, gold, brown, and green, with the color at times corresponding to that used for the decoration of the piece. An F in gold, a cursive M in black or red and an incised MW along with other unexplained marks also occur and finally there are many pieces not marked at all. Only one full signature by an artist is known and that is a tray signed "Schirmer."

There is naturally little reason to imitate this ware although pieces which brought 20 to 40 kroner in 1888 jumped to ten times that value in more recent sales. Soon we may be able to buy good fakes for equal prices, if this keeps up.

IRELAND

BELLEEK

The story goes that Mr. John Caldwell Bloomfield of the Castle Caldwell estate on the River Erne of County Firmanagh below the Donegal Highlands and about six miles from the sea directly west of Belfast, noted the exceptional brilliancy of the whitewash used on a tenant's house and discovered a limepit which led to the discovery that the whole estate rested upon a felspathic clay stratum. A factory was built, it is reported, in 1857 though just what the output was seems in some doubt. According to W. P. Jervis (*The Encyclopaedia of Ceramics,* p. 41), the so-called "parian ware" was first made by a William Bromley, a modeler named Gallimore and some workmen hired temporarily away from W. H. Goss of Stoke-upon-Trent who was supposed to have produced the ware there. Who Mr. Goss was and how he got the secret from William Taylor Copeland who invented the ware in 1846 I do not know. Jervis also states that the firm of Messrs. McBirney & Armstrong of Belleek, the town from which the ware takes its name, first made it popular in 1863.

The "inventor" of the pearly luster was J. J. H. Brianchou, a Frenchman who took out a patent in England in July 8th, 1857. Actually some biscuit unglazed pieces were made which might resemble the other "parian wares" but were quite different, due to the difference of local materials, and the Belleek usually known is glazed. I suspect that just as it was a vogue to make soft, white or cream biscuit in America and call it "parian" because it was supposed to be similar to marble in texture, so the Belleek potters also tried their hand at it. Of course, the Frenchman's patent is somewhat foolish in view of the fact that luster, or a thin solution of metal washed over a glaze and fired on, is one of the very ancient ways of decorating ceramic wares. However, it is probably true that no luster was used at Belleek until 1863.

The ware is made with the plaster casting process; after the clay has been ground and refined down to the consistency of cream, it is poured into a mold, turned this way and that and allowed to dry about 20 minutes. The mold can then be removed and appliqués of flowers, etc., applied by hand after having been hand modeled. The firing is done in troughs or long saggers and the best pieces are placed in sealed saggers inside of these same troughs. It is said that firing lasts about 56 hours and uses about 17 tons of coal per kiln. To form the beautiful baskets, the clay is put through a machine and comes out like spaghetti in strings which are cut to length and then woven by hand over plaster forms. A damp cloth keeps them the right consistency.

The glaze is of two sorts. The finest is of white lead, red lead, flint and borax while the coarser omits the red lead. The firing is done for less time and at a lower temperature and takes about 10 tons per kiln.

The painting is then done and fired again while the luster takes a fourth firing at very low heat. This luster is colorless or very pale primrose yellow. The most usual colors are pastel pink and green.

Fig. 1037. Belleek basket of typical type with beautifully even weave of strands. Length 10". W. S. Pitcairne Corp.

Fig. 1038. Irish Belleek flower-pot of better and simpler type of organic design which is sometimes ruined by application of modeled flowers, etc. Ht. c. 4". W. S. Pitcairne Corp.

Fig. 1039. Tea-pot "Limpet Cob" which shows a pleasant adaptation of sea forms. Ht. 8½". W. S. Pitcairne Corp.

Fig. 1040. "Nile Vase," an art nouveau design of more modern feeling which has been very popular and was made in three sizes. Ht. 10". W. S. Pitcairne Corp.

As the factory is so near the sea and the town lives through the kilns and fisheries, naturally the early pieces are of marine plants, sea shells, corals, mermaids, sea-dogs and such while later flat wares and flower vases were copied more or less from other kilns. However, a spirit of independence and the difference of the material makes these all quite distinct and easily recognized.

The early mark though not invariably used according to Mr. G. L. Pitcairn who represents the factory in America, is a round tower with an Irish harp to the left and an Irish Wolf Hound to the right. Beneath is a ribbon with the name Belleek and some shamrock ornamentation. On modern wares a circular Celtic symbol has been added. The basket pieces have a narrow, flat ribbon with the name impressed, stuck on the bottom.

As the factory is exactly on the border line between Eire and North Ireland it has had some troubles but fortunately appeals to both factions. It was also dependent on the River Erne for power until a board of fisheries recently made a grant of some machinery so that this power could be discontinued part of the year. It is, however, a beautiful place on this rushing stream amid rolling hills and I understand keeps some 100 to 150 men busily engaged in the making of this paper-thin, soft-toned and beautiful ware.

CHAPTER XXIV

ENGLISH "SOFT PASTE" AND "BONE CHINA"

OUR ceramic world centers seem ever to move westward and England took its turn after Crete, Greece and Rome but England was never an inspired disseminator of design so much as a repository into which was gathered much that went on on the mainland of Europe. Yet the English never made any real hard porcelain during the 18th century, and was still trying to improve soft porcelain after hard porcelain had about replaced it on the continent. On the other hand, being a tea-drinking nation, close connections were maintained with China and designs from the Far East as well as from the continent found their way there. However, even in the Far East the influences were not so much from the fine wares of Ching-tê Chên of the K'ang Hsi or Ch'ien Lung periods as from the later Canton decorated wares and those from Japan from Arita or "Imari" porcelain. Kakiemon ware had an influence both direct and from the European copies of it. The Tê-hua wares of Fukien province also were indirectly an influence though, through France from such places as St. Cloud.

Besides these we have the influences of the chinoiseries of later Meissen origin which look like German ladies dressed up in Oriental clothes, and the also strong influences of Boucher as found in Chelsea porcelain, and Meissonier, Watteau and the rest. We have "Indianische Blumen" followed by "Deutsche Blumen," by "Fantasievogel" (exotic birds derived from China), Sèvres influences superseded by pseudo-classicism and then Angelica Kauffmann. Only one major development took place and that was in the stoneware of Wedgwood which too was not true porcelain but which so caught the popular taste at the end of the century as to become very popular over many years.

CHELSEA, 1745–1751

The earliest dated piece of English bone china is a "Goat and bee jug" owned by Lord Fisher similar to the one illustrated. The design was taken from a piece of silver bearing a hall mark of 1724. This jug has incised in the paste before firing, the word CHELSEA, a triangle and the date, 1745. It is thought that the factory opened about a year preceding this date and was about contemporary with the Bow factory.

A tea-pot in the form of a Chinaman with a parrot in his lap and another

742

with a Chinaman bestriding a snake, both showing close influence by Kandler, are also known. A rare group which is also marked is of two lovers full of ardent feeling, the lady seemingly trying to press her beautifully rounded breasts to the cheek of her lover.

Other figures of the period are a "Waterman with Dogget's coat and badge," a fortune-telling group and a small figure of a girl dancing and a boy with a hurdy-gurdy; all of which have the same soft paste and distinctive bases cut at the corners and beveled wider at the top than at the bottom. It is difficult to tell these figures from the French. There are also cups with raised flowers and a tea-pot with moulded overlapping strawberry leaves.

Fig. 1041. "Goat & Bee Jug," Chelsea marked, with triangle and delicately colored. One in the British Mus. has no coloring as is rule with these pieces between 1745 and 1751. They are practically speaking simply an opaque yellowish-white glass rather than porcelain. Pair of swans, one with cygnets, of the raised anchor period of Chelsea. Frank Stoner–Stoner & Evans, Ltd.

The bodies of these wares are creamy and translucent with a glaze of yellowish cast. If held against strong light they show bright spots like pinholes and these are the prototypes of the famous "moons" of the ensuing period attributable to unincorporated frit or glass in the paste. Not all of these are monochrome for some have details painted in natural colors but this may have been done later. It is known that William Duesbury who later purchased the factory had, at about 1750, a large business in decorating various porcelains. Little strewn flowers served as they did in Germany to hide blemishes. Mr. Herbert Eccles, F.C.S., made an analysis of the ware and it shows a large percentage of lead oxide from which he concludes that a flint glass may have been used in the composition. There is an absence of bone-ash.

An advertisement of 1750 mentions a Mr. Charles Gouyn who might have been the founder. The marks are a triangle incised and a crown and trident in underglaze blue which occurs on the lover group described, though this color was not used in decoration. Also a small embossed anchor on a round button seemed to have been used. The period ends in 1751.

CHELSEA SECOND PERIOD, 1751–1753
RAISED ANCHOR AND OCCASIONALLY RED ANCHOR MARKS

Chaffers (3d edition p. 701) quotes Mason, a worker who wrote, "I think the Chelsea China Manufactory began about the year 1748 or 1749. I went to work about the year 1751. It was first carried on by the Duke of Cumberland and Sir Everard Fawkner, and the sole management was entrusted to a foreigner of the name of Nicholas Sprimont, report says, at a salary of a guinea per day with certain allowance for apprentices and other emoluments. I think Sir Everard died about 1755, much reduced in circumstances; when

Mr. Sprimont became sole proprietor; and having amassed a fortune, he traveled about England, and the manufactory was shut up about two years, for he neither would let it or carry it on himself. I then went to work at Bow for a short time, which was carried on by a firm, but I don't recollect their names. I went to work again at Chelsea for Mr. Sprimont, after being absent between two and three years, where I stopped till I engaged with Mr. (William) Duesbury to go to Derby, which was about the year 1763. I think there was very little business done after that time. What time Mr. Duesbury made a purchase of it I don't recollect, but some of the materials were taken to Derby." Another document says that the Duke of Cumberland was a great encourager of the Chelsea China and "bespoke a set for his own table."

Sprimont is thought to be a silver-smith. The eminent authority Frank Stoner says that Sprimont carried on until 1769, then sold to James Cox, who in 1770 sold to William Duesbury, who kept the factory between that date and 1784 during the "Chelsea Derby" period and then moved to Derby.

FIG. 1042. Chelsea raised anchor period figure of Chinese boy, c. 1750. One of earliest and rarest figures from this factory and one of rarest types in English wares. Attempt to imitate white Fukien wares though paste is grey, heavy and glaze shiny, of slightly cream tone and has many pits as of burst bubbles in firing. There are a number of fire cracks. Also a resemblance to St. Cloud soft paste. Ht. 8". Frank Stoner–Stoner & Evans, Ltd.

From 1751 the ware is thick, sandy and with a glaze like candle grease. It is sparingly painted in Oriental style. The added weight did not entirely prevent its warping in firing. Dr. Diamond has called attention to the "moons" or light discs in the body which were characteristic of the period. William Burton thinks that some of the frit was kept coarse to help prevent warping but actually I think it would act in the contrary way for it is the glass which melts and is soft in the kiln.

An analysis made by Eccles and published by King shows that the lead oxide is almost eliminated and a large content of lime introduced much as in the French soft paste, in a raised anchor marked piece.

With this mark there were busts in white glaze of the Duke of Cumberland, pieces of Imari (German influenced) style (and these occur also with the red anchor or in one odd case in the B.M. with an underglaze blue anchor). "Yellow tiger" and "red lion" as well as hexagonal jars were copies of the

Meissen designs after Kakiemon. The Meissen jars date between 1720 and 1725 while the Chelsea ones date between 1753 and 1758, the only change being the use of alternating panels of white strap work on coral red ground. The raised anchor also appears on copies of blanc de Chine in both Kwan Yin figures and cups with raised flower decoration, and these continued into the next period.

THE THIRD OR RED ANCHOR PERIOD, 1753–1758

The only differences now taking place are that the porcelain is a little better made, thinner, more translucent but blemishes still had to be covered by decoration. The Meissen influence was strengthened by the collection of Sir Charles Hanbury Williams, Plenipotentiary at Dresden, who allowed the factory to work with his German pieces. In 1748 Sir Charles was presented with a dessert service in the form of artichokes, laurel leaves, sunflowers and double leaves. The "Doctor" in the collection of Mrs. Radford is from the original by Peter Reinicke (1743–4) and is probably the "Italian Doctor" described

FIG. 1043. Hexagonal jar copied from Meissen which had in turn copied from Kakiemon in general style. Many have alternating light and dark ground panels. c. 1753–1758. Ht. 12″. Metropolitan Mus. of Art.

in the catalogue of 1755 though it has a raised anchor mark. The "Hurdy-gurdy Player" is also so marked. Besides the Meissen influence the engravings of J. J. Balechon after Boucher had an effect.

FIG. 1044. Two of the "Five Senses," "Seeing" and "Hearing" made c. 1755 at Chelsea. Ht. 11⅛″. Metropolitan Mus. of Art.

As the wares of the triangle period are easily confused with those of Chantilly and St. Cloud so those of the second and third period are with wares of Bow particularly the uncolored vases, cups and other vessels. Both the early and late wares of Chelsea have sealing-wax red, lemon yellow and milky blue but a pink used in the flower decoration of a small girl figure with the triangle mark is missing on later pieces and a pleasing dark red is peculiar. Parrots copied from Meissen were made in blue, purple and green and copied also by Bow but were discontinued by 1756.

The red-anchor figures were the best produced by this factory, and softer than their Meissen prototypes. Flat washed colors, large areas of white, touches of black and no gold made them tasteful. Plates were edged with brown, and underglaze blue is exceedingly rare. Applied flowers in full relief and reticulation were practiced. "A Pair of Peasants Dancing" are mentioned in the catalogue of 1756 and copied from Mandler, as were also the "Monkey Band" and tureens of sitting birds but perhaps the long-eared rabbit tureen was actually a Chelsea invention. Other figures are, "A Gardener and his Wife sitting with a Basket, River God, River Goddess, Ceres" (which gives the opportunity of a luscious nude in the flesh-like soft porcelain), "Map Seller, a Jew with his Box of Toys, Pierrot," and a typical subterfuge, "The Pedlar extoling his wares in a Box" which was copied from the Meissen "Man with a Tamed Rat" with omission of the rat. A "Maypole Group" belonging to Lord and Lady Fisher contains a figure exactly like a "Peasant Dancing" in the same collection. More elaborate groups are the "Madonna and Child on a Sphere" and two groups of three figures on rococo bases and equipped with candle sockets. The rococo bases are unusual for the period and one has a gold anchor mark which should warn us not to take the divisions of the period

FIG. 1045. Chelsea figure of duck painted with green back and pink wings dated by museum between 1750–1755. This may be one of "Stooping birds" mentioned in cat. of sale in 1755. Ht. 4⅜". Metropolitan Mus. of Art.

FIG. 1046. Nurse with child, Chelsea of the red anchor period about 1758. This group is from a continental prototype. Frank Stoner–Stoner & Evans, Ltd.

as too definite. King warns us as well that the "Persus Group" has distinctly the coloring of the gold-anchor period and is marked with a red anchor.

The useful china was taken from silver models and Meissen ones with often used relief borders and painting of German style. There was some spirit and even humor as may be seen by the "Nonsense panels" on the rim of a plate showing a lion scared to death with mane on end, a camel with stag horns and a twisted tail, etc. (See V. & A. Mus.)

Impractical "Crawfish Salts" were made and a "Sweetmeat Tray" is a pile of shells supporting a seven-shell group of cups painted with insects.

Blue and white specimens mentioned in the catalogue are difficult to identify. However, some with blue-anchor marks have pierced lattice rims with flowers in blue either in relief or flat at each intersection and crude center medallions of a "Willow Pattern," composed of Chinese rocks and trees. The sandy paste and spur marks are characteristic.

The useful wares were usually marked below the base while the figures were marked on the upper part of the bases. The anchor appears also in brown and purple. The two red-anchor marks are not established and their meaning is unknown. Occasionally the Meissen crossed swords were used perhaps when a set had to be filled out.

The catalogues of 1755 and 1756 mention an "exceeding rich blue enamel" and gilt edged plates which would seem to prove that the gold-anchor period began about this time.

THE FOURTH OR GOLD-ANCHOR PERIOD, 1758–1770

Spur marks continue but "moons" disappear. The paste now contains bone ash and is whiter and more translucent but tends to crackle. This is the great period of ground colors and gilding. On April 15th, 1763 two large vases said to have been made in 1762 were given to the B.M. and they have "mazarine blue" ground and reserve panels of the death of Cleopatra on one side and exotic birds on the other set off by elaborately chased gilding.

Horace Walpole wrote to Sir Horace Mann on March 4th, 1763, "I saw

FIG. 1047. Vase with blue ground and rich gilding after Sèvres style. Between 1765–1770, Chelsea. Ht. 9¼". Metropolitan Mus. of Art.
FIG. 1048. Vase with tall, comparatively pleasing form and rococo handles, between 1762–1770, Chelsea. Ht. 11⅜". Metropolitan Mus. of Art.
FIG. 1049. Vase and cover of heart shape with reticulated neck and raised flowers. Not enough technical stunts could be heaped upon these pieces. Chelsea, 1765–1770. Ht. 9". Metropolitan Mus. of Art.

yesterday a magnificent service of Chelsea China which the King and Queen are sending to the Duke of Mecklenburg. There are dishes and plates without number, an epergne, candlesticks, salt cellars, sauce boats, tea and coffee equipages; in short it is complete; and cost twelve hundred pounds! I cannot boast of our taste; the forms are neither new, beautiful nor various. Yet Sprimont, the manufacturer, is a Frenchman. It seems their taste will not bear transplanting." It is amusing to add William King's comment some 160 years later, "Walpole's failure to appreciate this triumph of rococo art, the Mecklenburg service, is a melancholy reminder that after the pseudo-classicism of the next ten years there was yet to dawn the day of Strawberry Hill and the Gothic revival." He might have added that there was to follow Modern Art, streamlining, and revivals of the Mid-Victorian and Empire! However, it was in this year 1763 that a trend started away from the over-elaborate.

Fig. 1050. Vase of involved form influenced by most decadent of Sèvres designs. Ht. 9¼". Metropolitan Mus. of Art.

Fig. 1051. Vases between 1760–1770 with heaped up molded decoration in worst possible rococo taste. Chelsea. Ht. 13¼". Metropolitan Mus. of Art.

It is to be noted that during the transferring of ownership from Sprimont to Cox to Duesbury in 1769 and 1770 a workman, Francis Thomas, stole a quantity of the porcelain from the factory, some of which may have been decorated elsewhere.

The gold-anchor wares contain about 40% of the bone ash, the paste is still sandy but the glaze is richer and collects thickly in hollows. The elaborate design and gilding were copied from Sèvres. William Burton says that the gilding was done in the Chinese manner; leaf gold ground in honey was applied before low firing. Gold so applied has a dull look not improved by burnishing. The later rich Chelsea gold was made in the modern manner; amalgam of gold and mercury ground fine with a small amount of glass or flux. In this way the gold can be laid as heavy as desired and then burnished and chased.

Figure modeling was improved. The "Pieta" was taken from a painting by Rubens in the Prado or from an engraving after the painting. Bernini did a similar subject at Doccia. The largest figure made by the factory is of Una or "Britannia" with a lion. This was listed in 1757 in the catalogue. Another group after Rubens was the "Roman Charity," and the series of Apollo and the Muses is well done. After Kandler were made little cupids and particularly one which is playing a bagpipe and controlling with a string a pair of lovers. "Bocages" or a "bosky grove" of flattened hawthorn leaves

"Roman Charity" group of 1765–70 based on engraving after Rubens with arrangement of feet changed. This group is a little different from one shown by William King in color (Pl. 4, *Chelsea Porcelain*) the robe of Cimon in this case being richly decorated and the bodice of Pera being spotted while they are plain brown and red in the other. Pera's skirt is also more richly decorated. The one in King's book is also shown on a blue and gold stand. Ht. 16¼". Irwin Untermeyer Coll.

CHELSEA GROUP, "ROMAN CHARITY"

PLATE 192

and flowers came into use behind the figures and among these is "L'agrèable Leçon" or the "Music Lesson" also rendered by Johann Friedrich Luck after Boucher in Frankenthal. These figures were done about 1765 and the colors were bright and growing brighter. A very ornate clock in rococo pink and gold; architectural, scroll and animal designs with a wing sprouting to one side to say nothing of cupids and flowers is in Buckingham Palace and is of the period. Other well-known pieces are a "Leda with Swan" after Boucher, "La bergère des Alpes" and "Le noeud de cravate" after Falconet from sketches by Boucher and dating from 1770 to 1784 depending upon the authority. There were also the "Seasons" and a series of portraits of popular Englishmen. These though childish in color and crude in modeling are better than the biscuit insipidity taking hold on the continent. The unknown modeler of the "Reaper" is somewhat better than average.

Vases and useful china with solid ground colors plain or patterned are chiefly of this fourth period. Polychrome flowers on bright gold grounds were used. In 1759 pea-green was added and in 1760 turquoise and the famous "claret" which is deeper than rose Pompadour and even than the Danish Rødgrød, and which was equalled only in rare Worcester imitations. The uneven bright blue and turquoise green were continued.

Fig. 1052. Vase in deep blue with gold decoration after Sèvres style. Chelsea, c. 1765. Ht. 8¼". Metropolitan Mus. of Art.
Fig. 1053. Gold Anchor period covered cup with scale pattern from Meissen in pink and gold. Possibly what was meant in cat. of 1756 by "oxe's eye pattern." c. 1760-1765, Chelsea. Ht. 5¼". Metropolitan Mus. of Art.
Fig. 1054. Plate with red ground, gilt decoration and natural colors. Chelsea c. 1765. Dia. 8½". Metropolitan Mus. of Art.
Fig. 1055. Toilet bottle with white ground and claret color on neck and base and gilt on handles and bordering medallions. Again shows French taste and neo-classicism though said to date c. 1760. Ht. 7". Metropolitan Mus. of Art.

"Chief among the masterpieces," says King, "of this period are the set of seven vases known as the 'Dudley Vases.' The ground is claret colored, richly gilded; on each are reserved two panels, one containing a mythological subject, the other panel of naturalistic birds in the style of Hondekoster. The painting is beautifully finished and the modelling a perfect expression of rococo feeling." If this is the Englishman's idea of perfect rococo feeling, it is quite different from that of the simple little tureens so classed on the continent. These vases are distorted monstrosities with weak, wobbly handles and I doubt that one put in a store on Broadway or at Atlantic City would bring $8 very readily though the actual price runs into four figures.

After the Boucher influence came a second-hand one first of Watteau and

CHELSEA: CHINESE GROUP AFTER BOUCHER.

Raised anchor mark Ht. 8⅞ Inches   Coll. of Alfred E. Hutton

then of Greuze. The Chinoiserie painting and Chinese shapes in beakers top-heavy and clumsy are characteristic, and some of these latter were inappropriately decorated with naturalistic German flowers. In fact naturalistic painting was very much in style. By 1763 the Mecklenburg service has plates with centers containing exotic birds and festoons of flowers on the rims, interrupted with five blue panels containing different butterflies. An even more ornate service has the same centers with claret rims heavily gilded and still another has a peacock-feather rim copied from the Meissen original and poetically called the "oxes eye" pattern.

A bowl of the general aspect of what is called "Lowestoft" has a scene containing two boats and the Chelsea Old Church.

Fig. 1056. Chelsea cachepot with gold anchor mark and decoration in turquoise and gold on handles and edge and naturalistic colors. c. 1760. Ht. 7". Symons Galleries.

Fig. 1057. Chelsea candelabra with gilt and bright colors, c. 1765. Ht. 13⅝". Metropolitan Mus. of Art.

As early as 1754 wares incorrectly called "toys" consisting of snuff-boxes, smelling bottles, "etwees," trinkets for watches and handles for knives and forks were recorded in a sale by a Mr. Ford. Bonbonnières and patch-boxes were also copied from the French. On some of these little pieces even the bottoms were painted and they frequently have mottoes of a gallant or sentimental nature in incorrect French.

CHELSEA-DERBY OR DERBY

Chelsea-Derby is a vague term only correctly used in referring to pieces bearing the official mark of the factories in amalgamation, an anchor traversing a D. Rackham has shown that the gold anchor was still used in 1770 and mentions it on a cup in the Herbert Allen Collection marked also with an N. used at Derby. The true Derby mark, a crowned D in blue, puce, purple and green having crossed batons and six dots between the D and the crown has never been found with a gold anchor.

William Duesbury, the new owner, had been an enameller and had decorated 382 pieces in 1751. He obtained pieces from Chelsea, Bow, Derby and Staffordshire. Jewitt claims to have identified the first maker of porcelain at the Derby factory as Andrew Planche, a Frenchman who is said to have made small animals in a pipe-maker's kiln in 1745 and also to have entered into an agreement with Duesbury and Heath in 1756. Another theory assigns the beginning to the Cockpit Hill Works, a pottery which also made porcelain. John Heath was one of the owners of this place. In 1758 Duesbury

Derby "Ranelegh" figures c. 1765 showing grace of modeling and usual colors
except for orange brown on skirt. Ht.
11¼". Frank Stoner–Stoner & Evans,
Ltd.

"Una with the lion" figure, largest and
most important made at Chelsea factory.
Made and listed in cat. in 1757. c. 27".
Frank Stoner–Stoner & Evans, Ltd.

Part of group of four elements, represent-
ing Earth and Fire, c. 1765 at height of
Derby factory. Ht. 14". Frank Stoner–Stoner
& Evans, Ltd.

Rare and lovely group of four seasons made at Chelsea, 1765. Frank Stoner–Stoner &
Evans, Ltd.

CHELSEA AND DERBY FIGURES

PLATE 193

and Heath bought the Longton Hall Works and they seemed successful in 1763 but Heath went broke and Duesbury gained control.

When he died in 1786 his son, William Duesbury, and the grandson, continued until 1796, when the latter was joined by Michael Kean, until 1811 when it passed into the hands of Robert Bloor. It closed in 1848. Much later a revival was attempted of the high sounding "Royal Crown Derby Porcelain Works," but the wares were inferior. The molds including those from Chelsea were sold to Samuel Boyle who sold them to Copeland of the Spode works where they were not used but remained piled up until discovered in 1924 by Mr. Frank Stoner.

Fig. 1058. Two musicians, Chelsea, 1765, and two children, 1780. Frank Stoner–Stoner & Evans, Ltd.

Not a single figure has been identified from Derby before the uniting of the factories in 1770 though some were made. The earliest identified piece is a white cream jug which has an incised mark D 1750. The paste is sandy and the glaze very white. The handle is a twig and the foot has strawberries in relief. Duesbury made many experiments and technically some of the wares are so much like Gold Anchor Chelsea that they cannot be so distinguished. D'Hancarville's catalogue of Sir William Hamilton's collection (1766-7) changed the style overnight to classical adaptations of Wedgwood and to spiritless figures of sentimental character in pale, thin coloring. From 1771 the innovations are biscuit and lacework. The first had just been taken up at Meissen and the second, which originated at Sèvres in the 1750's, reached Meissen in the 70's and did not come to England certainly until about the same time.

Of course the portrait biscuit technique made possible the patronage of famous people and royalty and it is largely for this that the factory became famous. The paste was soft and pleasing and clever modellers were hired such as John James Spengler, from Zurich, in about 1790. He worked from designs of Bartolozzi and Angelica Kauffmann, Coffee and Stephen though the latter went to Coalport in 1800. Coffee probably did copies from Meissen and Sèvres as probably did also John Bacon. Stephen made a figure of

Fig. 1059 . Bacchus, designated by Mus. as "Late 18th cent., Chelsea." Ht. 14⅛". Metropolitan Mus. of Art.

Fig. 1060. Pair of Chelsea candlesticks with *"bocage"* or bowers of flowers and figures with cupids, doves and swan. Marked with gold anchor c. 1765. Irwin Untermeyer Coll.

Fig. 1061. Sailor and lass, Derby c. 1795 showing ornate rococo bases. Glaze lightly crazed. Under bases are large incised marks "No. 316." Ht. 10". Frank Stoner–Stoner & Evans, Ltd.

Fig. 1062. So-called "Chelsea Derby" figures, c. 1780 and having soft coloring and pleasing modeling. Ht. 5¼". Frank Stoner– Stoner & Evans, Ltd.

Admiral Lord Howe and his well-known Four Elements. Spengler is well known for his Girl with Her Dead Bird, the Young Man Burying a Bird, Two Young Girls Waking Cupid, etc. During the Bloor period the biscuit became cold, hard and chalky.

Glazed figures from Derby are usually on simpler bases than those of Chelsea, the green used is washed out and pale, the color in general is soft and there is a lack of life and charm.

The decoration of the useful porcelain is symmetrical and weak in the best of taste for the finicky housewife who thought a great deal about taste

FIG. 1063. Biscuit group, by John James Spengler in "Crown Derby biscuit." Late 18th cent. Ht. 10¾". Metropolitan Mus. of Art.
FIG. 1064. Derby biscuit statuette of Lord Lyndhurst, c. 1810. Ht. 14¼". Metropolitan Mus. of Art.
FIG. 1065. "Gardener and Wife," Derby c. 1760. Ht. 8". John Gibbons Coll.

FIG. 1067. Derby 1780–90. "Crocus vase" beautifully painted with landscapes. In overglaze blue on bottom "Near Dalkeith, Scotland," beneath which is mark # 2 a crown with crossed swords below flanked by three dots and beneath which is a script D. Length 9½". Frank Stoner–Stoner & Evans, Ltd.

FIG. 1066. Baroque vase and stand of type called "Dudley vases," with turquoise ground and gilding. Chelsea c. 1760. Ht. 18". Symons Galleries.
FIG. 1068. "Chelsea-Derby" vase (c. 1775), soft paste decorated after Angelica Kaufman with stripes of blue, white and gold. Ht. 10⅜". Metropolitan Mus. of Art.

FIG. 1069. Chelsea 18th cent. boar in natural colors of general pinkish cast. Length 13½". Plummer, Ltd.

FIG. 1070. "Crown Derby" soft paste plate decorated in enamel colors of ocherous-red against rich green ground. 18th to 19th cent. Dia. 10". Metropolitan Mus. of Art.
FIG. 1071. Derby tureen c. 1770. Colors chiefly pink, purple and brown on white, with some added yellow and yellow green in the foliage. Length 9". Frank Stoner–Stoner & Evans, Ltd.

Crown Derby service of so-called "King pattern" (George III). Factory pattern # 1, c. 1780–90 and showing strong Imari influence. Philip Suval, Inc.

Part of Derby dessert service decorated in salmon pink and gold. c. 1800. Wm. H. Plummer & Co.

DERBY SERVICES

PLATE 194

in those days. A new lapis-lazuli blue and an underglaze blue replaced the warm "Mazarine blue." The canary yellow bettered the Chelsea but the claret color is less rich. During Bloor's time poor imitation Imari was made.

One cannot become seriously critical of the work of these factories for they contributed nothing to the art of ceramics. Their works are at times amusing but it is even then a second-hand amusement.

Bow

Edward Heylyn who had a glass factory, and Thomas Frye, an Irish engraver, took out joint patents in 1744 and started a factory in Stratford-

Harlequin and Colombine figures. Smaller ones made at Bow in 1755 (Stratford-le-Bow, Essex) are extremely rare. Larger ones are Derby of 1780. Note that postures are identical and that small figures have simpler bases while Harlequin has a typical square hole at back of base. Bow figures have glossy black, double outlines of patches, pale olive green, bright yellow and deep blue of gentian shade. Derby ones have mat black, poor drawing of details in light pink line, dull turquoise, dull orangy yellow. Hts. 6¼″ and 5¼″. Frank Stoner–Stoner & Evans, Ltd.

DERBY AND BOW FIGURES COMPARED

PLATE 195

Left: "The Cooks," Bow figures dating c. 1755, maid with leg of lamb and the boy with fowls. Note low, unscr bases having only a few strewn flowers. Frank Stoner–Stoner & Evans, Ltd.
Right: Bow figures c. 1765. Note high rococo bases hollowed beneath, typical of period. Irwin Untermeyer

Left: Squirrels, Bow 1760, rare and particularly vigorous and alive in modeling. Note raised roococo bases. F Stoner–Stoner & Evans, Ltd.
Right: Pair of Bow birds dating 1760 and showing good modeling and coloring. Frank Stoner–Stoner & Ev Ltd.

BOW FIGURES AND ANIMALS

PLATE 196

le-Bow, County of Essex, and Frye alone repeated the procedure in 1749. This is the factory popularly known as "Bow." He made some soft-paste ware which is the first we know to have contained bone-ash. The patent states that earth from America, "produce of the Cherokee nation," was used and called "unaker" by the natives.

From 1750 the owners were Weatherby and John Crowther with Frye as a foreman until 1759 when he retired. In 1762 Frye and Weatherby died and the year following Crowther went bankrupt, though he kept the factory going until in 1776 Duesbury bought it and took the models and molds to Derby.

We have little real data: excavations in 1868 and 1921–2, some note books, lists of sales, etc. The "Craft Bowl" is dated 1760 and Thomas Craft wrote about his bowl that there were some 300 workmen employed in this year, that the factory was started in 1750 and called "New Canton." A few

Fig. 1072. Unique Bow figure of Cleo, one of the Muses, c. 1765. There is a similar model in Chelsea but this is only one known in Bow. Note anchor and dagger mark under base in light red, also square hole at back of base for attachment of fixtures for candle sockets. Ht. 12½". Frank Stoner–Stoner & Evans, Ltd.

ink pots marked "Made at New Canton" and dated 1750 exist. I am happy to show one through the kindness of Lord Fisher. The ware was glassy, yellowish, thick, heavy and only slightly translucent having the general look of poor French soft paste which it imitated also in style. Small white statuettes were also made.

The Craft Bowl of ten years later shows that the ware had improved but was more chalky and white. However, a pair of octagonal plates in the B.M. one of which is dated 1770 shows the ware then to have become opaque, reddish-brown and covered with a bluish glaze full of black specks and such as to cease almost to resemble porcelain.

Vase shapes are a degenerate rococo with reserved medallions, applied flowers and twisted stem handles. There is a characteristic frilled collar

FIG. 1073. Plate with decoration in ochrous-red after Kakiemon in what is called the "Partridge pattern" made about 1760. Dia. 8⅜". Metropolitan Mus. of Art.

FIG. 1074. Rare type of early Bow dating about 1750 and probably representative of one of the Muses. There are other similar examples in the Victoria & Albert Mus. and all are thought to be the work of one man. Ht. 6". Frank Stoner–Stoner & Evans, Ltd.

FIG. 1075. Ink pot bearing the inscription, MADE AT NEW CANTON 1750 which is the earliest dated ware known from the factory at Stratford-le-Bow. It has been suggested by Lord Fisher that Mr. Crowther had seen a factory at Canton China and modeled the new one more or less after it, also that these ink pots may have been distributed to celebrate the opening of the "New Canton Factory." Similar examples are in both large British museums and this one came from the Mus. of the Worcester Porcelain Company. The property of Lord and Lady Fisher.

around the foot. This great addition to the ceramic arts seems to be an entirely original invention! A vase in the B.M. has handles formed as jets of water spouted by dolphins. And of this period 1760 to 1770 there were knife handles of plain white with rococo relief scrolls on them.

Figures from Kandler are a Harlequin and Colombine (see the compared Bow and Derby ones illustrated), a Gallant Kissing His Hand, a Negro with

FIG. 1077. Sauceboat of Bow ware made about 1770. Length 8¼". Metropolitan Mus. of Art.

FIG. 1076. Platter of famille rose type made at Bow (c. 1760). Length 12". Plummer, Ltd.

a Horse and a Turk with a Horse. English subjects include a stately "Britannia" with a portrait medallion of George II in one hand and a Union Jack on a shield in the other, a figure of John Manners, some of Woodward and Kitty Clive (the actor and actress) playing The Fine Gentleman and The Fine Lady in "Lethe," the farce by Garrick. A sphinx has the head of the actress Peg Woffington. These figures and those of male and female cooks are thought to be by John Bacon. They are sometimes white and sometimes colored in bright hues. The dresses are partly in plain colors and partly patterned. Whether the foliage backgrounds originated in Chelsea or Bow is uncertain but Bow did make the first pedestals divided into four curled feet which later became characteristic of much English porcelain. Bow figures also frequently have a square hole made in the back to hold metal branches with painted leaves and porcelain flowers and a candle sconce.

FIG. 1078. A rare example of a Sweet-meat dish set, Bow, 1755, decorated in famille rose enamels, the drawing in a flat brown, the rose pitted and duller than the Chinese, the green and yellow green dull and thin, the aubergine and blue about like the Chinese. The potting is very uncertain as may be seen by the foot of one dish shown and the center dish has evidently sunk in the middle during firing. There are also a number of fire cracks. Dia. laid out 15¼". Frank Stoner—Stoner & Evans, Ltd.

Animals and birds, particularly parrots, and pie-dishes in the form of partridges had strong colors often badly handled as were, in truth, also those on the figures copied from Watteau and on the pieces copied from the Kakiemon style. The usual Imari styles were followed as were those of famille rose and powder blue Chinese porcelain and it must be said that the

FIG. 1079. Group of parrots amidst foliage in bright colors made at Bow between 1755 and 1760. Ht. 9⅛". Metropolitan Mus. of Art.

FIG. 1080. Parrot with strong green color made at Bow about 1760. Ht. 6½". Metropolitan Mus. of Art.

underglaze blue was of good quality and a deep indigo tone. The transfer process was used but whether actually at the Bow factory or at nearby Battersea, where we know it was used as early as 1753, has not been determined. They were printed in black, red or purple and usually further painted.

The Bow wares were usually not marked but a red anchor with or without cable and usually accompanied by a dagger has been attributed to them and may have been from the arms of the City of London. Some blue and

FIG. 1082. Bow porcelain salt cellar of about 1750 colored in soft tones of pink and green. Ht. 4¾". Metropolitan Mus. of Art.

FIG. 1081. Male figure on rococo base made about 1760 at Bow. Ht. 8". Metropolitan Mus. of Art.

FIG. 1083. Group of two birds and a dog made at Bow about 1755 to 1760. Ht. 6½". Metropolitan Mus. of Art.

white pieces are marked TF in monogram standing for Thomas Frye, though Hobson has tried to call it a "maimed version of the Chinese character yu (jade)" and calls such pieces Worcester. Some figures bear the mark To possibly standing for Tebo, a French modeler who is supposed to have worked at Etruria, at Worcester and also Bristol, for the mark appears on these wares too. The figures marked B are supposed to be by Bacon.

The only other distinguishing characteristic is a maroon purple supposed to be unique.

WORCESTER

Bernhard Rackham, the editor of "Pottery and Porcelain" by Emil Hannover and author, for me, of the *Encyclopaedia Britannica* article on the sub-

FIG. 1084. Three Chamberlain Worcester plates, 1st with apricot ground and reserved medallions, 2nd with iron red and gold in a derivation of the Imari manner, and 3d with gold and Sèvres blue and flowers in natural colors in the Sèvres manner. Thus all sources were drawn upon. c. 1811–1820. Philip Suval, Inc.

FIG. 1085. Large 1785? Chamberlain Worcester vase of good proportions and well gilded. The flower paintings are beautifully executed. Ht. 17½". Frank Stoner—Stoner & Evans, Ltd.

FIG. 1086. Worcester dish of about 1770 to 1780 of soft paste decorated with enamel colors of blue, violet, copper red, green, black and gold. Dia. 7½". Metropolitan Mus. of Art.

ject, is the acknowledged authority on Worcester, yet even he has found little real data to go on. Worcester is supposed to have started in "Lowdin's China House," a glass manufactory which made "steatitic porcelain" as early as 1750. An advertisement found by William Pountney would seem to prove that the work was transferred to Worcester in 1752 where the factory was managed by Davis until his death in 1766. In 1783 the business was sold to its London agent Thomas Flight for his sons, John and Joseph. In 1790 Martin Barr was taken into the partnership and the following year John Flight died. Thus in 1791 the company was called "Flight and Barr." In 1807 a younger Barr came into the business and the name was changed

FIG. 1087. Chamberlain Worcester covered urn with entwined handles. Cobalt blue ground with rich gold. This was modeled after the famous Warick Vase in Worcestershire. Has script mark of Chamberlain Worcester c. 1810. John Gibbons.

to "Barr, Flight and Barr." In 1813 Martin Barr the elder died and his son George was taken into the firm which was then called "Flight, Barr and Barr" under which it continued until 1840.

In 1786 a second factory for the decoration of porcelain alone was started with wares from Caughley and called Robert Chamberlain and Son. It was fused into the other company in 1840 and in 1847 the older factory was given up and the new continued under the names of the Chamberlains. In 1848 Walter Chamberlain and John Lilly became the proprietors and in 1850 the

Plate in Kakiemon style painted in enamel colors at Worcester about 1770. Dia. 9". Metropolitan Mus. of Art.

Bowl of Worcester ware which looks like a Near Eastern copy of a Chinese one. The colors are blue and red. c. 1770. Dia. 5⅞". Metropolitan Mus. of Art.

Worcester milk-jug with design in pink, made about 1770 after continental style of Vienna of about 10 years earlier, Frankenthal, Gotha, etc. Ht. 4¾". Metropolitan Mus. of Art.

Worcester dessert basket painted in Chinese style with enamels, c. 1765–70. Length 9¼".

WORCESTER WARES SHOWING FOREIGN INFLUENCES

PLATE 197

son was taken in and W. H. Kerr, the name being in 1852 "Kerr and Binns" and from this time it so remained until in 1862 the "Royal Worcester Porcelain Co." was formed and existed up to a few years ago.

The earliest period is incorrectly known as the "Dr. Wall period" through the false idea that the apothecary William Davis and a Dr. Wall started the factory. During the time that steatite was used the ware was yellow or grey but of a fairly constant bluish-green tone by transmitted light. Not until 1800 did experiments lead to the adoption of modern Staffordshire body and chemical analysis at the V. & A. Mus. prove that Flight, Barr and Barr were still using a steatitic porcelain as late as 1823.

A considerable number of pieces attributed to the Lowden factory at Bristol or the earliest days of Worcester comprise pieces painted with Chinese

Worcester platter dating between 1770 and 1780. Length 11¼". Metropolitan Mus. of Art.

One of pair of Worcester "Glacières" or fruit coolers with "royal blue" ground enriched with gilding and surrounding panels with birds and flowers in natural colors. c. 1775. Philip Suval, Inc.

Worcester hexagonal vase with cover decorated in the typical style. c. 1770–75. Ht. 16¼". Metropolitan Mus. of Art.

Worcester platter painted with fruit and insects, made about 1780. Length 13½". Metropolitan Mus. of Art.

WORCESTER PORCELAINS

PLATE 198

figures in underglaze blue or enamels, cylindrical mugs widening out toward the base, jugs with ordinary lip and scroll handle and sauceboats in the form of two conjoined leaves the stems of which form the loop handle.

Such wares date about 1750 to 1752 and are generally marked with one or two short strokes or with a saltire cross incised in the paste before firing. They have also various painted signs including an arrow passing through a circle in either underglaze blue or overglaze red. Another general feature is a short incision made with a sharp instrument on the inner side of the foot-rim.

Fig. 1088. Bowl with relief and under-glaze blue decoration made about 1760–70. Dia. 4″. Metropolitan Mus. of Art.

Fig. 1089. Worcester cream jug with underglaze blue decoration and rococo relief scrolls, made about 1760. Ht. 2¾″. Metropolitan Mus. of Art.

The earliest porcelain definitely made at Worcester is from silver models with rococo relief designs painted in vignette style in reserved panels in under-glaze blue or polychrome. They resemble St. Cloud. Much early Worcester blue and white ware was formerly ascribed to Bow including some marked with TF. The Kakiemon style was copied with later (in 1765) other Imari designs. Some of these were marked with quasi-Chinese symbols including the "fretted square" in underglaze blue. At about this time the famille rose designs from Canton were copied.

At the early date of 1756 the bad practice of transfer printing was in general use in black, red and various shades of purple with, slightly later, under-glaze blue. Frequently supplemented with hand painting such wares show landscapes with ruins, portraits of Frederick the Great, George III, Queen Charlotte, the Marquis of Granby, the elder William Pitt, etc., and such subjects as a tea-party on a terrace, a gallant kissing a lady's hand, etc. Robert Hancock an engraver introduced the process and worked at the factory until 1774. The usual influence of Watteau, Boucher and Pillement were strong.

London dealers were able to dictate various subjects for treatment in their taste, but in 1768 some of the best artists from Chelsea were hired and the habit terminated. At this time the best period commenced with the famous colored grounds having reserved panels, gold bordered and painted with exotic birds, Chinese or natural flowers and scenes in the Watteau manner. The most famous color was the blue both in powder-blue form and laid in scales; but apple green, pea-green (sometimes over black scale outlines),

FIG. 1090. Plate in blue and white showing Japanese and Chinese characteristics, made at Worcester c. 1770. Dia. 7¼". Metropolitan Mus. of Art.

FIG. 1091. Plate decorated in enamel colors after Imari pattern, made at Worcester between 1770 and 1780. Dia. 8⅜". Metropolitan Mus. of Art.

turquoise, "maroon" and "claret color" and finally a pale canary yellow were also used. This last was used over a ground of basket work in relief to represent straw. An overglaze blue was rare but effective at times. A manganese violet is even more rare. Many modifications took place probably more or less accidentally just as the ware itself varied from greyish to yellowish. The underglaze blue is usually of indigo tone, the violet purple is "peculiarly misty" and a plum color is often predominant in the exotic bird panels.

Between 1768 and 1780 the "Blind Earl's pattern" of flowers and leaves in low relief was supposed to have been devised for the Earl of Coventry but he lost his sight in 1779 and both Bow and Chelsea used the design and technique much earlier. The green over black outline technique is known in Sung Chinese wares, of course. The use of diagonal gold stripes in the background was supposed to have been a real invention but the same were used in Meissen in the 1720's and were popular all over the continent, particularly in Sèvres. A design perhaps actually original was a "curtain of green leaves with little red berries among them, supported by a rococo trellis-work in gold." Artists were Donaldson about 1770 who did crude peasant scenes and clumsy exotic birds; O'Neale, Billingsley between 1808 and 1811; and Thomas Baxter between 1814 and 1821 with a gap between 1816 and 1819.

Between 1775 and 1780 the neo-classic influence stopped all originality and the Flights and Barrs coarsened the designs for mass production. Some odd pieces were decorated with trophies of feathers, the 19th century brought brassy gilding and the colors became strong and without meaning. Thus a factory that had been one of the distinguished ones of England became one of the most flagrant destroyers of good taste, and late Worcester is nothing for a collector to be proud of.

Before 1783 a crescent mark was used in gold, colors, printed in blue over the glaze but also painted in underglaze blue. The Chinese "fretted square,"

FIG. 1092. Worcester dessert basket in enamel colors, c. 1770–75. Length 10½". Metropolitan Mus. of Art.

FIG. 1093. Worcester pitcher dating about 1770–75 having bright coloring and a scale blue ground. Ht. 11⅝". Metropolitan Mus. of Art.

FIG. 1094. Flight, Barr & Barr 1807–13 tea cup and saucer with a dull rose Pompadour, gold and polychrome painting. The saucer has an impressed crown and F.B.B. The cup has "Flight, Barr & Barr, Worcester, London House, 1 Coventry St." in red script. Ht. 3½". Frank Stoner–Stoner & Evans, Ltd.

W, imitation Chinese characters, Meissen crossed swords with the unaccounted for numerals 9 or 91, and the Sèvres double Ls were common.

After 1783 the crescent was used at the old factory usually with the name of Flight.

From 1792 to 1807 the usual mark is Flight and Barr surmounted by a crown. Later marks are of no interest to collectors.

Figures were made but few have been identified.

CAUGHLEY SHROPSHIRE, 1772–1799

Thomas Turner, a pupil of the engraver Robert Hancock, settled in Shropshire near Broseley and influenced the ten year old pottery factory in 1772 to make china. It seems that Hancock went there too when he left Worcester in 1774.

In 1780 the well known "Willow Pattern" and "Broseley Blue Dragon Pattern" were made and probably originated with Turner. Both were printed in underglaze blue and touched with gold from the very first. The latter was printed in two blues, a cobalt and a more lavender color, and used for tea services. The willow pattern was used for whole dinner services. It was copied everywhere and an interesting chapter in "How to Identify Old China" by Mrs. Hadgson tells of its spread. Nothing could better exemplify the utter dearth of aesthetic consciousness than the stupid copying of this design which lacks every element of true Chinese painting and any real claim to beauty whatsoever, and the maudlin stories wrought about it to please the sentimental old ladies of the late 18th century.

The commercial chiseling in of Chamberlain in 1783 when he used Caughley to decorate was based upon a very inferior ware. The potting was bad and yellowish or brownish by transmitted light. The decoration at the factory

FIG. 1095. Dessert basket with underglaze blue decoration made at Caughley about 1775. Length 10⅝". Metropolitan Mus. of Art.

FIG. 1096. Caughley tea caddy with floral designs in gold alternating with vertical lines in dark blue. Ht. 4⅜". Metropolitan Mus. of Art.

FIG. 1097. Caughley dessert dish with cover and platter of soft porcelain decorated with polychrome and marked in underglaze blue. Length of tray 11¼". Metropolitan Mus. of Art.

chiefly was printed and often so badly that the background is not clean. The blue is strong and clean when it has not run. At times gold and gaudy colors were added in polychrome flowers. The "Salopian sprig" design about 1780 was done in blue with fine gold lines, "Salopian" being the name by which Caughley porcelain was known in the trade. The "Queen Charlotte's Pattern" used by both Caughley and Worcester was simply an elaborate "strohblumen muster" from about 1740 of Meissen, and later in Copenhagen, only that in this case the plate is divided into six panels instead of four. The flowers are large and scrolls and foliage fill the whole ground but each panel is exactly symmetrical and all life lost. Everything bigger and better but dead!

Caughley used the oil-spot ground of Sèvres rather than the scale pattern of Worcester.

The C for Caughley and S for Salopian were both painted and printed in underglaze blue. There are also crescents similar to the Worcester ones, numerals disguised as Chinese characters and the word Salopian which pertains to Salop or Shropshire.

COALPORT OR COALBROOKDALE

John Rose, a pupil of Turner's, set up a factory at Jackfield about 1780 but soon moved it to the Severn at Coalport opposite Caughley and in 1799 bought the older factory, managing both. In 1814 he gave up Caughley but subsequently absorbed both the Nantgarw and Swansea plants. Coalport exists today.

The wares were seldom marked and are hardly distinguishable from those they obviously copied. From 1810 to 1820 they copied the Swansea style. In

FIG. 1098. Coalport vase with turquoise blue ground, gold details and a medallion of flowers in natural colors. Ht. about 12″. Frank Stoner–Stoner & Evans, Ltd.

FIG. 1099. Coalport basket of about 1820 with the typically well modeled and delicately tinted flowers and touches of gold. Length 11¼″. Frank Stoner–Stoner & Evans, Ltd.

1819 William Billingsley, founder of Nantgarw introduced the body of this and the Swansea wares. In 1820 Rose "invented" a feldspathic glaze containing no lead which could be fired at low temperature. The usual styles were copied from Meissen, Sèvres and the Chinese as well as Chelsea.

The first wares sometimes bear C B D for Coalbrookdale and rarely the name of the factory. Imitations bore the marks of original factories forged. After 1819 CS stood for Coalport-Salopian and C S N for Coal-

FIG. 1100. A typically elaborate ink-well and candlestick made at Coalport about 1820. Length about 12″. Mrs. David Mahany.

port-Swansea-Nantgarw. From 1820 the new glazed pieces bore the imposing legend "Coalport Improved Felspar-Porcelain—J. Rose & Co.

NANTGARW, SWANSEA AND PINXTON

Nantgarw and Swansea were founded in 1811 and 1814 in South Wales and made the old glassy soft paste of France rather than the "bone china" invented by Spode about 1800.

In 1796 the wandering William Billingsley left Derby and with John Coke

FIG. 1101. Garniture of five Swansea vases dating 1820 and beautifully gilded and painted. A pierced gallery runs around the shoulder and lip and the covers are pierced as though they were intended to contain rose petals or other perfumed substance. This is the only set known. Frank Stoner–Stoner & Evans, Ltd.

started up in Pinxton in eastern Derbyshire. He had the old soft paste formula and between 1796 and 1801 made that. Coke didn't get the secret, for after Billingsley left the ware became clayey and opaque. Decoration of flowers, strewn roses, and landscapes in polychrome or in brown, pale yellowish-green and salmon pink were not unusual. Gold was costly and sparingly used, the edges of plates being finished in blue or red. Ground color of yellow and rarely salmon pink were the full range.

P and Pinxton occur as rare marks.

Following Billingsley's trail we find that in 1801 he left Pinxton for Staffordshire and after several unsuccessful attempts to set up for himself settled with Flight and the Barrs at Worcester. He had one stock in trade, his roses painted with the highlights taken out in the wet color. In 1811 he tried again to set up a factory in Nantgarw but gave it up in 1814.

FIG. 1102. Pair of delicate and thinly potted vases from Swansea (c. 1800) with decorations in natural colors. Ht. 8½". Plummer, Ltd.

Swansea had developed out of the "Cambrian Pottery" founded in 1764. In 1814 Lewis Weston Dillwyn, manager, sent for Billingsley and they worked together for three years. In 1817 the firm was taken by Bevington & Co. and Billingsley went to Nantgarw until 1819, then back to Coalport where he had set up a kiln in 1811. Nantgarw continued under Wm. W. Young and Thos. Pardoe, a flower painter from Bristol and Swansea until 1822. Bevington & Co. kept Swansea open until 1823 or 1824.

Billingsley's porcelain was cold white and translucent but hard to work and imperfect. At Swansea after 1817 steatitic ware was made with a mark of a trident and bone-ash ware was continued by Bevington & Co. During the delightful Mr. B's stay at Swansea the mark Nantgarw, NANTGARW or NANT GARW with or without the lettered C W for "china works" was also used at Swansea. The ware of Dillwyn is harder, less translucent and markedly greenish by transmitted light and is marked Swansea with or without crossed tridents or a single one. The Bevington & Co. wares bear the firm name in full. To add to the disorder, both firms also sold undecorated ware and various uninspired artists added to the general bad odor.

BRISTOL AND PLYMOUTH

Remembering "Lowdin's China House" we understand that it was difficult to tell Bristol and Worcester china of 1750 to 1752 apart.

About 1755 William Cookworthy, apothecary of Plymouth and possibly interested in the Lowdin plant, discovered the first kaolin known in England in Cornwall. A second factory ran from 1760 to 1765 in Bristol and in 1768 Cookworthy began to make a sort of hard porcelain in Plymouth. This plant

FIG. 1103. Pair of Plymouth (c. 1760–65) figures of "Antony and Cleopatra." Length 10¾". Plummer, Ltd. Note this model should not be mistaken for those of Ralph Wood, Jr., who made figures from the same moulds at a later date.

was transferred to Bristol in 1770 and in 1773 sold with all rights to Richard Champion who appointed John Brittan foreman. In 1781 it was sold to a syndicate of Staffordshire potters who continued the Plymouth-Bristol porcelain at New Hall, Shelton (Hanley).

A mug in the B.M. is dated March 14, 1768 and has the arms of Plymouth and name of the town. It is decorated in pale and blackish underglaze blue as might have been expected on a hard ware. The ware has many black specks and the enamels do not fuse perfectly with the glaze. Figures were made with greyish-yellow or greyish-blue tone, are mostly decorated and have bases touched up with red. Some are clumsy but some have finely modeled "bocages" and dresses with small patterns. The best are large figures representing the "Four Continents."

In 1770 some simple and well formed coffee pots and mugs seem to have been copied directly from Chinese examples. Garniture sets also seem to be fairly close in shape and design to Chinese originals.

The Plymouth mark is an alchemist's symbol which looks like a two or four and is in underglaze blue, red, blue enamel or gold.

Thus the later porcelain of Bristol is a continuation of Plymouth and not that of Lowdin. In fact the earliest hard paste of Bristol is not marked Bristol as at Lowdin's but sometimes bears the Plymouth mark alone or with the cross Champion used in overglaze blue. He also used the crossed swords of Meissen but with an overglaze B superimposed. He evidently had some conscience as compared with other Englishmen of the day.

Fig. 1104. Plymouth teapot decorated in red, blue, green, yellow and puce with gold on a hard paste crude porcelain discolored and pitted typically. Ht. 6¾". Metropolitan Mus. of Art.

The Bristol hard ware has a shiny glaze of milk-white and the enamels stand out in relief on it as they do not fuse with it perfectly, due to the too large difference in fusing temperatures. Wheel marks left showing are common to both wares. A transparent copper green is most characteristic and it was at times combined with painting *en grisaille*. Rare ground colors are yellow and "scale blue." Gilding is rich and often tooled. "Cottage china" had some underglaze blue and some polychrome decoration. Transfer printing, if used at all, was well handled.

Fair technical achievement was ruined by the English genius for the combination of unpleasant colors found nowhere else in the world. This has been explained on the ground that the climate was so dense and foggy that raw color was the only kind that would carry, but this cannot be so, for nowhere else in the world do we find such strong color as about the equator. No, it cannot be the climate. It is just a penchant for unqualified colors in a sometimes fresh and child-like effect but at other times the most unpleasant results. Hannover says of Bristol and Plymouth, "—As one of the most serious offences in this respect we may point out a hexagonal vase in the B.M. with applied flowers in relief painted in natural colors, further decorated with two landscapes in blue monochrome and two others in crimson, and two (with exotic birds) in natural colors."

Artists who worked for Champion were Henry Bone (miniature painter), William Stephens, the modeler Thos. Briand and possibly Tebo as at Bow and Worcester. The theory that these artists signed themselves with numbers is not correct. Of course Meissen and Sèvres came in for their proper and improper attention.

LOWESTOFT

Lowestoft turned out an agreeably decorated soft paste useful china entirely different from the "India china" made in China which was attributed to it. It was founded in 1757 and lasted until 1802, had no marks of its own and occasionally made use of those of other factories preferring those of Worcester. In 1902 some wasters were excavated along with moulds and sherds.

FIG. 1105. Lowestoft inkstand decorated in colors but without gold made about 1780 and showing very crude potting for that late period. Ht. 1¾". Metropolitan Mus. of Art.

FIG. 1106. Lowestoft cup decorated in a very crude Chinese style with enamel colors of blue, red and green, made between 1770 and 1802. Dia. 3⅜". Metropolitan Mus. of Art.

FIG. 1108. Tea-pot in underglaze blue and white ware decorated in "Chinese style" and made at Lowestoft between 1760 and 1770. Ht. 3". Metropolitan Mus. of Art.

FIG. 1107. Blue and white tea-caddy in Chinese style and with low relief ornament. Only two cup handles prove that this factory ever did even very crude modeling. Ht. 3⅞". Lowestoft. Metropolitan Mus. of Art.

It varies greatly in tone but has a greenish-yellow tint by transmitted light resembling Bow, and contains bone-ash. Painted and printed underglaze blue designs resemble Worcester from which some were copied direct. From about 1770 the decoration was in enamel colors predominantly red and violet in flowers and scrolls. Rococo lasted here longer than elsewhere, in fact until about 1800. A feather-like motive is characteristic and natural flowers including French cornflowers were done. Numerous examples are labeled "A Trifle from Lowestoft" and seem to indicate a souvenir trade. These are usually small ink-pots or mugs of the common sort.

LIVERPOOL

It is thought that Richard Chaffers was making porcelain in Liverpool in 1756. The "Printed Ware Manufactory" decorated many pottery wares and perhaps some porcelain from different factories. But later Samuel Gilbody, Philip Christian, Seth and John Pennington and Zachariah Barnes made porcelain.

FIG. 1110. Liverpool tea-pot with fluted body and flower decoration in natural colors (c. 1765). Ht. 8". Plummer, Ltd.

FIG. 1109. Early 19th cent. Liverpool jug with black printed design on cream ware, showing the American eagle and a map of the U. S. with figures of Washington, Liberty, etc. A bowl at the museum has the same circular medallion. Ht. 10⅛". Metropolitan Mus. of Art.

Excavations prove that certain poor porcelains formerly called Longton Hall are actually Liverpool.

The Herculaneum Pottery started about 1796 at Toxeth Park on the right bank of the Mersey near Liverpool and made porcelain from about 1800 to 1841 the ware being similar to Staffordshire and some of it bearing landscapes in black.

STAFFORDSHIRE, LONGTON HALL

(The pottery wares commonly known as "Staffordshire" are discussed in the Pottery section.)

At Brownhills near Burslem, William Littler had a factory which was moved to Longton Hall about 1750. About 1758 Duesbury is supposed to have added it to his combination of Bow, Chelsea and Derby.

The first Longton Hall ware is glassy and transparent resembling early Chelsea. Its later ware is hard and much like Worcester. The mark is two L's above a row of vertical dots. Forms comprise strongly veined leaves and rococo

FIG. 1111. Two jugs the one in black and colors and the other in black only. The first was of the sort made to catch American trade favor by heaping on patriotic pictures and legends and the other is a rare naval type. Liverpool. Hts. 9¼" and 9½". Ex W. R. Hearst Coll. International Studio, Inc.

FIG. 1112. Set of three Longton Hall (c. 1770) baroque vases with flowers in natural colors and shading in deep crimson of purplish hue. Hts. 6½" and 5". Plummer, Ltd.
FIG. 1113. Longton Hall (c. 1760–1800) watch-holder by Wm. Littler, having a deep cobalt blue glaze of almost Chinese richness. Ht 9½". Plummer, Ltd.

pieces painted in purple after Littler. Freely molded and applied flowers and even birds were highly colored and ornate in effect. White enamel like that of Battersea or Staffordshire was applied over a strong blue ground as in Ming wares in China, and blue and white stripes were used.

FIG. 1114. Tea-pot of New Hall style, 19th cent. Staffordshire. Length 8¾". Metropolitan Mus. of Art.

NEW HALL

Champion's factory at Bristol ended at New Hall and under the name of the "New Hall China Manufactory" it existed from about 1782 to 1825.

The early ware is like "Cottage China," hard and decorated with patterns found at Bristol and also Minton. Rarely the mark was an N.

LONGPORT OR DAVENPORT, 1793–1887

John Davenport, at Longport, made an old pottery into a porcelain factory. The mark was "Davenport" and its wares resemble Derby in paste, glaze and decoration. Ornate gilding, a blue or apple green ground and reserved medallions are typical.

MINTON AT STOKE-UPON-TRENT

Thomas Minton, pupil of Turner at Caughley, made porcelain at Stoke-upon-Trent in 1796. Later he worked under the first Josiah Spode. At his

FIG. 1115. Pair of "Spode" vessels called "fruit coolers" but actually made for boiled and chilled marons. Ice was placed around the inner containers and also on the covers. The ground is apple green and the colors natural. Ht. about 9". John Gibbons Coll.

death in 1836 the factory passed to his son and remained under him until 1883 when it became a limited company.

In 1798 it made bone-china after the formula by Josiah Spode 2nd, marked with an overglaze blue M between 2 crossed S's.

SPODE AT STOKE-UPON-TRENT

Of the three Josiah Spodes, the first had a pottery works at Stoke and died in 1797, the second made the first bone-china there and died in 1827 and the third died a few years after but the factory continued under the name until 1833 when it was bought by William Taylor Copeland. It still operates

FIG. 1117. Spode of the second member of the family or early 19th cent. with a pattern less Japanese than most of the earlier ones. It has a bluish body. Wm. H. Plummer & Co.

FIG. 1116. Pair of Spode c. 1815 vases marked in purple under the base "Spode 3802" with thin and translucent thrown bodies of fine texture and well painted with flowers on one side and landscapes on the other in natural colors. Ht. 6". Frank Stoner–Stoner & Evans, Ltd.

FIG. 1118. Tea-pot by Josiah Spode II, Stoke-on-Trent, 19th cent., showing the Imari style. Metropolitan Mus. of Art.

under his family name. The ware showed a leaning toward Japanese influence like Derby. The old mark was "Spode" with or without the addition of "Stone China" or "Feldspathic Porcelain."

About 1846 Copeland invented a ware called "Parian" after the marble but not resembling it and we will hear more of this in America. For further discussion of Spode wares see the Pottery section.

WEDGWOOD OR ETRURIA

Wedgwood's factory called Etruria made porcelain between 1812 and 1816. It is generally marked "Wedgwood" in red print. We have treated the well

FIG. 1120. Rockingham figure called "THE POT BOY" on the post on the back and inscribed, "I vish as there was a hact O'Parlement to make people find their own Pots—." Figures are rare from this factory. A peculiar indented mark under the foot looks like o—o or a key hole. The colors are yellow, mustard brown, light grey and black. Ht. 9". Frank Stoner—Stoner & Evans, Ltd.

FIG. 1119. "Spode" tureen of the late 18th cent. with "Imari" pattern. John Gibbons Coll.

known "Jasper ware," etc., under another section in this book. The porcelain, of the class of transfer printed wares with hand coloring in enamels, was unimportant.

ROCKINGHAM

The Rockingham works at Swinton in Yorkshire made porcelain from about 1826 to 1842 at a time when taste was at the lowest level, and it followed the other factories both in technique and in design.

This has been a story of the effect of commercialism and industrialism upon one art. The effect upon all arts and on the people themselves can be clearly seen in it; not only did the arts suffer but the very souls of the people suffered. Man does not turn back to Greeks and Chinese if he has gods and dragons in his own soul. He may look at them with interest but he has no time to copy them. In the 18th century man learned a number of negative lessons: 1.—That the dynamic curves of the Baroque were tiring, 2.— That the softening of them into Rococo made them weak and even less pleasant, and 3.—That the straight lines of Neo-Classicism were dead. He proceeded

FIG. 1121. One of pair of Rockingham vases with the griffin mark of the Marquis of Rockingham in puce. The ground color of the vase is a light apricot with rich gilding and flowers in rather strong polychrome. Ht. 11⅜". Made about 1825. Ernest F. Follows. The mark reads: Rockingham Works, Brameld. Makers to the King.

from the fat ladies of Rubens to the delicate and challenging ladies of Watteau and finally to the very pure ladies of David and sentimental ones of Angelica Kauffman. He turned from wine and beer drinking to tea drinking. But he also learned that factory workers have no incentive to become artists and are in truth afraid of losing their jobs, if they do so incline. He learned that short cuts like transfer printing kill beauty and life. He learned that the clever nonproducer could collect more pennies and set himself over the producer. Some declared that machines were to blame but no real artist would use a machine unless it could actually improve his art, if it were not that he was in fear of starvation. Thomas Carlyle in his "Past and Present" published in 1843, and Mill and many others saw it and tried to stem the tide. The French Revolution really accomplished nothing, for the rich bankers simply took the place of the old royalty. Actually gold getting became the acknowledged aim even of men who counted themselves respectable. This was the disease of the century and artists cannot think deeply about their work when they have to put their minds on the tricks of money getting.

CHAPTER XXV

EUROPEAN 18TH CENTURY POTTERY

THE technical development from the first crude neolithic potteries to the mastery of porcelain has been traced. We have seen how porcelain became the plaything of rich monarchs and died as an art, but in its development we have seen what man did with this medium of baked clay; how he made his vessels for eating and drinking from it; how he made images of his ancient gods, of fearsome monsters, of Christ and the Madonna, of kings and philosophers; images of all that interested him in life, of love making, of humor and of death; images of a whole town or of the tiniest blue flower, and in this one medium we see reflected practically all that man is and all that man does. Vessels to hold things and images to remember things by are perhaps two of the most important necessities of man.

Most potters of the 18th century had frantically tried to imitate the beautiful porcelain of China but a few resisted this impulse and adhered more closely to the art of pottery. In doing so they were perhaps a little less imitative; a little more inclined to keep their art a sincere expression.

NETHERLANDS

We return of course to the Netherlands where "Delfsche porsleyn," that is the faïence of Delft, had never given way to porcelain. Around 1700 the commercial influences began to control. There was a natural pressure for mass production regardless of artistic merit but the tradition was strong and integrity and quality of the wares was maintained for some time.

The first few real artists included Johannes van der Haagen of the "Jonge Moriaanshoot" or "Young Moor's Head Pottery" and he refrained from the competition in ever more ornate polychrome, adhering to painting in blue alone in the style of Hendrik Goltzius and influenced by the old Italian masters.

Piet Vizeer and Gijsbert Verhaast were two others. The latter, however, might better have been a painter on canvas for his landscapes in full color are of that nature and simply executed on faïence panels for framing.

Others are included in the following list:

LIST OF 18TH CENTURY DUTCH PAINTERS ON FAÏENCE

Gillis and Hendrik de Koning (1721) Style of *Pijnacker* and *Keizer*. Proprietors after *Louwijs Fictoor* of the "*Double Tankard.*"
Johannes Pennis (1725–1788) Blue and white and polychrome. We see his signature on "music plates" in the Rouen Museum and elsewhere. Founded the "*Porceleijne Schotel*" (*Porcelain Dish)* which later came to *Johannes van Duijn.*

781

Delft plate with buff body, tin glaze and poly-chrome decoration. Early 18th cent. Dia. 13¾". International Studio Art Corp.

Delft dish of tin-enameled earthenware in Imari style. 18th cent. Dia. 9½". Metropolitan Mus. of Art.

Armorial plate not unlike in design those painted at Canton and in red, blue and gold on white ground. 18th cent. Dutch and possibly from the Pijnacker factory. Dia. 8¾". Metropolitan Mus. of Art.

Coupe shaped bowl with buff body, tin glaze and blue, green, yellow and aubergine painting from an Italian original with a Biblical subject. Dia. 14". International Studio Art Corp.

DELFT DISHES OF THE 18TH CENTURY

PLATE 199

Hendrik van Hoorn (1759–1803) Blue and white and polychrome on rococo models. Was last proprietor of the *"Three Ash-Barrels"* factory. "The Three Porcelain Barrels" says Barber.

Pieter van den Briel (1759–   ) Blue and white. Last owner of the *"Fortune"* factory.

Justus Brouwer (1759) Blue and white and polychrome, enormous output. Made the *"Herring Fishery"* plates, the *"Months,"* etc., represented in many collections and was proprietor of the *"Porceleijne Bijl"* or *"De Porcilain Bgl"* *(Porcelain Axe)* factory.

Gerrit Brouwer (1759) Blue and white and polychrome of poor quality, proprietor of the *"Lampetkan"* (Ewer).

Dirk van der Does (1759) Proprietor of the *"Rose"* started by *Arendt Cosijn.*

Plaque of escutcheon shape with buff body, tin glaze and under-glaze blue and aubergine decoration, the border being in blue and white. The humor which may be intentional or unintentional or half and half, as expressed by the gent leaning against the sleigh drawn by a galloping horse and the skaters who seem to be enjoying all sorts of hazards, is nevertheless ticklesome. Width 15″. Early 18th cent. International Studio Art Corp.

Rare type of 18th cent. Delft dish having the usual tin glaze and turquoise, green, black, gold and iron red decoration. Dia. 8½″. Dia. of tub 4½″. International Studio Art Corp.

DELFT PLAQUE AND DISH (18th CENTURY)

Plate 200

Set of ten plates by Justus Brouwer called "De Haringvangst" (The Herring Fishery). Two are missing. Dias. 9". (1716-1770). From the W. R. Hearst Coll.

DELFT PLATES "THE HERRING FISHERY"

PLATE 201

Anthoni Pennis (1759) Blue and white, polychrome and plastic works. Founded *"Twee Scheepjes"* (*Two Boats*) factory.

Anthonie Kruisweg (1759) A number of pieces have been wrongly credited to him in *Sèvres,* the Victoria and Albert Museum, etc. Was supposed to have followed the tradition of *Hoppesteyns.*

Hugo Brouwer (1716–1807) Blue and white and plastic work, rococo feeling usual, directed *Pijnackers* old factory the *"Three Porcelain Flasks."*

Albertus Kiell (1764) Blue and white sometimes with good Chinese drawing, owner of the *"Star"* (or "The White Star," Barber).

Johannes van Duijn (1764) Large number of blue and white and plastic pieces, signed name in full, blue and white tureens and *"pike-dishes."* Took over factory of *Johannes Pennis,* the *"Porcelain Dish."*

Lambertus Sanderus (1764) Poor quality of blue and white, proprietor of the *"Claw"* factory.

Zacharias Dextra, owner of *"Two Ash-urns"* factory from 1720. And *Jan Theunis Dextra* who from 1759 on controlled the *"Greek A."*—Copied Meissen designs on butter-dishes, sugar-bowls and tea-caddies, etc., marked with VA or V or other letters or figures in usual way but meaningless to us now.

At Delft the faïence was made thinner and lighter and copies of Meissen were made with the muffle, or decorating kiln. The old technique of under-glaze decoration was therefore discarded and the technique began a decline. The competition with the cheap English cream colored earthen wares con-tributed. Of the 30 factories, 10 remained in 1794 when Gerrit Paape wrote his book. By 1808 there were only 8; the Ewer, the Flowerpot, the Claw, the Porcelain Bottle, the Greek A, the Three Bells, the Rose which made only tiles and finally Sanderson & Bellard who called themselves "Fabrikeurs in zoogenaamed engelsch aardewerk." By 1850 the Three Bells was the only

FIG. 1122. Early 18th cent. Delft money vase decorated in iron red, blue and gilding. Ht. 10¾". International Studio Art Corp.

FIG. 1123. Two Delft steins of the 18th cent., the left in yellow, and green with aubergine stipple, the right in yellow, blue and green which was a favorite combination toward the end of the century. J. Gibbons Coll.

one. In 1884 Joost Thooft and Labourchère started a place that made only slip-covered hard-fired earthenware with lead glaze which was not pleasing.

Holland was a country of painters but the shapes devised aside from the usual copies of Chinese and Italian ones were bizarre and sometimes amus-ing. "Finger vases" were probably inspired by Near Eastern ones but the ladies' shoes, sledges, monkey jugs, bird cages, violins, etc., were at least original. The modeled animals such as parrots after the Chinese, cocks, horses, cows, etc., were childlike and naïf, like wooden toys.

But the tiles show mastery and were sent even to Spain, a tile making country itself. They were sometimes framed but usually used about the stoves, in fireplaces, as dados or as a single row about the baseboard of a room.

FIG. 1124. Delft pot decorated in gold with the arms of England and Holland. Ht. 10". From the W. R. Hearst Coll.

FIG. 1125. Delft vase dating between "1675 and 1750 from the factory of Adrian Pijnacker" and of the usual enamels on thin body. Ht. 8⅞". Metropolitan Mus. of Art.

There were roughly three periods of tiles: First from late 16th to early 17th century they were of Italian type in yellow, dark blue, copper green and manganese purple and are about ⅜ inch thick. Second, from about 1650

FIG. 1126. Delft plate possibly by Anthoni Pennis depicting Christ's Entry into Jerusalem and made about 1759–60. Dia. 13". Metropolitan Mus. of Art.

FIG. 1127. Plate showing strong influences of the South Chinese blue and white wares made around Canton, of the early 18th cent., Dutch, of white enameled blue underglaze ware. Dia. 6½". Metropolitan Mus. of Art.

to 1750, is that of the best painting of ships, figures, landscapes or flowers usually in blue alone, and are about ¼ inch thick. The figures are often in the style of Palamedes or Peter Codde. The third period is from 1750 to around 1800 and the manganese purple of the rococo period becomes popular along with polychrome and the subjects are more pictorial such as landscapes with people in them, genre subjects, biblical subjects, etc. They are usually in a circle with the corners decorated. The rectangular ones have ornamental borders continuing from tile to tile. The thickness is still about ¼ inch.

Tile pictures of the 18th century covering four, six or more pieces are less well painted than the 17th century masters' works but still sure in drawing.

Fig. 1128. Pair of Delft 18th cent. plaques with embossed frames and paintings in blue of 1.—David & Abigail and 2.—Rebecca at the well. Ht. 20″. Metropolitan Mus. of Art.

"Useful Delft," "Boeren-delftsch" or peasant wares were often so cheap that the backs were left unfinished and covered with a yellowish half transparent lead glaze. The painting on these, either blue or polychrome, is usually too dull or too bright and sloppy. They have holes in the foot-rims for hanging.

Various Centers Outside Delft

Through the habit of calling all Dutch faïence Delft we may lose sight of the other potteries, a list of which follows:

Gouda—A few pieces with the name have been found and in about the middle of the 17th century there were supposed to be two potters there, one was *Cornelis Cornelisz van Dijck* and the other was *Michiel Wouters van Want*.
Dordrecht—At one time both of the above potters were working in this town.
Schiedam—A few pieces marked with the name are known.
The Hague—A 7 years' privilege was obtained by *Willem Jansz Lammerlaan* for the erection of a "*tegelbakkerij*" in 1644 and in 1680 or thereabouts two men from *Delft*, *Willem van der Lidt* and *Jeremias Godtlingh* went into partnership with a gold-smith, *Nicolas Keyser*.

Panel of tiles in manganese purple on white with floral corners and various landscapes. Each tile 5⅛" sq. Metropolitan Mus. of Art.

DELFT 18th CENTURY TILES

PLATE 202

Rotterdam—In 1627 a factory was in existence and running under two brothers, *Jacob* and *Henrick van der Heuvel,* and, as we know, in the middle of the century the city had so many *"plateelbakkers"* that they formed a corporation within the Guild of St. Luke. There were five or more factories here during the 17th and 18th century but only *Cornelis Boumeester* and *Jan Aalmis* have left behind recognizable signed work. *Boumeester* did marines with ships and landscapes of Italian type in the style of *Nicolaas Berchem. Aalmis* also did large tile pictures but was chiefly a figure painter and did allegories, pastoral subjects, military and tavern scenes, Dutch harbor scenes and even Chinese pavilions. His tiles decorating an old house at *Altona* are famous.

Utrecht—Seemed early to be a center for tile making and the museum there has many.

Arnheim—Was the place where fine *faïence* coffee-services, tureens and dishes in the style of *Pater* and *Lancret* were made and marked on the bottom with a cock. The factory was established in 1755 by *Johan van Kerckhoff* who did chinoiseries and polychrome painting in his first period, blue and white and pastoral genre in his second and then turned to imitating *Meissen* as did the *Dextras.*

Overtoom, near *Amsterdam*—Was called *"Blankenburg"* and later *" 't Fort de Eendragt"* and from there we hear from an old chemist who wrote in 1789. "I have seen many samples of the productions of this place. The material recalls *Delft* of the good period. . . . They made in this factory not only all sorts of table and kitchen wares, but also decorative articles, finely modeled and naturally painted birds, vases, candelabra, statuettes, groups. It is to be

FIG. 1129. Vase of late 18th cent. Delft pottery decorated in blue on white. Note crudity compared with 17th cent. one of similar shape with floral decoration. Ht. 9½". Metropolitan Mus. of Art.

FIG. 1130. Dutch 18th cent. bird cage decorated with floral design. Ht. 16½". Metropolitan Mus. of Art.

FIG. 1131. 18th cent. Delft cow with polychrome decoration. Ht. 3¼". Metropolitan Mus. of Art.

FIG. 1132. Horse marked with an AP monogram in blue and from Anthoni Pennis said to be between 1750 and 1775. The decoration is in polychrome. Ht. 9". Metropolitan Mus. of Art.

regretted that these things were excessively heavy. The enamel was white and brilliant, the colours as fine and vivid as on porcelain." The factory seems to have run only from 1754 to 1762 and used no mark and none of these pieces has been definitely identified.
Amsterdam—Unfortunately we have no examples we are sure of and there seemed to be no mark, though Barber says "Hartog v. Saten (1780–83)."

All of the marks found have not been deciphered and many are not to be depended upon for there were forgeries here as elsewhere and outside of Holland many attempts were made to copy the ware, in both the old days and recently. In Northern France factories have worked for years filling the market for "Old Delft." Hannover points out that a jug in South German style

FIG. 1133. A barber's basin of 18th cent. Delft in blue decoration. Length 11″. Metropolitan Mus. of Art.

FIG. 1134. Dutch late 18th cent. tea-pot and brazier with polychrome design adapted from Chinese porcelain. There is a lavish use of yellow. It is said to come from the Moor's Head and to be in the style of Gertrnij Verstelle. Ht. 14″. Metropolitan Mus. of Art.

Delft might bring $30 to $50 while a modern one might be had for $1 and he adds, "These ridiculously cheap Northern French imitations are by no means bad. The body is as light in color as it should be, the glaze satisfactory as regards pin holes, etc., the wearing of the glaze plausible—where found—the blue color excellent, the brush work bold and practised as in the old ware, the style of the figures often unimpeachable. The forgeries really betray themselves only in the ornamental designs, and sometimes by their 'crazing' (genuine Delft is as a rule free from this), and by a slightly excessive weight, the genuine wares being, thanks to certain properties of their clay, of a lightness that is often astonishing." He then continues, "Even so the Northern French forgeries of blue-and-white Delft are nothing compared with those made by Samson in Paris. He makes imitations of everything as is well known; but blue-and-white Delft is his specialty, which he has carried to the highest degree of perfection." These, however, need not be feared for they bear his own mark and bring quite as much as the old ones.

FIG. 1135. Panel of manganese purple decorated tiles of the late 18th cent. showing the influence of Indian palampores or cotton prints. About 20″ high. Metropolitan Mus. of Art.

The prices of Delft are varied from a few dollars to about $500 though never so much as Italian majolica or German Hafner ware. Its influence was a common one of pleasing the masses of people in many places.

BELGIUM

Belgium never did much but copy the Dutch faïence. There were two factories in Brussels known to have started as early as the 17th century and in 1705, Corneille Mombaers and Thierry Witsenburg founded a factory which only attained success when it was taken over by the son, Philippe Mombaers in 1724 who had been in France and Delft. This factory specialized in covered dishes in the form of pigeons, ducks, hens, etc., cabbages, melons and such. The marks B and K beneath a hay fork are not Brussels mark but refer to Abtsbessingen, near Sonderhausen and to some unknown painter. Authentic pieces have a tin glaze that runs with the colors and produces areas of agate-like veins, as has been pointed out by M. Marcel Laurent. The CB in monogram beneath a crown is the proper mark but is easily confused with that of Friedberg, Bavaria.

Another factory founded by Jacques Artoisenet in 1751 joined the older one in 1766. Laurent states that it is practically impossible to distinguish between these wares.

Stadtholder Charles-Alexandre of Lorraine erected a factory at Tervueren, near Brussels, in 1767 and it continued until 1781.

At Tournai, whence the clay for Delft came there had been potters from the 16th century and between 1698 and 1725 Joseph Fauquez had a factory there. He also had another at Saint-Amand from 1718 which was famous for its bianco sopra bianco ware with white on a slightly bluish ground. The wares of these two places are alike. In 1750 at this place another factory was started by François Carpentier and taken by Joseph Péterinck in the following year. It was reported to have imitated the wares of Strasburg, Rouen and Delft, and to have made "brun de Rouen," a brown ware white inside though that from Rouen is all brown. "Grès d'Angleterre" is also mentioned and was probably similar to the cream ware from England. After Péterinck's death, his son-in-law, Bettignies made decorated quart pots marked "Fabrique de Bettignies à Tournay," with a date later than 1800.

At Liège, Baron de Bülow had a privilege for 30 years and it must have run out by 1767 for Lefébvre and Gavron then obtained one. The former is said to have turned out 150,000 pieces but not one has been identified. One interesting point is that at Tournai, Lille and Brussels the clay was supposed to have been stored for at least five years, and this probably permitted the full oxidation of all iron and rotting of all vegetable and animal matter. This habit was also found in many of the German and Dutch factories. Liège finally came into the hands of J. Boussemaert of Lille, the son of the well known potter of that city, and he made good wares marked L.G. or with L.G. on either side of the arms of Liège which is a stone pillar on two steps. These wares are often decorated with polychrome flowers in Strasburg style.

At Andenne, Joseph Wouters of Louvain started two factories in 1783 and 1787 and from the latter come the little figures by Guilain Richardot. After 1800 they made a large amount of lead glazed ware with or without printed decoration along neo-classic lines and marked AD W (Andenne-Wouters).

At Septfontaines, near Luxemburg, the Boch brothers began in 1767 and in 1795 the owner was Pierre-Joseph Boch. He made a white ware that looked like soft paste. The shapes were "elegant" and the decoration was in cobalt blue usually of flowers which have three petals and long branching stamens. In the 1780's Dalle made faïence landscape panels there. Biscuit groups copied from Sèvres were thought to have been made there but this is not likely. The factory still operates under the name of Velleroy & Boch.

FRANCE

Though the Far Eastern contacts were not great in France, and she misunderstood Chinese design, the desire for color brought about the discontinuance of painting the design on the unfused tin enamel of faïence and the adoption of painting on a fused tin enamel surface with muffle-kiln colors of

Rouen platter decorated in blue and red with a "lambrequin" design. It dates about 1705–1720. Metropolitan Mus. of Art.

Sinceny plate of about 1750 with polychrome decoration of lambrequin type. Metropolitan Mus. of Art.

Rouen platter of about 1750 decorated in polychrome and showing Italian influence but the weakness of the center landscape and the spiritless composition are lacking in all vitality. Metropolitan Mus. of Art.

Moustiers plate dating between 1738 and 1749 and attributed to the Olerys. Metropolitan Mus. of Art.

FRENCH FAÏENCE ROUEN, SINCENY, MOUSTIERS

PLATE 203

greater variety in a technique more like that of China. This change took place about 1750 but it did not entirely displace the older method of Nevers, Rouen and Moustiers. After all, the art of porcelain was an off-shoot from the main stem of pottery making; a rich man's plaything for many years before the common people could touch it, while the art of faïence continued to develop along its own lines until the end of the century.

ROUEN FAÏENCE

With Edme and his son, Louis Poterat, shortly after 1644 when they took over the privilege taken out originally by Nicols Poirel only a short while before, begins the real history of Rouen faïence which was destined to become important in several ways.

The oldest dated specimens are two dishes at the Musée Céramique, Rouen, marked "fait à Rouen 1647." One is painted in the center with what appears to be a female winged centaur holding an arrow, and about the rim four octagonal panels alternating with flowers and containing a design of probably Near Eastern influence. The other is in the style of Nevers with polychrome figures and flowers and the arms of the Bigot family of Rouen in blue and yellow.

There are also some unmarked pieces with quasi-Chinese figures in blue camaïeu which may be either Rouen or Nevers, of about this period.

An Italian style cistern of poor quality and having the arms of the Duke of Luxemburg may also be from Nevers. Thus there is no distinguishing characteristic between the two wares to begin with. Nevers was first in point of time and Rouen in importance and the workmen went from one to the other factory.

Rouen was the first factory after the Medici one to make soft paste and there seemed to be more interest in this than in the pottery which copied the Italian and Dutch styles. But soon competition with Nevers began and several potters who set up in Saint Sever in spite of Poterat's privilege showed that something had to be done. The war had exhausted finances so much that in 1709 everyone was obliged under a penalty of 6,000 livres fine to send their silver to be melted down. By 1722 people had to have pottery to take the place of the plate and some 2,000 men were at work in Saint Sever. Therefore the new design necessarily had to be simple and easily taught to workmen. Figures are difficult to draw so they were dispensed with. The elegance and formality of silver had to be carried over. The solution had been reached in China in Ming times of the Wan Li reign (1573–1619) or before in the "sceptre" or "Ju-i" design used about the shoulders of vases. Somehow it came to these French potters and "lambrequins," named after the pieces of cloth with various shaped bottom edges that were hung over windows and

FIG. 1136.

doors, were employed. The designs are of perfectly spaced alternating symmetrical units consisting of one larger and more important and one smaller used as a sort of filler in. They were adapted to borders of plates and to centers where they formed star-like medallions. The alternation was also used in technique, one unit being in blue on white while the other was in white on blue.

Fig. 1137. Lambrequin design on a plate of blue and white which shows a tendency to bring the border and center medallions together. Metropolitan Mus. of Art.
Fig. 1138. This plate decorated in the typical Rouen manner in blue and red, shows the enlarged medallion reaching all the way to the border lambrequins. Metropolitan Mus. of Art.
Fig. 1139. In this example the center medallion is replaced by a flower but the radial lines have become heavy. (1705–20). Metropolitan Mus. of Art.

The Rouen white was bluish or greenish in tint. In the earliest example known, inscribed "Brument 1699," there is an odd and fanciful psuedo-Chinese design. It has lambrequins about the rim in blue and a red which Nevers could not obtain even in later copies, for the color is replaced by a dark ochre. The blue could easily be copied, and was at both Nevers and St. Cloud, but it was stiff to draw with and in both places the outlines were in black. Most Rouen pieces have an ornamental motive, rosette or basket of flowers but in the early 18th century they are all perfectly symmetrical.

Fig. 1140. Polychrome plate of Rouen of 1710 to 1712 showing an adaptation of Chinese design of the worst sort which was made up in and about Canton to appeal to western merchants. Metropolitan Mus. of Art.

Fig. 1141. Rouen plate decorated in blue and yellow (1705–1720) with a chinoiserie figure in the center and the typical hatching in the border. Metropolitan Mus. of Art.

This best period ware reaches its culmination between 1720 and 1740 in large dishes about 20 inches in diameter of the "style rayonnant" in which the center design has spread outward and the border inward until they meet and interlace.

Hannover quite rightly suggests that the designs all came from those of engravers of ornament, book-binders, decorators of Boulle furniture, textiles, wrought iron, etc., but never from nature. Thus life and new ever-changing interest were not present and the germ of death lay in the ready limitations of such research. When each field had been mastered to its limit there lay

Fig. 1142. Rouen polychrome plate of about 1750. Metropolitan Mus. of Art.
Fig. 1143. Plate said to date 1725 but of the general style termed, "a la corne" which was very popular by 1750. Metropolitan Mus. of Art.
Fig. 1144. Rouen jar of about 1750 with polychrome decoration on blue ground. Note: The stupid quality of this painting is typical of the decadent results of factory work. Metropolitan Mus. of Art.

ahead only further complication and elaboration. Yet within this ever thickening crust was born, probably from Delft, the powerful Chinese and Japanese germ of life which was destined to burst it apart.

CHINESE, JAPANESE AND ROCOCO DESIGN AT ROUEN

The first we know to make use of these Far Eastern motifs was Guillibaud who made a platter shortly after 1720 with a rococo scrolled rim, the arms of

Fig. 1145. Rouen plate of 1720 to 1750 which has a little style but shows the beginning of the decadence in its weak landscape and set quality of the border. Metropolitan Mus. of Art.

Fig. 1146. Rouen, Levavasseur of about 1780, platter decorated in colors and following the style of "German flowers" strewn on its surface. Metropolitan Mus. of Art.

the Duke of Luxemburg and a center filled with flowers, insects and birds, faintly Chinese in character but perfectly symmetrical which is opposed to Chinese tradition in painting such objects. Guillibaud also used cross-hatching in panels alternating with sections decorated with flowers which is another Chinese custom. The hatching is usually green with little crosses in red at the intersections or other little red motives and the rest is in polychrome colors often with flowers alternating in red, blue and green.

Another rococo type has what was known as "décor ferronnerie" with scenes of "pastoral gallantry" and all in the coloring of Guillibaud. Still another group has chinoiseries after Watteau, Boucher and Pillement freely adapted and set in solid borders broken by alternating panels. Again there were those decorated "au carquois" ("quiver"), etc., with trophies, horns, torches, bows, birds and flowers dully drawn without perspective, modeling, or composition. By 1750 the most popular were called "à la corne" and had a horn of plenty sprouting flowers and surrounded by birds and insects. By this time everything has become asymmetrical and the borders are wavy. It was not that the artists knew anything at all about the laws of Chinese arrangement but simply that they were tired of the dead symmetrical and broke it up.

Porcelain competition by 1770 forced the kilns at Marseilles and Strasburg to turn to overglaze painting in similar technique and soon Rouen followed. Of course earthenware could not compete with porcelain in finesse of detail but only sold as something similar at a lower price. M. T. Ph. Levavasseur started the change and it was not for the best. In 1786 there were 18 factories with some 1,200 employees. By 1802 there were only 6, by 1807 there were 4 and they were making the common "grès à l'anglaise."

A few odd styles are known such as the "Boulle style" and Rouen copied the Nevers "bleu persan" but with a more opaque blue of greyish tone and the designs outlined in red. Similar ones were made with yellow and green on a thick white ground. Delft "music plates" were also tried but with polychrome borders and, of course, such a good idea was not neglected at Nevers, Lille and Moustiers.

At Sèvres there is a large set of floor tiles in carpet design supposed to date about 1730 and to have been made at Saint Sever by Sieur de Villeray, one of the largest manufacturers, who made it for his own use. Another group was made at Lisieux by a Rouen worker, Joachim.

Everything was made; drug-pots, chamber-pots, church lamps, miniature commodes, "guéridons" (stands for the center of tables), watch-stands, mirror frames, weather-vanes, sconces, chess boards, maps of France and even bellows. Of these things Hannover says, "The Rouen potters showed their wonderful genius by decorating their ware in such a manner that even in senseless articles it became at least a delight to the eye." He also claimed that their appeal to the "artistic sense can disarm the intelligence." Well we are less disarmed!

Four polychromed busts of the seasons in the Louvre attributed to Fouquay (1725–1740) brought 2,646 pounds sterling at the Hamilton Palace sale in 1882. Fairly good plates can reach a few hundred dollars but the taste for such things has changed. However the prices were high enough to attract many forgers. Some of these have a red with orange cast, the blue and white pieces often have too much crackle and foot rings have been added to the round dishes while the originals were without them and slightly concave or flat. Any marked piece is not early Rouen. The fleur-de-lys was a later mark and never used in the early period. Imitations were made at Gien and Orleans about 1875 but marked with the town name.

The general characteristics of old Rouen are: 1.—They are thick and heavy, 2.—the glaze is greenish and less often bluish and always tends to crackle, 3.—the outlines are always in blue or red and never in black, 4.—the yellow color is always greenish and 5.—in the red there are always small pits where the color fails.

SINCENY (AISNE)

Other places made faïence similar to that of Rouen but quite honestly and one of these was Sinceny (Aisne) which was founded in 1733 by Fayard and placed under the management of Pierre Pellevé, who brought with him from Rouen workers and artists. The prices are about the same for these wares and the differences slight. A few of these may be noted: 1.—The Sinceny glaze is usually more bluish, 2.—the blue pigment stronger, 3.—the red is slightly glazed and not so inclined to bubble and pit. In the style of Guillibaud the quasi-Chinese figures have bright yellow garments and also similar figures were made as statuettes. The marks are an S with dots in color and the signature of Pellevé.

About 1775 artists from Lorraine did muffle-kiln decoration in the style of Strasburg, after the Rouen method, so well that the wares cannot be distinguished.

FIG. 1147. Sinceny plate of about 1750 with polychrome decoration. Metropolitan Mus. of Art.

ROUY AND SAINT-DENIS-SUR-SARTHON, QUIMPER (FINISTÈRE), ETC.

Pellevé went from Sinceny to Saint-Denis-sur-Sarthon (Orne) taking his followers and there in 1750 and later in 1790 at Rouy wares were made which can hardly be distinguished from each other or from Rouen. Again at the Loc-Maria factory in a suburb of Quimper (Finistère) founded in 1690 and taken over in 1743 by Pierre Caussy (son of a worker at Rouen who stole many quasi-Chinese designs from the older factory), a ware was made which can only be distinguished by its thick and dirty glaze and strongly accented drawing in manganese. By 1809 this place turned entirely to ordinary earthenware. Later a stoneware was tried and marked with an H in a triangle below a fleur-de-lys. In 1872 old models were tried from tracings of Caussy. He also used the mark in old style and Hannover points out that Graesse includes it as really old.

SAINT CLOUD

Even at Saint Cloud which we respect for its development of soft paste the lambrequins of Rouen were copied, using a different black instead of blue for the outlines. Later the faïence freed itself for there are blue and white pieces with pictures of workmen, craftsmen, etc., crudely painted which seem original. These are marked BV, CR and T with crowns for the château at Bellevue, Choisy-le-Roi and the Trianon, for which they were made.

THE PARIS FACTORIES

Most of the Paris wares are distinguishable from Rouen only by their marks. The quality was not high. The red was replaced by ochre of a poor quality as at Nevers. More manganese and yellow were also used with the latter thinner and more transparent than that of Sinceny. The drawing was in black and none too good. Some of these factories are listed below:

The Factory of Oliver, rue de la Roquette, made stoves, drug vases and turned to the Strasburg colors and then to English ware.

The Pont-aux-Choux Factory started in 1772 and made wares cast from silver in Rouen-like material and then English ware.

The Factory of Digne, also rue de la Roquette, made apothecary jars for a monastic pharmacy at the order of the daughter of the Duke of Orleans after Rouen style of decoration.

CLAUD MICHEL (CLODION) (1738–1814)

Of course, not in glazed faïence and neither in biscuit porcelain, there were works done in low fired terracotta in France and particularly in Paris that were of great importance, in fact of such importance that they are thought of as sculpture and not ceramic art, which, however, they certainly are. Perhaps the greatest artist of this type was Claud Michel (called Clodion) who was born in Nancy in 1738 and came to Paris in 1755, a young man of only 17 years of age, to work in the shop of his uncle Lambert Sigisbert Adam, J. B. Pigalle. In 1759 he won the grand prize of the Académie Royale and in 1762 went to Rome. In 1792 the revolutionary agitation drove him back to his birthplace and he remained in Nancy until 1798. There is no positive record that he ever worked for any of the ceramic factories and the authority Mr. George Wildenstein is certain that he had his own kiln and did his own firing contrary to the way Falconet worked. Certainly his figures rank among the highest products of the century and of all time in his country just as did those of Luca and Andrea della Robbia in 15th and 16th century Italy.

MOUSTIERS (CLERISSY FACTORY)

The third large center with Nevers and Rouen was, of course, Moustiers-Sainte Marie (Basses Alps) where the sons Joseph and Pierre of the potter

FIG. 1148. A group in terracotta by the famous "Clodion" (Claud Michel) called "The Intoxication of Wine," which shows his full, rounded modeling and the sex appeal almost always present. Ht. 23¼". Metropolitan Mus. of Art.

FIG. 1149. A group by Clodion showing Bacchus and a nymph with Cupid, in terracotta. Ht. 18½". Metropolitan Mus. of Art.

Antoine Clerissy seem to have started in 1679. Joseph went to Marseilles to manage the Saint-Jean-du-Désert Factory and Pierre I, as he was called to distinguish him from the later Pierre, started at Moustiers. An Italian monk helped him and he hired the artists Gaspard and Jean-Baptiste Viry. The son, Antoine II, succeeded his father upon his death in 1728. Honoré Clerissy, whose relationship is not known, was also active there. The place did so well that in 1736 Antoine II retired and turned the plant over to his son, Pierre II. Under him it improved still more and when he was ennobled as a landed proprietor in 1783 he lost interest and sold out to Joseph Fouqué.

Another factory at Moustiers was started in 1738 by Joseph Olerys who had probably worked at the Clerissy place, had then gone to Marseilles and thence to Alcora in Valencia, Spain, in 1727 or 1732 (depending upon the authority) where the Count of Aranda had established a factory. His brother-in-law, Jean-Baptiste Laugier started with him, and when he died his son, Joseph II, took his place until 1771 when he sold out to Laugier, though the factory used the old name until 1790 as is proven by the mark, an O crossed with L on decadent wares. It occurs in yellow, orange, black or blue along with painter's marks.

There were still other factories but they were all small copyists. The Ferrat toward the end of the century copied Strasburg and then the English ware. Revivals were tried but by 1874 all work stopped.

Moustiers is light in weight as compared with Rouen. It is resonant and milk-white with slightly pinkish tone. There seem to be three generally accepted periods:

1.—Wares decorated in blue only from the beginning to 1738.
2.—Polychrome period from 1738, called the "Olery's period."
3.—Decadent period, in which both types were made, from about 1770.

FIRST PERIOD OF MOUSTIERS (1680–1738)

The Clerissy blue is lighter and brighter than Rouen blue. The only similar blue is that of Saint-Jean-du-Désert but there the outlines were in manganese while at Moustiers the blue was used for outline also. Gaspard Viry probably started the style of large dishes with hunting scenes after engravings by Antonio Tempesta and biblical subjects after Matthieu Mérian. Some have no borders while others have rims of lambrequins or motifs from Italian grotesques such as griffins, masks, etc.

Contemporary are those said to be of the style of Bérain though prototypes are found in the work of Sebastien le Clerc, Bernard Toro and others. In fact the style goes back to Roman wall paintings and had developed through the Renaissance and Baroque periods. It consists of airy and fantastic architectural members assembled without any thought of structure into patterns of delicate dreamlike arches with pedestals on leafy scrolls, awnings partly suspended by ribbons, balustrades guarding nothing, baldacchinos, terminal figures, consoles, brackets and such showing no slightest pull of gravity. However, gravity is taken account of in the draping of these things with garlands, hanging trophies, draperies, festoons, etc., of rich materials and flowers, not to mention lanterns. Then again it is not regarded, for there stand about in mid air or upon cushions of flowers with floating ribbons all manner of beings such as nymphs, genii and vaguely mythological personalities surrounded by flaming urns, fountains and vases of flowers among which are monkeys and parrots, cupids, satyrs, etc. It was great fun and led to many fantasies until the lambrequins surrounded it and slowly smothered it out of existence. The early ones with groups of goddesses, the Judgment of Paris or something of the sort are alive and sometimes even playful with contemporary dress included. They are generally rectangular with "broken" edges and come first to mind when Moustiers is mentioned.

SECOND PERIOD (1738–c.1770)

It is fairly certain that Olerys came back from Alcora and started the polychrome style. The "hunt dishes" stopped but the blue and white continued for a short while. The colors introduced were brown, yellow, green and purple. The style of Bérain was adopted but also cross influences seem to have continued between Alcora and Moustiers. Soon both used "décor à quirlandes" or small garlands alternating with medallions about the rim while in the center is another medallion with garland treated edges. In the medallions mythological subjects are used. The colors were usually blue, yellow, brown, black, green and purple in various shades. Those which are warmer and have no marks are usually attributed to Alcora, though this is a some-

FIG. 1150. Moustiers plate decorated in blue only and dating between 1738 and 1749. Metropolitan Mus. of Art.

FIG. 1151. Faïence coffee-pot decorated in yellow and attributed to the Olerys and Laugiers. It is said to date between 1738 and 1749. Metropolitan Mus. of Art.

what arbitrary rule of thumb. Some have rococo designs instead of the flower garlands and these can be easily told apart because of the different treatments between Spanish and French scrolls. These commence about 1745 to 1750.

The "décor à la fleur de pomme de terre" (decoration of potato flowers) is used with both garlands and scrolls or alone and is of bouquets of flowers of symmetrical form separated by single flowers. This has a strong East Indian feeling explainable through Spain. Potato flowers could have had nothing whatsoever to do with the origin because they were unknown in France in 1750. The constant use of alternation is Near Eastern (see section on Ashur) and it is interesting to see it so strong in this Spanish influenced French place.

Finally the "genre Callot" design is of strewn grotesque figures faintly reminiscent of Callot, flowers, fragments of landscapes, etc., more or less, and chiefly less, in "Chinese style" in yellow, green, orange, blue, manganese and black combinations, usually the first three but sometimes all. This style lasted from about 1750 to 1770.

THIRD PERIOD OF MOUSTIERS (c.1770–)

When the decadence set in of course Meissen and Strasburg were copied but at Moustiers at least no more was taken than given for it had been considered a sort of school of potters for years. However, perhaps the real credit should go to Alcora for it was the source of much at Moustiers. There were also many small hangers-on such as Angoulême (Charente) founded c.1750 which with dull colors also copied Nevers and Rouen, Ardus (Tarn-et-Garonne) c. 1737 with red body and strongly crackled greyish glaze and stiff drawing, Aubagne (Bouches-du-Rhône) near Marseilles, c. 1782 where there were supposed to have been two factories, Auvillar (Tarn-et-Garonne) where several factories copied Varages, Rouen and Moustiers, Avignon (Vaucluse), Castilhon (Gard), Clermont Ferrand (Puy-de-Dôme) where the blue is more indigo than at Moustiers c.1730–1740, Goult (Vaucluse) c. 1740, La Foret (Savoy) 1730 by Noël Bouchard where Nevers was also imitated, Limoges (Haute Vienne) 1736 which changed in 1773 to porcelain making and then was an annex to Sèvres. (The faïence is poor. It is in manganese, light blue and green.) Lyons, 1733 by Joseph Combe and Jacques-Marie Ravier where the enamel was slightly bluish, Montauban (Tarn-et-Garonne) 1770 where Armand Lapierre did polychrome coats of arms with borders in blue and yellow and other imitations, Saint-Jean-du-Désert, Samadet (Landes) 1732 which copied the "Chinese style" and "genre Callot" along with imitations of Marseilles and Sinceny, and Varages (Var) where six factories between about 1740 and 1800 all made clumsy imitations.

About Alcora we have spoken of the attempt of the Count to have porcelain made and before that soft paste. We know that he encouraged only the best of craftsmanship and highest conceptions of the artists. It is told that he started a school and made each workman take several apprentices under him. He hired only Spanish artists after Olerys left up until 1750 when he gave up the factory entirely.

STRASBURG

Next in importance is probably Strasburg. It has often been mentioned in connection with the decline but, of course, in all fairness the decline was due to the general influences toward the end of the century and not to any one place, and it was the copyists of Strasburg rather than Strasburg itself which were responsible.

In 1720 a factory was established there by J. H. Wachenfeld of Ansbach. In 1721 a partnership was formed with Charles François Hannong who was a maker of clay pipes and stoves in Maestricht. In 1722 the partnership was broken and Hannong carried on. In 1724 he founded a new factory at Hagenau and in 1732 he turned both over to his sons, Paul Antoine and Balthazar. A price list of the time proves that they were active in making table services, coffee and tea services, knife handles, dishes, drug-vessels, doll's house sets, chimney sets, etc.

FIG. 1152. A typical Strasburg plate with the famous flowers casually laid askew. They are in natural colors with strong carmine and green. 18th cent. Metropolitan Mus. of Art.

The confusion about the early wares was dispelled by Brinckmann when they were found among those formerly called Rouen, Höchst, Ansbach and Hanau but chiefly among the first named. They are blue and white in much the Rouen manner, but with flowers more natural and fewer lambrequins. The next period shows "Indian flowers" in the Meissen manner.

In 1737 Balthazar Hannong took the business at Hagenau. In 1739 this factory came into Paul's hands and the next ten years saw its best and greatest production. Later Löwenfinck, having fled from Höchst, prevailed upon him to try "true porcelain" and this awakened the jealousy of the Vincennes factory which was making soft paste and they urged the ruling powers to call Alsace "foreign" and impose duties. Paul tried his best to sell the secret of hard porcelain in Paris but did not succeed and at last was forced to leave Strasburg. He then went, as we know, to Frankenthal where he made faïence and porcelain until he died in 1760.

His sons, Pierre Antoine and Joseph Adam stayed in Strasburg in the faïence business and later on Joseph was alone and tried again in 1774 to make porcelain, was hit by the drastic tariff and ruined, and thrown into debtor's prison. He died in Munich about 1800 in misery and want, a victim of jealousy in trade.

The history of Strasburg is that of the Hannongs solely and the style was entirely the one they adopted. Attempting to imitate porcelain they used muffle-kiln colors fired at low temperature on an already fused tin glaze. This glaze was not greenish like that of Rouen nor bluish like that of Nevers nor yet pinkish like that of Moustiers, but a fresh, soft, pure white without any brilliance. The colors were remarkable; especially a carmine-red which has never been matched and which was generally used. Flowers were gathered into loose bunches and laid coquettishly askew while similar smaller bunches were employed to obtain balance and individual blossoms covered imperfections. A beautiful copper-green, a violet, a light yellow and a blue were also used but the carmine and green predominate. Paul Hannong was the first in Europe to use gold on faïence and it is reported that in 1744 he showed Louis XV "gilded faïence" which is assumed to mean faïence with gold decoration only.

A few odd pieces have Chinese figures and these together with ones having flowers in crimson monochrome, also others imitative of Rouen blue and white, are signed by Joseph Hannong.

In the better ware the flowers are painted without outlines and with simple brush strokes modeling the petals with vitality. This must have been arrived at as a sort of invention because there is no evidence of Chinese or Japanese models having been seen or copied and the style is different also. On the shadow side the pigment may be laid so heavily that it stands out like enamel. The green was used pure and then shaded with black so that it has weight and acts as a foil for the delicacy of the flowers. Often the colors are not mixed but used with one over another to obtain blended effects. To the layman this may not seem a vitally different method but when a painter gets to thinking in masses rather than in outlines filled in, he has passed the first stage of his development. (See discussion of Sung, Chinese Tz'u Chou wares.)

In the cheaper and less good Strasburg wares the outline is thin and stiff as though done with a pen. This took longer but was safer for untrained artists.

Besides flat wares the usual odd pieces such as clock-cases, frames, etc. and some figures were made the latter being after Meissen ones but with more crudity and vigor.

These figures occur with the mark of Paul but not with the mark of Joseph Hannong. Paul's mark PH is never accompanied with other marks but Joseph's JH in monogram form usually has also numerals 1 to 1,000 in blue, below which is usually another number in blue or black. The first referred to the model list of the factory and the second had a meaning unknown. It did not refer to any sequence, date or quality as some dealers have tried to claim. A fiction grew up about the number 39 and imitators readily supplied the demand. Samson makes the body a little too light a grey and even he does not get the carmine. Strasburg glaze seldom crackles. But the collector must handle a number of pieces to make sure. No other faïence has been so much copied.

NIDERVILLER

One of the factories to be early influenced by the success of Strasburg was that of Niderviller in Alsace Lorraine also, near Sarrebourg. It was founded by Baron Jean-Louis de Beyerlé in 1754 with workmen from both Strasburg and Meissen. He and his wife loved the work and for some years their faïence wares were nearly as delicate as the porcelain of Meissen. The place came to Comte de Custine in 1774 and he placed it under François Lanfrey who allowed a slow decline to the final production of "English ware." In 1793 the comte was executed and Lanfrey became owner.

FIG. 1154. St. Clement jardinière with white tin glaze and decorated in natural colors. c. 1750. Metropolitan Mus. of Art.

FIG. 1153. Niderviller faïence plate decorated in cerise and having a crudely pierced rim. It is said to date between 1760 and 1780. Metropolitan Mus. of Art.

Table wares very much like Strasburg are cleaner but slightly yellowish. The painting is delicate and good but the colors less fresh, particularly the carmine.

During the time of Beyerlé wood-grain effects were accomplished in grey, brown and yellow and the usual stunt of indicating an engraving pinned on it was faultlessly rendered. Some are signed "Kirian pinxit 1764," etc., and he may have been the originator of the idea in this particular factory. Framed panels with landscapes were also made and large drug vases, center pieces, etc., came in time. There are also biscuit and painted figures by Charles Sauvage Lemire and others.

Rarely the mark is "Niderviller" in full while again it may be BN (Beyerlé-Niderviller) or two C's set back to back for the Custine period.

LUNÉVILLE & SAINT-CLÉMENT

Jacques Cambrette founded three concerns, two at Lunéville and one as an offshoot at Saint-Clément, all of which he left his son, Gabriel Cambrette, and son-in-law, Charles Loyal, at his death in 1758. Stanislaus Leozinski gave the two permission to use the "Manufacture Royale" but the business declined and Cambrette declared himself bankrupt, whereupon Loyal took over the business but had to sell the Lunéville holdings in 1778 to Sébastien Keller & Guerin, whose descendants were recently still owners. At Saint-Clément, Loyal formed a partnership with Mique and the sculptor Paul Louis Cyfflé but this was soon broken up and the place went to the stock-holders until 1824 when Germain Thomas got hold of it. (See below for description of wares.)

BELLEVUE

In 1758, Bellevue near Toul (Meurthe) was founded by Lefrançois and in 1771 transfered to Charles Bayard and François Boyer and, like Lunéville, also obtained the title of "Manufacture Royale," and here too Cyfflé worked. He was born at Bruges and was a well known sculptor and his figures at both places became famous.

Lunéville made copies of Strasburg and also "English ware," but also large couchant lions with yellow jaws, and hounds of heraldic character which were used in the 18th century in halls in pairs to guard the vestibules. In biscuit there is a large statuette of King Stanislaus and at Sèvres there is also a cream colored bust of Louis XV, with a lion beside the pedestal.

Saint-Clément copied Strasburg and also the "English ware" as did Belle-vue. At the latter place there are large figures such as "The Gardner," the "Little Savoyard" and the "Abbé Reading his Breviary," figures such as were used to "beautify" gardens in the 18th century.

The white and buff wares from Lunéville are often stamped "Terre de Lorraine" but the other wares from this place and all of those from Bellevue and Saint-Clément were not marked.

Thus the wares might not have been known had it not been for the fact that Cyfflé's style is recognizable. He did such things as "A shoe-maker whistling a tune to a starling in a cage above him," the "stocking-darner listening to a bird in a cage," and other small tradesmen or craftsmen in sweetly moving situations showing their kind hearts and causing all who observe them (providing of course that the observers could get themselves

FIG. 1155. Tall vase and cover made at Lille in 1767 and having polychrome decoration. Ht. 21″. Metropolitan Mus. of Art.

FIG. 1156. St. Amand-les-Eaux tureen and cover dating about 1750–1775 and decorated with the usual polychrome flowers. Metropolitan Mus. of Art.

into the right state of mind) to feel a sad compassion. The supreme compliment of the 18th century, namely forgery, was granted them also.

Many other factories should be mentioned but we can content ourselves with those of the following chart:

CHART OF MINOR FAÏENCE FACTORIES OF FRANCE

Place	Mark	Dates & Founder	Description of wares
Aprey near Langres (Haute-Marne)	AP in monogram or APR	*Jacques Lallemand de Villehaut,* the Baron of Aprey, and his brother, *Joseph*	Early wares rococo and painted on a previously-fired tin glaze which is likely to chip off. Decoration is usually in blue and is of flowers, birds and Chinese figures or landscapes either free or in medallions.
	Also used on late imitations from old moulds	1769 Jacques died and his brother called in *François Ollivier* from Nevers	A tureen in colors with a good brown and of pinkish cast in Cluny. A Jardiniere with red shell edge picked out in green and flowers in colors is in the *Camando Coll., Louvre.*
	Samson also copied	Closed about 1860 Then owned by *Abel Girard* who copied old wares.	*Aprey* recalls the work of *Strasburg, Niderviller* and *Sceaux.* Colors are used in broad and strong work inclined to run.
	From 1772 no mark.		In 1772, according to *Paul Deveaux,* the painter *Jacques Jarry* influenced the work to be fine and delicate. These wares are not ever marked.

CHART OF MINOR FAÏENCE FACTORIES OF FRANCE—*Continued*

Place	Mark	Dates & Founder	Description of wares
Les Islettes (Meuse) *Bois d'Epense* (Marne)	No marks	1785 *François Bernard* took over factory from his father. *Jacques Henri Bernard,* his son, made great success.	It has fresh color and strong outlines of brown or black. The motives are large bouquets tied with red ribbons or in baskets, birds, poultry, Chinese landscapes and figures, and landscapes with military figures in them.
Lille	Lille between two palm-leaves under a crown and date Many fakes are on the market,— particularly on pieces with Dutch landscapes and on snuff-boxes looking like porcelain. FB in Monogram ? Fleur-de-lys?	Founded in 1696 by a modeler, *Jacques Feburier,* of Tournay, and a painter, *Jean Bossu.* After Feburier's death in 1729, his widow and son-in-law, *François Boussemaert* 1773 After the death of Boussemaert his widow married *Philippe-Auguste Petit,* who carried on until 1802.	Two altar pieces one in private possession and one in Sèvres, marked, "*Fecit Jacobus Feburier—Insulis in Flandria—Anno 1716—pinxit Maria Stephanus Borne—Anno 1716.*" Painted in indigo tinted blue and touched with yellow. Rococo cartouche with cupids holding a ribbon inscribed *Maitre Daligne* with three scrolls and three insects alternating on rim all in colors on a plate in *Sèvres,* marked *Lille—1767.* Tea-pot marked *Lille—1768* in Cluny painted with rococo ornament in color with landscape on one side and two cupids in pale violet on other. Plates with playing cards on them.
Lille		1711 founded by *Barthélemy Dorez* and his nephew, *Pierre Pelissier* 1749 came to *Michel Joseph Herreng* and his widow carried on until 1780, when it went to *Hubert François Lefebure* Closed about 1820.	Founded for making soft porcelain but also made *faïence.*
Lille		1740 founded by *Jean Baptiste Wamps,* who worked for first factory. 1755 after his death it went to *Jacques Masquelier* who let it go in 1808.	Tiles only of rather Dutch characteristics. *Wamps* was Dutch.
Lille		1773 founded by *William Clarke* from Newcastle Only lasted a short time	Claimed he had a *faïence* "which is otherwise produced only in England and is very nearly as beautiful as porcelain."
Lille		1774 founded by *Charon* Only lasted a short time	Brown ware called "*terre de Saint-Esprit à la façon d'Angleterre et du Languedoc.'*

NOTE:—There are other wares attributed to Lille but upon what would seem to the author unsound grounds and the characteristics which *Jaennicke* points out are not worth consideration for they do not even wholly coincide with those of the very few known or fairly certain specimens.

CHART OF MINOR FAÏENCE FACTORIES OF FRANCE—*Continued*

Place	Mark	Dates & Founder	Description of wares
Saint-Amand-les-Eaux	PF in a double monogram	1718 founded by *Pierre Joseph Fauquez* from Tournay. 1741 on his death his son, *Pierre François-Joseph Fauquez* who died and passed it on to his son, *Jean-Baptiste-Joseph Fauquez.* During Revolution he fled to Germany but returned to try to set the factory up again and died in Tournay 1804.	Imitated *Rouen* and *Strasburg.* Wares painted in an opaque white over a grey or grey-blue glaze, at times alone or sometimes as a ground for a floral or lace pattern in several colors, such as the wall-fountain at *Sèvres,* in blue monochrome and *"blanc fixe."* Also at *Sèvres* is a tureen with white branches and flowers over a grey ground and with added colored flowers over it, a plate with flowers in pale indigo blue in center and the rim in opaque white, a sauce-boat with grey-blue ground striped in white with flowers in colors over it, etc.
	Late mark same but flanked with an S and an A		Blue monochromes probably came first, then pieces with decoration in opaque white and finally the ones imitating Strasburg or borrowing from it. Last of all imitations of English ware which are generally yellow-glazed and painted in one or more colors with occasional gold edges.
Bailleul (Nord)	Marked Jacobus Hennekens		A tureen at *Sèvres* is oval and partly painted over a relief decoration in blue, grey and a good yellow.

Note:—Most of the factories in the west and south-west parts of France are much the same, perhaps having some one little specialty but otherwise following the current trend and their wares are difficult to distinguish one from another.

Place	Mark	Dates & Founder	Description of wares
Rennes Brittany *Pavé Saint-Laurent* factory		c. 1745 by *Forasassi,* a Florentine.	Various clays from different places and also glazes of various tones. The tureens were moulded from silversmith's ones like those of many places and the decoration is similar to that of *Rouen, Moustiers* or *Marseilles.*
	Chiefly no marks, others are questionable	1759 came to *Dubois de la Vrillière.*	Manganese-purple is supposed to be more pronounced than elsewhere but this has been claimed elsewhere as we know. It also is all inclined to "blister" or "boil" so this is not a distinguishing feature.
		Jean-Baptiste-Alexis Bourgoin came from Rouen about 1755.	No red at all was used and the green is darker and duller so that the wares are somber.
	The inkstand is marked *"Fecitte. P. Bourgoiin A Rennes ce.12.8bre 1763*		A large inkstand at *Sèvres* has drawers and decoration in blue and manganese. (See mark.)

CHART OF MINOR FAÏENCE FACTORIES OF FRANCE—*Continued*

Place	Mark	Dates & Founder	Description of wares
Rennes *rue Hü*	*Francois-* *Alexandre* *Tutrel* Some painter's signatures Chiefly no marks	1749 founded by *Francois-Alexandre* *Tutrel*	Earliest known piece is 1769 and latest 1774. Perhaps here or at another factory was a painter named *Hirel de Choisy* who signed some of the best wares including a polychrome tureen in *Rennes Museum.* There was also *Michel Derennes* and perhaps *(Jean) Baron.* See also wall cistern in colors dating about 1760 at *Rennes Museum.*
La Rochelle *(Charente-* *Inférieure)*	*Rochelle* *1777*	1743 founded by *Bricqueville* and another factory was working until 1789.	Imitations first of *Nevers,* then of *Rouen* blue and white, and then of *Moustiers* and finally of *Strasburg* wares in the usual sequence. Dishes with birds in center and rims with butterflies and other insects and flowers. Urn-shaped *"vase sur terrasse"* with freely modeled and painted flowers is typical and one at *Sèvres* is marked Rochelle 1777.
Maran	Maran and date No mark on fountain Another fountain is marked Maran 1754 of latter type.	1740 by *Pierre Roussencq*	Possibly, a wall fountain in the *Musée des Arts Decoratifs in Paris,* with a garland of flowers freely modeled and painted around the upper part of the body and within the garland a few fishes in brown colors. Other pieces have heavy and violent color with an intense red.
Angoulême *(Charente)*		*(See Moustiers)*	
Cognac *(Charente)*		End of 18th cent.	Center of *"Faïence parlante"* during Revolution similar to that of *Nevers,* etc.
Bordeaux	Clock dial marked Hustin 1750.	1711 *Jacques Gautier* who took in *Hustin* from Lille	Copies of *Moustiers, Nevers* and *Rouen.* Colors bad; blue is blackish, and there is no red. Some of the largest pieces of *faïence* ever made such as the clock dial from the city exchange.
Montauban *Auvillar* and *Ardus* in Tarn-et-Garonne			Strongest *Moustiers* influence.
Montpellier		1750—*Andre Philipp* from Marseilles	Fine *faïence* with flowers on yellow ground extending to back. These were models for *Moustiers.*

MARSEILLES
SAINT-JEAN-DU-DÉSERT

Perhaps ranking next to the greatest factories is Saint-Jean-du-Désert. In the 16th century some Italians were making faïence there but in 1677, 1678 or 1679 a factory was started in this suburb of Marseilles, by Joseph Clérissy, a son of Antoine Clérissy of Moustiers, or, if it was not started by him at least it came into his hands. When Joseph died in poverty in 1685 the direction of the place was under his eldest son named Antoine after the grandfather and he held it until 1733 when he went to Marseilles. From about 1750 there were about 10 factories selling to the Levant and French Colonies. By 1756 a school of painting unique in excellence had sprung up which produced a fresh and sincere sort of flower painting though landscapes were not improved much and figures not at all.

Among the places influenced were those of Louis Leroy (1741), Antoine Bonnefoy (1777), Fauchier, Veuve Perrin, Joseph Robert and Honoré Savy. Fauchier took over the factory of Etienne Héraud at Saint-Lazare in 1711, carried on with his nephew, Joseph Fauchier II, who finally inherited it in 1751 and his son carried on until 1794. The wares from the factory were just recently recognized among Moustiers types. A centerpiece in the Limoges Museum inscribed, "Joseph Fauchier à Marseille à la Bourgade," set us right.

In 1740 Claude Perrin founded a factory which did not gain distinction until after his death in 1748 when his widow ran it. Later she joined with Honoré Savy until about 1770 when she formed another company with François Abelard and her son. This latter made some experiments with porcelain up to about 1793 when she died.

Joseph Robert had started with a porcelain factory but in 1754 turned to faïence. Both were successful.

Honoré Savy after the partnership with Madam Perrin was dissolved, started in for himself around 1777 and became so successful that he even had a ship of his own for exporting.

Hannover says, "Like all the wares from Saint-Jean-du-Désert, everything from the factory of the elder Fauchier is painted in grand feu colours." This meant, of course, a limited palette. The oldest wares are in blue generally outlined in manganese. There is a dish signed by Antoine Clérissy in the style of the Moustiers "hunt dishes" and dated 1697. Another dated 1718 is in the style of Bérain of Moustiers but thinner and less vigorous. Large baluster jars of about the beginning of the century are in Nevers style following the Chinese but having taller and more flaring feet and angular curved covers with double knobs. The decorations on these are of a wide band containing figures from mythology and smaller borders of the dry arabesque style. The styles of Rouen and Savona were also employed. Under the young Fauchier the wares were muffle-kiln decorated and similar to those of other factories.

Around 1750 the Veuve Perrin factory took the lead in producing wares selected from all the best factories, copied in a highly developed technique.

It was particularly strong in colored grounds among which were the yellow of Montpellier (transposed into overglaze painting), a transparent water-green and a copper green which Honoré Savy brought to it. The gilding was fine. The sea motives predominate and marines and airy landscapes are characteristic decorations.

This could not have been due entirely to Madam Perrin for Joseph Robert achieved the same results and the wares of the two places cannot be told apart unless marked. The whiteness and refinement of his porcelain was also

FIG. 1157. Marseilles plate of about 1760 with a polychrome landscape. Metropolitan Mus. of Art.

FIG. 1158. Veuve Perrin late 18th cent. barber's basin from Marseilles with polychrome decoration. Metropolitan Mus. of Art.

obtained in his faïence and the richness of the glaze was even more pleasing, as is often the case. He was not quite so ambitious for variety but had a fairly wide range of shapes. His most appreciated work was decorated in monochrome, sepia, blue, or gold alone and the green and pink decoration he himself had a special affection for, but there were many styles. The flower modeling was done with style and beauty and not overdone. In general the plastic work of his factory was not quite so good as that of the Veuve Perrin one, though it is only fair to say that the confusion in attributions may have confused this issue.

Honoré Savy did plastic work but was a better painter and was a member of the Academy at Marseilles. Many of his plates are painted with poly-chrome in the center and green ornamentation on the rims. Another rich effect was obtained with dark green, light green and a purplish red. He was visited by Monsieur (the brother of the king) who obtained for him the use of the fleur-de-lys as his mark in 1777.

The Veuve Perrin mark was VP and Clérissy sometimes signed his name or the word Marseilles and the date, the earliest being 1681. An upright or horizontal F is supposed to be a mark of Fauchier, when on pieces of his style. The VP is easily confused with the IP of Store Kongensgade factory at Copenhagen and Madam Perrin's initials are sometimes detached from one another. Black and red were often used. At the time Robert worked, in his earliest period, with Etieu, the founder, they signed "Robert et Etieu"

sometimes. He also signed R or JR or RX ? in monogram. Other marks
attributed to him are not correct. Most of the finer pieces have no mark
and forgers are always ready to add a mark for good measure.

SCEAUX

Even the Marseilles wares were surpassed by a factory at Sceaux, near
Paris (Seine), founded in 1750 under the protection of the Duchess of Maine,
and then under that of Marie de Bourbon, the Duke of Penthièvre and High
Admiral of France (1725–1793). The first director was Jacques Chappelle,
who was both a chemist and member of the Academy, and its next was
Richard Glot who had the reputation of being the greatest modeler of his

FIG. 1160. Sceaux (1753–1795) jar which is one
of three designed as a garniture and decorated in
polychrome. Metropolitan Mus. of Art.

FIG. 1159. Sceaux vase possibly of the 18th cent. but more likely early 19th cent. Ht. 20″.
Metropolitan Mus. of Art.

time. Chappelle made porcelain and tried to make faïence just as refined.
He was also a man of business and in 1763 he retired with a fortune leaving
the work in charge of Jullien and a sculptor, Charles S. Jacques. It was they
who sold the factory to Glot for 40,000 livres in 1772 after having owned it
for nine years. Under him and the Duke's protection it achieved great fame.

The wares are mostly services of the period just preceding and of that of
Louis XVI. They are simple, formal in outline and decorated with pastorals,
cupids among clouds (often in crimson monochrome), flowers, birds, etc., set
in panels with molded borders of laurel leaves twisted about with ribbons.

The carmine-red is less pure than that of Strasburg and softer. They had a fine ultramarine blue.

Glot was mayor of Sceaux and was arrested by the revolutionists. This broke his spirit and he finally sold the factory for an amount equal to one year's rent in 1794, to Antoine Cabaret who did nothing of note.

Chappelle did not seem to mark his wares. The SP (Sceaux-Penthièvre) was used after 1772 when the Duke became patron. It is in colors with or without an anchor referring to his being Admiral. Later the mark was Sceaux impressed and also with or without an anchor.

The body is maize-yellow and very light in weight. The glaze is white or slightly yellowish. It is one of the most costly of faïence wares and at the Bordes sale, 1911, a pastille-burner with decoration after Greuze of birds and festoons about a genre subject brought 10,100 francs.

"ENGLISH WARE," "FAÏENCE FINE," "STEINGUT" OR "FLINTPORSLIN"

We have had to end the histories of a number of factories with a disparaging reference to "English ware" which was often their last product. This is not due to the material itself which was in some ways an improvement over faïence, but to the use to which it was put, the way the market was flooded with it and the decadent period in which it was made. The French called it, "faïence fine," the Germans called it, "Steingut" (Steinzeug meaning the Rhenish stoneware), and the Swedish, "flintporslin." It originated in England but the continental imitations are of a blend of plastic clay with flint or quartz pebbles and often some kaolin. This produces a white body and thus the tin, necessary to make a white opaque glaze, was eliminated and an ordinary lead glaze took its place. As the result was too glaringly white, yellow-staining metallic oxides were mixed with the glaze. Sometimes the body was also colored and, naturally, this led to the mixing of two or more colored clays to produce the old marbled effect, wood graining, agate and tortoise-shell. This ware could be decorated on the biscuit and then glazed and given one firing, or a second or even third firing could be given it allowing the use of muffle-kiln colors. It was, unfortunately, peculiarly fitted to transfer printing. The temperature needed was not high and it could be fired with coal instead of wood, thus it was cheap. It was light and durable and, when chipped, the broken place remained white.

At first the effect of this ware was not bad for it brought along the designs of Wedgwood, though even these were cold and hard. Then France made a trade treaty with England in 1786 very much to the benefit of the latter country and entirely ruinous to the potters of France. Thus the ware was not taken up with enthusiasm as an artist might welcome a new material, but through the force of circumstances. It was one more insidious way in which the pressure of the penny might be applied. It is not interesting to us from any aesthetic viewpoint and I, therefore, simply append a list of a few of the most prominent factories which made a feature of it:

"ENGLISH WARE" OR "FAÏENCE FINE" FACTORIES

Douai (Nord)	*"Leigh & Cie— Douai"* *"Leigh 17 Douai"* *"Martin Dammann"*	1784—*Charles* and *Jacob Leigh* from England had managed two places in Staffordshire, formed the company *Houzé de l'Aulnoit & Cie.* Was hard hit by treaty of 1786 but lasted till 1820. 1799—*Martin Dammann* started a new factory but failed in 1804. 1800—*Boulé* brothers until 1806.	They obtained a privilege to make, *"fayence en grès pâte tendre blanche connue sous le nom de grès d'Angleterre."* Cream colored ware of English type mainly, and like that of Leeds particularly with pierced type of decoration, and with braided or twined handles and flower knobs. (See Sèvres) Red stoneware, black stoneware with garlands in relief after Wedgwood and jasper colored ware as well as polychrome wares with gilding. At time of Revolution they made the first orignial wares of the *"faïences parlantes"* type, snuff boxes, plates, etc., and busts of such people as Voltaire and Rousseau.
Choisy-le-Roi	*Choisy*	1804—Brothers *Paillart* started a factory which in 1824 came to *V. Paillart & H. Hautin*	Plate at Sèvres with printed medallion in black portrait of Marie Antoinette with an inscription on the rim reading: "Marie Antoinette d'Autriche Reine de France—*Impression sous couvert par Brevet d'Invention."*
Sèvres		There were seven factories by the end of the 18th century. 1806 *Clavareau Lambert & Cie.,* etc.	Painted decoration type. One with yellow ground with goat's head handles, festoons, medallions in relief and partly colored in blue and manganese. Another in same shape is pale green with black decoration. (Both at Sèvres)
Longwy (Lorraine)	Longwy incised and stamped	End of 18th cent.	Bust of Bonaparte and a tureen with imperial emblems, the handles being eagles with outspread wings.
Sarreguemines (Lorraine)	"Sarreguemines"	1770—*Paul Utzschneider* to present.	About 1800 great production of marbled wares. At *Sèvres* one brown jar of earthenware color in body.
Orleans (Loiret)	"Orleans" (stamped) "Grammont Laine' (Paine) Fabqt A Orleans"	1753—*Dessaux de Romilly* was authorized to set up a factory. 1757—Followed by *Gerault-Deranbert* who hired the sculptor *Jean Louis* End of 18th cent. *Grammont Laine* was there.	To make *"faïence en terre blanche purifée."* Statuettes of children, marbled and agate ware. In *Sèvres* there is a cream colored jug with flowers in relief.
Apt (Vaucluse)	No mark R is not correct	1780 and earlier factory amalgamated by *Bonnet.*	Earthenware of yellow body and also yellow and brown marbled ware.

"ENGLISH WARE" OR "FAÏENCE FINE" FACTORIES—*Continued*

Montereau (Seine-et-Marne) No mark Criel marked:—*"Manufacture de décors sur porcelaine et fayence* *—Rue du Cadran No. 9 à Paris"* also:—"Creil" or LCS (Legros-d'Anizy-Coquerel-Stone)	1775—*Clark, Shaw &* *Cie* amalgamated with Criel factory.		Transfer printed landscapes, etc. At *Creil* the first transfer-printing in France was done on earthenware under *Stone, Coquerel* and *Legros d'Anizy.* Scenes from French History, Fables of Lafontaine, etc., and portraits of great men, views of Italy, etc. At *Sèvres* there is a cup with red and green flowers among black-dotted clouds.
Chantilly	Hunting horn in gold *"Chantilly"* with P.......... below		V.A.M. there is a tea-pot with raised flowers and gilt lines. At *Sèvres* an oval dish painted in blue under a yellowish glaze, with a pair of lovers, and an octagonal dish with circular center and moulded rim. At *Rouen* a tureen in silver style of Louis XVI.
Loire (Nièvre)	*"La Charité"* may be the mark	1802—*Francis War-burton* from Staffordshire and later successor *Michael Willis*	English models in "faïence fine" and also "*biscuits noirs égyptiens*" after Wedgwood's so called "Basalt ware."

The makers of porcelain had worked under the retarding influences of "arcanists," rich dilettantes of the nobility and then commercial competition of a cut-throat variety. The makers of faïence did fully as important and perhaps more interesting things in their more honest appeal to the common people but were finally met by the competition of "English ware."

Delft had been inspired by the Far East and was also strongly influenced by the Near East in a roundabout way. The faïence of France was more strongly influenced by Italy and the Near East until later when naturalism and the Chinese motives came from the north and low countries. However, it was Delft and French faïence which had the strongest influence on the whole world of design until Wedgwood and the other classical influences became dominant.

GERMAN FAÏENCE

Nowhere nearly so important nor original a source of design as Delft and French faïence, yet German faïence had some charm of its own. Its chief early influence readily traceable is that of Italian majolica as it affected Hirsvogel of Nuremberg who made the little owl jugs, the Pfau family and the peasant potteries of the Salzkammergut, the Alpine regions and south central Europe. These latter are not considered important by some general writers but I find in them a vitality and real joy of creation which is most stimulating. They are also most interesting in their relationship to the American wares incorrectly called "Pennsylvania Dutch."

The earliest dated examples of faïence in these regions are blue and white jugs from Franconia some of which bear the monograms LS for Lorenze Speckner of the Vest family factory at Kreussen. These all have metal screw tops. Another possible piece is a jug in the form of a dove with plumage in blue outline in the Victoria & Albert Museum. All of these pieces have designs that are similar to each other and unlike anything else in European faïence. These designs are of three large flowers arranged symmetrically

with sometimes a fourth hanging straight down. The flowers and foliage are composed of curved lines terminating in spirals and the earliest ones are amplified with graduated dots in the background. It is difficult to explain this characteristic design for although the spiral was a heritage of Central Europe since Halstadt times, the symmetrical arrangement had been dropped since the Gothic period, and only in Spain in the 15th and 16th centuries

FIG. 1161.

was there any sign of it. Only one other place on earth showed this tendency strongly at the commencement of the 17th century and that was Central India, as may be seen by carpets, metal works, etc. This would seem an entirely impossible source of design for Bavaria until we read that, "During the 16th century Bruges, Antwerp and Amsterdam became the great emporia whence Indian produce, imported by the Portuguese, was distributed to Germany and even to England," in the article by Meston in the 14th edition *Encyclopaedia Britannica* (Vol. 12, p. 191 b). He continues with, "Private companies for trade with the East were formed in many parts of the United Provinces, but in 1602 they were all amalgamated by the states-general into the *'United East India Company of the Netherlands.'* Within a few years the Dutch had established factories on the continent of India, in Ceylon, in Sumatra, on the Persian Gulf and on the Red Sea, besides having obtained exclusive possession of the Moluccas."

Mr. Quill Jones, the eminent authority on Oriental carpets, tells me that in Holland, England and Germany worn fragments of the Central Indian rugs, which are now almost priceless, were used by some people for common floor coverings. He further confirms the fact that the metal work from Central India and of this period is found in use in the same countries and states that the bringing of such objects down to the coastal cities of India for trade was comparatively easy and typical of the people. He even relates a story of finding a very heavily woven rug some 75 feet by 40 feet which had been brought hundreds of miles over mountainous country by a trader on camel back to show him. Thus these objects once landed in Holland would have been easily carried up the Rhine to Frankfort, into the foothills of the Vosges and east to Nuremberg.

Why did we not find more definite trace of these things in Holland design? Well, on looking back we do see some in the work of Pijnacker and earlier wares, and it may have been that the painter nation was appealed to more by the naturalism of Italian painting than by the primitive designs of India, while the contrary was the case among the Austrians, German peasants and Hungarians.

The use of these designs continued over a long period of time from about 1618 to well toward the end of the century; Speckner died about 1670 and

Three krugs with pewter covers and feet, the first from Kreussen dated 1701 painted with enamels. Ht. 9½". The second from Saxony and of the late 17th cent. It is brown glazed with enamel decoration of madonna and child in relief. Ht. 11". The third is either Frankfort or Hanau of the last quarter of the 17th cent. It is blue and white with Chinese influence. The cover has initials K. R. Ht. 12". From W. R. Hearst Coll. International Studio, Inc.

Two *kanne* and a *krug*, the first from Hanau of the middle 18th cent. painted in blue, the second from Nuremberg and said to be about 1730 and the third a *"walzenkrug"* also from Nuremberg of about 1725-50. Hts. 12½", 13" and 8¼". From W. R. Hearst Coll. International Studio, Inc.

GERMAN DECORATED WARES LATE 17TH AND 18TH CENTURY

PLATE 204

some may have been his work though no one man could have turned out all of them. Fragments have been found in excavations in Copenhagen. A large alberello type vase and an inkstand were found there and in Christiania. At Lübeck were discovered a pair of drug-pots dated 1660. Others from Nykøbing are dated 1668.

As time went on the glaze becomes coarse and glistening while at first it was mat and fine. The blue pigment also becomes heavier and the brushwork is more clumsy.

HAMBURG FAÏENCE

Temporarily we will now skip the South German wares and turn to Hamburg where specimens even when rarely marked are not identified, though some bear the arms of Hamburg or Hamburgers. Jugs found here seem to be prototypes of blue and white Hamburg stoves. These jugs have flat conical bases, inverted pear-shaped bodies and narrow cylindrical necks supported by a sturdy handle. Some have pewter lids but they were for containers and were too heavy and large, and too small of mouth to drink from. The body is heavy, the glaze opaque and cream and the design in bright blue with touches of strong yellow at times. The front side opposite the handle was the decorated surface and had a shield of arms, a merchant's mark, and an emblematic subject such as "Fortune" or the "Fall of Judith," etc. This panel is generally surrounded by a frame of leaves or wreath and outside of that small leaves springing from below the handle and spreading upward and outward toward the front.

Hamburg Jug

FIG. 1162.

Hamburg or South German

FIG. 1163.

The only similar example with flowers alone is a more softened form with neck curving into the body instead of cylindrical and set on it and the base missing and a metal one added, which is in the Copenhagen Museum. The body too is more sagging and perhaps this is a South German form, for again the flowers are symmetrical Indian ones, this time set on rock formation of Chinese character. Dishes are rare but there is one in the Hamburg Museum with a shield of arms within a wreath and a rim of Chinese flower forms, but set in un-Chinese symmetrical manner. The Hamburg factory seemed to reach its height about 1640 while the last dated piece is of 1656.

The stoves started about 1700 and have strong baroque forms enclosing subjects from Greek and Roman mythology, the Bible, views of the town and marines and landscapes. The best known makers were J. H. Volgrath, Cord Michael Möller, H. D. Hennings and Johann Otto Lessel.

At about 1775 the blue and white style was petering out and white stoves or white and gold stoves in the classic manner stopped the cheerful painting of the older artists. Wilhelm Tischbein at Eutin (c.1810 to 1820) made the best of these with friezes of figures from Greek vases in light colors inlayed in an ingenious manner on a dark brown clay.

HANAU WARES

For what may be considered our third oldest factory we return to the southwestern part of Germany to Hanau near Frankfort-on-the-Rhine. Here two Dutchmen, Daniel Behaghel and his son-in-law, Jacobus van der Walle, having tried to get a concession at Frankfort, started in 1661. They imported Dutch workmen. In 1679 one of these workmen Johannes Bally took away the privilege. In 1689 he died but his widow carried on until 1693 when the factory returned to Daniel Behaghel in company with the widow of Walle. After further changes it came to Heinrich von Alphen in 1726 and between 1740 and 1745 to his son. In 1787 the company, Martin, Dangers & Co., in 1794 Daniel Toussaint and in 1797 Jacob Achilles Leisler owned it until its end in 1806.

T'ang Chinese

Hanau

Fig. 1164.

Ernst Zeh, authority on these wares, divides them into three general periods as follows:

FIRST PERIOD OF HANAU WARE (1661–1700)

Between 1661 and 1700 the ware was entirely Dutch with blue outline and blue painting but without the use of "kwaart" which gave to the real Dutch faïence its brilliant color. The shapes are new and were later copied at Frankfort. They consist of "Enghalskrug" or long necked jugs with thick lip-rim which is pewter covered, and a globular body on a shallow but widely flaring foot, often bound with pewter for reinforcement, which might have been a help to some of the weak Greek prototypes; a similar form but with horizontally fluted neck and helically fluted body and a twisted handle extended on the body in two curls; radially fluted plates with small flat or slightly convex centers; and plates with nine lobes together with other common forms.

I have pointed out that the little T'ang bottle from my collection and now in the Metropolitan Museum has a horizontally fluted neck which originated as an Indian design. These ewers or jugs are closely similar to forms which we see carried out in metal in India and the Near East and even the fluted plates recall Near Eastern wares.

The decorations on the plain surfaced jugs are usually shields of arms but those of the fluted jugs are strewn flowers, possibly partly inspired by India cotton prints, or more formally arranged flowers in large symmetrical bunches, and having background filled with groups of dots. Sometimes these dots are replaced by a ring, a cross or a bird with outspread wings. This is the most typical feature of the factory and occurs on plates also. At times both plates and fluted jugs have interpretations of Chinese landscapes and figures.

Second Hanau Period (1700–1740)

The second period of Hanau carries on the designs of the first but the sprigs become smaller, the birds more numerous and the groups of dots closer.

FIG. 1165. A krug of pale blue glazed earthenware with blue design of the typical transition period 1700–1740, the flowers still showing Chinese influences but also the new symmetry of Indian flowers. Hanau. Ht. 14″. Metropolitan Mus. of Art.

Both Zeh and Hannover saw only the two influences: 1.—Chinese and, 2.—indigenous naturalistic, and neither of them properly account for the symmetrical Indian influence which evidently never dawned upon them. Goodness knows, there was enough talk in the period of "Indian flowers" to give them a clew even though most people entirely misapplied the term; there was so much smoke that one could not help but guess that there might be some fire, but, having seen Chinese design miscalled Indian, they looked no further for the real Indian influences.

During this period the Chinese influence in figures and landscapes continued but with much more European modification.

A new development is the lobed plate with radially arranged design and small center flowers, landscapes or fruits. This again speaks eloquently of Western Asia. One plate and a few odd jugs have muffle-kiln colors but these may have been made outside the factory for generally the color is blue alone or other of the high fire colors. The glaze is greyish, greenish or bluish and at times it was sprayed with manganese and had masked medallions in reserve.

The Third Period of Hanau Ware (1740–1786)

Zeh calls this the height but Hannover points out that the old designs are not even improved, and that the "German flowers" used are not so good as those of the French factories, while the same is true of the experiments with muffle-kiln colors. I quite agree that this period ushers in the decline.

The Fourth Period of Hanau Ware (1787–1806)

Zeh lists 109 marks and Graesse 101, many of which are not of the factory at all. The general mark found on hundreds of pieces from the beginning of the 18th century is an incised crescent. Another typical characteristic is the impression of a tool by which the base of the handle is pressed into the body on the shoulder. Most pieces have unglazed bases underneath.

This last period is really simply a final continuation of decline and nothing new was done that I know of.

No clear demarkation has been established between Hanau wares and those of Frankfort-on-the-Main which have no general mark at all and the chief authority on the latter, Stoehr, differs with Zeh on a number of points. As an instance, Stoehr attributes the jugs with plaited handles to Frankfort excepting only three. He also says the jugs with the depressions mentioned above on the handles are Frankfort ones, while Zeh also admits that this does occur infrequently on the Frankfort wares, and on those of Florsheim as well. Where such specialists disagree it is well to tread lightly.

FRANKFORT-ON THE-MAIN

The factory at Frankfort-on-the-Main was established in 1666 with a privilege to Jean Simonet of Paris who had previously been a Hanau workman. In 1693 the patron Johann Christoph Fehr died and the factory was held by the widow and two sons until 1723 when it went to Georg Haszlocher. Between 1732 and 1742 it changed hands many times until Johann Heckel bought it and he and his son kept it until 1772 or 1774 when it was finally closed down.

I hazard one guess about the new type symmetrical design and that is that it would be more likely to have started in the parent factory. Otherwise what we have said just above held true and the wares cannot be distinguished from those of Hanau.

The chart below lists the other more run-of-the-mill factories and we need mention only that we find more Western Asiatic

Depression

Frankfort or Florsheim Jug

FIG. 1166.

FIG. 1168. Small tureen of Höchst faïence decorated in natural colors by Danhofer and signed with red wheel over line with D under it, 18th cent. Mrs. Bruce.

FIG. 1167. Bavarian stein with pewter cover and base, having polychromed decoration. Ht. 8". J. Gibbons Coll.

FIG. 1169. Mug with coat of arms on manganese ground attr. to Bayreuth c. 1720. Ht. 10¼". W. R. Hearst Coll. International Studio, Inc.

traces at Nuremberg, almost perfect copies (except for the ware of course) of Chinese blue and white K'ang Hsi wares at Dresden and nothing much else of interest unless it be a new method of heaping vegetables to the side of a dish or flowers to the top of a vase at Proskau.

FIG. 1170. Pitcher with pewter cover and foot attr. to workshop of Cornelius Funke. Powdered manganese ground with blue painted monogram A.W.M. and windmills on side. Cover marked MEA 1745. Ht. 16". Krug with pewter cover and foot from workshop of Cornelius Funke, decorated with monogram and crown supported on sides by two eagles. Cover marked CES 1725. Ht. 11". W. R. Hearst Coll. International Studio, Inc.

FIG. 1171. Mug of blue and white tin glazed earthenware with Chinese figures, Potsdam, c. 1720. Ht. 10". W. R. Hearst Coll. International Studio, Inc.

CHART OF GERMAN AND CENTRAL EUROPEAN FACTORIES

Nuremberg	N or NB in monogram only occasionally	1712—*Johann Caspar Ripp*, a potter from *Hanau*, manager for three merchants, *Christoph Marx*, *Heinrich Godfried*, *Anthon Hemmon* and the guardians of *Johann Conrad Romedi*, who died and his share came to *Johann Jacob Meyer*.	*Marx* got other good talent such as *Johann Wolff*, who later founded the *Copenhagen* and *Stockholm* factories, *Valentin Bontemps*, *Wenzel Ignaz Proschen*, *Adam Schuster*, *Andreas Tauber*, etc.
	often with name or initials of artists.		Glaze is white, pale blue or greenish decorated with monochrome blue generally but also in other high temperature colors.
		1720 this had taken place and *Hemmon* had sold out to *Johann Andreas Marx* who was a good painter at the factory.	Manganese occurs in all shades from light to nearly black. Also bright yellow and yellowish-green. Red and pure black very rarely.
			Later muffle colors.
		Later owners were *Kess*, *Kordenbusch*, an artist, *Eckert* and finally *Struntz* until about 1840.	Motives are Chinese, a feather-like foliage, designs are arranged radially or symmetrically, small detached flowers occur on jugs of *Hanau* type, and a basket of fruit with birds is a favorite. The *Vögleinkrüge* or jugs of *Hanau* form with strewn tiny birds and flowers in blue on slate blue are typical.

These last jugs are even made to the present day as a tourist ware and were produced also in the 18th century at *Hanau*, *Frankfort* and *Ansbach*.

Landscapes of local character, biblical scenes and genre are typical of *Nuremberg*.

Rococo is seldom used and when it is it follows the engravings of *Nilson* and *Augsburg*.

Another specialty is the *Sternschüssel* a large or small round dish with a sunken star in the center and six depressions of heart shape around it. Here again we find a typical Near Eastern "sweetmeat dish" such as were made at *Rhages* and *Sultanabad*.

Still another type are the "rosette jugs" with *Hanau* shape but what Hannover calls "pierced Gothic rosettes" on either side of the globular body. We find their prototypes in the metal ones of Persia in which charcoal was placed to keep the contents warm.

WR is one of their signatures but we do not know which.

Purple pictures and those in *"Schwarzlot"* were done mostly by the outside painters or *"Hausmaler."*

Bayreuth	*"Bayreuth. K."* or *Bayr. K.* or *B.K.* for (Bayreuth-Knöller) or *B.F.S.* for (Fränkel and Schreck) *B.P.F.* for (Pfeiffer and Fränkel) or *B.P.* plus painter's marks	c1720—erected by *Johann Georg Knöller* 1745—purchased by the *burgomasters Fränkel* and *Schröckh.* Later came into the hands of *Johann Georg Pfeiffer* who held it until 1767 then to *Wetzel.* 1767 to 1783 it was managed by *Oswald.* 1735 to 1763 at its height but was still esteemed in 1795.	Shapes were usual jugs, lobed body and plaited handle jugs, pear-shaped jugs and cylindrical tankards, waiters or trays, inkstands, candlesticks, etc.

Pale blue glaze like that of *Nuremberg*. The chief color being a light blue veiled by many small white specks.

Decoration of *Laub-und Bandelwerk* forming a rim around the dishes similar to the *lambrequin* designs with a monogram or shield of arms in the center. (See *Hamburg Museum*)

Muffle color was employed earlier here than elsewhere. Scattered flowers and birds occur. (See *Würzburg Mus.*) Some of the colored wares were painted by *Joseph Philipp Danhofer* and are very like *Vienna* porcelain in the period of *du Paquier* (1718–1743).

CHART OF GERMAN AND CENTRAL EUROPEAN FACTORIES—*Continued*

			Another type is in shiny brown stoneware decorated in silver or, infrequently, gold which it will be remembered was made in imitation of *Böttger's* early ware.
Amberg (Upper Palatinate)	Name of *Amberg* and *date*, 1774. *AB* in monogram	1759—*Simon Hetzendörfer* and now exists.	One coffee-pot known at *Sèvres* painted with polychrome, a butterfly and flowers. (See also *Luitpoldmuseum, Würzberg*)
Ansbach or *Onolzbach* (Middle Franconia)	Ansp:popp— 1768	c1710—*Matthäus Bauer* also *Johann Caspar Ripp* 1747 worked but became the proprietor in 1769, *Georg Christoph Popp*. *Georg* took also *Johann Gottfried Popp* as partner. 1791—*Johann Julius* and *Georg Ludwig* Popp. Ended in 1807.	Not only *Ripp* but also *Johann Georg Toglieb* was an artist there. Copied *Rouen* but in 1730 probably under *Georg Christoph Popp* gained some difference in style, also *Bayreuth*. Chinese *famille verte* made as well as at *Delft* and many other classes of Far Eastern porcelain and in bright colors including a brilliant emerald green. Some rims of dishes were made in the *Laub-und Bandelwerk*. Coats of arms in *famille verte* colors. *Imari* ware with red and gold with deep strong blue glaze and frequent relief ornament in vases, tureens, bottles and bowls—also with *unfired* gold and cinnabar which is mostly worn off. Rarely they were made with lacquer alone and not on the blue glaze. Of course these are copies of the "Canton Mandarin wares." The blue is deep and heavy and often outlined with blackish manganese. Blue and white tureens and tankards of c.1730 have border ornaments of concentric semicircles. On the front of the tankards is generally a pink with petals striped lengthways in yellow and green in high temperature colors, there are also figure subjects of a crude type and a tree of the palm type is set on either side of the handle. The last known piece is a little jar painted with common polychrome flowers and inscribed: "*Abschiidt der Porzelainmahllerey in der Feijange-Faberick in Ansbach den der 13 Febr. 1804.—Der He(rr) ist gestorben, drum sindwir all verdorben.*"—

			"Farewell of the porcelain painters in the *faïence*-factory at *Ansbach,* 13 Feb. 1804— The master is dead, therefore we are all ruined."
			But the factory struggled on for a few years more.
Höchst	Not always marked Wheel and painter's mark *JZ*—Johann Zeschinger *FH*—Friedrich Hess *I.H.*—Ignaz Hess *AL*—Adam Löwenfinck **B.B., G.C.,** M.S., LR and AMB are not yet known. (See porcelain section)	1746—*Adam Friedrich von Löwenfinck* with help of *Christoph Göltz* and *Johann Felician Clarus.* (See porcelain section) c1760 *faïence* seemed to have been discontinued. 1798 the factory was sold at auction but some moulds were evidently saved by the workmen and eventually went to *Damm.*	Ducks, geese, turkeys, partridges, pheasants and boar's heads in natural size and colors,—also lettuce, melons, artichokes, bunches of grapes, cabbages, etc.—better it is claimed than those of *Delft, Brussels, Proskau* and *Holitsch, Strasburg* and *Sleswick, Eckernförde* and *Kastrup* (near *Copenhagen*). Muffle-kiln colors like those of porcelain,—same artists did both. Baroque services (See tureen at *Troppau Museum*) *Hess* type rococo bordered dishes in yellow and black with crossed ears of corn in the center and a wreath around them (See *Strasburg Mus.*)
Damm near Aschaffenburg	*Wheel* of Höchst and a *D*	1827—the mother of *Forstmeister-Daniel Ernst Müller*	"*Fin Fayence*" or lead glaze earthenware. Many figures from the *Höchst* moulds (See *Frankfort* and *Würzburg Museums*).
Fulda	*Fuld* or FD with painter's marks or *black cross on white shield* and the signature F.v.L. for (Löwenfinck)	1736—*Adam Friedrich von Löwenfinck* having just escaped from *Meissen* and become Court enamel-painter.	Finest quality of muffle-kiln decoration with gold. It is said that 10 guilders worth was used on one set of vases by *Löwenfinck* in 1744. Great richness of coloring. (See gourd vase in *Hamburg Mus.*) Another fine vase by him is in the *Berlin Museum.*
Cassel	*HL monogram for* (Hesseland) *IHK—1719* (Johann Heinrich Koch, who rented the factory from 1719 to 1724.) "*Steitzische Vasenfabrik in Cassel*"	1680—*Georg Kumpfe* founded. Changed owners several times. 1724—*Johann Christoph Gilze* 1735—Inherited by *Ludwig Gilze*—Later financial difficulties to *Landgrave of Hesse* to 1766 when porcelain took its place. (See that section) 1771—another factory by *Simon Heinrich Steitz,* Court Confectioner Also there were other factories making the common English wares toward the end of the century.	Earliest wares unknown. Wares of blue and white like *Delft.* Copies of *Hanau* and according to *Brinckmann,* table services painted in colors. Toward the end also made stoves. Imitations of agate and jasper after *Wedgwood* (See *Hamburg Mus.*)

CHART OF GERMAN AND CENTRAL EUROPEAN FACTORIES—*Continued*

Offenbach	*O* followed by two *F's* written in one. (See porcelain section) *Offenbach 1807—Frantz G. Jülb*	1739—*Philipp Friedrich Leyh* (or *Lay*) with workmen from *Hanau* 1762—*Georg Heinrich Leyh,* his son. 1765—*Christoph Puschel* and then many others. 1807—still in existence	Decorated with flowers and among them tulips are prominent in four high temperature colors. Dish with bird in middle at *Landesmuseum, Cassell.* Also pieces at *Frankfort Museum.*
Kelsterbach and *Flörsheim* between Frankfort and Mayence		1758—*Kelsterbach* by *Johann Christian Frede* 1760—took in *Kaspar Maintz* Later made porcelain it is supposed	Wares of everyday use,—some like latest wares of *Hanau,* others like imitations of porcelains with blue flowers. In *Hamburg Mus.* there is a statuette of *Judith* with the head of *Holofernes* marked HD (*Hessen Darmstädtische.*)
Flörsheim	FH (Flörs Heim) monogram Same but with an impressed bunch of grapes, surmounted by his initials MJW	1765—*Georg Ludwig Müller* 1773—sold to the *Carthusian Monastery at Mayence,* who had it managed by *Kaspar Dreste* of *Hofheim.* 1781—leased to *Matthias Joseph Weingärtner.* 1797—*Kronenbold* and his nephew *Machenhauer* to 1846 and is still operating	At best resembles that of *Hanau* and simple peasant wares with more than usually smooth glaze. A center piece at *Hamburg* in high temperature colors is better than ordinary. *Weingärtner* produced "English" ware painted with roses and other flowers in blue on shapes of earlier wares.
Durlach	No identifying marks. Numerals from 1 to 8 painted in black which seem to indicate size. Also names of painters Löwer, Keim, Dumas and Karl Wettach Only in 19th century *"Durlach"* impressed on "English" ware.	1749—uncertain beginnings before this date (See *Stoehr-Der Cicerone* II. (1910), p. 310.) * *Johann Adam Benchiser* (or *Benckieser*) Did not end until about middle of 19th century	*Brinckmann* tells us the body is pale yellowish-grey sometimes of reddish cast. The tankards and jugs with the exception of the earliest are unglazed on the bottom and show rough string marks caused in separating them from the wheel. Blue is pale and washed out in earlier pieces and stronger later. Much manganese was used and often has white specks. The green is pale, bluish and dim. The yellow is lemon color shaded with ochre. In earlier pieces there is a brownish-grey and in later a dry brick-red. Black outlines and inscriptions are usual. Mostly the wares are jugs with pewter cover and foot-rim decorated with figures employed in industrial work framed in slight rococo frames on front. There is generally an inscription—name of person who ordered the piece, date, an aphorism in rhyme or something of the sort. On either side of the handle are flowers, roses,

			tulips or forget-me-nots. This type lasted into 19th century even with asymmetrical framework to the pictures long after they had gone out of style.

"English ware" buff or rarely white, with yellow, yellowish-brown or white (rarely) glaze. White wares as a rule are unpainted or with landscapes in blue or flowers in colors. Yellow has frieze of vine leaves in brown or black. |
| *Mosbach* in Baden | T for (Tännich) ? *MB* below an electoral hat like a *crown.* Also *"Mossbach"* and *date.*

CT for (Carl Theodor) in Monogram as on the Frankenthal but without crown of latter.

In 1806 when Mosbach was made part of Baden, the mark was CF for (Carl Friedrich)

"Steingut" is stamped *M* or *Mosbach* | 1770—*Pierre Berthevin* (See *Marieberg*) and *Johann S. F. Tännich* from *Meissen* and *Strasburg* who later went to *Jever* and *Kiel,* before coming to *Mosbach.* 1774—*Tännich* was manager and 1781—*Carl Theodor* put *Johann Georg Friedrich List* in charge and *Tännich* went to *Mannheim,* and *Frankenthal.* 1787—*List* departed with most of the capital and *Roemer & Co.* had it until 1828. Still in existence with commercial wares. | None of the earliest wares are known. After *Tännich* arrival there is a rococo clock in the palace at *Karlsruhe* marked "*Mossbach . . . 1774*" At *Munich* is a portrait medallion of *Elector Carl Theodor* done in 1783 and at *Würzburg* are parts of a service with polychrome landscapes.

The jugs are much like those of *Durlach* and tankards are done with a name or motto enclosed in a wreath of flowers, and plates with mottos.

The latter more ordinary wares are frequently painted with forget-me-nots and cornflowers.

The factory also tried to make the "English" *"Steingut"* but they have a grey or dirty white glaze and are not painted. |
| *Ludwigsburg* | Two *C's* crossed but without the crown which is on the porcelain. Similar to Niderviller mark of the Comte de Custine

Or crossed C's above a W.

Or crossed C's above a B. | 1763—Also made *faïence* (See porcelain section for full story of factory.) | Rare and uncertain because of confusion of marks.

Colossal white bust of Charles I *Duke of Württemberg* now at *Stuttgart.*

At *Sèvres* a covered jar marked with crossed C's above a W and decorated with muffle-colors and partly worn off lacquer gilding.

In *Hamburg* is an oval dish with large floral monogram in middle and four blue cartouches with groups of fruit on a black ground while there is a similar one in the *V.A.M.*—Also at *Hamburg* a tureen with branch of lemons on lid and painting in high fire manganese, yellow and green, marked with B under the crossed C's. |

CHART OF GERMAN AND CENTRAL EUROPEAN FACTORIES—*Continued*

Göppingen in *Württemberg* Do not confuse with **Göggingen** in **Bavaria**	*Stag's horn* from the arms of *Württemberg* sometimes with IMPH which may mean (*Johann Matthias Plieder-Häuser*) ?	1741—*Andreas Pliederhäuser* 1749—took partner, *Christian Rupprecht* from *Hamburg, Delft, Fulda*, etc.—Later, *Cyriacus Loubert* and *Adam Fichtmayer*, painters from *Hanover* were employed In 1753 *Andreas Pliederhäuser* died in poverty and his son, *Johann Matthias* inherited the privilege. Nothing is heard for 35 years, in 1788 there is record of tariff troubles. End unknown.	Reddish-buff body with thick greyish glaze. The decoration is in blue and sometimes of two shades as a special feature. Later pieces of the stag's horn mark are chiefly of peasant pottery and no really artistic wares seem ever to have been turned out.
Schrezheim near *Ellwangen*	*B* under a small *arrow*.	1752—*Johann Baptist Bux* and carried on by his heirs after his death in 1800 to 1872 when it was destroyed by fire.	In the *Chapel of St. Anthony* at *Schrezheim* is an altar-tabernacle of great size and bold rococo design. In *Würzburg* is a large statuette of *St. Nepomuk*. Also made vegetable tureens in shape of cabbages, melons, etc. Most productions available to collectors are artless and homely. One group has a pale blue glaze but white is more usual. They are painted in blue or the high-temperature colors with a yellow. The designs are of "Indian" or "German" flowers and in the style of *Rouen*.
Crailsheim about 12 miles south of *Ellwangen*	"*Crailsheim*"	Not known	Tankard with man waving a moss-green flag and gripping a man who stands at his side. Others have bouquets of flowers in *Strasburg* style in moss-green and yellowish-brown.
Oettingen *Bavaria* later, transferred to *Schrattenhofen*	"*Oettingen*" or an L over an Ö separated by a stroke Later wares are marked *Schrattenhofen*	1735—Not known 1740—*Johann Ulrich Sperl* 1748—taken over by *Köhler*.	In *Berlin* is a good tankard of about 1750 and with the L-Ö mark which is ascribed to Gottfried Leinfelder. It has a fine rococo feeling of scrolls and sprigs of foliage around a sort of shield holding a center medallion of flowers. The foot has a typical Chinese cross-hatched band with open panels. They made also a brown stoneware of Bayreuth style.

CHART OF GERMAN AND CENTRAL EUROPEAN FACTORIES—*Continued*

Göggingen not to be confused with *Göppingen* Was later transferred to *Friedberg*.	*CB* with or without a *crown* may be a correct mark? for (Chur-Bayern) also JH for (Joseph Hackl) ?	1748—*Prince-Bishop of Augsburg* 1749 *Joseph Hackl* was made modeller 1752—He owned it.	Pieces painted with flowers in soft, subdued, high-temperature colors. Chinese flowers of really good character were done here in blue and also in high-fired colors. (See oval platter in *Gewerbemuseum*, at *Reichenberg*.) In *Lund, Sweden*, there is a marked oblong dish with wavy edge and painted in blue with shield flanked by lions and a mottled band along the edge. *E. W. Braun* shows besides the Chinese decorated dish spoken of a wavy edged one with a basket of flowers in the center in typical South German style from the *Hamburg Museum*.
Künersberg near *Memmingen*	Usually fully marked "*Künersberg*" or *KB*	1745—*Jacob Küner* and lasted until about 1770.	Imitations of ornamental designs of *Rouen* in a strong blue on a perfect white glaze on some dishes with deep curved edges and a conventionalized edge Other pieces have yellow and green. Others have several colors with a yellow-green predominating All simple and well made. Also vases with rococo relief ornament probably by *Johann Ulrich Sperl*. Gold was also used. A wide variety of design including almost all styles.
Coburg		1739—	Only a few isolated pieces known.
Dorotheenthal near *Arnstadt*	*AB* monogram for "*Augustenburg*" where *Elizabeth Albertine of Schwarzburg-Sondershausen*, had her seat as dowager. She was a patroness for some time. *J. G. Fliegel Arnstadt d. 9 May 1775*	1720—*Johann Theobald Frantz, Wilhelm Kanja* and *Johann Schnöter* are mentioned as manufacturers but the factory had already been known from around 1707 or a little later by workmen from *Brunswick*. (See *Max Sauerlandt*) There were some fifty known painters, which include *Alex, Wellendorf* and *J. G. Fliegel*.	*Laub-und Bandelwerk* dish at *Bremen* is typical as is also the blue and white wine-cooler at *Nuremberg*. Blue and white and polychrome, the blue chiefly for European designs and the polychrome for Chinese. All are high-temperature colors. No muffle-kiln painting was used in any of the Thuringian factories. Vivid iron-red verging on orange plays a large part but is never used on an extended surface. The green is grey-green or blue-green and the yellow approaches dark ochre. Jug with the figure of St. George in *British Museum*, is signed by *Fliegel*

CHART OF GERMAN AND CENTRAL EUROPEAN FACTORIES—*Continued*

Erfurt	Town mark a *wheel with six spokes* and painter's marks, one exactly like that of Joseph Hannong	There were three factories:— 1717—*Johann Gottfried Vorberg* and *Johann Ludwig Schumann.* 1719—a concession was granted for a new factory. 1734—Still a third was granted to *Johann Paul Stieglitz* and later his son, *Johann Christoph* between 1750 and 1754. 1791—His son in turn *Friederich Christoph Stieglitz* 1792—no mention and must have ended its work.	Colors same as those of *Dorotheenthal* but brighter, a fine brick-red, light olive-green and bright lemon-yellow with rich use of blue while the manganese is less prominent. No new shapes. A design much like that of Persian 17th century wares is seen around the edge of plates and on cylindrical tankards. It is a series of graduated strokes forming four "suns" with intermediate play of the same sort of strokes:— A typical plate in the *Museum Fredericianum in Cassel* shows also a triple fish motive much like that of the Persians and certainly not indigenous to this inland town. Others have ships or landscapes reserved on manganese grounds. One small group has grass-green designs outlined in manganese. Also fine flower painting was done in imitation of porcelain.
Abtsbessingen about 12 miles south-west of Sondershausen	*Hay-fork* from *Schwarzburg* arms	1766 or earlier—*Heinrich Christoph Muth* The last owner was supposed to be named *Wolff* and died in 1816.	Vases with reserved panels painted in blue on a yellow ground, a pyramid of modelled flowers painted in green, red, yellow and blue, a blue and white garden vase and also a stove in the same treatment, jugs, tankards, inkstands, etc. can be seen at the castle at Gehren and in the museum at Halle. They have a thick, low-fired, pale clay body with soft cream colored glaze and may be painted either with blue only or with several color combinations.
Dresden Saxony	No marks in first period	1707—It will be remembered that *Böttger* sent for *Peter Eggebrecht* (See Porcelain) and later he left the factory at *Dresden* to him and it passed down through the *Eggebrecht* family until in 1768—it became the property of *Christiane Sophie von Hörisch.* 1782—it was taken over by her son, *Carl Gottlieb Hörisch* 1783—it stopped.	*Brinckmann* at the *Hamburg Museum*, and *Zimmermann* conclusively respectively guessed at the wares and finally proved them definitely to include:— A 32 inch blue and white cylindrical vase with tall cylindrical neck very close to the Chinese shape and decorated with reserve rectangular medallions holding the "precious things" and flower decorations all in perfect Chinese style, with an uneven glaze with a tendency to "slide off" as Hannover says, and a blue with a tendency to form "eyes" or bubbles.

CHART OF GERMAN AND CENTRAL EUROPEAN FACTORIES—*Continued*

			Some covered vases more of Italian style, and a series of jugs with the arms of *Poland* and *Saxony* and the AR for *(Augustus Rex)* on them all in the same blue on the same glaze.
			Other small vases have lacquer colors of the type used before fired colors were produced here.
			And finally other faïence figures from *Böttger's* models.
	D.H. for (Dresden-Hörisch)		Later wares include similar drug-jugs or vases marked D.H. and dated 1781—long after *Augustus the Strong* had died. They must have been made to fill in sets by the later owners. Also pieces had high-fired colors; cornflower-blue, and yellowish green being characteristic. Became poorer and poorer in quality.
Hubertusburg	A *tree* surrounded with *three stars* with "*Hubertusburg*" below it, and below this T for (Tännich) Also H with T below it.	1770—*Johann Samuel Friedrich Tännich* backed by *Count von Lindenau* till 1774—then the count took over full management —But *Count Marcolini* and his *Meissen* factory made so much trouble that *Count Lindenau* finally placed his factory at the feet of the Elector asking only for a service as a "gracious memento"	A few pieces of *Tännich* period are known (See Dresden Museum) one is a vase painted with muffle-kiln flowers over a lemon-yellow lead-glaze, while another is painted with a bouquet in tones of purple on a sea-green ground. On a white plate painted with flowers scattered in the porcelain manner, is an H and a T below it.
	19th century "*Wedgwood*" stamped.	1776–1835 it was under *Marcolini* and made "English" earthenware From 1814 to 1835 it was named:— "*Königliche sächsische Steingutfabrick Hubertusburg.*" In 1835 it was sold to a man of business from *Leipzig* and declined until 1848.	Best wares were imitations of *Wedgwood* (See *Dresden Mus.*) but they are hard to classify being like many others made in German factories and stamped "*Wedgwood.*" Of brittle material and with a glaze likely to crackle. Ordinary useful ware only.
Funke in Berlin		c1700—*Cornelius Funke* was not the first but was the first we know much about	A large center piece in the palace of *Charlottenburg* has the eagle of *Brandenburg* on it. Jardinieres and plates with the monogram of *Frederick III at Berlin* in the *Hohenzollernmuseum.*
		1756—*Carl Friederich Lüdicke* obtained another privilege.	Wares are not surely identified.

CHART OF GERMAN AND CENTRAL EUROPEAN FACTORIES—*Continued*

Potsdam	"*Potsdam*" —*1740* *P* with an *R* beneath it for (Potsdam-Rewendt)	c1740—*Christian Friedrich Rewendt* 1768—His sons, *Friedrich Wilhelm* and *Johann Christian Rewendt* inherited. 1770—*Johann* was full proprietor. 1775—bankrupt, and *Sartory* took over factory 1790—sold to wife of *General von Linckersdorff* 1790—*Sartory* founded a new factory 1800—sold to *Gottfried B. von Eckardstein.*	Most excellent imitations of *Delft* (were actually thought to be *Delft* for many years) but with a special character of their own. *O. Riesebieter* on the evidence of the one vase at Berlin in the *Schlossmuseum* marked "*Potsdam*—*1740*" set aside in 1912 a group that had been called *Delft*, with the following characteristics: Strongly reddish-toned body, shapes are ribbed or fluted inverted pear shapes with flaring feet and are more narrow than the corresponding *Delft* wares and finally a special decoration from *Delft* but differing and more constantly used is the peacock among Chinese flowers, with also a band of spirals such as we see on some *Ming* porcelain of the *Wan Li sur biscuit* type. The colors are intense blue alone and the high-temperature colors:—yellow, green, iron-red, along with a few in seagreen ground and some in cold lacquer colors.
Danzig	No marks	1658—There is mention of glazed wares made there. 18th century had several factories but wares are not differentiated.	Partly blue and white and partly polychrome and some are plastic but all are crude and, as Hannover says, "boorish." The stoves are better and the tiles for them have raised in relief like frames.
Königsberg	Stamped *HE* for "*Hofrath Ehrenreich*" The "*Hofrath*" is a title bestowed on him in *Sweden*. Also dated with day, month and year and has painter mark. "English" wares stamped with a K, sometimes several times.	1776—*Johann Eberhard Ludwig Ehrenreich*, after having gone broke at *Straslund*. 1788—Sold to *Provinzial-Controller, Buvey* at auction. Changed owners several times and about 1808 *Ehrenreich* died at 80 and the factory ended in 1810.	Blue is the leading color and only a sparing use of manganese. The decoration is all of "German" flowers; no Chinese. The glaze is greyish or grey-blue in cast. The blue is intense. Later "English" wares.
	"factory of the *Brothers Collin*"	1776—Another factory was started by *Paul Heinrich Collin* and his brother. c 1786	All its efforts were directed to the imitating of *Wedgwood*. (See large brown vase in the *Prussian Museum at Königsberg*) Portrait medallions of black "basalt" ware and white in *Berlin Museum*.
Zerbst Duchy of Anhalt	*Z* in combination with other letters. *La* or *J.C.La* is for the painter	1721—*Johann Caspar Ripp* of *Nuremberg* fame, *Ansbach* and *Frankfort* as well as	Blue and white and high-fired polychrome colors and too various to bring out any characteristics.

CHART OF GERMAN AND CENTRAL EUROPEAN FACTORIES—*Continued*

	Johann Christian Langendorf	*Hanau* and *Brunswick.* Closed in 1861 (See *Stieda's* history)	A greyish-green color apparently painted over a bluish foundation, the use of yellow in combination with red, which is rare in north German wares, the use of applied and painted flowers with a flower acting as knob for tureen covers—are typical. Later did the usual lead-glazed wares.
Bernburg Anhalt	*"Bernburg—1725 Freytag"* VF monogram for *Victor Friedrich prince of Anhalt-Bernburg* from 1721	There must have been a factory in the early 18th century but we have, as yet, so little data that no history is possible.	Set of three vases of *Delft* shape and painted with Chinese designs in blue and manganese with the middle piece bearing the mark opposite. (See *Sauerlandt* report.) A plate in *Halle* and a foot warmer in the castle of *Dessau* marked VF. Also other wares such as the oval dish in *Hamburg* with blue and white foliated scrollwork or *Laub-und Bandelwerk.*
Magdeburg	*"J. P. Guichard"*	Not known	"English" earthenware with or without the name mark and a white glazed portrait medallion in the Berlin Museum.
Mecklenburg		There were places which are still not known. (See *F. Schlie*)	Renaissance period glazed stoves and unglazed architectural pieces 18th century wares unidentified.
Schwerin	*Z-like sign* and *A Sverin* with *K* below **also** *A.S.-K.*	c1760—*Appelstädt* founded and later it came to his son-in-law, *Malon,* and exists even today.	At the *Schwerin Museum* there is a collection including "tureens after pewter models," and that is about all we know. (See *Brinckmann*)
Brunswick		1707—*Duke Anton Ulrich* with *Johann Philipp Franz* from *Saxony* as mgr. 1711—*Heinrich Christoph von Horn* and his partner *Werner Julius Günther von Hantelmann.* Then changed hands repeatedly.	Began with blue and white but soon developed several colors.
	VH for von Hantelmann	1744–1749—two brothers, *Heinrich Werner* and *Christoph Friedrich Ludwig von Hantelmann.*	Took up plastic work, modeled and colored fruit, asparagus, melon, grapes, etc., tureens and others in shape of birds on dishes amongst fruit.
	R & B *J.E.B.* *J.H.R.*	1749–1756 *Johann Erich Behling* and *Johann Heinrich Reichardt* 1756–1773—*Duke of Brunswick* 1773—let to *Johann*	At *Hamburg* a plate after *Nuremberg* with a basket of fruit and ornamental designs on rim in vivid blue, dark manganese and lemon-yellow, green and brick-red.

CHART OF GERMAN AND CENTRAL EUROPEAN FACTORIES—*Continued*

	J.B.R.	*Benjamin Rabe* who bought it in 1776. 1803 *Rabe* died and it came to an end.	
	Two *C's* crossed like those of *Ludwigsburg* and the *Comte de Custine*	1745—Another factory by—*Rudolf Anton Chely* till 1756.	Vegetable and animal tureens as above
Hanover at Wrisbergholzen	*WR* in monogram with painter's marks of *letters* or *numerals*	1737—*Vielstich* probably a relative of *Johann Christoph Vielstich* c1800—*L. V. Gerverot* who was for many years director of *Fürstenberg,* the porcelain factory. Lasted until about 1830.	*Kestner Museum at Hanover* —a large octagonal covered vase in Chinese-Dutch style with flowers in bluish-violet, —also a blue and white globular vase on high stand painted in similar manner. Combinations of blue, manganese, yellow and green were used. Also certain porphyry-colored tankards with panels reserved in blue. No muffle-kiln colors were used.
Münden	*M* or three *crescents* taken from the arms of *von Hanstein* and painter's marks	1746—Grew out of early pipe and pottery factory of *Carl Friedrich von Hanstein* 1775—Moved nearer to town and was inherited by his son *Johann Carl Friedrich von Hanstein,* and was soon extended for manufacture of the "English" ware.	*Faïence* with pierced decoration having double walls, the outer being perforated in the case of vases or other vessels and the rims of the plates being perforated. At the point of intersection of the mesh is usually a forget-me-not or other small flower in slight relief and colored. Manganese-purple and a dull green are more conspicuous than the blue, which, however, is sometimes used alone. There is also a yellow and all colors are high-fired; no muffle-kiln colors were ever used. Also wares in green and purple alone painted with landscapes or flowers in *Meissen* style. Plain white stones and also ones with gallant scenes in blue.
Aumund northwest of *Bremen*	M.T.T. D. & W.T. A v E	1751—Three merchants *Johann Christoph Mülhausen,* and *Diederich* and *Wilhelm Terhellen,* organized it with *Johann Christoph Vielstich* as mgr. 1757—bankrupt and sold to *Albrecht von Erberfeldt* who got a *Strasburger* mgr. and workmen from *Swabia*	A melon in natural colors marked M.T.T. *at Hamburg.* (Ill.) Blue and white tureen at *Kunstgewerbemuseum, Bremen* marked D. & W.T. (For *D. & W. Terhellen,* after the death of *Mülhausen* in 1775) Also a polychrome tankard in the same museum with Chinese figures, which has A v E (for *Albrecht von Erberfeld*)

CHART OF GERMAN AND CENTRAL EUROPEAN FACTORIES—*Continued*

Lesum	*V* or *Vi* The painters marked the wares "putting a stroke under the name of their employer and the first letter of their own name under the stroke," as Hannover says.	1752—*Johann Christoph Vielstich* after working one year at *Aumund* settled at *Lesum* until he died in 1792.	Tureen with flower sticking up on cover similar to the way they were made at *Zerbst* (mentioned above) and painted with a shield of arms in blue, at *Hamburg Mus.* Tops of tea-tables, ink-stands, *potpourri,* vases, melon-shaped boxes, fruit baskets, wall and stove tiles, etc., according to *Brinckmann,* the last brown and black as well as marbled and blue-and-white. In the *Vestlandske Kunstindustrimuseum* at *Bergen* is a stag lying down, in manganese on green grass. At *Bremen* is a similar hound and also some tankards sprayed with manganese and with galloping horses and flowers in reserve,—ink-pots painted with flowers and a pierced basket with stand, but far better than these are the blue and white stove and some tiles in purple and green with *Hamburg* influence. (Ill. several and stove) The body is reddish, its glaze usually yellowish or bluish but infrequently pure white. The colors are blue, an insipid bluish green, several yellow shades, and—*no red.*
Jever	*Jev* or *Jever*	1760—Our old rambling acquaintance, *Tännich* turned up here and started a factory that had a difficult existence and lasted until 1776. *Sebastien Heinrich Kirch* who had worked at the *Chely* factory at *Brunswick* is, according to the authority *Riesebieter,* the sculptor.	A very few high class works such as the blue and white center piece of a boy with a basket on his head from the *Reisebieter Collection, Oldenberg.* Butter-dishes in the shape of swans and heavy tureens with freely modeled flowers and foliage show *Brunswick* and *Zerbst* influences.

There are perhaps a dozen other unimportant factories for which Graesse gives more or less well founded marks but their wares are very few and not distinguished.

It is strange upon reflection that we have found a strong Near Eastern influence and Indian influence in the faïence factories and that none of this was reflected in the porcelain of the day. Also the authorities became so absorbed in the correcting of the wrong habit of calling Chinese design "Indian" that they completely overlooked the fact that there really was Indian design in use. In fact the dilettante decorators of the 19th and 20th centuries have forgotten, or never heard of any Indian design in the 18th century in Europe at all.

Though it may be said that on the whole the workmanship in faïence was not so perfect as that in porcelain yet it must be said that the taste shown by the faïence potters or their common customers was superior to that shown in porcelain. There was a more reasonable approach and the medium was better expressed. The limited number of colors obtained brought about a natural harmony or at least safety of color scheme. Many of the factories never used muffle-kiln colors which broadened the palette but often brought unpleasant effects. Then again there were fewer forgeries because faïence did not as a rule command such high prices. The art of faïence did not wholly escape the attentions of the forgers, however, for Fleischmann of Nuremberg copied Hanau, Nuremberg, Frankfort and Bayreuth but his work is so cheap and badly made that it could not fool anyone who had seen the originals.

SWITZERLAND

The Swiss wares offer little but reflections from those of Italy and the other large surrounding countries. Most of the early work was in the form of stoves at such places as Winterthur where the Pfau, Ehrhart, Graf, Volger and Sulzer families worked into the early part of the 18th century. Other

centers were Stechborn, where Daniel Meier worked, Zurich and Berne, where Emmanuel Jean Früting (1745–1798) made blue landscape tiles and polychrome flowered ones. Probably other wares were made at these places but not many have been set aside. They were smoky in tone and had subdued colors though some had charm and delicacy. The factories at Beromünster and Lenzburg made household wares. At the former Andreas Dolder started at the end of the 18th century while at Lenzburg one factory was started in 1763 by A. H. and H. C. Klug and another later by Hans Jacob Frey. Most unmarked Swiss faïence is attributed not entirely correctly to one or the other of these factories unless it is the "Winterthur" type in which case it may not have come from that place either. This type consists of plates with broad rims decorated with arabesques in blue or with large flowers or fruits in colors or left plain, while the center has a shield of arms. The colors are high temperature ones only.

Fig. 1172. Swiss stove of 17th cent. decorated in blue, red and yellow, from mansion of Col. Von Sprecher Maienfeld. Ht. c. 8'. International Studio Art Corp.

Zurich wares are not easily identified unless marked Z. Both porcelain and faïence were made at the same factory and by the same workmen. The factory was not in the city but at Schorn near Bendikon. It was founded in 1763 and lasted until 1766. The poet and painter Salomon Gessner lost most of his fortune in the venture. The technical director was Adam Spengler, the same who discovered a way of printing pictures on porcelain after the English invention. After the initial failure the company dragged along into the usual decline and making of common "steingut," or lead-glazed white earthenware.

Swiss stove of 18th cent., decorated in blue on white. Made for a Basel Bishop in 1722. Ht. 4′ 5¼″.
International Studio Art Corp.

SWISS FAÏENCE STOVE (1722)

PLATE 205

AUSTRIAN TERRITORIES

The central location of the Austrian territories made them naturally absorb the various impulses. Wares from Italy, Nuremberg and other South German places, and even those of Delft had a stimulating effect on the peasant wares. There was nothing exclusive about them for most were turned out by the gross and peddled by the "Haussirer" and sold at country fairs but they were individual pieces instead of sets and made to commemorate some occasion such as a wedding, baptism or birthday and many had inscriptions and mottos. These were made at Graz, Gmunden and Salzburg among many other places in the Alpine districts. They were also extensively turned out in Moravia and Hungary. These peasant wares of Slovak or non-Slovak sorts with their simple flower ornament in enamel-like colors of yellow, green, blue and purple, even in the 19th century had more life and interest than those wares done for the Imperial and Royal Austro-Hungarian nobility at the "Majolika-Geschirrfabrik" at Holitsch.

This peasant ware is commonly known as "Habaner ware." I have been unable to obtain pictures of it for this book but the principle of alternation is well understood, the spacing is original and effective, the drawing is swift and direct as though the design had been well thought out in advance. These plates change their tempo much as does the Tzigane music and after the commercially choked stupidity of many of the better known wares they bring a joyous life that moves us and is lost like the music itself for they existed only from about 1635 into the early 19th century and had little after effect. They were started by Anabaptists who settled in the 16th century on the border between Moravia and Hungary and had with them potters who at first seemed influenced by the "Winterthur" wares of Switzerland.

The "Majolika-Geschirrfabrik" was at Holitsch near Göding straight north of Pressburg. The factory was founded in 1743 by Francis of Lorraine, consort of Maria Theresa. The wares were strongly influenced by those of France probably because Nicolas Germain, the foreman, had come from there. In 1750 Charles François Leduc was director and between 1756 and 1760 they even called the wares by such names as, "Strasburg salad-bowls," "Strasburg tankards," etc. But the factory also obtained models from Vienna and some plates are in the style of Castelli and show that the factory also kept its eyes open to the south. It imitated Meissen, Rouen, Nevers, Niderviller, Marseilles, Moustiers and Montpellier as well as Chinese and Japanese wares. Also many of its things were copied from Proskau as they were in turn copied there from workmen who had left the Hungarian factory.

In general the wares are decorated in both high-fired and muffle-kiln colors, the body is red and fine grained but otherwise there is no distinguishing characteristics unless it be the mark, which is generally HF standing for "Holitscher Fabrik." The H also occurs alone or accompanied by another H, a P, etc. Generally the mark is in clear blue but it was made also in manganese and rarely in light green.

The tureens in the form of birds are best known but these were copies as all else. From about 1786 the factory made "English ware" stamped

"Holitsch," and in 1827 it closed. Fakes of even these uninteresting wares were made and marked H.

POLAND

PROSKAU FIRST PERIOD (1763–1769)

With the help of workmen from Holitsch, Count Leopold von Proskau started a factory in 1763, in the village of Proskau near Oppeln, southeast of Breslau. The first wares are closely like those of Paul and Joseph Hannong of Strasburg and are painted in muffle-kiln colors in large flowers, especially carnations, in strong and heavy colors including sulphur-yellow, crimson and lifeless pale green. Another type seems to have copied porcelain with plastic flowers. The first period came to an end when the count fell dead in a duel in 1769 and the estate came to Johann Carl von Dietrichstein, who was an excellent patron. The mark of the first period was a P in baroque style.

PROSKAU SECOND PERIOD (1769–1783)

The second or "Dietrichstein Period" is strongly plastic in its flowers for decoration of vessels and its figures, of allegorical, mythological and such subjects. Many animal, bird and vegetable tureens were made as well as dishes in the form of leaves and candlesticks like trees. The colors are much as before except that the yellow is subdued and the yellow-green becomes dark green. The red becomes duller and duller until in 1780 it is a reddish-brown. The blue also became less and less conspicuous until it finally is lost entirely. The mark is D P in manganese brown or dark grey-blue.

PROSKAU THIRD PERIOD (1783–1788)

In 1783 the count sold the estate to Frederick the Great of Prussia having transferred his own undertaking to Weisskirchen, Moravia. Frederick appointed Johann Gottlieb Leopold, the district councillor who in 1786 took the factory on lease. The wares are now changed, being only useful things decorated in monochrome, chiefly pink. Some colored wares were made but they were dull in color and dry of design. They are all marked with P in manganese brown or blue.

PROSKAU FOURTH PERIOD (1788–1850)

English models in white, red or black clay, the latter without glaze were now made. The classic Empire was taken so seriously that real Greek vases were closely copied in 1793 under the direction of Prof. Bach of Breslau. In 1796 transfer printing was introduced and the plates were supplied chiefly by Degotschon and Endler whose names are sometimes seen on the wares. Brown-glazed ware decorated in silver, or plain in the style of Bayreuth was also made but not marked. Perhaps it was not a stock product. All the late "steingut" is impressed with "Proskau."

About the only partly original thing that the factory was noted for was the heaping of vegetables, fruits or flowers on pieces in the second period.

This went so far that on one egg-shaped tureen in Copenhagen, with fruit and flowers on it, a bunch of grapes is at one end and divided also so as to form a bowl and receptacle attached. Another idea was shown in a vase which was kept fairly plain but the cover is smothered under a large bouquet of flowers.

The Belvedere factory produced a service in 1776 which King Stanislaus Augustus Poniatowski sent in 1789 with a special mission to the Turkish Sultan. This is decorated in enamel colors and gold and inscribed in Turkish, "These gifts are sent to the Tsar of the race of Osman by the King of the Lekhs in proof of his most complete affection and utter devotion—in the capital of Warsaw." In Hamburg there is also a pair of covered "temple jar" vases with flowers and rocks in something like the Chinese manner. They also have bright colors. In Berlin is another vase with famille verte bird, rock and tree designs on a yellow ground in reserved medallions. Others are known with freely modeled flowers of Marieberg and Chinese "hawthorn" patterns.

One other factory of note was erected at Telechany by Michael Oginski toward the end of the 18th century. From there come vases with exotic rams' heads and human faces in relief. Also at Warsaw was another factory erected by a Saxon named Wolff in 1775 which copied Chinese vases in Delft style decorated with birds, flowers, etc., in blue. The Belvedere factory mark is B or "B-Varsovie" over the glaze. The "Fabryka Wolfa" used W alone. The Telechany wares are generally marked CO for Comte Oginski in dark brown.

A number of insignificant places made the "English ware" toward the end of the century.

RUSSIA

Peter the Great engaged potters while he was at Zaandam and installed them in Petersburg. The museums so far as I can find made no classifications of the early wares but Hannover says he visited there in 1913 and he describes stoves as follows, "Enormous and often magnificent flat faïence stoves, painted in some cases with flowers in colors, in others entirely in manganese with a figure enclosed by ornament on each tile, in others again with figures in manganese within ornamental framework in copper green; some of them are blue-and-white in the manner of Hamburg stoves, and some of the Empire period entirely white with a figure standing free between two columns." He continues, "Some of the blue-and-white examples are perhaps to be attributed to Hamburg potters, others to Dutchmen," but this is only a guess on his part, of course.

Also at Petersburg there was a factory which made cheap household wares.

At Reval was a factory at least as old as 1773 for it is mentioned in the "Connaissances politiques" of Beausobre, though Von Manteuffel dates it 1780. The marks are R with an F below it, or Re-Fi, or Reval-Fick (for Carl Christian Fick who had studied pharmacy at Keil and practiced in Stockholm). He settled about 1765 in Reval taking over a chemist's business and later started the pottery factory. Most of the output extant is in the possession of the Fick family with a few in the Esthonian Museum at Reval and some in Petersburg and Riga. The pieces are of richly developed rococo much like those of north Germany of this time and earlier. They are in green and yellow with natural flowers in colors similar to Marieberg and Stralsund. There are also "network" wares like those of Münden, and animal, human figure and fruit and vegetable boxes of a sort of Dutch type. The most remarkable and unforeseen development is that they also made "Toby-jugs" after the English ones.

DENMARK

In Store Kongensgade, Copenhagen, the Delfs Porselins eller Hollandich Steentøys Fabrique was established in 1722, with as manager Johann Wolff, a painter from Nuremberg, but he was dismissed in 1723 and went to Stockholm. In 1727 Johan Ernst Pfau became manager and stayed until 1749. The brewer, Christian Gierløf became owner in this time and there was a suit between him and Pfau in 1752 when the latter died. Other suits seem to have taken place between this place and Kastrup and also Østerbro established by Peter Hofnagel. In 1772 or 1773 the factory began to feel the competition from England but stuck to its blue and white wares to the end. These are high fired, buff and coarse of body. The glaze is white and only occasionally tinged with greyish-blue. It has pin holes like Delft which it most resembles and at times appears to have been "gekwaartet" like that ware. The blue is strong and clear but broken into minute specks. All drawing was done in blue. The general mark appears to be VP with at times a dot over the P, between the letters or over the down stroke of the V. Hannover suggests it should be read JP for Johan Pfau but it was also used after his time.

FIRST STORE KONGENSGADE PERIOD (1722–1727)

In Copenhagen is a beaker of vaguely Chinese feeling marked "Copenhagen J W" with the crown and cipher of Frederick IV of Denmark in the decoration. The reserved acanthus leaves, spirals, festoons of flowers and flower filled lambrequins are all typical Copenhagen in design. A similar piece shows the chequer pattern after Rouen and a Chinese emblem of four parts within a circle which also became a stock pattern of the factory. A plate marked "W-Kopenhagen-Anno 1726" has the so-called "parsley pattern." The W does not stand for Wolff but for Peter Wartberg who controlled the place after Wolff left.

SECOND STORE KONGENSGADE PERIOD (1727–c1750)

Wolff undoubtedly provided many of the designs of Nuremberg origin used by Pfau such as the basket full of flowers for plate centers. An amusing little piece of rather ingenious workmanship is a spice cabinet having four drawers and decorated in blue flowers. It is signed J. F. Pfau and dated 1737. Stars and dots were used after the Delft notion between flying birds, flowers and in the "parsley pattern." There are numbers running from 3 to 119 but their meaning is not known. Some pieces have freemasonry emblems for decoration and are dated 1747. Other "royal plates" or "Konge-tallerkener" sometimes have the monogram of Christian VI and are dec-orated with well painted lambrequins while those with the cipher of Frederick V are not so good perhaps indicating a decline. A rectangular tray and single candle wall sconce are dated by Hannover as of 1730. Both have Chinese influence. The baroque and rococo motives are to be seen on the "bishop bowls," etc. Figures and general modeling were badly done and avoided. The "bishop bowls" were in the shape of a bishop's mitre with a design of a drinking party on them and served a derisive purpose as well as being useful, as—"who should not put a cabbage in a bishop's hat or fill it up with Koldskaal?" The Roman Catholic church had abused its power and misused its riches and after Luther's time and the last defenses of Helgesen, it had fallen into disrepute.

An often used motif was that of the arms of noble families.

THE THIRD OR GIERLØF PERIOD (c 1750)

At just about the time that Gierløf came in 1750 there was a change to rococo style. Asbjorn was one of the chief artists as was also M. Momtoft. The new style was used chiefly on trays and not at all on the rococo modeled tureens. Some designs were also like those of the Japanese artist Korin consisting of large flowers drawn in the flat and well spaced, with the use of reeds and bamboo in the background to give slightly curved perpendicular lines in contrast to the rounded masses. Where Gierløf got this design we do not know but to say, as Ch. A. Been and Hannover do, that it is "merely a modification of the peonies, lotus and bamboo of Chinese porcelain," is not true for it is too well organized to have occurred in so immediate an application and is so close to the Japanese solution of the problem, arrived at over a period of years, that it would be a miracle if two so widely different people attained so close a result.

Craftsmanship fell off but the design was more broad and direct. Han-nover scorns it somewhat in his description of a plate in Copenhagen, saying, "Even in the simplest among them, such as the plates painted with three pears or apples lying down or in the air, the slapdash manner of the brush-work may often be combined with a lively sense of the decorative effect of the great, broad strokes." Little did he know what we would become used to after Picasso! But whatever the likes and dislikes are concerning this technique, it was new to Europe and I believe it came somehow from Japan. In Seto since the early 13th century had been kilns turning out "Ishizara" or kitchen ware which is used all over Japan. An article in the *Eastern Art Annual,* Vol. III, p. 45 by M. Yanagi describes this ware and illustrates some pieces which strongly resemble the Store Kongensgade pieces. He says, "The date when these plates were made is not yet known precisely, but it is fairly certain that they were of late Tokugawa period, that is from the end of the 18th century to the beginning of the 19th." Later he says, "A Seto potter told me that 300 such plates can be made on a wheel within a day by one person, and more than that number can be painted."—"The kilns are built densely along the slope of the surrounding hills like labyrinths and their chimneys in great number stand like a forest. The sky is always black with smoke and the river is always white with clay. Even now from this old pottery town an immense number of wares are distributed all over our country." This is a little like the Chinese description of Cheng-tê Ching but probably a fair report, and some of these plates must have found their way into Gierløf's hands, just as Imari found its way to other parts of Europe.

We learn that the glaze became dull and that experimental use of the sponge was made, to give the texture of foliage. This too is a Japanese stunt.

It was thought that all of the Store Kongensgade wares were decorated in blue until the Hamburg Museum found an ink-well of the Pfau period (1727–49) with high fired colors bearing the mark and of unmistakable style. The colors are two shades of yellow, greyish-green, manganese brown and blue. In Copenhagen is also a tankard with the mark and a Japanese painting in yellow, blue, green and iron-red reserved in a white ground on a manganese background.

HP is a usual mark perhaps referring to the son, Johan Heinrik Pfau. B, C or H also occur. Note our reference to marks under each period. Pieces have brought as much as $250 or $300 but these wares are not so high class as the wares of Rörstrand, Marieberg or the Norwegian faïence of Herrebøe.

ØSTERBRO FACTORY

Peter Hofnagel established a factory in 1763 at Sortedamssø, now called the Østerbro factory. He was the Norwegian founder of the Herrebøe factory and some of his workmen came from Store Kongensgade and Kastrup, including his manager, Heinrich Wolff (not to be confused with Johann Wolff). A series of law suits with Gierløf wasted much of the substance of both places, though the final decision was in Hofnagel's favor, and he had to close down for lack of money. His advertisements show that he made all kinds of wares including blue-and-white until 1765 despite Gierløf's claim to have the sole rights to make them. At this time he turned to manganese purple and later he included blue decorations again, but it is almost impossible to identify his wares. Thor Kielland has brought together some pieces marked Ø:B:F interpreted as meaning Øster Bro Fabrik by J. Olrik, and one, a tureen with manganese flowers marked Hasrisz and IH in the cover and on the stand. This name also occurs on a rococo candlestick and blue-and-white dish among other pieces. The tureen is like wares from Sleswick and Hofnagel did advertise "tureens after the Sleswick fashion with embossed stand." The clay is grey or greyish-yellow and the glaze closely "smutted" without tendency to craze.

KASTRUP FACTORY

Jacob Fortling erected a factory in Kastrup on the island of Amager between 1749 and 1754. He was the court architect and was given permission to make every sort of ware except the "so-called Delft porcelain or Dutch stoneware which Christian Gierløf and his associates alone are permitted to

make." As Fortling wanted to copy the wares of the Westerwald, three pot-
ters were brought from Coblenz and Joseph Adam Hannong was called from
Strasburg to supervise the building of the factory, but Fortling found him
"unyttig" or useless and appointed Heinrich Wolff, who later went to
Østerbro, as manager. Frederick V was sponsor and he appointed Johann
George Richter to keep Strasburg spirit alive.

In 1761 Fortling died and his widow carried on for a year and then sold
out to Jacob Stentzler and Jes Diedrichsen, who kept Richter on as art
director. As late as 1772 it had two kilns, one for faïence and one for stoneware, and set about building another for "English ware" but in 1776 Stentzler
died. In 1777 a creditor of Diedrichsen sold the factory to Christian Detlew
Westerholdt who took in as partner N. C. Høpffner. From this time the
place became entirely commercial. In 1781 Jacob Casper Leopold Mantzius
took a lease and tried to revive the faïence but he died in 1794.

The Fortling mark was F and the wares are naturally much like those of
Strasburg on a greyish-buff almost white body not so highly fired as the Store
Kongensgåde. The glaze is thick and reddish or bluish-grey tinged and often
full of "pin pricks" and other flaws and is sometimes crazed. The red is dull;
the blue-green uneven and inclined to volatilize and settle on the white glaze;
an aquamarine seems to be of similar composition; and the yellow and other
colors are about as usual. Butter dishes in the form of an artichoke on a
saucer are in a deep blue as are also the leaves veined in black with the
floral painting. Large full blown roses and yellow parrot tulips are favorite
rococo designs, as are also pansies, honey-suckle and fanciful strewn flowers.
Tiles were also made with good figure painting. Large baroque vases surmounted by figures too big to be regarded simply as finials show good modeling. Many of the usual birds were made and there are two fine busts after
models by Saly, of Christian VI and Frederick V.

Hannover points out that the wares known as the "watchstand group" and
little dishes with high-fired colors also attributed by Frohne to this factory
do not belong here.

A price list of 1784 tells us that wares similar to "English ware" were
being made and stamped with an oval stamp with the letters CW and M
for Christian Westerholdt—and Mantzius. Many plates have fine perforated
rims with little flowers at the crossings of the strands. Slight relief was also
practiced.

The lesser Danish factories are given in the following chart:

LESSER DANISH FACTORIES

Hestkiøbgaard near *Birkerød*	1807—*Dybvad* founded as a contin- uation of the factory at the *Vesterbro*, in *Copenhagen*, which was destroyed by the English in that year. Closed about 1819	Stoves ?
Antvorskov near *Slagelse*	c 1810—*Haagen* *Christian von Astrup* Closed about 1820	We read that its sales were "endless" in 1812 *Faïence* ——— ?

LESSER DANISH FACTORIES—*Continued*

Søholm	"Søholm"	1826—A company started	Bowls with roulette-impressed borders in brown glazed, yellow glazed and in glazed red earthenware to be seen at the *Royal Porcelain Factory, Copenhagen.*
Farm of Hesbjerg west of Odense		1810—*A. C. de Heinen,* who was *Chamberlain.*	None yet identified.
Mors	Plate is marked L and ΛM below	1774—*Thomas Lund* 1779—*Saxo Aschanius and Hans Meulengracht.*	*Frohne* illustrates a plate dated 1782 and inscribed with the name of the owner within a leaf wreath and a tea-pot with poor flower decoration. Both are in blue.
Gudumlund nine miles south-east of Aalborg	A bee impressed usually with a number 1, 2 or 3. From 1808 three brown spots or a bee. Later no mark.	c1805—*Count Schimmelmann* established various industries which included a faïence factory which lasted until 1820.	Clay and its manager came from *Bornholm* and workers from Germany. It was very unskillful. Part simple *faïence* and part cream-colored earthenware like that of the English. Slight scattered flowers, etc., and all in defective high-temperature colors. The later unmarked wares are hardly distinguishable from those of the English.
Øland Island in the Limfjord	Øland—*E. Beck* 1818—B written and incised within a circle Øland—B	1814—*Eskild Beck,* from *Bornholm* and mgr. of *Gudumlund*	Ink-stand painted in blue and green with the name of the owner "*Ole Jensen Rønne*—1819" at the *Dansk Folkemuseum,* also two plates with crowned initials and the date 1820 within a wreath of flowers and another with a flower in the middle in purple, yellow, green and blue. Two are unglazed on the back. The clay is grey. Four pieces at the *Kunstindustrimuseum* are marked "Øland—B" and have slight blue patterns.
Bornholm Island, Rønne	"Spietz" impressed on body Not usually marked	*James Davenport* came in 1789 to dig coal there but failed and started a limeworks and brickworks and pipe and *faïence* factory. All failed. *Johan Spietz,* a German set up an earthenware factory on his own at *Rønne*	Pretty cream colored ink-stands sometimes picked out in green or blue see *Dansk Folkemuseum, Copenhagen.*
Sleswick	SO with L below (for *Slesvig Otte* and *Lücke*) in monogram	1755—*Ludwig von Lücke* but had to give up because of "Thoughtlessness, folly and lack of good conduct." 1758—*Johan Rambusch* became sole proprietor 1773—His son *Friederich Vollrath Rambusch* inherited.	Predominant use of manganese purple and plastic usage. The clay is pale buff almost white and the glaze is discolored almost to a grey. One small group of wares with Chinese plant ornaments after the *Meissen* style is thin and light but most of the other wares are thick and heavy.

LESSER DANISH FACTORIES—*Continued*

SO with S below and R (for Rambusch) below that.

S alone and often left unmarked.

Lohmann was one of the figure painters who signed a "bishop bowl" in the *Dansk Folkemuseum*.
Meyer is another who signed a rococo dish in the *Frohne Collection* with flower decoration.

One of the marked pieces is a relief decorated rococo tureen with the design picked out in manganese and a knob of strange twisted form, a helical round pyramid.
The factory also did "bishop bowls" as is proven by the one in *Hamburg* bearing the mark.
Another quaint conception is a punch-bowl in the form of a warship resting on rococo volutes, picked out in manganese and having scattered flowers in blue (at the same museum).

In the *Rambusch* period a grey green of either bluish or yellowish cast became a favorite color, also muffle-colors for *Meissen* type flowers came into use, but the grey green was high-fired and generally occurs with a manganese outline. There is also a slight resemblance to *Moustiers* wares, *Brinckmann* has observed. There was also a pure yellow-green of lower temperature but often used with manganese and this combination occurs on a "bishop bowl" in the *Folkemuseum* with figures and trees the trunks of which are in manganese and the foliage in the green.
There is one tray known in the Louis XVI style painted in yellow, green, blue, violet and black, and which must have been made between 1775–80.

Criseby later transferred to *Eckernförde* in 1764

C with L or AL in a monogram and also an E added.

1758—*Johann Nicolai Otte,* having sold his portion of the *Sleswick* factory to *Rambusch* when his two brothers did, set up on his own account.
1764—Transferred to *Eckernförde,* and came to a syndicate but in
1771—returned to *Otte*
Had modeller *Johann Buchwald* and painter *Abraham Leihamer,* who left c.1769.

O (for *Otte*) and E (*Eckernförde*) with B below (for *Buchwald*) and AL or L (for *Leihamer*) or other painter's marks below

A delicately painted plate in manganese is signed by both artists and *Otte* and dated 1761 (in *Hamburg*) as is a dish painted delicately in blue and two rococo candlesticks in the *Folkemuseum* and the *Kunstindustrimuseum*.
Many imitations of foreign models, for *Buchwald* had been to *Holitsch, Hungary, Rörstrand* and *Marieberg*. Later he went to *Kiel* and *Stockelsdorff*. Boar's head, cabbage, etc., tureens in the *Holitsch* manner, muffle-kiln colors and freely modelled blossoming sprays in the *Marieberg* manner and blue painting of all the others, were favorites, and a powerful blue is characteristic just as manganese is at *Sleswick*.

One small group has blue painted flowers with manga-

LESSER DANISH FACTORIES—*Continued*

again and numerals (66, 67 or 68) designating the year below again is the full mark but it also occurs in various parts.

All pieces signed AL or L may have been supervised by Leihamer but not necessarily painted by him. Sometimes his full name is signed and these are probably his own handiwork.

nese over them. These are thought to include certain watchstands that might otherwise be from *Kastrup* with the same color combination. (See *Nationalhistoriske Museum,* at *Frederiksborg.*) *Hannover* says, "the motives of decoration on *Eckernförde* faïence are about as many as the wares themselves." Had both high and low temperature colors.

The clay is higher fired than Sleswick and is warm grey with very slight greenish or reddish tone and the glaze clean white with only a slight tendency to craze.

Leihamer painted flowers, figures and also landscapes.

Also *Jahn Zopff* probably from *Meissen* was a good flower painter.

A restless rococo movement was characteristic, a spray with full blown rose is often used and a snail or butterfly among the flowers on blue and white plates is favorite.

Also occasionally plain white faïence.

Flensborg	c1764—Developed from an earlier tile works	Large garden-vases of heavy body with coarsely painted garlands in the style of *Rouen* are thought by *Brinckmann* to come from here but *Dr. Sauermann* claims that there is no supporting evidence.
Holstein Kiel	The mark was a 3 storeys mark: K on top, T (*Tännich*) below and some painter such as P below. The others were A, R, M, and B for flowers. P did figures.	1758—*Peter Grafe* later became a ducal possession and was placed under *Tännich* 1766—Sold to two *Hamburg* business men *Reimers* and *Neumann* who let *Tännich* go and appointed *Buchwald* and *Leihamer.* 1769—Came to *C. J. Richardi* and both artists went to *Stockelsdorff* 1793 or earlier ceased.	Low-fired, soft, pale buff, nearly white with faint reddish cast body, with glaze smooth and cold white but uneven and may vary from a bluish to reddish tone on same piece. It often has small holes which fill with dirt and show black but no crazing and many of the best pieces are quite perfect. Muffle-painting was favored and though not quite so good as some French factories, it is better than most German ones. Not so fine as Sceaux and *Marseilles* but bold and decorative.
	In the *Tännich* period there were also numerals such as # 1 and # 5		*Kiel* dishes always have the wavy edge of the rococo period and are edged with brown.

LESSER DANISH FACTORIES—*Continued*

In *Buchwald* period a B replaces the T.

Tännich developed a *"Potpourri-vase"* called "lavender-jar" which seems to be a new form consisting of an ovoid body on concave foot with flaring base, the body cut flat across the top to form a wide, squat concave neck and the cover is tall with concave sides and dome top surmounted by freely modeled plant forms or flowers often oak or cherry branches. The cover is perforated in six or eight holes to allow the fragrance of flowers placed inside to escape. The decoration is of flowers, landscapes or less often of small cupids (See *Kunstindustrimuseum*) (Also *Dansk Folkemuseum* also *Hamburg*)

One tea-tray has on it, *"Abr. Leihamer fecit, 1769—Buchwald Directeur—Kiel."* (See *Hamburg*) Only infrequently did *Leihamer* sign with full name. At *Hamburg* is also a fine *"Potpourri-vase"* by him.

During *Buchwald* times blue was freely used but *Tännich* seems to have scorned its use.

There is only one plate known with a Chinese figure on it, but many figures from everyday life were used in landscapes also from the immediate surroundings.

In *Hamburg* is one plate with Chinese flowers but that is the only one known; and copying was not so prevalent as elsewhere.

The gilding is handled with taste.

Beautiful wall cisterns with bowls below were made and are among the finest productions of the whole North. They are in natural colors of the fine flower painting and sometimes edged with blue. The modelling is the best of the rococo period. (See *Hamburg, Kunstindustri* and other museums.)

The *potpourri* vase by *Leihamer* has a landscape from an etching by *J. de Vischer* after *van Goyen*, as *Brinckmann* found out, and many were taken from copper plates but flowers seemed to have been done largely from nature.

Rendsburg	1765—*Christian Friedrich Gottlob Clar* and *Jesper Lorentzen*, an apothecary and a merchant 1772—When	A list of the wares of 1767 says they produced all types of wares from *"Pot-pourris"* and *"Bischofshüte"* or "bishop bowls" to cane handles, snuff-boxes, etc.

LESSER DANISH FACTORIES—*Continued*

Lorentzen died *Clar* tried to make "English ware" and turned the business over to a company 1784—*Clar* went bankrupt and the company declared itself insolvent. The business was then turned over to the judge and shareholder, *Johann Heinrich Hallensen* in 1788 who kept *Clar* on.

The pierced baskets are marked in stories: At top a **D** reversed or a rectangle combined with the R, below a painter's letter and below again usually 67, 68, **or** 69 for the date.

Stamped **with** cursive RF at times followed **by** a numeral, but this was often omitted to fool the customers into thinking that **they** were "English wares."

English black "basalt ware" and a slightly glazed red terra-cotta of *Clar's* own were produced.

First period (1765–72) whitish-buff body with soft white glaze. There are only a few pieces known: a small dish in *Hamburg* has a rose and an anemone in green, purple and yellow. A wash basin in the same museum is in natural flowers in blue only. Chinese flowers also in blue were used. (See *Folkemuseum* dish) Manganese was also used alone as on a teacaddy in *Hamburg*.

Rendsburg pierced baskets touched up with blue and with a bouquet of flowers in blue are not rare.

The lead-glazed earthenware is after 1772. It has flowers in blue and landscapes but is often simply picked out with blue. It is too strongly straw colored or too white and generally muddy and densely crazed in glaze. Its forms are an urn with mask handles, a blue lined basket with grapes and other fruit in relief springing from the handles, a large pierced basket with inner container and plain cover with holes for flower stems and a tulip-bowl supported by three boys.

Brinckmann claims that a large center piece of yellowish ware with three nearly nude ladies on a pedestal, two supporting an open-work basket with a strange bird on the cover, is from here. *Hannover* says, if so, it is the largest piece yet known that this factory could handle.

Kellinghusen in Holstein

Magretah Stemman

c1760—*Carsten Behrens* dreamed of a porcelain factory and got some men from *Saxony* to come there. Soon he was forced to convert the porcelain factory into a faïence factory and form a company. Technical manager was *Sebastian Heinrich Kirch.* 1765—the factory was granted a privilege 1768—*Kirch* departed

Kirch introduced the plastic trend of *Jever* and it became popular. *A large Venus* in the *Gewerbemuseum* at *Bremen* is proven by *Karl Schaefer* to have come from the factory of *Behrens.*

The hair is applied with a painting-horn in lines as thin as thread. It is similar in feeling to the *"Clutie"* wall-plaques with a head in high relief and a sunburst above, left open to hold a watch. (*Hamburg* and *Folkemus.*)

KH—B (for *Kellinghusen-Behrens*)

KH—M (for *Kellinghusen-Møller*)

KH—Dr. G but as a rule it is not marked at all.

for places unknown and the company was dissolved so *Carsten Behrens* had to carry on alone. At his death it went to his heirs and lasted at least until 1825.

1783—Meanwhile two workmen, *Christian Heinrich Geppel* and *Georg Geppel*, who had been with *Clar* at *Rendsburg*, had established at *Kellinghausen* and were given a privilege for the making of white wares only.
1785—a royal resolution was given the old factory and *Dr. Joachim Møller* obtained a share in it and with it freedom to make every kind of earthenware at the new factory which he now owned also.
His widow married one of his workmen, *Jacob Stemmann*.
1800—it is still called, "*Doctor Grauers Fayence-Fabrique.*" *Dr. Grauer* was a practicing physician and owned the factory only as a side issue.
1822—it went to *Nicolai Friedrich Mohns* who left it to his son, who sold it to *Martin Püssel* of *Lehmberg*.
1787—A third factory was set up by *Georg Geppel*.
Others tried as the clay from *Ovendorf*, nearby was excellent.

The pair in the *Folkemuseum* are inscribed "*Magretah Stemman*" and are of the *Dr. Grauer* period. These were among the commonest wares made at the place.

A bucket with flowers in colors at *Bergen* is marked KH-B.

Wall flower-holders and wall-plaques dated 1794 must be from the factory of *Joachim Møller*, as does also a cream jug in the shape of a satyr's head marked KH-M.

Local factories all used same clay and all used same rustic painting in high-temperature colors so that they cannot be told apart. Hannover says that the wares attributed to *Kastrup* and having large, coarsely-painted yellow and purple flowers with feathery greenish grey leaves and thread-like stalks in manganese are really from some factory here at *Kellinghusen*.

The ordinary peasant wares of *Kellinghusen* are more vigorously painted and have an iron-red added to the colors. The flowers are similar to those described above and also landscapes, ships, galloping horses or such subjects as a saint in her cell are used. Of course, the single colors were also used alone.

Stockelsdorff near Lübeck

* *Stockelsdorff* 1773—*Buchwald* Direct.—*Abr. Leihamer fecit.* ** A similar inscription. *** *Buchwald* Dir.—*Creutzfeldt fecit*—*Stockelsdorff* 1776.

Grew out of an earlier stove factory, owned by *Peter Graff* or *Grafe*, who founded the *Kiel* factory.
1771—obtained privilege for *State Councillor, Georg Nicolaus Lübbers.*
c1773—*Johann Buchwald* is director and *Abraham Leihamer* as decorator from *Eckernförde* and *Kiel*. But left in a few years and the painter *Creutzfeldt* took his place.

Under *Lübbers* and *Buchwald* stoves were the main output as they were in the time of *Graff*. They were in the rococo and "*Zopf*" styles and had grates of iron. All are painted in muffle-kiln colors in marbling and figures or landscapes with figures in them. They are real works of art and are signed with care as on the rococo *Hamburg* one with Chinese genre scenes,* and another in the early "*Zopf*" or classical style of the death of *Caesar* in the *Lübeck Museum,*** and still another in the *Folkemuseum*

LESSER DANISH FACTORIES—*Continued*

* *Stockelsdorff*—
1774—*Leihamer
fecit.*

St or Stoff on
blue and white
wares

1788—*Lübbers* died
and the son of
Johann Buchwald
carried on.

with subjects from the
Iliad.***

Next to stoves come tea-trays
in importance. One with cows
in a landscape within a rococo frame * and another
with blue and white land-
scape at *Hamburg* are typical.

The factory used both high
and low fired colors and services in manganese are known
(See tureen at *Lübeck*) Very
poor plates in blue are also
found rather plentifully.
The clay is lightly fired pale
yellowish-white sometimes almost pure white.

The above plates are poor indeed but some wares in well
painted blue show that it was
also used in the best period.
(See wall cistern and vase at
Bergen.)

Among the colored wares are
helmet jugs, jardinieres, etc.
in splendid green, beautiful
yellow, soft violet (for lining
and shell borders) and a mat
red.

Thus Danish wares contained little that was original but there was a tendency to simplify the too florid foreign wares to their simple components with a beneficial result. Surprising and rather refreshing it was to find here a Japanese influence. Of course the end was in sight when the "English ware" began to be made but here again the penny-pinchers had less to do with faïence than with porcelain so that there was less stealing of ideas and workmen and a consequently more original outlook in most of the factories. Of course we run across the trails of such secret-peddlers as Tännich and Hannong but the air smells generally sweeter than elsewhere. The appeal of the beautiful is an elusive thing and it sometimes settles upon the more lowly material in spite of every effort to capture it with the most costly of webs.

SWEDEN

RÖRSTRAND

We need not give in detail the unpleasant reports of Johann Wolff. Aereboe would have us believe that he was a thief and betrayer of trusts; that he brought to Stockholm materials and workmen from Copenhagen and it is true that he offered a considerable consignment of cobalt blue supposedly bought from Elsinore, but he was not unlike the other "arcanists." He came to Rörstrand in 1725 and was followed by Anders Nicolaus Ferdinand. In 1729 a privilege was granted and by that time Wolff had been dismissed. Ferdinand too was soon replaced by Christoffer Conrad Hunger who had been at Meissen, Vienna and Venice. In 1733 he was dismissed and replaced by Johann Georg Taglieb from Ansbach until 1739 or 1741.

The factory did a fair amount of work though it was financially unsound. The manager Anders Fahlström helped a bit but reorganization was necessary in 1753 after which he with Elias Magnus Ingman as director brought it to success. However Marieberg began to bring competition in 1758 to 1759 and the quality fell off. At the death of Fahlström in 1760 the management went to Jonas Tåman then to Erik Fahlström, Jacob Öhrn or Øhrn in 1763. Johann Buchwald introduced high temperature colors but by 1758 went to Marieberg. Anders Stenman invented a method of printing on faïence independently of the English but he and Henrik Sten about 1766 or later also went to Marieberg where the latter became manager and then director.

Ingman was enobled in 1758 and he became sole owner of Rörstrand by 1773 when he died. In 1782 his son, E. M. Nordenstolpe bought up the factory but a few years later closed it. Finally it was sold in 1797 to Bengt Reinhold Geijer and he made "English ware" or "flintporslin" as it is called in Swedish. The factory still continues.

WOLFF PERIOD (1725–?)

The only pieces of this period, and they are doubtful, are some walkingstick handles marked (Stock)?"*holm Anno 1725*," a plate having a view with buildings in the center and a rim with alternating design of trellis and flowers in the Chinese manner, other similar plates and two blue and white vases in early Ming style. All but the first are marked "Stockholm."

FERDINAND PERIOD (1729–)

By 1729 Wolff had "long been under arrest" and Ferdinand was in charge. A jar and cover is the only example known. It has blue and white decoration like that of Rouen and Dorotheenthal, consisting of a monogram in a medallion surmounted by a crown and with lambrequin borders on the cover and top and bottom. It is dated 1729.

HUNGER-THELOT PERIOD (1733–)

Hunger and a man named Thelot seem to have turned out pieces together, and signed some stove tiles. They signed also an octagonal tray dated 1733 and painted in blue with a picture of "the feast of the Israelites at the foot of Sinai with Moses kneeling on the mountain—a subject conceived in the profane South German spirit," as Hannover describes it. This is a lively bit with musicians in the foreground, an old girl getting water and much other action set within a stupid floral border. Other pieces show a man with a trained bear, and some have lambrequin borders. Also there are some bowls with feet having landscapes with lovers, hunters, etc. The old Laub-und Bandelwerk was as popular as in Germany. Plates with biblical texts on a banner held by an angel and armorial pieces were made, one of which was signed "Anders Fahlström—Stockholm 1739." All are in blue on white.

From the early 1740's the Chinese influence becomes strong. One typical motive is of a bird with a long tail while others show a beflagged pavilion and a weeping willow. A very queer one shows a dead bird with its head hanging over a ledge while over it is a large flat umbrella. To one side is a tree while to the other is a dart. Perhaps Dali had ancestors! Actually Pillement, Oudry and Boucher were behind much of this, and the latter is said to have invented the "swan spouting water," though a very similar design occurs on two incised Sung period vases (A.D. 960–1280) (see Chinese section) in my collection. This design represented ducks eating greens.

The ground of all these wares up to c. 1750 was white of varying tone but at this time they began to add a bluish-grey tinge and decorate in white on it in the technique called in Italy, "bianco sopra bianco." But this was always much more crude and broad than the Italian examples. The earliest is a plate dated 1745. Later the technique was tried a little at Delft, Bristol and Saint Amand-les-Eaux, all in about five years. New stunts soon got around in the 18th century.

Hannover gives four supposedly original designs from Rörstrand:

1.—The scattered trefoil.

2.—The "blue leaf" which is also like a flower and appears in a center decoration and looks like "large twisted catkins (of hop?)."

3.—The "polestar motive," a sharp five pointed star with a space around it and five heavy rays with about eight or nine graduated lighter rays between them. (c 1748)

4.—The "Rehn design" supposed to have been devised by an architect named Jean Erik Rehn. It is a sort of bursting pomegranate centered and with a rococo border of three wave-like scrolls with three smaller ones between them (1745). This occurs in manganese and sometimes yellow too was added.

Marieberg had started with muffle-kiln colors in a style of painting like that of Strasburg and to meet the competition, Rörstrand made some trials on panels adding even gilding. These are dated 1758. Within a year plates were made with bird designs in colors similar to those known as "famille rose" of the Ch'ien Lung dynasty, China (1736–1796). A foliated butter dish copies Delft and has a decoration of small scattered roses after Meissen and marked as a real Delft one would be with an unintelligible rake and bird's head, and it might even be confused if it did not also have a mark "Stockholm 2/5 9/5 59. There are also some light, thin snuff boxes almost like porcelain.

The brushwork of the 1760's was broad and good and flowers and butterflies are well drawn in a sort of fluttery style. Toward the end of this decade flowers in the round were applied boldly to three sides of a temple jar shaped vase with a scalloped foot.

Marieberg forced the old factory to find a sort of half-hearted interest in plastic work. There were center pieces with half figures holding a shell supported on rococo scrolls and tureens had modeled flowers or fruits for the knob handles. On one there is a reclining lobster and on another a cauliflower. The jars with roses on three sides give somewhat the effect of a fat lady with a large corsage pinned on her great bosom. These were done both in muffle colors and in high-fired colors. But the factory concentrated chiefly on the latter. A red was never developed. The manganese purple was usually broken up into many small circles where bubbles had broken. The green is greyish or yellowish with a tendency to part in small fissures so that the white glaze can be seen through. The yellow is pale and has the same tendency. Therefore, the result is pallid but giving an antique and harmonious result. The blue alone is pure and strong and it was not overdone. The four designs listed continued, at least until 1773.

By this time there seemed to be a change of taste and polychrome was discontinued entirely in favor of black design. Many of the old forms were revived and so treated.

The stoves are copies of those made at Marieberg but of fine quality. This is not to say that sincere flattery was not returned in good measure by the younger factory. Punch bowls were made to imitate wooden tubs with vines and grapes applied about them and two vases in the Rörstrand Museum are five feet high. They are decorated with Chinese figures and landscapes. These seem to date about 1765.

The Rörstrand marks are complete and until 1773 the name of the factory, or the city, the day, month, year, the painter's mark and frequently the price of each piece or of a dozen was added. To 1758 "Stockholm" was used. Then "Rörstrand" and in 1758 and 1759 "Rörstrand-Stockholm" is found. Odd exceptions dating 1760–61 may also have just "Stockholm" on them. The date may be "–18/4. 52." The painters do not interest us as there were none of outstanding merit. Stråle and also Looström have made extensive studies but allowed their enthusiasm to run away with some of their conclusions.

MARIEBERG

Marieberg was founded on the island of Kungsholm off Stockholm by Johann Ehrenreich, court dentist, jack-of-all-trades and the same referred to in Königsberg and Stralsund. He had applied for a privilege to make porcelain in 1758 but his factory burned down in the following year. He then started on faïence and the first firing took place in April, 1760, bringing an immediate success for by 1762 he had 6 designers and 248 workmen. In 1766 the financial crisis forced him to give up his post to a Frenchman, Pierre Berthevin who came from Mennecy and went later to Mosbach. He tried to make soft porcelain for about 3 years and then Henrik Sten was director and soft porcelain was continued until the "English ware" was adopted. When Nordenstolpe the younger from Rörstrand bought the factory, he put Philipp Andrea Schirmer in charge until 1788 when it closed.

Probably the first wares were not marked and were decorated in rich colors in the manner of porcelain applied as enamels. Landscape and figure subjects were popular while modeled fruit, vegetables and flowers appear often. A little group of the "comedy figures" are in yellow or natural colors. The old stunt of marbling or making wood grain was done but in several colors used together such as red, yellow, blue, brown and violet. These pieces may have bird or flower finials on the vase covers or tureens.

Another group of wares are called the "violet group" though they are predominantly white with touches of violet. There has been some speculation about these pieces but it is fairly certain that the color was added intentionally and was no accident of the glaze. Hannover says, "Rörstrand faïence has not infrequently such an even faint violet tone, and it was perhaps this that the Marieberg factory sought to imitate." This same lavender tone does appear also on Sung Dynasty (960–1280) Tz'u Chou wares and seems to be due to small patches or specks of impurity in the body or slip. Perhaps there are tiny bits of manganese or iron in the clay. They are sought after by Chinese collectors and these or brown stains are often pleasant relief to the white. If, therefore, it occurs on Rörstrand, it may have originally been unintentional. Other examples of this staining appear on the "Tu Ting" wares also of the Sung Dynasty. Examples of plastic work of Marieberg are a pair of wild swine, rococo cachepots, women or a triton supporting a shell-shaped bowl, etc., and are often not decorated. On the other hand colored pieces are candelabrum, boxes and figures.

Blue and white was done with a bright blue tinged with ultramarine giving it a purplish tint and only seldom inclined to run. With it cornflowers, roses and convolvulus were painted on a service dating 1765. Again tureens were made with vegetable and lobster knobs or handles. All manner of natural shaped boxes were made in the forms of artichokes, melons, birds and fruits. One odd one is like a bunch of grapes. All were in natural colors.

About this same time the modeled and applied flowers were popular. One at least was done in black, brown and green. Many were in polychrome but all were in good taste due to Ehrenreich.

Ehrenreich also brought certain ideas to the factory including the tureens in rococo style with flowers in Strasburg manner, the use of a dolphin or bird for the cover handles, and the "terrace vase," "rabbit vase," etc. The "terrace vase" was a simple and pleasant inverted pear shaped jar with dome cover and decorated up each side and on the cover with flowers modeled in the round while the whole stands upon a large swirling baroque scroll perhaps five times larger than would be expected and having in its curves a bunch of grapes. This does sound terrible but somehow the effect is to give a preciousness to the jar. The "rabbit vase" we may at least commend as original in this age of worn out ideas and it was popular, for many examples exist. It consisted of the same shaped vase decorated with muffle-kiln colored flowers and the cover surmounted with a bunch of berries. This vase is set on a rock-like base around which and tapering upward to accent the perspective, goes a staircase with railing, while at the foot of this sits a rabbit about to ascend. Later the rabbit was replaced for some unknown reason by a boar.

Again we exclaim, by all the shades of poor unbalanced Dali, his brethren surely seemed to have existed back in those days, and we are led to believe that perhaps we should add another human appeal to the possible armament of the artist, namely that of *shock*, during the bored and despondent times of decadence; of unexplained and unexplainable and unrelated objects which, if not alluringly satisfactory as possessions for ourselves, are, at least *talk creators;* challenging conundrums and the sought-after symbolical representations of those who wish to appear mysterious and strange. Such extroverts.

who always make great pretense of being introverts, cannot stand life, if they are not noticed and, no other means being easy for them, will play up their personal oddities. I remember when I was very young I had a great desire to have a black room, in which there was to be a black piano upon which would rest a bleached human skull. This room was a dream of mine for months until I suddenly awoke to the fact that I wanted it to impress a young lady with whom I was very much in love and who did not seem sufficiently impressed to return my love in like measure. My dreams always ended in picturing her astonishment when the door was thrown open and somehow I felt that *then* she would appreciate the dark depths of my soul. I spited her by not thinking of the room any more at all and by adopting a very flippant and shallow manner. She never knew what she missed! So it is with melting watches and rabbit vases. Can you imagine the astonishment of a proper young man left in a waiting room in a tasteful mansion to contemplate what at first glance appears to be a suavely perfect vase quite expensive looking and up to the taste of the moment when suddenly, penetrating his thoughts of the lady for whom he is waiting, he sees that the vase has at the bottom a rabbit or a boar about to ascend a staircase? He looks more closely for a hidden meaning. He wonders if there is some significance perhaps a symbol of the thwarted ambition for, of course, neither a rabbit nor a boar could go up a staircase and why should they anyway? He thinks all pottery is somewhat crazy and remembers the Wettergren's soup tureen with a lobster and cauliflower on the cover and how he tried hard to think of two foods that would go less well together and be more indigestible. Well artists are certainly crazy, but why should his Anna fall for a thing like that? It must be the influence of that fellow Erik who thinks he is artistic! And then she comes and says, "Why Johann, why are you sitting and frowning so at my new vase? What is the matter with you?" And he answers, "What is the idea of having such a crazy thing? Rabbits don't go upstairs. Why should you buy anything so silly?" And she, "Because I like it." And that is that.

Yes we have something here, something which Poe played at, something which is part of the old "groteschi" of Urbino and which Grünewald, Bosch and Brueghel seemed to know; the tales of strange things, the figures part animal part human, the danses macabres and such may not be able to move us to tenderness, to tears or to happiness, but at least they command attention and have been known to lead to fear, sexual desire and a sense of superiority, though usually those who practice such art are satisfied with obtaining attention alone, and if notice is taken of them that is sufficient.

MARIEBERG FROM 1766—BERTHEVIN

So much for our court dentist and his rabbits! When Ehrenreich departed in 1766 no great change took place. In 1768 a pompous and not too good service was done for Louis Auguste le Tonnelier de Breteuil, French Ambassador to Stockholm, each piece of which bears his arms printed with the transfer process while the rest is of flowers poorly painted. The handles are of bent vegetables. Many museums have parts of this service and the best that can be said of it is that it did have a clear porcelain-like white glaze.

Berthevin brought a spirit of imitation of porcelain not at all suitable to the material of faïence. Anders Stenman from Rörstrand started much printed design and Henrik Sten introduced classical shapes. Another service with pierced rims and scattered flowers was done in 1773 and in 1774 another was in much the style of Joseph Hannong. Just as Rörstrand was famous for its blue, so Marieberg was famous for a crimson about as good as that of Strasburg. Bianco-sopra-bianco was copied from Rörstrand. In 1764 an attempt had been made to handle the high temperature colors but it failed.

Hannover wisely says, "Nothing follows in history more surely after love of colour than colour-weariness and a tendency to renunciation of colour." Thus the chief characteristic of the Sten period was a demand for austere vases decorated after engravings after Boucher in black or brown and the same colors in renderings of trophies. Thus we approach the deadly Empire with its chinoiseries and neo-classical treatments in grey or red, its imitations of jasper or agate and its final descent into "English ware" or the "flint-porslin" and imitation of Staffordshire so good that without the marks one can hardly tell the difference.

The mark is of three crowns of Sweden above a line, below which is MB in monogram or not and an E (for Ehrenreich) or B (for Berthevin) followed by the date and a painter's mark. Johann Otto Franzén wrote his name in full on a terraced vase of 1766 (30/8) but this is not usual. The "flintporslin" is usually simply impressed with MB. Other marks are usually in blue under-glaze, and rarely in black.

The body is buff with slight greenish tint. The glaze is very white and not inclined to craze. The flintporslin ware is astonishingly light, yellowish and with a close, fine crackle. Gilding is uncommon except as an edging but was combined at times with grisaille painting. Very infrequently it was combined with blue and white.

CHART OF SMALL FACTORIES

The following small factories are interesting only to a few readers. Of them Stralsund is the most important for it is there that Ehrenreich went when he left his post as director at Marieberg in 1766.

CHARTS OF SMALLER SWEDISH FACTORIES

Stralsund	*Three nails* of the Crucifixion from the arms of the town, with an *E* (for *Ehrenreich*) followed by the date and often the painter's mark. Sometimes the E is replaced by a C (for Carl) or a B (for *Buchwald*)	1757—*Councillor von Giese* with largest kiln to hold 6,480 plates. 1766—*Ehrenreich* took over management with help of *Johann Buchwald*. 1770—Was blown up by powder magazine explosion and *Ehrenreich* bankrupt, but stayed and *von Giese* put the factory on its feet again. 1780—*Giese* died and there were many disputes about the money with heirs.	Buff body with greenish tone with sometimes a grey and cold glaze. The colors are heavier, harder and more dead than those of *Rörstrand* and *Marieberg*. *Bianco-sopra-bianco* technique was copied. Also the *Rehn pattern*, the blue leaf and others among all the popular models of *Marieberg* including the boxes with recumbent figures, the "rabbit vases," etc. Early in the 1770's were made about the only original things: monumental *potpourri* vases with a nude woman and

CHARTS OF SMALLER SWEDISH FACTORIES—*Continued*

		1785—When an agreement was made the resources were so depleted that it had to close. It was revived by *Carl* but had further troubles and closed for good in 1792.	other figures modelled in the round about the bases.
Pålsjö north of Helsingborg	*P F C* (for *Pålsjö Fabrik-Cöster*)	1765—*Michael Anders Cöster,* the district magistrate under direction of *Fröling* a *Swede* from *Stockholm,* until 1770. 1770 to 74—was under *Hindrich Wulph* our old acquaintance, *Heinrich Wolff*	See *Sigurd Wallin*—Undamaged pieces are among the greatest rarities. Sherds of flint porcelain moulded from English originals, have been found in large quantities at the site. The *faïence* body is pale buff and rather fine in texture. Another type is coarser and reddish-buff. The glaze is crazed and faulty. The decoration is in blue or manganese of very variable tone. There is one example of polychrome, a tankard in the *Kulturhistoriska Museum, Lund.* Motives were a spray of five petalled flowers and small scattered clover leaves and flowers with among them tulip-buds with stalks bearing similar clover-like leaves. These occur sometimes alone or sometimes in wreaths around royal monograms,—that of *Adolf Frederik* of *Sweden.* Another motive is a small view of buildings similar to those of *Copenhagen,* and these are probably from the *Wolff* period.
Sölvesborg	S B for (Sölves-Borg) with numbers 1 or 2 added.	1773—*Major Gabriel Sparre* and managed by the painter from *Marieberg, Peter Akermark.* Later went to *S. Fr. von Ziepel,* a Prussian officer. 1793—closed	Buff lightly fired and fine clay. The glaze is inclined to craze. Decoration in blue or manganese and exceptionally in several colors, see large tureen with dolphin on cover in *Rörstrand Museum.* No independent style for shapes, taking all from *Rörstrand* or *Marieberg.* Motives of flowers not original and are different only in being more hastily and commercially painted. Most of the wares were without decoration or with the conventional "blue leaf" of *Rörstrand* in blue and also in manganese. Trees were also sometimes printed with a sponge. Also copied English earthenware.

CHARTS OF SMALLER SWEDISH FACTORIES—*Continued*

Ulfsunda in parish of Bromma in the district of Sollentuna province of Stockholm.	C A L *Linning's* initials stamped and sometimes name of factory	End of 18th cent. *Christian Arvid Linning,* a sculptor of little ability. 1819—Was called "*Wedgwood-Fabriken paa Ulfsunda.*"	Appropriation of models by *Wedgwood* and *Flaxman* for useful wares of classical style. (See blue and white drug jar in *Lund*) Less hard fired than real *Wedgwood* but occur in black "basalt," buff terra-cotta with applied reliefs in brown or red, etc., cast from the prototypes direct. The largest piece is a clock in the *Nordiska Museum* signed by *Linning* but copied from a French model (See Hannover "Pottery and Porcelain," p. 497)
Gustafsberg		1827—May have had a predecessor at 1780–90	Typical of the times and of no interest

There were also several other late factories such as that at *Malmö*, another at *Höganäs* as well as *Norrköping* and *Norrtälje* the outputs of which are of very modest description.

NORWAY

C. Nyrop gives the following list of Norwegian factories though the wares are known from only one:

1741—Didrik von Cappelen at Dorholt near Skien
1753—Johan Heinrich Schwabs and Oluf Falch at Styrstuen
1758—Peter Hofnagel at Herrebøe (which we will speak of later)
1760—D. P. Fasmer at Bergen (stoneware and faïence)
1778—Iver Bredal and Gunner Eide also at Bergen

HERREBØE (1758–1770)

The wares from the factory at Herrebøe far from being unknown are among the most interesting of Scandinavia. Peter Hofnagel started the factory here near Frederikshald in 1758 and he obtained a privilege to open a factory at Drammen in 1762. He was a lawyer then a merchant after trying to become the postmaster of Arendal and he bought an estate where he took up agriculture. In 1757 he founded a tile factory and the next year a stoneware and stove factory from which the faïence factory developed. The director was Georg Kreibs, probably a Dane or at least his family was at Copenhagen. Two stepsons partly Scottish, named Joseph and Gunder Large, became artists at the ages of sixteen and eighteen in the year 1760 but the early painting was probably due to Heinrich Christian Friedrich Hosenfeller of Berlin.

The common mark is HB with at times an H below probably standing for Hosenfeller. Another was H K L with a slanting stroke below, standing for Herrebøe Kreibs Large. The often seen A and R and AR are identified. Finally we are sure at least of the full name of the factory and the name Large but they are rarely used. There are also numerals which do not refer to size (0 to 4).

The earliest piece is a large wall cistern inscribed Herrebøe 1760 and a similar one signed Large, probably of about the same date, now in Oslo. These are usual in shape and have a medallion in low relief with slight painting of flowers and a figure. Hosenfeller's style is supposed to have broad, free brush work with claw-like terminations to the rococo scrolls according to Thor Kielland but soon the young apprentices also did things in his style.

The body is fine-grained, buff and lightly fired. It is porous and the glaze tends to crackle and is of bluish or palest buff tint. It is only a little less opaque than oil paint white so the blue or manganese decoration were used above the unfired tin glaze. Outlines were not used but sometimes a detail is handled with a fine brush. Almost nowhere else and certainly not in Germany can be found such masterful handling of the best that the rococo style could give; there is a daring swing in the movement, a better accented rhythm and a more capricious viewpoint easily evident. Here once again we find appreciation of swift brushwork as in the Danish factory of Store Kongensgade in the 3rd or Gierløf period (c1750) though used not so much in a Japanese sort of technique as pure rococo. Undoubtedly this sort of technique occurred from time to time because the unfired glaze sucked up the paint almost as fast as would a blotter and *forced* a sure, swift stroke. Sometimes this is overdone in a work of art while again we all can recognize a too labored painting but once in a while an artist will gauge his tempo so perfectly that he will "hit it right on the nose" with all the sting and follow-through that is necessary and not a jot too much. It is then that the opponent in the prize ring unexpectedly collapses and the critics speak of timing. It is then that the golf ball sails further down the fairway. And in art something of this mastery was to be seen at Herrebøe though it was never anything like as fine as in the Sung Tz'u Chou wares, because of the inherent deficiencies of the whole rococo style.

The breaking up of the surface of the ware with indentations and convexities helically twisting about them, with melon-ribbed modeling or well spaced and sometimes alternating slight ribs and grooves, gives the design a less obvious rhythm as it plays a leitmotif over the undulating swells like ripples over waves. It is not a question of painting a flat design on an uninteresting surface or trying to make such a surface appear uneven; the pieces would be plastically beautiful in themselves, the designs would be beautiful in themselves, and the two are perfectly harmonized so that, as a rule, neither the one nor the other dominates and even when this does occur it seems intentional.

As an example of one piece which may be considered overmodeled, we can take the largest example known, a center-piece with cruets, mustard pots and salt cellars grouped around the figure of an almost naked baby boy holding a pierced basket for fruit. The modeling of this object is surely overdone and the anatomy of the boy is none too good but what gives it a peculiar charm is the vigorous painting and the bubbling overjoyed intoxication of the boy as he prances through the scrolls and scallop-shells, the foliage and pots, as though gaily bringing the pièce de résistance of the whole dinner. This work of art has been called "the jolliest figure in the whole art of faïence" which it certainly well may be. Who gives one small damn for anatomy and perfection of modeling if an artist can catch that illusive charm that makes men smile thereafter? Here is something that the merchants and copyists cannot catch any more than they could lay hold of a sunbeam. I wonder if this is not always true and that *those who lost the most through forgery had not actually the least to lose*. Meissen, Sèvres and Wedgwood are names that collectors conjure with but we might enjoy ourselves far more with the real things from odd places such as Store Kongensgade, Herrebøe, South Germany and Hungary as well as the Far East of pre-Ming days.

Large trays, wall cisterns, "bishop bowls" (which became more bowl and less mitre) and round tureens comprised most of the wares. A simple, well proportioned and undecorated turned candlestick of 1770 is signed Gunder Large and is in the church at Id.

Odd examples show that gold was tried and the bianco-sopra-bianco. Chinese designs occur on a few plates while swift and direct little landscapes and large flowers never lost the life of the place. Yet Herrebøe was not successful; it soon had to have sales at sacrifices and by 1772 it had about failed. Not until 1900 did the Kunsindustrimuseum of Oslo have an exhibition which led to modern appreciation with pieces bringing from 4,000 to 12,000 kroner. How much one such sale would have encouraged the factory! Hofnagel tried again in Drammen but again without success. He then went to Copenhagen in 1763 where we know he opened Østerbro sometime around 1764 or 1765. In 1770 he was obliged to return to Norway where he died in 1776 a sad and disconsolate failure.

Conclusion of Continental Faïence

The fate of Hofnagel was no different from that of most of the other "arcanists" of the day such as Tännich, Johann Wolff, Ehrenreich and all. They, after all, earned their way by the misappropriation and sale of the secrets of one factory to another and were naturally mistrusted. And so they moved from place to place establishing the manifold crossings of their art, losing manhood, individuality and personality, probably hating themselves in their innermost hearts, and giving up to a hang-dog existence until what was at first a clear desire to create faïence or porcelain was transformed into a mere struggle to get money by hook or by crook. Some hated themselves so much that they were discharged "for riotous living." Some were partly successful due to dual personalities because they were able to play the artist and creator on one side and the businessman and accumulator on the other. These men are none of them pleasant to contemplate and their mongrel art is no more pleasant. Of course there was greater skulduggery in the field of porcelain because there were more secrets to know and more rich patrons to work on, but all arts of the 18th century were similarly handled.

Despite all this and the misfortunes that visited the "arcanists," faïence had become a living art in some places and grown into the hearts of men. Some modernists think that plastics may supplant it but this is simply another material with completely different expression. Faïence will not be discarded any more than wood will be discarded for the manufacture of furniture and that will not be for many a year to come. The handful of clay which can be modeled or thrown on the wheel and painted with colors that never fade and given a glaze pleasant to the touch will always have its appeal to artists and to public alike and its possibilities for expression have only been half explored.

It was the penny piling business men who really harmed the ceramic arts and man had to live to the 20th century to find that gold is as worthless as words and words are as worthless as arms in the gaining and holding of power over fellow men. There is no such a thing as a burglar proof lock and no shield has ever been invented that cannot be pierced by some future weapon. The "arcanists" were not different from other men of the period.

Lincoln Steffens says in his autobiography, "The great corporations, called syndicates, are essential parts of the business political machinery in France, where the tendency to merge business and politics has gone further than anywhere else. We in America have what all those countries once had, a dual government, the political establishment and business, and the theory is that the government exists to regulate, control, and adjust the conflicting interests of these businesses as against one another and as against the people. Apparently this is a theory in conflict also with the facts of economic growth. The economic forces, therefore, cause in the United States that political corruption, which we regard as an exceptional evil, which in England has gone on to the point where it is quiet, decent and accepted, but which in France has succeeded in uniting the management of business and the direction of political policies into one government. The syndicates have divided France into spheres of influence, financial, industrial and political, which are not identical with but as governmental as departments; and in practice, a political leader can have a man appointed to a business job just as he can to a political office. The effect on business is the same as on political administration with us: inefficiency, dishonesty, the retardation of enterprise." This is the best description I know of just how it works. We remember all the granting of privileges and organization by royalty first; then the business men who ran the kilns for what they could get out of them; then we saw that the men who actually devoted their whole lives to doing the work in the factories, after the stockholders were paid, the landlords paid, the merchants taken care of, etc.—obtained nothing in the end.

But let us continue with Steffens, "The ownership of big business in France (in England, in Europe, too, but most clearly you see it in France) is in the hands of the third and fourth generation of the descendants of the great founders and builders. There are literally princes of business in France as there were princes and descendants in politics, and they are alike, these two kinds of privileged descendants. They want security, income, profits; not adventure enterprise, new machinery and methods. How the Europeans ever came to say that Americans worship money when they sell everything for money—the state, honors, business, the arts—is a mystery; and another is how they can see standardization 'in the States,' when they have it in their very bones. The general effect of European political business corruption has been to make everybody think of money, and not as with us as capital to build with and give away, but as cash to get, hold, or waste, to standardize dress, conduct, customs, and all thinking." Here though Steffens knew nothing about pots he has most clearly told us just what is the matter with them.

It is significant that only in odd places have we seen any originality at all as in South Germany, Hungary and Norway. Such spots simply were less touched by the blight. Other originality will be found in America but first we turn to England, the furthest western point of European culture, the latest to be affected but the final focal point of all this commercialism in the next century.

CHAPTER XXVI

THE POTTERIES AND STONEWARE OF ENGLAND AND WALES

IN THE excellent book "English Pottery" by Bernard Rackham and Herbert Read an introductory statement says that the English are likely to dismiss their earlier potteries as "mere peasant work" not to be compared with the stoneware or faïence of Europe. Of course Roman kilns are found there but during the wars of the Saxons and Normans the art seems to have been lost, and in the middle ages little was done of importance. Hannover points out that in the upper classes only pewter and silver were used to any extent while in the lower, bowls of wood seemed to take the place of pottery. He jumps directly to "Toft ware" of the 17th century as a beginning. Mr. Ferrand Hudig's handbook to the English wares in the Nederlandsch Museum at Amsterdam dismisses the 17th century slipware with, "It may on patriotic grounds have a certain attractiveness for the English collector; for the foreigner it is a backward production, destitute of aesthetic worth, and by no means so purely English as British writers would like to assume." Actually Rhenish stoneware, the Delft and other faïence products of both the north countries and of France, the wares of Spain and even Italy all had their influence in England. No art in this world can be called "pure" any more than any blood can be so termed for the peoples of the world did quite a bit of getting about from time to time. The degree of purity interests us, of course, as do all influences which go to make up any work of art, but this degree is nothing to boast about. England is, after all just one more European state separated by a creek which a number of people have swum across. It has dabbled with a number of European countries and been dabbled with in turn. Any isolation in an Englishman's mind is merely a defense mechanism as the last war has well proven.

ROMAN INFLUENCES

The Romans brought the use of the wheel in potting though for some unknown reason glaze was not also imported. Therefore, of course the crude pottery could not compete with wood, metal or leather for bowls and containers. At once the urge of the potters was expressed in scratching of designs and only a little later clay of a different color was applied to make a design or a slip covering was applied and scratched away to give a two colored effect. The trend toward painting, as we see it on the continent was retarded so that the plastic outlet was a natural one for the artist. Of course, pieces found in England do not materially differ from other Roman wares and they were strong in plastic expression and nondescript color. In fact we are not entirely certain as to just what pieces were made in England and what imported.

THE "DARK AGES"

Rackham and Read suggest that we term the period between the Roman occupation and the 16th century the "Dark Ages," although I wish to point out that the name should be granted, as on the continent, more because of our lack of knowledge than as a condemnation of the times. After the Romans withdrew there was no contact with the Near East as in Venice, no Islamic conquest as in Spain so that painting with enamels, lustre and all such did not influence England. Thus a natural development of the Roman trends; a coarse body, thin lead glaze and simple clay applications for ornament we find all the way through. R. L. Hobson says in his *Catalogue of English Pottery*, "Pavement tiles are the only form of pottery made in this country in mediaeval times which can claim any artistic qualities," but then we have also found Mr. Hobson unappreciative of the early Chinese wares and his code of beauty was perhaps so refined as to eliminate a number of wares we feel most worthy and strong. Sir Arthur Church in *English Earthenware*, p. 15, says of the Tudor costrels, that their forms are, "perhaps the least inartistic of any native ceramic vessels of the time which have come down to us," as though all were bad and these only less so. But let us examine these wares with an open mind:

12TH TO 14TH CENTURY WARES

On fairly certain circumstantial evidence we find the following:

1.—A jug of unglazed grey earthenware in the B.M. (No. B11) found with coins of Henry III and Edward I in it. This oviform body with spreading foot and lip-rim establishes a common form, reasonable and good. It has dignity and some vitality; stands well and is easy to pour into and out of; has a handle which grows out of the curves pleasantly and structurally. The form recalls certain ones from Hamburg and Kreussen of the 17th century. It has no relationship with South European forms or Western Asian ones but seems to have been evolved by an original craftsman.

2.—The ewer in the Salisbury Museum representing a knight on horseback so armed as to date it about 1200 is original though not commendable.

3.—Another aquamanile in the form of a bearded man on horseback, is of buff ware with dark brownish green glaze and is in the Sussex Archaeological Societies' Museum at Lewes.

4.—Other aquamaniles are in the form of rams and one is overlaid with chain-like spirals, a design found also on a spreading footed pitcher in the

Left: Buff earthenware jug decorated with green clay ridges and red clay roses under yellowish lead glaze. Found on site of Christ's Hospital (Greyfriars Monastery) London. 14th cent. Ht. 12⅞". London Mus.

Center: Buff earthenware jug covered with white slip and painted in brown, amber and dull green under transparent lead glaze, uncrackled. Found at Bishopsgate Street, London. 14th cent. Ht. 12". Guildhall Mus., London.

Right: Red ware jug with red slip under greenish-yellow glaze. 14th cent. Ht. 15¾". Found on site of Civet Cat, Oxford. Ashmolean Mus.

Left: Cistern with heraldic achievement of Henry VII and Elizabeth of York. Early 16th cent. Ht. 13". Sir Henry P. Harris K.B.E.

Right: Tyg and mug of Cistercian ware having red body and dark glaze but no slip decoration. Hts. 8¼" and 5⅝". London Mus.

Left: 16th cent. jug of buff earthenware partly covered with green, lead glaze. Ht. 5⅛". Victoria & Albert Mus.

Center: Jug of buff ware painted in brown under yellowish glaze in spirals. Found at kiln-site at Cheam, Surrey. 14th cent. Ht. 10¾". Cheam Parish Council.

Right: Red earthenware jug with white slip design under deep yellow lead glaze, found on site of Master's Lodge, University College, Oxford. 14th cent. Ht. 12½". Ashmolean Mus., Oxford.

EARLY ENGLISH POTTERY

PLATE 206

Ashmolean Museum, Oxford. This is a design common to 13th century stained glass, illumination and murals. Of course we have spirals emanating from the "Black Earth Region" and central Europe thousands of years before and spreading in all directions but the application of this motive with slip did not come in the western hemisphere until it appeared on the Hafner ware around 1550. Therefore this 13th century appearance might be a direct Roman development saved over as it were.

5.—There is a stag with yellow glazed body and green glazed horns which is probably 14th century and shows one of the earliest developments of diversity of color. It is in the V. & A. Museum.

Though Hobson claims metal prototypes, Messrs. Rackham and Read speak of stone and wood carvings as also having given ideas to the potters. Some are ornate and mischievous while others are dignified and not unlike Han pieces with strong shapes, though these potters had certainly never seen the Chinese tomb wares. Yet here we find the horizontally ribbed body suggestive of metal types, the heavy rim and well formed handle. Strangely we even find the glaze covering the whole of the inside and not the whole outside as in Near Eastern and some Han examples.

The tall spindle shaped jugs, roughly potted and without decoration but of unusual grace of form are 13th century also and those with the slightly dented lip to aid pouring are perhaps a little later. The bases of these are generally thumbed down, giving a gadrooned effect and making them stand firmly. This technique appears only again so far as I know in Siegburg faïence of the 16th century, but there was no connection. In 1923 a kilnsite was opened in Cheam, Surrey where examples were found including some with freely painted foliage and one with spirals between border lines. The body is buff, the design in brown slip and the glaze yellowish and thin. Probably those with chevrons and trellis work are earlier. Still another found on the site of the Master's Lodge of University College, Oxford, has a red body with complicated spiral design and pendant points on the neck in white slip under a deep yellow glaze. Also at Oxford was found a trellis type with red body, red slip and greenish-yellow glaze. This one has been called 14th century after a study of its potting, though few of this type are later than 1300.

14TH AND 15TH CENTURY WARES

By the end of the 13th century the lip-spout had been made and turned grooves about the neck with also a further development of the different colors of clays for ornamentation. The height is a little less in proportion to the width. A fine example is the one in the London Museum with chevrons and perpendicular lines about the neck in green dented with a tool and dull red roses applied on a greenish brown body, while another in the British Museum is a jug with nearly globular body and of red earthenware while two diamond shaped panels contain a dragon and a lion in lighter clay on reddish brown ground while black is used in a crisscross pattern about the neck; and eagles, leaves and studs appear in brown. Naturally it was not long before such treatments led to purely painted techniques but it was a parallel development perhaps because so much of the Roman influence to model had

Fig. 1175. Red ware jug with applied studs partly covered with grey-green glaze, found on site of Crown and Cushion Inn, Weekday Cross, Nottingham. 15th cent. Ht. 7½". Castle Mus. and Art Gallery, Nottingham.

Fig. 1174. Red ware jug with relief decoration on reddish-brown ground in panels between which are eagles, leaves, etc., in black under transparent colorless glaze. 14th cent. Ht. 10¾". British Mus.

Fig. 1176. Jug of red ware with white slip decoration under yellow glaze. Found at Whittington Park, Buckinghamshire. 15th cent. Ht. 9¾". Victoria & Albert Mus.

been absorbed. A good example is one in the Guildhall Museum, London and found in that city. In this the lip-spout has become exaggerated and the neck loses definition. It is of buff earthenware with white slip painted in green, amber and brown. It begins to show the decadent result of a more facile medium and is not so beautiful as those with applied design.

Plain bodied wares with wheel marks and also simply carved patterns continued and had copper green glazes of a simple lead type. These are well established through having been shown in manuscripts of the period and not in the 15th century ones.

At Ipswich Museum are fragments with boss-like handles and projecting human faces which are called 14th and 15th century probably correctly. Another example, of the anthropomorphic type, is in the B.M. It has a human face molded on either side of the neck and a globular body with upside down pine-cone-scaled carved body. It is of buff clay with green glaze. The use of the faces seems to disappear later.

Rackham and Read also mention 14th century examples at Oxford which are buff with pale yellow or greenish-yellow glazes and decoration of strips or trellises in dark red clay, some of which have a short tubular spout springing from the front of the shoulder and attached by a strap to the neck. This we have seen in Italian majolica of the 14th and 15th centuries, at Siegburg of the latter half of the 16th century and in Near Eastern metal examples which are probably the source of the idea, though this may not be true for the development may be listed as follows: 1.—The rounded lip which does not pour well, 2.—The pinched up or V spout which pours well but makes covering more difficult, 3.—A tubular spout which overcomes both of these difficulties but breaks off easily, 4.—An added support and the troubles are over. However the abutting line like a check-rein on the spout is not pretty or simple and the whole thing is better in metal than in pottery.

16TH CENTURY WARES

A large number of pieces with bright green glaze are assigned to the 16th century:

1.—A small "bleeding-cup" of the B.M. with fleur-de-lys horizontal handle from the rim which might be Roman or Chinese in character but simple and sturdy in design.

2.—Small pitchers with glaze running down unevenly on the outside.

3.—A large variety of costrels and pilgrim-bottles with loops for straps for suspension.

4.—Others with lion head modeled handles.

5.—The natural evolution into marbled wares of red and white (or nearly white) clays as slips on buff body clay. And this again may have been a long suspended idea inherited from Rome, in turn from Crete and from there back to Egypt where it seemed to have originated.

FIG. 1177. Bleeding cup of buff ware with green lead glaze, of early 16th cent. Dia. 6¼". British Mus.

FIG. 1178. Jug and two tygs, 17th and 16th–17th cent. showing typical appliqués of white slip under brownish-yellow lead glaze. Hts. 6¼", 6¾" and 6⅜". C. J. Lomax and Yorkshire Mus.

6.—During the 16th century the mould came into use and we have stove-tiles, candle-sconces, etc., with the royal arms of the Tudor period (1485–1603) in relief.

7.—A fine and well-known example of this work is developed as a cistern (again the earliest we know), and it is about 20 inches by 13 inches at the front and filled with the heraldic achievement of Henry VII and his queen, Elizabeth of York. It is of red ware glazed in green.

There has been some doubt cast upon these wares and it has been suggested that they were not made in England. However a costrel in the B.M. shows the same quality of fine modeling and the style of lettering and the form of the rose would hardly have been learned by a foreign workman.

CISTERCIAN WARES

The "Cistercian wares," found chiefly on the sites of the abbeys, were made by monks and are technically excellent. The ware is red and harder than the other wares. It is covered with a dark iron-brown glaze and sometimes decorated with white slip or again incised. The cylindrical mugs are full of strength and vitality.

These early potteries of England are the ones which many Englishmen have been apologetic about and which Hannover does not even deign to mention, while Wedgwood and Ralph Wood pieces make them enthusiastic. To deny the potters have humor, strength and vitality is as foolish as it would be to say one does not like Shakespeare, and these wares prove that slip-ware was continuous from Roman times in England and perhaps a more characteristic craft than any other. Of course there were copies at odd times of continental things such as the jug in the Dr. J. W. L. Glaisher Collection which has an inscription about the neck: G. R. WROTHAM WAK, and which looks like a crude cast from a Raeren piece but these last Cistercian wares include pieces which form the prototypes of the tygs and posset-pots which are definitely English forms, just as is also the cup with two low handles which is like the Tickenhall tyg type. Tygs or tigs were cups with two or more handles so that they could be passed from hand to hand among several people. We must therefore conclude that slip-ware descended directly from the 16th century wares of the Cistercian monks, without halt, in a continuous line.

TICKENHALL WARES

Perhaps the crudest way of using slip is to apply a little cut shape like a cookie to a pottery surface and then cover the whole with a glaze and this is the way it was done at Tickenhall, Derbyshire where the wares resembled the Cistercian wares. A favorite shape was a cylindrical cup rounded at the bottom and fitted with a sturdy foot-rim. Opposing loop handles are placed low extending from near the bottom to about two thirds of the way up. A primitive flower or animal was usually applied. The ware is red and fairly hard, the slip white and the glaze brownish-yellow. They date from late 16th through the 17th century.

The later type it is said is a globular jug with cylindrical neck and handle. These seem to be of brown ware with chevron design hatched and fronds all in white slip under a yellow glaze. In these the technique is improved. That this ware extended into the 18th century in a less sincere and degraded form is proven by a dish marked E.W. 1796 owned by Mr. C. J. Lomax.

WROTHAM WARE (c1612–1721)

Dr. J. W. L. Glaisher has made a special study of the pottery made at Wrotham, Kent, and his collection includes one showing slip tracery and dots and dated 1656 on an applied pad while the initials probably of the owner are on another. An earlier one in the V. & A. Museum is dated 1621 and is simpler being decorated with pads only. Soon the pads included such designs as angels, masks, stars, etc., and some were "stitched" on with little dashes of slip, a technique hardly suitable to the medium. One technical stunt that was attractive and, so far as I know, not practiced elsewhere, was

FIG. 1181. Loving-cup with badly restored foot and picture of Charles II between the handles. Ht. 7⅝". Yorkshire Mus., York.

FIG. 1179. Wrotham (Kent) slipware candlestick with four handles, light taffy colored earthenware with white slip decorations. Note ingenious inlays in handles of white and taffy rope-twisted clay. Late 17th or early 18th cent. Ht. 6⅜". Ernest F. Follows.

FIG. 1180. Jug and Tyg of Wrotham ware covered with brown glaze having greenish tinge over red body. Jug has inscription reading "G R WROTHAM WAK" and relief casting about neck from Raeren piece. Tyg has initials M^{S}M and inscription, "DECEMB: THE FIRST 1645." Hts. 12" and 6". Ex Dr. G. W. Glaisher Coll.

that the handles were made with a groove along the length and filled with a straight cord of slip, or a twisted one of white slip or even of white and red slip twisted together. The handles were usually double loops and there may be three or four with each mounted with a knob finial or knobs in the V of the loops, showing no practical purpose and a bad tendency to heap ornament. Some had incised slip and some simple incised decoration without slip. Many bear the name WROTHAM.

These date from about 1612 to 1721 and the earlier ones are better craftsmanship and also simpler. It has been suggested that the handle inlayed decoration and the use of the prunts or dots come from earlier leather techniques while Rackham and Read suggest that the shapes are not unlike the mortars of bell-metal; which are contemporary. The Spanish and Italian bronze mortars also of the period were made with appliqué pads so that the designs could be changed and probably this technique also was taken from them.

NORTH STAFFORDSHIRE AND "TOFT WARE" (1676–1707)

Thomas and Ralph Toft, who may or may not have been brothers, rate high in English ceramics. Other potters in Staffordshire imitated their wares such as Richard Meir, Ralph Simpson, Robert Shaw and Ralph Turner.

"Highwayman" dish with raised outlines, white slip and two-toned brown slip decoration, Staffordshire, c. 1640. Dia. 9". Mr. and Mrs. Frank P. Burnap.

Red earthenware dish decorated in white slip under yellowish glaze, made in Staffordshire (1670–1680). Mr. and Mrs. Frank P. Burnap.

Two Wrotham tygs showing pads of white clay stamped with relief design, upper 1656 and 1621. Hts. 7" and 6⅝". Dr. J. W. L. Glaisher and Victoria & Albert Mus.

Left: Buff earthenware dish with brown slip and combed decoration of white slip over it and under yellow glaze, Staffordshire, 18th cent. Dia. 13½". Mr. Frank Falkner.
Center: Beautiful bowl of hard chocolate-brown earthenware covered with white slip through which design is incised. Salt glaze. Made by Ralph Shaw, Burslem, Staffordshire, c. 1733. Ht. 3⅝". Mr. Wallace Elliot.
Right: Dish of dark brown ware covered on front with white slip having incised design and dabs of slate-blue under yellowish glaze. Staffordshire, 1753. Dia. 14½". Central Mus., Northampton.

Left: Dish of red ware covered with brown slip and decorated in white and olive-green slips under yellowish glaze. Inscribed *Thomas Toft,* c. 1670. Dia. 22". Dr. J. W. Glaisher.

Right: Brown ware dish decorated masterfully in white slip under yellow glaze. Staffordshire c. 1700. Dia. 13". Central Mus., Northampton.

ENGLISH SLIP WARES OF 17TH AND 18TH CENTURIES

PLATE 207

There is a large loving cup in the Yorkshire Museum, belonging to C. J. Lomax, of brown ware with decoration in dark brown and white slips and the legend, THOMAS TOFT ELIZABETH POOT, but most of his work was on large 18 inch plates, made for a marriage, christening or some other occasion. It is suggested that Toft was the manager of a factory that turned out ordinary pots and did these things himself only for such occasions. However, there must have been quite a trade in them too. His decoration was of very spirited animals or beautifully arranged plant forms such as those on the dish in the Central Museum, Northampton. The animals are as alive and vigorous as those on 12th to 13th century wares of Western Asia or the "Scythian" bronzes and one can say no more in praise.

The technique was difficult consisting of the pouring out of a pipette or long-spouted can the almost liquid clay. The longer one's hand hesitated, the wider became the line, as the liquid continued to flow. Thus the constant speed of drawing had to be maintained. Moreover the beginning or termination of a line would have a blob unless the attack and withdrawal were done surely and without hesitation. This is much like the technique of batik

Fig. 1184. Earthenware covered with white slip. Decorated in red slip under clear glaze, inscr., MARY PERKINS, 1704. Staffordshire. Dia. 19".

Fig. 1182. Two pieces of buff earthenware decorated in brown and white slips under yellow glaze. Upper 1704, lower 1697. Hts. 8¾" and 5½". Dr. J. W. Glaisher and Mr. C. J. Lomax.

Fig. 1183. Dish molded with raised outlines, covered with white slip and decorated with light and dark brown slips. Made by William Bird, Staffordshire c. 1751. Dia. 16¼". Manchester Art Gallery. Beneath is mold of hard brown earthenware incised to produce raised outlines. Incised on back: William Bird made this mould. In the year of Our Lord 1751. British Mus.

Fig. 1185. Brown earthenware decorated in white slip stamped with cross pattern, signed about neck SAMVEL HVGHESON 1678. Ht. 7⅜". Formerly Dr. J. W. Glaisher Coll.

(see article in 14th edition Ency. Britannica by the author) but the fabric in this case is stretched flat while a pottery vessel has a curved surface. With the pencil or etching-point, the brush or carving tool one can go slowly through a difficult passage, therefore, in one sense they are much more easily handled. However, the real artist does not, of course, want a line of constant width and Toft, just as Miss Ethelyn Stewart, makes the lines taper and grow and taper again to bring life and vitality like that of nature itself into the drawing.

The perpendicular brush of the Far East is surely a wonderful instrument and with it more sensitive expression can be achieved, but closely akin to it is this pipette technique and it imposes one more difficulty which drives the artist to great achievements in some ways. Thus the beautiful dish illustrated is decorated with only nine strokes and seventeen dots. It could not have engaged the artist more than ten minutes of actual work. The dish with a running hare which I believe now belongs to Mrs. Frank Burnap of Kansas City is as economically rendered and these things almost approach the wonderful work of the Sung period Tz'u Chou artists. Yet it is this ware which Hannover dismissed with, "There was no future for the ceramic art proper in peasant-pottery in England any more than in other countries. Here as elsewhere, it was from without, from the centers of ceramic culture, that the decisive fertilization came, after being awaited for a remarkably long period." How totally blind the porcelain-minded gentry are to art!

Of course, to be quite fair, it depends upon what Mr. Hannover was searching for; if he was looking for the beauties he does somewhat appreciate in Rhenish and Delft wares, he could find them in England only later and adulterated, but, if he had appreciated the wonderful brushwork of the Far East and the superb animal design of the Near East, he could hardly condemn Toft ware as mere "peasant-pottery" without a future.

These artists also invented other effects such as the outlining with dots on a dark slip giving a soft and yet brilliant result. This we have not seen elsewhere. Another stunt was to fill the design with a colored slip and grain it to look like matting or material. This was, of course, one of the first ideas in potting but it had long been lost and this occurrence without knowledge of the former wares is interesting. Another Staffordshire process was to make mound shaped molds of baked clay with the design incised, the lines often roughened by many tiny notches at right angles to them on the outside edge of a design. Over these the clay was patted and smoothed in exactly the same manner as was done with Ting yao, Sung period Chinese bowls. When the clay was removed ridges or cloissons were left standing outlining the design, and the areas between them were filled with different colored slips after which the whole was glazed and fired. These bowls with cloisonné technique were continued some years after the period of Toft ware. In the B.M. is one of the molds. Some had unnotched lines and some were notched on both sides. The notching was simply a method of softening the effect artistically. The former is well illustrated by a dish with St. George and the dragon and the latter by another with a spirited "Highwayman" brandishing sword and pistol, in the collection of Mrs. Frank P. Burnap. Most of these dishes are of buff body covered with white slip and decorated with light and dark brown slips and sometimes with red or reddish-brown. Some authorities attribute these wares to Derbyshire but most have been found in Staffordshire.

The "Hugheson Group"

Another type of wares was found marked "HUGHESON" or "SAMUEL HUGHESON" and the earliest of these is dated 1677. A typical example marked 1678 has an ovoid body of brown, a heavy foot-rim, short, sturdy wide cylindrical neck and heavy curved loop handle. The inscription is about the neck in white slip unimpressed, but the design on the body consists of diamond forms and scrolls with spots, stamped with a cross pattern throughout. Rackham and Read say, "On the earlier of these jugs manganese has been added over the impressions before glazing." This is the first use of manganese that we find, though some of the browns may have been partly and unconsciously due to it. A posset-pot of the Glaisher Collection was dabbed with bright green before the slip lines were applied. A similar one dated 1691 and with the name IOHN HUGHESON also on it, has green and cream slip dragged in alternating directions much as we see the designs of Egyptian glass, which, of course, these potters had never seen.

Fig. 1186.   Posset-pot of red earthenware with combed white slip decoration and inscription reading, "IOHN HVGHESON 1691." Glaze yellowish streaked here and there with green of copper. Staffordshire. Ht. 9¼". Dr. J. W. Glaisher.

There are other names which occur such as on the example in the B.M. dated 1686 with "IOHN WENTER" and one in the Ashmolean Museum, Oxford, with "ANN BENOM F.K." and 1687, but whether these are names of the potters or of prospective owners we do not know. Some have doubted also that these are Staffordshire wares but we believe the evidence supporting that attribution is secure.

Fareham near Southampton

Posset-pots of red body with band decoration and inscriptions in crinkled strips of clay of white, dull red or stained green are attributed to Fareham, near Southampton.

"Metropolitan" or London Ware

A very simple sort of jug of red body with slight design and sometimes inscriptions trailed in white slip and covered with yellow glaze is found in and near London. These have all the appearance of the late Tickenhall group or even less well developed ware and one owned by B. T. Harland is inscribed "BE NOT HY MINDED BUT FEAR GOD, 1638" bearing out the earlier dating. A few examples are in the London Museum.

A still cruder and more summarily designed ware may come from London or from Staffordshire though the former seems more likely. These are thinly potted in buff clay, covered with a white slip, and dabbed with large spots placed in an irregular row and streaked with crude stripes. Rackham and

Read place them as late as the 17th century but, if this is their date, they show a definite decadence.

"Feathered" or "Combed" Wares

On the posset-pot above mentioned we spoke of dragged or "combed" design. This dated 1691 but the technique became popular about 1680 to 1700 or later in general, and "marbling," "feathering" and "graining" methods were devised. The technique was not used much at all in the North Countries of the continent where modeling made the surface textures, but here again it picks up the ancient stunt and carries it on probably not through any connection with Egyptian or Chinese or Near Eastern wares but just as a natural development arrived at through playing around with colored slips. Various rows of spots of slip were applied and while still fluid were dragged with a point or comb. This again appears easy enough but one should try it on the curved surface of a vessel to see how tricky it really is. The slip has to be just so moist and the body just slippery enough and the touch must be exceedingly light. Hannover's "peasant wares" forsooth! He should have tried it.

The method was used in various parts of the country. Some are known as "Welsh ware" and were made at Hounslow while others come from the northern potteries. In the V. & A. Museum is one marked "SCOTTS SUPERIOR FIRE-PROOF, SUNDERLAND."

Of course the more direct and primitive process of mixing clays together like marble cake produced the "agate ware" in the late 17th century but both seem to have not been copied from any known imported examples.

Incised, Graffito or Sgraffito Wares

A potter named Ralph Shaw of Burslem took out a patent in 1733 to make chocolate brown and white striped curious pottery with a salt glaze but three years later Mr. Shaw's patent was taken away from him, so some of the large number of pieces known must have been made by others. A salt glazed bowl from the collection of Mr. Wallace Elliot is hard chocolate brown, covered inside with white slip, and outside with a band of the same through which a design has been scratched. Every other piece known has lead glaze with nowhere nearly such artistry. The un-, initiated might even think this bowl to be Sung Chinese, so good is it. Very likely this is a real Ralph Shaw piece and it is a pity that he was not allowed to continue.

FIG. 1190. Devonshire jug of red ware with white slip and greenish-yellow glaze, much in style of certain South China, Ming wares. Inscribed, "Now i am come for to supply your workmen when in haruist dry when they do labour hard and sweat good drink is better far than meat. In winter time when it is cold i like wayes then good ale can hold all seasons do the same require and most men do strong drink desire. W H 1724, 1724, 1724." Ht. 13½". Ex Dr. J. W. Glaisher Coll.

The later type such as that shown with a bird design and dated 1753 shows strong resemblance to South German wares and the "Gabri" 10th to 11th century ones done with a light slip over a dark body with dabs of color on the slip in this case slate blue, to relieve the hardness. Of course it is not possible that these English potters had ever seen the Persian or Sung wares.

The incised method was used also in the West Country and Wales at such places as Donyat, Somersetshire and Crock Street where the thicker and more crude ware even more resembles "Gabri." The latest date found on any of them is 1779. But in many places in Devonshire and elsewhere about the country the method is used even to-day. A Devonshire one also from the Glaisher Collection looks very much like a certain type of Ming example from China, and by 1724, its date, there were quite possibly imported pieces to work from.

From about Salisbury are pieces of red body and with a very iridescent manganese glaze and these are variously dated between 1603 and 1800. The decoration is incised and several bear the initials W.Z. followed in one case by the word "MAKER." A fine covered goblet in the Salisbury, South Wilts and Blackmore Museum is inscribed "HERE IS THE GEST OF THE BARLY KORNE GLAD HAM I THE CILD IS BORN, 1692 I.G.R.K.S.K." and this is typical for most of these seem to have been made for christenings.

At many other places red bodied ware had brown or manganese glaze over simple incising. Some odd conceptions seem to have been favorites such as the modeled bear-holding-a-

FIG. 1191. Buff earthenware jug with thick, glossy dark brown glaze. Head forms cover. Midlands 18th cent. Ht. 11". Mrs. J. W. Gaunt.

cub jug with detachable head cover and a small monkey on the handle. This sort of jug was also made in the white Staffordshire ware and elsewhere. Little molded plaques were continued in use and undoubtedly gave Wedgwood his ideas later.

Finally Rackham and Read state that the wares of the 19th century were made in Blackburton in Lancashire, Pot-Howcans, near Halifax, at Midhope near Sheffield and at Polesworth in Warwickshire. They also state, "It is also interesting to note the spread of this technique to the United States, where pottery quite similar in technique was made in the early 19th century at Huntington, Long Island. This New England ware is quite distinct in character from the slipware made in Pennsylvania by German Immigrants." Of course we now know that the English were also partly responsible for the Pennsylvania wares and they need not have been so much on the defensive. In fact the plate with bird design is very much like both Long Island and Pennsylvania ones.

Here again we have found an unsullied art practiced by free men who were not forced to copy and could suit themselves.

FIG. 1194. Red-ware ink-well with rich chocolate-brown slip decorated in white slip under usual transparent glaze. Dia. 3″. Plummer, Ltd.

FIG. 1192. Red earthenware jug with inlayed design and inscription reading, "Mrs. SHOO-SMITH? CATERBURY? 1809," in white slip, Sussex. This is a technique chiefly of Korea, of course, but arrived at here without outside influence. Ht. 12⅜″. Coll. of Mrs. Hemming.
FIG. 1193. Cup with four handles and a whistle, of brown ware with incised decoration under lead glaze with flecks of iron. Inscribed, "HERE IS THE GEST OF THE BARLY KORNE. GLAD HAM I THE CILD IS BORN I G 1692," and on foot, "RK SK." Found at Mere, Wilshire but made near Salisbury. Ht. 8½″. Salisbury, South Wilts and Blackmore Mus.

ENGLISH FAÏENCE OR "DELFT"
AND THE FOREIGN INFLUENCE

The first direct foreign influence was indicated, of course, in the Tudor period (c1428–   ) with the green glazed heraldic wares but these did not continue much beyond the start of the 16th century. The general use of the word "Delft" is misleading, though it is customary in England, for the first wares of this sort came direct to England from Italy even before Delft was started in any great degree. Guido di Savino, from Castel Durante, went to Antwerp and was established by 1513. He has been linked with Guido Andries and Jacob Janson who left Antwerp to avoid persecution and settled in Norwich, later in 1570 moving to London. From this date, presumably in the "waterside" parishes Southwark and Lambeth, tin-enamelled wares were made. At Norwich we hear they made tiles and apothecaries' jars. (Cf. John Stow, "A Survey of the Cities of London and Westminster and the Borough of Southwark, 1598," 6th ed., London, 1755, Vol. II, p. 327.)

Some wares found in London, Oxford and elsewhere might almost be thought to be Italian majolica. They are decorated in polychrome, or are blue and white with the same bright colors but are somewhat different in form. For instance vases were made with a wide neck and bulbous bodies having two small loops, useless as handles or for tying on a cover, neither original nor sensible shapes. They often have the sacred monogram "yhs" in Gothic characters or at times a bird recalling those of Faenza ware. A polychrome tile showing a man in the dress of about 1530 is in the Guildhall Museum, London and is of the same class exactly as tiles with busts from the Herckenrode abbey, Belgium, Limburg, now in Brussels. Duplicates are also found in the bed of the Scheldt, Antwerp and in Brussels itself. Another from the house of Sir Nicholas Bacon built between 1563 and 1568 is in the exact colors of the Flemish tiles, blue, green and orange. It seems likely that this is of the early work of Jasper Andries and Janson.

A group of wares showing Italian influence are glossy enameled plates with foliage painted peculiarly with each leaf one half yellow, one half orange, with green and blue added. Another type has fruit including pomegranates bursting. A fine jug of the Early Stuart Period bears a picture of a youth in the dress of James I, fruits, flowers and foliage, in yellow, brown and blue. This has a medallion encircled with an English inscription and three initials in triangular arrangement, which is peculiarly English.

MOTTLED IMITATION STONEWARE

Similar in shape to the stoneware jugs of Cologne and Frechen are earthenware enamelled ones with globular bodies and cylindrical necks quite different in substance from any European ones. The glazes are brown, tawny yellow, dark green, purplish black and dark blue usually, though other odd colors do occur, and all seem to have been daubed or splashed on, combined

FIG. 1195. Earthenware jug covered with mottled purplish blue enamel, having chased silver-gilt mounts bearing London hall-mark for 1550. Ht. 7½". Lord Swaything.

FIG. 1196. Raeren (c. 1580–1600) stoneware flagon with brown mottled glaze and renaissance silver mounts. Ht. 9½". Plummer, Ltd.

FIG. 1197. Enamelled mug sprayed with purple in which there is a band about top reserved in white and painted in blue, "ELIZABETH BROCKLEHVRST 1628." London (Lambeth or Southwark). Ht. 5". Victoria & Albert Mus.

with a flux. They are usually mounted with English silver or silvergilt covers and bases, the hall-marks of which show them to date about the middle of the 16th century.

These were not made by foreign workmen as they are technically entirely different from anything on the continent. The English silversmiths did seek the continental "tiger ware" to mount and these were probably used for models for general shape.

ENGLISH FAÏENCE
"LAMBETH DELFT WARE"
OR
"METROPOLITAN TIN-GLAZED WARE"

Around 1630 we find that there were kilns at first in London and then a little later in Bristol and the nearby village of Brislington, Liverpool and a small place at Wincanton in Somersetshire. The products of the London potters came to be called "Lambeth Delft Ware" which is doubly wrong for Delft was not yet known as a pottery center and all the potters were not in the Lambeth parish of London, but in Southwark and Bermondsey where some sherds were found near a street called "Potter's Field." In 1690 there was also a potter at Aldgate. It is difficult to argue against even an incorrect tradition in England, however. Rackham and Read have suggested the term "Metropolitan tin-glazed ware" which, though grand sounding, is no more sensible. As the word faïence is generally accepted for this type of ware, and, as we cannot list all the places where it was made, I suggest that the ware be simply called "English Faïence."

FIG. 1198. Rare English faïence shoe decorated in blue with yellow heels, 1759. Length 8". Courtesy—A Collector.

It is argued that as Joseph Medway, an Englishman, was employed as a thrower in Rotterdam in 1649 and Andrew Morton was a foreman in 1629 in another factory in the same city, the making of the ware must have preceded these dates in England. Of course, both may have been entirely foreign trained in their work. However, a piece recorded by B. J. Warrick and shown at the Burlington Club in 1914 has a silver collar on which in Latin there is a report of having bought it in 1618. This is decorated with mottled manganese and cobalt sprayed on the surface of the enamel, a process not found exactly the same on the continent. The same technique is found on a barrel-shaped mug in the V. & A. Museum clearly dated 1628 together with the English name ELIZABETH BROCKLEHURST. This technique is in the line of general development and was probably not copied from anywhere, though it has been used almost everywhere.

Also in 1628 is a globular jug so dated in the Collection of B. T. Harland which is near white with blue decoration of birds and flowers. Others of similar decoration date around 1631 or 1632. The designs are described as Chinese but are very much more crude and have some different characteristics from even the worst of the Canton wares of the time. By 1640 no more such

Group of "Lambeth delft" chargers partly blue and white and partly polychrome, all dating in late 17th cent. Upper left is Duke of Monmouth, center below is identical figure serving for Prince "Eugin." This was often done. Probably upper right is James II fleeing and lower right is William of Orange. Average dia. 13½". Guitel Montague.

Enamelled earthenware plate painted in blue, yellow, orange and green outlined in deep purple, inscribed, "THE ROSE IS RED THE LEAVES ARE GRENE GOD SAVE ELIZABETH OVR QVEENE." London, 1602. Dia. 10⅛". London Mus.

Enamelled earthenware jug painted in blue, yellow, orange and dull yellow-green. On front is youth in dress of early Stuart period in medallion about which is inscribed, "I AM NO BEGGER I CAN NOT CRAVE BVT YV KNOW THE THING THAT I WOVLD HAVE." On the neck are the initials $_R^C$ E. Lambeth or Southwark, London c. 1630. Ht. 12½". Colonel John Parker.

Platter of relief and polychrome decoration called "Lambeth Delft." Mark on back is A–NLP. Length 20½". International Studio Art Corp.

ENGLISH FAÏENCE ("LAMBETH DELFT") OF THE 17TH CENTURY

PLATE 208

designs are used and only later was there a return of Chinese influence through the copying of the Dutch so-called "Nanking blue ware."

From about 1632 Italian designs came in at first through the Low Countries and these were most popular in Bristol. They are largely of fruit, flowers, etc. and have formalized borders usually edged with diagonal blue strokes for which they have been called "Blue Dash Chargers" by Ed. A. Downman. Some of these too were made in Brislington and London. The wares are buff, covered on the front only with tin enamel, while the backs have only a transparent lead glaze of yellowish or greenish tone. The enamel is white and the painting is in orange, yellow, purple, green and blue. The drawing was

Fig. 1199. Posset pot of "Lambeth Delft" made about 1700–1720. Ht. 5¾". "Liverpool Delft" mug with handle in blue and white made in early 18th cent. Ht. 4¾". Owl after those made in Germany. Ht. 4 Guitel Montague.

crude and the anatomy particularly of the Bristol and Brislington pieces is bad. The foot-rim was flared outward and made fairly deep so that a cord could be tied around it to hang the piece on the wall. The earliest is one owned by Dr. Glaisher dated 1628 which has a design of all-over foliage with spiraled stems and conventionalized flowers reminiscent of Spanish lustre decoration. Some have portraits of sovereigns and important personages, others the Temptation of Adam and Eve while fruit heaped on a high footed dish seems to have been a later motive. They lasted at least until 1674 for there is one so dated also in the Glaisher Collection.

URBINO AND FAENZA TYPES

Another group in softer colors of purple, brownish-orange and blue have grotesques, caryatids, winged beasts, etc., in the styles of Urbino and Faenza but more crowded and loosely painted. These are not copied from Dutch "Urbino Delft" which is quite different. The Glaisher group includes one dated 1649 with the initials $_{E\ M}^{\quad B}$ in the center of the front and the added colors of yellow and yellow-green.

A cistern dated 1638 and with the initials $_{T\ I}^{\ I}$ had a modeled figure,

English faïence dish showing Urbino influence, painted in blue, yellowish-green, yellow, brownish-orange and purple. In center is $_E^B$ M and date 1649. Made in London at Lambeth or Southwark. Dia. 15¼". Ex Dr. J. W. Glaisher Coll.

London faïence dish painted blue, green, yellow and orange. Inscribed on back under lead glaze: $_R^A$ M 1640. Dia. 17". Mr. J. H. Taylor.

Dishes showing "The Fall." Upper one London, painted in blue, yellowish-green, yellow and brownish-orange. Lower, Bristol ware painted in blue, yellow, green, dark purple and dark red, trees being "sponged." Both are middle to late 17th cent. Hts. 14" and 13¾" W. M. Beaumont.

Left: So-called "Lambeth Delft" said to be rare in this size. Portrait, James II. Ground pale turquoise, drawing in plum and bright orangy yellow. Note three spur marks. Dia. 7¼". Frank Stoner–Stoner & Evans, Ltd.
Right: Faïence cistern described in text. Ht. 15¼". Hanley Mus.

English "delft" or faïence flagons with tin glaze and lettering in light blue on first reading WHIT 1651 and on other monogram of Queen Mary. Hts. 5½" and 6¾". Guitel Montague.

ENGLISH FAÏENCE (17TH CENTURY)

PLATE 209

flanked by two pilasters, paintings on the sides of the Spinario and Cupid
and panels of allegorical figures in landscapes above panels of grotesques in
the Urbino manner. The colors are partly blue and white and partly blue,
purple and brownish yellow. But the interesting thing about this mixed up
piece is that the back has a typical symmetrical "Indian flower" design like
those of South Germany or the Kreussen c. 1618 to c. 1660 ones even to the
spirals. This piece seems to have borrowed from everywhere. It is in the

Fig. 1200. English faïence pharmacy jars inscribed in blue, c. 1720. Ht. 12″. Probably Lambeth. Courtesy—A Collector.

Fig. 1201. Small feeding-cup of English faïence, probably from Lambeth with relief Tudor Rose decoration and white glaze. c. 1645. Mrs. Bruce.

Hanley Museum. Generally speaking these designs are found only on Bristol
pieces and never on the London ones which is strange and can be accounted
for only by some now unknown potter having gone there.

OTHER TYPES

A number of the Adam and Eve plates were made and it is conceded that
the London ones are far better than those from Bristol and thereabouts.
One in the collection of W. M. Beaumont, due to a notch in the tree excused
by a notch on the other side, and some cleverly placed foliage, gives Adam
quite a masculine look, which shows the playful and not too touchy humor
of the period.

A few were of religious nature showing the Nativity, "Prodigal Son feasting
with harlots," etc. One in the V. & A. Museum, painted in blue, green and
yellow shows a figure of St. Mary Magdalene with crudely drawn house and
castle in the background in the style of the period as can be seen in embroideries.

TECHNICAL CHARACTERISTICS

As we have said most of these wares are only lead glazed on the back, not
like the good Delft but like what the Hollanders call "schotelgoed." They
had no protection of saggers in the kiln and were simply fired like tiles. Of
them Hannover says, "This English 'Delft' is in every respect inferior to
the genuine article, and is obviously quite different from it from a technical
point of view. Whereas the true Delft is so soft in body that it can be cut
with a knife, it is difficult to scratch the English variety with a steel point."
(I fail to see how this is an inferior characteristic.) "Genuine Delft is of a
porous clay, which drank up the enamel far more readily than the English, and

is therefore completely and evenly covered with glaze in quite another manner than the latter. Lastly, English Delft is often much crackled in its glaze, whilst the Dutch, as has been remarked on an earlier page, hardly ever has this defect." In other words the English material is put in the strange category of being a copy of Delft, which it is not, and then declared to be no good because it is not. Certainly hardness is not a bad point; crackle is considered pleasant in texture and all told the English seem to have pulled down such criticisms because of their unfortunate choice of the name "Lambeth Delft."

Some of the shapes not used on the continent are: barrel-shaped mugs, truncated egg-shaped mugs, wine bottles with wide body and narrow necks, posset-pots usually with spouts for sucking the liquid and slabs for pill-making decorated with the arms of the Apothecaries' Company.

Fig. 1202. English faïence wall-pocket, c. 1730. Courtesy—A Collector.

Posset, according to the *Century Dictionary* is, "A drink composed of hot milk curdled by some infusion, as wine or other liquor, formerly much in favor both as a luxury and as a medicine." L. Jewitt in his "Ceramic Art of Great Britain" (first ed.) I., p. 108 says, "Posset is an excellent mixture of hot ale, milk, sugar, spices and sippets or dice of bread or oat cake, almost if not quite universal for supper on Christmas eve." It is evident that such a mixture could not be drunk from a spout unless the liquor was simply drained off from the bottom. Perhaps the earlier sort was not thickened with bread and such.

Of continental type wares there are those similar to the late ones of Bernard Palissy, square salt-cellars and various dishes molded with the subject called "La Fécondité" ranging from about 1659 to 1697 according to the dates on them.

The wine bottles were labeled SACK, WHIT, CLARET or RENISH WINE with sometimes a personal coat of arms and name added. They may have been used for samples as they seem to contain too little for table use in those days, at least this suggestion has been made by Mr. Frank Falkner. The apothecaries' jars had the names of drugs on them.

Fig. 1203. Mugs covered with dark and light blue enamel respectively, decorated with white slip. Upper London, lower either London or Bristol. Hts. 3½" and 5¼". City Art Gallery, Manchester. Mr. Edward Sheldon.

WHITE ON BLUE WARE

Infrequent Italian majolica and Delft but a usual technique of Nevers, France, was that of staining the enamel with cobalt and then applying the design in white arsenical slip on it. At Bristol this was done with a blue of dark inky tone, while at London it was lighter showing up the crackle even through the white. The designs were of crude Chinese character. There were also wares of a similar nature with blue combined with manganese.

ORIGINS OF BRISTOL WARES

In speaking of the cistern above we mentioned that the symmetrical flowers must have been brought by some individual potter or group of potters who came to Bristol not by way of London. The factories seem to have started from one of Edward Ward, "galley pot maker," in Brislington. Rackham

FIG. 1204. Enamelled earthenware plate of greenish tone, painted with deep yellow, dull red, blue and dull yellowish-green. Probably by Michael Edkins (c. 1760). Bristol. Dia. 9″. Brig.-General Sir Gilbert Mellor K.B.E.

FIG. 1205. Plate by John Bowen of Bristol painted in blue on white. c. 1760. Ht. 8¾″. Mr. R. Hall Warren.

FIG. 1206. Enamelled earthenware dish painted in blue, yellow, orange and clear turquoise-green, 1676. Probably Bristol. Dia. 12¾″. Dr. J. W. Glaisher.

and Read say the word "gallipot" occurs in 1465 and was thought to have been used to designate pottery of all shapes that were brought from the Mediterranean in galleys. I think this theory unsound. They further say, "Dutch writers of the 17th century interpret 'glei' as meaning porcelain clay" (that is clay used for making tin-enamelled ware, then not distinguished from true porcelain). The general idea to-day seems to be a small mouthed

FIG. 1207. Dish, Bristol (?), painted in dark and light cobalt blue, yellow and turquoise blue outlined in purple, inscribed S and dated 1676. Dia. 8¼″. Ex Dr. J. W. Glaisher Coll.

FIG. 1208. English faïence pilgrim bottle roughly decorated in purple or aubergine of manganese. Bristol (?) Early 18th cent. Ht. 7¾″. Plummer, Ltd.

jar such as would be *used* on a ship. In any event Ward went to Bristol and built a pottery at Temple Back which remained in his family until 1741. It was the parent of the present Bristol factory at Fishponds. Ward's pupil, Thomas Frank, opened a factory at Brislington at Redcliff Back and his son worked at both places. Still another pottery was opened at Limekiln Lane by William Pottery, and John Bowen began his apprenticeship here in 1734. He worked later for Joseph Flower and others.

CHARACTERISTICS OF BRISTOL

We have said that the drawing of anatomy at Bristol was less good than that of the London wares and that the symmetrical flowers are characteristic. The colors include a slaty blue, "quaker green," dull yellow, brownish-orange and occasionally manganese and pale turquoise blue and are softer than the colors used at London. Plate edges are often scalloped, foliated or octagonal. Punch bowls had flattened flaring sides tangent to the curve of the bottoms. Posset-pot lids sometimes took the form of the royal crown with open-work bows, and the handles were in the form of snakes or rolls of clay twisted into the shape of coiled tendrils. Oblong flower holders with holes in the top for stems (see our illustration) were characteristic. Even tea-table wares were attempted toward the end of the 18th century but were clumsy and not popular.

FIG. 1209. "Bristol Delft" "crocus-pot" with polychrome decoration. c. 4″ high. Guitel Montague.
FIG. 1210. English "delft" crocus pots with grids and decorated with almost identical scenic subjects. Even when art was not wholly mechanical such was dearth of imagination that painters copied their own work over and over. c. 1730. Lengths c. 6″. Guitel Montague.

Perhaps the best painter was John Bowen who confined himself to blue on white wares and created an odd fairyland with stately ladies and gentlemen strolling among tall and misty trees and gaunt houses all in the most economical brush work, while on the other hand his ships show accuracy and attention to detail.

Michael Edkins is reported to have been a scene-painter, enameller of both faïence and Bristol glass and a good musician. Most of his known things are of chinoiserie character.

Joseph Flower started a factory at Redcliff in 1743. He painted in imitation of engravings and showed more skill than taste but at times also a naïve simplicity. He made starch-blue and lavender blue plates with broad white flowers on the rims in the bianco-sopra-bianco style and having centers of landscapes in blue or flowers in purple-blue, olive green and brownish orange. The same blue enamel with white flowers in borders is used inside

Bristol posset-pot painted purple, blue and yellow in pseudo-Chinese style. Late 17th cent. Ht. 9½″. Brighton Mus.

Posset-pot and tray of pale blue faïence decorated in cobalt-blue with border of tray in purplish-blue. Both pot and tray have   and are dated
T
C A
1685. Ht. 13½″. Ex Dr. J. W. Glaisher Coll.

Right: Punch bowl covered with pale lavender-blue and painted by **John Bowen** with **white slip** borders and Swedish ship inside with landscape with figures outside. 1728. Bristol, factory of Joseph Flower. Dia. 11⅜″. City Art Gallery, Manchester.

Left: Bristol mid-18th cent. tin enamel plate painted in blue, brown, dull, dark red, yellow and olive green. Dia. 12½″. Warren E. Cox Coll.

Center: Bristol plates, upper in blue, green, yellow, orange and dark purple (c. 1670). Lower in blue, orange and olive green (last of 17th cent.). Dias. 16½″ and 14½″. Mr. B. T. Harland. Mr. W. W. Beaumont.

Right: Bristol faience plates, upper in blue, yellow, dark orange, green and dark purple with figure of William III, c. 1700. Lower in blue, green and brownish red with portrait of Dr. Sacheverell c. 1720. Dias. 14″ and 11″. Mr. B. T. Harland. Brighton Mus.

BRISTOL FAÏENCE (17TH AND 18TH CENTURIES)

PLATE 210

of bowls having ships in blue with touches of color for the flags, the sea, etc. He liked conical trees like the clipped boxwood ones one sees in England. Tiles were made at all the factories but were a feature here and were both individual and with grouped designs.

It has been claimed that Liverpool wares are thinner than the others and that Bristol is slightly more bluish or greenish in tone but neither rule is entirely true. In fact it is difficult to distinguish between Bristol and Liverpool wares for the flowers are identical except for perhaps a greater stiffness of stem and more direct brush work, less inclined to curlicues and scratchiness distinguishes Bristol work.

London plates were made in blue decoration of formal wreaths with legends, often beginning, "What is a merry man, etc.," including also ones which refer to the frailty of earthenware, expressions of sentiment, etc. At Bristol a special group includes a bowl of lavender grey with painting in white and inscription in blue celebrating the candidacy for Oxfordshire, 1755, of Viscount Wenman and Sir James Dashwood, Bart. The outside of this bowl has Chinese decorations in heavy manganese-purple and blue. This was a type often found.

FIG. 1211. Two plates from factory of Joseph Flower covered with pale lavender-blue, with borders of white and center painting in purple, blue, olive-green and dull, brownish orange. c. 1760. Dias. 8¾" and 16¼". Bristol Mus. and Art Gallery. Mr. W. R. Ackland.

SPATTERED GROUND WARES

Evidently suggested by the Chinese powder blue was a speckled ground used in the same way about reserve medallions. They date around 1754 and were in blue, manganese-purple, brown or yellow, not made by blowing powdered color onto a glaze but by spattering with a brush. Round, fan-shaped and shell-shaped reserved medallions were used both in Bristol and Liverpool.

Generally speaking Bristol took more interest in Chinese design than the other places. John Niglett who had a factory at Redcliff had an original color scheme of mahogany-red of

FIG. 1212. Bristol "delft" pomegranate tea-pot with yellow stippled ground. Ht. 4½". c. 1730-40. Guitel Montague.

sticky appearance, blue, sage-green and bright lemon yellow. His designs include the "long Lizas" of the Chinese, happy boys, rocks and palisades in a sort of clumsy imitation of K'ang Hsi style. Both John Flower and Edkins also made attempts after the same style. Of course, these all lacked the beautiful brush work and brilliant but harmonious colors of the Chinese but they should not be compared for they were not so much copies as individual works of art inspired by the Chinese and they have an appeal of their own in the soft qualified colors and almost childlike drawing.

HUMANISM IN ART

There is also a homely humanism in this art. When we think of humanism we think of Will Rogers, Mark Twain, the present etcher S. Van Abbe in England, of Hogarth, Franz Hals and Will Shakespeare. What is this element which occurs in such different arts?

One may argue that all art is human as it is done by humans and for humans. Yet we think of some people as being more human than others even though they are of the same flesh and blood. If one is too alive he is not so human; if one is too dull, too careful, too good or too bad, he loses some of this human quality. Are we to come to the conclusion that to be human one should be just average or as Will Rogers said it, "know only what he reads in the papers"? Well hardly that. I think he said that just to make people more comfortable. I heard him in Cochran's Review in London kid the people about paying their war debt to the United States, kid about the Prince of Wales falling off his horse and say things that you would think quite impossible. Yet they liked it and paid him a high salary to come back and give them more. Perhaps this was because he said, "I never saw the man I did not like." Perhaps they felt his sympathy with all people underlying his kidding.

A human man is liked by dogs, children and cats. He has a sense of humor and not too much regard for himself. He will often play with an idea for some time before coming to any definite, hard and fast conclusion. He is seldom a religionist, though Christ was perhaps one of the most human of people. He is seldom a business man or scientist for their codes, ethics, rules and principles are too set and formalized to ever catch the fluid character of the really human world. He is interested in a *man* not in some one idea which represents that man, and he expects and allows for many contradictions in the thoughts and character of a man. And then fundamentally, of course, he has no fear for himself or his position or his reputation. He can smile at the world for he is not afraid and not very serious about it. He is willing to give up himself and even to give up any idea or any cause because of his breadth of vision. The army men used to express it by saying, "A hundred years from now nobody will know anything about it." And by this very attitude a number of men will be remembered for many centuries though they did not expect it or aim for it.

Perhaps we are trying to say something very similar to the ideas and beliefs of the Taoists and Zen Buddhists of the Far East; a human man is one who does not try to buck the current but stays in the flow of the universe.

It is fear that makes an artist copy another artist. It takes courage, that many men lack, to sing a song. The very courage of a man is in his approach to other men, to animals and to children, and it can be seen in the carriage, the look of the eye and, it is said, animals can even tell it by the smell of a person. This simple courage to do something of one's own was evident in the early potteries of England but it was lost by the 18th century porcelain makers to a great extent. They were frail but certainly not human in the large sense.

WINCANTON

Potters from Bristol established that less good factory at Wincanton, sherds of which were discovered by William Pountney. Blue and white, and manganese and white were of common style except for some which were sponged or splashed with reserve medallions in the usual manner. Some plates have a brown line at the edge. Again the design is scratched out of the colored ground and this was also done earlier at Liverpool and Bristol. An accidental strong pinkish tone occurs on many pieces.

FIG. 1213. Speckled purple ground plate with reserves painted in blue. Inscription reads: WINCANTON 1738. Somersetshire. Dia. 8¾". Ex Dr. J. W. Glaisher Coll.

Chinese plants with frond-like leaves set in trellis borders are typical. Dr. Glaisher has two plates dated 1738 and 1739 having St. George on one and a Chinese pavilion on the other. Both are marked WINCANTON. Other examples have the usual arms, etc.

STAFFORDSHIRE

To quote Rackham and Read, "More satisfactory evidence than has yet been brought forward will be needed to prove that delft ware was ever made in Staffordshire."

LIVERPOOL

Liverpool did not become a pottery center until well into the 18th century and had not the early tradition that Bristol had. Its chief outlet was American

FIG. 1214. English faïence puzzle-jug decorated in blue and inscribed, "HERE GENTLEMEN COME TRY YOUR SKILL I'LE WAGER IF YOU WILL, THAT YOU DON'T DRINK THIS LIQUOR ALL WITHOUT YOU SPILL OR LET SOME FALL." Attr. to Richard Chaffers, c. 1750. Ht. 7¼". Plummer, Ltd.

FIG. 1215. One of pair of Liverpool "delft" sitting dogs on moulded bases made hollow and with slot in their backs as though intended for banks but so small a slot that few coins could be inserted. Underglaze blue, green and aubergine stipplings with overglaze yellow. c. 1730-40. Ht. 8⅜". Ernest F. Follows.

and other foreign markets. The best known potters were Alderman Thomas Shaw, who made ship punch-bowls, Seth Pennington, Richard Chaffers and Zachariah Barnes who made tiles.

The secret of transferring of copper plate etched or engraved designs onto paper and then onto the faïence was discovered by John Sadler and Guy Green in 1749. At first this was done only on the fired glaze but later they accomplished it on the unfired body. The paper was thin and soft so that when wet it would readily bend over the curved surface. Only a press, a little soap and the usual color to be fired on are necessary. One can begin to understand what happened to the art of faïence when it is understood that in 1756 they claimed they could print 1,200 tiles in six hours. The prints were in black, red or purple.

Rackham and Read say, "The mechanical process coming between the designer of the decoration and the finished product robs this type of ornamentation of any great aesthetic value," and this is putting it mildly and not quite right. Actually it was nothing more nor less than the temptation to make cheap things ever cheaper that ruined all chance of real art. Artistic things have been done in etching and artistic things could have been done in this medium, but they were not.

A chief product of Liverpool was the punch-bowl variously decorated with a ship in full sail and an inscribed ribbon. The outside was usually treated with the old designs of flowers, birds and insects. Such bowls may have been used to drink the luck of a voyage. They certainly were not used on board. John Robinson, apprentice of Seth Pennington, did one with the fleet and the legend, "Success to the Africa Trade." The Liverpool purple was almost black at times and the red was more russet than that used at Bristol. Other colors used were blue, yellow, olive green and occasionally brown. Trophies of weapons or naval gear in blue only around the borders or on the outside are also characteristic.

Some ship-bowls have Chinese landscapes on the outside and

Fig. 1216. Six tiles about 5" square all from Bristol except the one with children dancing and "Mr. Woodward in the character of Razor," which are Liverpool, the first having been printed by Sadler & Green in red c. 1755 and the second by the same people printed in black. Victoria & Albert Mus.

some bowls were Chinese in character throughout. One in the Glaisher Collection and dated 1724 has lambrequins of the Rouen type. Another dated 1760 and wishing "Success to the Monmouth" has cranes on the outside similar to the "Fantasievogel" of German porcelain and to the exotic birds of Chelsea and Worcester, painted in yellow, dark purple and orange amidst purple and olive-green foliage.

Large flowers were painted on mugs in slate-blue, brown-orange, violet and olive-green on a bluish toned ground. Whole services carefully copied Ch'ien Lung contemporary blue and white ones of the South Chinese type with peonies, etc., but were so bad as to do no harm.

The tiles have an almost child-like simplicity of design and were often done in blue with the addition of just one other color. This was rather typical of many Liverpool wares. Sadler and Green made a series of actors in character. Others copied Chinese birds, French prints, etc. Bowen made some with his personal landscapes having tall feathery trees. Of course Sadler and Green printed designs for other factories and the process was not long kept a secret so that sure attribution of the printed wares is difficult and perhaps not worth the trouble anyhow.

By 1800 the lead glazed cream wares made all over England crowded out all worthy endeavor at Liverpool as elsewhere.

English Stoneware

There is some looseness in the application of the term "stoneware" as there is in porcelain, faïence and the other branches of ceramic arts. Hobson says stoneware is a partly vitrified earthenware attained by hard firing, that it is frequently translucent in its thinner parts, is impervious to liquids and able to resist acids. Burton simply says that stoneware consists of those varieties of earthenware which when sufficiently fired for use are practically impervious to liquids and so do not need a coating of glaze. Actually translucence, though it may be present, is not at all necessary as a characteristic. Furthermore there are some earthenwares, not stonewares, such as those made by the Cistercian monks, which hold liquids without having been glazed. Actually any or all wares are attacked by some acids such as hydrofluoric and this depends also upon the strength of the acid, the temperature, the length of time the application is made among other factors. Let us say then that all stoneware is vitrified sufficiently to ring when struck, to be impervious to liquids even when unglazed, to show translucence occasionally and finally to be harder than earthenware, though there are borderline wares which could go into either category.

Just as England was influenced in faïence by Italy and later by Delft so she was quite naturally influenced in her stoneware by the wares of Frechen, Raeren and Cologne during the 16th and 17th centuries. Licenses were petitioned for by William Simpson during the reign of Queen Elizabeth (1558– 1603), by Thomas Rous in 1626 and by three associates, Ramsey, Arnold and Ayliffe in 1635 who wanted to make, "pantiles, stone jugs, earthen bottles, and other earthen commodityes nowe made by Straungers in Forraigne Partes." Yet we cannot find these wares and it is hardly likely that real stoneware was made until the latter half of the 17th century.

JOHN DWIGHT AT FULHAM

In 1671 and again in 1684 John Dwight obtained a patent to open a factory in Fulham near London. He claimed he could make "opacous red and dark coloured porcellane or China and Persian wares." By the first it is supposed he meant something like Yi-hsing wares or similar to those the brothers Elers made, which were unglazed, but he never really accomplished the "transparent earthenware commonly knowne by the names of porcelaine or china," and we cannot guess what he had in mind as Persian wares, unless they were the contemporary 17th-century porcelaneous ones, which again he never approached.

In 1661 he was registrar to the Bishop of Chester. We hear of no former kiln training. Therefore it is believed that he opened his factory with the help of German potters, and his first wares are very much like those of Frechen and Cologne, wine jugs called "Bartmann" by the Germans with small necks and loop handles and a bearded face on the front of the neck with a rosette or crude shield of arms on the belly. Among some of these found in a walled up chamber at Fulham in 1866 was one with the crowned double C of Charles II, while another has the CR cipher and fleur-de-lys of the same king. A sherd of the ware made at Grenhausen, Nassau, with typical blue and manganese purple coloring was found also in Fulham. Similar wares were made by Symon Wooltus the younger and older in Southampton.

Dwight then developed a white or ivory body which he used for jugs of

FIG. 1219. Fulham stoneware plaque of tobacco-brown with relief bust of cavalier, early 18th cent. Dia. 8¼". Plummer, Ltd.

FIG. 1218. Jug of salt-glazed grey stoneware stained brown near top and decorated with appliqués after Hogarth, etc. Fulham c. 1740. Ht. 7". Brighton Mus.

FIG. 1217. Brown stoneware jug streaked with variegated colors (brown, white and mouse-grey) and decorated with appliqués in white including double bust of William & Mary, Fulham, c. 1690. Period of John Dwight. Ht. 6¾". Ex Coll. Dr. J. W. Glaisher.

German shape. Two of these mounted in silver are in the V. & A. Museum and are dated 1682. Another has dabs of brown and blue on it.

He also developed a marbled ware which was similar to that found in several other countries. Dr. Glaisher has one which is brown streaked with two bands of brown, white and grey, between which are appliqués of white figures, birds and a double bust of William and Mary over which is an angel's face with

Left: Mug of grey stoneware partly covered with brown glaze. Body has double walls with outer reticulated in flowers and foliage with stems incised. Fulham in period of John Dwight, late 17th cent. Ht. 4¾". Mr. Edward Sheldon.

Center: Neptune of grey stoneware covered with brown salt-glaze in imitation of bronze, Fulham, period of John Dwight, late 17th cent. Ht. 12¼". Victoria & Albert Mus.

Right: Fulham grey stoneware mug stained tobacco-brown on upper part as customary, and with interesting trees applied. Foliage made in simple and direct technique. Ht. 7½". (c. 1750). Plummer, Ltd.

Tea-pot of Astbury type and possibly by him. Glaze manganese and appliqués white under lead-glaze. Ht. 5". Guitel Montague.

Interesting oval plaque of chocolate brown ware with bust in white under greenish-yellow, crackled glaze. Attr. to Astbury c. 1740. Plummer, Ltd.

Coffee-pot with molded handle and spout and all-over incising of greatest technical skill. Potting thin and of reddish brown, hard ware. Bottom has psuedo-Chinese square mark. Probably made by Thomas Astbury c. 1740. Ht. 8½". Plummer, Ltd.

Staffordshire salt-glaze bowl of Elers style, c. 1730–40. Ht. 3½". Plummer, Ltd.

Left: Nottingham mug with incised stag-hunt decoration about the center and bands of applied clay grit over which is salt-glaze. Early 18th cent. Ht. 8¼". Brighton Mus.

EARLY ENGLISH WARES OF DWIGHT, ASTBURY AND ELERS
(c. 1700–1750)

PLATE 211

two wings. Others are simply marbled in black and white, brown and grey or brown and white.

Another technique was perfected, that of making double walled jugs with the outer wall perforated. This was done in China and Korea as well as on the continent in a crude way and also later at Nottingham. The appliqués were not always white as mentioned above; a mug in the collection of Edward Sheldon is light brown with stamped spots and pear shaped applied bosses in blue and chocolate colored clays. The process was described by Dwight in 1691 in one of his note books and these also prove that Dwight used flint in his mixture and also made an unglazed stoneware of reddish color.

Hannover and other authorities have said that the unglazed red ware had not been certainly identified but Rackham and Read show one "(period of John Dwight)" (Fig. 133) and say that they think among those now attributed to the Elers brothers we are likely to eventually find Dwight examples.

Some figures were done by Dwight and are of white or slightly buff stoneware, translucent in thinner parts and covered with a salt glaze of uneven thickness. Four other pieces are known which are dark brown and were copied from bronzes. One of Charles II and others of Mars and Jupiter show traces of unfired gilding. A light colored figure of Dwight's daughter inscribed, "Lydia Dwight, dyed March 3, 1673," dates these surely but none were possibly original works of art. Possibly young Grinling Gibbons did the modeling, or Italian sculptors may have been hired.

After John Dwight's death in 1703 the Fulham pottery was continued by his family but the figure work ended except for a possible few buff colored ones with cream colored tin enamel, reflecting the style of Queen Anne.

Beer jugs of the 18th century become more truly English. The grey or buff body is exposed on the lower half while the upper has a brown salt glaze. They are usually cylindrical with rolled and grooved mouldings near the top and bottom and have a grooved handle pinched where it joins the side near the bottom. Appliqués with arched or square shapes, oval or cut to fit the outline of the figures were used for decoration. From about 1720 there were busts of kings

Fig. 1220. Figures of "a sportsman with hound," and "Meleager," of white stoneware with salt-glaze, Fulham of period of John Dwight, late 17th cent. Hts. 9½" and 11". British Mus. Franks Coll.

Fig. 1221. Mug of grey stoneware with brown salt-glaze and applied reliefs. About top is inscribed, "GOD PRESERVE KING GEORGE AND ALL THE ROYAL FAMILY, EDWARD VAUGHAN, 1724." Ht. 8½". Fulham. Brighton Mus.

and queens such as Charles II, William III, Queen Anne, hunting scenes, beef-eaters, hares, stags, etc., all in settings with trees and church spires. On one dated 1729 is the "Midnight Modern Conversation" after Hogarth's well known print. Others had representations of the owners. The inscriptions are stamped on and the whole effect is commercial by the middle of the century.

The factory continues to-day and makes commercial wares and sanitary equipment.

MORTLAKE

At Mortlake a stoneware factory was started about 1800 by Joseph Kishere and in passing we may note also that a faïence kiln was started about 1750 by William Sanders. The former turned out many jugs with reliefs of Toby Filpot, groups of topers and hunting scenes but none are worth study.

YORK, THE MANOR HOUSE

At York in the Manor House, Francis Place had a small factory in the early part of the 18th century. A small cup in the V. & A. Museum proves that the ware was much like Dwight's marbled ware of light grey with markings in dark grey and brown. The potting seemed good and thin. After Place, Clifton made a white ware in imitation of Dwight's also.

NOTTINGHAM AND THE MIDLANDS

In the 14th century Nottingham had earthenware kilns and in 1693 James Morley was named in legal proceedings by Dwight. Morley had worked for Thomas Harper of Southwark. The earliest dated piece attributed to him is

FIG. 1222. Molded Nottingham tea-caddy of brown stoneware inscribed, "Wm. & Ann Lockett, Jan the ye 6:1755. Also tea-pot with incised and brown slip design of same period. Castle Mus. and Art Gallery, Nottingham. Dr. E. J. Sidebotham Coll.
FIG. 1223. Nottingham bear-jug with removable head. Typical clay-grit and salt-glaze. Ht. 10". (c. 1760–1770). Plummer, Ltd.
FIG. 1224. Nottingham mugs of brown stoneware with incised and milled decoration covered with lustrous salt-glaze. Upper, 1720. Hts. 4½" and 8". Castle Mus. and Art Gallery, Nottingham.

a posset-pot of 1700. The carved walled double potted wares seem to have been a pet stunt at Nottingham. The stoneware is light, neat, suave in form and is brown or russet-brown of deep tone on a salt glaze of almost metallic sheen. At times a dark brown slip was used to accent incised designs as on the puzzle-jug shown, but this is the only sort of painting attempted.

The puzzle-jugs were taken from an idea of the Chinese and will only pour in a certain way if the finger is held over certain holes and the vessel is turned in a certain series of motions. Any other attempt will spill the contents. The usual incising and stamping was employed but one characteristic was the close stabbing of the ground with a sharp point, the use of this same technique in borders, designs, etc., and the use of the roulette. Again tiny sherds of clay were sprinkled evenly on parts to give a rough texture. Only later did appliqués come into use.

The Nottingham designs are usually floral though stags, trees, etc., do occur and when not crowded, as they were later, have an honest and direct look. There is a definite resemblance to the pewter designs of Holland and Germany. Many of the forms also suggest metal in their thinness and elegance though all were heavy enough to be suitable for stoneware.

In the Midland, Swinton, later to become Rockingham Porcelain Works, Belper and also Brampton and Chesterfield all copied Nottingham more or less well but none were so good.

INDUSTRIALIZATION IN STAFFORDSHIRE

All the wares described to date were made in England for the use of the common man. The rich people did not use these wares because they drank from silver or glass and ate from silver or imported porcelain. It was tea and coffee which made the rich man become interested in the poor potter, because glass or metal was too hot to hold and there was also a tradition from the Far East that tea tasted better from pottery containers.

The East India Company of England imported a great many of the miscalled "buccaro" tea-pots made at Yi-hsing and elsewhere, even in Japan. (See those sections.) These fetched high prices and it is only natural that the potters of both Holland and England should try to imitate them. From Holland two men came shortly after the revolution in 1688 and settled in Bradwell Wood near Burslem, working as silversmiths in Fulham until they could start themselves as potters. They were the brothers, John Philip Elers and David Elers and whether they had anything to do with Dwight or brought their secrets from Lambertus van Eenhoorn or Ary de Milde in their homeland we do not know for they were masters at surrounding themselves with mystery. It is claimed that they hired only weak-minded workmen whom they locked up each day and searched before they left in the evening. They must have heard about some of the continental "arcanists!" They turned out teapots, cups, jugs, mugs and beakers with stamped appliqués in a pseudo Chinese style and with little figures in the contemporary style of England. Their wares were refined as might be expected from silversmiths.

The English potters seeing the competition tried to make their own wares neater and more refined. The adoption of salt-glaze, instead of the earlier lead glaze, in London, from Germany, led to the making of the famous "Staffordshire salt-glazed wares." Rackham and Read point out that the idea did not take hold in London because of the lack of brushwood and coal. Colonel J. C. Wedgwood said that the lack of large estates in Staffordshire helped and that the "Five towns" section near Burslem was made up of many small holdings on which workmen could have each his own little plot of ground.

For a time the wares of such men as Twyford, Astbury and the Wedgwoods kept their quality in being wheel-shaped and of natural colors, but soon the porcelain competition made for a desire to obtain white wares even though they lost much of their warmth and charm thereby. Early in the 18th century Thomas Astbury brought from Bideford in Devonshire the method of covering the body with a thin, white slip. Of course this lost much modeled detail and the natural plastic quality of the body. Probably either Astbury or Thomas Heath found that calcined flint added to the body would make it white and from then on the colored wares were second rate.

Earthenware, metal or stone molds had been used in making earthenware and not accomplishing any higher quality of aesthetic appeal. Now models were carved from alabaster and a series of clay impressions were made to form a master mold from which working molds could be made in any quantity. The pouring was done with liquid clay and washed around the inside, then left to dry. Any thickness could be obtained by repeating the process. When all is finally dry the mold is taken apart, the sutures trimmed but the original artist's work is thrice removed from the finished article and shrinkage and loss of detail and loss of all the subtle hand quality was the result.

This was bad enough but about 1750 Ralph Daniel brought "Plaster of Paris" which was the final step in the industrialization of the Staffordshire potteries, that industrialization which was the main cause of the death of ceramic art in so many places, as we have found out. It would certainly have been far better had tea never turned the eyes of rich men upon the humble pottery wares, for it was this which made the "improvements," the methods of quantity manufacture and the final squeezing of it for pennies that ruined it completely as an art in the short space of time between 1750 and 1800.

The Elers brothers are thought perhaps to have been at Cologne and they spent a short time at Fulham. About 169[7] they came to Bradwell Wood, so it is supposed. Yet with all the talk of them there is not one piece which can surely be attributed to them. All that we judge them by are pieces which, as Rackham and Read say, "may with probability be attributed to them." Hannover says, "Connoisseurs of the subject, which will hardly be regarded outside of England as a profitable one for study or the activity of collectors, declare that they can distinguish genuine Elers ware from the slightly or much later imitations by the fact that in the former the handles, spouts, etc., show marks of having been made by hand, whilst in the latter they are made in moulds." Yet forgers would hardly overlook such a simple point. David became a merchant in London and a rich lady set up John Philip in the glass and earthenware business in Dublin, according to reports. They had used the lathe. They had or had not used molds, according to the authority whose word you wish to believe. But they certainly did not add one jot to the art of ceramics.

Tradition has it also that John Astbury and Joshua Twyford pretended to be half-wits and succeeded in getting into the Elers' place to obtain the secret of the red ware. In any event Twyford did make a red ware more human and less neat than the other type. He is supposed to have applied vines in relief and crabstock handles. Astbury made similar things in red stoneware we are told. At any rate he set up a factory for the purpose where either his son Thomas Astbury or Thomas Heath made the discovery of white wares with flint added.

Let us examine the dates: In 1710 it was, according to Hannover, that John Philip left for Dublin and his brother is supposed to have gone to London about the same time. It must have been before that date that the red ware was made. Yet the inventor of the red stoneware, Böttger, made his discovery in 1708 or 1709 at the earliest. Fast work! Just how much was due to Böttger, how much to the Elers and how much to Dwight who died in 1703 it is difficult to determine but it certainly seems likely that Böttger and Irminger must have received some impetus from Fulham and one need only look back upon the floundering around of the Meissen factory with its use of lacquer colors, cut glass technique, casting of Chinese figures, etc., to see that the *art* was secondary to the discovery and very uncertain indeed. Surely Dwight must have learned something from Germany, though hardly from Böttger, surely the situation is much like that where most "inventions" are concerned; uncertain to say the least, but surely the art which consisted of appliqués, incising, etc., was simply and soundly developed in England while it was not in Germany, although the very techniques used in England had appeared on much earlier ordinary stoneware in Germany. It seems to have been one of those borrowings back and forth.

SALT GLAZE AND "CROUCH WARE"

Josiah Wedgwood states that the Elers were responsible for the introduction of salt glaze and it may be true. The earliest examples are still in the first half of the 18th century, have a grey body and small white pads pressed on and stamped to form leaves, flowers, berries, etc., connected by thinly rolled stems, all in much the same technique as that of Dwight and the Elers. This is called "Crouch ware," a name which derives from the clay from Derbyshire which was used in the composition. Dr. Thomas Wedgwood seems to have been making this ware as early as 1710 in Burslem. Rackham and Read state positively that the mug dated 1701 in the Stoke-on-Trent Museum is German. But Wedgwood did not sign his wares and it is difficult to know whether many are from him or from the Astbury factory.

Thomas Astbury established a factory in Lane Delph, now Fenton, in 1725 and at this place the father and son made red, buff and brown wares with stamped relief ornaments applied and glazed over with a fine lead glaze. They also made marbled wares and scratch-ornamented wares. The "Portobello bowl" commemorating the capture of Portobello by Admiral Vernon in 1739

Interesting group of salt-glaze teapots from Staffordshire. First, second and sixth of bottom row by Whieldon and have usual "tortoise shell" glazes of yellow, green and brown. Fifth in bottom row has portrait of Frederick the Great and "black arrow" ground. Handle of this one is sort known as "crabstock." Hts. c. 4"-6". Guitel Montague Coll.

Left: White salt-glazed jug with dressing of cobalt-blue. Inscr. "G. E.," Staffordshire c. 1750. Ht. 8½". Col. John Parker.

Center: Early Georgian salt-glaze coffee pot after silver model. Color off white due to many small pores in glaze which give effect of light brown dust over surface. C. 1730. Ht. 5¾". Frank Stoner—Stoner & Evans, Ltd.

Right: Salt-glazed molded mug with bust of King George II and legend, "GOD SAVE THE KING AND MY MASTER," also arms of Leveson-Gower, Staffordshire, c. 1750. Ht. 4⅞". City of Manchester Art Gallery.

Staffordshire salt-glazed tea pot with pale aubergine spout and handle, green ground and turquoise and pale rose flowers with yellow centers surrounding medallions of sketchy character. Chinese influence obvious. Length 8". C. 1770. Frank Stoner—Stoner & Evans, Ltd.

Staffordshire cream jug with salt glaze and enamel floral decoration in bright blue, rose, green and yellow and mat iron red inclined to chip off. c. 1770. Ht. 4". Frank Stoner—Stoner & Evans, Ltd.

SALT-GLAZED PIECES (c. 1730–1750)

PLATE 212

FIG. 1226. Tea-pot of white salt-glazed stoneware with decoration of blue relief appliqués, Staffordshire, early 18th cent. Ht. 5½". Three pieces of "Crouch ware," of drab color with white appliqués, Staffordshire, first half of 18th cent. Hts. 3", 4¾" and 3½". Mr. Edward Sheldon. Mr. C. F. C. Luxmoore.

was made there and is typical, being of red-brown clay with small ships, etc., in white clay applied.

The introduction of flint to the body which we mentioned above occurred about 1720 and this made the body nearly white so that it could more or less imitate porcelain. The reliefs were stained blue with cobalt. The results obtained were not good.

FIG. 1229. Staffordshire loving-cup with incised design filled with blue slip, salt-glazed. c. 1750. Ht. 4¾". Wedgwood Institute, Burslem.

FIG. 1227. Lead-glazed red earthenware tea-pot of Astbury type (c. 1750) painted with enamel colors and gold. Initials M.E. appear on it. Ht. 4¼". Harland Coll.

FIG. 1228. Astbury 2nd mug dating about 1750–55 of red ware with coat of arms applied in white slip and yellow glaze over all. Potting thin. Ht. 5½". Frank Stoner–Stoner & Evans, Ltd.

In the "Scratch blue ware" however the results were better. There are really two distinct types: the first being to scratch a design in the white ware, rub blue into the scratches and then fire it with a salt glaze; the second consisted (not quite so successfully) in applying blue to an area and then scratching through to the white. Both processes had existed in Germany in the Westerwald and had, of course been known for centuries in China. The second is much the rarer, perhaps because the potters were not quite satisfied with it. In fact Rackham and Read are not quite sure they have ever seen a piece

FIG. 1230. Late 18th cent. salt-glazed wall-pockets which are fairly rare. Wm. H. Plummer & Co.

and the one they illustrate may have been done this way or simply incised and then given a light wash of cobalt for instead of the lines being white, the blue has gone into them. This may, possibly, however, in due justice, have happened in the kiln. It is hard to say.

FIG. 1231. "Crabstock" lead glazed tea-pot of tan body with appliqué flowers touched with purple, green and bluish-grey. Ht. 4½". J. H. Taylor Coll.
FIG. 1232. Salt-glazed jug with enamel design after Tenier, c. 1770. Colors blue, rose, green and yellow but clearer and brighter than in many examples. Ht. 6¾". Frank Stoner–Stoner & Evans, Ltd.
FIG. 1233. Fox-head cup of late 18th or early 19th cent. in natural colors. Length 5¼". Plummer, Ltd.

Block-cutting for the molds for salt-glazed wares was done by Aaron Wood, apprentice to Dr. Thomas Wedgwood. Some of these were used also in lead glazed wares. In circles about medallions in much the sort of plan that was used in the Stuart period stumpwork embroidery, we find the various fanciful ideas carried out. A certain amusing association of ideas occurred in these but it was soon lost in the prevailing rococo art.

Enamel decoration was also applied to salt glaze. The earliest examples

"The Fall" in white touched with brown, first half of 18th cent. Ht. 6¾". Ex Col. Dr. J. W. Glaisher.

Unique Staffordshire figure c. 1740. Wallace Elliot Coll. Victoria & Albert Mus.

Cat of red earthenware partly coated with white slip through which floral pattern is incised, then touched with blue and purple under lead glaze, Staffordshire, c. 1750. Ht. 5¼". Ex Coll. Dr. J. W. Glaisher.

Large, important group of light buff earthenware figures with greenish white and brown craze glaze, 1740–50. It is claimed these are some times reproduced in modern days, but I hav never seen one. Length 9¾". Plummer, Ltd.

Whieldon dove cote with typical "tortoiseshell" decoration. Continental model popular for its child-like "quaintness." c. 1760. Ht. 10". Guitel Montague.

SALT-GLAZED FIGURES AND ALSO THOSE OF ASTBURY AND WHIELDON TYPES

PLATE 213

were sent to Holland to be decorated and closely resemble Delft of the Meissen influence in general appearance. The colors of this type are not so bright and vivid as those made after 1750 by the two Dutchmen of Hot Lane and Daniel of Cobridge, who were early "hausmaler" or artists working at their own homes. Some of these wares were sent to London for decoration and also the influences of Chelsea and Worcester porcelain were felt. They were cheaper than porcelain and the colors were made garish to appeal to the lowest taste. Oil gilding was employed. One type had thick white flowers touched with black or gold on a blue ground. This is said to have been the noble invention of Aaron Wedgwood and his brother-in-law William Littler, the porcelain maker of Longton Hall. Then, of course came the transfer printing which we have described.

STAFFORDSHIRE FIGURES

In the first half of the century about 1740 or a little earlier salt-glazed figures were made of delightful charm. "Pew-groups" consisting of a lover and his sweetheart or two elderly people seated on a bench or pew about five or six inches long were made of white clay and decorated with dark brown. Again the figures would be set under a tree very crudely resembling the Chelsea ones. But these were real potters' wares and showed exuberant humor, invention and a childlike simplicity that is most appealing. Note the treatment of the hat on the one shown which was bequeathed by the late Wallace Elliot to the V. & A. Museum. As Mr. Frank Davis has suggested, she seems distantly related to the snake-goddess of Crete, and perhaps in thousands of years when the strange people who excavate the British Isles and try to piece together

Fig. 1234. Lovers under tree and "agate ware" rabbit in white and brown salt-glazed stoneware. First half and middle 18th cent. Hts. 7" and 2⅜". Ex Dr. J. W. Glaisher Coll. City Art Gallery, Manchester.

Fig. 1235. Hand made salt-glazed figures with impressed and also added brown clay touches. Owl-mugs recall those of Germany and China. Hts. 5⅜" and c. 8½". Ex Dr. J. W. Glaisher Coll.

the story of their 18th century inhabitants come across her, they will conclude that the natives bound their breasts very tightly, hid their limbs and worshipped birds but would not admit it, just as their men actually love flowers but would feel embarrassed if caught with one in hand.

Owl jugs were copied but improved upon from the more wooden models of 200 years before made in Germany about 1540. No shields were used but the plumage is ruffled and smart and the claws curl characteristically.

The eyes of all the figures are touched with simple dots of the dark brown which gives them a staring and often foolish expression. The tendency was to become more and more naturalistic which lost them much of the earlier life, and then came the use of the mold, copies of Tê-hua, Fukien, Chinese figures, added details, etc. By the middle of the century the "Astbury type" of lead glazed figures more or less supplanted them and then came Whieldon and Ralph Wood; the former preserving a little of the first charm but the latter losing it all.

LEAD-GLAZED POTTERY

Contemporary with these salt-glazed wares and, in fact forming a continuous series from the earliest days, were wares of red, various shades of brown from mahogany to light buff or faun, and almost white wares decorated with all manner of techniques and covered with lead glaze often inclined to crackle where it runs thick. They made no effort to imitate porcelain and therefore avoided the fate of the salt-glazed wares.

"Crabstock wares" of about the middle of the 18th century were made in the Astbury factory after Chinese models, but these are miscalled for the actual crabstock wares had the handles and spouts made to look like short lengths of wood with branches and twigs twined about them and the ornamentation was of the usual leaves and tendrils in relief. The thinly rolled stems, we have spoken of, were called "vineing" and this word was taken incorrectly to mean veining by Jewitt and others.

Fig. 1236. Whieldon horse with underglaze green and tortoise-shell colorings on cream ground, c. 1770. Cow jugs c. 1760. Voyez figures of sportsman and wife in mottled colors, Staffordshire c. 1780. Philip Suval, Inc.

Silver influences were quite natural and at first had simple charm but then the potters made "head and claw feet" and fragile finials so that stability was lost and inappropriate tours de force attempted.

In the Toft type occasional use of underglaze green occurred. Now manganese and iron were also used along with cobalt blue, grey, ochre yellow and orange, etc., on the applied reliefs on red-brown grounds and covered with the lead glaze. These date about 1750 and Twyford made some of them.

THOMAS WHIELDON—"AGATE WARE,"
"VEGETABLE WARES," ETC.

Considered a genius of the day, Thomas Whieldon made cream-colored ware not long after 1725. He was one of the most enterprising of English potters between 1740 and 1770 at his place Little Fenton or Fenton Low and it was here that many of the other potters received their training.

Yet his strange conception seemed based on the idea that pottery should be made to look like anything but pottery. He had never heard about "expression of material" or at any rate he discarded the idea. He made agate ware of

Fig. 1237. Whieldon type bull and dog of cream colored earthenware dappled with slate-grey and green under lead glaze, 1750. Ht. 4¼". Mr. C. J. Lomax.

Fig. 1238. Three cavalrymen in red, brown and white clays, stands splashed in slate-blue and purple under lead glaze, Staffordshire, Astbury type, c. 1750. Hts. 8". Mrs. Arthur James.

Fig. 1239. Tea-pot of earthenware with reticulated outer wall, glazed in green, mouse-grey, yellow, purple and blue, inner wall being light brown clay, Staffordshire, Whieldon, c. 1750. Ht. 6". Mrs. Arthur James.

mixed clays with a clear lead glaze over them a little like the T'ang Chinese ones, but by cleverly bluing the glaze a little he came really closer to the appearance of agate. Knife handles, tea-pots, snuff boxes, etc., were made of this product. "Clouded wares" included "tortoise shell" with oxides of manganese, cobalt, copper, antimony and ochre dabbed on his creamware.

But the "vegetable wares" in the forms and colors of various vegetables and fruits such as pineapples, etc., were most famous though they seem to burn our good old friend Hannover in aesthetic indignation as nothing of this sort on the continent ever did. I think that they are really better for they do not pretend to imitate natural forms but rather adapt them loosely to the forms of the vessels and conventionalize them somewhat. In fact Hannover seems to have an antagonistic attitude toward all of these English wares which

Fig. 1241. Late 18th cent. figures probably made in Whieldon factory. Wm. H. Plummer & Co.

Fig. 1240. Whieldon tea-pot c. 1765 of a so-called "pineapple" type. Glaze rich yellow and yellow green and finely crackled particularly where it runs deeper. These teapots extensively copied in America later. Length 7". Frank Stoner-Stoner & Evans, Ltd.

somewhat colors his critical sense and his translator, Bernard Rackham, takes quite justified exception to it. The walls of these wares are thin and the detail good. The colors are not objectionable though the glaze is somewhat shiny and sticky looking.

Reticulated and double walled wares were well made by this versatile potter also.

Fig. 1242. Woman with bucket and dog in brown and ivory glaze, Staffordshire, c. 1740. Ht. 4¼". Plummer, Ltd.

Fig. 1243. Musicians in various colors but having typical crackled lead glaze, Staffordshire, c. 1740. Hts. 4½" to 6¼". Plummer, Ltd.

When Josiah Wedgwood was 24 years old he became a managing partner of the Whieldon plant. Others to profit from the place were Daniel Bird who opened a factory at Cliff Bank near Stoke-upon-Trent, where he produced another agate ware, and John and Thomas Alders (or Aldersea) who made "tortoise shell ware."

Both at Little Fenton and Jackfield in Shropshire from about 1750 a black glaze was used over the red ware probably following Böttger's idea of black ware. The decorations were in relief with oil gold decoration. It is to be remembered that another imitation of the ware was made at Namur, Belgium. The county of Shropshire was a great stronghold of the Jacobite cult and the

Fig. 1245. Prattware pottery cows in stippled decoration of blue, green and yellow, and two jugs of same ware with relief decoration and same colors. c. 1790. Philip Suval, Inc.

Fig. 1244. Grotesque pottery pitcher of seated figure on obverse side holding "Horn of plenty" from spout of which issues a dolphin. Handle is a panther. On reverse side is young faun. Blue, dark green, yellow and deep orange. Ht. 12". "Pratt ware" c. 1800. Plummer, Ltd.

decoration from there was made to appeal to the supporters of the young Pretender in a brownish and less brilliant sheen.

In Staffordshire and particularly in Little Fenton was also made "Pratt ware" a lead glazed ware named after the potter who worked there from about 1780 to 1800. This was colored with high temperature colors of blue, orange, black, purple, brown, green, etc., on a white ground.

"Astbury and Whieldon Figures"

It was probably Dwight at Fulham in the last of the 17th century who began to turn out little figures for more commercial purposes than simply as trick pieces for the potter's own amusement. Rackham and Read seem inclined to give some credit to the Elers but I think the playful spirit of the Staffordshire potters was actually responsible. In any event many red or light colored clay figures were covered with a lead glaze. Some had brown or yellow-buff clays added for ornamentation. On the slender and unsound reasoning that some details are something similar to those of the vine decorated tea-pots which may or may not have been made at the Astbury factory, these are called "Astbury Figures." The reasoning is doubly foolish and there was probably no connection whatsoever but the figures, though most of them are somewhat later and never so stylized and charming as the early salt-glazed ones, are nevertheless direct and living art portraying characters just as they were in the small towns; musicians, gamekeepers, soldiers, etc. The Mrs. Arthur James Collection is excellent and odd examples can be found now and then on the market. Once in a while the artists strayed to foreign subjects and a Buddhist sage or Italian comedy character might be tried but never were these actual copies. Plain white hussars made at Delft closely resemble certain models but it is likely that they were copied from the English in this instance.

Among them we are suddenly confronted with a totally different color scheme which was attributed to Whieldon. In Brighton Museum is a pillion group showing blending and spotting of purple, green, grey and blue. The cobalt was sometimes blended with the purple to form violet and dabbed on the figures before glazing. The first of these were hand made but soon they, like the salt-glazed ones were molded, but the potters seem to have sensed the pitfall and kept them simpler. Thus of the figures the salt-glazed early ones are by far the finest, the lead-glazed, not so good to begin with, but hold out and are better toward the end.

It has recently been claimed by an English dealer that some of the very few on the market are "fakes." Of course, there are none of these figures which are actually proven to have been made by Astbury. Rackham and Read along with other authorities call them simply "Astbury type," quite likely incorrectly as we have explained, but I venture to say that there are no fakes of this type of ware. My reasons are simple: 1.—Naïve art is the most difficult to fake convincingly and the ones doubted are full of the more or less careless but at the same time effective simplicity that cannot be assumed by a sophisticated artist trying to be childlike. 2.—I have compared the quality of the glaze with particular attention paid to the size and form of the crackle of the doubtful ones with undoubted ones and I find it identical in thickness, color, glossiness, crackle and number of bubbles. (It is impossible to duplicate a given type of crackle unless all the various elements which enter into the making of it are perfectly duplicated both chemically and physically. The glaze fractures in certain forms due to its structure plus the way the fractures are caused by the body; and even the same glaze fractures differently under slightly varying firing conditions.) Thus a forger would have had to perfect every detail beyond human possibilities. 3.—These figures do not bring very large amounts on the market, seldom going over a few hundred dollars. Therefore the reward to a forger would not be great unless he did a great many, and there are, and have always been very few indeed available. I, therefore, come to the conclusion that the doubted pieces are quite all right and are of the period, also that nothing resembling them is being made to-day.

Animals too were made with excellent life and spirit. Later on Crucifixions in various forms and other more pretentious things were made. The animals are not sufficiently appreciated because they came along when the people of England were talking of *Art* quite seriously. I can only say that they often rank very close to the beauty of the Egyptian and T'ang Chinese ones.

Ralph Wood

Rackham and Read only touch lightly upon them and many authorities skip them entirely. The former gentlemen then say, "Staffordshire figures reach their zenith in technical skill and artistic quality in the pottery of Ralph Wood and his son of the same name, of Burslem, brother and nephew of the block-cutter Aaron Wood." The senior was also a block-cutter. Thus it may be said that the family was born and bred to the mold and I shall probably call down the wrath of the dealers, and the chilling breath of British contempt, by declaring that the works of the two and of the nephew of the younger, Enoch Wood, are worthy of no more attention than is given to them by old Hannover in his statement, "About this class a long chapter could be written, extending from the still sound old-English joviality of the 'Vicar and Moses'

Fig. 1246. "Farmer & Wife" and "Old Age" (smaller ones) by Ralph Wood, having usual transparent underglaze colors. Said to have been made c. 1750. Philip Suval, Inc.

Ralph Wood and Whieldon toby jugs decorated with colored glazes c. 1765. Almost identical in form though not from same mold. Flesh parts of Wood one of pale aubergine tint and britches grey-blue while color is better controlled. Mug of Whieldon one is cinnamon-rufous brown and dark parts are very dark aubergine rather than brown black as on Wood example. Hts. 9½". Frank Stoner–Stoner & Evans, Ltd.

On left, Wilson toby-jug, 1810, with typical stippled base and modeled handle while flesh parts are white. her is Davenport, 1820, marked with name and anchor flanked by 3 and 6. Flesh tone appears on face and nds. Both have enamel colors of blue, yellow-green, yellow-tan, black and rose-red. Hts. 9¾". Frank Stoner– ner & Evans, Ltd.

TOBY JUGS (c. 1765–1820)

PLATE 214

of Ralph Wood to the 'Toby jugs' already somewhat less funny and thence to the great mass of thoroughly talentless and finally even tasteless Staffordshire figures—" and, "The same chapter relating to the peasant strain in English pottery of the period, about 1800 and afterwards, would also include another class of ware made to be sold at fairs—earthenwares with copper, silver and gold lustre, for the most part tea and coffee-pots, which from about 1790 onwards, were produced not only in Staffordshire, but also at Swansea, New Castle, Liverpool and Sunderland." Thus he makes his one statement about the Woods and concludes, "But in pursuance of the programme set before this book we may release ourselves from describing all these ugly things,

FIG. 1248. "Haymaker and Companion," in glazed white earthenware, by Ralph Wood, Burslem, Staffordshire, last half of 18th cent. Hts. 9½" and 9¼". Mr. W. Sanders Fiske.

FIG. 1247. Boxer by Ralph Wood, Sr. Cream colored clay glazed with translucent vinaceous-fawn on britches, chrysolite yellow green coat and fluorite green base. Fire crack and incised X are shown under base. Ht. 8". c. 1760. Frank Stoner–Stoner & Evans, Ltd.

and make our final halt." I dislike only his term "peasant pottery" for these wares had outgrown in their rank commercialism their original peasant stock.

The facts are these: The colored glazes had been fully developed in general

FIG. 1249. "Madonna and Child" by Ralph Wood the younger. Almost identical figure illustrated in last work of Wedgwood except that hand of child is below madonna's chin. c. 1785. Ht. c. 12". John Gibbons Coll.

FIG. 1250. Figure of Newton with telescope, globe and books. Remarkable modeling full of vigor and yet sensitive. Signed *R. WOOD, Burslem*, at back of base. Ht. 12". c. 1785. Frank Stoner–Stoner & Evans, Ltd.

in Staffordshire, as we listed them above. Rackham and Read liken them to those of poor Palissy of 200 years before and this is not saying much though even this is not true for they are different in colors and more glassy; really not so pleasant even as these. In other words there was no technical accomplishment other than the simple art of block-cutting of greater detail. Of the "Toby jugs" there had been a long tradition based upon Toby Philpot, as Rackham and Read point out, he of the song "The Brown Jug" and not Uncle Toby of Laurence Sterne, and certainly the Woods lowered the standard rather than added to it. Of the "Vicar and Moses" and other kindred subjects there is proof that they were taken from contemporary engravings with nothing more than a common exercise of the block-cutter's art. But the majority of the figures are not even English in origin and were stolen from continental models of Paul Louis Cyfflé, Palissy, etc. Among the classical figures, the Diana is the Diane Chasseresse of the Louvre, etc. Other figures were taken from Dwight.

Mr. Frank Falkner discovered that the younger Ralph Wood shared a tenement at Burslem with the French modeller John Voyez, and the jug with figures in relief signed Voyez and dated 1788 together with his medallion of the Judgment of Paris have led to this statement by Rackham and Read. "The treatment of the figures upon these works is so similar to that of the statuettes bearing the impressed mark of Ralph Wood or his son (or the stamped mould-numbers of a series to which such statuettes belong) THAT THERE IS LITTLE ROOM FOR DOUBT THAT THE WOODS OWE THEIR FAME, AS FAR AS MODELLING WAS CONCERNED TO THIS FRENCH IMMIGRANT." (The capitals are mine.)

Thus there is not much interest or beauty in the products of these block-cutters who stole their technique and even their modeling, giving no credit to Voyez in the purely industrial manner of their class.

Of the portrait busts of Enoch Wood after this or that real source, often with enamel colors to imitate porcelain and of such figures as that of Benjamin Franklin which was miscalled and inscribed "Washington," perhaps the least said the better.

JOSIAH WEDGWOOD

Josiah Wedgwood was born at Burslem in 1730 and died in 1795. He was the youngest son of Dr. Thomas Wedgwood and soon after his father died, which was in 1739, the boy was apprenticed to the brother Thomas, the oldest of the family and it was he who taught him the technique of ceramics. In fact the family had been more or less noted since the 17th century.

In 1752 he became the manager of a small factory at Stoke-on-Trent, known as "Alders" or the Cliff Bank Pottery and was a partner of Harrison and Aldersea, but moved on in 1754 to join Whieldon at Little Fenton, where he made his experiments with salt glazes to no very good purpose. In 1759, disappointed as he said in the "conservatism of Whieldon" whom, God knows, we never would have thought of criticising for conservatism, he started his own place at "Ivy House" in Burslem where he chiefly made salt-glazed wares and green and yellow glazed wares. In 1762 he leased in addition the "Brick House," called the "Bell Works" also in Burslem, just about at the time the English cream-colored earthenware was reaching perfection and he became one of its chief makers with the result that he received the patronage of Queen Charlotte and the ware was called "Queen's ware," becoming Wedgwood's financial support. It is not true that he "invented" this ware as we are led to believe by some "authorities."

FIG. 1251. Marbled ware candlestick said to be, "typical of very early period, c. 1769." Josiah Wedgwood & Sons, Ltd.

Now at 32 years of age he became a social leader of his community, improving roads, taking interest in the construction of the Trent and Mersey Canal, founding schools, and in time becoming "potter to the King." He traveled extensively visiting London, Liverpool, Manchester and Birmingham. When he left Whieldon in 1759 he opened a shop in Newport Street, London, and the merchant Thomas Bently became his friend in Liverpool in 1762, later to aid him in many ways particularly in supplying a classical training which Wedgwood lacked. He also acted as his only agent for some years, in which he sold the wares extensively to Sadler and Green who decorated them with transfer prints. His was undoubtedly the influence that started Wedgwood to making "artistic classic stoneware."

FIG. 1252. "Black basalt" candlestick marked "Wedgwood & Bentley," c. 1770. Josiah Wedgwood & Sons, Ltd.

In 1767 he was introduced to the Comte de Caylus' work called the "Recueil d'Antiquities Egyptiennes Etrusques, Greques, Romaines et Gauloises" and became enthusiastic about using the designs reproduced therein. Miss Meteyard also states that he became acquainted with the works of La Chausse, Laurent, Berger, Montfaucon, Dempster, Gori and Winkelmann. In a sense he was really a pioneer of the adaptation of classic designs to potting though, of course, some such influence had begun to be felt in design in general on the continent of Europe. Of course, the influence was not felt in England until about 1770 or the Chelsea-Derby times. Actually at Sèvres, although the Louis

XVI style made some use of classic design, there were no real imitations of antique models until Napoleon's time. In Germany the style came later than in France.

In 1773 he transferred all of his plant to "Etruria" and his products included both earthenware and stoneware for useful wares and stoneware of an ornamental nature. Rackham and Read say, "Before Wedgwood we may almost say that there was no such thing as 'ornamental pottery' in England." Later a branch of the factory was established at Chelsea for enamel painting on the earthenware and "encaustic" painting on the black stoneware. Bently had become a partner but he died in 1780. In 1790 Wedgwood took his sons John, Josiah and Thomas, and the cousin Thomas Byerley into partnership forming the company which is still moderately successful.

Hannover wrote an oft quoted passage which seems just, "On his monument in the parish church at Stoke-on-Trent are chiselled the words, 'Who converted a rude and inconsiderable Manufactory into an elegant Art and an important part of National Commerce.' Some have thought that he did the opposite, converting an art, perhaps rude and inconsiderable, but nevertheless always an art, into a manufacture. The truth is that he did both, creating a great manufacture with an incontestably artistic stamp." Hannover tried his best to give Wedgwood the benefit of the doubt but when one is acquainted with Hannover's feelings about the whole classical movement, one realizes just how charitable he was being.

Rackham and Read, being English, are of course more laudatory but they say of Greek ceramics which Wedgwood copied (*English Pottery*, p. 122), "From the point of view of the potter it was a misfortune for Wedgwood that the pottery from which he chiefly drew his inspiration for his innovations—whatever virtues it may possess in exquisite beauty of draughtsmanship and gracefulness of shape—was not good pottery." It is a little difficult to understand how all this "gracefulness" and "beauty" could exist without its being good pottery unless one takes account of the classic attitude which dreams its dreams unhampered by any structural or functional criticisms. But these two were on the track for they continue, "In ceramic qualities, Greek vases of the 'best' period stand far behind the ancient wares of Egypt, Persia and the Far East, and are inferior even to the unpretentious pottery made far and wide by aborigines in the provinces of the Roman Empire. Their shapes are copied from, or intended to emulate metalwork; nor do they depend for decoration on the plastic possibilities of clay." So, having laid the blame on the Greeks, firmly but somewhat dressed for those classic minded people whom they did not wish to offend, they say of Wedgwood, "It is to these circumstances that we owe the fact that in his ornamental stoneware Wedgwood drifted altogether away from the conception of pottery as a branch of plastic art. In actual appearance his jasper and other stoneware speaks far more of the art of the sculptor and the gem cutter than that of the potter." My readers know my feelings in the matter but I am willing to let the indictment stand just as it comes from the mouths of his countrymen. He can be forgiven the art-for-art's-sake creation of "ornamental" meaning *useless* wares for that was the trend of the day, but other students of the antique have gained immeasurably from their studies while he grasped the shell only and understood none of the inner life or meaning. He was a good business man and perhaps should be mistrusted even in any sincere attempt to do better than make saleable merchandise.

Prodigious were the technical processes practiced at this factory. Wedgwood was a genius at getting other people to work for him. In 1771 he got an order to do a huge table service of some 1,000 pieces for the Empress of Russia and each piece was to have on it a view of an English castle, monument or landscape and, on the strength of this he was able to get a large staff of the Chelsea porcelain painters. From Sheffield and Birmingham metal workers he learned methods for making his wares thinner and piercing them more successfully. Unglazed red and black stonewares called "rosso antico" and "basaltes" or

FIG. 1253. Three plates from "Catherine II of Russia" dinner service said to have been "executed by Josiah Wedgwood in 1774." Josiah Wedgwood & Sons, Ltd.

"Egyptian black" were simple adaptations of wares which had long been made in Staffordshire and which he simply improved and named. The "basaltes" ware was used for panels in relief, portrait medallions, life-sized busts, gems copied from antique ones, lamps, ink-stands, salt-cellars and vases among other things. He is quoted as having said that he could copy any of the "Etruscan" vases (which, of course, were not Etruscan at all) and improve them by giving, "higher artistic value by the addition of light and shade, which are entirely lacking in the old vases."

Besides the red and black wares he made a number resembling stone by the admixture of various oxides. "Jasper ware" is perhaps the best known and was obtained by the adding of carbonate and sulphate of barium to a semi-porcelain clay. The result is translucent when thin, hard enough to grind and polish and yet soft enough to be stained throughout with the metal oxides. In 1775 when it was first made, the body was so stained but almost at once in 1777 the process was cheapened by dipping the body (before firing, of course) so that only the surface was stained. There are seven colors all of which are mixed with sulphate of barium: lavender-blue of three shades, lilac, pale pink, greyish-green, olive-green, yellow and black. The rarest is yellow and the most difficult to get and most variable is the lilac. Usually the relief decoration contrasts in color with the ground and often the decoration is white. Sometimes rare examples combine three colors such as the pair formerly in my own collection which are lilac, with small green medallions and white ornaments over all.

Nothing seemed too small or too ambiguous for Wedgwood's attention and he made buttons, ear-rings, finger-rings, beads, knife handles, shoe-buckles, panels for furniture, etc.

Many Italian modelers were hired along with such English ones as James Tassie and William Hackwood, who did many portraits, etc., but far better known is John Flaxman who was a great sculptor in his own right. He was born in 1755. His father was a molder and kept a shop in Covent Gardens for the sale of plaster figures. It is said that by his own efforts he learned enough Greek and Latin to read the poets. At 15 he entered the Royal Academy and in 1797 was elected associate and in 1800 a full member. In 1810 he was appointed Professor of Sculpture there. In 1787 he went to Italy for a few years where he made illustrations of the Odyssey, and Aeschylus and Dante. Wedgwood captured him and some of the portraits are by him as well as some of the best vases, one of which is the "Apotheosis of Homer" known as the "Pegasus vase" from the finial on its cover. This vase was given to the British Museum in 1786 before the Italian sojourn.

The original "Portland vase" was of glass and was discovered in the course of excavations in Rome toward the end of the 16th century. After having been in the possession of the Palazzo Barberini in Rome, from which it is also called the "Barbarini vase," it was sold in 1786 for 1,000 guineas to the Duke of Portland. It is now in the British Museum in a restored condition as it was smashed to many pieces by a madman. The original is, of course, glass with an almost black ground and is one of the masterpieces of the glass cutter's art. Wedgwood copied it sometimes in blue-black and sometimes in blue jasper and looked on these copies as the crown of his life's work. There are about 20 examples, but some of these were not turned out until after Wedgwood's death. He sold them for 50 pounds sterling while one fetched £215.5s in 1892. Actually the copies are pretty bad and even the simple

Fig. 1255. "Warwick vase," 1880, a reproduction of a silver piece in Warwick Castle. Josiah Wedgwood & Sons.

Fig. 1254. One of reproductions, somewhat distorted, of the "Portland Vase." Josiah Wedgwood & Sons, Ltd.

FIG. 1256. Set of flower vases of white earthenware with brown slip through which pattern is cut while festoons are in relief appliqués. Over-all lead glaze. Josiah Wedgwood, Etruria, Staffordshire, late 18th cent. Middle vase 11⅛". Wedgwood Institute, Burslem.

FIG. 1257. Example of well-known "Queen's Ware" which flooded market. Said to be, "hand embossed" but most of design on this ware is simply cast in mold. Josiah Wedgwood & Sons, Ltd.

shape of the original was not followed perfectly. In the Wedgwood copy the handles do not follow the curve of the body but sag inwards and the upper parts of these handles do not meet the neck horizontally as the original ones do. The shoulder is also more rounded and not so strong and the neck is slightly shortened. The result is dumpy and not of the aristocratic stance of the original. Is this criticism picayune? I assure you that it is just such subtle lines which make or break a work of art, and it is in just such things that the copyist fails.

Thus in general we find that Wedgwood lost all of the warmth and interest of the touch of the human hand in potting. In the freest things he ever did there is a tightness which shows that, had he really known the Greeks, he would have been shocked at them. Wedgwood erected the final cold slab over the tomb of all the appeals of ancient pottery. As Hannover says, "Even

FIG. 1258. Wedgwood game-pie dish with glazed inside oven dish. Outer dish and cover of terracotta which looks like pie crust. Made in four sizes for Trinity College, Cambridge. c. 1850. John Gibbons Coll.

FIG. 1259. "Queen's Ware" plate, part of service called "Hampton Court" with rather stiff flower said to, "bespeak, through the intricate detail and beautiful underglaze enamelling," (whatever that may mean) "the craftsmanship for which our artisans have been renowned for six generations." Josiah Wedgwood & Sons, Ltd.

to the method by which he stamped his wares, instead of marking them with a name written by hand in the manner of the old faïence, we trace the factory spirit in his activities." This mark was WEDGWOOD. Later between 1768 and 1780 it was WEDGWOOD & BENTLEY-ETRURIA or at times the ETRURIA was left off. Pieces marked simply WEDGWOOD-ETRURIA are later and from about 1840. Small pieces sometimes have W & B̶. There are many workmen's marks such as letters, figures, flowers, etc., some impressed and some painted, which have no importance. Hannover says, "We should note, however, that three large letters such as OTN or ALX in combination with the factory mark indicate that the piece in question is not older than the period after 1860, the factory indicating the year with an O, the following with a P and so on." The first letter refers to the workman, the second to the month and the last to the year.

Fake marks are WEDGWOODE and WEDGWOOD & CO. which he did not use. Pieces so marked were made by William Smith about 1840 at Stock-on-Tees. Of course we have said that many continental factories copied the wares before they were snowed under by them and there was hardly a factory in the whole of Staffordshire which did not follow suit, while others in England were not far behind. The factory still turns out all the same wares more crudely made save that the "jasper" was discontinued for the war period. In the modern ones the blue color is often paler and dryer and sometimes darker and less grey, the green is too fresh, the white reliefs are rougher and not so soft to the touch. In the latter part of the 19th century pieces brought over $2,000 and now a tenth of that would be fairly high.

Leeds' Swinton and "Don" Pottery

About 1774, according to Messrs. Kidson, a firm by the name of Humble, Green & Co. was established at Leeds. Hannover says two brothers by the name of Green founded it around 1760. Sometime in the 70's Hartley joined and the firm was then known as Humble, Hartley, Green & Co. and then later as simply Hartley, Green & Co.

Hartley set out to copy Wedgwood and did succeed in spreading his wares all over the Continent. The firm changed hands several times, having its prime between 1781 and 1805 and went out of existence in 1878, though several revivals have been attempted up to this day.

Some catalogues and drawings show little of what might have been original. Nearly everything was copied including "agate-ware," "Tortoise-shell ware," "basalt," etc., but the specialty seemed to be a cream colored ware which was now made everywhere. Some of the forms were simple but they grew progressively worse and worse in greater complications. The ware is a little yellower than

Fig. 1260. Reticulated Leeds earthenware piece with impressed mark, "LEEDS POTTERY." A most delicate and accurate piece of work. Ht. 11". c. 1780. Plummer, Ltd.

that of Staffordshire and may look slightly greenish where the glaze runs thick. It is harder and never quite so thin as the Wedgwood glaze. As duty was charged by weight, the Leeds kiln tried to make theirs lighter and succeeded better than any other place but not satisfied with this they commenced to pierce every possible surface such as the rims of plates, covers, etc. This work was done hole by hole with individual punches. Wedgwood caught the idea and improved it by making block punches which killed even the slight unevenness which still expressed the hand made article. Much of the cream ware was left undecorated and it is preferable that way. Some, however, was painted in black, red, brown or blue and some was painted in subdued colors of enamel, green, red, lilac and yellow.

FIG. 1261. Leeds, late 18th cent. pair of rabbit candlesticks of cream colored earthenware touched with copper-green, with bases in yellow "tortoise-shell." Ht. 5½". Mr. Victor Gollancz.

FIG. 1262. Chestnut-bowl of Leeds pierced earthenware of cream color. c. 1800. Ht. 9". City Art Gallery, Leeds.

Figures were also made which Rackham and Read are enthusiastic about but which have little to recommend them except their subdued colors. They seem to represent most of the bad points of their Staffordshire predecessors and no good ones. In fact these authorities seem unaccountably enthusiastic about all the Leeds work; they say, "The pierced ornament is executed with a care and delicacy never equalled by any other pottery." I think that as long as they are quibbling about so unimportant a technique they might be referred to the "ling lung" or "devil's work" done in the latter part of the Ming Dynasty in China, or some of the K'ang Hsi and even modern examples. Englishmen seem to enjoy making such flat statements concerning their own excellence.

John Green started another factory in 1790 near Mexborough in South Yorkshire known as the "Don Pottery," and some of the partners had an interest in Swinton from about 1787 to 1806. We suppose the wares made in both places were closely like those of Leeds, which were closely like others. Several places such as Castleford in 1790 and Ferrybridge in 1792, followed suit. The only recorded mark of distinction that Castleford could claim was that a blue outline was used and the tea-pots were rather oblong or squarish.

Still other factories were:

Shelton (1774–1816) by Samuel Hollins which made red and brown unglazed stoneware.

Lane End (1739–1786) John Turner, friend and rival of Wedgwood with "jasper," "Black basalt," and a "cane colored ware." The blue "jasper" was better modeled than Wedgwood's.

FIG. 1263. Late 18th cent. Leeds figure of musician with greyish-white crazed glaze. Ht. 11¼". Plummer, Ltd.

FIG. 1264. Ambitious cruet-stand of typical cream colored Leeds ware with names of condiments in German in reddish-brown. c. 1800. City Art Gallery, Leeds.

Neale & Palmer (1760–1776) Henry Palmer took workmen and models from Wedgwood including John Voyez.

Josiah Spode (three individuals) The eldest served with Whieldon, did painting in blue underglaze and printing in underglaze colors, though this was done first at Caughley and brought to Spode by an engraver named Lucas and a printer named Richards.

Elijah Mayer (1770–1813) at Hanley copied black Wedgwood ware.

William Adams of Greengates, Staffordshire (1745–1805) was a pupil of Wedgwood and made "jasper." His blue is more violet and shiny. He himself modeled and Enoch Wood worked for him for a while.

Herculaneum (1796) An old factory was taken over and given this name and the business of copying the wares of Etruria.

Swinton (mentioned above), near Rotherham, made a "brown china" that is called "Rocking-

FIG. 1265. Castleford tea-pot of ware almost like so-called "parian body" of some American wares, decorated in dark blue enamel. Ingenious slotted arrangement holds slide cover in place even when pouring. Bottom has impressed 22 as only mark. c. 1820. Length 9". Frank Stoner–Stoner & Evans, Ltd.

ham glaze" from the estate of the Marquis of Rockingham upon which it is located. This type was later very popular in America, as at Bennington.

Jackfield, in Shropshire, made black glazed tea-pots, etc., painted in oil colors which are usually worn off to no great loss.

Joseph Ring at Bristol made a cream-colored ware the color being due to the glaze and not the body which was dark.

Cambrian Pottery, at Swansea, made all kinds of Staffordshire wares and particularly an "opaque china" which is whiter than most of the cream wares and owes its reputation to:

Fig. 1266. Staffordshire figure of "Flora," possibly Wedgwood, c. 1800. Ht. 11". John Gibbons Coll.

Fig. 1267. One of pair of Staffordshire groups "Peace and Plenty" set upon hollow bases with vent hole in bottom. Bright green, iron red, blue, yellow and tan. c. 1800–10. Length 9½". Ernest F. Follows.

Fig. 1268. Staffordshire girl with doll (unidentified) with enamel decoration and costume which dates it c. 1830–40. Vermiform motif dress is typical. Ht. c. 11". John Gibbons Coll.

William Weston Young, a painter of flowers and landscapes.

Derby made the cream wares and a "brown ware" it is thought though this has not been definitely proven and some found about the site may have been sent in for decoration.

Shore & Goulding at Isleworth made a copy of the "Portland vase" of a red earthenware also used for tea-pots in Chinese style.

We have given too much space to the sad tale of the 18th century, but it was necessary first in order to set right many misled collectors who are still impressed, as the English were, by the continental vogue; secondly to gain a proper perspective on the porcelain achievements of Europe; and finally to help us understand our modern age. The trend was ever westward and finally, of course, it jumped the wide stretches of the Atlantic to America. One wonders, if after this last war or within another few hundred years, the complete circuit of the globe will have been accomplished and China will again take the lead.

Conquest of arms had to do with the 18th century in the introduction of the neo-classic through Napoleon, if nowhere else. Actually it had much to do with the North Countries also. Conquest by religion had little or nothing to do with the 18th century art of ceramics. The old kings and popes had little power, but conquest by pennies was all important and it brought disaster to most of the factories by 1850 because it brought about the very antithesis of all art appeals.

FIG. 1269. Staffordshire Obediah
Sherratt group c. 1830 showing bull
baiting. 3-color stippling of base is
typical. Length c. 11″. John Gibbons
Coll.

FIG. 1270. English stoneware jug of cream white with neck, lip and upper part of handle in
cobalt blue, late 18th to early 19th cent. Brought to Newburyport, Mass. c. 1763, it is reported.
Ht. 9½″. Metropolitan Mus. of Art.

As the art of ceramics moved west to America it had little chance to accomplish great works of art. The machine had done all it could; mass production had worked its greatest harm and soon there developed the era of sanitation; of the making of whole facades of buildings sheathed in tiles such as the Near Easterners or Chinese never dreamed of, the era of fuller knowledge of all art of the past, and then the inevitable turn of fate; depression, war and the attendant troubles. In art the greater knowledge of ancient arts did not become strong enough to bring the enthusiasm and love for art in general that one might have expected; instead the use of machines, the habit of mass production and the urge to sell ever cheaper to satisfy the penny gatherers, overcame our possible rennaisance almost at once and withered it as soon as it sprouted here in America. Every means of cheap short cuts were employed to develop a psuedo art called "modernistic." This had no strength during the boom days but gained powerfully when the final depression of 1929 came along. Thus the story of American ceramics is also sad in conclusion.

However, before the European came to this country some really great things were done and in the beginnings we shall find much to interest us.

CHAPTER XXVII

AMERICAN INDIAN POTTERIES

Along the great Siberian plain eastward following the Arctic Circle and crossing such great rivers as the Lena and the Kolima, in highlands, river valleys and frozen salt marshes, and at times north of Sakhalin, and north of the Sea of Okhotsk along Kamchatka and down the river Anadir out onto Cape Deshnef (East Cape), came various waves of migratory people, not travelling but drifting as would flotsam on the tide, sometimes advancing, sometimes retreating, following their hunting. Life was very hard in these far northern latitudes, for they lie at about the same latitude frozen most of the year and open only during July, August, September and sometimes part of October with temperatures usually not more than ten to fifteen degrees above freezing even then. Hunting and fishing were the only livelihood and the providing of shelter and food took all of man's time. Accidents were swift and terrible and courage was not a seldom used and talked about embellishment of character but the simple necessity for survival.

The Bering Strait is only 56 miles across and ice extends the shorelines in the cold season. Moreover, there are two bleak granite domes of islands, between which the boundary line between Russia and the United States now passes, which have no harbors but upon which live about 80 Eskimos. These islands, with their ice flanges must have been stepping stones so that at times, when conditions were right a small trickle of the peoples of Asia came to America. At times some must have returned while at times also some penetrated up the Yukon valley or even further east and south to the mouth of the Mackenzie. The ice cap moved north and south imperceptibly to them and with this movement all flora and, therefore, all fauna either gained further north or was pushed south. We must not think of the ice cap as a hard and frozen line of solid ice; there were simply harder and harder winters or more and more, what we might call, heat spells. During the harder winters the rivers froze deeper and the glaciers pushed further and, as the cap moved south, they did not retreat so far and the herds which grazed right up to the foot of them and all around them found better pasturage a little toward the south.

So it was over a short period in the life of man, a mere few 100,000 years or so, or perhaps a bit more, no time at all in our history for the "Java Man" is said to have lived some 450,000 years ago.

Down the coast to the Columbia River they came, up the Mackenzie to Great Slave Lake, on to what is now California on one side, and into the head waters of the Missouri and Mississippi on the other side. Into these warmer, easier lands moved the strong men who had survived the hardships of the north, very slowly and perhaps even holding still a subconscious mistrust of the too good lands which greeted them. They didn't bring much of culture along. The journey had been far too arduous or it may be that the culture of the old world had developed elsewhere or later than the waves of migration. It is true also that they did not seem so very capable in developing certain cultures of their own as fast as some other groups of men. Even when they did settle down in one place for a while, they were very slow to learn the benefits of agriculture and animals were only to be hunted so far as they could see, excepting the dog, of course, which was a fellow huntsman. They had no cattle, sheep, goats, pigs, horses, camels or reindeer, no wheat, barley or rice and they knew nothing about the plow, the wheel in any form, or iron, and stringed instruments seemed never to have occurred to them at all.

But certain things they did develop in common with all mankind of the Old World. They knew about fire and how to make it, the spear and spear thrower and probably the harpoon and bow, the making and use of cordage and nets as well as baskets, the implements of stone for cutting, scraping, piercing and hammering, and finally they brought with them the shamanistic practices and beliefs, and rites for adolescent boys and girls. But beyond all this they brought one more thing with them and that was a well developed sense of conventionalization of design. In an earlier chapter I have explained how this was developed by nomads through the urge to record important things on the very confined space areas available to the men who have to carry all their worldly goods through many hardships on their own backs. Here we have a race of men which has crossed the ice fields and the strait, has ascended great rivers and seen many hardships. A square inch of leather or small piece of bone would have a value to them, and they had learned well to be brief in their expressions, they could conventionalize a world of meaning in a small space. Nothing was drawn naturalistically for ages until the building of civilization had changed things in many aspects.

We were taught in school to think of the American Indian as of the "red race" as though they were a race apart but actually they are chiefly of the Mongoloid division of the human species, having brown skin, straight, stiff, black head hair and little beard or body hair. Their faces are broad and they have shovel-shaped incisor teeth as well as bluish pigment spots in the sacral region during infancy. All of these are common also to their Mongolian cousins and not to other humans. At first the French school of ethnology explained much of the settlement of the country as from Polynesia, but this was discarded and then it was believed that *all* of the American Indians came by way of the north, if not across the strait at least by way of the Aleutian Islands. Now certain head formations and other characteristics have introduced an element of doubt best expressed by Dr. A. L. Kroeber in the 14th edition *Encyclopaedia Britannica*, Vol. 15, p. 505, "There are some interesting but as yet insufficient indications of Australian or Melanesian Negroid influence on the physique of the American Indians of certain localities. The very long and low skulls of the south end of Baja California may represent a colony or infusion of such immigrants. Similar conjectures have been advanced about the long headed peoples of the Atlantic sides of both North and South America." Of course, these "infusions," as the Doctor calls them, must have been very slight and certain it is that they brought few traceable art motives or trends with them, though a perusal of "Elephants and Ethnologists" by G. Elliot Smith, most convincingly demonstrates that some motifs came even from India to our west coasts.

And so our migrations wandered further and further south, some settling along the Pacific coast, some in the great central plains and a few drifting off to the east. Living conditions became comparatively easy and the migrants multiplied, finding their way down through Central America and finally into South America. In the area from Mexico to Peru agriculture did begin with the partial cultivation of certain indigenous plants such as the squash, pumpkin and beans. Maize, probably native to the highlands of Mexico and Guatemala was slowly altered and domesticated to man's use, spreading over all the Americas from the St. Lawrence to the La Plata. In the tropical regions other plants were cultivated such as the potato, sweet potato, manioc, tomato, pineapple, tobacco, chocolate and chili pepper, but all of this agriculture was hand done with no help but that of a rude hoe or sharpened stick. Eventually the turkey was partly domesticated in Mexico and the llama and alpaca in Peru. Cotton, of another species than that of the Old World, came to be used and true fabrics were made. The bronze age probably developed before this and we soon find that in "Middle America" copper, gold, silver, platinum, tin and lead were smelted, cast and plated. Whether these arts were in any part brought from the Old World and, if so how much, are most interesting speculations which we cannot enter into here. And, just as we would expect, pottery was made in just about the same places as agriculture was practiced and at just about the same time. Finally masonry began and spread as far as the southwestern United States and south to northwestern Argentina, and a civilization was launched and under way.

When we stop to think of the hazards of the way, we can easily see how little, how very very little of culture could possibly have been brought by the various migratory peoples and, bearing this in mind, it is amazing to see how alike the mind of man is in its natural development. Each phase of the Old World culture is, in a way, duplicated by that of the New World.

Naturally those who had come first had had longer to enjoy the benefits of this virgin continent of North America and naturally it was they who, in their drifting, had moved furthest south until met by delaying obstructions. Thus we find the greatest advancement in Central America where the Isthmus of Panama pinching down had helped to stop them and where the approach to the Equator slowed the progress. Some overcame the difficulties and reached South America to be lost in the valley of the Amazon and others luckily drifted along the Pacific coast to Peru and there we find a closely following culture just a little later but quite as great.

Thus our culture in the Americas traces its course geographically and chronologically from the most primitive of the far north, the most recent arrivals, through the next in culture, the eastern wandering tribes of North America, through the more advanced Central Plains Indians and Southwestern Indians, to the Mexican and South American peaks of culture represented by the Mayan and Inca civilizations. And peaks they were, as great as those of Egypt and Iran in a not very different way, and after them came the natural and inevitable decadence; the story of the history of man's progress and stumbling, much as it occurred in the Old World, written for him again that he might see it and have a second chance to learn his lessons from it. Then the Spaniards and the English and the French burst upon the New World and swept all this away caring nothing for it and wanting only gold and the fountain of youth and to impose their well earned and magnificently developed culture of the 16th, 17th and 18th centuries upon these "poor benighted heathens" and we come to our modern era.

Eskimo Pottery

The Eskimos are racially no different from other American Indians, though we now find them mixed with the whites in certain areas, but by and large, from Greenland to Siberia they are the same and even in Siberia are many who have actually come back from the North American continent. We need not go into a description of them and their life habits except to say that they live largely upon fish and meat and have little use for pottery particularly in that they do not as a rule cook their meat. What pottery they did make has long been obsolete except for the making of rude clay oil lamps where stone for the purpose could not be found. Along the coast as far east as Franklin Bay heavy pottery has been found of good sturdy form and some

Fig. 1271. Pottery lamp for whale oil, probably most primitive in our book being simply a hand patted shallow bowl fired in an open fire. Ht. c. 4". Crude pottery cylindrical cup of hand patted clay impressed possibly with dim recollection of mat-made wares brought from Asia or possibly given the treatment simply through a desire for texture. Ht. c. 7". Both are made by Eskimos, first from Cape Prince of Wales, second from Point Barrow, Alaska. Mus. of Am. Indian.

surprisingly large in size and ornamented with incised and impressed designs. This pottery is altogether further advanced than we would expect to find as a natural development of the people themselves particularly with the consideration of their hunting habits and lack of interest in such things, and must have been made by men who had learned their art in Siberia. This theory is borne out by the total lack of pottery of any kind made by the central Canadian country Indians of the Athabascan and Algonkin tribes and also by the fact that there is no pottery made from southern British Columbia to Alaska on the Pacific coast, where vessels of bone, wood and horn serve instead. We do find along this coast traces of advanced Asiatic art occasionally, though these have not been planted by any planned invasion and we do have the strange similarity of design, called "Pacific Art" by Ernest Fenellosa. But this all came later than the time when these potteries seem to have been made, and they stand interestingly alone in themselves as an isolated development.

NORTH ATLANTIC INDIAN POTTERY

From Newfoundland to South Georgia on the Atlantic coast is an area which may be considered as a whole though there are many subdivisions unnecessary to our survey. These Indians were of the Algonkin, Iroquois and, further south, Sioux stocks of historic times. They lived a little on agriculture during certain times but more largely upon fishing and hunting. One shell mound known on the Potomac consists of oyster shells which covered about 30 acres to a depth of some 15 feet. In the lower Penobscot Valley in Maine dwelt a people who strangely placed large quantities of red hematite paint in their graves and so were called the "Red-paint people" by archaeologists. These people have long slender celts and slate points resembling those of the Eskimos and even those of Northern Europe and Asia. They are not related to the Indians of Colonial times who had similar burial customs, but seem to form a link with a more distant past. The pottery is of the simplest of the Algonkin type.

ALGONKIN POTTERY

The Algonkin pottery chiefly of the marginal regions such as New York bay, Long Island, Connecticut and Rhode Island is primitive in form and decorated with incising, cord-marking or mat impressions very much as we find it thousands of years before in China.

IROQUOIS POTTERY

The Iroquois pottery is more interesting and shows a primitive virility and originality. The vessels, found chiefly in New York and Pennsylvania have a rounded conical base, constricted neck and high straight collar *square in plan* or sometimes slightly inward slanting, the sides of which are usually incised with a rectilinear or triangular pattern or both, or sometimes with modelled figures or heads in relief, giving a strong and not unpleasing effect. Why and how this peculiar form came into being I cannot seem to find out but I venture the guess, and that is all it is and all it should be taken for, that in propping such a vessel up on its point leaning against a mat wall, the round mouthed type was found to roll and fall over unless a corner could be found for it. Certainly this type with its square mouth to steady it would

FIG. 1272. Primitive jar from Suffolk County, N. Y., which lacks rim of any sort and has simple incised design about shoulder. Of dark gray clay. Ht. 8¼". Mus. of Am. Indian.
FIG. 1273. Large jar seemingly comb impressed and similar in shape and treatment to those found in Western Asia. Ht. 15⅞". Found in Clinton County, N. Y. Mus. of Am. Indian.
FIG. 1274. Pottery jar from Fichers Island, Suffolk County, N. Y. showing Iroquois squared mouth which seems a more or less local idea. Dark brownish gray clay. Ht. 12½". Mus. of Am. Indian.

lean well against any wall. In other words we have here a mat-leaning-surface decorated with a sort of incised mat design. Also *two* of these vessels would lean together over a fire. This seems to be one that the Chinese did not think of!

Trumpet-like smoking pipes were beautifully shaped and often also well ornamented with modelled life forms. Dr. Kroeber says, "The typical Virginia pipe with long stem and upturned bowl, taken to England by early colonists along with the first tobacco, gave form to the common clay pipe of the present time." These would have been made by the antecedents of the Sioux Indians we suppose.

GEORGIA AND FLORIDA INDIAN POTTERIES

This section is naturally somewhat complicated by various influences such as the Muskogin family in southern Georgia and northern Florida, the traces of Calusa and Timucua further down, and on the west coast early Arawakan

FIG. 1275. Pottery jar fror Bronx County, N. Y. which shows further development with actual figures modeled and stuck on corners. Slow transition from beginnings of incising to first appliqués. Mus. of Am. Indian.
FIG. 1276. Pottery burial urn from Bryan County, Georgia, with interesting stamped design probably made by wooden stamp. Proportions good and graceful form has been evolved. Ht. 16½". Mus. of Am. Indian.
FIG. 1277. Jar from Calhoun County, Florida, with interestingly developed incised design which had evidently been conceived before the vase form because neck and mouth curve to harmonize with it. Amazing how few vases are so conceived. Even finest Greek ones seem to have designs which are after-thoughts. Ht. 7¼". Mus. of Am. Indian.

from the West Indies. Here again naturally fish made up the chief diet as is proven by hundreds of shell mounds but agriculture was also practiced where the country was suitable.

On the Florida peninsula it was the custom to bury the dead, either extended or flexed depending upon the region, or sometimes exposed until the flesh had gone and then the bones only were buried—together with many crude figures of animals or things, vessels of fanciful shapes, etc., made of fired clay, as mortuary offerings. On the west coast especially large deposits of earthenware utensils are found with the dead and the forms suggest a distinct type of vessel. In other words we find here the beginning of the customs which gave us so much pottery in Egypt and China and it would not have been

Fig. 1278. Left, a square jar from Calhoun County with figure moulded on one side. Ht. 7″. In center an odd idea of a vase in form of grub or perhaps a sea-worm. Ht. 6¾″. Right, cylindrical jar with incised design and several colors employed as with "three color" wares of China. This jar had been "killed." Ht. 8½″. Mus. of Am. Indian.

so very long, comparatively speaking, before this art would have developed perhaps along similar lines. It is impossible to date any of these Indian potteries closely for there are no historical records kept by the tribes, but they cannot be over 2,000 years old and the customs probably did not change materially from 1,000 years back up to historical times. We must remember the slowness of the development of the same primitive cultures in other countries such as Egypt in which a mere thousand years did not greatly change the look of things.

GEORGIA AND GULF COAST POTTERIES

It is interesting to note that these mortuary vessels were "killed" by putting holes in the bottom. In Georgia urn burial of either cremated or non-cremated remains is rather common. Along the Gulf coast, where pile dwellings were used as protection against marauders human or animal, an unpainted pottery was made of good and pleasing form and in the western part of this area we find well modelled life forms and pottery with engraved or indented designs.

An interesting group of potteries is decorated with figured stamps or paddles with designs so like those of certain West Indies wooden objects that they

FIG. 1279. Pottery vessel of animistic form from Hardman Mound, Nacoochee, White County, Georgia. Dark clay with white decorations. Very like those found in Western Asia dating c. 3000 B.C. though made thousands of years later and thousands of miles from there showing how much man's development takes similar trends. Mus. of Am. Indian.

seem to prove a connection of some sort though these pieces are found not only on the coast near Mobile but also all the way inland to near Knoxville, Tennessee.

Pipes were usually of trumpet shapes with the bowls expanding into animal and human heads or bird shapes, those in most of the territory being beautifully designed and well made though those on the West Coast are less so.

On the Florida keys the pottery was similar to that of the peninsula but showing stronger West Indies influences as we would expect. Cutting tools of shell and shark's teeth were mainly used.

Thus we see that the South Atlantic Coast is advanced over the North Atlantic Coast and this is probably due to the more nomadic tendencies of the hunters in the northern region, as well as their somewhat later arrival.

GREAT LAKES AND UPPER MISSISSIPPI POTTERIES

The Great Lakes and Upper Mississippi area also belonged to the Algonkin and Sioux stocks and its culture is similar to that found to the eastward and not so well developed as that further south. Wild rice, hunting and fishing supplied the food wants and agriculture was practiced in favorable parts. Evidently two important industries were undertaken, for in Minnesota, in Pipestone County, there are evidences of the mining of catlinite or "red clay-stone" which was made into pipes, ornaments and ceremonial objects which were spread far and wide, and the copper of the Lake Superior region was battered out of pits by rude stone hammers. This copper was used for the

FIG. 1280. Three pieces found at Big Bend Bank Cemetery, Posey County, Indiana, near junction of Wabash and Ohio Rivers. Human effigy bowl, complicated and far from easy to pot, bottle and animal effigy bowl show considerable development. Dias. c. 8". Mus. of Am. Indian.

Fine strong pottery bowl from Nacoochee Mound, White County, Georgia. Dark clay with well drawn spirals spaced about rim and typical space-filling device. Ht. 7¼". Mus. of Am. Indian.

Left: Jar from Cayuga County, N.Y., with not only Iroquois squared mouth but suggestions of faces at corner designs suggesting further development. Ht. c. 12".
Right: From Cross County, Arkansas, comes this animal vessel which, though primitive, is amusingly decorated.

Left: Pottery jar representing human head, from Mississippi County, Arkansas, which gives feeling there might have been a prototype of stone.
Center: Pottery jar from Natchez, Mississippi, truly potted, of hard nearly black ware with beautifully worked out spiral design masterfully applied to form.
Right: Fully developed basket technique as applied to coiled pottery. From Apache Co., Arizona. Ht. 13". Mus. of Am. Indian.

making of ornaments, tools, etc., and the sheet copper with repoussé designs on it found in Illinois and even in Florida came from these mines. This is outside our field of pottery but is mentioned to show the degree of culture and also of intercommunication which prevailed.

FIG. 1281. Water bottles from Lafayette and Miller Counties, Arkansas, of hard black ware which appear to have been carved after firing, then polished. This would account for scratchy look of design. Hts. c. 8″ to 9″. Mus. of Am. Indian.

The pottery was frequently incised and indented with figures and painted pottery is rare. The shapes are more primitive than those to the south, but distinctive.

MISSISSIPPI POTTERIES

The "Mound-builders," as the Indians of the Mississippi basin are called, show evidences of higher culture than any other group north of Mexico as we would expect, for have we not found that all the great cultures of the world were likely to center about the fertile basins of great rivers? Here life was

FIG. 1282. Three-lobed water bottle from Ozan, Hemstead County, Arkansas, which suggests use over fire and recalls some of two-lobed ones of South America. Ht. 9½″. Mus. of Am. Indian.
FIG. 1283. Pottery jar from Arkansas with pinched-up applied bosses and incised design. Mus. of Am. Indian.
FIG. 1284. Animal effigy bowl with incised decoration after firing. Length 9½″. Mus. of Am. Indian.

comparatively easy and became sedentary. At first these mound-builders were thought to have been a race apart but it was found that the tumuli were entirely the work of the Indians, that many in the Ohio Valley were in use and even in process of building after the arrival of the Europeans. Some of the mounds are complicated in form and show considerable engineering knowledge. They were used for living quarters, burial, defense and also religious and civic purposes. There are evidences of cultural relations with Mexico and the influence of these people extended into the coastal region of Georgia and north into the Great Lakes region. We don't know what the houses and temples were like but there is evidence that they were of wattlework faced with clay and perhaps with bark thatched roofs. Remains of stockades have been found.

These people worked stone masterfully as is proven by the fine tobacco pipes with animal figures on them. In the Hopewell mounds in Ohio was found a head-dress "consisting of a high frontal piece made of sheets of copper cov-

Fig. 1285. Female effigy jar from Crittenden County, Arkansas, which again shows parallel development to those of South America. Possibly such jars started as ritualistic vessels having to do with fertility. Ht. 7". Mus. of Am. Indian.

Fig. 1286. Water bottle from Ouachita Parish, Louisiana. Hard dark gray ware in form and design which, though well related, are beginning to show an over-sophistication and perhaps tendency toward unstructural. One could imagine points being easily knocked off. Ht. 5¾". Mus. of Am. Indian.

Fig. 1287. Bowl from Ouachita Parish, Louisiana. Well formed, shows beginning of definite foot treatment, body and rim, and which has well worked out snake-like incised design. Ht. 2¾". Mus. of Am. Indian.

ered with indented figures out of which rise a pair of wooden antlers neatly plated with sheet copper, etc.," as is said by Frederick W. Hodge in the article on North America in the 14th edition *Encyclopaedia Britannica*. He continues further by quoting Holmes, "The sword-like blades of Tennessee approach the highest place among American chipped products and the agricultural implements of the Illinois region constitute a unique and remarkable class without parallel in any country." So much for their general culture. Their pottery is not quite up to that of the ancient Pueblos of the Southwest. Yet it is certainly far advanced. We find elaborately engraved and painted vases. Effigy vessels are full of character and even humor, though we should be careful not to confuse our own sense of humor with that of distant peoples as we well know that the dealings with humor, even between such closely allied people as the English and Americans, are precarious; that which seems funny to one man may seem deadly serious to another. The basic roundness of a pot is carried out in the effigy ones by making the body very fat and the appendages closely pressed to it. Of course, the roundness of heads as related to the roundness of pots did not escape them and we have some which are indicative of a portrait approach. These occur in the middle Mississippi region. In the lower reaches of the river and on the Gulf Coast a most beautifully proportioned and decorated scroll-decorated pottery was made with particular use of the spiral, that ever recurring design like that of the swastika and vine border or wave border, which we find sooner or later on all primitive wares. These are largely incised and with a considerable degree of accuracy. There are globular and bottle shapes along with others. In the Southern Appalachian region between this culture and that of the Southern Atlantic there was made a good stamp-decorated ware.

GREAT PLAINS AND ROCKY MOUNTAIN POTTERIES

The nomadic Indians of the Great Plains did little farming except in the valleys of the eastern part and that was very minor; their livings were made through the abundant herds of bison and antelope and other game. We should not think of the Apache or Comanche stock as having been there for these tribes are comparatively recent comers but the Pawnee of Nebraska, the Wichita of Kansas and the Caddoan of Arkansas, Oklahoma and Texas were earlier, although we do not know just how early. Pottery is rare throughout the whole area except at the eastern fringe where it is probably partly that of the Mound-Builders. In the Ozark rock shelters a late pottery is infrequently found associated with the bow instead of the earlier *atlatl*.

BASKET-MAKER I (1500–2000 B.C.)

In the arid region further west it is said that maize agriculture was derived from Mexico as much as 1500 to 2000 years B.C. The people made beautiful coiled basketry and the *atlatl* or throwing stick was used instead of the bow. There was no pottery made in this time.

BASKET-MAKER II AND III PERIODS

Pottery of the so-called "Basket-maker II and III periods" may have been invented or have been introduced. It was of a most primitive and rude type. "Slab-houses" with pole and brush roofs over a pit were made in villages and the bow was used in Utah, Colorado, Arizona and New Mexico areas.

PROTO-PUEBLO OR PUEBLO I

Rooms of the Proto-Pueblo period became rectangular and emerged from the ground. Heads were deformed by pressure. It is believed by some that a new race of broad-headed people supplanted the former long-headed people coming from the South but this is debatable to date. Pottery was made by the coil method much as the baskets were made and left, the structural coils unobliterated, in what we term "corrugated pottery." Here we see almost as though unfolding before our eyes the slow development from basket to pottery taking place. At once black-on-white and neck-coiled pottery was made because the people were accustomed to see the natural designs developed in their basketry and felt a need for them on their pottery. This culture took place in the San Juan drainage, parts of the Rio Grande, Little Colorado and upper Gila valleys. It became rapid spreading geographically. The *kiva* or

Left: Animal jar like those of Western Asia in general conception and decoration, from Arizona. Ht. 8". Mus. of Am. Indian.

Right: Only a painter of the bowls found at Nishapur, Persia, or a Sung, Chinese artist could render a parrot with such simplicity and spirit as is shown in this fine bowl from Hawikuh, New Mexico. Dia. 10". Mus. of Am. Indian.

Left: San Domingo Pueblo pottery jar, New Mexico, which may even have had Spanish or Mexican prototype. Stag drawn in X-ray style with intestines and arrow of spirit within. Stag's head inside seems to be giving up spirit and god on mountains may be representative of thunder, lightning and rain with mountains of clouds above. Mus. of Am. Indian.

Right: Bowl with design of ceremonial dancer. Dia. 8". Hawikuh, New Mexico. Mus. of Am. Indian.

Left: Typical late Zuni jar of sort made even today. Ht. c. 10". New Mexico. Mus. of Am. Indian.

Right: Pottery jar from Hopi tribe, Arizona, with design of ceremonial mask and head gear. Late piece and even modern ones are similar. Mus. of Am. Indian.

NEW MEXICO AND ARIZONA PAINTED POTTERIES

PLATE 216

FIG. 1288. Right, from Hawikuh, New Mexico, typical primitive coiled pottery jar with outside untouched, inside smooth. Left, jar from Chaco Canyon, N. M. grooved to satisfy coiled texture which had become habit. Center, partly coiled, partly smooth surfaced jar. Note that device very like twisting reed in basketry was used to make design. Hts. c. 3½" to 5¾". Mus. of Am. Indian.

ceremonial chamber was started which implies certain solid developments of priest-craft which is to have as much influence upon this hemisphere as it did upon the other.

THE GREAT PERIOD OR PUEBLO III

Some geographical contraction took place but the great architectural and ceramic achievements were accomplished about which I shall have more to say later.

FIG. 1289. Bowl with interesting head and shoulder picture of man in ceremonial trappings, much conventionalized. New Mexico. Mus. of Am. Indian.
FIG. 1290. Zuni, New Mexico, jar with stags. Late type not well potted and sloppy in design. Ht. c. 9". Mus. of Am. Indian.
FIG. 1291. Mimbres Valley, New Mexico, bowl with designs of what appear to be dead stags with large targets on them, perhaps for easy shooting? Mus. of Am. Indian.

PROTO-HISTORIC OR PUEBLO IV AND HISTORIC OR PUEBLO V

A definite cultural degeneration set in and large areas were abandoned in the Pueblo IV and V periods. Corrugated pottery disappeared and the arts all became less certain and in the first of the 17th century the colonization of the Spaniards began. Up to this time, over long periods, were gradually developed small masonry houses on the sites of which we find black-on-white pottery which evidently originated in the San Juan drainage country of Colorado and spread as far as Salt Lake, almost to the Texas border, and south through New Mexico and Arizona, or—did it come up through the South and reach as far as Colorado and Utah? We cannot be too sure of such origins. Then began the period of contraction and defense. Large pueblos or group houses were built on mesa tops or in valleys and protected at places with walls. The entrances were gained by ladders and hatchways and only in the latter decades were ground floor openings introduced.

Fig. 1292. Bowl from Mimbres Valley, New Mexico, with grasshoppers for decoration. Note that they have very full stomachs. Mus. of Am. Indian.

Fig. 1293. Jars with spiral treatments, one square and other round. One on left with knob handle like those seen on Chinese eating bowls of Han period, but decorated to represent bird's head. Ht. c. 5½″. Rio Puerco District, Arizona. Mus. of Am. Indian.

FIRST PRIMITIVE START TOWARD BRICK MAKING

Where there was stone it was used but where it was lacking a form of concrete was employed and even in prehistoric times mud mixed with sage was rolled into loaf forms and used for wall building. Here we see our natural steps in brick making which leads to tile making, etc. First man makes two rows of posts and wattles or osiers between which he pounds mud. Then it occurs to him that mud can be made into loaves and so more easily transported to where he wants to build his walls. And finally it occurs to him to fire the loaves and we come to a stage of brick building. This must always take place in a section which is lacking in stones, for bricks are simply man made stones. The bricks were not used in prehistoric times by the Pueblo Indians, but some of the primitive pueblos would house several hundred persons, and were wonderful pieces of construction with the means in hand.

The pottery was made, as we have explained, without the wheel but was true and fine in workmanship. It was graceful and well proportioned and beautiful in color in the later periods. During two periods the decoration was in glaze. In the Mississippi valley and again here we find the natural inclinations of the people for conventionalized design of ancient derivation meeting the desire to expand the arts into more and more naturalistic forms. The animal and human and bird figures are beautifully developed, side by side or actually knitted in with the conventional. Given a few thousand years more the conventional would have disappeared entirely or been reduced at least to odd symbols such as the crescent, the cross, etc., for these people had space to develop naturalism. As life becomes more and more sedentary there is less danger of breakage and even the basketry gives way to earthenware.

So much for our North American Indian pottery which does no more than approximate the earliest known painted pottery of China dating some

3000 years B.C. (and the string decorated or impressed wares of such times).
It is less like that of ancient Egypt or Crete and, in fact, is interesting to us only
because it helps to show us better how such stages were arrived at.

CENTRAL AMERICAN CERAMICS

ARCHAIC

An archaic people in Central America left traces from the Valley of Mexico
to Salvador under volcanic ash and lava flows. We know little about them
except that their culture was not of a low grade, for they understood the arts
of weaving and of pottery making and may be compared to the Pueblo Indians
of later date and further north. Some time before the Christian era there came
an influx of people from South America, a sort of backwash of earlier migrations, which settled practically all of Panama, and Costa Rica, parts of
Nicaragua and also Honduras and these sections show closer analogies to
South American culture than do the others. Some believe that the first of these
may have been the Mayas while others are inclined to believe that the Mayas
developed from strains which had stayed in place during the earlier drifts
southward, remaining in the Huasteca country around Tampico and then moving southward and eastward.

MAYAS AND CHOROTEGAS

By the beginning of the Christian era two more or less definite linguistic
groups had assumed a historic pattern owing to their use of writing and of a
calendar. Dr. Herbert Spinden has shown that the Maya calendar was put
into working order between 613 and 580 B.C. Our earliest Chorotega records
are considerably later, but it seems that this linguistic group preceded the
Mayas and was forced by them to move from Western Honduras north and
south so that they finally came to settle in parts of Southern Mexico and along
the south coast of Costa Rica. They are of comparatively little importance.

THE MAYAS—OLD EMPIRE (A.D. 50–700)

Centering in northern Guatamala and within an inverted triangle the points
of which are in Palenque, in the Mexican state of Chiapas, a point somewhere
about in the northern part of British Honduras and southward to Copan in
the western part of the Republic of Honduras was the earliest phase of Mayan
development. Dr. Sylvanus Griswold Morley believes that the Mayas originated on the Atlantic Coast about Vera Cruz and points out that the earliest
dated object is the Tuxtla Statuette of 98 B.C. found at San Andrés de Tuxtla
which is roughly half way between this place and the site of the Mayan Old
Empire described above. Two objects bearing the earliest dates found within
the area of the Old Empire are the Leyden plate dated A.D. 60 and Stela #9
at Uaxactun dated A.D. 68. We may think then of the rise and fall of the Old
Empire of the Mayas as being roughly between A.D. 50 and 700, the original
area being occupied continuously up to about A.D. 450 at which time a period
of the greatest vigor occurred and movement north into Yucatan took place

Sculptured (before firing) pottery jar which, contrary to method of modeling, is actually carved with much same technique as stone carving. From San Agustin Acasaquastlan, western part of El Progreso Province, Guatemala. Ht. 7¼". Mus. of Am. Indian.

Pottery figure of baby owl probably used as ritual vessel, recalling again prominence of owl in ancient Chinese bronze forms. Probably c. 10th cent., Colima, Mexico. Ht. c. 8½". N. M. Heeramaneck Coll.

Small jar found at Costa Rica. Red ware. Bears close resemblance, save for wide mouth and flaring lip, to Yüeh vessels in form of frogs of 6 Dynasties and T'ang times found just west of Hang Chou at Chiu Yen site. Dia. 3". N. M. Heeramaneck Coll.

Pottery or terra-cotta dog of Toltec Civilization from Colima, Mexico c. A.D. 800–1300. Length 15¾". Brooklyn Mus.

MEXICAN PRE-COLUMBIAN POTTERY

PLATE 217

where the New Empire was founded. At the same time a body of the populace must have traveled west and the culture in an attenuated form even reached to the Valley of Mexico where it was developed by the Toltec, later immigrants from the North, the first of many waves all speaking the language known as Nahuatl.

NEW EMPIRE

From about 450 to 700 oversophistication and internal crumbling of the morale brought about the decline. But the art of pottery, that of stone and also wood came to equal "any work of Europe up to the Industrial Revolution and is worthy of comparison with any of Asia or Africa," as has been said. In the New Empire all became extravagant and flamboyant.

From about 690 to 990 is a period analogous in many ways to the Dark Ages of Europe. What brought this about we do not know but Dr. Morley and Ellsworth Huntington have suggested that climatic changes took place which caused far greater humidity and also that a system had been started for the burning off of the luxuriant growth. This was found at first to benefit the crops but they did not realize that the fire also consumed the humus in the soil itself and after each burning it took a longer and longer time before regrowth took place, therefore, living became more and more difficult. A strong centrifugal movement took place perhaps something like that of the colonial enterprises of the Ancient Greeks and finally the great cities, some 25 of which existed, were encroached upon by the jungle and fell into decay so that now the immense pyramids and temples are overgrown. I need not describe these as it is out of our field but these people had made the pyramid of the Sun in Teotihuacan with a larger base and nearly the same height as that of the Great Pyramid of Egypt, and many other surprisingly great works.

Fig. 1294. Pre-Toltec figure c. 8th to 10th cent. found at Colima. Ht. 12". N. M. Heeramaneck Coll.

Fig. 1295. Terra-cotta female figure in Tepic style with painted and modeled ornamentation, from Ixtlan territory, Mexico. Ht. 16¼". Brooklyn Mus.

Renaissance Period (990–1200)

From 990 to 1200 a great recrudescence of the old spirit took place; new cities were built, art was more virile and forged forward and a period of excellence occurred.

Toltec Invasion (1201–1458)

This period was closed by internecine strife and the setting up of the Toltec hegemony which was in itself a period of brilliant achievement and showed that these invaders from Mexico were in themselves a strong and cultural force but new intrigue took place and new revolutions occurred until after

1458 the Maya-Toltec culture burst into many hostile parts and so it was when the Spaniards found them.

THE POTTERY OF THE MAYAS

Whole lifetimes of study will be necessary to work out all the phases of the material we even now have in hand from this section and in our brief survey we can only pause to glance quickly at it. Here too the wheel was unknown though, strangely enough, certain altar stones and the so-called "Calendar stone" are made and designed on the circular principle, but the potteries were true and well formed without its use. Modelling, coiling and even molding were practiced from early times. Stamping, incising or engraving and painting with slip were methods well understood for decoration. The paste is fine and hard. Tripod bowls and vertical-sided beakers are characteristic. Vases in animal form are also common. Only rough chronological classifications can yet be attempted. There seem to have been definite pottery centers from which the wares were distributed and these should in time be investigated and their wares traced. Among the amusing pottery wares are the ocarinas made in human form. Large idols were also made.

TOLTEC AND AZTEC POTTERIES

It is not necessary to go into the formations and developments of the Toltec people in Mexico for there is much the same stock underlying all and the Aztecs may be looked upon simply as a final wave of many of the Nahuatl-speaking tribes who came from the North and broke up the Toltec clans which were pushed further south and east resulting in the introduction of Toltec art into Yucatan and Salvador and in time even into Nicaragua and Panama. It seems that these Nahuatl-speaking tribes were the ones that introduced the bow into the Mayan culture and that this aided the conquests. How like our history of the other hemisphere where the northern bowmen–hunters overcame the southern agriculturists!

To the Aztecs, the Toltecs were known as master stone cutters, while they themselves were warriors and political organizers. But the art of the potter also flourished in Mexico through the means of the coiling process and moulds, though the pottery of the Aztec is inferior in every way. Toltec pottery naturally shows close affinity with the Mayan but certain techniques were developed of their own. Primary is the method of adding a dark slip to the body and carving it out to form outlines between which slips of other colors were laid, the favorite being a turquoise blue. Ware of this sort, a kind of champlevé, is found about Vera Cruz in the Totonac area and shows a close connection between these people and the Toltecs. But in form and finish all of these wares are fine though in polish they are not equal to those of the Maya or Zapotec type, nor those further inland in Puebla where there were also Toltec people. Later under the Aztec reign the Toltec potters of Cholula were considered the great masters and were supposed to have received their traditions of color from the Mayans. It is said that the table ware of Montezuma and the Aztec nobles was made there. (See pl. 224A)

NICARAGUA, COSTA RICA AND PANAMA

The southern limit of Mayan culture is unknown. Nahuatl-speaking colonies are to be found in the Rivas Department of Nicaragua and on the Nicoya Peninsula of western Costa Rica. The potteries from these places also show strong Nahuatl influences even when found in what appear to be early sites, and these potteries are far finer than any of that of the Aztecs. They are decorated with polychrome designs in slip and so is that on the mainland found in the graves of the Guetar people.

In Southern Costa Rica and Western Panama where there are Talamancan tribes the pottery was developed to a degree which is equalled only by that of Peru. It has been said that in the "biscuit-ware" they have never been surpassed in the history of hand made pottery. I suppose this means pottery made without help of the wheel. The forms are beautiful in the extreme and the colors are also fine but less brilliant than those of Cholula or Oaxaca, and, especially of Southern Peru. The Talamancans were also masters of what is called the "lost color" process. This consists of painting designs in wax on a slip of a certain color after which a slip of another color is applied by dipping. When the piece is fired the portions covered with the wax release the last applied or upper slip which comes off leaving the first showing through. This process was practiced also by the natives of Ecuador and Colombia and at times in Peru and ties up our present territory closely with these sections.

And thus we see what took place on the North American Continent. One might almost say that culturally as the land tapers down we come to higher and higher achievements and there are all indications of a sort of clogging up of the processes of migration in the tip of the Central American cone with only one major back-wash in Yucatan, but such hindrances as the equatorial heat, the dangers of the sea, of the jungle and of marshes among many others could not stop such a movement in the conquest of this globe by the ever restless races of man.

SOUTH AMERICAN CERAMICS

Onward they came down the West Coast of South America in their canoes to avoid the jungle and marshes, though they had no seafaring technique to speak of, or over to the East coming up the Magdalena and Cauca rivers into the highlands of Colombia and southward into the inter-Andean plateau, or along the Atlantic sea coast.

THE COAST

In Ecuador on the coast were steaming hot jungles full of yellow fever, malaria, tangled forests and carnivorous animals. This was no place for man to stay. Certainly no civilization could be built here at least for millenniums to come.

At Tumbez the hills divide the hot and humid coast from the more southerly hot and arid coast which stretches for some 1500 miles on to the south into Peru and Chile, cut only by the swift and turbulent small rivers rushing down from the mountains and the verdure which clings to their banks. From June to November the country is repellent and forlorn, cloaked in fog and desolate, without movement or life though the sea teems with gulls, ganets, pelicans and cormorants, and fish of many kinds as well as dolphins and seals. This did not look like a promised land, and one wonders what urge there was behind these people to drive them on, but they came and they settled and they lived on fish and what small game there was, and finally came to grow cotton, maguey and tequilla, from which they wove baskets and of which our "Panama" hats are largely made. In the southern part the desert plain lies 2000 or 3000 feet above the sea down to which the rivers make their ways in narrow canyons which 20 miles back from the coast are 1000 feet high and closely shut in. Here they could go no further inland and survive.

THE CORDILLERA

Down this coast run the three great Cordillera or mountain ridges, the East, the West and the Central with *hoya* or valleys between them. In Ecuador are about 25,000 square miles between 7,000 and 14,000 feet high which are suitable for pastoral or agricultural societies. Roughly this equals Massachusetts, New Hampshire, Connecticut and Rhode Island. In Peru there is three to four times as much livable area, the Marañón on the northwest being too hot and enervating for any great development, the Huallaga and the Maritime Cordillera south of the Knot of Pasco being better, though even the passes through the Maritime Cordillera are higher than Pike's Peak or Mont Blanc.

THE CEJA DE LA MONTAÑA

The *Ceja de la Montaña* or "eyebrow of the woodlands" links the mountains with deep valleys to the eastward which descend among high ridges of barren stone to plunge into the dense wilderness of roaring streams and thundering water-falls, impenetrable and terrifying jungle and savage animal life, insect life, reptilian life and all that goes to make up one of the most unconquerable parts of the world's surface, the great Upper Amazon. The Incas even tried to dominate this country at one time but never succeeded.

CUZCO THE CENTER OF THE INCA EMPIRE

In south central Peru is Cuzco, the home of the Inca Empire, the capital of *Ttahua-utin-suyu* or the "land of the four sections" among the head waters of the Amazon. The small streams drain into the Urubamba, which drains into the Ucayali, which in turn drains into the Marañón turning east from a long journey north, which finally drains into the great Amazon. The Urubamba, on an average of about 11,000 feet above sea level, has a valley of temperate climate rich in the necessary raw materials for making pottery, textiles, metal-work, stone architecture and all that goes to produce a civilization.

LAKE TITICACA BASIN

South of Cuzco is the knot of Vilcañote and then the basin of Lake Titicaca stretching south to Lake Poopó at about 12,100 feet above sea level and on south to the salt beds of Coipasa and Uyuni. This is the cradle of the great *Tiahuanaco Empire*. Still further south is a tangle of mountains known as the Desert and Puna of Atacama in South Bolivia, Northwest Argentine and North Chile which is a continuation of the Peruvian coastal region ethnologically speaking where there are only traces of a few backward people.

This is the background of one of the greatest cultures that man has ever known. There are alluvial plains for agriculture and steppe conditions for herds. There are *viscacha,* large edible rodents, deer, edible guinea-pigs or *cui,* partridges and good lake fish. There is gold, silver, lead, tin and—a queer distinction but a good one, *checorumi,* or large working stones for building and *vini,* or small heavy stones. Here sometime and probably some considerable time before Christ came an almost primitive race of men, probably drifting down from the earliest beginnings of the Central American culture which was always a little ahead in both development and decline, of the South American culture. Through the legends of the natives and the writings of early European scholars we are led to the same conclusion. Father Cabello de Balboa writes between 1576 and 1586 the report as given him telling how the strong ruler Naymlap arrived from the North with his wife and many concubines, retainers, officials and soldiers. These followers worshipped an idol made in his likeness from a green stone (jade?). When he died he was interred in the room in which he died, and his followers gave out the story that he had taken wing, because of his goodness, and flown away so that the people went in every direction searching for him to bring him back. Father Antonio de la Calancha tells of a chief named Chimo who ruled the section around what is now Trujillo, on the northern coast of Peru, and founded a strong and rich empire which lasted so well that it took the Inca, Topa Yupanqui, a long time with many troops to conquer it.

Chimu Culture

This refers to the early culture which existed in this section, it is thought between 200 B.C. and A.D. 200 and up to Inca times with a dark age period of decline between 800 and 1100 after which there was a "renaissance," the Early Chimu period. It will be interesting and instructive to pause to note indications as to what this culture was, so far as we can piece it out from present beliefs, legends and archaeological evidence.

The Moon

The Indians of Pacasmayu or Pacasmyo just north of Trujillo worship the moon and built her a temple called Sian or "House of the Moon" for they saw that she controlled the movements of certain fish, the periods of their women, and caused crops to grow. She is greater than the sun for she can be seen both day and night and sometimes eclipsed the sun while the opposite never occurred. Dances and sacrifices of children five years old were held to her

Early Chimu water bottle of man on llama with stirrup-shaped spout handle. Am. Mus. of Natural Hist.

Left: Early Chimu water jar with single spout stirrup-shaped and paintings of men carrying others in litters, etc., in red on buff ground. Am. Mus. of Natural Hist.

Owl, in red and white Chimu pottery of fairly early period. This bird had significance to worshipers of moon, and is probably one of symbols brought from China. Ht. 7½". N. M. Heeramaneck Coll.

Fine Chimbote, Chimu red and white ware portrait. Ht. 9". Alice Heeramaneck Coll.

PERUVIAN CHIMU POTTERIES

PLATE 218

THE SEA

The sea they naturally worshipped and called it *Ni* making sacrifices of maize-meal and ochre to it, for it was the source of much of their food, but fish were looked upon only as food. The whale, because of his size, was respected and adored and we see numbers of pictures of him in their art, and even pottery vessels made in his shape.

STONES

A certain sort of stones called *Alecpong* was holy and to quote one of our most excellent authorities, Mr. Philip Ainsworth Means (p. 61, *Ancient Civilizations of the Andes*), "They were regarded as the progenitors of the people among whom they stood, for it was thought that the stones were sons of the Sun who, in a rage because of the death of the woman by whom he had had them, had turned them into stone, commanding later on when his anger was past, that the descendants of each stone adore it."

THE STARS

Three stars were deified and called *Patá*. The Spaniards call them *"las tres Marías"* and there is a story about one having been a thief and the other two commanded to lead him away to be devoured by vultures. They also believed that the human race descended from four stars, two of which conceived the Kings and Chiefs, while the other two conceived the poor and lowly. Also both the Indians of Pascasmayu and those of Yungas around northern Bolivia east of Lake Titicaca calculated the year by certain stars called *Fur* and which the Spaniards called *"las Cabrillas"* which were so honored because of the good they had done for the people.

MARRIAGE AND RELATIONS WITH WOMEN

The marriage custom was to fill a newly made pot with maize-flour and tallow from young llamas and place it before the man and woman. It was then set on fire and they poked and stirred until it was entirely consumed. Then they were told, to quote Means again, "Now you are married, but bear it in mind that you must always be equally industrious and equally ardent in love, for you must always be equals in the state into which you are entering." It is not clear whether this means personal equals or equally balanced in the two endeavors or perhaps both, the woman representing the industry and the man the ardor.

Adulterers were thrown over the cliffs.

During times of drought or famine fasts were held and the animals were forced also to fast. Intercourse with their wives was also denied the celebrants of the fast.

DOCTORS

Doctors had become skillful in the use of herbs and simples and were highly respected but they might be beaten to death if a patient died or tied to the body which was buried while they were left above ground to be devoured by the vultures. Many of the potteries show easily recognized symptoms of various diseases.

DEMONS

Demons were thought to be present at the dances and feasts of Pacasmayu and other parts of the coast and would make replies to questions asked idols and "guacas," or idol houses—temples.

FIG. 1296. Red and White Chimu pottery vessel showing remarkable drawing of running demon. Ht. 7". N. M. Heeramaneck Coll.

All this Means tells us from the account given by Father Calancha.

We learn also that these people used javelins in their wars, probably nothing more than well developed fish spears which had been necessary to them in their migrations for thousands of years back along the coast. The people of the highlands used slings.

They were not bound by strict rules of primogeniture. The chiefs chose their heirs to the throne from among their sons or brothers beforehand and the chosen one was especially trained for the position. In the very most northerly section between Piura and Tumbez the Tallanas Indians had chieftainesses or "*capullanas*" as the Spaniards called them.

All accounts agree that these coastal tribes were more advanced in the early times than those of the highlands.

CHAN-CHAN

The capital of this empire, Chan-Chan, was between the sea and the present Trujillo on the right side of the Moche River. All the lords of the shore country built their palaces on the summits of hills or, if no suitable hill was available, artificial ones were made by piling up earth to the required height into mounds or "*huacas*" like flat topped pyramids. At Chan-Chan the capital of the empire there were reservoirs and aqueducts. Beautiful gardens flowered about the palaces. The interiors were of cool white plaster painted with frescoes. Some of the *huacas* were 200 feet high so that advantage was taken of the sea breezes when the rooms were opened. From the sea the aspect must have been one of charming beauty and the life could not have been very different from that of the Egyptians or the Greeks.

CHIMU POTTERY

Dr. Alés Hrdlička found in the Chicama Valley in Peru a very old *huaca* in which were two vessels, one a pedestal-foot dish and the other a tripod dish,

Right: Interesting little bowl from Chimbote, Peru, in form of bat, with head for handle. Am. Mus. of Natural Hist.

Left: Bowl of the red and white ware of Chimbote of the Chimu period, called a "jaguar bowl." Length 11". N. M. Heeramaneck Coll.

Left: Peruvian pottery sandalled foot modeled hollow for bottle. Am. Mus. of Natural Hist.

CHIMU POTTERY FROM CHIMBOTE

PLATE 219

Fig. 1297. Early Chimu water bottles one showing demon head above ears of corn and flanked by lesser deities, other showing a full hamper. Mus. of Natural Hist.

both of definite Central American type both as to form and decoration, just such as are found in Panama, Costa Rica and Nicaragua. With these pieces were brachycephalic skulls of the Central American type, proving beyond a doubt the tieup already outlined.

Thus we find out at once that pottery is one of our chief sources of infor-

Fig. 1298. Water bottles from Chimbote, first being portrait of diseased head, second looking like man without teeth and with puffed cheeks and third holding stump of one leg and cup or perhaps tip of wooden leg. Am. Mus. of Natural Hist.

mation as to the origins of these people but pottery tells us much more that is interesting for this pottery particularly with its highly realistic paintings and well modelled figures possesses a great documentary value besides its aesthetic aspect. Mr. Means has grouped it into four definite classifications as follows:

1.—Scenes and landscapes showing ceremonial and daily life (painted and modelled).

2.—Portraits single or in groups (chiefly modelled).

Fig. 1299. Early Chimu pottery bottles, one painted with warrior in full regalia, another modeled as fine portrait and third painted and in relief showing fight between mythical beings. All have stirrup spouts but portrait one is inclined toward back. Am. Mus. of Natural Hist.

3.—Decorative designs, naturalistic, formalized and also conventionalized (predominantly painted).

4.—Miscellaneous (painted and modelled or plain).

SUBJECTS OF CHIMU POTTERY

He then illustrates various examples similar to those in our own illustrations showing battle scenes, the effigy of a man on a raft with swimmers, a warrior showing his arms and body and face painting, men killing a deer in a netted enclosure, fishing scenes showing boats with carved bow and stern in the form of animal heads, ceremonial dances and a fanged warrior against an aureole-like "sun" design. Others show that the mighty were carried in chairs or litters elaborately decorated, there are also houses, meeting houses, open pavilions and other buildings. The portraiture is life-like and shows excellent characterization.

WOMEN IN CHIMU POTTERY AND DISCUSSION OF OBSCENITY

Women are seldom shown and this is peculiar for all recently nomadic groups value their women highly as is only natural, for women could not

FIG. 1300. Portrait bottles from Chimbote, Peru of type after handle-spout had moved down to back. First and third might well be of same person. Am. Mus. of Natural Hist.

stand the hardships of nomadic life as well as men and slowly become scarce as they are now in Tibet and Mongolia. When the sedentary life is taken up they are preserved carefully and, one might say, collected by the more powerful members into harems much as we found them with the Crusaders in Western Asia. Father Cabello's account proves that this was also the case

FIG. 1301. Chimu bottle in the form of a bird, in red and white. Ht. 10″. N. M. Heeramaneck Coll.

in Peru. When shown at all in the pottery they are hard at work, in the practice of witchcraft or else in acts of a physiological sort peculiar to their sex such as child bearing. Perhaps they were so precious that religious taboos had been built up about them, though in all of this art we do not find much evidence of servitude to priestcraft, or decadent introspection. Rather, there is a healthy and straightforward viewpoint which may be difficult even for us of today to grasp. While I am on this subject I want to point out that it is frequently impossible for members of our own society to gather clearly the pure simplicity of such societies. To them it is no more interesting to depict the processes of body elimination than those of body replenishment and one is no more obscene than the other. The processes of life, birth, sustenance, procreation and death are all simply part of living and, if anything is set aside as different, it is invariably death for the simple reason that death is sometimes difficult to understand as to cause, etc. The pleasures of the chase and of war are also those of the feast and of copulation; cause and effect, they are all one. We saw how in the Philippines the water sold from a vase was used indiscriminately to aid fecundity of the soil and of the women, and this is ever the sound and healthy attitude of man until he is persuaded by the religionists, or those who make power out of his weakness for being taught introspective questionings, to taboo this or that and anything may be tabooed for their purpose, anything which is more or less necessary for natural existence; the chase, war, food, sexual relations or anything else in part or even in the whole at times. Obscenity cannot be ill-omened until the priests have pointed out the omens, it cannot mean moral impurity until the priests have drawn up the lines of what they call morality and, as there is nothing impure in nature, obscenity does not exist for those who live closely and understandingly with nature. These Peruvians could not have come thus far without living closely and very understandingly with nature in both her hardest and softest moods.

CONVENTIONALIZED DESIGNS IN CHIMU POTTERY

The conventionalized designs are not so vital as those further to the North in Middle America and here we have a transition period in which they are being lost. It is evident that they are continued simply as ornament and that the significance has been lost, but so bred into the past are they that the people felt a certain subconscious satisfaction in them.

CHIMU TECHNIQUE

The Early Chimu emphasis is on form rather than color. The wares are of a reddish clay, much like those of Central America though somewhat lighter and cleaner looking, are covered in part with a white or cream colored slip and maybe painted in black, brown or red-brown slips. On the effigy pieces the hands and faces are sometimes left uncovered by the slip and well burnished with an advanced technique. We have seen how those of T'ang China were left exposed but they were never burnished. Very rarely other colors were used such as crimson, yellow, orange and blue.

EARLY NAZCA CULTURE

So far as we know the Early Nazca people, who were in the Pisco and Ica valleys on the coast of Peru about two thirds of the way toward the south, were of an even earlier culture or the finds represent a later date (probably the latter) for they had progressed to the point of coming under the influence of a priestcraft-religion the mainspring of which was terror and from which the Early Chimu people seemed still to be free.

GENERAL CHARACTERISTICS OF EARLY NAZCA POTTERY

Means gives three main differences between the Early Nazca and the Early Chimu potteries as follows:

1.—Realism survives but is rare and to be seen only in occasional examples.

2.—Color is far more varied and important including—crimson, scarlet, pink, yellow, orange, green, various blues, brown, grey, black and white.

3.—Stylistic dogmas of design are all powerful "with an increase of beauty." The last remark being a simple statement of Mr. Means' own taste without the support of argument, but perhaps it would be better to say—with a *different* beauty appeal.

FIG. 1302. Two beakers the one on the left being strangely close in general feeling to a Chou period (1122–249 B.C.) Chinese Tsun. Am. Mus. of Natural Hist.

FIG. 1303. Water bottle from Pachacamac which shows Nazca type highly conventionalized figures and an angular feeling not seen in Chimu pieces. The double spout with bridge handle is a later development. Am. Mus. of Natural Hist.

Dr. Eduard Seler in his excellent treatise on Early Nazca art describes the following fabulous personages which are depicted:

The Spotted Cat—called "the Bringer of the Means of Life" which may

FIG. 1304. Two cups from Nazca, Peru, the one having a conventionalized face painted on it, the nose and ears of which form three perpendicular flanges set at even intervals about the center. The other has a strangely camel-like animal and what appear to be figures with their heads bent over. Am. Mus. of Natural Hist.

FIG. 1305. Nazca jar with bridge handle and oddly arranged figures. Am. Mus. of Natural Hist.

Large cup found at Nazca, Peru similar to other shown from the museum. Ht. 7½". Nasli Heeramaneck Coll.

A rare pottery dish from the Valley of Nazca, Peru with a realistic human figure much less often seen than in Chimu wares. This is really Tiahuanaco in style. Ht. c. 16". Am. Mus. of Natural Hist.

Rare Nazca pottery jar with two posts which probably fitted into ring supports. This is very similar in style to the dish with figure and is also Tiahuanaco in style. Ht. about 8". Nasli Heeramaneck Coll.

NAZCA POTTERIES

PLATE 220

or may not be so, but he brings in his paws frequently what appear to be seeds, leaves and pods, although sometimes they are lacking.

The Cat Demon—a demon which brandishes a club and clutches one or more decapitated heads by the hair or at times whole figures by the waist which in turn seem to hold a mummified head by the hair. Many of the heads seem to be mummified for they are drawn or modeled with thorns passed through the lips. He seems to be a sort of war god and similar to, or perhaps the same as, the god with a bird head or that of a masked man.

The Bird Demon—seems similar to that above though sometimes more conventionalized. The feet are never those of a man and it does not, therefore, seem to represent a man with a mask.

The Multiple-Headed God—has attached relaxed (perhaps dead) spindly legs and puny weazened arms. The faces are all highly conventionalized but give, nevertheless, unpleasant leers from their lozenge shaped eyes.

The Centipede God—seems to derive from the centipede figures on Early Chimu pots which perhaps indicate that the Early Chimu culture was before that of the Early Nazca for the Nazca ones are far more detailed and complicated.

Fig. 1306. Two Nazca bottles the one with a painting of the Centipede God and the other a crudely modeled staring figure. It is to be noted that this head is very small in scale and the handle approaches that of the double spout. In other words first came the stirrup spout-handle, then the heads pushed it back as it were, and then the modeling of heads became less important and the double spout came into being. Hts. about 10″. Am. Mus. of Natural Hist.

Mr. Means says concerning the Multiple-Headed God: "It seems to me quite possible that this personage is a late development in Early Nazca art, perhaps of the late 5th or early 6th century."

Mouth-masks like cats' whiskers seen on these faces have actually been found made of copper and gold and Means points out that they seem to be the peculiar property of the dead and of the gods or demons. A tongue-like long flat band hangs down over the chin and seems to be supported by two pin-like points into the septum of the nose.

Headdresses are ornamented with secondary faces, "human, feline or nondescript."

Hands and feet with too few digits are found in large proportion and others have too many digits. The significance of this is not known. It could hardly be a simple disregard of detail for these people seemed to love detail.

The figures hold what seem to be ceremonial staffs, clubs and similar weapons, spears and spear-throwers and also slings such as Dr. Hrdlička found on the southerly borders of the Early Nazca region.

There are other similarities of design to be noted: Where there is realism it is much like that of the Early Chimu culture and we find a spout situated back of the heads set at an angle away from them on the effigy pots and attached to them by a bridge which forms a sort of carrying handle. The Early Chimu pots have a stirrup spout. Later the Nazca spout develops into a double one with bridge between. These narrow openings were used because of rapid evaporation from larger mouths even though they must have been exceedingly difficult to pour into without spilling. A most interesting development is the whistle spout which comes along later.

Chimu

Nazca

Fig. 1307.

HIGHLAND CULTURE TO A.D. 600
TIAHUANACO I

In Peru Means mentions only one structure which seems to be pre-Incaic and that is at Vilcashuaman. Of it he says, "Save that it is built of stone and not of adobe it closely resembles the pyramids so common on the coast." Near the southern end of Lake Titicaca in Western Bolivia were two easily distinguishable cultural periods which we may term Tiahuanaco I and Tiahuanaco II. The structures of the first are of the local reddish-brown sandstone and of the other of hard stone which must have been brought from some distance.

TIAHUANACO I POTTERIES

The potteries are very crude and are coarsely incised or painted.

TIAHUANACO II

The Tiahuanaco II section is the most important excavation site in the mountains though this section may have been ruled at times from Cuzco in Peru. In the earliest times the people could hew stone and make buildings huge but very rough. Then trade of coastal cotton with highland wool must have acted to bring the Early Nazca culture to these people and, to a lesser extent, even that of Early Chimu some thousand miles or so to the north. Father Cieza de Leon, writing between 1540 and 1550, tells us that even in his day the great structures of this people were known to be more ancient than the Incas who imitated their masonry in building the city of Cuzco. He describes in some detail the tremendous size of these works including doorways carved out of a single stone "30 feet broad, 15 feet or more long and 6 inches in thickness." Father Diego de Alcobasa wrote, "There are also many other stones carved into the shape of men and women so naturally that they appear to be alive, some drinking from cups in their hands, others sitting, others standing and others walking in the stream which flows by the walls. There are also statues of women with their infants in their laps, others with them on their backs and in a thousand other postures—" Mr. Means says that the statues of women do not now exist and discredits some of the other things said, but the full allowance for enthusiastic exaggeration deducted, we still have a very interesting account which probably had some foundation, and we know from the accounts of Father Cobo and in these days of Dr. González that far more remains underground than above. (See also reports from Pennsylvania University Museum work, etc.)

"The Weeping God of Tiahuanaco"

Means says a general conspectus of Tiahuanaco II art may be seen in the monolithic gateway at the northwest corner of Calasasaya, which has on it what is well known as "the Weeping God of Tiahuanaco." It is not necessary to trace a full description of the piece here but briefly it has a central figure with large square face and elaborate headdress from which project many snake-like parts terminating in conventionalized puma profiles and circular patterns of unknown significance. From his large round eyesockets tears course down his cheeks. There is no doubt but that he is Viracocha, the chief god of these mountain people. His hands have only four digits and hold a highly conventionalized spear-thrower in one and in the other a quiver containing two spears. His rich dress and girdle are decorated with puma heads. Every part of the frieze is laden with ornamental detail representing men, animals, birds and fish as well as many symbolical motifs the significance of which we do not yet know. There are 24 attendants on either side arranged in 3 rows of 8 each, the upper and lower rows having winged men with spears while the center row is of birds or men wearing bird masks. Below is a maeander border seemingly of heads like the god's. The arrangement is symmetrical in general scheme but there is considerable vigor and some variation. Everything seems to be thought of in squares broken by jagged angles. This is probably because of the fact that in their stone building they were necessarily very conscious of the square and the jagged angles may represent fractures or thrusts of which they were also conscious. No one can say for sure but the association seems likely.

Tiahuanaco II Pottery c. a.d. 300 to 600

The bowls, jars, bottles and vases of this people are strictly consistent. They are decorated in rich sombre colors with pumas and other creatures much like those on the gateway. Many shapes are simple and well proportioned but some found at Cuzco are involved and poor. Typical are the ornamentation of the nose and forehead of the faces and ornamentation of the rim of the pot. Fanged mouths recall those of the Early Chimu art. Hands with too few digits and grasping decapitated heads are reminiscent of Early Nazca art. These pieces date back from about a.d. 600. Means thinks, namely to a.d. 300 or thereabouts.

Later Tiahuanaco II Art

At Chavín de Huánter in the valley of the Puccha River, a tributary of the Marañon, was found a monument called the "Raimondi Monolith" after the discoverer. This stone has the same god represented on it but the face is absolutely square and strangely made to appear like a face from either above or below. From above it looks like a highly conventionalized feline face or two snarling feline faces nose to nose and in profile. Means points out that we have something rare here in Andean art but a trick which can be duplicated in Mayan art, in Alaskan art and he says doubtless elsewhere in ancient American art. He might have also added in Chinese art of the Shang Yin and Chou periods and gone on around the Pacific and added in the tattooing of the islands of the South Pacific.

This piece has the same characteristics of Early Nazca art as found in the gateway but it is interesting to note that the art has now become in every detail perfectly symmetrical. Early Nazca art was strongly so, Tiahuanaco at first was more symmetrical and now it has frozen into the rigid convention so that a line drawn down the center will have exactly the same on one side as on the other. The fangs and the feather-like ornaments are from Early Chimu art and not indigenous. The multiple headed headdress is typical of Early Nazca art, as we know. Mr. Means says about it, "Its style is decidedly more mature—one might almost say more nearly senile—than that of the Monolithic Gateway." He places it about A.D. 800.

In describing another find made by Dr. Tello called the "Chavín Obelisk" in the Museum of the University of San Marcos, he says that Dr. Tello says it is a dragon eating fish, serpents and condors all highly conventionalized. From the photographs I must admit that the good doctor can see in it more than I can. However, an interesting comment concerning the genital organ of the creature is made by Means. It is in the form of a fanged puma-head from which issues a plant-like object which Tello says is perhaps emblematic of fertility. Means says, "In this element we have a faint suggestion of that wistful phallicism which so often accompanies the degeneration of art among people desirous of fertility who dimly realize that their vitality is at a low ebb."

Some finds have been made from the mountains of the Department of Piura in the north and Means shows a piece of polished black pottery from the Elías Collection which he claims is the earliest artifact known to us from that region dating between A.D. 800 and 1000 and showing Chavín Tiahuanaco art in its last stages. The decorative band he says represents birds with only the beaks showing and we hope he knows that they are birds but at any rate they show, he says, "the ultimate stage of aesthetic disintegration."

Symbolic Conventionalization

Previously we outlined a theory which so far as I know has not before been suggested, namely that conventionalism in art came from the necessity to make records on small areas. Here we come to another type of conventionalization, that of symbols which at first are abbreviated without the slightest loss of meaning, then are carried on to a degree more simplified because all know what they mean, and finally end up as meaningless designs used solely for ornamentation until they pass out of existence, the public slowly having forgotten what was at first a perfectly clear shorthand.

It is not always easy to distinguish between the two kinds of conventionalization when seen on an individual example, but there is no trouble at all when we have a group of the one to compare with a group of the other. The living conventionalized art of the nomads is always strong and dynamic and would suggest to the uninitiated that it held a meaning and a vital one. The dying conventionalization of decadent-art-symbolism is really a sort of laziness or lack of interest on the part of the artist and it is always marked with the signs of short cuts to effects and poorer craftsmanship. As an instance we have here the perfect symmetry which no living art would tolerate but which the lazy and uninterested craftsman finds saves worry and the effort of thinking on his part. There is as much difference between the two as there is between infancy and senility. There are likenesses but also great differences which can best be sensed when we ask if the artist was doing his best. Sometimes today artists like to assume a primitive pose. Between their assumed simplicity and that of the simple man expressing himself earnestly to the best of his ability is all the difference between charlatanism and sincerity. So it is with conventionalization and purposeless conventions in art; conventions which have lost their purpose are useless and dead.

ECUADOR

In Ecuador, the Kingdom of Quitu, at first a seafaring people, moved up into the highlands to escape the heat. They were warlike and reached from

FIG. 1308. Pre-Conquest red pottery vase from Ecuador ingeniously designed with the body of a seated figure as neck and the head as stopper. This piece undoubtedly shows a closer relationship with the Peruvian potteries than is usual. Ht. about 14″   Brooklyn Mus.

FIG. 1309. Native pottery bottle decorated with "negative painting" from El Angel, Ecuador, pre-Conquest. Note the similarity to some neolithic European and also some Egyptian forms. Ht. 25½″. Brooklyn Mus.

an archaic culture more closely associated with that of Colombia and Central America than with the Peruvian culture, up to about a par with Tiahuanaco II. In general they showed some traces also of influence from the latter in some of their potteries.

The highland culture was not very unlike that of Peru but always less advanced. The coastal culture is more like that of Colombia. A few odd outstanding pieces show that their art as potters was not of much consequence except where influenced by outside sources. A bowl with a rather well conventionalized bird in white on a black ground is crudely made and probably fairly early as is also a vase with face and arms on the neck, perhaps of Early Chimu times. Later wares are represented by the typical Inca "aryballus" and the refined small jar of good shape with two loops and no decoration. The tall vase shows a grace of form which would also indicate a period of about Inca times. It is an excellent piece of work.

THE PERIOD OF DECLINE (A.D. 900–1400)

The Tiahuanaco II culture has shown us that a decline had set in. The central government now showed the same weakness, and conflicting groups set up innumerable small tribal communities throughout the highland zone while the coastal people returned to their original condition. Dr. Max Uhle has invented a term "Epigone Style" from the Greek meaning "one born afterwards" for this time, and describes it as follows: He says it resembles the Tiahuanaco II but "is inferior to its famous prototype in almost every respect." Means thinks that the specimens Dr. Uhle offers are actually "integral parts of Tiahuanaco II art" and that others are "unskillful attempts by coastal artists to copy the characteristics."

The states which were now separated from the central government and cultural life soon fell into degeneracy themselves. The Chimu one extended from the Gulf of Guayaquil to Parmunca and conquered up into the hills but the rulers whiled away the time with buffoons, concubines, dancers and all such court parasites and gave themselves out of boredom to unnatural vices, the worship of animals and human sacrifices, much as we have seen about the Mediterranean in ancient days.

POTTERIES OF THE DECLINE

The argument about general characteristics suggests to us how difficult it is to tell about individual examples. Dr. Kroeber says of all we have, 3% are Early Chimu and 97% late in the black style pottery. In other words, there is practically no Early Chimu black pottery. In the red type 25% are early while 75% are late. The stirrup handle with spout is common to both periods as is also the double bodied jar.

Late Chimu features which are not found at all in the Early Chimu period are:

This ceremonial urn of the Tiahuanaco Epigonal Period is from the Nazca Valley and shows the symmetrical style with some Early Chimu characteristics. The figure is Viracocha, the creator god worshipped in pre-Inca times. Am. Mus. of Natural Hist.

Three bottles from Tiahuanaco sites dating about 6th to 7th cent. and typical in style. Hts. 5″ to 6″. N. M. Heeramaneck Coll.

TIAHUANACO POTTERIES

PLATE 221

1.—Double spout linked by bridge (which came from Early Nazca via Tiahuanaco to coast again).

2.—Flattened oval rather than globular bodies.

3.—Absence of spirited and beautiful realistic paintings of genre-scenes or persons, etc.

4.—There are cases of Early Chimu whistling jars but they are exceedingly rare while in Late Chimu times they are common.

5.—Stolid modeling which attempts to be lifelike and is not.

6.—Formalized wares showing Tiahuanaco influences.

Fig. 1310. A group of Peruvian late period black clay potteries showing the decline in the art. Am. Mus. of Natural Hist.

Fig. 1311. Black pottery bottles, the one on the left of two parrots about 8¾" high, the center a whistling bottle (Chimbote) showing a man in a shelter, and the right one also a whistling bottle with a man on the shoulder seated in a contemplative attitude. Am. Mus. of Natural Hist.

WHISTLING BOTTLES

The whistling bottles are most amusing and typical of this period of non-sense and funmaking. I show an example which was in my possession

which has two spouts connected with a bridge in typical Late Chimu style. One of the spouts is closed by a top on which is perched a monkey with his tail arched high and when one either pours liquor into or out of the other the air is forced through a small hole so cleverly designed that a mournful whistle results. The obscene nature of this piece is such that it would never have occurred to the Early Chimu people and what early examples there are represent birds or other things.

FIG. 1312. Late Chimu whistling bottle of black clay. Ht. about 6".

THE RIMAC VALLEY ABOVE LIMA
CHANCAY AND NIEVERÍA

Found at Chancay by Dr. Uhle and classified by Dr. Kroeber are the following types of pottery:

1.—"Interlocking ware" of the various surrounding types.
2.—White on red ware.
3.—"Epigonal" 3 and 4 color wares.
4.—Three color geometric ware (red, black and white).
5.—Black on white ware.

Means says that #1. is pre-Tiahuanaco of a mixed Early Chimu and Early Nazca type, that 2, 3 and 4 are Tiahuanaco II provincial wares influenced by 1, and that 5 is post Tiahuanaco yet pre-Inca. The latter is a very crude ware realistic in modelling though geometric in painting and

FIG. 1313. Figures from Recuay, Peru, of a man with a llama, a jar, and a woman with a water jar. Am. Mus. of Natural Hist.

Means cannot explain this strange crudeness unless it is perhaps "an artistic mannerism." It seems hard to believe that these people had descended to our modern plane wherein crudity could be assumed, as simplicity is assumed, simply because the artists can think of no more shocking type of self-advertising, but this may be the case.

Of the black-on-white ware Means has to say that it has also been found at Ancón and as people came from all about to visit the oracle-god at Rimac-Tampu, it would not be surprising if pottery from every region of the Andean area were found there.

NIEVERÍA POTTERY

Higher up the Rimac Valley at Nievería and Cajamarquilla is found a post-Tiahuanaco ware with elements from earlier coastal wares again taking the modelling from Early Chimu and the painting from Early Nazca.

CHINCHA, PISCO, ICA AND NAZCA LATER WARES

After the Early Nazca period there were Tiahuanaco influences strongly throughout all of this war loving section. When the realm of Chuquimancu divided up war was constant but brief periods of peace were procured by the expedient of exchanging of women. The wares of the later periods continued rich and somber in color with the same methods of depicting human and animal life. The most distinctive of these wares of what may be called the Late Nazca period were decorated with designs inspired by textile art. Such designs constitute a new type of decorative art and are peculiar to this region during this time.

TIAHUANACO-EPIGNOL PERIOD A.D. 600–900
ATACAMENO PERIOD A.D. 900–1100
CHINCHA-ATACAMENO PERIOD A.D. 1100–1350

Dr. Max Uhle makes a somewhat different classification which consists of the Tiahuanaco-Epignol period (A.D. 600–900), the Atacameno period (A.D. 900–1100) and finally the Chincha-Atacameno period (A.D. 1100–1350). He says that the first pottery in north Chile in the Tacna and Arica region was much like that in Peru. The second period is marked by influences from the South and Southeast and he calls it by the name of a more southerly section in Chile. The pottery is coarse and heavy with ill arranged designs of vigor. Means says about these that they have some relationship with Inca pot shapes as we shall see later. The last period has the same shapes but the designs have become more refined doubtless because of the influence of Chincha or late Nazca art.

In the highlands after the Tiahuanaco II period from say 600 the arts declined to an uninteresting level. Thus we conclude that after this period there was a distinct decline throughout the whole of Peru and Bolivia but a decline far greater and more telling in the highlands.

THE INCAS

Mr. Means points out an unhappy truth in his "Ancient Civilizations of the Andes" (p. 205) and that is that the historians of Peru fall into two biased schools: the one he terms "Garcilasan" and the other "Toledan." The Inca, Garcilaso de la Vega, tells of the creation of man and woman by the sun and the placing of them on an island in Lake Titicaca whence they travelled with a staff of gold seeking a place where with one blow it would sink out of sight in the ground. This was a story he had from his maternal uncle. There are others concerning shining youths in golden mantles that so blinded the people that they gave homage. Of the "Toledan" school he says, "The underlying objective of this school was to justify the establishment of Castilian power in the Andean area and elsewhere in America, this end to be served by showing the Incas to have been bastards and usurpers whom Charles I and Philip II of Castile, descendants of those questionable sovereigns, Sancho IV and Henry II of Castile, had every right to supersede, not only because they were so much superior in their hereditary right to rule, but also because America was only a fitting reward for the services rendered to God during the eight centuries of the Reconquest in Spain—and also because Alexander VI—that holy pontiff—had given them the right." This school was represented most loyally by Viceroy Don Francisco de Toledo, Capitan Don Pedro Sarmiento de Gamboa, in his history of the Incas, 1572, and by Cieza de Leon who tried to be honest and unbiased but bases his work upon that of Sarmiento.

The Incas themselves have a story which is related from their royal *quipus* or knot-records something as follows: In A.D. 945 a barbarous family of four sons and four daughters lived in the highlands. The sisters made beautiful raiment heavily spangled with gold and they all stole by night to some deserted buildings about five leagues from the present city of Cuzco. When dawn came they entered the market place telling the villagers that they had come from Heaven and were children of the Sun and such was the awe caused by their shining beauty that they were hailed as rulers.

Another story is that Mama Ocllo became pregnant by her brother Manco Capac, that another of the brothers disapproved and was killed by Capac who then gave out word that Mama Ocllo had become pregnant by the Sun and so Sinchi Roca was born. Here we have a Zeus-like myth taken in much the same spirit as that of the early Greeks.

Then there is the legend of Mama Huaco, who was mannish and warlike as well as wise and prudent. She threw two golden rods in such a way that one fell two cross-bow shots from Matahua while the other landed at Huaca Pata (Holy Terrace or Square) in the city of Cuzco. The first entered the earth only a little, while the other buried itself so deeply that it was argued that at this place the group was destined to go.

We find then, 1.—simple migration myths and 2.—memories of astuteness and chicancery of the shining mantle type.

Dr. Uhle, supplementing his study of the languages has made a thorough study of the pottery found in the Yucay, Urubamba and Arequipa sections among other places in southern Peru which have yielded up not only the beginnings of the ceramic forms later perfected by the Incas but also the incipient decorative motives which were later to become the developed indicators of the highest art of the Incas, and he has found out and satisfactorily proven that it is likely that the Incas were originally simply a small tribe of "llama-tending, potato-growing mountaineers" no different from hundreds of others at the time of the collapse of the Tiahuanaco II culture. They probably lived south of Cuzco or Tampu (now Ollantaytambo) on the Urubamba River, though this is not definitely established. Other small tribes were forming alliances and engaging in conflicts, building dynasties, etc., and as Means says, this was much the same as the conditions which produced Genghis Khan, "for the rivalries resulting therefrom engendered recurrent struggles for mastery, and the struggles bred strength and ever more strength in the victors."

CHARACTERISTICS OF INCAS

These Incas were not luxury loving rulers but soldiers and wise administrators and their glory was not expressed in bodily comfort so much as in a "superlative aesthetic glory." They were not far advanced in certain things; the arch was unknown, glass was unknown, the wheel had not been invented and they could not, therefore, harness natural water power. Iron called *"quillay"* was, alas for their hopes of opposing the Spaniards, not known but as workmen in gold, bronze, silver, pottery, textiles, and stone sculpture or architecture they were as fine as any known up to the time of the Renaissance, at least.

INCA POTTERY

We cannot be so definite about the Inca potteries as we can about those of Greece but excavation and study is going on and this is one of the richest fields of present day investigation. It is a field in which that master archaeologist and critic of aesthetics, Mr. Horace H. F. Jayne, has shown considerable interest and leadership as well as those others of whom I have spoken and who are mentioned in the bibliography. A number of our museums are rich in treasure such as The Museum of The American Indian, The American Museum of Natural History and the Pennsylvania University Museum, but so far all too much interest has been expended upon the ethnological and archaeological aspect to the exclusion of the aesthetic, except only in the last mentioned museum which was in charge of Mr. Jayne. Our great but somewhat unbalanced Metropolitan Museum does not even deign to show this art, though most of the larger museums of Europe have specimens of which they are justly proud.

INCA FORMS—THE "ARYBALLUS"

Probably the best known and appreciated shape of pottery is the "aryballus" because of its general similarity to some Greek forms though it has ever been more structural than they. The base is a shallow cone, point downward.

INCA POTTERIES

Inca potteries from Peru, a flat dish with bird head handle, an "aryballas," a graceful flaring cup which is a form also made of wood, and a small jar with typical loop handle characteristic of these wares. Am. Mus. of Natural Hist.

PLATE 222

The body arches up from this in almost a deep parabolic curve and from this comes a cylindrical neck flaring to a fairly wide mouth-rim. There are two loops low down on the sides and they are small and strongly made. Most are yet intact in place on those found. A small nubbin either plain or with roughly indicated animal head (usually feline) is frequently seen on the

FIG. 1315. Small flat pottery dish which seems a typical Inca form. The double loops on opposing sides suggest a possibly arched handle. Dia. Am. Mus. of Natural Hist.

FIG. 1314. Two pieces found on the island of Titicaca in Bolivia just over the border of south east Peru. The "aryballas" is said to be of Cuzco type and the one handled vessel is similar. Am. Mus. of Natural Hist.

shoulder at the base of the neck. Concerning this Means says, "This nubbin and the two handles at the widest part of the pot served to hold the carrying-rope in place when the aryballus was carried upon someone's back, the rope being passed through the handles and over the nubbin, after which the ends of the rope fell over the carrier's shoulder and were held by his hands on

FIG. 1316. A very large "aryballas" with the neck broken and sitting upon the sort of stand which was probably used. It is my contention that the loops were used also to sling these vessels from above and to aid in tipping them for pouring. This vase would have been well over 4 feet high. Am. Mus. of Natural Hist.

FIG. 1317. Stem coupe with cover and an "aryballas" of good proportions and conventional decoration. These latter range in size from about 6" high to huge examples about 4 feet high, and far too heavy for any man to carry even partly filled. Am. Mus. of Natural Hist.

his chest. This arrangement brought it about that the side of the aryballus which would rest upon the carrier's back was left undecorated, all the ornamentation being concentrated on the other side, that which bore the nubbin, though some have decoration on both sides." I frankly admit that I am not satisfied with the description for most of these vessels are only from about 9 to 12 inches high, though there are larger ones, of course, some of which are about 40 inches high and which, if filled with water could not be carried by any man of ordinary strength. It seems in fact that they were made in about three sizes: 1.—small ones 8 or 9 inches high which could be carried easily by simply grasping the neck, 2.—fewer middle sized ones about 12 inches high that are at least a good size for carrying with cord slings, 3.—even fewer very large ones that few men could lift when filled. There are practically speaking none in between these sizes. Therefore, at once we see that most of them are not even appropriate sizes for carrying vessels. A man would certainly look like a fool with one of the little ones on his back and I doubt he could even hoist one of the big ones. I have carefully computed the capacity of one of the larger jars and find that it would hold about 21 gallons of water which would weigh approximately 186 pounds avoirdupois plus the weight of the jar itself which is about 40 pounds making a total of 226 pounds. Quite a load to carry any distance in mountainous country!

Another thing is clear and that is that the two loops are generally below the center of gravity. If then the vessel were to be held on the back by means of cord at all, the cord would have to pass around the back at the widest part (where it would rub well into the carrier's back), come through the loops and cross at the base of the neck to keep it from tipping outward before going around it and over the shoulders. This would mean that the nubbin had no reason for being at all, and it would also mean that a man was carrying a most unpleasant and awkward burden. Of course the cords could cross *under* the knob instead of simply at the neck, but there would be no particular reason for this and any such arrangement would press the lip-rim into the carrier's back in a way that would be hardly comfortable to say the least.

I think, therefore, that considering sizes, the possibilities of cord arrangements and the shape we must reach the definite conclusion that these are not carrying vessels at all. Perhaps the consensus has been reached by our authorities because there is some evidence such as the picture or model of a man carrying one of these vessels which I have been unable to run down, but it can have been reached only because our authorities are not pot carrying people and did not think of the difficulties involved. Furthermore I have searched in vain for the natural wear of chafing of cords on the decorations of these vessels and have found none. We might as well conclude that an amphora or a hydria was a carrying vessel because we have pictures of Greeks carrying them in various ways, or that a modern ice-water pitcher is a carrying vessel because we see people carry them from the kitchen to the dining room.

What then is the nubbin for? Let us pause to consider how often we see in these wares a man's head, a god's head, a puma head or some other animal head projecting in relief from one side of a vessel. In fact this was one of the chief characteristics not only of South American wares but also of Central American wares. Could the nubbin not, therefore, simply be an atrophied form of the same thing? I feel that it is and that a series could be arranged showing the prototypes of the "aryballus" in rounded bodied jars with loops and more prominent and detailed heads upon them.

The pointed bottom, which is never decorated, by the way, would raise another question were it not for the fact that in the American Museum of Natural History there is an actual clay rest which was found on the Island of Titicaca and with an "aryballus" fitted nicely into it. The pointed bottom would make another inconvenience for any possible carrier as he would have to stand and balance the jar, if he put it down, as the width of the body makes it a shape that will not lean nicely against a wall or other object. Naturally the carrier, if he could hoist one of the big jars, would not mind carrying also a clay base of a few pounds more, but he might forget it and that would be a pretty fix.

Everything helps to make us believe that these jars were used on stands in the homes of well-to-do Inca people. They were occasionally against a wall and therefore in such cases decorated only on one side. I believe that for the larger ones, which probably stood on the floor, there may have been rope hoists attached in some way to the loops which are nicely placed just about at or sometimes slightly under the center of gravity, to aid in pouring from them. The pointed base would also make it easier to tip them in their circular stands sufficiently to pour from them. The small ones can be nicely handled by the two loops, which were perhaps actual handles. By this means pouring from them, as a servant might pour wine into a cup, is not an ungraceful movement.

Some of these vessels have two more much smaller loops, one at either side of the lip and just under it immediately above the large loops. They can be used only for tying a cover on although there is no evidence of a rim for a cover inside the lip. They are too small and the location too dangerous at the fragile edge of the lip to have supported the weight of the vessel in any way.

Generally cylindrical but slightly flaring wooden cups were made and decorated with fine painting. These were also copied in pottery and, in fact the size was sometimes increased to make a fairly large and deep vessel.

DISHES AND BOWLS

Small and very shallow dishes were made frequently with little double loops at the rim arranged horizontally and opposing each other. Larger dishes have often a more bowl-like form and an animal or bird head as handle or ornament on one side only.

Really much more like an aryballus (I think the larger vessel might better be called an amphora, if we have to go Greek in our naming of these unrelated wares. I continue the custom simply because it has become so definitely grounded that otherwise misunderstandings might arise.)—is a small globular vessel with horizontally placed loop handle and excellent all-over decoration. Another is similar but has a narrower mouth and beveled bottom, the decoration consisting simply of a band about the body at the height of the handle. A third shape which seems fairly common from Cuzco is a pear shaped bottle with small straight, unflaring neck and the same sort of loop handle.

General Characteristics

Dr. Bingham in his recent work shows pedestal cooking-pots, bowls, jars, kettles, ladles, plates, jugs and cups and says that they are found from North Ecuador down to Northwest Argentine and Central Chile and that they are always at the top of the archaeological sites.

These potteries are all thin walled and extremely good. Some are of brown or buff color, though most are grey. The coloring is good though chiefly geometrical, limited in range and low in tone nowhere nearly approaching the Early Nazca wares or those of Mexico with their brilliant and dynamic painting, or even those of the complicated Tiahuanaco II patterns. Means says, "In the later reigns from the death of Pachacutec to that of Huayna Capac, Incaic art fell away from the austere but beautiful geometric ornamentation and became increasingly flamboyant, and increasingly naturalistic due probably to traditions of peoples brought into the empire."

An interesting case in the American Museum of Natural History shows examples of all these periods and a classified listing on the card something as follows:

Early Nazca—polychrome designs of mythical figures on globular vessels with double spouts connected by a bridge and also vases with curved sides.

Early Chimu—realistic figures modelled in reddish-brown ware with light buff or white slip, portraits and models of houses typical, the stirrup spout typical, and also delicate painting in red on white.

Middle Chimu—curvilinear style design in red, white and black.

Epigonal or Tiahuanaco—Tiahuanaco bird and animal design combined with coastal styles.

Late Nazca or Ica—designs in black, white and red from textile patterns.

Late Chimu—typically black ware modeled and incised.

Early Tiahuanaco—incense bowls with modeled puma heads and zoomorphic figures in burnished colors.

Classic Tiahuanaco—the puma, condor, and warrior figures in black, white and yellow on red ground are seen, and flaring sided goblet is typical.

Decadent Tiahuanaco—general breakdown of classic designs.

Chavin—designs copied from their famous sculpture.

Recuay—(central highlands of Peru)—Tiahuanaco influence with the jaguar predominant as an art motive and the use of a "negative" painting technique.

Inca—geometrical designs and animal handled dishes and loop handled bowls along with some poor head-cups.

COLOMBIA

The Colombian culture is naturally strongly influenced by Costa Rica and we find strong modelling such as is shown by the face with protuberant eyes on the fragment of grey pottery shown. Small figures were made, seemingly of a female deity. A finely incised and rather ornate jar has an owl-like face on it and another of good angular shape fitted with four loops for suspension is painted in black, orange and white with a well conventionalized but probably meaningless design. The plinth loaned to the American Museum of Natural History by A. F. Tower is an excellent example of powerful work and may be compared with some of those from Costa Rica.

FIG. 1319. Two jars of red ware decorated in black from Colombia. Hts. 9¾" and 9¼". Am. Mus. of Natural Hist.

FIG. 1318. Pre-Columbian pottery burial urn from between Ocana and Puerto Mosquito on the Magdalena River near Los Angeles, Colombia. Ht. 27⅛". Am. Mus. of Natural Hist.

FIG. 1320. Large pottery jar from the Island of Marajo in the Amazon, Brazil. Note the crudely modeled but highly conventionalized faces on the neck. Ht. 19¼". Brooklyn Mus.

FIG. 1321. Red pottery jar from Colombia which shows a close association of ideas with some of the North American incised and partly modeled wares carried to further development. Am. Mus. of Natural Hist.

BRAZIL

In Brazil the Carib and Arawak stocks in the North and the Tupi-Guarani and Ges in the South did work much as they do now with painted, moulded, applied and engraved techniques. Their potteries do not as a rule interest us although two or three beautiful examples of an incised slip ware are interesting in both decoration and form. But as I have said before, the conditions climatic and otherwise were not particularly conducive to the making of good pottery.

AFTER THE SPANISH INVASION

The "Great Inca" Huayna Capac died in 1526 and in the following year Pizarro appeared at Tumbez, to return again in 1531 and finally treacherously seized the Inca, Atahualpa in 1532. In 1533 Almago brought reinforcements

A large lavatory made of polychrome tiles of majolica type. About 7' long. Made in Mexico about 1830. Metropolitan Mus. of Art.

Jars of about 1700 made in Mexico and showing Spanish (Talavera) Influence. Metropolitan Mus. of Art.

MEXICAN POTTERY AFTER THE SPANISH INVASION

PLATE 223

and Pizarro entered Cuzco. Troubled times were brought by the "men of God" from Spain. Pizarro executed Almago in 1538 and was himself assassinated in 1541 by "Almago the Lad," half caste son of Almago. In 1542 Vaca de Castro beheaded "Almago the Lad."

FIG. 1322. Mexican faïence or majolica laver showing the influence of 17th cent. Persian design through Spanish influence. (c. 1660–1680). Metropolitan Mus. of Art.

FIG. 1323. Mexican majolica plates made about 1840 the one on the right showing a design of symmetrically arranged "Indian flowers." Metropolitan Mus. of Art.

Naturally some trickle of Spanish potteries were brought in but it was no time for the development of the unwarlike arts and it fell upon unfertile soil.

In Mexico things were a little different; the Spaniards came in 1519 and in 1521 Cortes hired some 400,000 natives to rebuild the city. I show a large blue and white Spanish type majolica bowl from the Metropolitan Museum,

FIG. 1324. Early 18th cent. majolica flower-pot made in the form of a Chinese garden seat of drum form. Ht. 18". Metropolitan Mus. of Art.
FIG. 1325. Flower-pot made about 1830 with polychrome decoration and faintly reminiscent of Chinese form and decoration. Metropolitan Mus. of Art.
FIG. 1326. A set of blue and white tiles of late 17th to early 18th cent., Mexico. 53" by 43½". Metropolitan Mus. of Art.

of about 1660–1680. Other European influences came in later although still through Spain. The barrel shaped flowerpot of Dutch-Chinese influence appears of this varied type about 1700 to 1750, while the three jars of somewhat Near Eastern flavor after the Talavera influence show that the Moorish style

Coiled snake vase, two headed, ceremonial, glazed, deep intaglia surface design 8″ dia. (Acambra).

Jointed ceremonial doll with eagle claw and jade bracelet, 11″ tall.

"God of Fire" funeral urn, full standing figure front, vase concealed, all-over glyph intaglia over painted. Terra cotta, 2′ 2″.

"Goddess of Agriculture—Xipe" and deity funeral urn, vase concealed, terra cotta.

Tepic Clay Figurines, male and female, phallic.

MEXICAN POTTERIES

(See text p. 940 et seq.)

PLATE 224

had not been lost and the tiles show a rather crude style which might be Spanish. This same Talavera influence appears as late as 1800 and even a little afterwards as can be seen in the dishes shown. These are of no real importance but some large endeavors were attempted as can be seen by the lavatory in polychromed majolica dating about 1830 at the Metropolitan Museum. The colors are crude and bright and not very pleasant and the style had become florid and softened without the dynamic qualities of the Spanish.

Then troubles increased: the American army at Ayotla, a treaty in 1848, then the French under General Forey took possession in 1863 and Maximilian, Archduke of Austria, was crowned Emperor of Mexico in 1864, and finally Diaz captured Mexico City in 1867. The wares are a poor quality of peasant pottery with vague Indian or Spanish designs, flowers, some Christian symbols, etc., badly potted and unpleasant in tone, then things to sell to the tourist trade.

Sculptured head, high glazed clay, 6″ high.

Left: Portrait of Deity, full figure, terra cotta.
Center: Left—Seated Deity figure, 4½″. Right—Portrait of Deity, full figure, terra cotta.

(Left) Laughing mask, terra cotta, 2½″ high. (Right) Death mask, painted surface, 5″ high. Note the wonderful studies of expression in this plate.

Right: Head, sculptured clay.

ALL FROM PERMANENT COLLECTION OF INTERNATIONAL BUSINESS MACHINES CORP.

TOTONACAN CULTURE POTTERIES STATE OF VERA CRUZ, MEXICO

(See text p. 942 *et seq.*)

PLATE 224A

Ceramic bottle from the Santarem region (Amazon River). Exuberant detail. Procession of animal figurines. Mouth of bottle well turned and ornately decorated with incised designs. From Permanent Coll. of International Business Machines Corp.

Vase executed by Marajo Indians who lived at mouth of Amazon, showing the use of geometric design and fine bold potting. National Mus. of Rio (Quinta Boavista).

Idol of red polychromed clay, anthropomorphous figure, representing a chieftain or person of very high dynasty among the Chibcha personages. Found in the neighborhood of Tunjaque, a city which belonged to the reign of the Chibchas. From Permanent Coll. of International Business Machines Corp.

SOUTH AMERICAN POTTERIES

PLATE 225

CHAPTER XXVIII

AMERICAN COLONIAL TO 19TH CENTURY WARES

Pre-Revolutionary Wares

No one knows when the first attempts at pottery were made in America by the European colonists. We suppose about the first Monday after father had shot a rabbit and mother had declared that she would not cook in those poisonous looking Indian pots, the idea began to take hold. Anyhow not later than 1650 there were several potteries in Virginia making crude household wares. Records are scanty and though we hear about the distilleries and grain mills nothing much is said of pottery. Probably it was not even thought worth decorating.

We would have expected an earlier start in New Amsterdam but the first record is of a list of burghers of the city of "Amsterdam, New Netherland," including Dirck Claesen, "Pot Baker," 1657. We do not even know whether or not he followed his trade and we hear nothing again until 1697–8 when three more names are so listed. Edwin Atlee Barber, in his "Pottery and Porcelain of the United States," credits Prof. Isaac Broome with the discovery of an old kiln a few miles south of South Amboy, N. J. and suggests that perhaps the first Dutch pottery was located there. John Spargo, in his "Early American Pottery and China," (p. 54), says, "So far as the present writer knows, there are no records bearing on this point, nor are there any specimens of pottery bearing the mark of Dirck Claesen or any of his contemporaries or credibly attributed to any potter of this period."

He does say, however, that there was a pottery "at least as early as 1684 at or near Burlington, N. J." No piece has been attributed to this place either but there is a record in the Bodleian Library, Oxford, concerning a Daniell Coxe which proves some such place existed, and that it made "Pottery of white and China ware," though this seems highly doubtful to say the least. The manager is thought to be James Budd who is mentioned in a suit against the potter Edward Randall in 1685. Some believe that Coxe was merely an owner and that he never came to America at all. In any event we can only surmise that the report was exaggerated and not to be taken seriously. Spargo argues that it was not translucent and could not, therefore, have been "china ware" but this is a waste of time, and a futile argument.

Let us try to clear up some of the odd habits of collectors of Americana.

979

It is not necessary to go far back, for Spargo is typical. In his "Early American Pottery and China" (1938) (p. 7) he says, "All wares produced by the potter's art which are not pottery are china. That is only another way of saying that wares which are not absolutely opaque, but possess the quality of being translucent in any degree, are to be classified as china and not as pottery." Thus he would call stoneware "pottery." And all the translucent wares such as Medici, French soft paste, Belleek, English "bone-china" would be called "china." Again he states that "china" and porcelain are synonomous and continues, "They both equally designate any product of the potter's art which is translucent." Actually translucence is not present to any appreciable degree in many of the original, real China wares as we find in many of the Wan Li late Ming period. Any ware in a thin enough piece will be translucent as we find in some of the non-kaolinic early Sung wares. Many translucent wares are more glass than "china" or porcelain, and contain no kaolin at all. Also even thin sheets of so dense and opaque a material as gold are translucent, and he would have to get down to micrometer measurements to make his definition stick. Also all dictionaries give the term pottery as meaning a non-kaolinic ware made of clay and hardened by burning, but also as *any ware* so hardened, covering the whole of ceramic products. Thus we may call porcelain, soft-paste, stoneware, terracotta, faïence, etc., all pottery in general. Thus confusion reigns! I have tried hard to give concise definitions at the back of this book and the composition of each ware has been given, when it could be found, under its description. Generalities are misleading and should be avoided as much as possible.

Having decided arbitrarily in his own mind that only porcelain can be translucent, and knowing that porcelain was not invented in Europe until much later, Spargo concludes in backward reasoning that the Burlington ware could not be translucent even though, as he himself admits, it might resemble Dwight's white ware which *was* translucent in thin parts. If he has ever seen any of the Dwight type ware, he blinded himself to its translucence because it did not fit his definitions. But Spargo is not the only one to blame for this confusion; four or five of the leading authorities in this field wander about just as vaguely. And, if on the shelves of any collector today there is a piece which seems to answer the description of the Coxe pottery and which has been condemned because of being translucent, that collector may take hope again and continue his comparisons and research along the lines of Dwight type wares of about the same period in Staffordshire.

Virginia Kaolin or "Unaker" (c. 1744)

Edward Heylyn and Thomas Frye of the Bow factory took out a patent in 1744 for making "China ware" in which they state that the material to be used was, "an earth, the produce of the Cherokee nation in America, called by the natives 'unaker,'" and we believe that the Bow factory actually used this material at least for some time, at least until the discovery of china clay in Cornwall in 1768, perhaps. William Cookworthy in 1745 wrote a letter which mentions a person who had discovered china-earth in the back of Virginia and who had gone for a cargo of it. He says that both petuntse and kaolin were discovered and says, " 'Tis the latter earth is the essential thing towards the success of manufacture."

SOUTH CAROLINA CLAY (c. 1765)

About 1765 clay was sent from South Carolina and it is supposed that pottery making started about when it was discovered. Even true porcelain might have been made for we know that Wedgwood was alarmed that the industry might rival his world monopoly. He said, "They had an agent amongst us hiring a number of our hands for establishing new Pottworks in South Carolina; having got one of our insolvent Master Potters there to conduct them." Also, "They have every material there, equal if not superior to our own," and again, "As the necessities of life and consequently the price of labor amongst us are daily advancing, it is highly probable that more will follow them, and join their brother artists and manufacturers of every class, who are from all quarters taking rapid flight indeed the same way! Whether this can be remedied is out of our sphere to know, but we cannot help apprehending such consequences from these emigrations as make us very uneasy for our trade and Posterity." Wedgwood himself used some of the clay for some years, and later some from Pensacola, Florida. However, the existence of the Carolina potteries was precarious and left no trace.

NEW YORK CITY (1735)

In New York, John Remmey (1735) had a pottery on Potter's Hill near Fresh Water Pond not far from the site of the old City Hall. Barber wrote that Clarkson Crolius was a partner but Spargo, who has done some excellent researches in the historical field, states this to have been impossible, though he does say there was a William and Peter Crolius (or Croylas), potters who became freemen in the city in March, 1729. He also says the wives of William and of John Remmey were sisters and that the two properties were contiguous. He is sure there was never any partnership though both Dr. Stillwell and Barber thought there was. Spargo goes on to say that John Remmey had a son John Remmey II and William Crolius had a son John who had a son Clarkson.

A stoneware batter jug now in the New York Historical Society is inscribed "New York, Feb'y 17th, 1798—Flowered by Mr. Clarkson Crolius." This is a brownish grey stoneware with the design incised and a deep blue color applied here and there. It has a typical salt glaze. Barber claims, "John Remmey, one of the partners, having died in 1762, the second partner appears to have carried on alone, as indicated by a salt glazed stoneware jug or batter pot." Spargo points out that Clarkson Crolius was only born in Oct. 5, 1773 or about ten years after the death of his supposed business partner. I also point out that one of the owners of a kiln would hardly be inscribing himself as having "flowered" a pot.

After the death of John Crolius, the son, Clarkson Crolius took over the management of their kiln and in 1812, when Potter's Hill was leveled and Collect Pond filled in, he moved to 65 Bayard Street where he continued until 1848. Meanwhile his son, Clarkson Crolius II joined his father and

Stoneware butter churn made by Clarkson Crolius, Sr. c. 1800. N. Y. Historical Soc.

Salt-glazed stoneware batter jug dated Feb. 17, 1798 and made by Clarkson Crolius, Sr. N. Y. Historical Soc.

Salt glazed grey jug with blue decoration made by John Crolius. Dated July 18, 1775. Metropolitan Mus. of Art.

Teapot made by Clarkson Crolius, Jr. Flower and acorn design, with squirrel on lid. 19th cent. N. Y. Historical Soc.

Late 18th cent. Crolius stoneware jar. N. Y. Historical Soc.

CROLIUS (NEW YORK) POTTERIES

PLATE 226

signed "C. Crolius, Manufacturer, New York" impressed into the clay just as his father also did.

John Remmey II had a son, John Remmey III, and it is possible that Barber may have been right about some financial connection between one of the Crolius and one of the Remmey boys, though it could not have been the

FIG. 1328. Left, stoneware jar covered with light brown slip, an unusual treatment; inscribed: "Paul Cushman's Stoneware Factory 1809." Cushman, so far as is known, was the first Albany, New York Potter. Right, Gray salt glaze stoneware jug with incised and cobalt blue decoration; inscribed: Commeraw's Stoneware N. York." 1802–1820. McKearin Coll.

FIG. 1327. Salt-glazed stoneware jug, stamped J. Remmey, Manhattan-Wells New-York and with U. S. coat of arms which establishes this was not the work of the first John Remmey but either the second or third, probably the latter. 19th cent. N. Y. Historical Soc.

first two in the business. John Remmey III was a good potter and also wrote articles and a book, "Egypt as It Is," (1799).

PENNSYLVANIA WARES (1683–)

Pennsylvania was first settled along the Delaware River by English, Dutch and Swedes, the latter making the first settlement. In 1655 there was Dutch control, while in 1664 it was English. The William Penn petition to Charles II was made in 1680 and his treaty with the Indians was in 1683. To this land came many of the oppressed and among them were the Quakers of Welsh stock and formed the "Welsh Barony" in Delaware and Montgomery counties. Also about this time came the Mennonites (1682–3) and settled in "Germantown." They were Germans from both sides of the Rhine and were followed by Lutherans and Reformed Church people from the Palatinate, Bavaria, Austria, etc. Swiss came in great numbers around 1727 and later. Scotch-Irish Presbyterians arrived and took up the back country along the frontier and finally in 1770 Connecticut "Yankees" came to the beautiful Wyoming and Muncy valleys. Thus we have a melting pot and the people are not "Pennsylvania Dutch" at all.

The earliest established piece was found by Dr. Edwin A. Barber in 1891 and is a shaving dish dated 1733, but of course these various peoples must have made much pottery before that, and the first must have been made about 1683 or fifty years earlier. It must have been some of the simple wares with plain surfaces or incising as slip would not have been attempted at the beginning, though it may have occurred within a very few years. The settlers from England may well have included some potters who knew the techniques, both of trailed and incised slip, from Staffordshire, the West Country or

Plate of slip-ware with incised decoration. Parts of the design are colored in green. Penn. late 18th cent. This is not unlike the Staffordshire ones though a bit more ornate than most and the American potters seemed to use green rather than blue. Similar German examples more often have several colors employed. Metropolitan Mus. of Art.

Irregular octagonal plate with yellow slip on a dark chocolate ground, from Penn. and made about 1800. Ginsburg & Levy. Dr. Smith Coll.

Incised slip-ware plate with "Indian flowers" and dated 1805. Dia. 12". Metropolitan Mus. of Art.

Crude trailed slip decoration of cream and green on red ware of the early 19th cent. Penn. Dia. 7⅝". Metropolitan Mus. of Art.

PENNSYLVANIA POTTERIES

PLATE 227

FIG. 1330. Red earthenware jar with yellow and green slip as well as incised decoration, made by Christian Klinker c. 1792. Ht. 10″. Metropolitan Mus. of Art.

FIG. 1329. Penn. bowl with cover, of red ware mottled glaze and modeled applied decoration. This piece is very like the wares found in England near Salisbury, Wiltshire. This is late 18th or early 19th cent. Ht. 5¾″. Metropolitan Mus. of Art.

Wales. Some Toft wares are similar (1676–1700) and on these tulips seem also to be a favorite design. A dish supposedly from Somersetshire dated 1725 and in the Glaisher Collection has an attached cup in the center and an incised slip design including a bird in just the style and colors of the Pennsylvania wares. Actually the retarded English development just about occurred at the right time to bring about prototypes of the American wares, while in Germany the development was far advanced. In Hesse at Frankfort and elsewhere there are odd instances of similar wares but even in the first half of the 17th century the designs are more ornate, involved, executed in various colors and often including incising, spotting and trailing of the slip all on the one piece. To be sure, the symmetrical "Indian flowers" are there but by the end of the 17th century they had become quite detailed and showed signs of decadent overloading.

Spargo goes to great trouble to prove the source as Germany. He says, "Neither in the color of the body or the glaze nor in any other

FIG. 1331. Rare Pennsylvania earthenware covered jar, colored slip and incised decoration. Probably late 18th cent. McKearin Coll.

feature does the sgraffito ware of the German potters of the middle nineteenth century differ from that of the earlier German potters who settled in Pennsylvania." He then says the roulette used in making a band of regular indentations around the edge of a piece is common to German and Pennsylvania potters but neglects to say that it was also used commonly in Staffordshire. He also

Fig. 1332. Pennsylvania, Montgomery Co., jug inscribed "Whitpain Township" and "Henry Dull" as well as with the county name. It is dated under the handle with what appears to be 1805. Geo. S. McKearin.

states that the late Albert Pitkin told him that he had examined *two*, no less, "sgraffito plates, both brought from Germany within twenty-five years, which were identical with one in his collection made by Troxel, in Montgomery County, Pennsylvania, bearing his name and date." Neither Pitkin's notes nor his widow who published them in "Early American Folk Pottery," (1918) mention this astounding coincidence or even touch upon the exact duplication of both materials and works of art being made thousands of miles

Fig. 1333. "Tulip ware" incised slip Penn. plate of red earthenware dating about 1800 and showing the typical "Indian flowers," symmetrically arranged. Dia. 12". Metropolitan Mus. of Art.

Fig. 1334. Slip-ware plate in cream and black on red ground. Penn. 18th cent. Dia. 12". Metropolitan Mus. of Art.

apart. Spargo, who has been often quoted as an authority, throws all reason to the breezes when he raves on, "The writer of these pages believes that

Pitkin's conclusion in the case of this single experiment would have been the same if the experiment had embraced three thousand pieces instead of three." But the whole is just plain nonsense and I note that Spargo does not even show ONE of these duplications in illustrations. Barber also says the wares were quite similar and that he could tell them apart because the backs of the German ones were, "a lighter and brighter red color than any of the Pennsylvania ware."

FIG. 1335. Nearly every country has made marbled ware since it was first devised to imitate stone in Egypt. This example is decorated in cream and green glazes on red ware. It has a coggled rope border. Dia. 15¾". Penn. c. 1800. Metropolitan Mus. of Art.

FIG. 1336. Slip-ware plate with brown ground and yellow and green decoration. The inscription reads, "In this plate stands a star; brandy I drink gladly." Dia. 13⅛". Metropolitan Mus. of Art.

FIG. 1337. Jug by Jacob Schall of Montgomery Co., Penn. It is of red earthenware with incised design of three doves with cream and green glazes lightly brushed on. Ht. 6¾". (Probably about 1830.) Metropolitan Mus. of Art.

Actually no two of these freely hand done things could be alike. There may be a very close similarity to a half blind man of little background or experience between some Ming wares, the "Gabri type" Persian incised slip wares, those of Germany, those of England and those of America. Such similarities do not go very far and the different characteristics of the artists cannot escape the eye of the careful observer.

One element of design they did owe to the people of the Rhine or possibly the Dutch, and that is the symmetrical "Indian flowers" which were actually originated in India and brought direct to these northern countries, not into Morocco and Spain. These designs may be seen in the "Lorenz Speckner Group" (c1618–1670), which are, by the way, excellent blue and white. They are seen also in some of the "Habaner ware" of Austria of the late 17th century and early 18th century, which were richly colored; and in Hesse about Frankfort in incised examples painted in with slip (seldom incised through the slip to the body) and in slip trailed designs. They are known also in England though there the symmetry was less popular and is seen only in such odd pieces as a cistern of faïence and a Staffordshire dish figure. After the Revolution these designs gave way to poorer yet more ambitious ones such as the one Spargo illustrates with a fiddler and two dancing couples, the men wearing "Washington hats," and which is dated 1786.

The mariner's compass design in the form of a star with added points is, so far as I know, entirely English and does not occur on German wares at all. Spargo says, "Toward the middle of the 17th century it was made in England, and it is a remarkable fact that the designs used by the English potters at that time, and the ware itself, were practically identical with those made familiar by the work of our Pennsylvania potters during the 18th and 19th centuries." The gentleman seems to have what might be called an "identity complex," such as some people who see in every one on the street a close resemblance to some friend or acquaintance!

FIG. 1338. Typical cream slip over red ware dish signed "Gemacht oon Samuel Paul, 1798." Penn. Dia. 12½". Metropolitan Mus. of Art.
FIG. 1339. Plate somewhat in the style of Hessen ones but different in color. It is of red ware with cream slip and a strong green glaze over it. Made by Geo. Hübener (1785–1798). Dia. 10½". Metropolitan Mus. of Art.
FIG. 1340. White slip and red ware plate from Montgomery County, Upper Hanover Township and made by Samuel Troxel (c. 1823). Dia. 11¼". Metropolitan Mus. of Art.

Most of these wares were not made so much for use as for gifts much as in Italy and later in England. It is also to be noted that most of them were simply two color in effect, though green splashes were added in the glaze as in the Near East and T'ang China (A.D. 618–906).

FIG. 1341. Cistern of stoneware molded and pressed with appliqué bosses and leaf forms in blue on a grey ground. Penn. Franklin Co., Waynesboro, by Salomon Bell, early 19th cent. Ht. 14½". Metropolitan Mus. of Art.

FIG. 1342. Early in the 19th cent. some had grown tired of the dead symmetry of the "Indian flowers," and turned to such arrangements. This piece is from Montgomery Co. near Tylersport and was made by Johannes Neesz (1775–1867). It is inscribed, "There is meat and sauerkraut. Our daughter is a bride in the year 1810." Dia. 10". Metropolitan Mus. of Art.

Among the known names because of signatures of makers are John Leidy, one of the best who died in 1838 (this name has a possible English sound to it), David Spinner, a Swiss (1758–1811), George Huebener, John Neesz (or Nase) (1775–1867), Jacob Schell (or Scholl) (c1830), David Haring (c1840), Samuel Troxel and Jacob Taney, but often the piece would have not the name of the maker but of the intended owner on it, as in England.

Most all of the so-called "scratch wares" were made in Pennsylvania but there is a local tradition around Bennington, Vermont, that a few were made by German potters employed there. Perhaps this was only because the Bennington people wanted to say that every type of American ware had been made there. Others were said to have been made in the Pruden pottery in Elizabeth, N. J., but none have been so identified.

OTHER PRE-REVOLUTIONARY POTTERIES

In Quincy, Mass., which used to be Braintree, Joseph Palmer, a Devonshire man, started a pottery in 1753. He brought his brother-in-law, Richard Cranch, who was only 20, in with him and they started salt factories, chocolate mills, spaghetti factories and finally a glass and pottery works, and, as they hired largely German labor, the settlement was called "Germantown" again as in Pennsylvania. Cranch sold out in 1760 and Palmer became fairly important although we have no specimen of his pottery recognized. It was supposed to have been a heavy stoneware and a salt-glazed cream-ware.

PHILADELPHIA

A pottery was opened in 1769–70 in Philadelphia with a Frenchman named Gousse Bonnin from Bow and a George Anthony Morris, who seemed to have put up the capital. It was on Prime St. near the present navy yard. They announced in 1769 that they were ready to sell porcelain as good as Bow, and advertised for workmen and for bones as well as "Zaffer" or "Zaffera" for making blue ware. In 1772 they wanted more workmen and "fifty wagon loads of white flint stone." In the Pennsylvania Museum is a piece which is probably authentic. It is an openwork or latticed sided fruit bowl with flowers at the corners and intersections in relief. The decoration is of a large rose and foliage in the bottom and this and the flowers in relief are in underglaze blue. In 1774 the factory failed and Bonnin went back to England.

MASSACHUSETTS POTTERIES

In Boston a factory was established in 1769 and made "tortoise-shell" and "cream-and-green" wares for table use, so it was claimed.

Other early Massachusetts places were at Salem, 1641, by John Pride; in Danvers by William Osborne shortly after; and finally in Peabody where in 1730 earthenware was commenced by Jonathan Kettle, Joseph Osborne, Joseph Whittemore and Miles Kendall. Later in Peabody (1759–1828) William Southwick made pottery with red body and almost black glaze. The ware was what might well be termed "Kitchen American" with nothing to recommend it. At Weston, Abraham Hews (1765) made domestic wares and moved to Cambridge later.

CONNECTICUT POTTERIES

At Litchfield (c1753) John Pierce had a place as did also Jesse Wadhams and Hervey Brooks. Jonathan Durell started here about the same time and moved to New York in 1774 where he opened a kiln near "Kitechemet's

Mead House." He may also have drifted to Philadelphia and worked in the Southwark Pottery of Bonnin and Morris but this is not surely proven. He seemed to be a bit along the "arcanist" type.

CHART OF PRE-REVOLUTIONARY KILNS

Burlington, N. J.	1684	Daniell Coxe absent prop. Edward Randall William Winn	Salt-glazed white stoneware
Peabody, Mass.	1730	Jonathan Kettle	Black glazed red ware
New York City	1735	John Remmey I	Stoneware—salt-glazed grey type
Huntington, L. I.	1751	Adam States	Red ware and stoneware
Braintree, Mass.	1753	Joseph Palmer Richard Cranch	Stoneware—grey type
Litchfield, Conn.	1753	John Pierce Jesse Wadhams Hervey Brooks	Red ware and Stoneware
Peabody, Mass.	1759	William Southwick	Redware with black glaze following Kettle's
New York City	c1762	John Remmey II John Crolius	Stoneware—grey type
Also son of Clarkson, etc. Either together or separate but at any rate upon friendly terms we would suppose.			
Weston, Mass.	1769	Abraham Hews	Red ware
Philadelphia, Pa.	1769	Gousse Bonnin George Anthony Morris	"Bone-china" white and decorated
New York City	1774	Jonathan Durell	Probably copies of Bonnin's wares
East Greenwich R. I.	1775	—Upton	White ware of some sort
Pennsylvania	1733 or earlier		The scratchware or slipware of engraved type described

All of these wares seem to fall into four simple groups, only one of which has any real artistic merit:

1.—Common lead glazed red or reddish brown ware of purely utilitarian type with slight decoration or none, of which one can only say that they are sturdy, honest and direct. A few show good proportions and some have wheel grooves. Impressing had just begun a little. Slip trailing was done infrequently. There was little inclination to exchange the colors so that wares from one section are much like those from another.

2.—Grey stoneware which was much the same in use and spirit but more durable and cost more. They are a little stronger in form and show the first traces of incised technique. Soon afterward they used rather hastily and scantily applied blue color.

3.—Imitative wares from the English such as the Philadelphia type and of salt glaze which are near white and with polychrome decoration. They are poor imitations at best.

4.—The Pennsylvania slip wares which are real achievements of the potter's arts.

LATE 18TH AND 19TH CENTURY AMERICAN POTTERIES
AFTER THE REVOLUTION (1775–1783)

Wedgwood is thought to have sent his best wares to the colonies and was worried about the possible competition there, but he need not have worried for soon after 1783 the flood of "English cream ware" from his factory and others swamped the market. The case of Bonnin and Morris in Philadelphia was typical for no sooner had they made American "bone-china" than large cargoes were dumped, and brought about their bankruptcy.

When the war spirit swept the country there was no liking for the English wares and small potters again sprang up and the larger places were able to pay expenses, but the result of this boom was a cheapening of the qualities because of the financial conditions and because some of the good English potters living here withdrew and went home. In 1783 when the war of arms ceased, England again commenced the economic war. Huge amounts of transfer printed wares were sent over with portraits of Washington, Franklin, Jefferson and other national figures. This was not, of course, very patriotic of the English merchants but they have always been broad-minded and have had the "progress of mankind" in mind. They even went further and wrote mottoes on pieces expressing British humiliation and American exultation over victory.

So clever were they that soon the Americans actually became ashamed of home products and thought that "imported" things were the only ones worth while. Even the excellent wares made at Bennington were demanded by dealers unmarked so that they could be sold as English. By the end of the 19th century there was hardly a factory worth mention left in America.

BENNINGTON, VERMONT (1793–1839)

Captain John Norton came from the "Litchfield Group" of potters having worked at Goshen, then later at Williamstown, Mass. before he settled in 1785 in Old Bennington, where there had been a settlement less than twenty years. In 1793 he built a kiln opposite the Hinman house. To this date he only made common red pottery and at his last stop probably salt-glazed stoneware. He died in 1828. In 1831 his son, Judge Lyman Norton, moved to the present Bennington village and built on the present site. He and his son, Julius, continued stoneware and made a new "yellow-ware" in imitation of the English "cream ware" or "Queen's ware," adding also imitation "Rockingham ware" which is about the same as the "cream ware" spattered before firing with a brown glaze similar to that used at Swinton on the estate of the Marquis of Rockingham and not unlike the "tortoise shell ware" of Whieldon, all of which simply made use of manganese with lead spar and flint.

Up to this time all was entirely utilitarian, but because of the growing middle class market, salesmanship became exuberant. Notable for this exuberance were the large wagons painted dark green and lettered in yellow,

Left: Fine example of a so called, "handwarmer," but undoubtedly a flask mottled in green, yellow, brown and white made by the U. S. Pottery of Bennington, Vt. (c. 1853–1858). Ht. 7⅝". Metropolitan Mus. of Art.
Center: A Bennington "hound handled pitcher," with the usual mottled glaze. Geo. S. McKearin.
Right: So-called, "celery dish," of Bennington ware mottled a beautiful black, brown and yellow on brown pottery. c. 1850. Ht. 9¾". Metropolitan Mus. of Art.

Left: Two good old New England bean-pots made by Lyman & Fenton about 1850 at Bennington, Vt. Ht. 7⅝". Metropolitan Mus. of Art.
Right: Curtain knobs made at Bennington about 1850 and mottled in black, brown and yellow. Length about 4½". Metropolitan Mus. of Art.

Left: Bennington candlesticks in various mottlings of green, black, brown and white. c. 1850. Ht. about 8". Metropolitan Mus. of Art.
Right: Bennington pottery stag with the mottled "Rockingham" glaze made by Lyman Fenton & Co., 1849. Ginsburg and Levy, Inc.

BENNINGTON (VERMONT) POTTERIES

PLATE 228

Fig. 1344. A grey stoneware jug signed J. F. Fenton and made at Bennington, Vt. Ht. 18". Metropolitan Mus. of Art.

Fig. 1343. A "Toby jug," and bottle in the form of a man, made at Bennington with what was called "flint enamel." Geo. S. McKearin.

"BENNINGTON STONEWARE," "NORTON POTTERY." These wagons were drawn by four perfectly matched horses, and with a smart young man handling the horses, talking up the wares, collecting the money and creating a demand.

Norton & Fenton, East Bennington (1839)

In 1839 Judge Norton took his son-in-law, Christopher Webber Fenton,. in with him. Fenton had made red pottery at Dorset, Vermont, where Jonathan Fenton had established a pottery in 1801. The firm was now, "Norton & Fenton, Bennington, Vermont" (the first mark), and this was impressed on some of the octagonal pitchers of "single glaze," "Rockingham ware." It also appears in an elliptical form on similar pitchers supposed to be a little later, while mark 3, a few years later still, "Norton & Fenton, East Bennington, Vermont," showing that at this time they moved to what is now Bennington and what was then derisively called "Algiers." In 1828 Fenton married Judge Norton's daughter and the first "down town" pottery was erected, the mark being simply "Norton and Fenton." This year Captain Norton died. The association was between Fenton and Judge Lyman Norton, the captair.'s oldest son. Still later the firm was Julius and Edward Norton and about 1865, Edward and Lyman P. Norton, and again later Edward Norton & Co., when Thatcher (C. W.) became partner.

Meanwhile the younger men wanted to go into the making of "Parian ware" and though the judge did not care about it, Mr. Fenton, Julius Norton and Henry Hall started the work in the north wing of the pottery, bringing

FIG. 1346. A "Cow Creamer" with the imitation Rockingham glaze made at Bennington, Vermont about 1850. Length 7". Brooklyn Mus.

FIG. 1345. Sugar bowl with "flint enamel glaze" marked *Lyman Fenton & Co., Bennington, Vermont* and made about 1840. Ht. 4¾". Brooklyn Mus.

FIG. 1347. Bennington mottled "flint ware" or "Rockingham" glazed book flasks. The titles are such as, "Bennington Companion," or, "Departed Spirits." Hts. 5" to 11". Ginsburg & Levy, Inc. Dr. Smith Coll.

FIG. 1348. A well made jar with cover of about 1850 by the Lyman, Fenton & Co. kilns. It is black, brown and yellow on brown ware. Ht. 10¼". Metropolitan Mus. of Art.

John Harrison from England to do the modeling. The partnership lasted only a few years and then Fenton leased the wing from the Nortons and went into business alone, his mark being "Fenton's Works, Bennington, Vermont." During this period we find the mark on a great variety of wares such as Rockingham, Cream ware, Parian ware, glazed and unglazed and with elaborate ornamentation.

Shortly afterward Fenton obtained another partner, Alason Potter Lyman, who despite his middle name was a lawyer and the firm was now known as "Lyman and Fenton." Then Mr. Calvin Park came in and it was, "Lyman, Fenton and Park."

Meanwhile the Nortons made a new partnership but relinquished their interest in 1881 when they sold to C. W. Thatcher who used the name, "The Edward Norton Co." This later company seemed to make only stoneware.

Fenton, though a real artist, wore out the patience of his several partners by his expensive experiments. A patent was issued #6,907 on Nov. 27th, 1849 which tells of a process of immersing the article in transparent glaze and sprinkling colors on it with a small box with holes in it to obtain variegated effects. This would seem to be simply another method similar to the Chinese "powder blue" process but Fenton and the Patent Office probably did not know that.

THE UNITED STATES POTTERY

The United States Pottery was formed by Fenton and his partners in 1852 and was directly across the street from the Norton Stone Ware Works. It had six kilns. Finer wares were made including soft-paste, elaborately decorated "Parian ware" and "white granite." Fenton's ware was supposed to have been an improvement over Rockingham and was harder with also a greater variety of color. It was plain, mottled and "scrodled," the latter meaning a sort of mottling or marbling. The wares were known as "Fenton's enamel," or "Flint enamel," and the colors were black, yellow, olive green and other greens, browns and dark red and blue which were sparingly used. He found a fine kaolin deposit in Vermont which brought the kiln prosperity.

Workmen came from Germany and England and the payroll jumped to $6,000 a week. Theophile Fry and Daniel Greatbach were the chief artists. The latter had worked for the Jersey City Pottery and he made the first "hound handled pitchers," there. The idea was far from original, however, for fox handled ones had been made in Hungary and dog handled ones in Brampton, Derbyshire, and Doulton. But when he joined the U. S. Pottery he altered the design slightly and again when he went to Trenton he altered it again. The U. S. Pottery ones have a spirited deer hunt on one side and a boar hunt on the other. A grape vine covers the neck and shoulder and it was made in three sizes and usually brown. The head of the dog is free of the forepaws, while the Jersey ones do not have the vines and are heavier.

When the U. S. Pottery closed Greatbach went to South Carolina and then to Peoria, Ill., where he sold the mold for his jug. It then came to the Vance Faïence Co. which made a few copies but honestly signed them with their name. Greatbach came from England where he had been a mold maker as were also Charles and William Leake, John Leigh, Enoch Barber, Joseph and Henry Lawton, John Harrison, Alsop, Molds, Cartwright, Turncliff, etc.

"PARIAN WARE"

The "Parian ware" was an imitation of that made in England. It is an unglazed more or less soft porcelain or bone china of fine near-white body

FIG. 1349. Superb "Parian ware" 19th cent. Bennington vase of blue and white showing all the beauty of proportion and ornamentation. Ht. about 9". Brooklyn Mus.

FIG. 1350. "Parian ware" pitcher of about 1850 with molded relief decoration of corn. Ht. 9". Brooklyn Mus.

out of which small figures, vases and pitchers were made. Cows, Toby jugs, etc., were also made. The ware was supposed by Copeland to be so fine grained that it looked like Parian marble (which by the way is neither white nor close grained). Many imitations of the Bennington output were made and few real originals are to be found. Fenton may have invented the idea of making it with blue ground which was perhaps suggested by Wedgwood "jasper ware." The ground which was usually blue was pitted. The model was made and pitted by hand. Then the mold made from it had small projections corresponding with these pits. These points were covered with blue or grey slip with a brush so that when the white clay was poured in, it took up the color from the points and left the relief design in white. Sometimes a velvety surface was obtained by coating the interiors of the saggers with glaze which vaporized with the heat and gave the piece a glossy sort of half glazed look. As a rule, only the pieces intended to hold liquid were glazed on the inside, not on the outside. The original ware of Copeland's was invented in 1846. Silly quibbles have come up and some purists claim that the blue and white ware should not be called "Parian," but once he stole the name, I see no reason for Fenton not having used it on both colored and uncolored wares which were otherwise identical. Spargo is very confusing about it, calling the ware a "true hard-paste porcelain," and then adding, "It was mellowed somewhat by the use of bone-ash." Of course the latter would immediately make it fall into the "bone-china" classification.

Some of the pieces bore a raised ribbon mark but most were unmarked. Even the originals did not continue a constant level of quality. After the factory was closed the workmen went hither and yon and the molds were stored and used time and again.

A few added notes from Pitkin may be of interest: The "white granite" ware was chiefly for toilet sets but occasionally for mantel ornaments. The "scrodle" or "lava" wares were not popular and are the rarest. In making it the "wedging process" was used. Clays came from Long Island, New Jersey and South Carolina, chiefly as ballast for ships from abroad, and "blue" or "ball clay" came from Woodbridge, N. J., while the stoneware clay was from South Amboy. The "Parian ware" was both pressed and cast.

Fig. 1351. Bennington American Eagle with Parian body and white transparent glaze with gilding. (c. 1840–1850). Length 4". Ginsburg & Levy.

A marvelously horrible statue was made by Fenton, Greatbach and others and shown in the Crystal Palace in the New York World's Fair of 1853. The base is "lava ware," the second section "flint enamel," on which is a bust of Fenton caged in by eight "Rockingham" columns, and the whole is surmounted by a madonna and child in "Parian ware." It is now on the porch of Fenton's former residence for all to admire.

Fig. 1352. Grey stoneware salt glazed jug with blue decoration over incising, made by Daniel Goodale of Hartford, Conn., between 1818 and 1830 and inscribed *D. Goodale, Hartford.* Ht. 15". Brooklyn, Mus.

Fig. 1353. Pitcher of grey stoneware decorated with dark blue while the inside is brown and yellow, made at Hartford, Conn. early 19th cent. Metropolitan Mus. of Art.

Fig. 1354. Pottery jar of brown with lighter brown glaze, incised "GOODWIN & WEBSTER," Hartford, Conn. 1830–1850. Ht. 9½". Metropolitan Mus. of Art.

I refer those who would seek further to the excellent book by Pitkin and his widow and to their collection in Hartford.

OTHER VERMONT FACTORIES

Jonathan Fenton started a small kiln in 1801 in Dorset and Spargo describes an inkwell from it as being extremely hard in body, almost black and covered with a green glaze.

In 1806–1809, Norman L. Judd started a place in Burlington, and later again in Rome, N. Y., c1810. In the place of Samuel Woodman who made a crude ware at Poultney around 1800 to about 1820 there was nothing of interest. Neither was there in the Middlebury kiln of Caleb Farrer (1812–1850). Many other towns had kilns where useful wares were made.

I think little came of this art because America had bitterly cut off all traditions between 1776 and 1783. Also conditions were bad and there was the English competition. In any event no real works of art were made.

CHART OF OTHER AMERICAN KILNS

Hartford S.E. Corner of Park St. & Quaker Lane	Marks none	c1790—Nathaniel Seymour—Employed 4 men at wheel—kiln 10′ diameter and fired about 50 times a year. Retired in 1825—but the kiln was carried on by grandson Major Seymour until 1842. 1840 Moved "Up the lane." 1849 Major Seymour joined Stedman at Ravenna, Ohio in making stoneware.	Used clays from outside the state (Spargo p. 107)—But this was after 1825. Before entirely Conn. clay. Glaze of red lead and sand half and half. Ordinary red ware. Dishes of 1 gal. were $1 per doz. Milk pans 2 gal. $1.50 per doz. After 1830 they made chiefly unglazed flower-pots
Hartford N.E. Corner of Potter & Front Sts.		(c1790—heresay—) John Souter, who was English. 1805—sold out to Peter Cross who moved in a few years to 38 Front St.	Earthenware. Boston got most of her earthenware from Hartford, such as pots for beans, cake, butter, tea, and beer bottles, mugs, fountains, butter-pails, water coolers and milk pans.
Norwich, Conn.	"Norwich" and dated from '794 to 1812	1792—Charles Lathrop	Salt-glazed stoneware and also red ware.
Norwich	None	1796—C. Pott & Son	A few found about Norwich Ring-shaped bottles wrongly called "haymaker's" bottles. Were neither carried by haymakers nor, as Spargo says, carried over the arm when riding. It was originally a Western Asian design and idea. Spargo claims they were made in Conn., Vermont, West Virginia, Maryland, Ohio and South Carolina though he gives no evidence.

CHART OF OTHER AMERICAN KILNS—*Continued*

Huntington, L. I.	Report quoted by Spargo from investigations by Mrs. Irving S. Sammis: .... "Lewis and Gardiner"	1751—Adam States Idle for some time after war then came to Jonathan Titus 1805—sold to:— Timothy Williams Scudder Sammis Samuel Fleet Samuel Wetmore Later Williams sold his quarter share for $65.25. Scudder bought out the lot and ran until 1825 then sold to Benjamin Keeler 1827 sold to Henry Lewis and Nathan Gardiner	Lead glazed red ware c1758–60 added salt glazed stoneware "Crocus jar" before 1813 and inscribed in yellow slip with name of Iantha Sammis who was married in 1813 to Abner Chichester.
Morgantown West Virginia		c 1784—Foulke who was probably foreign trained. c1800—James W. Thompson took over, had been working for Foulke	Slip-decorated ware ranking with the best from Pennsylvania, not scratched but trailed. Also lead glazed red ware. Grey stoneware.
Philadelphia Sugar Alley	None	c 1790—Andrew Miller 1810—retired and left to 2 sons Abraham and Andrew who moved to 7th & Zane Sts. c 1817—Abraham sole proprietor. He was leading member of Franklin Institute. 1858—Died and business passed to ?	Wares not known but supposed to be red ware and "slip covered ware"—without decoration or with simple decoration ? Pure speculation. Abraham Miller, an enthusiastic potter, is supposed to be first American potter to make silver lustred ware. First piece exhibited in 1824 in Franklin Inst. Also red and black glazed tea-pots, coffee-pots, etc. Also a specimen of porcelain and of cream-ware. The porcelain was never sold on market. In 1835 he had an exhibit showing all steps of pottery making. In 1842 he showed earthenware plates, vases and ornamental flower-pots.
	Never marked		He originated the "Tam O'Shanter mugs" in Rockingham ware popular from c1840 to 1850. Modelled figures in creamware for friends. Dipped lace into slip and applied so that lace burned away in kiln leaving slip pattern, an old and not good "art."

CHART OF OTHER AMERICAN KILNS—*Continued*

Philadelphia	None	c 1790—John Curtis 1811 was still in city directory	Supposed to make "pottery of good quality?"
		Perhaps his was the place where a murder occurred in 1800 ?	Supposed to be cream-ware?
Elizabeth, N. J.	"Samuel Dunham"	1816—John Pruden old red ware pottery made till 1876 slipware Samuel Dunham was potter	"Quaint" slipware trailed technique. Some inscribed "Shoo fly"
Philadelphia	None	c 1808 or perhaps a few years before— Alexander Trotter Head of the Columbian Pottery c 1813 retired.	Cream-ware or "Queen's ware" No pieces authenticated
Philadelphia S. Fifth St.	None	c1810—Daniel Freytag	Cream-ware elaborately decorated also with silver and gold—overglaze colors, of course. No wares identified certainly
Philadelphia		1816 or 1817, or 1822 or 1823—David G. Seixas	Such good copies of "Liverpool wares" i.e. cream-ware as not to be distinguishable. So we hear.
Philadelphia	Called the ——	1809 or 1810—Capt. John Mullowny 1816 "Washington Pottery"	Common yellow and black glazed red earthenware. Teapots, coffee-pots, pitchers, etc. Advertised, "any device, cypher, or pattern put on china or other ware at the shortest notice by leaving orders at the warehouse." (This is important for collectors to bear in mind.)
Philadelphia South St.		1809—Messrs. Binney & Ronaldson	Same as above with slip decorations, trailed.
Philadelphia		1812—Thomas Haig 1833—succeeded by his two sons James and Thomas who carried on till about 1883.	Earthenware with red color and also black, tea-pots, coffee-pots, cake moulds, pitchers, strainers bowls, mugs, plates, etc. Perhaps also cream ware because the judges at the Franklin Inst. said his ware was better than that brought from England. "Believed" Haig made a Rockingham pitcher with Washington full length and shown as a mason, wearing his regalia in the act of presiding over his lodge ? ? ?
South Amboy, N. J. Old Bridge now *Herbertsville*		1800—Van Wickle's	Stoneware
Roundabout now *Sayreville*		Another in 1802–	Same

CHART OF OTHER AMERICAN KILNS—*Continued*

South Amboy and on other side,—"Liberty For Ev	"Warne & Letts, 1807"	Another in 1807—Warne & Letts S. Amboy. Ne Jer'sy."	One marked crock owned by William Goedecke, Esq. of N.Y.C. Is crudely potted Ordinary Jersey stoneware.
South Amboy		1828—John Hancock, English, from Cobridge, Swansea, South Wales, etc.	Stoneware similar to Van Wickle's it is thought, and yellow ware similar to Locker's.
South Amboy		1849—Thomas Locker	Yellow ware
East Liberties, Pa. now part of *Pittsburgh*		1827—Jabez Voudry, English, with a partner named Frost	Earthenware and stoneware Yellow ware and possibly some white ware Perhaps Rockingham (Spargo says he saw a pitcher marked Voudry & —— and the rest of the mark was not legible.)—But he thinks it may have been made in East Liverpool, Ohio "and that the mark was really that of Voudry & Brothers, sons of Jabez Voudry.
Whately, Mass.		1802—Thomas Crafts 1821—He took in partners 1833—New partner and plant enlarged 1847 or 1848 closed.	Coarse red earthenware Black tea-pots added Stoneware They made jugs, crocks, churns etc. Cider pitcher with face odd example

Note:—Spargo says, *"Assuming some or all of them to have been made at the Whately pottery, it has not been possible to tell whether they were made as early as 1805 or as late as 1840, for example."* He continues, *"Nor could the most careful examiner point to a single feature of the ware, whether a quality of the material used or a marked individuality of workmanship, demonstrating that they could not have been made anywhere else."* And again, *"The same thing might be said of the stoneware that was made at Whately from 1833 to 1847."* So far as can be learned, it was as undistinguished, and as undistinguishable from the product of scores of contemporary potteries, as the red ware."

James Clews, an Englishman, worked at Cobridge where he succeeded Andrew Stevenson in 1818 and continued until 1829. He made a deep blue transfer-printed ware showing American historical events, scenery, etc. Two series called the "Syntax" and "Quixote" were in much demand. He came to Louisville, Ky., in 1836 and joined Jabez Voudry and Jacob Lewis, Voudry having left Pittsburgh and the Lewis Pottery Co., which had been established in 1829 and made "cream ware." They went to Troy, Ind., and were incorporated in 1837 absorbing the Lewis Pottery Co., but Voudry immediately withdrew and remained in Louisville.

The Troy pottery found that the wares were not white as Clews had promised they would be, so a yellow ware and "Rockingham" were made, both of inferior grade. In about two years Clews went home and Voudry had to close his successful place to try to pull the Troy kilns into shape. In 1846 the business was abandoned.

THE JERSEY PORCELAIN AND EARTHENWARE CO.
THE FIRST REAL PORCELAIN

There had been many claims to real porcelain but none had been made until the Jersey Porcelain and Earthenware Co. was incorporated in 1825. None of the firm had any records as potters. They were George Dummer,

FIG. 1355. Jersey City c. 1850, "Hound handled pitcher," on the front of which is a mask and the body is decorated with a hunting scene on one side and an American Eagle pulling the tail of the British Lion on the other. Note the handle form as compared with the Bennington one. Ht. 7 3/16". Metropolitan Mus. of Art.

Henry Pots, Jr., Timothy Dewey, Robert Abbatt and William W. Shirley. In 1826 the Franklin Institute awarded the firm a silver medal for "the best china from American materials." The ware was a true white porcelain decorated chiefly with gold. A yellow ware and cream ware were also made and in 1828 the real porcelain was given up because of competition with the imported cream ware.

The works were finally bought by Henderson and were known as the D. & J. Henderson Co. They made cream ware, yellow ware and a good grade of "Rockingham" marked with the firm name and Jersey City impressed in circular form.

The American Pottery Mfg. Co. was formed in 1833 with David Henderson at the head, and the new mark was a flag with "Am. Pottery Manufg. Co., Jersey City," also an elliptical design elaborately drawn with the same legend, both printed and never impressed. Still later the mark of the American Pottery Co., 1840, was impressed. About 1839 it is said there was a print of a "Casanova pattern" stolen outright from John Ridgway of Staffordshire. Pitchers have been found with the portrait of Harrison who ran for president in 1840, but these may or may not have been made at Jersey City. Daniel Greatbach was there in 1839 before going to Bennington.

In 1845 the business came into the hands of Messrs. Rhodes, Strong and McGerron who made only cream ware until 1854 when it closed. Later a new firm made only commercial wares marked with a British coat of arms, a lion and unicorn and the initials R.T.

PHILADELPHIA. WM. ELLIAS TUCKER

Benjamin Tucker, c.1815, opened a china shop at 324 High St., Philadelphia (later Market St.) and carried it on until c.1823. His son, William Ellias Tucker played with a decorating kiln in the back room, painting floral and other designs rather badly on English china. In turn he learned to make cream ware, a fairly hard bone-china, at any rate harder than the English product, and in 1825 or 1826 he started to erect a kiln. His brother Thomas Tucker said that he had many failures because of the sabotage of Englishmen sent over as workmen. However, he overcame the difficulties and made a gilt decorated "bone-china," with poor decoration.

FIG. 1356. Porcelain pitcher by Tucker & Hemphill, Philadelphia, and decorated in gold and blue, dated 1828 in red. Ginsburg & Levy, Inc.

FIG. 1357. Pitcher dating about 1828–1838 made by Tucker and Hemphill works. It bears the incised mark of Andres Craig Walker, W, who was reported to be one of the best workers in the factory. Ht. 9¼". Lent by Arthur W. Clement. Brooklyn Mus.

In 1828, when the Jersey firm was failing, Tucker and Thomas Hulme showed at the Franklin Institute and took a prize. The mark was "Tucker and Hulme, Philadelphia, 1828," pencilled in red under the glaze with at times the addition of "China Manufacturers." In 1829 Hulme withdrew his support, and Tucker wrote to President Andrew Jackson who complimented him but gave no support for his work. In 1832 he found a new partner, Judge Joseph Hemphill. Meanwhile a strong competitor had sprung up.

Judge Hemphill kept Thomas Tucker, the son, and sent to France, England and Germany for men. An imitation of some Sèvres wares was made with borders of roses and other flowers. Elaborate monograms, coats of arms, portraits of noted men, etc., were all made and later copies of well-known works such as the Vaughan portrait of Washington by Gilbert Stuart and the Charles Wilson Peale one of Wayne ("Mad Anthony"). One ambitious piece shows Napoleon watching the burning of Moscow.

Some were unmarked and some had Hemphill's name in red. At least one

Fig. 1358. Tucker & Hemphill pitcher of the 19th cent. with usual white ground and flower decoration in bright colors. The banding is in gold. Ht. 9⅜". Metropolitan Mus. of Art.

Fig. 1359. Glazed white pitcher made about 1862 at Kaolin, Southern Porcelain Co. in South Carolina. Ht. 9½". Metropolitan Mus. of Art.

writer states that the wares were as fine as those of Sèvres but they were not, neither technically nor artistically. Hemphill could have brought over every brick of the old factory, all the workmen, their wives, children and sweethearts as well as all the personal enemies and casual acquaintances of the workmen. He could have enclosed the whole in a dome of soft French atmosphere and made settings of the surrounding country and yet he could not have captured the real Sèvres, for such is art.

In 1837 the judge sold his interest to Thomas Tucker who kept up only about six months and then Abraham Miller bought the machinery and molds while Tucker opened a shop and began to sell imported wares. The kaolin had come from Chester County, Pa., the feldspar from Newcastle County, Delaware, near Wilmington and the blue clay from Perth Amboy.

SMITH, FIFE & CO.

In European style a couple of workmen left Tucker and started a place known as Smith, Fife & Co. The money was put up by Jason Fennemore and he had a lady friend to whom he sent representative pieces and she preserved them so that we know they made pitchers, smelling bottles, leaf shaped dishes, etc. The ware (though less white) and decorations were almost identical to Tucker's of the same period. They were marked with underglaze red. The little piracy expedition did not last long. This was about 1830.

WILLIAM H. FARRER AND KAOLIN, S. C. (1856)

From Bennington a seed was planted in South Carolina when William H. Farrer withdrew his interest and went to Kaolin. This place was the source of some of the Bennington clay and it was thought that money could be saved in not having to ship this product. Alexander H. Stephens, later vice-president of the Confederacy, was a member of the company. Though Farrer had taken some workmen with him when he left Bennington, he was no potter and soon found himself in trouble. The start was in 1856. In 1857 Decius W. Clark and Christopher Webber Fenton went down to advise him. The designer and modeler Josiah Jones advised him to use mixtures of other clays but Farrer stuck to the native product.

They made common earthenware, poor "Rockingham," fairly good cream ware and yellow ware, along with a fairly good porcelain. Attempts were made to imitate the pitted ground "Parian ware" but nothing of real quality was ever turned out.

The place operated through the Civil War but gave up in 1865 when a new firm was formed by R. B. Bullock, later governor of Georgia. After about 12 years it was turned over to McNamee & Co. of New York. The original company marked with "S. P. Company, Kaolin, S. C." or "S. P. C."

GREENPOINT, L. I.
CHARLES CARTLIDGE & CO. AND HERBERT Q. FERGUSON (1848)

Charles Cartlidge came here from England in 1832, worked at Jersey City under David Henderson, became a manager for wholesale distribution of Ridgeway's china and finally formed the Charles Cartlidge Co. in partnership with Herbert Q. Ferguson, at Greenpoint, L. I. in 1848. They began to make buttons. Cartlidge sent to Staffordshire for his brother-in-law, Josiah Jones and Elijah Tatler, china painter. In 1853 at the fair they showed table ware, drawer pulls, door knobs and plates, escutcheons, etc., in bone-china and earthenware. They also made busts and small figures, all from the work of other sculptors, and these were in "Parian" or bisque. Several of these of about 6 inches to 11 inches in size are in the museums. The firm closed in 1856.

WILLIAM BOCH (1850)

Also at Greenpoint, William Boch, a German, and his brother started a kiln in 1850, and made bone-china. In 1857 Thomas C. Smith became manager and part owner, then sole owner and in 1864 or 1865 he started to make real porcelain. In 1866 he began to decorate his ware. In 1874 Karl Müller joined him as modeler and designer. The period was bad and this Müller was typical of its worst aspects. "The Century Vase" is typical with bison-head handles, portraits on two sides, modeled animals' heads on a rib of gold, pictures of Indians, a "Revolutionary Soldier," the Boston Tea Party and God knows what on it. We understand that Müller did some worse things but let us pass them swiftly. He also did Forrest acting William Tell and some figures illustrating Hood's "The Song of the Shirt."

The factory also made some poor copies of Sèvres from 1876 down to our days. The mark has been an eagle's head with S in the beak. See also Union Porcelain Company of Boston.

TRENTON, NEW JERSEY
OTT & BREWER AND THE "ETRURIA POTTERY"

In Trenton the Etruria Pottery which came into charge of John Hart Brewer hired Professor Isaac Broome to work in "Parian ware." John Spargo says, "His bust of Cleopatra and his various baseball designs rank in the best ceramic sculptures of the 19th Century." The statement covers very well the artist, the critic and the century.

EAST LIVERPOOL, OHIO

James Bennet with the help of Anthony Kearns and Benjamin Harker started in East Liverpool, Ohio, in 1840. There may have been some small potters of kitchen ware before this time. He had worked under David Henderson in Jersey City and in 1837 for James Clews in Troy, Indiana. The first firing netted $250 and he promptly sent to England for his brothers David, Edwin and William who arrived in 1841 and brought along John Tunnicliffe. They all made yellow pottery until 1845.

FIG. 1360. An Ohio stoneware jug made to demonstrate the technical proficiency of one E. Hall of W. P. Harrises Factory and dated 1856. Ht. 18". Chas. W. Lyon, Inc.

Benjamin Harker was paid off and started a kiln of his own. Also in 1842 James Salt, Joseph Ogden, John Hancock and Frederic Mear started the "Salt and Mear Works." In 1844 John Goodwin, another of the original workers, started still another kiln. All of these places made yellow ware and "Rockingham." Of course they were far from the first to make it even in this country but "Rockingham" was largely made popular from East Liverpool and Bennington.

In 1844 the Bennet brothers sold out to Samuel, Jesse, Thomas and John Croxall. In 1847 William Brunt started a kiln and again in 1848 Jabez Voudry started "Wood & Voudry." This place burnt down in the first year and then "Woodward, Blakely & Co." rebuilt it in 1849. In 1847 George S. Harker, Benjamin Harker's son joined James Taylor and this firm stole the already stolen Greatbach hound handle pitcher model, which they changed slightly. This firm was "Harker, Taylor & Co." and they ceased in 1851.

Isaac W. Knowles, who sold down the river for James Bennet the first year set up in 1845 with Isaac A. Harvey, then bought him out and reorganized with John Taylor and Homer S. Knowles. The firm in 1870 was "Knowles, Taylor & Knowles." They made the usual wares and started with cream ware in 1872. In 1873 they started to make "ironstone china," or "stone china," or "white granite," as it was variously known.

TRENTON, N. J.

Returning to Trenton, the first pottery was established in 1852 by James Taylor and Henry Speeler, both of whom had been in business in East Liverpool. The usual common yellow and "Rockingham" wares were made and another design of the hound handled pitcher and a cow creamer in both wares. There are no pieces bearing the mark of this place.

In 1853 Richard Millington and John Astbury opened a small kiln which made the same wares and also white ware. No trade-mark was used until 1859 when the firm took in Mr. Poulson and became, "Millington, Astbury & Poulson," marking their wares with an impressed M.A.P. in an ellipse. Among other things they made in 1861 a pitcher with relief design showing the shooting of Colonel Ellsworth at Alexandria, Va. It was of white with garish polychrome painting. This wondrous work of art may have been made by Jones at Greenpoint but that is uncertain.

Charles Hattersly in 1852 started and at once leased to William Young & Sons. Some pitchers seem to prove that they made the first cream ware and porcelain in Trenton.

In 1855 Taylor & Speeler made "white granite" and in 1859 Rhodes & Yates followed.

Thomas Maddock and William Leigh started decorating china in New York in 1847 and later Maddock was in the crockery business in Jersey City. In 1873 he started selling and making sanitary wares and Trenton and East Liverpool made a great industry of this.

BALTIMORE, MD.

Edwin Bennet, one of the East Liverpool brothers, set up in Baltimore in 1846. In 1848 he was joined by his brother William and they marked their wares, "E. & W. Bennet, Canton Ave., Baltimore Md." In 1856 William withdrew and the initials E.B. were used. This firm made all the wares. Charles Coxon joined them in 1850 and made the "Rebekah at the Well Tea-pot," copying the design from a jug made by S. Alcock & Co. It has white figures on blue ground. Also the "Wild Boar Pitcher," and the "Stag Hunt Pitcher" were made there. Another had a standing stork. A hound handled pitcher had game hanging around the sides while another with dolphin handle had fish. The "Daniel Boon Pitcher," was another. All of these wares are difficult to tell from Bennington.

So much for the highlights of an inbred and decadent art which really never had a chance to develop. It was never anything but a sprout from

the already failing English ceramic art and everything from the beginning was done for commercial reasons—enough to kill an art. Aesthetics are not of so much interest to the collector of Americana as history and popular interest in little facts. Quaintness is its chief appeal to such collectors. Humor was heavy as may be seen by the beer mugs made with a frog in the bottom, the "monkey-jugs," etc.

Then came the days of the scroll-saw-gothic, the mansard roofs of elegance from France and the iron stags on the front lawn. America came of age and a very rough and selfish age it was, characterized chiefly by money grabbing, ruination of natural resources

Fig. 1361. "Stag pitcher" designed by Charles Coxon in copy of the Rockingham ware of England. Made possibly at South Amboy, possibly at Baltimore. Ht. 10". Brooklyn Mus.

and boisterous debauchery set off against stiff-necked narrow mindedness. Some of the people had come here because of religious principles, yet we find no great religious thinkers as in China and Italy. There was no incentive to do religious art. The country had political leaders but none who offered the artists patronage. This was a great country of bourgeois and the 19th century art was the worst of bourgeois art.

CHAPTER XXIX

CONTEMPORARY CERAMICS

IN ALL ages the term "MODERN" has been used to designate every *revolt* against accepted tradition. The underlying psychology is easy to understand: tradition is difficult to learn and understand; it takes long to ground oneself and many will not put in the effort to do so, therefore, they take the short-cut of modernism thinking it an easier path. An architect has to adhere to some traditions of building or his structure would fall down. A lawyer must at least know the procedures of the courts and a doctor must have some knowledge of medicine or he would be a menace to the race. An artist, however, is looked upon as harmless and is, therefore, free to do as he likes. Only very rarely do we find, as in the case of Picasso, an artist who is well grounded in the various elements of his art turning to a revolt against some of its phases. In this sense most "modern art" exponents are really charlatans or at the very least people who wish to reap rewards for the least possible endeavors.

Our commercial attitude and industrial attitude are chiefly responsible for the large number of such artists in the past fifty years. If the business man tries to get all he can for the least possible effort, so, it is reasoned, should the artist. The eye has been focused upon the results and the results have been largely measured in pennies.

Any revolt will do and we have had many in the past years: 1.—The revolt against the machine and its corollary, the revolt against those who revolted against the machine, as represented by the "handicraft" movement in England and America of William Morris, Elbert Hubbard, etc., and those who preached that the machine, properly mastered, would lead to new arts such as Edgar Brandt in France. 2.—The return to simplicity in America after the renaissance between World War I and 1929. 3.—The discovery after the Paris Exposition of Japanese art, a revolt against European tradition. 4.—The new ways of seeing light expounded by the impressionists. 5.—The new ways of drawing by the post-impressionists, the vorticists, the cubists, the futurists, the da-daists, etc., which revolted against drawing anything as it is seen. 6.—The revolt against the classic movement of the end of the 18th century and the beginning of the 19th century by reverting to naturalism. 7.—The revolt against natural forms imposed by the architects of skyscrapers who had found their soap-box forms imposed by the zoning laws of New York City. 8.—The revolt against this soap-box design imposed by the

1009

streamline experts who streamlined not only moving objects but all manner of static objects for no reason at all. 9.—A revolt against all of this cold design by a return to Victorian horrors which were at least human. These and many other revolts have been tried in the last twenty-five years to such an extent that "modern art" is impossible to define. This impossibility is well demonstrated by the New York Modern Art Museum which has had to fall back upon Italian masters, various primitive arts and all manner of twisted versions and roundabout reasons to prove its reason for being.

The history of modern art as outlined by Rudolph Rosenthal in the December, 1935 *Parnassus* is, to quote, "Briefly, the first period of modern decorative art lasted from 1860 to 1893, beginning with Morris and reaching the continent through Van de Velde of Brussels. The second period came in 1894, lasting until 1925 when the Decorative Arts Exposition was held in Paris. The third is the one that began with 1925 and is still continuing." We might split hairs about the last statement but it is on the whole quite right.

The Paris exhibitions of 1867 and 1878 featured Japanese art. Whistler was doing his nocturnes and Degas his dancers. Carlyle had written his warnings. The adjustment had to be made and industrialism could not win out. But the germ of our present revolt against the factories and the whole system of heckling, money grubbing, stupid and yet powerful parasites was born.

THE FRENCH "GRÈS POTTERS"

One potter was Ernest Chaplet (1835–1902) a champion who made all his wares by hand and sometimes without even the aid of the wheel. His "flammés" and "grès" stonewares and porcelains of blues, violets, greys and copper reds were beautiful. He worked at Sèvres where he revived the old barbotine technique, at Laurin's at Bourg la Reine, and was later manager of the Haviland factory. Finally he went to Choisy le Roi where he worked until he died. His mark was the chaplet or rosary.

Chaplet won the heart of the sculptor Jean Carriès (1855–1894) who gave up his art to carry on ceramics. He set up his kiln at St. Amand en Puisaye and Montriveau, near Nevers and in the exhibition of 1889 his results brought universal admiration. The Japanese had inspired him but his work is very much his own and he did not only vases but also masks, figures, heads, animals, etc. His architect friend, G. Höentschel, who was a similar potter, gave a collection of his work to the Musée du Petit Palais, Paris. Another disciple was Paul Jeanneny (1861–1920) who adhered more closely to the Japanese wares, which by the way, were the early type and not the Arita or "Satsuma," things.

L'Art du Feu was a school started by Chaplet and among the pupils was the great artist Auguste Delaherche, who worked with running glazes at times over relief designs and obtained effects of velvety richness. Others of the group were Adrien Dalpayrat, who worked with Voisin Delacroix and later with Mlle. Lesbros, and who did glazes of opaque blood-red, deep blue and soft yellow which were not very beautiful but technically interesting. Edmond Lachenal used relief foliage under dull green glazes which he etched with hydrofluoric acid to produce a velvety surface known as "émail velouté."

Left: Pair of Limoges vases by Ernest Chaplet of about 1870 to 1886 with relief decoration and copper-red glaze. *Center:* Stoneware vase by Emile Lenoble. *Right:* Earthenware plate of the early 20th cent. by André Methey (1871–1920). Metropolitan Mus. of Art.

Left: Beauvais stoneware bowl by Auguste Delaherche in the 20th cent. *Center:* A typical stoneware vase by Emile Decoeur of the 20th cent., Fontenay-aux-Roses, Siene. *Right:* Plate made by Haviland & Co. of Limoges and designed by Felix Braquemond (1833–1914) and probably made between 1872 and 1880. Metropolitan Mus. of Art.

THE FRENCH "GRÈS POTTERS" AND OTHER EARLY MODERNISTS

PLATE 229

FIG. 1363. Bottle of 1899 by Alexandre Bigot of stoneware glazed in light grey streaked with blue, brown and tan in the flambé manner. Metropolitan Mus. of Art.

FIG. 1364. Stoneware vase by Adrien Dalpayrat made at the end of the 19th cent. This, of course, shows the uneven potting and glaze mannerisms of some Japanese potteries. Ht. 8". Metropolitan Mus. of Art.

FIG. 1362. Stoneware jug made at Limoges under the technical direction of Ernest Chaplet around 1882 to 1886. It is a teutonic thing somewhat sweetened up with French Art Nouveau style. Ht. 9". Metropolitan Mus. of Art.

Albert Dammouse at Sèvres did more naturalistic and accidental things of similar feeling. His "pâte décor" made use of glaze and paste used side by side or over each other. The only reason that the business men at the factory could not grasp his art and ruin it was that no two pieces came out alike so that the merchants could not reorder and, too, the colors were dull while merchants like bright colors that arrest the eye—though they may tire of it later. Taxile Doat, an Englishman, at Sèvres made among other things some small insets of animal heads, etc., in porcelain and stoneware.

FIG. 1365. The two upper pieces are by Raoul Lachenal and the lower ones by Claude Lévy of France. In the 1939 Exhibition in New York the latter's style had become greatly exaggerated.

FIG. 1366. Stoneware vase with the well known "engobe" glaze treatment undoubtedly inspired by the Sung, Yüan and Ming or later wares of Tz'u Chou. This is certainly no improvement even upon the latest and worst of the type. Emile Lenoble. Metropolitan Mus. of Art.

Among the younger men was Emile Lenoble, Chaplet's son-in-law, who inherited his kiln and practiced with "engobes" which he cut away to the biscuit in straight line decoration. These engobes were glazes of dark brown, grey, deep blue, green, orange-red and white, all of which contrasted well against stoneware of grey. Many of the things remind us of Sung incised "Tz'u chou yao" and here a truly great art might have been born but times were not right and not many of the finest of these wares were then available.

Emile Decoeur produced the soft, thick and rich glazes of modified color which he used over the simplest of relief decoration in the best of taste. The colors were brownish-yellow, delicate grey-blue or green and his glazes all run slightly in firing. There is a suave, sure strength in his work which is not immediately obvious.

Young Raoul Lachenal, the son of Edmond, followed Decoeur and sometimes his work is as fine as is also at times that of Henri Simmen.

Another group led by Jean Mayodon followed the figure decoration of Syrian and Persian wares, such as slender leaping deer and gracefully drawn birds. René Buthaud worked in large, flat figures in strong relief with deep incising.

None of these "grès potters" were really great artists but they obtained beautiful textures and very simple and pleasant forms and France has a right to be proud of them for they faced the flood and stood out as a hopeful light in the darkness until they were extinguished.

FIG. 1367. Sèvres pieces exhibited in the Paris 1925 Exhibition. The art-nouveau stunts are well represented and in the first piece, upper left, we see superimposed rosettes of Edgar Brandt iron-work fame.

FIG. 1368. Vase of typical Art Nouveau type designed by Georgês de Feure about 1898–1904 and potted by E. Gerard. Metropolitan Mus. of Art.

FRENCH EARTHENWARE

There had been various half hearted attempts to revive lustre but André Methey really did some pleasant things with simple repeat patterns of natural forms. Etienne Avenard followed him and Félix Massoul used deeper colors and more geometric patterns. Jean Besnard also made lustre. But all of these were inclined to cover the whole vessel with lustre rather than using it sparingly as in early works. The result is a bit like a metallic vessel or Christmas tree ornament rather than a pot decorated with simple brush strokes.

No earthenware of merit was turned out at Sèvres. Gordon M. Forsyth wrote in 1925 that Sèvres had "become artistically mute." Raoul Kachenal and Claude Lévy made decadent things in which the shapes boast without being strong and the colors do not suit either the designs or the shapes. Sentimental sculpture was made by E. de Canto and Marcel Renard.

MODERN GERMAN WARES

The revival in Germany is associated with Max Läuger and Schmuz-Baudisz both of whom are strongly influenced, and to good purpose too, by the peasant wares of Bavaria and the Black Forest region.

Läuger's jugs and vases are of deep, even color with natural slip decorations in contrasting color, as he made them at Karlsruhe. More recently he worked at Kandern for C. Mayer making tiles, and still later he made strong colored majolica for the Maiolica Manufaktur at Karlsruhe. Ludwig Koenig and Georg Schrimpf followed him but fell into the modern pose of trying to appear naïve.

This is an interesting characteristic of much modern art. There is an appeal of a sort in it. Some men love innocent, doll-like little girls with starry eyes and not a thought in their heads. Some women like naughty, boyish men whom they can mother. The instinct is a perverted one similar to that of a capon which likes to take care of chicks. It recalls the story of De Maupassant of the fat inn keeper who came to enjoy hatching out chicks in his own bed. The objects of such affection in art are those who just never came of age and are still in adolescent stages and they prefer to be thought cute.

There is no doubt but that this instinct to play motherly protector and to play child is strong in all decadent societies. Note for example the Roman phases and the "puttis" of the days of Louis XV. It is also strong in our days, up to World War II.

The artist who consciously makes this appeal is begging to be protected. He says, "Here, this is my little effort. I know, of course, that it is nothing," and he puts his head on one side and smiles coyly, hoping that you will answer, "But my dear fellow, it is charming and so, so clever!" Others less obvious but of the same ilk are those who never get beyond the sketch stage. Everything they do is, "just a sketch," said in a deprecatory yet hopeful manner. Modern ceramics are full of such works done by little old ladies who turn out the cutest donkeys in bright blue glaze purchased in a package from Drakenfelds, or perhaps they are foreign gentlemen with souls which they can only express in the most charming and child-like manner by scratching clay as though they didn't really half mean it, or again they may be the daughters that mothers are proud of (for their age) and who do children's lamps and ash receivers for nit-wits.

"But," one may argue, "you have said that you find an appeal in naïveté as found in the simple savage or primitive people such as that shown by the Chimu or Han cultures. Why not then appreciate it in artists of today?" My answer is that it represents sincerity *today* in this sophisticated age only among the members of the grammar schools or asylums and that people who find their mental enjoyments in associations with children up to 10 years of age or the inmates of special homes for feeble minded can and should enjoy the arts of such undeveloped or distorted minds of today. I personally take a rather objective viewpoint of such intelligences and find them somewhat depressing. Each man to his own tastes. Just as a fine savage differs from a retarded or perverted civilized man so does his art differ from that of the feeble minded. The one is at least healthy while the other implies disease of one sort or another.

Th. Schmuz-Baudisz painted in Munich and only after 1896 became interested in ceramics. He covered his vessels with engobe and incised animal and floral designs in highly stylized manner. In 1902 he became director of the Staatliche Porzellan Manufaktur, Berlin, after being at Swaine & Co., Hüttensteinach. In Berlin he tried large tiles with landscapes in color which are poor.

Dr. Seger in 1884 used copper oxide glazes and made some plastic things of fair quality, as did also Franz Metzner, Anton Pachegger and Herman Hubatsch. In 1918 Max Adolf Pfeiffer directed at Berlin and some fair things were made by E. P. Borner, Max Esser and Paul Schuerich.

All the factories tried to give some little flavor to their commercial endeavors by attaching a few artists as appendages. At Nymphenburg, Albert Bäuml was director in 1888, and Jozef Wackerle made fine peasant type potteries and humorous figures deriding 18th century life. He mastered both porcelain and faïence techniques and did not allow his things to become crude but took from the peasant wares their directness. Theodor Kärner and W. Neuhäuser made animals well. Much of the work was influenced by Copenhagen or by the peasant wares. Most of these moderns fall into schools or copy each other outright more slavishly than did even the Chinese who had traditions but also a basic originality.

Ernst Barlach set a new style with his Russian peasants full of life and plastic good sense. He worked at the Schwarzburger Werkstätten für Porzellan at Unterweissbach. Others there were Hugo Meisch, Arthur Storch and Hans Poelzig. At Nymphenburg Fraus J. Biehler and M. Goossen did reliefs.

At Munich George Kemper made rather effeminate putti, etc., and Königsbauer did double walled medieval looking jugs with outer walls pierced. Otto Müller made similar faïence things after Chinese ideas. Kurt Feuerriegel also shows 16th century characteristics. Perhaps the best in this part of the country is Frau Auguste Papendieck, whose kiln was near Bremen, who did

POTTERY AND PORCELAIN

monochrome and slightly glazed vessels of simple form and good honest potting.

In the Villeroy & Boch firm J. Kühne and Jean Beck along with Ernst Riegel worked, the latter doing fair modeling.

It has been said that Germany showed the greatest hope during this time but we find a dull and uninteresting art there. The pots were made for no common use and were looked upon as art, separated from the life of the people and from their tastes. This divergence of artist from the course of the times was brought about by his revolt against what the people were being educated to like and to use by the industrialists. No art can grow on mere revolt. No artist can thrive if he does things which the people about him do not want. And yet what was the artist to do in the dilemma in which he was placed? He had either to go along with the industrialists or oppose them, and they had sold the public a bill of goods through their ballyhoo on cheapness and the pressure of their everlasting noise in advertising. Of course the public would regret its purchases, for a thing which is not honestly made is an outrage and offense forever, but who could outshout the money makers?

AUSTRIA

Only in the 20th century did any movement start in Austria. After the Viennese Secession, 1902, Bertold Löffler worked in terra cotta, and Michael Powolny joined him to form the Wiener Keramik. The latter's things are in common clay with bright, opaque, low fired glazes. In 1907 they collaborated with the Wiener Werkstätte which the architect Josef Hoffmann was fathering and Kola Moser, who died in 1918, joined. The Werkbund Exhibition of 1912 showed the crude putti set among flowers and the black and white underglaze wares which became well known. Also in 1912 the Wiener Keramik collaborated with the Gmünder Keramische Werkstätte and made peasant pottery under the direction of Franz and Emile Schleisz. Powolny made tiles for Hoffmann's use as did others also. Otto Prutscher was a designer and also pottery maker. But this work as art is all affected, sloppy and undisciplined. In 1925 at the International Exhibition the faïence stove by Gmünder and the large figure by Dina Kuhn were typically loose. Why Hoffmann, whose own work is the essence of simplicity, could not hold down the exuberance and childishness of these young potters has always been a mystery to me. He wrote for me in the *Encyclopaedia Britannica*, 14th edition, "Sound development does not lie in a mere production of novelties; the whole circumstances of the age must lead in a natural line to new form."

HOLLAND

About 1884 the German potter, W. Von Gudenberg and artist, Th. Colenbrander commenced original work at the Rozenburg factory, The Hague. The latter shows Japanese influence but also did things with leaf decoration which may be said to be his own, if there is any glory in that for the glazes are unpleasantly crude and bright and strive to be "futuristic." He left the place in 1889 and all such work stopped.

In 1916 pseudo-porcelain in pale colors was shaped and painted in the "Jugend style." Japanese influence was great. The material was thin as paper, and not porcelain in any sense. E. L. F. Bodart and L. Senf made earthenware with brown glazes scratched with designs after the Sung and later Chinese techniques. They also made faïence with non-stanniferous glazes of transparent colors allowing Near Eastern sorts of designs to show through, and gold and silver lustre ware.

William Morris and Walter Crane of England started a movement first at Amstelhook then at Distel, which consisted in the use of simple materials and old techniques. W. C. Brouwer made original shapes covered with home made glazes giving accidental effects. The sculptor, J. Mendes De Costa, made small groups of Jewish women and also animals in lead glazed grès. C. J. Lanooy made imitation French grès and used flambé glazes. B. Nienhuys, a teacher, turned out some vases of simple and fairly strong shapes with soft harmonious glazes.

In 1912 Colenbrander, using chiefly blue and brown in dull tones, painted designs on faïence while by 1925, in his old age, he designed unglazed wares for the Arnhem factory at Ram. There was a great leaning toward dull and sombre colors which were considered "good taste" as a revolt against the splashers in bright colors, just as these splashers were in revolt against "antique colors."

H. Krop, at Eskaf, made really pleasant domestic wares with rich white glazes sometimes over relief decoration and sometimes painted in black.

BELGIUM

From Belgium about the only good work shown at the Paris Exhibition, 1925, was that of Ch. Catteau with fine white glaze and designs of flowers, birds and animals. From the Boch Frères the work of Domergue and Sandoz was better than anything else shown but the whole of Belgium endeavors were copyist and poor.

SCANDINAVIA
THE ROYAL COPENHAGEN FACTORY, DENMARK
(See Earlier and Later Sections)

At the Royal Copenhagen Factory, Denmark, Arnold Krog toward the end of the 19th century introduced white porcelain with underglaze design

FIG. 1369. Jars # 1, 3 and 4 are from Boch Freres while # 2 is from the Faiencerie de Keramis, Belgium. All show the peculiar angularized convention then thought "artistic."

which had to be in blue and other soft, cool colors. This led to painting of birds and flowers, etc., because the effect was so thin that the use of mere design would have been uninteresting. There being no accidental texture in the surface, texture had to be introduced into the painting itself. The modeling of animals and other forms was entirely naturalistic but of fine quality from

FIG. 1370. Two plates by Arnold Krog who was at the factory from 1885–1890 and, as these show, was strongly influenced by late period Japanese art.

FIG. 1371. Group of vases, the flowers and fish showing Japanese characteristics and the two with boats showing the naturalistic trend. These were designed by Arnold Krog 1885–1890 in underglaze colors.

the start. Henning used overglaze painting on his "oriental figures" and obtained a not at all unpleasant delicate sex appeal. The Danish peasant figures by Carl Martin Hansen are sensitive and charming and the ethereal figures by A. Malinowski again are very beautiful. He worked in a cream biscuit which gave warmth to his figures and the decoration was confined to slight touches of sepia and gold as a rule. Also a grey crackle was developed in various patterns, large and small, squared and rounded, and used by such artists as Thorkild Olsen and the excellent draughtsman N. Tidemand.

A "celadon" was practically a factory material and too glossy and vivid a green to be pleasant. Few artists worked with it but some figures were made recently.

The stoneware, however, attracted some of the finest artists and Jais Niel-

Fig. 1372. Jar by Jais Nielsen, a dish from Herman A. Kähler designed by Jens Thirslund and another by Chr. Joachim from Kobenhavns Fajancefabric, all Danish.

Fig. 1375. A Silenus group by Kai Nielsen of Bing & Gröndhal, Denmark. Metropolitan Mus. of Art.

Fig. 1374. Fine, strong works by Jean Gauguin wrought in perfectly suitable rough surfaced pottery. The animal forms are dynamic and alive, a quality which they strangely lost in the 1939 Exhibition in New York.

Left to Right: Two plaques, the upper by C. F. Liisberg who worked at the factory from 1885 to his death in 1909, and the lower by A. Smidth (1885–present).

Plate with low relief design which seems to have been taken from a Japanese bronze and a plaque with a very sentimental mysterious scene quite in keeping with the feeling of the period. The first between 1885 and 1890 and the second 1896 to 1900 both by Arnold Krog.

Jar and cover which was shown in the Exhibition of Brussels, 1910, the leaves on the shoulder in low relief and the border on the stand rather typical "Art nouveau."

Also shown at Brussels this jar has a fine adaptation of swimming mackerel and sea-weed.

ROYAL COPENHAGEN PIECES MADE BEFORE 1910
BY KROG, LIISBERG, SMIDTH

PLATE 230

Two small figures by Carl Martin Hansen. Ht. about 4". George Jensen, Inc. Note: These have the black crown and three lines of blue, for marks.

Left: This figure called "Ave Mari" is said to be the first by Henning and was shown in the Paris Exposition of 1925. The head is nicely balanced so that it sways from side to side. Ht. 12½". George Jensen, Inc. The mark is the black crown with three wavy lines in blue. Ht. *Right:* Typical of Malinowski is this dainty figure which is touched with sepia and gold only. 8½". George Jensen, Inc.

ROYAL COPENHAGEN FIGURES BY HENNING, MALINOWSKI AND HANSEN

PLATE 231

sen particularly did some beautiful things with strong turquoise-blue glazes.

The "faïence" was frequently covered with lead or hydric borate transparent glaze and painted with underglaze colors. Of course, this is not faïence technique strictly speaking, but is exceedingly effective. Joachim is the best master of this ware and his work is gay and lively with rich assemblings of colors.

BING & GRÖNDAHL AND OTHER DANISH FACTORIES

About as large as the Royal Copenhagen factory is that of Bing & Gröndahl also in Denmark and established in 1853. The first good artist hired by Harald Bing was Peitro Krohn who did the "heron set" combining underglaze colors with gold. In 1900 this firm showed at Paris the work of two

FIG. 1376. A charming figure by Knud Kyhn of the Royal Copenhagen Porcelain Factory and figures of the usual great beauty by the late Kai Nielsen of the Bing & Gröndahls Porcellainfabrik, Denmark.

really great artists, Kai Nielsen and Jean Gauguin, the son of the painter. Kai Nielsen's Venus is truly (as Dalgas, the then director of the Copenhagen works told me) "a symbol of complete harmony between the art and material." In the 1925 exhibition he showed "The Grape Gatherers, The Birth of Venus, The Christians v. Saracens," and his latest at the time, "The Sea." Everything he ever touched was alive and full of charm. His accenting of certain proportions was masterful. This was a great artist now unfortunately no longer alive.

To Jean Gauguin I give the palm as the greatest of artists at that time. Of him Gordon M. Forsyth said, "He is undoubtedly one of the greatest artists that have ever worked in pottery." At the exhibition was a bull rampant with the power that one would expect to find in the work of a Western Asiatic bronze artist. Another piece is of a satyr reeling on the back of an ass which is shrieking and stumbling to its feet. Two large jars with covers and finials, one of another bull and the other of some strange animal would add dignity to any collection of pottery of any age. Here is no pose but a real dynamic working out of all that the material affords in expression.

At Copenhagen, Jais Nielsen (not to be confused with Kai) really belongs to this small group of the really great. His work gives one a sense of tremendous scale, though it be small. Some trick of proportions is responsible. Perhaps he is a little mannered but certainly his things carry the manner.

At Nastved, Herman A. Kähler used the local clay and applied lustres. Jens Thirslund also made some interesting dishes, one of which was triangular and with a stag design.

At the Kobenhavns Fajancefabric, Chr. Joachim made decorative things with strong overglaze colors and on the island of Bornholm, at the Hjort's pottery they made some beautiful small vases and figures with thick glazes. Hansen-Jacobsen also made some beautiful but not great things.

SWEDEN & NORWAY

Sweden shows much less of the creative spirit and copies of peasant pottery are about all that was shown. The same is true of Norway and of the "Arabia" factory in Finland.

ENGLAND

Some private decorators in England worked at the Wedgwood factory on cream ware but to no good purpose. Alfred and Louise Powell are typical.

FIG. 1377. William de Morgan of Fulham, Sand's End Pottery (1839–1917) made these ruby, and other toned, lustre pieces of glowing, rich color but rather mussy design. Metropolitan Mus. of Art.

FIG. 1378. Two plates by Alfred Powell and Louis Powell respectively showing St. Paul's and the "Badge of Aldeburgh, Suffolk." The two jars are from Stabler and Adams.

Whether the "Flambé movement" started in France or England is of no moment. But transmutation glazes of Chinese type became a vogue and they were made by Doulton of Burslem, W. Moorcroft of Stoke-on-Trent, W. Howson Taylor of the Ruskin Pottery, Smethwick in Pilkington's of Manchester, Bernard Moore and many others. The only thing that kept this sort of thing from becoming a real bonanza in the commercial field was that every piece turned out different.

Among the best known early modern potters were Gwladys Rodgers at Pilkington's who used lustre and in 1928 turned to a grey glaze with slight designs in black, Gilbert Bayes and Mr. and Mrs. Harold Stabler at Doulton's who made figures of fair interest, Charles Vyse and Gwendolen Parnell, who did traditional 18th century things and finally John Skeaping who used glazed pottery as a medium for sculpture.

OLD NOTES ON 1925 EXHIBITION AT PARIS

As I go over the old catalogue of the 1925 exhibition at Paris I find these marginal notes: The whole English section was heavily commercial. The wares were well enough made but lacking in the textures of the French wares and the skill and beauty of the Scandinavian, and particularly the Danes. Gordon Forsyth wrote, "The British section as a whole was inclined to be rather staid and dull. There was in the pottery section a real lack of spirit of adventure on the artistic side." He also said, "If British potters are to lead in the various markets of the world, they must be creative artists and not complaisant tools of the retailers." Amusingly, his British mind in his very statements gives away the attitude, for he speaks of the "artistic side," (as though there were any other for an artist to follow!) and he sets the ambition of achievements as "the markets of the world."

FIG. 1379. Doulton & Co., Ltd., wares by Hy. Simeon, Vera Huggins and Wm. Rowe. Including salt glazed stoneware and a crystalline glaze so popular at the time.

Opposite the Wedgwood exhibition I noted, "Not a spark." Powell had some sloppy silver lustre service designs. The "jasper ware" had become poorer in craftsmanship and positively sentimental. J. E. Goodwin made unobservant and badly shaped copies of Sung and later Chinese wares. It was interesting to note that some of these were made for lamp fittings. England had awakened to the American lamp business!

W. T. Copeland & Sons, the descendants of the Spode factory simply showed more underglaze transfer prints, some exotic flower decorations and some stupidly modeled birds and animals.

Doulton & Co. had a fountain by Gilbert Bayes in stoneware with colored glazes that blended well with the foliage about it. If more of our great sculptors would let themselves go and make use of a bit of color here and there (not flesh color to imitate life but patterns) the art would become more interesting to the average man. I once heard a critic say of a man's paintings that they were as dull and lifeless as an exhibition of sculpture. This Doulton firm made use of the term "Sung glazes" which they were not and which I resented. Actually these were flambé, crystalline, etc. Hy. Simeon used some peacock tail patterns in soft colors and with salt glazes on safe and uninteresting shapes. Vera Huggins tried to be primitive in a nice way. William Rowe was "just too too sweet!" I also made note that the pinwheel roses with stiff foliage seemed to be the rage in Liberty's batiks. The general impression was, "Arts and crafty."

At Pilkington's, founded in 1900, a small department was formed for artists including Walter Crane and Lewis F. Day. All pottery was wheel made. Lustre was favorite. The shapes in the 1925 show came nearly up to the Danish ones. In Richard Joyce's work there was a too close adherence to Renais-

FIG. 1380. Pilkington & Co. vase of about 1906 decorated by G. M. Forsyth in purple and gold lustre somewhat following the style of de Morgan's things.

FIG. 1381. Examples from the Pilkington Tile & Pottery Co., Ltd. 1.—Silver and blue by Richard Joyce. 2.—Underglaze and lustre decoration, W. S. Mycock. 3.—Bowl in silver lustre on ruby ground by Gwladys M. Rodgers. 4.—Mottled glazed effects. 5.—Similar to # 3 also by Gwladys M. Rodgers.

sance design. W. S. Mycock got away from this effect by allowing his glazes to run. Gwladys M. Rodgers got patterns which seemed to drip with the fire of lustre, and there was nothing effeminate about her shapes.

Of Worcester I found nothing to look at.

Of Minton one could only say that since M. Arneaux there was a weak following of the French.

The Cauldon Potteries, Ltd., were entirely commercial.

Also exhibiting was Wm. Moorcroft & Co., run by Moorcroft himself who is an accomplished potter with real feeling and perhaps a too great worship of the Chinese without a clear understanding of them.

One of the best known and appreciated of the English potters in his own country is Bernard Moore who makes a piece now and then and obtains beautiful effects in lustre, flambé glazes and various slip treatments. A case full of these pieces shows like the smouldering of lambent fire.

John and Truda Adams' firm is Carter, Stabler & Adams, including the Stabler couple as well. It was originally a tile making firm under the super-

Fig. 1383. A group from the Ravenscourt Pottery and two pieces from the Ruskin Pottery made by W. Howson Taylor and glazed with flambé effects.

Fig. 1384. Slipware plate by Bernard Leach and a rather insecure small bottle by the same artist. The large bowl is of "Kuan type", made by W. Staite Murray who often came fairly close to Sung wares or at least Yung Chêng copies of them.

Fig. 1382, Figures by Gwendolen Parnell, the "Atalanta" far from sound but the two lower ones showing some good qualities of observation and humor.

vision of Mr. Adams. The Stablers make stoneware figures of some charm and decorated by Mrs. Adams. The firm also makes a "Della Robia" ware for architectural purposes which is gay in spirit. Messrs. Carter of Poole, Dorset aid. They do much underglaze decoration with a mat surfaced glaze and also have a brilliant fine blue with a greenish cast which is used over a red earthenware body. The shapes are not so good as those of Pilkington and the decorations are less sure but at times Mrs. Adams turns out a rather sweetish Persian sort of thing that is not too bad.

M. W. Howson Taylor, Birmingham, makes the well-known Ruskin Pottery which is not happy in shapes but well potted and sometimes surprisingly thin in the egg-shell bowls. Again flambés, lustres, etc., were favorites.

Among the individual potters the best known are probably W. Staite Murray and Gwendolen Parnell. Miss Parnell used porcelain body and a full palette of colors. She did figures of British characters successfully but at times overreaches herself as much as does her running figure of "Atlanta." Someone has said that her British types are, "dainty rogues in porcelain," and this well describes them.

W. Staite Murray studied the Ming Tz'u chou potteries and thought them Sung. His ware has a stoneware body and the glazes are thick and rich and of soft ivory, buff or grey. The decorations are in black, brown and white in the Chinese manner though painted without benefit of the perpendicular brush. Mr. Bernard Rackham, however, has one so close to the Chinese that it might well fool some incautious collector.

Bernard Leach does similar things again but his shapes are less good. He also worked in slip after the technique of the old Staffordshire potters but captures none of their real qualities. There are a host of others who are more or less amateurs and none of whom are of any interest to us.

CZECHOSLOVAKIA

At this Paris exhibition of 1925 the Czechoslovakian part showed a fine fireplace in cream white by L. & C. Hardmuth of Prague and some commercial wares challenging the English.

BELGIUM

Though a good part of the modern movement started in Belgium it never got more than a start there. At the exhibition Ch. Catteau had some ware with an opaque crackled glaze. Boch Frères had some things by Domergue and Sandoz with soft and bad forms suggesting glass by Galle or Lalique and designs that would go well with "Mission furniture" the Roycroft movement, etc. It is hard to say why these designs are so sickening. Perhaps they are most expressive of schoolteacher-conventionalization or the stencil patterns sold by women's magazines.

ITALY

In the Italian section Richard Ginori of Colonnata, Firenze, had services decorated with simple lambrequin patterns in one color or in gold on white.

One design is of a reclining classical lady with draped cords above and below her.

SPAIN

There were several pieces in the Spanish exhibition from Daniel Zuloaga's Sons of fair merit.

LATVIA

Strangely in Latvia there were some of the best ultra modern things such as cubist designs not at all unpleasant and not so demanding as they would be on canvas. These were made by A. Sutta, and Vidbergs did some charming and rather sexy plates with plain broad rims and center decorations of simply drawn nudes reclining amongst huge blossoms and foliage. There were also the peasant types of wares.

A FEW NOTES ON DESIGNS IN OTHER MEDIUMS

In order to understand that ceramics are often influenced by other mediums as they in turn affect other mediums, a note or two here may be of help. This had become a time of artificial fabrics, which needed to be sumptuous and rich looking. Perhaps this explains the vogue for transmutation and lustred effect in part. Again the modern process of autogenous soldering made possible Edgar Brandt's metal screens of various combinations of brass, copper, silver, etc. Cheney Bros. have a pair of doors here in New York done by him and they adopted some of his rosettes in fabric design. I have never seen it exactly copied in ceramics but have no doubt that it was and perhaps our stiff pin-wheel rosettes are owed partially to him.

Of course the newly discovered Han tomb potteries and those from Mesopotamia along with greater interest in archaeology brought about a semblance of the sort of enthusiasm that was shown in Renaissance times and again in those of Napoleon just preceding this modern era.

Finally trade had become so international in character that, had not the wares been labeled, it would have been difficult to tell what country they were made in. American influences were not shown because Mr. Hoover had made up his mind that America had nothing worth showing.

AMERICA, THE ART CENTER OF THE WORLD

The Ruskin, Burne-Jones, Rosetti and William Morris influences had reached America from England, more as a revolt against classicism than anything else. There were three revolts: that against the machine, that against commerce and that against classicism and naturally America did not feel so strongly against the first two because they had benefited this nation while they had harmed England in many ways. Even classicism had not bothered us as much as others. The Art Nouveau hardly touched us. But what did suit our taste was the Arts and Crafts movement. The ideas were good: 1.—The use of the hand instead of the machine. 2.—The idea of building furniture to function. 3.—The idea of not disguising materials, all suited the practical American way of thinking and people like Elbert Hubbard boosted them. "Mission furniture" and "Colonial mahogany" became popular and were set upon "Turkish carpets." Rich people even had Turkish dens dimly illuminated with pierced brass lamps lined with red. Sanitation, air and light had not yet become words to conjure with.

In the finer homes the great decorators were doing "period rooms" with a leaning toward the heavier styles. Wm. Baumgarten & Co., White, Allom & Co., etc., were making the American millionaire conscious that he could spend money for antique furniture and ornaments. Some of the great collections such as those of Morgan, Altman and Mellon were well under way and fine tapestries, bronzes, porcelains and all manner of great works of art were being brought to this country. These had such a strong influence that the craftsmen were busy translating harmonious characteristics into their own works and very little was heard about art movements in modern Europe. There was a market and it created no revolts. Such firms as Tiffany Studios and Edward F. Caldwell & Co. were making the finest craftsmanship almost regardless of cost.

The masses knew and cared nothing about art and men of commerce only turned to it after their fortunes had been made. Art in business had not been thought about.

Two architects, iconoclasts in our midst, were condemning all this and trying to get down to first principles. They have been much overrated by some but they did exert some influence. One was Louis Sullivan who died in 1924 and the other Frank Lloyd Wright. It is argued that Wright brought about much of the modern movement in Germany but it was too complicated for any one such influence to be solely credited. Wright is not a profound man though there is little doubt that he considers himself a prophet. Broadly speaking, his houses fit into a landscape about as well as would a large tombstone in a living room. They are angular and textureless with queer jutting shelves and planes. Color means little to him. Yet, having worked in Japan, he places in these houses, without understanding of the highest elements of Japanese economy in art, fussy spots such as few Japanese would tolerate, of wood carvings, screens, ornamented vases, etc., in "artistic groups." On a cement shelf that is as uncompromising and unpleasant in texture as only a block of cement can be he will have a vase with dried grasses and a paper fan. His masses are as assertive as his speech and his taste as erratic as his reasoning. But this man did start something, of that there is no doubt, for many of his ideas were taken up in Europe far more than here and have much to do with the "modern movement."

The "skyscraper" design came about through the drawings of Hugh Ferris for Harvey Wiley Corbett which showed the "envelope" allowed by the zoning laws. These drawings had hardly been shown at the Architectural League of New York before many other architects developed the style in their work. Such men as Raymond Hood, Ralph Walker and J. Ely Kahn developed the "setback" style which had its advantages in buildings but no reason at all to be copied in furniture and potteries. Everything became angular and squared except, of course, the human body which did not feel comfortable in the chairs, while at the same time the eyes became tired of such hard angularity.

A few potteries were making fair wares and people paid high prices for Rookwood, Roseville and even Fulper jars of which we shall speak later.

At the same time the "Boom" was in the making and American millionaires had started to clean the art out of Europe in earnest. The auction galleries were selling "Ming vases" for $25 to $50 and "Corot paintings" for a few hundred, although the real things were bringing hundreds and thousands of dollars. Every salesroom hummed and fakes supplied the market. Living artists and popular craftsmen were only just surviving for the larger American homes had Tudor living rooms, Spanish patios, Grinling Gibbons mantels in pine incidental rooms, Chippendale upstairs sitting rooms, Louis XV and Louis XVI bedrooms and Modern bars. Thus the poor craftsman had to work in every sort of period. It was educational but not soundly so. More money was spent for faked antiques and for liquor (for this was the prohibition era) than for honest craftsmanship.

Due to the fact that Americans did not think modern craftsmanship sufficiently expensive, there was no interest in the potteries of contemporaries. About the only modern wares which were sold in large quantities were those imitating old Chinese wares and made in China and Japan. At least 75% of the pottery lamps were made from these. In making lamps we tried to widen the taste and attempted to sell Persian wares, East Indian brasses, Italian potteries, etc., but with no very great success.

The genius of one man, Mr. Edward I. Farmer, led to the selling of fine antique Chinese wares as lamps and it was also he who taught the American public that they could spend thousands of dollars for lamps made with bases of fine jades and other hard stones. His shades were rounded and soft in tone, often made from embroideries or tapestries of Chinese origin and hung with thick fringes. I do not know what Farmer's highest priced lamp was but he sold many for $10,000 or more. Vase lamps became a sure and definite style trend.

A reaction against the overcrowding of rooms with many decorative objects led to the revolt against Victorianism and no objects of art were permitted. Thus lamps became about the only art objects in many modern rooms, retained simply because they are of use. An amusing sidelight was that the most modern of modernists did not give up vase lamps despite all their theories of functionalism, etc.; they simply used modern looking vases and shades.

In our own studio which started immediately after World War I in East Orange, N. J. and moved to New York in the following year, we made lamps of every period (Farmer had never stepped out of the Chinese field.) and we tried to do all decorating of shades by hand instead of using the fancy fabrics which Farmer had used. All of the graphic arts have been employed and our chief artist, Miss Ethelyn C. Stewart, is a master of etching, lithography, the oriental perpendicular brush, the tjanting used for batik, etc. She is also quite able to demonstrate the differences between Meissen flowers of various periods, Vienna flowers, Sèvres, Chinese of various periods, Japanese,

Rakka jar of 12th to 13th cent. mounted as a lamp with shade designed by Warren E. Cox and made of hand blended velvet by Ethelyn C. Stewart.

Sung Dynasty Tz'u Chou lamp with shade designed by Warren E. Cox and hand painted by Ethelyn C. Stewart.

Late Sung to Early Ming Tz'u Chou vase of unique character but with neck cut slightly and therefore made into a lamp by Warren E. Cox. The shade has alternating panels of hand painting on silk and batiked design (to reproduce the incised parts) on velvet by Ethelyn C. Stewart.

17th cent. Hispano Moresque lustre jar with shade designed by Warren E. Cox and batiked by Ethelyn C. Stewart.

Late Ming "Three colored" vase with shade designed by Warren E. Cox and batiked on velvet by Ethelyn C. Stewart.

K'ang Hsi (1662–1722 A.D.) porcelain vase with famille verte enamel decoration mounted as a lamp. The shade is designed by Warren E. Cox and decorated with hand colored etchings printed on the silk by Ethelyn C. Stewart.

ANTIQUE POTTERIES AND PORCELAINS INCORPORATED
IN LAMP DESIGNS BY WARREN E. COX

PLATE 232

Modern Sèvres porcelain lamp with shade designed by Warren E. Cox and decorated with a hand colored etching printed on silk by Ethelyn C. Stewart.

Takatori 18th cent. Japanese saki-bottle with shade designed by Warren E. Cox and batiked and hand painted by Ethelyn C. Stewart.

A porcelain dish mounted as a lamp by Warren E. Cox and the shade hand painted by Ethelyn C. Stewart.

Sèvres lamp with shade designed by Warren E. Cox and etched and hand painted by Ethelyn C. Stewart.

Modern Wedgwood vase with shade designed by Warren E. Cox and decorated with an etched and hand painted border by Ethelyn C. Stewart.

Modern reproduction of a Sung Tz'u Chou incised slip vase somewhat modified and designed by Warren E. Cox, fired by Walter Howat and with shade hand painted by Ethelyn C. Stewart.

LAMPS DESIGNED BY WARREN E. COX USING ANTIQUE AND
MODERN CERAMIC PIECES

PLATE 233

English, etc., etc. A hundred or so of her etchings made for lamp shades have become truly famous.

Meanwhile a large collection of fine potteries and porcelains was made. The less good pieces were sold as lamp bases and the finest have been put to one side for sale to collectors. We became interested in a kiln and made many reproductions for less expensive lamps.

Many other lamp firms followed. Roland and Mrs. Moore copied Farmer's shades and lately the crushed velvet ones which we designed for Persian wares mottled to pick up the texture and iridescent tones. Mrs. Moore died some years ago and since that time less attention has been paid to the shade art in his establishment although many fine antique Chinese ceramic wares have been sold. The more commercial and larger firms, such as Yamanaka & Co., Long Sang Ti Co. and others, built large lamp departments until more vases were sold for this purpose than for any other. Edward F. Caldwell & Co. mounted many ordinary 17th century Persian oil jars with their superb champleve enamel work.

Such was the many sided and diverse "modern art" of the period after World War I up to the depression. No two people could even agree as to what was modern and it was really a free-for-all with plenty of money behind it.

REPORT ON THE 1939 POTTERIES SHOWN IN THE NEW YORK EXPOSITION

FRANCE

Robert Bloch, Paris, showed some wares strongly reminiscent of the Victorian era, with heavy body and thin, frosty, mat glazes of pastel colors with often decorations in chocolate brown and gold. Dishes in the form of ostrich feathers, stupid chess-men and pairs of negro figures led me to note that a great effort had been made to obtain a soigné effect of chic, and had failed.

There was nothing of note in the table wares of Charles Ahrenfeldt, Au Vase Etrusque, L. Bernardaud, The Porcelain Manufactury of Limoges and Robert Haviland & Le Tanneur. The block-like and gaudy colored figures of Breton peasants made by Hanroit of Breton had little charm.

Germany and Austria were, of course, not exhibited.

HUNGARY

In Hungary the Herend pieces were the most ordinary but even these were alive in spirit. The bird and flower decorations were gayly painted with clear, fresh but harmonious colors. A nude figure some twelve to fourteen inches high was beautifully modeled by Lux Eleby and the broad touches of color, a yellowish buff for the hair and a light, dull red irregularly brushed on the drape showed a perfect understanding of just how much and just how little color to use. No attempt had been made to touch up the high places with natural pink but the warmth of the off-white glaze itself adds feeling of life.

Madam Olga Braun told me about Géza Gorka who has spent many years in recovering the lost arts of the Hungarian peasant potteries. In the Christmas Exhibition of 1938 he and his brother received honors for this ware which is direct and strong like that of long ago. The colors are rich blues, greens, dull yellows and the ground frequently buff. This kiln which is at Nógrádveröcze, near Budapest, will bear watching, if it survives the war.

Lili Márkus had a large, cylindrical dark jar with circular concavities in

FIG. 1385. Dish by Mrs. Truda Adams of the Carter, Stabler & Adams company, which is pleasant in its pseudo Persian design but overly weak and delicate.

FIG. 1386. W. Staite Murray not only made Tz'u Chou type things but also attempted the Chün glazes with some success. Metropolitan Mus. of Art.

FIG. 1387. Tz'u Chou type jar by W. Staite Murray owned by Bernard Rackham. Comparison with Sung examples is hardly fair, but the form is too fat and rounded and the brush-work too much organized in the swirl of the fish and repetition of the V marks. However, it is better than most modern pottery.

which were tiny crude models of things in bright enamels sunk quite deeply as though in little inch wide caves. The overmantle of a mountain with figures on it in relief and enameled with soft colors is not a new idea but was well done. Another large jar reminds us a little of those by Gauguin but is less dynamic.

FIG. 1388. Large jar by Lili Markus in glazed earthenware of dark brownish black and greyish blue. Ht. about 16". Note: The feeling of this piece is not unlike that of some of Gauguin's but it is weaker.

FIG. 1389. Faïence Madonna and Child by G. Y. Eleöd which is typically sweet, and even somewhat flippant. Ht. 16". Modern Hungarian.

FIG. 1390. Technically the lustre effects of Zsolnay Gyár are very excellent but the results are somewhat thin and glassy, like Christmas tree ornaments and the forms are uninteresting. Ht. 15½". Modern Hungarian.

Jenö Eschnebach had only been out of art school for a short while but had made a small crucifixion which was outstandingly beautiful and sensitive, though done in what at first appears a sketchy style. It looks to have been done by a great artist in haste and totally without pose.

Margit Kovács works in heavy pottery which has a mediaeval feeling in its slip decorations and dark glazes of gold, red and blue. The sculptors B. Markup and Béla Ohmann had good figures in faïence, one of a mountaineer on a donkey and another of a rather sweet and willowy Madonna and Child.

Of poorer effect there are the sloppy modeling and potting of István Gádor and the overornate lustres of Zsolnay Gyár much like the English 19th century ones.

Fig. 1391. Margit Kovacs medieval sort of things in dark glazes, gold, red and blue. Ht. 12½". Modern Hungarian.

Fig. 1392. By F. Borszéky—A bonbonnière in various soft colors of glazes on what appears to be a hard porcelain ware. Dia. 7". Modern Hungarian.

HOLLAND

The Royal Delft Factory in Holland has gone in for some Persian shaped pottery having rather indefinite patterns in well blended and deep colored lustres. They are also making some very thin white wares after the Chinese. There were also a dull continuation of the blue and white and polychrome "Delft wares."

The factory Zaalberg "de rinj," Leiderdorp, had some heavy and medium red pottery prominently scored with wheel marks and covered with a thin and often partly wiped off glaze of pale green, blue, lavender, yellow, grey or a thick, deep blue of unpleasant reddish tone. The shapes are tall beakers, one well formed pitcher and platters. This all appears to be a great effort to be primitive.

BELGIUM

The S. A. Faiencerie de Nimy had some ordinary cream ware and some with blue glaze. There were also some very poorly modeled animals in lumpy sugary white glaze, a Belgian artist's conception of a negro jazz-band and some figures in sets of five or six all of poor quality and no redeeming features.

P. Paulus had some poor copies of 17th century "Kashan" potteries in brown and green and cream and rust.

Marcel Wolfers found a new texture, something always dear to the mind of a modernist, and it consists of a thick brown glaze in which are sprinkled many pieces of mother-of-pearl giving somewhat the effect of some Ming Chinese lacquer only that in the latter case the pieces are not scattered but laid carefully like mosaic. Again Wolfers uses what appears to be flecks of egg shell set in a dark brown glaze though I should imagine that real egg shell would calcine and crumble with the heat. Another trick is on a large jar which seems to have been stippled or sponged on a thick glaze which after firing was covered with gold and rubbed so that the gold does not adhere to the high ridges. There was also a large plate treated this way and with coral red on the inside.

Van Nerom has a jar and dishes with cute little figures in child-like drawing and colored with pale blue, pink, etc., rather carelessly so that it runs over the edges. It is strange that we don't mind a bold splash of color that breaks carelessly over a strong outline but we resent the transgression of a weak and uncertain hand.

Pierre Caille probably thinks of himself as a great humorist when he does his badly modeled animals in unpleasant yellow, green and rose glazes; and his lumpy birds are well frosted. He has also copied some of the Austrian, Wiener Werkstadt techniques and some pie-faced lions of Italian heritage.

The Belgian artists were on the wrong track in 1925 and they certainly lived down to expectations.

DENMARK

The Hegnetslund Lervarefabrik showed some vases, jugs and figures in red iron rust glazes, some majolica pigs and jugs by Anker Nørregaard and some pottery in dull green glazes. Nothing new in any way approaching the fine wares from this country was shown.

Saxbo work was marked by refined and beautiful shapes and among them one, so far as I know, new treatment for a jug so simple and so fundamentally good potting that it is a wonder it has not been used for centuries. The pear shaped body has a fairly wide neck which is cut down the middle, one half curving forward to form the lip or spout while the other is extended and curves backward to join the body and form the handle. This seems to be a real invention.

Nathalie Krebs and Eva Wilhjelm together with Erik Rahr all had beautiful shapes in their wares with the finest of glazes of buff, brown, cream and white as well as pale blue running to deep blue. Nathalie Krebs was manager of the factory and is an especially able potter.

There was a strong Japanese influence in the "temmoku" flat straight-sided tea bowls actually invented in China but given a more popular flare and weaker character in Japan. Some of the tea-pots could have been shown by Japan and not thought misplaced. They had glazes of brown, pinkish white and buff.

The sculptors, Hugo Liisberg and Olaf Staehr Nielsen, work well but were not particularly thrilling, though I did note with pleasure a charming faun in brown glaze which was gentle, alert and living.

If this factory would turn a little more toward the strength of Chinese

Vigorous animals full of life are modeled by Knud Kyhn in solid stoneware of great weight and glazed in dull brown, bluish or green tones. The power and life in his work are well shown in this old bear. Length 13". Frederick Lunning, Inc.

Left: The most beautifully potted and decorated Royal Copenhagen porcelain bowl I have seen. There is a pale grey-blue shading about the stand and the design inside which was painted by Bertha Nathanielsen and signed by her. Dia. 5½". Mrs. Warren E. Cox.

Right: Large modern Copenhagen underglazed decorated jar of the type made by The Royal Copenhagen Manufactory and copied somewhat weakly by Bing & Grondahl. Ht. 31". Frederick Lunning, Inc.

MODERN ROYAL COPENHAGEN WARES

PLATE 234

sources rather than the already second-hand ones of Japan, it would benefit. Yet there was nothing that one would not be happy to own and I believe that over a period of years one would not grow tired of any of the pieces. I do not know of any stoneware of finer quality though than that of Axal Salto, the painter, and Bode Willumsen perhaps rates as high.

The Herman A. Kahler factory has two fine artists in Svend Hammershøj and Jens Thiirslund who do what are almost classic shapes but with strange and pleasant distortions that are so sure that they are entirely convincing. The ware is lightweight and high ringing stoneware of grey or black and thinly made. The glaze is greyish white of dull surface and crackled and wiped off in places so that the body shows through. There is real textural charm very hard to put in words.

FIG. 1393. This cup shows one style of Thiirslund of the Kähler pottery, Näestved. It is of light grey with black decoration swiftly and none too surely applied. Metropolitan Mus. of Art.
FIG. 1394. Two pieces of the new red glazed ware which is more mat than a sang de boeuf glaze and more closely approximates the Yung Chêng sang de pigeon. Hts. 8″ and 3″. Frederick Lunning, Inc.
FIG. 1395. So well known are the animal figures from Copenhagen that it is unnecessary to show more than a few. This was taken from the figure in the fountain in the Peace Palace, Hague. Ht. 11″. George Jensen, Inc.

The L. Hjorth's Terracottafabrik, Rønne, Bornholm, had some cylindrical jars with covers in dark brown, dull glaze on thin but heavy stoneware and a few heavy vases in pleasing transmutation glazes but uncertain in shape. There was also a small figure of a woman with a jar but poor in modeling. This ware is called "iron glaze ware," which does not seem particularly original. Much of the glaze is actually olive green which might include some iron along with copper or other green producing elements.

A. S. Michael Andersen & Søn of the same place, also showed some simple vases of good quality stoneware with transmutation glazes of brown to blue. A terra-cotta bust of a girl is piquant and illusively charming with suggestive shrug, secretive smile, and off the face hair treatment. This last is worth note for the artist has simply pressed the clay up into small rounded waves with the thumb and then incised them with lines producing a convincing texture.

The Royal Copenhagen Porcelain Manufactory had a few of the older type underglazed painted porcelains of beautiful craftsmanship and some perhaps overchaste table ware, but other things were more interesting. The heavy stoneware thickly potted of roughly modeled animals glazed in buff, mottled

FIG. 1396. A group of the grey crackled wares decorated in a peculiar and none too pleasant orange color, black and gold. Royal Copenhagen. Hts. about 2″ to 13″. George Jensen, Inc.

grey, cream and iron rust were vigorous and strong. Some rich brown glazed pieces like the "Tsung Sê," "Chien yao," or "Temmoku" Chinese type are good but have less lustre and variation than the Far Eastern ones.

FIG. 1398. Christian Thomsen did a series illustrating the Hans Christian Andersen fairy tales, of which this, "The King's Nightdress," is one. Ht. 8″. George Jensen, Inc.

FIG. 1397. A group of modern plates decorated with natural flowers somewhat in the old style of about 1780 to 1800. George Jensen, Inc.

A new ware to me was of superb beauty and was shown in only two pieces. It is of pure white porcelain body which shows an "iron foot" and "brown mouth" as in some of the Kuan and Ko wares. The glaze is cloudy, pale greyish, greenish blue like that of the finest "kinuta" celadon and is as soft and unctuous and pleasant to the touch. This is perhaps the most beautiful ware the factory ever turned out.

One of the best artists is Hans Hansen who does vessels which O. Mathiesen glazes though the two work so closely in mutual understanding that the glaze

FIG. 1401. This lovely little dog has a silky and soft colored glaze. It is interesting to compare it with the dog by Edward McCartan (see modern American section.) Length 13". George Jensen, Inc.

FIG. 1399. Ducks by G. Herold of the Royal Copenhagen Factory, 20th cent. Metropolitan Mus. of Art.

FIG. 1400. Typical underglaze painting of ship on Royal Copenhagen jar. The colors have to be blue, gray, lavender, etc., to stand the high temperature in firing. They are both decorative and beautifully detailed. Courtesy of George Jensen, Inc.

FIG. 1402. Bing and Grøndahl porcelain vase by Mrs. Jo Hahn Locher in low relief with mat glaze. Metropolitan Mus. of Art.

is always perfectly suited to the shape. One particularly fine one was a tall slightly bulging cylindrical vase with perpendicular grooves covered with an olive green glaze. A smaller jar and cover had a most ingenious hexagonal design in relief on it and a finial in the form of an animal which looks to have been inspired from a Ming period jade carving.

Niels Thorsson is another strong modeler and his pieces are glazed by H. Madslund in a new and very rich glaze of copper red which varies from bright and strong color to dark blackish red and slips from the edge as do the sang de boeuf glazes of China, though it is thinner and less glossy than these, which is after all more pleasant and less assertive.

The other things were of little note such as the set of plates with silhouettes from Hans Christian Andersen's fairy tales, etc.

This factory has always maintained such a high standard of technique that there could be little improvement but the trend away from the more pictorial things and toward the stoneware and beautiful glazes is a good one, if the public will support it. After all it does take a more sophisticated and better trained taste to appreciate a small white or green bowl with wonderful glaze than it does to like a big vase with boats or flowers painted on it, and the public appeal for fine things will probably always be a narrow one.

Bing and Grøndahl also at Copenhagen, which calls itself "The National Factory of Porcelain," has become perhaps as important as the older factory, due to a few great artists who have been on its staff.

Kai Nielsen, who died, I understand, in 1934 or 1935, had developed his talent even further. A life-sized statue of Venus was full of sexual charm and very lovely. This had been pushed over by a drunken woman who reeled against it at the fair and had been broken but I inspected it in a closet and found the modeling wonderfully sure and knowing. Another charming piece was the "Venus with the Apple." Nielsen's proportions are purposely changed but add to the vitality of his work somewhat as do "El Greco's."

FIG. 1403. Stoneware vase from Bing and Grøndahl by C. Olsen. Metropolitan Mus. of Art.

I was disappointed in Jean Gauguin. His jars were similar but less strong and a life-sized tiger's head was naturalistic and without power as though modeled from the head of a fur rug. A small model of a tiger showed poor and uncertain knowledge of anatomy. A rhinoceros head looked so good that it might have been sliced off a real animal but one wonders what the purpose might be. A couple of faun heads were stupid and dull. As I wrote this I wondered, if I might have been wrong in my first impression at the Paris show but going back over old photographs I find it was not so; it is he who simply seems to have dried up. Perhaps all his strength was borrowed from Han potteries and now that he has drifted away from them he has lost his source.

Professor Hans Tegner did a group of hard porcelain small figures with bright and deep overglaze colors representing various characters from the Andersen fairy tales. There was the "Nightingale," "Swineherd," "Chimney Sweep and His Princess," the "Emperor's New Clothes" (showing his majesty in crown and shirt tails), and "Big Claus and Little Claus," among them. They are all full of humor and delicacy and are also fine craftsmanship, but similar subjects had been treated by Christian Thomsen at the Royal Copenhagen works.

Axel Locher has a few rather 18th century-like little figures such as, "The Girl with Sheep," etc.

The vases and other vessels of this factory are of the finest of modern wares and rate very close to the Royal Copenhagen ones. Both of these places have withstood the withering effects of industrialism probably because of the royal patronage and the intense national pride which all Danes take in them.

ENGLAND

In England it is a different matter. We walked past the throne on which the Magna Charta was displayed and watched the faces of the people who were disappointed to find they could not read it. We crossed an immense room which contained racing automobiles and engines of other sorts, then after climbing some stairs to a balcony where there were many ship models, statistical charts, etc., and following directions to turn to the right, we found tucked away in the furtherest corner a half dozen little cases chock full of "china," for the most part as ornately bedecked as an officer of the Palace Guard on dress parade. People were passing these cases in double line, each fellow pushing his girl along before him and not giving her any too much time to look at anything. The exclamations were typically preceded by exhaled or aspirated exclamation so common to the British, "Ooh! Aren't they wonderful? Ho! That's a fine one!" all very much as though fireworks were being displayed. And the wares themselves really called for something like that.

Royal Worcester China was in the first case and along the top was a row of plates in red with one in blue so heavily encrusted with gold filigree that you could hardly make out the color under it. Below this was a large porcelain sign with the words Royal Worcester China and a row of life-sized birds contorting themselves as much as possible beside a nice large flower on each piece. The birds looked overstuffed and the colors dull. On the bottom shelf was a well modeled but cheaply colored group of three circus horses and some smartly, flatly conventionalized hunters showing the style common to advertisements for men's clothing. (See any copy of Esquire.)

The Wedgwood case showed not one new spark and a muddy copy of the same old "Portland vase."

The usual floating ladies in flowing drapes in pâte sur pâte on shiny olive green and dull blue grounds were proudly shown still again by Minton. A cup was delicately decorated with light gilt tracery about two photographic portraits of George VI and Elizabeth with many legends so that no one could mistake who they were. These commemorated their trip to the United States. There were also services in heavy colors and with too much gold surrounding too small medallions in which were painted birds and flowers.

Royal Doulton has tried pitifully to copy dogs in Copenhagen style and this factory too showed encrusted gilt plates. Some dainty and sweet little girl figures were shown but no artist's name was given, and a "balloon woman" may have been by Gwendolen Parnell, though the humor was missing and it may have been just a stylized copy of her work.

Royal Crown Derby rehashed the same old Imari designs in Derby red, gold and blue, tightly painted flowers in pasty colors and having much of the too red blue which would go well only in petunias, and a small cup in celebration of George VI's visit.

Spode had some plates with the stiffest flowers yet seen and the most opaque colors. They had left off the gold but the very broad rims were finished in heavy rose de Mantenon.

That was all. I asked the manager why they had not sent over some of their artists' work and was told that the exhibit represented the best work in England. They had never heard of Staite Murray. Where were the Adams, Hy. Simeon of the Doulton Co., Gwladys Rodgers and the rest? In the true British disdain which covers uncertainty I was looked upon as though I had mentioned the names of foreigners.

ITALY

The Societa Ceramica Italiana, Laveno, had some heavy potteries particularly some 16-inch pilgrim bottles with a large clumsy child with a goose on them in horrible, bright orange and other colored glazes that hurt.

The Melandri Pietro, Faienza, had some ordinary lustre and some grotesque shaped and bizarre pots of large scale. It seemed that Italy was trying to gain notice by scale alone.

Ivos Pacetti had some crude modern sculpture with sticky brown and blue glaze.

Pietro

But when we come to Richard Ginori, Milano, there is a new and charming note. The shapes are restrained and yet they are all quite different. Some are of neo-classic feeling as in a large cream mat glazed vase with two acanthus scroll handles in gold, and two smaller vases of the same ware with female figures riding dolphins done in burnished and mat gold. Another was in a soft grey blue of beautiful tone. But though classic these pieces are all original in proportions and details of treatment.

A number of bottles are tall and simple being modeled in helical convex ridges some of equal width and some alternating wide and narrow. These are very thinly potted and covered with a pearly grey glaze, a greyish white and a pinkish white not at all iridescent but seemingly glowing like the surfaces of real pearls. A small cylindrical jar with narrow neck was alternately convex ribbed with soft, dull red and pearly grey. Some similar wares were in mat black and one such jar had a wide rolled up lip curving back over the shoulder and colored in light terra cotta.

A large jar was in underglaze blue and gold on white porcelain body and the blue looked almost exactly like real lapis. The form was simple and quite satisfying.

There were also some photographic gold portrait plaques, service pieces with purple landscapes, etc., but they did not harm the real joy found in the work of other artists at this factory, though these artists remained nameless.

POLAND

Ginori

FIG. 1404.

Poland showed a couple of saints in badly modeled, low-fired cream pottery of pinkish hue, some heavy stoneware plates, vases of amateurish shapes, metallic lustres with blended effects, mannered "modern" vases and various copies of Persian wares. Nothing approached their embroidered arts or the other crafts.

CZECHOSLOVAKIA

Czechoslovakia had some faïence of the usual sort including a puzzle pitcher with three spouts and pierced neck, but nothing of interest.

RUSSIA

Russia has had a strange turn for the literal and naturalistic. The artists seem to have so much of a story to tell that art is forgotten. This artistic hysteria is like that of a public speaker so unsure that he heaps statistics, fact upon fact, until he bores his audience. And again there seems to be little of the true bourgeois appeal for only the British can surpass their wares for royal ostentation and bad taste.

Nadezhda Zamyatina had some small female "Tartar Dancers," very sexy but I had to examine them with care to determine in the case whether they were porcelain or actually carved out of ivory. There was also a "vase for desk" in the form of a book case with a girl sitting in front of it with an open book in her lap. Can anyone imagine a more appropriate subject!

The Dulevsky Porcelain Factory had a well modeled figure of "Chapayev on Horseback" by Alexander Sotnikov and some "Cossack Dancers" by the same artist. The first figure was also done by Orlov with overglaze colors.

Dulevsky had some dinner services much in the late 18th century French style with the "Order of Lenin" and the "Red Banner" motives.

FIG. 1405. Typical "Ku-Yüeh Hsüan type" eggshell vase with carefully shaded painting in delicate famille rose enamels and a square Ch'ien Lung seal mark in blue enamel. Ht. 7½". Ex Warren E. Cox Coll.

FIG. 1406. Reproduction of incorrect shape and too sweet colors of famille verte porcelain. It has a double ring underglaze blue mark. Ht. 11¼". T. C. Lee–Warren E. Cox Coll.

FIG. 1407. Modern Tz'u Chou pottery vase with sandy buff body, a sort of sticky cream slip and glaze, and too sharp, crowded black design. The form also is not Sung. Ht. 11". Warren E. Cox Coll.

FIG. 1408. Reproductions of "peach bloom" vases of crude potting, the smaller having a dull, spotty glaze while the larger has a too glassy pale yellowish green glaze with traces of pink and an odd crackle. Both have six character K'ang Hsi marks in the underglaze blue. Hts. 6¼" and 7¼". Perry Moore–Warren E. Cox Coll.

There were several large vases a yard or more in height. One had views of Moscow, parades, etc., on it and was by Tamara Bezpalova. Another with hunting scenes by Ivan Riznich looked much like the chromos of the early 19th century calendar art. Others were called, "Twenty Years of the Red Army," "The Mosco-Volga Canal," etc., and were by Ludmila Protopopova.

Left: 19th cent. beautiful figure of Kwan Yin in brown-crackled glaze and face and hands in ivory white. It is very large. Ht. 53". C. T. Loo & Co.

Right: Modern eggshell porcelain vase of the so called, Ku Yüeh Hsüan (See Ch'ien Lung section) type with a seal mark of that period in blue enamel. It has a coral red ground over which is delicate tracery of gold and in which are reserved medallions beautifully painted. Ht. about 8". T. C. Lee–Warren E. Cox Coll. Now in Nai Chi Chang Coll.

CHINESE 19TH AND 20TH CENTURY PORCELAINS

PLATE 235

So much for the various sections of the New York 1939 Fair. It is obvious that our times will not go down as a great era of art achievement but there were some fairly nice things here and there.

The Far Eastern exhibitions had little to show but the Japanese continue to make copies of both the Chinese wares and their own which are altogether too good and sometimes really dangerous to the unwary collector, while China turns out some perfectly beautiful modern wares among which are very fine egg-shell bowls marked with Yung lo characters delicately incised in the inside of the bottom and dragons about the sides in good style. Among the

FIG. 1409. A modern Japanese reproduction of a Korai "mishima" bowl too glassy in appearance, fired on a foot-rim instead of spurs and having three spots of red in the center flowers, all of which are not characteristic. Dia. 7". Fritz Low–Beer Coll.

FIG. 1410. Paper-thin egg-shell bowl of slightly greenish white beautifully incised with clouds and dragons and on the bottom inside a four character Yung Lo, Ming mark, before glazing. This type does not, so far as I know, copy any existing Yung Lo type of bowl but some unwary collectors have been taken in by such pieces. The difference in price is about $15 against a minimum of several thousands. Dia. 5". T. C. Lee–Warren E. Cox Coll.

FIG. 1412. Modern porcelain bowl made at Ching-tê Chêng and decorated with too brilliant famille rose enamels. The marks are six character Ch'ien Lung ones in script in faint iron red. Dia. 6¾". Perry Moore–Warren E. Cox Coll.

FIG. 1411. Vase of the K'ang Hsi famille verte style of pure white porcelain (too white and glossy) and well painted in too brilliant enamels. Has a green enamel leaf mark. Ht. 6½". Modern Ching-tê Chêng. T. C. Lee–Warren E. Cox Coll.

FIG. 1413. Modern vase made at Ching-tê Chêng of the heavy "Ku-Yüeh Hsüan" type and with the usual square seal mark of Ch'ien Lung in blue enamel. The ground is dull iron-red with gold tracery and the reserved medallions are beautifully painted in the shaded style influenced by western painting. Ht. 9¾". T. C. Lee–Warren E. Cox Coll.

excellent wares are also "Ku Yueh Hsüan" wares of fine porcelain beautifully painted and all properly marked in blue enamel or lavender enamel marks. Potteries and stonewares are no less generally good and modern celadons, Tz'u chou wares and Tsung Sê wares are deceiving. I show a few for comparison. In Korean celadon and "mishima" again excellent copies are made by a factory there but the tendency with these wares is to introduce too much red and make the designs too overdone. Only once in a while does one come along which is an exact copy of some fine old piece.

Japan also has copied "Lowestoft" and other commercial European wares very crudely for the decorative market.

Again there is a thriving business in the Near East copying the "Kashan" oil jars and one can find the results in almost any rug shop window, but these lack all the true character of the 17th and 18th century specimens.

CHAPTER XXX

CONTEMPORARY AMERICAN CERAMICS

MUCH has been said as to the sources of modern design in the preceding chapter but the development here in America is somewhat different from that of Europe or Asia. There are three pretty well defined classifications:

1.—Commercial suppliers of building materials and table ware.
2.—Individual potters both amateur and professional.
3.—Sculptors who work more or less in ceramics.

There is practically no artistic merit left in the first classification for obvious reasons. So far as the architectural suppliers are concerned there is a noticeable attempt to try to make pottery tiles look like wooden ones or asbestos ones or any other medium other than what they really are. Stone, gold and other substances are copied probably at the direction of the architects. Thus the Ludowici Celadon Co. got out a booklet showing "Georgian" and "Provincial Shingle Tiles," etc. Again the Gladding McBean & Co. advertising speaks of "Granitex-finish ceramic veneer," for steel sheathing.

Another characteristic is shown by this same company which gets out a booklet telling us that the company was founded by Peter McGill McBean in 1875 and showing "improved Hermosa tile" and "Franciscan table ware" with pride, but not mentioning one word about any artist that may have worked for them. The architects are given ample mention even when the lowly urns are spoken of in connection with the Beverly Hills Post Office. The designer of the "Franciscan ware" is said to be "one of America's foremost merchandise stylists." In the Northwestern Terra Cotta Corp. material we find two artists mentioned, J. H. Lambert and B. Leo Steif neither of whom are Americans and both of whom are architects. These gentlemen and Mr. Andre Alizier did doorways very much reminiscent of Edgar Brandt's metal work with flattened rosettes and wavy lines. Even this sort of imitative trash was slapped around two reliefs of Will Rogers for the high school of his name in Tulsa.

The Northwestern claims that, "Chicago's Michigan Avenue is virtually a 'Terra-Cotta Boulevard'" implying that it is largely theirs. Why they do not pay more attention to the quality of their quantity I do not know. Other such companies are the older Atlantic Terra Cotta Co., the Federal Seaboard Terra Cotta Corp., the Galloway Terra Cotta Co. of Philadelphia, The Mosaic Tile Co., Ohio, Conkling Armstrong, etc. The materials that these companies turn out or turned out could produce really beautiful effects. Once in a great while a really fine work of art is made such as the pediment for the Pennsylvania Museum which I shall describe under the work of C. Paul Jennewein and which was executed at the Atlantic Terra Cotta Co., but it is seldom the case.

It is not necessary to go into detail about the "Kitchen and Garden" pottery such as that made by the Galloway Terra Cotta Co. and Homer Laughlin China Co. The latter is making simple and heavy ware colored with plain light and dark blue, yellow, green and orange glazes, the idea being that one should mix the colors in setting a table.

FIG. 1414. A simple and well designed set called the "Rancho pattern" made by Gladding, Mc-Bean & Co.

Also in the commercial field is the Fulper Pottery started in 1805 in Flemington, N. J. In 1928 a larger plant was built in Trenton, N. J., and a claim is made that many pieces are hand made though this is not obvious from looking at the wares. J. M. Stangl has been president for about 30 years and the wares are marked "STANGL." They claim to have made the first solid color ware; a modest boast! And also claim the very practical feature that the ware is "oven proof," that is, it will not crack from fairly quick transitions between heat and cold. They also make wares of a "peasant type" which, however, are of no particular note. "Art ware, lamps, vases, flower pots, ash trays and countless other items in all shapes," cater to the small gift shop and store trade. The wares are called pottery but are said to be fired at 2200° to 2300° Fahrenheit which would be a fair heat for stoneware or even porcelain.

Fig. 1416. Fulper pottery sent as examples of their best work, "very simple but effective patterns."

Fig. 1417. It will be noted that both of these very simple designs are on the same shapes.

Fig. 1415. Terra cotta panels made for the Will Rogers High School, Tulsa, Okla. which do not bear the artist's name and which show somewhat inappropriate use of designs obviously taken from Edgar Brandt's iron work which have nothing to do with either Mr. Rogers or Oklahoma. Northwestern Terra Cotta Co.

LENOX BELLEEK

Walter Scott Lenox worked as an apprentice in the Ott & Brewer factory and Willetts Pottery, Trenton, and became manager of the former. In 1889 he formed a partnership with Jonathan Coxon, Sr., in the Ceramic Art Co. until 1894 when he acquired his partner's share and continued until 1906 when he organized the Lenox Co.

His intention from the first was to make a similar ware to the Irish Belleek and he employed two potters who had worked at Castle Caldwell and were in this country. Actually what he did is more pleasing than the original Belleek in some ways. The Irish ware is very thin, cold white and covered with a lustre which has a high sheen. Dainty things were done with it and it seemed to escape much of the blight of the period but it was at times overornate. The Lenox ware is warmer in tone, perhaps even more translucent and not so lustrous, being more like highly polished ivory.

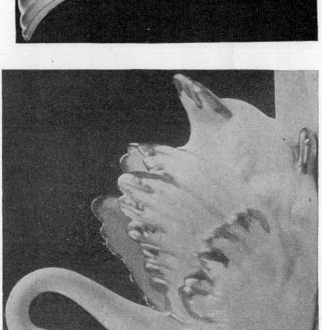

Left: The two color effects are well carried out and one wishes only for a somewhat more characterful design than such things as these little flowers. Lenox Co. *Center:* Swan bowl made by the Ceramic Art Co. of Trenton, N. J., about 1889–1896, the immediate predecessor of Lenox, and marked *C. A. C. Belleek.* Ht. 4¾". Brooklyn Mus. *Right:* This simple shape is beautifully proportioned and lends itself to charming flower arrangements. Lenox Co.

LENOX BELLEEK

Plate 236

Harry A. Brown managed the factory for some years before the death of Lenox in 1920 and carried on after that time. Frank G. Holmes has been the chief designer for many years and he is responsible for the simplicity, grace and restraint which have marked the products. William H. Clayton who was an apprentice of Lenox has also been a powerful factor.

This ware is made of clay, feldspar and flint mixed with filtered water. The feldspar comes from New England and after being reduced to a fine, white powder by grinding under an ancient millstone is mixed with the clay and

FIG. 1418. Mr. Holmes often uses even thinner and more sparse decoration for the Lenox services. Of course this does show off the beautiful material to advantage.

FIG. 1419. Frank G. Holmes employs fluting in a great many of his designs for Lenox and it has a sort of neo-classic charm. One must admit that the factory always carries it out accurately.

FIG. 1420. A simple neo-classic feeling makes this service very chaste and in good taste in a formal way. Lenox Co.

placed in a large revolving cylinder, lined with porcelain blocks and containing some water and flint pebbles, where they are, "pebble ground." Even the number of revolutions is counted so that all results will be entirely uniform. It takes fifty hours to complete the, "pebble grinding," and then the mixture is forced by compressed air through a fine wire screen containing 200 meshes to the square inch and the slip is produced. But it is not finished for it then passes over electro-magnets which remove all iron particles and enters into an aging process. We do not know what this aging really accomplishes, though many opinions have been advanced but it is an old process and the results are certainly better when it is followed. At Lenox it is "aged" for only a few days (not years as in ancient China) when it is ready for casting or for the "jiggering" machine. This is simply a wheel, power driven, and upon which cups and plates are made over a plaster mould or into a plaster mould. A "profile" is necessary in many cases. The elaborate shapes are, of course, moulded, as has been done for years, in a plaster mould.

Firing is done in saggers and the men have become expert in balancing them upon their heads as they climb the ladders to stack the kiln. The heat is brought to 2200° Fahrenheit and it is interesting to note that the kilns would burst, if not bound with steel bands. Cones which wilt under certain heats are no longer used, their place having been taken by pyrometers. The firing is done for 30 hours and cooling for two days.

This produces the biscuit ware which is then sand blasted to remove any irregularities. Finally they are cleaned of any particles by compressed air, and dipped into the glaze. The second firing is done at 2100° F. and in a kiln called the "glost kiln."

Decoration is all surface and consists of the old processes of etching with hydrofluoric acid, and applying of gold and overglaze colors. Some powdered colors are applied and both etched outlines and transfer prints are used though these are often touched up by hand. All imperfect ware is destroyed and not offered for sale.

Obviously this factory aims toward a super perfection which is undoubtedly achieved and for the small flaw-finding mind of the commercial buyers it has great appeal. That the material is beautiful no one can deny but just as obviously the "jiggering machines," use of molds, etc., eliminates all expression of the hand and though these things are simple and pleasant they are far from inspired works of art. The table ware is tasteful and has charm.

ROOKWOOD

One factory which did overlap the commercial and artistic field was the Rookwood Pottery of Cincinnati. It was started in 1880 by Maria Longworth Storer after experiments in the Dallas Granite Ware Factory where she noted that the high fire destroyed all colors except blue and black. The factory was financed by Mrs. Storer's father to, "give employment to the idle rich." In 1883 William Watts Taylor became a partner and in 1890 Mrs. Storer retired. Later John D. Wareham became president and treasurer.

From its earliest days the decoration consisted in "the application to wet clay pieces of metallic oxides mixed with clay and water or what is technically known as slip, so that the colors become of the very substance and fibre of the piece." Low relief simple modeling is often used. About 1883 "tiger-eye" and "goldstone" glazes were used. Less kindly critics called this "the molasses period," but these glazes did have a depth seldom equaled. Crystalline effects

FIG. 1421. Rookwood vase decorated with various colored porcelain glazes. It will be noted that in this and other pieces from this kiln an artistic effect is sought by a softening of the line somewhat as early photographers obtained it by throwing a picture out of focus.

FIG. 1422. "Sung Plum (reduction)" glazed vase so named but, if it is meant that it has any relation to Chün yao, we must disagree for neither in shape nor in glaze is there any slightest perceptible similarity. Rookwood c. 1935.

FIG. 1423. Weak and wandering pseudo Chinese design motifs, applied in a way that shows lack of understanding, have been used for years by Rookwood on very safe vase forms. This vase shown on a cheapest possible teakwood stand is typical and one dislikes seeing such technical skill so misused.

An early Rookwood jar showing the Japanese influence which was popular at the time, dating between 1880 and 1884.

"Tiger eye" Rookwood ware made from 1884 to the present and rather typical of the factory.

"Mat glazed" type of Rookwood which shows considerable influence of the French pottery of the time, 1896, made by Emile Decoeur and his followers. The soft texture and color has some appeal.

"Iris type glaze" of the type made between 1900 and 1920. It has a certain depth but is glassy and unpleasant in some ways. However, the vase is nevertheless well designed and well decorated to suit the shape.

Contemporary jar with red clay and porcelain glaze by John D. Wareham. The sturdy shape is well related to the very impressionistic bull and flower design.

"Vellum glazed" or transparent mat glazed vase over design of colored clay. This type was done from about 1900, the particular one shown dates 1904. It is evident that more attention was paid to the texture than to the design.

ROOKWOOD POTTERY
PLATE 237

were obtained in the glaze and not on the surface as in the Copenhagen wares of this nature.

In 1896 mat glazes were produced and "Iris" of pale tone and "Sea Green" were first shown in Paris in 1900. In 1904 the first "Vellum" glazes were made by Stanley Burt, while later came "Ombroso" 1910, "Soft Porcelain" 1915 and a revival of "Tiger-eye" 1920 along with "Oxblood," "Flambé," and a "special red" following the European and English enthusiasm for these effects.

In fact there was probably too much following of the "early modern" French potters.

The firing was done around 2000° F. for a period of 24 to 36 hours and allowed to cool for three or four days. Later the piece was glazed and refired.

Artistically speaking the product was probably about as high as any turned out in America though all the ills of the times are also reflected in it. Artists were largely from the local Cincinnati school and among them were Valentine, Daly, McDonald and Shiryama. Mr. Wareham also has made some fine pieces. A celadon was unpleasantly overglossy and the shapes are often arty though some good strong ones do occur. An idea can be obtained by noting the fine jar with a bull on it and the celadon both by Mr. Wareham which are illustrated.

FIG. 1424. An early Rookwood piece by Mrs. Storer and called "Limoges painting" though why it is so called escapes me.

FIG. 1426. Mat glazed Rookwood vase showing influence of Emil Decoeur and his French followers but fairly strong in shape and having a design with concavities well designed to catch and hold the glaze interestingly.

FIG. 1425. "Celadon and turquoise glazes" are used on this vase by Mr. Wareham which in its glassy slickness has all the unpleasantness of modern Japanese commercial celadons with only the advantage of a turquoise note introduced, perhaps not so very much to its benefit.

Unfortunately this factory has been closed recently and I doubt that it will ever again be reopened. A Mr. Walter Schott, dealer in second-hand automobiles in Cincinnati, has purchased the stock and is trying to give the impression that the kilns are still working in order to help sell it off, but nothing new comes out of the place. If our government had been as far sighted as that of Denmark, this establishment might have rivaled that of the Royal Copenhagen one in foreign propaganda and building of a pride in home products.

KENTON HILLS

Meanwhile some of the men from Rookwood have started the Kenton Hills Porcelains factory in Erlanger, Ky. Harold F. Bopp was listed as production manager and chemist, David W. Seyler, art director and sculptor, William E. Hentschel, designer, and Rosemary Dickman and Alza Stratton are down as decorators. These are all Art Academy of Cincinnati people except Bopp, who, I believe, is no longer an associate.

Their work is very much along the lines of what they were doing at Rook-

FIG. 1429. Small Kenton Hills jar called "Ox blood" but really of a crushed straw-berry color. Ht. 4¼".

FIG. 1427. Kenton Hills small yellow vase with white and brown decoration signed Hentschel. Ht. 5¼".

FIG. 1428. Kenton Hills porcelain vase with starch-blue glaze and well designed form and decoration. Ht. 12¾".

wood and Mr. Seyler has told me that they still regret conditions at the older pottery. Due to the war and draft, this organization has closed temporarily but plans to continue when hostilities cease. They also are trying to straddle the commercial fence and on which side they finally alight will be interesting to note.

INDIVIDUAL AND AMATEUR POTTERS

Certainly one of the most fundamental of our modern potters is Leon Volkmar of Bedford, N. Y., whom I show here at work in a few stills from his wonderful moving picture detailing every step of the making of a vase. He was born in France, 1879, studied in the National Academy from 1898 to 1901 and the year following took up the career of potter. His father, Charles, was a well known painter. He joined the Durant Kilns in 1911 and continued after the death of his associate Durant Rice in 1919, discontinuing the trade name in about 1928. His glazes include the copper blues and reds, aubergine, yellows, etc., and some browns and blacks. Applied designs, crystalline glazes, etc., never interested him as he was always trying for simple forms with fine color and texture. The Near Eastern influence was strong but never that of Japan. He says, "I have since held quite steadily that an artist's work that stems out of the historic past need not for that reason be lacking as an expression of that artist's personality; that originality does not consist in seeking out ways, types and processes that have never been thought of before for this way lies the 'novel,' the 'bizarre' and not least the 'commercial' in the commoner sense." He has done work for some of the finest patrons and is represented in several museums and has taught in Pratt Institute, Penn. Museum School of Industrial Art, Teachers College, Columbia University and was Professor of Ceramics in the University of Ceramics, Cincinnati.

It is impossible to give an idea of the depth and beauty of the glazes he has devised but the pieces shown will speak for themselves as to the integrity of his work and the fine sturdiness which most everything he touches seems to develop.

In the building of a vase we see him at work first "wedging" and "kneading" the clay to get it entirely a smooth and homogeneous mass. We will remember that this was all done with machines at the Lenox plant and the mass was kept thin for molding. The turning process demands infinitely more manual labor.

FIG. 1432. Copper reduction glaze of the texture of some Chün or flambé types. The form is also somewhat reminiscent of the Chün hexagonal flowerpots. Leon Volkmar. Cranbrook Foundation Mus.

FIG. 1430. Pottery with enamel decoration in turquoise, cobalt, yellow, aubergine and cream. Leon Volkmar.

FIG. 1431. Jar in turquoise, cobalt and cream which won the bronze medal in the Paris Exposition 1937. Leon Volkmar.

Next we see him carefully centering the lump of clay on the wheel and then, by foot power alone because it can better govern the speed, the turning begins and the lump is brought upward, while, at the same time, the inside is hollowed out. As the pressure from within might break through, the outer wall must be supported with one hand while the other works its way downward. Then a scraper is used to even the surface. (You will note that this is not a template with the form of the side already determined.)

The finishing touches are those in which the final refinements are accomplished and they take great care. I show Mr. Volkmar shaping a lip-rim. Later the surface has to be more or less smooth, the foot-rim must be shaped, etc., before the start of decoration and glazing and final firing during which, of course, the whole may be lost.

When one knows how thorough and painstaking the craftsman must be, what a skillful and tricky business it is to turn well on the wheel and how little the appreciation for honest craftsmanship is felt in this country; when one considers the knowledge and training necessary to make one good pot and the hard work involved in making every single good pot even after one knows all about it—then one can appreciate the courage that it takes to give a lifetime to this art, but, one way and another, many work at it.

In nearly every small town and in all the cities there are individual kilns

The clay has to be left out in the sun to dry partially after it has been put through a sieve and carefully strained. Here it is being picked up out of the container. Leon Volkmar.

A few steps in the making of a vase from a handful of clay. The pounding and wedging. Leon Volkmar.

Centering the lump on the wheel is a careful business the lack of which may end in catastrophe due to centrifugal force. I have seen a piece fly across the room. Leon Volkmar.

Here the actual turning has progressed somewhat and the clay has been pressed upward. Leon Volkmar.

LEON VOLKMAR SHOWS STAGES IN VASE-MAKING I

PLATE 238

Pressing from within and also from the outside, the hollowed cylinder is taking form. Leon Volkmar.

Here the scraper is brought into use to even up the grooves made by the fingers. Some Chinese potters feature these very grooves. (See Sung T'zu Chin wares.) Leon Volkmar.

As the neck takes shape the lip-rim is treated. When one notes the delicate handling in mid air and without arm rest, one begins to appreciate some of the paper thin lips of Ying Ching and other Chinese wares. Leon Volkmar.

The master-potter, after the tense effort, is putting the final surface touches upon his work. Through his mind is going a series of questions: Should the neck be pulled up and elongated a trifle? Does the lip flare sufficiently? Has the body enough lift in it? etc. Now everything is in a fluid moment of conception. Tomorrow it will have become a hard and well nigh permanent achievement. Leon Volkmar.

LEON VOLKMAR SHOWS STAGES IN VASE-MAKING II

Plate 239

in operation. In the times of our grandmothers when ladies painted pansies on everything from the coal scuttles to the bottoms of frying pans the artiness led to much china painting, and when the Japanese influence was felt from the Paris Exposition many went in for potteries. In time the Syracuse Museum of Fine Arts, whose director is Anna Wetherill Olmsted, became a sort of center.

In 1932 a small exhibition was organized in "Memory of Adelaide Alsop Robineau," and in 1936 an exhibition was organized to send to Kunstindustri-museum in Copenhagen, which later went to Stockholm, Gothenburg, Helsingfors, Stoke-on-Trent and the Whitney Museum, New York. It was financed by the Rockefeller Foundation.

The aims of this society are "To improve ceramic art in America, to educate the American public and to make sales for ceramic artists." A greater concentration on the first might further the latter projects. As sales made

FIG. 1434. "Student Singers" by Russell Barnett Aitken which has some element of cartoonist humor of a broad nature.

FIG. 1433. "Europa" by Russell Barnett Aitken.

FIG. 1435. Russell Barnett Aitken's cartoonist qualities again appear in "The Hunter."

Miss Olmsted mentions: 1.—The securing of a job with the late Dwight James Baum, architect, for "Edward Winter's enamels on sheet metal." 2.—The sale of a chess set by Peter Ganine for the purpose of manufacture in bakelite. What these did to further ceramic arts is doubtful. Miss Olmsted says, "Visitors have been frankly amazed after coming in a trifle high-hattedly with the expectation of seeing rows upon rows of dinnerware when they discover instead Archipenko's glazed terra cotta life-sized figures," and I should think they might be for I have heard of those who were amazed at almost anything done by this artist. By "glazed terra cotta," we suppose Miss Olmsted means pottery. The statement preceding this quotes, " 'More beautiful things for everyday life' runs the Swedish motto—and if Sweden, why not America?" What on earth would one do with a life-sized Archipenko figure in everyday life?

The paper ends with the flat statement that "American ceramic art has come of age and can hold its own with the contemporary output of any country in

the world." This is, of course, ridiculous for we cannot match either technically or artistically the modern wares of China, Japan, or Denmark. But let
us see the wares on which Miss Olmsted's boast is made.

Russell Barnett Aitken was given the frontispiece in the catalogue of the
last show before the war for a childlike bit of humorous cartooning called

FIG. 1437. Salt glazed stoneware
jar and cover by Charles M.
Harder. A good, sturdy job.
Charles M. Harder, Alfred, N. Y.

FIG. 1436. Jar and plate by Edgar Littlefield which won a prize in 1935. The forms and decoration are sound and the glazes appear interesting particularly in the mottled quality of the jar.

"Student singers." Besides this he also had two other of the sixteen illustrations. I leave the reader to judge the "Europa" and "Hunter" for themselves.

Edgar Littlefield received the first prize given by the Onondaga Pottery
for the fourth annual exhibition with some heavy but well formed pieces with

FIG. 1438. "Fish scale"
crackle glaze with slip decoration in gray and black.
This has nothing to do with
the Chinese "fish roe"
crackle, of course. The design gives good texture to
the piece. Charles M.
Harder, Alfred, N. Y.

FIG. 1439. This group of pieces by Gertrude and Otto Natzler are well potted and show a sensitive appreciation of form but the glaze in its weak interpretation of the rough Japanese feeling is
neither practical nor attractive. Syracuse Mus. of Fine Arts.

geometrical designs and soft glazes very reminiscent of the wares of Decoeur and other French followers.

Charles M. Harder's work is similar in its simplicity and attention to textures. He is the head of the department of industrial design at The New York State College of Ceramics at Alfred, N. Y., was born in Alabama but lived in Texas and graduated from The Art Institute of Chicago, the same school in which he is now teaching. He writes me, "When I do break down and decorate, I try to 'ram it into the wet clay' while the pot is fresh, and tie it up with the glaze treatment in such a way that it can't get away from the form." He likes, "plastic quality" and "function," as who does not. Glen Lukens is of simi-

FIG. 1440. Deep cup by Mary Yancey Hodgdon which has some good qualities though strongly influenced by the Japanese mannerisms of the 19th cent. The dish is by Glen Lukens. Syracuse Mus. of Fine Arts.

FIG. 1441. Two fairly well formed but thick and clumsy pieces by Glen Lukens finished in what he calls, "Death Valley raw yellow alkaline glaze." Syracuse Mus. of Fine Arts.

lar persuasion but covers his wares with what he calls, "Death Valley raw yellow alkaline glaze." Gertrude and Otto Natzler won another prize with some thin and well potted bowls with dry and what appear to be only partly fluxed glazes roughly applied to bowls and dishes which would certainly be hard to wash clean. Mary Yancay Hodgdon showed a wheel marked cup of Japanese style with a rich glaze inside and running irregularly over the lip. She also showed a dish with thick scratched out glaze design. Carl Walters in the eighth show had a plate reminiscent of 9th century Rakka ware and a weak imitation of the Egyptian hippopotamus with foliage patterns on the sides and top. Karl Drerup had a tall grey porcelain vase fired by Von Tury. Josef von Tury has made an ingenious arrangement with the Ford Works of New Jersey to use the space between toilet seats, and other large pieces which they fire, for his vases in the kiln. Tury is a well trained European ceramist and like Walter Howat has really been responsible for much that appears under the names of others.

None of the above work is any more than less-good imitations of styles already established by others, but Harold Riegger received a prize for a stoneware bottle unglazed, which is sure and has fine points. It recalls no ancient ware. The form is pleasing, the wheel marks well related to it and the whole

Three thinly potted and very beautiful small cups made by Frank Reuss Kelley, having underglaze decoration, slip and blended glaze decoration fired at about 2470° F. The slip-ware piece on the right has some characteristics of the Sung though it is in no way a copy. The center piece of softly blended ivory and dull brown tones is an example of the finest potting in all respects. Hts. about 2½" to 4".

Two charming cups by Paul Freigang showing fine porcelain forms and simple well related and original design.

MODERN AMERICAN PIECES

Plate 240

Left: Deep cup by Frank Reuss Kelley decorated with some of his own crystalline glaze which is deep blue with rose crystals evenly distributed and graduated from large to small at the top. Ht. about 5".

Right: This fine, sure piece of potting by Harold Riegger is one of the best examples of use of wheel marks for ornamentation that I have ever seen. Its proportions give it a towering upward lift, it has a good sturdy neck to grasp, a practical mouth for pouring and a well proportioned practical base. Syracuse Mus. of Fine Arts.

Left: Vase of beautiful form and fine proportions covered down to near the bottom with a transmutation glaze. Leon Volkmar. Mrs. Beagle Coll.

thing very satisfying. I shall be interested to see more of this man's work.

Henry Varnum Poor also won a prize for an oval bowl which is typical of his style. Mr. Poor is a painter of fair success in a modern manner and his wares are more interesting to him as presenting a surface on which he can draw or paint than objects conceived as beautiful entities in themselves. The quality is that of faïence or majolica, the clay he uses is local from Rockland County, N. Y. Though the craftsmanship is rather sloppy, it is sincere work and he may do something really fine yet.

Fig. 1442. The Hippopotamus is a frank copy of the Egyptian ones and shows a flowery character which is no improvement. The plate is strongly reminiscent of 9th cent. Rakka ware but lacking in the original vitality and strength. Both are by Carl Walters. Syracuse Mus. of Fine Arts.

Fig. 1443. Platter by Henry Varnum Poor which shows more promise than any of his earlier work. Syracuse Mus. of Fine Arts.

Sculptural work seems to take up fully half of the work of the Syracuse group despite their ambition for usefulness and perhaps the best is by Way-lande Gregory an erratic and changeable sort of man in both personality and work. It is hard to describe his endeavors for his restless virtuosity is now sensitive and delicate as in the "Head of Child," in this exhibition, now humorous as in the figures representing octaves in a "Musical Fountain," or the very baroque figure he has in the pool at his own home or again fearful as in his "Fountain of the Atom," at the New York World's Fair. He has told me that "Sex is the motive power," of much that he does and yet his work is so purposely distorted in most instances as not to make this element at all moving to the ordinary man. He has a kiln of his own and boasts that he does his own firing. I do not rate him as a first class sculptor but his things are amusing and he understands the medium, though it is his temperament to exaggerate.

Of the others, Paul Bogatay shows little. Sorcha Boru's naïve short-legged animals with stupid expressions are uninteresting, Carl Walters' similar ones are better designed and more interesting and a host of modelers of small figures such as Thelma Frazier, Alexander Blazys, Walter J. Anderson and Viktor Schreckengost have done things which are full of the tiresome cuteness called

FIG. 1444. These two things by Sascha Brastoff actually were awarded a prize for "unusual humor or whimsy" and Miss Olmsted says "they may well be in advance of their time." Syracuse Mus. of Fine Arts.

FIG. 1445. "Smoked Ham" is by Viktor Schreckengost and shows a very cute humor. Syracuse Mus. of Fine Arts.

"exquisite humor," by Miss Olmsted. It is to be noted that the general trick of the babies as seen in Frazier's, "Pegasi on Tracks," is very close to that

FIG. 1447. I do not know whether Thelma Frazier did this "Pegasi on Tracks" before Schreckengost's "Smoked Ham" or after but it is cute in an almost identical manner except that it is not carried out in true pottery, the structure being so conceived as to necessitate the use of a metal rod. Cup by Josef Von Tury who is a well-known technician and gets some pleasant, interesting glazes. Excellent form. Syracuse Mus. of Fine Arts.

FIG. 1446. Thelma Frazier seems to have paralleled another potter's perhaps too original idea for certainly there is here a similarity in what might be called baloney sausage forms to those shown by Brastoff. This is found "an outstanding piece of whimsical sculpture," by Miss Olmsted. Syracuse Mus. of Art.

on Schreckengost's "Smoked Ham." Another similarity is noticeable between the figures of Frazier's, "Marguerita and the Jewels," and Sascha Brastoff's, "Emergence." I sincerely hope that this is not going to be the commencement of a whole school or style of what Miss Olmsted says is "always delightful and with no trace of vulgarity."

This society represents a fair cross section of what is being done among independent and amateur potters of the country but there are a few more about whom we should have a word. Paul Freigang is an European trained

FIG. 1448. Cookie-jar by Arthur E. Baggs of salt-glazed stoneware. No new invention in loop handles but they are adequate to get fingers into which was not always the case even in Greek wares, and knob on cover is beautifully harmonized with them. An honest, intelligent piece of craftsmanship which rises to a degree of really fine art. Syracuse Mus. of Fine Arts.

FIG. 1449. Three pieces by Maija Grotell. Large cylinder 21" of dark grey body with semi-opaque white mat glaze. Two firings at 2400° F. Shape recalls Chinese "symbol of earth" save that it has not proper eight divisions and is round. Small cylinder 14½" is in blue-grey, tan and brown slip decorated and having "an ash glaze." One firing at 2450° F. Globular jar 12" has an "inlayed crackle glaze in pastel colors." It is a borax glaze and had two firings at 2400° F. Recalls spotted Yüeh and Lung-ch'üan wares.

FIG. 1450. Charming bit of reticulated ware surely and expertly handled, not quite the "devil's work" of the Chinese masters but having considerable charm of its own, by Paul Freigang.

FIG. 1451. Large and well modeled vase of sturdy proportions and interesting design by Paul Freigang. Stoneware.

potter who has been practicing in this country for many years and is not only a top notch technician but a very real artist The three vases, one with incised slip, one with low relief modeled design and one reticulated, show sturdy and sound form and well adapted design of original character. The bowls are charming in form and color. The two cups are exquisite in every feature. He is not active just now but has plans for starting a new kiln before long.

Maija Grotell is another excellent potter. She graduated from the Academy of Art and Industrie, Helsingfors, Finland, has taught in a number of good centers including the Henry Street Settlement and Rutgers University, and is now instructing in the Cranbrook Academy of Art, Michigan. The Metropolitan Museum and Detroit Institute of Art own examples of her work. She works largely in stoneware and seems to like the rough textured surfaces of a "modern art" vogue but understands good potting and some of her things have considerable charm.

Fig. 1452. Well made flower bowl of pottery showing Japanese influence but distinctly original in its carrying out. Mrs. Mary Door.

Fig. 1453. Well conceived and beautifully made bowl for flowers. Glaze is mat type well suited to form. Mrs. Mary Door.

A man who grew up in potting is Arthur E. Baggs born in Alfred, inoculated and partly educated by Charles F. Binns, Founding Director of the N. Y. State School of Clay Working and Ceramics, now the N. Y. State College of Ceramics at Alfred. He developed and finally became owner of the Marblehead Potteries, Mass., assisted in the development of the Cowan Pottery Studios, Rocky River, Ohio and taught at Ethical Cultural School, N. Y., Cleveland School of Art and finally at Ohio State University, where he now is. Mr. Baggs says his chief interests are: 1.— Creative experimenting in design and technology of ceramics, and 2.—trying to interest recruits in the same absorbing job. His cookie-jar of salt-glazed stoneware shows fine structural form and a useful and beautiful development of the old-time loop handles, and the cover-knob.

One of our best American potters, a great technician and true artist is Frank Reuss Kelley

Fig. 1454. Porcelain jar by Frank Reuss Kelley fired at about 2470° F. and decorated with his own glazes. This piece shows his fine feeling for good structural form. Ht. c. 9".

of Norwalk, Connecticut. He studied in Alsace and has made many hundreds
of experiments with various body clays and glazes with the result that he can
actually produce some of the most surprising and beautiful of effects. He tells
me that he has an open method of firing without a sagger. But his forms would
be outstanding alone for their vigor and sure potting sense. Unfortunately Mr.
Kelley is somewhat disgusted with the uphill job of earning a living at making
pottery and has now ceased to work. I sincerely hope that someone will come
along and make it possible for this truly fine artist to continue.

FIG. 1455. Modified
T'ang amphora designed
by the author and fired
by Walter Howat. Color
is dull chartreuse.

A few pieces which I have designed are also shown.
These were fired by Walter Howat as were most of the
following sculptured examples. Mr. Howat is a chemist
who worked at the Atlantic Terra Cotta Co. and then
set up a kiln in his own back yard at Tottenville, S. I.
He is aided by his wife and daughter and employs a
number of other assistants. Technically I believe he
knows more about the obtaining of various glazes in
textures and colors to suit the piece than any other
potter in America. These pieces of ours are designed
for lamp bases and the glazes are an excellent celadon
of both the Lung Ch'üan and "northern Sung" types,
"imperial yellow," coral red, starch blue, a Ming type
lead glaze, and the transparent type used on Tz'u Chou
forms over slip. Some of my forms are traditional, some
are adapted and slightly changed and some are entirely
without precedent. These are, of course, all molded
pieces though we have attempted to get some hand work
into the incising of the slips, making of handles, etc.

SCULPTORS

Lu Duble is a sculptress who spent several years in Haiti and has caught
the feeling of the natives very well in her "Head of a Young Woman" and

FIG. 1457. "Agriculture" by Henry
Kreis. Only 15″ long but has an almost
monumental feeling. Masses simply
handled and slight flattening of surfaces
and economy of detailed decoration give
it power.

FIG. 1456. Life-sized study of young woman in Haiti by Lu Duble. A good portrait, full of the
movement of these people. An outstanding terra cotta.

Original design Tz'u Chou type bottle by the author, carried out by Agnes and Walter Howat. Body buff-grey, the slip hand carved by Mrs. Howat.

A helical twist bottle designed for use with a celadon or thick yellow glaze which accents form and surface texture.

Small Tz'u Chou type vase having incised slip executed by Agnes Howat. Bold crackle stained after firing.

Original "fig formed" vase designed particularly to be used with celadon glaze which runs thin on high ridges and deep in grooves.

Yung Chêng vase form slightly modified. Colors yellow, iron red, pale blue and celadon.

Ming form modified and carried out in celadon, cream, coral red and imperial yellow glazes.

PORCELAINS DESIGNED BY WARREN E. COX AND
MADE BY WALTER HOWAT

PLATE 241

Right: Kneeling figure by Carl L. Schmitz, full of beautifully rounded masses showing fluid softness appropriate to terra cotta. It is interesting to compare this figure with the very similar one, in pose, of Mr. Snowden's which is more fleshlike and perhaps less expressive of the medium being not so heavy and potterylike in its development.

I have seen nothing which so well swung the animal rhythm of Negro dancers as this figure in terracotta by LuDuble.

Left: Interesting small terra cotta by George Snowden makes use of a modern sweater, and its removal, to build a figure composed of all fairly large masses, eliminating the smaller details of face and fingers. A lovely composition.

Right: "Mimi" by C. Paul Jennewein is a charming small glazed head of a baby with a delicate and elfish smile full of character and charm.

AMERICAN SCULPTORS' CERAMIC WORK

PLATE 242

"Dancer." She does not do her own firing as in fact do none of the following sculptors who look upon terra cotta simply as one medium in which to have their work carried out. However, these are well trained artists who perfectly understand the characteristics of the medium.

W. T. Benda has done some charming little heads which were fired by Walter Howat.

Henry Kreis, from Essen, worked at stone carving and other sculpture crafts in Europe and then for Joseph Urban, Carl Paul Jennewein and Paul Manship here. From about 1933 he has made terra-cotta figures which have a simple strength and a somewhat carved feeling. He prefers the medium because it is less expensive than bronze or marble—perhaps $10 cost for a portrait (for material and firing) against $200 for bronze and $500 for marble.

FIG. 1458. "Accordion Player," by Helen Clark Phillips in waxed terra cotta. Ht. c. 15".
FIG. 1459. Girl with a lute is graceful and noble in bearing. It has a monumental quality and is yet alive, expressing terra cotta and also flesh. To my mind the best of the figures Schmitz has done.
FIG. 1460. George H. Snowden certainly gets a fleshlike softness with all its appeal in many of his figures.

He writes me, "Besides, bronze and marble look very pretentious in the average home, while a terra-cotta portrait fits everywhere from the furnished room up. Furthermore a terra-cotta keeps the touch of the sculptor and is therefore a real original and this is not the case with the other materials. I would rather have a terra cotta of, let us say, Rodin, than a bronze cast, which on top of it all might exist 100 times."

He also writes, "I model a portrait by building it up hollow, usually a day previous. This way I do not lose any time in making the model wait, while the clay turns slightly harder." His firing was done by Paul Freigang.

Carl L. Schmitz is a friend of Kreis and was born in Metz. He studied in Munich under J. Wackerle and H. Hahn, came to this country in 1923 and became a citizen. He attended the Beaux Arts Institute and worked for Jennewein, Carl Milles and Paul Manship, opening his own studio in 1930. Here we have a most interesting contrast between the carver in Kreis and the modeler in Schmitz. Both are strong and sound men. Both have cast off all mannerisms, if they ever did have any. Both express themselves beautifully in the medium yet a little study shows that Kreis likes planes while Schmitz prefers rounded forms. Schmitz too has Freigang do his firing.

George H. Snowden was born in Yonkers and went to Yale, the Academy at Rome and the National Academy. His figures, particularly the female ones,

Perhaps the greatest ceramic achievement of our day is the tympanum done for one of the pediments of the Pennsylvania Mus. of Art by Mr. Jennewein and executed in colored glazes by Mr. Leon Solon of the Atlantic Terra Cotta Co.

Right: Wheeler Williams is a most alive and promising sculptor but uneven in his work. This baby's head with its damp, curly hair and eyes slightly out of focus is as fine as anything Houdon ever did.

Beautiful "Madonna and Child" by Helen Brett Babbington which shows fine composition and a full understanding of terra cotta in the surface modeling.

Left: The architect, Harry Lindeberg, was a fine subject for this terra cotta head by Wheeler Williams.

AMERICAN SCULPTORS' CERAMIC WORK

have a soft natural feeling almost alive and yet not entirely naturalistic, for they all seem to have fallen by chance into designs of real charm. A startling yet perfectly sound one is of a girl pulling off a sweater over her head. The conception is daring, for it might appear overmannered and smart but the direct and sincere treatment saves it from all of this, and the elimination of the features and hair brings the whole thing into a system of large curves. The body divides itself into three sized groups of masses: 1.—the smallest are the fingers, toes and features. 2.—The medium sized masses are the arms, lower legs and neck. 3.—The largest are the torso and thighs. Snowden by this natural and clever subject eliminates the details and keeps the larger proportionate masses. This figure is wonderfully modeled for one at once feels the softness of the breasts, the firmness of the thighs and the hardness of the ribs.

A true potter-sculptor who does his own firing is Albert Drexler Jacobson who studied at the Beaux Arts Institute, New York, the British Academy, Rome, etc. He was greatly influenced by the Post Impressionist movement in France and has done a number of things influenced by such artists as Brancusi, but also does very direct and excellent portrait work in terra cotta such as the head illustrated. He also makes some well potted vessels, strong in form and well decorated in both single and double firings at 2000° F.

Fig. 1461. Madonna from "The Shrine of the Americas," by Frederick Allen Williams and executed in glazed white porcelain by Walter Howat.

Fig. 1462. Two flower boxes made in 1914 by Paul Manship, showing some influence of Western Asia and one might also say of Japan in spacing and arrangement of figures. Very pleasant moving designs and suit their purpose well.

Marion Lawrence Fosdick graduated from the Museum School of Fine Arts, Boston, put in a year at the Kunstgewerbe Museum Schule, Berlin, was a pupil of George Demetrios, Hans Hofmann, etc., and then went to Alfred University where she has taught drawing, design and ceramics. She has exhibited widely and several of the museums own her work including the Metropolitan Museum of Art, New York.

Paul Manship is one of America's best known sculptors and I need not go into his history, for it is well known. I was disappointed to find that he had only done a little in ceramics. However, the flower boxes shown, which are in his "antique style," are sufficient to show that he could do great things in the medium.

There are many less well known individuals, too numerous to attempt to represent in full but about whom a whole book could be done. Just by chance I discovered the very lovely "Madonna and Child" by Helen Brett Babbington of Detroit, Michigan and although the problem of the hands has not been happily solved in this piece, the general modeling and composition is very fine and I think it a beautiful work of art. Again by chance alone, I found the work of Helen Clark Phillips who, having studied at the Paul Revere Pottery, Boston, and at Henry St. under Maija Grotell and T. S. Haile has done a very expressive Basque accordion player, and a number of well designed incised slipware pieces showing various animals, and some well designed stoneware. It is a good sign that these who do not profess to be great are, nevertheless, sound craftsmen.

FIG. 1463. Portrait by Albert Drexler Jacobson showing direct and proper plastic handling of terra cotta. Life size.
FIG. 1464. Jar by Albert Drexler Jacobson decorated with brown and black glazes and some green and white drips about lip-rim. Sturdy in form, design well related to form. Ht. c. 10".
FIG. 1465. "Memory" is classic in feeling but one is sure that it is because the subject actually had classic features. The glaze forms a soft haze about the lines that is appropriate and moving. By C. P. Jennewein.

C. Paul Jennewein was born in Stuttgart but came to this country when he was seventeen, studied painting and did some good mural work, served in the army in World War I, received the Prix de Rome and studied there also serving in the American Red Cross in Rome. The three heads of "Mimi," "Marietta," and the one called "Memory," show the wonderful genius of the man and would rank with anything of the sort that had ever been done. The first is mat and the other two in a sort of soft glaze that does not harm the modeling, which, it should be noted, has been kept simple and undetailed so that little crevices would not catch and hold too much of the glaze. These are emotional and lovely.

However, special attention should be drawn to the tympanum panel by Mr. Jennewein placed in one of the pediments of the Pennsylvania Museum of Art in Fairmount Park, Philadelphia, the figures for which range from 2 feet 1½ inches to the center one of Zeus or Jupiter which is 12 feet tall. Much has been published about this greatest achievement of architectural sculpture in pottery in America and it is not necessary here to go into detail, but when one realizes that the figures had to be made in several sections, that the shrinkage is about 1 inch to the foot in the material used in firing, that the glazes had to be sprayed on evenly and could not be touched by fingers before firing, and that all had to be so planned that perfect drainage could be obtained, as ice would chip and finally destroy the work, otherwise, you can begin to realize some of the difficulties encountered. Mr. Leon V. Solon handled the coloring with the aid of Walter Howat, and the Atlantic Terra Cotta Co. of Perth Amboy did the firing at 2300° F. The red and gold similar to that used on Lenox china had to be fired again at lower temperature, of course.

Frederic Allen Williams was a Beaux Arts and National Academy student and though born 1898 in West Newton, Mass., has been associated in the public mind largely with the West, for he has been in various localities there and lived in Taos. He also has a great interest in American Indians as can be seen in his "Madonna," "Maid of Taos," etc. His animal figures are also excellent and some have been designed and rendered in glazed porcelain. Walter Howat again does his firing.

Wheeler Williams was born in Chicago, attended the Art Institute and Yale, served in World War I, received his master's degree in architecture at Harvard and in 1922 started as a sculptor. The large terra-cotta figure with the dog is somewhat overstylized and not convincingly so. His glazed porcelain table decorations of police dogs and the four standing figures are fairly good decorative art but we see his real strength in the head of Harry Lindeberg, which is, as the saying goes, a speaking likeness. The head of Helen Wills Moody is again well done but lacks all the brilliance of McCartan's. Williams has seen the face as more fleshy, there are suggestions of rings under the eyes and a

FIG. 1466. Good design but never as good as that of McCartan, monumental quality yet not to be compared with "Girl With Lute" by Schmitz, parts of this figure are almost naturalistic while other parts, such as the breasts are rather poorly conventionalized, yet—it has a charm which lies perhaps in the lift of the head and the movement and this may be more of the model than of Wheeler Williams himself. It is life size.

relaxed almost dreamy expression not exactly as we worshippers of our great tennis champion would expect to see her. In his baby's head "Diana," he has struck the truest note so far in his ceramic work. In the slight pout of the lips, the sleepy, dreamy expression of the eyes which do not quite focus, the moist curls on the towseled head and the suggested faintest shadow of a smile he has caught everything in the mood of the just awakened baby. I feel that this head ranks with that best one by Houdon and who could say more? It is a superb example of terra-cotta art. The firing of this piece was by Paul Freigang and the other things were by Walter Howat and Von Tury.

At the same time Mrs. Moody posed for both McCartan and Williams and I am delighted to be able to show here the work of both men. Edward McCartan was born in Albany and studied under Herbert Adams, George Grey Barnard and Herman MacNeil. He also worked at the Beaux Arts, Paris. Probably everyone has admired his "Diana with Grey Hound," bronze but his terra cottas are no less beautiful. The dachshund, "Jonas," is one more which shows his love for and understanding of dogs. The portrait head of Miss Ruth Fletcher is one of the most brilliantly alive and vital little heads, for it is just under life size, that I have ever seen, and the head of Helen Wills Moody shows the keen alertness and moral stamina of this great champion whom we used to call "Little Poker Face." Again Howat does McCartan's firing.

FIG. 1467 "Jonas," by Edward McCartan, a fine terra cotta and all dog, an utterly simple piece of modeling but as vigorous as are the little dachshunds themselves.

These then are our great ones and Modern America need feel no lack of pride in them, for they are doing really living art which will last down through the ages and always give enjoyment. There are many others no doubt and it is a strange thing that one only hears by chance of this or that one having done an odd bit in fired clay. Perhaps this is the fault of the public.

America then has very bad industrial ceramics, rather poor individual and amateur ceramics but some great sculptors who have done wonderful things. Of course, the less strong artists of the second and first category took the pleasant short cut to various sorts of "modernistic art," but it is gratifying to see that the great and truly successful men have avoided these stylizations as they have in fact avoided any and all superficial stylization. A man's style should grow from the heart of his work outward and not be put on like a coat of many colors.

With the ironing out of our cities by air travel which certainly will flatten the present huge piles of skyscrapers and with the great wealth which this country is sure to enjoy after World War II it is hoped that a new renaissance will take place in the arts and that the ceramic arts will benefit with the others. There is no doubt but that Americans will have to learn how to use

Left: I do not know Ruth Fletcher but Mr. McCartan has certainly made me want to with this wonderful portrait. Terracotta, fired by Walter Howat after careful finishing of the cast by Mr. McCartan.

Center: Compare this head with that of Wheeler Williams of Mrs. Helen Wills Moody and you will see part of the reason that I hold Mr. McCartan as our present greatest sculptor. "Mac" saw not only the girl posing for him but the vital, piercing intelligence, superb muscle control and brilliant outguessing of an opponent which made this true and superb specimen of American womanhood the so-many-times champion.

Right: The Williams head of Mrs. Helen Wills Moody accents her classic beauty but gives her a dreamy look and shows a tired sagging of the muscles under her eyes and on her cheeks which perhaps might have been present as she posed. Her sensitive yet resolute mouth is beautifully rendered. Perhaps the hair is a little too wavy and too much conventionalized.

AMERICAN SCULPTORS' CERAMIC WORKS

PLATE 244

their leisure better, for they are going to have plenty of it along with plenty of everything else. Perhaps some of the now inarticulate masses will find means of becoming articulate. Meanwhile the plate for steaming food, the cup or mug for brimming drink and the image of clay may continue to charm a few simple souls like myself.

THE MARKS OF POTTERIES AND PORCELAINS

INTRODUCTION

My FIRST inclination was to exclude marks from this book entirely, for, as the reader will have gathered from my often repeated statements to that effect, *marks cannot be trusted*. The true collector is impressed first by the style, second by the paste of the ware where it is exposed at the foot-rim or elsewhere, third by the type of glaze, its condition, etc., fourth by the colors used, the slips if any; the details of decoration, etc. and finally, if he finds everything else characteristic and correct, the mark adds perhaps 1% more conviction in the attribution. Most marks are easier to copy than a single good, vigorous brush-stroke and perhaps that is the reason that many artists, as on the Caffaggiolo wares, painted the marks with a swift spontaneity. It will be remembered that in our section on Hispano-Moresque lustre potteries we have pointed out that the backs of the plates often show the quality of the artist who painted them better than the fronts for, "No imitator can get the same swift feeling in his strokes as can a man who has done hundreds in his own way." Thus in looking at a mark its style of drawing and character must also be taken into consideration and a swiftly drawn mark is more difficult to counterfeit than a careful and meticulous one, paradoxical as that may seem at first. Practically all marks have at one time or another been copied and particularly those of costly wares receive the attentions of cheats and fakers for obvious reasons.

Marks may refer to any one of a dozen different things: the name of a factory, the name of a manager of a factory, the name of an artist, the name of a town (and there are often more than one potteries in a town), the name of a certain potter, a series date, a formula of one sort or another, the trade mark of a merchant, an intended owner's name, etc. Many places in the 18th century purposely made their marks look as much as possible like those famous ones of Dresden and Sèvres to add to the confusion. Thus the meanings of marks in the study of ceramics have varied from authority to authority and from year to year, in many instances. I have mentioned in my text here and there the scorn with which Emil Hannover treats the inclusion of certain marks by Chaffers. Barber mentions a number of contradictions between Jacquemart and Fortnum. And all writers include a large number of marks the meanings of which are entirely unknown.

Such are the difficulties but so long as these pitfalls are borne constantly in mind, the study of marks is no doubt fascinating and to some people affords as much enjoyment as might the working out of a cross word puzzle. It, of course, has little to do with the appreciation of a true collector for those illusive appeals, a few of which I have attempted to point out in this book, may exist in large number and great strength on a piece with a certain mark, while they are entirely nonexistent in another piece which perfectly authentically carries the same mark. Again, of course, many of the very finest things have no marks at all. One thing, however, may be said with certainty and that is that no piece that carries a faked mark can possibly be a great work of art for sincerity is one characteristic that is absolutely necessary. Thus in a negative way the study of marks may benefit a collector, if he learns something about the imitative and downright counterfeit ones, for it stands to reason that the pieces which bear them are also imitative or counterfeit and to be avoided.

Just as there are some people who know the names of all the flowers but never actually perceived the beauty of one, so there are those who know where most pots are made but never really appreciated the beauty of one. Yet we cannot deny that taste and appreciation are fed by knowledge. Contrary to the self-flattering popular belief, no one was ever born with good taste. It is just that we must not confuse the food of knowledge with taste itself. Facts as to where a work of art was made, by whom and under what conditions all add to our understanding of it, to our final appreciation and in turn to the enlargement of our general taste just as food aids the athlete to build a strong body, *but the food is not the body* and a wealth of training, of spirit, of both inherited and environmental influences in addition to the food go to make the athlete. If this is true with the body of an athlete, certainly it is a thousand times more true with the mind of a man of taste.

At least a mark will show what a piece is supposed to be and that is a beginning. In the various comments which I have added to our section on marks aid will be found and, if the student reads that such and such a mark was "of Duesbury's time," he can look up Duesbury and find out who he was and when he lived, and will probably go on from there to find out more and more about Derby wares. Nearly every mark has a whole history behind it and only by finding out about that history can one be truly said to know a mark. Most students prefer to get a picture in their minds of the development-in-general of a certain sort of ware and leave the details of the marks to be looked up when they are confronted by a certain piece. That is just why such a list of marks as we have brought together is useful. How, then, does the collector go about this?

It will be noticed that we divide the wares described in our book into several large groups as follows:—POTTERIES, GLAZED POTTERIES, SLIP COATED POTTERIES, TIN GLAZED POTTERIES, LUSTRED POTTERIES, PAINTED FAÏENCE, MODELED POTTERIES AND STONEWARES, PORCELAIN and BONE CHINA. The first thing to do is to determine whether a piece is *pottery, soft paste, porcelain* or *stoneware*. The latter need not trouble us much for it is seldom marked anyway. Pottery is readily distinguished by its softness and usually heavy potting. But between real porcelain or "hard paste" and the various approximations of it called "soft paste," it is not always so easy for the inexperienced to judge. There need be little difficulty in this, however, if one once takes a small file and tries to cut the foot, where the paste is exposed, for it will be found out at once that real porcelain is very hard and the file makes no impression, while soft paste can readily be cut. The only exception to this rule is that the Chinese soft paste is so nearly like porcelain, it being, in fact, porcelain with a little steatite added, that it also resists the file. One having determined which type of ware one is looking up, the field is cut down to a far more narrow search.

Next considerations should have to do with style and here we run into some difficulties, but usually one can at least determine whether a piece is actually Chinese or Japanese on one hand or European on the other. This is not invariably so easy as it would appear, but usually it can be done. If it is Far Eastern and has a mark, there is nothing for it but to search through those marks of the different reigns until one finds it, remembering such points as that famille rose enamel did not occur until the very end of K'ang Hsi so that, if a piece appears earlier but has rose enamel on it, it must be actually later or have been redecorated. In general the wares available to western collectors and made in the Ming dynasty are heavy, far heavier than Ch'ing wares of later period, but this is not always so as we find bowls of the Yung Lo reign very early in Ming times to be exceedingly thin. In general K'ang Hsi and later wares have the foot-rims turned in grooves to fit stands but this does not say that all Ming pieces lacked this characteristic or that all later pieces have it. In general the painting of Ming pieces is more bold and direct than that of later pieces, but once again there are many exceptions to the rule. Only study can give the student a sort of sixth sense about such things. The same thing is true about European wares and only by comparing can one tell the differences between English wares made to copy Sèvres or Dresden, and the real thing. Many of the soft paste wares such as St. Cloud and Mennecy in France copied Chinese wares of Tê Hua, Fukien, white porcelain and others. Light transmitted through the Chinese specimens is warm while light through the French ones is greenish. Of course the first cannot be cut with a file while the latter can. The amazing thing is that the poorly modeled French ones bring prices often into four figures, the originals can be bought for a few hundred or sometimes even below $100. However, in general again, the difference is not hard to tell.

If a piece is European or English the next step is to run through the marks of this field until something is found that seems to compare. Then read the comments on it to determine whether or not there were variations. Beware of pieces which bear the well known marks of the best and largest factories for these are the ones most often imitated. Also look carefully at the drawing. For crowns, as an instance, occur on potteries of Italy, porcelains of Italy, Sèvres, certain Paris wares and some German porcelains, as well as on English wares. Anchors occur not only on Chelsea but also on wares of Venice, Sceaux, etc. quite naturally, and shields, fleur-de-lis and suns or stars are often encountered on wares that were not intended to be imitative in any way. Sometimes even the size is tell-tale.

When this is all accomplished and you have coldly weighed the evidence, it is often wise to get the opinion of your curator at the museum, of some reputable dealer who handles the type of wares you are interested in or of private collectors who have handled many similar specimens. Opinions may differ here and there but it is surprising how very much alike are the opinions of those who really know. Such opinions are well worth paying for, for it is evident that the pitfalls are many and varied. However, the sport is worth the chance and the hazards only add to the enjoyment of victories attained.

We have listed here all the important marks, the basic ones and only those marks that are generally accepted as authentic. A few doubtful marks are included, but they are so designated.

Numbers at the top of the page in the following index of marks refer to the pages where the corresponding marks are illustrated. Similarly, numbers accompanying the illustrated marks refer to the pages on which the marks are discussed.

INDEX OF MARKS SECTION

* BARBER'S MARKS WITH NOTES, AND WITH THE NOTES ALSO OF
CHAFFERS, HANNOVER, ETC.

1.—Marks on Pottery of Italy.
2.—Marks on Wares of Italy, Persia, Rhodes, Hispano-Moresque, etc.
3.—Marks on Pottery of France.
4.—Marks on Pottery of Belgium and Holland.
5.—Marks on Pottery of Switzerland and Germany, Sweden, Spain and Portugal.
6.—Marks on Porcelain of Italy, Spain and Portugal.
7.—Marks on Porcelain of Sèvres.
8.—Marks Used by Painters, Decorators and Gilders at Sèvres.
9.—Artists' Signatures Found at Full Length on Sèvres.
10.—Marks on Porcelain of France.
11.—Marks on Porcelain of Germany and other European Countries.
12.—Marks on Pottery and Porcelain of England.
13.—Marks of Pennsylvania Potteries.
14.—Marks of New Jersey Potteries.
15.—Marks of New York Potteries.
16.—Marks of New England Potteries.
17.—Marks of Ohio Potteries.
18.—Marks of Southern Potteries.
19.—Marks of Western Potteries.
20.—Private Marks of Rookwood Decorators.
21.—Marks on Chinese Wares.
22.—Marks on Japanese Wares.

---

* Barber's Marks by courtesy of A. M. Maddock.

MARKS ON POTTERY OF ITALY

1-25.—*Caffaggiolo,* Caffagiuolo, Cafaggiolo or Cafagguolo. The most frequent form of the mark is seen in Nos. 1, 4, 5, 6, 7, in which a P has a dash across the upright, while the curved line at top is continued upward to make an S, thus forming a monogram which includes S.P.F. Senatus Populus Florentinus ?) or S.P.R. (Senatus Populus Romanus ?). Both these inscriptions are of frequent occurrence in Caffaggiolo decorations. Molinier suggests the meaning as an abbreviation of "Semper" one of the mottoes of the Medici and Hannover says, "The interpretation is the more probable as another of these mottoes, the word 'Glovis' (*si volg* read backwards) occurs on Caffaggiolo wares." The form of the mark varies widely often being little more than a P with the lower part crossed by a wavy line. It is found in one instance on Damascus ware.

3.—Doubtful. Fortnum says it is from Faenza.

5.—On a plate also marked *In Caffagiuolo.* Hannover says the monogram is sometimes accompanied by a trident, but of the trident, which also occurs among Faenza marks, absolutely nothing is known.

6.—On a plate also marked *Cafagioli* and on a dish marked *In Caffagiuollo.*

9.—The usual mark with C or G and under it *In galiano nell ano 1547;* under this the artist's initials A F *f (ecit),* possibly, suggested by Hannover, *Antonio Fattorini.* Galiano is a village near Caffaggiolo, where the artist may have worked.

11.—An undeciphered mark on an early plate with the Virgin and Child. This is not certainly of Caffaggiolo, but possibly of Faenza.

12.—Three marks uncertain. One on a plate in the collection of Baron Gustav de Rothschild is dated 1507.

21-30.—Caffaggiolo. Marks 24, 28, 29, 30 are doubtful. 26 occurs in a very large size on a dish attributed by Delange to Faenza, by Fortnum to Caffaggiolo.

31, 32, 33.—SIENA 31 is on a plate painted in blue *"a porcelan"* and is a mark of *Maestro Benedetto,* chief potter and artist there. Douglas states he was the son of a certain Maestro Giorgio of Faenza. A plate in the Victoria and Albert Museum is signed in full: *fata ĩ Siena da m⁰ Benedetto.* 32 has been mistaken for a mark of Pesaro. #32 and 33 are also assigned to Benedetto, but Fortnum thinks them initials of owners of the objects. (See 200)

34.—PISA.

35.—Unknown. On a box with emblems of Cosmo de' Medici.

36, 37, 38.—MONTE LUPO. 38 is on a dish dated 1663, and has been assigned by some to Monte Feltro.

39-47.—GUBBIO. These are various forms of the signature of *Maestro Giorgio Andreoli;* 43 is perhaps the most frequent. The marks are frequently very large. The upper initials in 39 are, perhaps, those of the owner.

47.—Mark of *Maestro Giorgio* in very large size on a dish with bathing scene, called "Diana and her Nymphs surprised, etc." Hannover says, "Maestro Giorgio signed his name in full only on his most important works; thus we have M⁰ Giorgio 1520 a di 2 de O'tobre in Ugubio. As a rule he signed himself merely M.G. or M.G. *da Ugubio* in a large careless hand. His latest dated works belong to 1541; he seems to have died in 1552." Pieces also bear the initials M,R,D and more often N but, as these never occur with the master's signatures, they may be the initials of assistants.

48.—A similar form of mark was used in the 16th and 17th centuries on goods, etc., by merchants; also found on merchant's seals. More commonly the top forms a figure 4. Perhaps it is a trade mark of a merchant. A similar form occurring in mark 52 is thought by Jacquemart to indicate ecclesiastical dignitaries, or pharmacies attached to Monasteries. The mark 48 occurs on several pieces.

49, 50.—Maestro Giorgio

51.—G.A. for Giorgio Andreoli

52.—Maestro Giorgio, with mercantile or religious sign. (See 48)

53, 54.—Maestro Giorgio: some read *Maestro Gillio.*

55.—Gubbio, supposed later than Giorgio.

56.—On a dish by Giorgio dated 1518.

59–61.—Marks assigned to *Maestro Vincenzio,* or *Cencio.* Hannover says, "His son, *Vincentius Andreoli,* is commonly regarded as identical with the *Maestro Cencio* mentioned by Piccolpasso as the only possessor in his time of the secret of red lustre."

62.—Gubbio

63.—Gubbio. Mark of the master *Prestino,* whose signature also occurs in full. A relief of the Madonna in the Louvre is signed *1536 Perestinus* and Hannover gives another example signed: *1557 in Gubbio per mano di Mastro Prestino* (that is "the Rapid Painter") and adds about his works that, "We may suppose that they were typical of the period of decadence."

64.—Gubbio. Probably *Maestro Vincenzio.*

65.—Gubbio

66.—Gubbio or Diruta. Uncertain.

67.—Gubbio

68.—Gubbio. Jacquemart thinks the letters mean *Mater Gloriosa,* not *Maestro Giorgio.*

69.—Gubbio. Probably *Prestino.*

70, 71, 72, 73.—Marks found on Gubbio wares.

74–85.—CASTEL-DURANTE

74, 76, 77, 78, 79.—Trade marks perhaps of dealers, found on Castel-Durante wares. (See #48)

81.—Signature of *Giovanni Maria, vasaro,* and date 12 Sept., 1508. Note:—Hannover says, "It is signed: *1508 a di 12 de Seteb. facta fu i Castel Durāt. Zona Maria Vro;* that is to say, it was made at Castel-Durante, on September 12, 1508, by 'Zona Maria Vasaro (The Potter'." (See text.)

83.—Doubtful. Castel-Durante or Fabriano. Mark of painter or owner.

85.—On cups, etc., made of dust of the Santa Casa at Loretto.

86.—URBINO. Mark on inferior work. Mr. Fortnum thinks of a young artist.

87–111.—Urbino.

87.—Attributed to Flaminio Fontana. Note:—Hannover says, "This style," (That of the Gonzaga service c.1519), "passed from Nicolo Pellipario (this was really his name)," (Not the usually used *Nicola da Urbino* who was really a native of Castel-Durante.), "to his followers, who assumed the name of Fontana." The first was Guido who signed *Guido da Castello Durante, Maestro Guido Fontana Vasaro,* and *Guido Durantino in Urbino.* "However this may be, Guido Fontana, son of Nicola da Urbino, had himself three sons, Orazio, Camillo and Nicolo. Of the last two nothing is known." Who Flaminio Fontana was I do not know.

88.—Unknown artist on a plate with St. Luke.

89, 97.—*Nicola da Urbino.*

90.—*Orazio Fontana.*

91.—Attributed by Passeri to Orazio Fontana, but #93 is on work much later.

92.—Unknown artist.

94.—On work of *Orazio Fontana.*

95.—Orazio Fontana.

96.—Orazio Fontana. The Greek *Phi* may be a monogram of O *f* and the *Delta* mean Durantino.

98, 99, 100, 106.—Signatures of *Francesco Xanto.*

101.—On one of the pieces of the Gonzaga-Este service, by Nicola da Urbino.

102.—On a dish painted with St. Jerome.

103.—*Francesco Durantino.*

104, 105, 109, 112.—Found on Urbino work.

107.—Initials of Gian. *Maria Mariani,* dated 1542.

108.—Attributed to *Luca Cambiasi.*

110.—*Alfonso Patanazzi.*

111.—CITTA DI CASTELLO. On a plateau sgraffiato.

113.—VITERBO. Date 1544.

114, 115, 116, 117.—DIRUTA.

118, 119, 120.—Diruta.

121.—FABRIANO.

122, 123, 124.—ROME.

125–141.—FAENZA. 125 and 126 are typical marks of the Casa Pirota. 127 is a frequent mark. 131 is the date 1491 between the letters M and G, which may imply *Mater Gloriosa*. 134, 135, 136, 144 are all of the same workshop.

142–156.—Faenza.

142.—On a plate with allegorical subject. B.M. for *Baldasaro Manara*.

143.—Casa Pirota. A frequent mark in similar form. (c.1525). Note:—Hannover mentions two plates of fine workmanship signed *Fata in Fae*(nza)—*Josef I* (n) *Ca*(sa) *Pirota 1525*, and *Fato in Faenza in Caxa Pirota*, respectively.

144.—On a plate representing Solomon. Lazari reads the mark G.I.O., but Fortnum thinks it is T.M. in antique letters.

145.—Doubtful. Faenza or Caffaggiolo.

155.—Said to be on a piece with the name of Giovano of Palermo, and the words *in Faenza*. Doubted by Jacquemart.

157.—FORLI. On a plaque date 1523.

158, 159.—Forli. Signatures on Forli wares are known also of *Moiero da Forli*, and *Leuchadius Solobrinus* 1564.

160. RAVENNA.

161.—*In arimin. Rimini.*

162.—RIMINI.

163–168.—VENICE.

165.—On a plate from the botega of *Mo Ludovico*. Other Venice pieces are marked *In Botega di Mo. Jacomo da Pesaro;* and *Jo Stefano Barcello Veneziano pinx.*

Note:—CANDIANA 1620, is a mark on a plate. There is no such place as Candiana. The word may be Venetian.

169.—Venice.

170.—On a plate seemingly Venetian.

171.—CORNARO.

172.—TREVISO.

173, 174, 175.—BASSANO. The *Terchi* family. The mark 173, which is the iron crown, is also on other fabrics.

176.—VERONA. Illegible mark, the enamel being broken. It occurs on a plate under the words 1563 *adi* 15 *zenaro. Gio Giovanni Batista da faenza in Verona.*

177, 178.—PADUA.

179.—GENOA. A lighthouse hanging out a signal.

180.—Attributed to Genoa by M. Demmin.

181.—SAVONA. The shield mark is drawn in various shapes, often with a few dashes of the brush, and is accompanied by a variety of letters.

182.—Savona.

183.—Savona. *Gio. Anton. Guidobono.*

184.—Savona.

185.—Savona. Solomon's knot.

186.—TURIN. Escutcheon of Charles Emanuel, 1638.

187.—Turin. Escutcheon of Victor Amadeus, 1713.

188.—Turin. Cross of Savoy and trumpet.

189.—MAURIENNE.

190.—MILAN.

191, 192.—Milan. *Felice Clerice?*

193.—Milan. *Pasquale Rubati.*

194.—Milan.

195, 196.—LODI.

197.—TREVISO.

198, 199.—NOVE.

200.—SIENA. Initials of Campani?
201.—PESARO. *Casali and Caligari,* 1763.
202.—SAN QUIRICO. Arms of Chigi. Date 1723.
203.—NAPLES. Vases; one inscribed *Paulus Francus Brandi Pinx.*
204, 205, 206, 207.—On same class of Naples vases.
208, 209.—Naples. *Del Vecchio* fabric, impressed marks.
210.—Naples. Attributed to Capo-di-Monte.
211.—Naples. *Giustiniani,* impressed. Other marks of this fabric are the name in full; the letter G, the name with I.N. and a vase.
212.—Attributed to Naples and to Castelli. We have it on wares found in Germany. Mr. Fortnum thinks German.
213, 214, 215.—CASTELLI; 213, *Saverio Grue;* 215, *Liborius Grue.*
216–230.—Unknown marks on Italian pottery.

MARKS ON WARES OF ITALY, PERSIA, RHODES, ETC.

231.—Persia. Painted in blue on a hard paste porcelain bowl.
232.—Unknown. On a hard paste porcelain bowl. Engraved through the glaze.
233.—Unknown. The square mark painted in blue, the characters engraved through the glaze, on a hard paste porcelain bowl.
234.—Persia. In blue on hard paste porcelain bowl.
235.—Persia. In blue on hard paste porcelain vase.
236.—Persia. In red on vase, apparently soft paste porcelain.
237.—MANISES, in Spain. On copper lustred ware. (Chaffers.)
238.—On a Hispano-Moresque plate, 15th century. (Chaffers.)
239.—On a Hispano-Moresque dish, gold lustred. (Chaffers.)
240.—On a Persian or Damascus ware jug.
241.—RHODES. Given by Marryat as found on Rhodian wares, supposed to represent the cross of the Knights.
242.—On a flask of "artificial porcelain paste, perhaps engobe," with design eminently Persian, but showing Chinese influence, brought from Persia. (Fortnum.)
243.—Persia. Name of maker, *Hatim,* on Persian pottery.

MARKS ON POTTERY OF FRANCE

1.—On a green enameled plate are escutcheons of arms of Frence provinces, and the one given here, which contains part of the arms of Beauvais and the name of *Masse,* perhaps of the artist. An inscription ends with *Fait en Decembre* 1502, or as Jacquemart reads, 1511.
2.—POITOU. The Goose of Thouars, found on a vase; supposed reference to Orion.
3.—AVON. Mark on the Nurse and other figures which were formerly attributed to Palissy.
ROUEN. All other marks which are not numbered, are found on pottery of Rouen. Many of these are similar to marks on Delft. The only artists' signatures known are the two, easily read, of *Dieul,* who decorated *faience a la corne.*
Still other marks painted, sometimes rudely, on Rouen were as follows (These are not in facsimile.): Ro, Go, G₃, DV, Gm., M, RD, GL, PP, Mo, HC, Mv, P.D, GMd, R, DL, HM, WGt, G., GW, S., Gi, HT and Mrs. Guillibeaux.

1, 2, 3.—LILLE. François Boussemart.

LILLE. Note:—Hannover mentions the five factories and the earliest pieces which date 1716 (See text.) and over 50 years later.

4.—Lille. Féburier and Boussemaert (or Fevrier and Boussemart).

5, 6.—Lille. Barthelemi Dorez, 1709–'15. His grandson signed N. A. Dorez, in 1748.

7, 8, 9.—Lille; 7, about 1788; (?) 8, Petit?

10.—VALENCIENNES. *Louis Dorez.*

11, 12, 13, 14, 15.—ST. AMAND LES EAUX. *P. J. Fauquez.* (Pierre Joseph.)

16.—PARIS. *Claude Reverend's* mark.

17, 18.—Paris. On ware resembling Reverend's.

19.—SCEAUX. Mark of Glot (Richard), who also marked with the word *Sceaux.* Prior to 1772 the mark had been S X.

20.—Sceaux? or Bourg la Reine? Doubtful.

21.—Sceaux. Glot's period. (Hannover says this SP was after the Duke of Penthièvre had assumed patronage. It stood for Sceaux-Penthièvre.) It occurs with or without anchor, referring to the Duke as Grand Admiral.

22.—BOURG LA REINE.

23.—ST. CLOUD. *Trou's mark.*

24, 25, 26.—SINCENY. 25 is signature of Pellevé (Pierre) who came from Rouen with workmen and artists, and later founded Saint-Denis-sur-Sarthon.

27, 28, 29, 30, 31, 32.—APREY. The factory monogram Ap, with initials of Jarry and other artists.

33.—MATHAUT.

34, 35—NIDERVILLER. Beyerle period. The mark is B N in monogram.

36, 37, 38, 39.—Niderviller. Custine period. These are very similar to the marks of Kronenburg and Ludwigsburg.

40.—SARREGUEMINES. *Utzchneider & Co.*

41.—STRASBOURG. *Charles Hannong.*

42, 43, 44.—Strasbourg. *Paul Antoine Hannong.*

45, 46, 47.—Strasbourg. *Joseph Adam Hannong.*

48.—Strasbourg or Hagenau. Possibly *Balthasar Hannong.*

49.—PREMIERES, in Burgundy. *J. Lavalle.* Other marks are J L P in a script monogram.

50.—MEILLONAS. *Madame de Marron.*

51, 52.—VARAGES.

53, 54, 55.—TAVERNE. *Gaze,* director.

56–86.—MOUSTIERS. The marks including a monogram of O L are attributed to Joseph Olery. Some are his but Jacquemart doubts many. 86 is supposed signature of *Foque,* successor to *Clarissy.* Names, perhaps of Spanish artists—*Soliva, Miguel Vilax, Fo Gianzel, Cros*—occur. A potter, *Ferrat* about 1760 signs his name. *Pierre Fournier* signs work dated 1775; *Antoine Guichard,* in 1763; *Thion,* in the last century. *Moustiers* appears as a mark written and also applied through pricked points. Viry, painter, signs a plate.

87–95.—Moustiers. 87 and 88 are marks of *Feraud,* potter. 95 is probably Olery. The others are uncertain.

96–98.—MARSEILLES. The fleur-de-lis is attributed to *Savy* after 1777.

99–102.—Marseilles. *J. G. Robert.*

103, 104.—Marseilles. *Veuve Perrin.*

105.—Marseilles. *A Bonnefoy.*

106.—Marseilles. *J. Fauchier.*

107.—MARANS. *J. P. Roussencq.*

108, 109.—Marans.

110.—RÉNAC. (Jacquemart.)

111.—ORLEANS.

112–123.—NEVERS. 112 is the earliest known signature; 113 Denis Lefebvre; 114, Jacques Bourdu; 115, 116, Henri Borne on statuettes; 117, Jacques Seigne; 119, Dominique Conrade, third of the name, 1650–'72; 120, Etienne Born; 121, François Rodriguez; 122, Nicholas Viodé; (?) 123, from the Conrade arms.

124.—LIMOGES. Massié.
125.—LA TOUR D'AIGUES.
126.—*Avisseau,* modern potter at Tours (Died 1861.)
127–146.—Unknown marks on French pottery.
147–183.—Unknown marks found on French pottery. On a basin is the mark ALEX 1724. On a bas-relief is the name *J. Alliot.*

MARKS ON POTTERY OF BELGIUM AND HOLLAND

1–3.—TOURNAY. Marks probably of *Peterynck.*
4.—TERVUEREN. ?
5.—MALINES. Attributed by Jacquemart.
6.—BRUGES. *Henri Pulinx.* (or Pulinckx) (1753– ?) Graesse gives 8 unsubstantiated marks for this place.
7.—LUXEMBOURG. Mark of the brothers *Boch* before the French Revolution.
8.—Luxembourg. Subsequent mark impressed.
9, 10.—Luxembourg.
11–19. Unknown marks on Flemish pottery.
20.—AMSTERDAM, 1780–'83. *Hartog v. Laun.*
21–40.—DELFT.
21.—*Samuel Piet Roerder.*
22, 23, 24.—*Suter van der Even,* 1580.
28.—Factory with the sign of *De Metaale Pot,* 1639.
29, 30.—*De Paauw* (The Peacock), 1651.
31.—*Jacobus de Milde,* 1764.
32.—*Martinus Gouda.*
33.—*Q. Kleynoven,* 1680.
34.—*Cornelius Keyser, Jacobus Pynaker and Adrian Pynaker* 1680. (or Pijnacker according to Hannover).
37.—*Jan Jansz Kuylick,* 1680.
38.—*Johannes Mesch,* 1680.
39.—*T'Fortuyn* (The Fortune), 1691.
40.—Widow of Pieter van der Briel.
41–81.—Marks deposited in the Hotel de Ville, Delft, in 1764, by potters designating their shop names. These are not always given in facsimile.
41–45.—DE WITTE STER (The White Star). *A. Kielle.*
46.—IN DER VERGULDE BOOT (The Gilded Boat). *Johannes der Appel.*
47–49.—DE ROOS (The Rose). *Dirk van der Does.*
50.—DE KLAAUW (The Claw). *Lambertus Sanderus.*
51, 52.—DE DRIE KLOKKEN (The Three Bells). *W. van der Does.*
53–56.—DE GRIEKSE A (The Greek A). *J. T. Dextra.* 1765, the works passed to *Jacobus Halder Adriaensz* (M.56).
57.—DE DRIE PORCELEYNE ASTONNEN (The Three Porcelain Barrels). *Hendrick von Hoorn.*
58, 59.—DE ROMEYN (The Roman). *Petrus van Marum.* The same year the manufactory passed into the hands of *Jan van der Kloot Jansz* (M.59).
60.—T'JONGUE MORIAANS HOFFT (The Young Moor's Head). Widow of *Peter Jan van der Hagen.*
61–63.—IN T'OUDE MORIAANS HOFFT (The Old Moor's Head). *Geertruy Verstelle.*
64, 65.—DE PORCELEIN BYL (The Porcelain Axe). *Justus Brouwer.* Occurs frequently.
66, 67.—DE DREI PORCELEYNE FLESCHJES (The Three Porcelain Flasks) *Hugo Brouwer.*
68–70.—T'HART (The Stag). *Hendrik van Middeldyk.*

71.—DE TWEE SCHEEPJES (The Two Ships). *Anth. Pennis.*

72–74.—DE PORCELEYNE SCHOOTEL (The Porcelain Dish). *Johannes van Duyn.*

75.—DE VERGULDE BLOMPOT (The Gilded Flower Pot). *P. Verburg.* The mark is not facsimile.

76.—DE PORCELYN FLES (The Porcelain Bottle). *Pieter van Doorne.*

77.—DE DUBBELDE SCHENKKAN (The Double Pitcher). *Thomas Spaandonck.*

78–80.—DE LAMPETKAN (The Ewer). Widow of *Gerardus Brouwer.*

81.—DE TWE WILDEMANS (The Two Savages). Widow of *Willem van Beek.*

Note:—All the unnumbered marks are found on pottery apparently of Delft; but their signification is unknown. It is important to note that similar marks are found on wares of Rouen, and other factories. The collector will exercise judgment as to paste and style of decoration before assigning specimens, and will frequently find it impossible to decide where a piece was made.

MARKS ON POTTERY OF SWITZERLAND, GERMANY, SWEDEN, SPAIN AND PORTUGAL

1, 2.—ZURICH.

3.—WINTERTHUR. On an escritoire. (Jacquemart.)

4.—Anspach (Bavaria).

5, 6, 7, 8, 9.—BAIREUTH. Sometimes the name in full.

10, 11, 12.—FRANKENTHAL. 10 and 11 are marks of *Paul A. Hannong;* 12, of *Joseph A. Hannong.* It is not possible to distinguish the first mark from Hannong's when at Strasbourg.

13.—GOGGINGEN, near Augsburg, established about 1750.

14.—Harburg. Initials of *Johann Schaper.*

15, 16, 17.—HÖCHST. 15 has the G for (Göltz) *Geltz;* 16 the Z for Johann Zeschinger; 17 is the wheel alone, the arms of Mayence. (Also note Hannover states the FH is for Friederich Hess, the I.H. for Ignaz Hess, the AL for Adam Löwenfinck and there are others such as B.B., G.C., M.S., L.R. and AMB which "await interpretation.")

18.—POPPELSDORF. Wessel's manufactory; impressed. Also found impressed with the name *Mettlach* on pottery of that place.

19, 20, 21, 22, 23.—NUREMBERG. M. Demmin gives a monogram of H C D, and date 1550, as on a stove. *Glüer,* probably an artist, signs a dish with *Nurnberg 1723.* Plates are signed *G. F. Greber Anno 1729 Nuremberg. Stroebel* signs a bell, with date 1724, and a dish painted, with date 1730. A stove of green tiles, with religious subjects, has the signature of *Hans Kraut,* and date 1578. *Hans Kraut* was the great potter of Willingen.

24.—SCHREITZHEIM.

25, 26, 27.—STRALSUND.

28–43.—Unknown marks on German pottery.

44–56.—Unknown marks on German pottery.

57–62.—RORSTRAND. According to Mrs. Palisser 61 and 62 are probably signatures of *Arfinger.* Chaffers gives a mark, *Storkhulm 22, 8. 1751 D H B,* as of the factory after Rorstrand was united to Stockholm. The marks include the date, price and signatures of artists. *Stockholm* is found, and also *Rorstrand,* impressed.

63.—Rorstrand, or Marieberg, or Kiel ?

64–69.—MARIEBERG.

70.—Swedish ?

71.—KÜNERSBERG.

72.—Künersbarg.
　　GUSTAFSBERG, 1820 to 1860. The mark is the name with an anchor.
　　HELSINBURG. Given by Chaffers as on stonewares, made from 1770.
73–79.—KIEL.
80, 81.—ALCORA.
82, 83.—Attributed to *Seville*.
84, 85.—LISBON.
　　For marks on pottery of Russia and Poland see porcelain section.

MARKS ON PORCELAIN OF ITALY, SPAIN AND PORTUGAL

1.—FLORENCE. On Medicean porcelain. The arms of the Medici and initials of Franciscus Medici Magnus Etruriae Dux Secundus. (Hannover gives it Franciscus Maria Medicis Magnus Dux Etruriae Secundus, but also illustrates the six palle with the two upper ones only bearing Ms.)

2.—Florence. On Medici porcelain. Dome of the cathedral of Florence.

3.—Tablet held by a lion in the decoration of a bowl. (This I do not think a Medici mark.)

4, 5, 6, 7.—DOCCIA. Near Florence. (Hannover says, "Among the earliest of its productions are certain cups signed by *Anreiter*.") (He also adds, "As early as 1821, when the famous Neapolitan factory closed down, Doccia acquired the models for the relief porcelain of Capo di Monte, and for the past thirty or forty years has copied them en masse, unscrupulously adding the mark of the originals.")

8, 9, 10, 11.—LE NOVE. 10 and 11 are signatures of *Gio. B. Antonibon*.

12, 13.—VENICE. *Vezzi*; impressed or in red.

14, 15, 16.—Venice. *Cozzi*; in red, blue or gold. This mark must be distinguished from that of Chelsea in England.

17.—Venice.

18–26.—NAPLES. CAPO-DI-MONTE factory. 18 is supposed to be the earliest mark, in blue. (Hannover says, "The mark of the factory during the first period (that of Charles III) was the Bourbon fleur-de-lis, either uncolored (Impressed) or painted in blue, more rarely in red or gold.") The fleur-de-lis was also used at Buen Retiro factory in Madrid, as given below. 21, 22, 23, 24 are marks of Ferdinand IV. in and after 1759. The crowned N is often reversed in the mark. The marks are sometimes in color, sometimes impressed.

GIUSTINIANI, of Naples made hard paste porcelain, using the same marks as on pottery. (See 211 in section on wares of Italy, Persia, Rhodes, etc.—pottery.)

27–31.—MADRID. Marks of the *Buen Retiro* factory. This factory was an outgrowth of Capo-di-Monte in Naples, and used the fleur-de-lis mark also. 27 and 28 are the cipher of Charles III. 29 is M, for Madrid.

32.—VISTA ALLEGRE, near Oporto, Portugal.

33, 34, 35.—TURIN, Italy; *Vineuf* factory of Dr. Gionetti, impressed or scratched. The cross is also sometimes accompanied by scratched lines, forming VN in monogram.

MARKS ON PORCELAIN OF SEVRES

1.—VINCENNES. The interlaced double L, the initial of the king's name, was adopted by the Vincennes factory shortly after its foundation, and used until 1753. The mark, unaccompanied by other letters, is rarely, if ever, found on porcelain made at Sèvres. After the removal of the factory to Sèvres, this mark, accompanied with date letters, as hereafter explained, continued the typical mark of the factory down to the Revolution.

2.—Vincennes. The mark was usually in this form, with a dot in the monogram. Marks 1 and 2 should be found only on pieces made prior to 1753.

3.—Vincennes and Sèvres. In 1753, at Vincennes, the system of dating by letters of the alphabet was adopted, A being 1753, B 1754, etc. (See table in text.) (Note:— Barber here gives QQ-1794 and RR-1795 which Hannover omits.) This mode of marking the date fell into disuse, and, from this period until 1800, it is found only on rare examples. In 1801, the custom of dating was resumed. (See our text.) Here again Barber differs from Hannover whose system we have shown in the text:—as follows –//– he gives as 1804, an arrow for 1805 and slanting parallel lines with dots at the center at the outer edges for 1806. From there on the two systems are the same.—Barber adds, "From 1818 the year is expressed by the two last figures only. Thus: 18–1818, 19–1819, etc. and is so continued to the present time." A further note adds:—The *Guide* published for the Sèvres factory still adheres to the old system of dates, which rejected the letter J, and regards K as 1762, and the letters which follow representing, L,1763, and so on. This system is abandoned by all authorities, French and English, and we do not know why it is retained in the guide. In addition to the above tables, it is necessary to add that 1811, 1812, 1813 are sometimes indicated by 11, 12, 13, and possibly other years were occasionally so indicated to 1817: 1769, the year of a comet, was sometimes indicated by a comet rudely painted, instead of Q. The factory was removed to Sèvres in 1756. A, B, C, D, therefore date Vincennes wares. D also dates work at Sèvres. The date letter is placed either within or outside of the monogram, and is sometimes a capital and sometimes a small letter.

4.—The crown was adopted over the monogram as the mark of hard paste porcelain after its introduction. Forms of this mark are 5, 6 and 10, showing accompanying signatures of artists. Thus, mark 10 includes the factory mark, the device of the artist *Vieillard,* and the date DD, 1781. This mark on a service in the T.-P. collection has also the mark of another artist, *Baudoin,* on each piece.

7.—The letter Z having been reached in 1777, double letters were used thereafter, AA being 1778, etc. A difference of opinion existed as to whether the letter J was used for 1762, but the best authorities now agree that it was used.

8, 9.—In the Republican period the royal initial was abandoned and the mark R. F., for *Republique Francaise,* was adopted (1792–1800), always accompanied by the word *Sèvres.* The R.F. was in monogram, as in mark 8, or in one of the forms in mark 9. Dates were not used from 1792 to 1801.

11.—About 1800 the word Sèvres was used alone, without the R.F. It was usually in a form similar to mark 11, but varied as made by different hands. This mark was in use from 1800 till the end of 1802.

12.—In the Consular period, 1803, the mark 12, for *Manufacture Nationale,* was used, stenciled in red.

13.—In the Imperial period, beginning May 8, 1804, mark 13, for *Manufacture Imperiale,* was adopted, and used until 1809, stenciled in red.

14.—The imperial eagle was adopted as the mark in this form in 1810, printed in red, and continued in use till the abdication, in 1814. Date marks were used from 1801, for which see our text chart.

15.—Mark of the period of Louis XVIII, used from May, 1814, to September, 1824, the date indicated by the last two figures of the year. This mark was printed in blue.

16, 17, 18, 19.—Marks used in the reign of Charles X., from 1824 to 1828, printed in blue; the figures under the mark indicating the year of the century.

20, 21.—Marks used in the reign of Charles X., in 1829 and 1830. Mark 30 was used on decorated wares; 21 was used on pieces which were gilded only.

22.—This mark was used only in 1830; under *Louis Philippe*.

23.—Used from 1831 to November, 1834, under *Louis Philippe*.

24.—Used from November, 1834, to July, 1835.

25.—The cipher of *Louis Philippe*, used from July, 1835, to 1848.

26.—Used under the Republic from 1848 to 1852.

27.—Used under the Empire of *Louis Napoleon*, from 1852 to 1854.

28.—Cipher of *Louis Napoleon*, used from 1854 to 1872.

29, 30.—These marks have been used in addition to the factory mark since July, 1872, usually printed in red.

31, 32.—The letter S with the date of the year of the century, in an oval, was adopted 1848 as the factory mark on all pieces, and continues in use. On white wares, sold without decoration, it is cut across by a scratch through the glaze. It is printed pale green. Mr. Chaffers says it has been used on white wares since 1833. This may be taken for what it is worth. Many modern pieces with this mark cut across are decorated by amateurs and others. None have any particular value.

33.—Marks of this kind, containing names of chateaux or palaces, were placed on pieces, table services, etc., made for use in the royal residences thus indicated.

34.—Monogram of Catherine II of Russia, in flowers, laurels, etc., on a service made for her.

35, 36.—*Visa* of Alexander Brongniart, the director, occurring on several fine pieces in the T.-P. collection. It does not appear as an intentional mark, but as if the artist's work had been submitted to the director, and he had written on the back wih a lead pencil *Vu Alex B* or *Vu B*. In the firing this has become a yellowish mark with some metallic iridescence.

37.—Marks stenciled in red on a plate dated 1811, decorated with a view of the Palace of St. Cloud, signed *Label*. The visa of Brongniart in form of mark 36 is also on the plate. (T.-P. Col.)

Many hard paste specimens of Sèvres which originally bore the marks of the Imperial period prior to 1814 are found with the letters M. Imple, or the eagle, ground off on a wheel, leaving only the words De SÈVRES OF SÈVRES. The wheel has removed the glaze.

MARKS ON PORCELAIN OF FRANCE

1, 2.—Unknown marks on early French porcelains, given by Jacquemart as possibly Louis Poterat, of Rouen, 1673–1711.

3.—Unknown, on similar porcelain.

4.—ST. CLOUD.—Two forms. Pierre Chicanneau, 1702–'15.

5.—St. Cloud. Trou, 1706.

6, 7, 8.—Uncertain. On porcelains resembling.

9.—PARIS. *Marie Moreau*, widow of Chicanneau's son.

10–13.—LILLE. 10 is the earliest mark. In 13 L is on a saucer, and B on the cup.

14, 15.—CHANTILLY. 15 is Pigorry's mark since 1803.

16, 17.—MENNECY—VILLEROY. In gold, color and later impressed.

18, 19, 20.—VINCENNES and SÈVRES.—See marks of Sèvres above.

21, 22, 23.—SCEAUX. 21 usually scratched. 22, later, painted in blue. 23 scratched.

24.—ORLEANS.

25.—ETIOLLES.

26.—LA TOUR D'AIGUES.

27.—BOURG-LA-REINE.

28, 29.—ARRAS.

30–39.—Unknown marks on early French porcelains, resembling St. Cloud, given by Jacquemart. 33, 35 are doubtless the same as 6, 8 above.

40–46.—Unknown marks on hard paste porcelains. 44 attributed by Riocreux to Fontainbleau. 45 resembles the mark of a Sèvres painter.

47.—Paris. Pierre A. Hannong's mark, 1773.

48, 49.—Paris. Same factory. Charles Philippe.

50.—Paris. Gros Caillou. Established by Lamarre, 1773.

51.—Paris. Morelle à Paris. Established 1773.

52, 53.—Paris. Souroux, potter. Established 1773. His successor was Ollivier.

54.—Paris. De la Courtille factory.

55.—Paris. De la Courtille. This mark, torches or headless arrows, is made in various forms, and somewhat resembles the Dresden crossed swords, which probably did not bother the users of it.

56.—Paris. *Dubois.* This mark—two branches, alluding to the maker's name—often resembles the previous one. Also assigned to De la Courtille factory.

57, 58.—LIMOGES. Factory of Massie. The earliest mark was G.R., et Cie.

59, 60.—LA SEINIE. Established 1774.

61.—Paris. J. J. Lassia, 1774.

62–70.—CLIGNANCOURT. The windmill is the earliest mark, rare, used only in 1775. 64 is stenciled on a specimen. 65, initial of *Monsieur,* the king's brother; 66, 67, 68, initials of Prince Louis Stanislas Xavier; 69, initial of Moitte, director, used with the name *Clignancourt;* 70, initial of Deruelle, director.

71.—Paris. *Manufacture du petit Carousel.* Mark used with the name of the factory variously abbreviated.

72, 73.—BOISETTE.

74, 75, 76.—Paris. Lebeuf. *Porcelaine de la Reine.* Initial of Marie Antoinette.

77.—Paris. *Porcelaine de la Reine.* Initials of Guy & Housel, successors to Lebeuf. These occur with *Rue Thirou à Paris.* LEVEILLE, 12 *Rue Thiroux,* is the latest mark.

78, 79, 80.—Paris. *Porcelaine d'Angoulême.* Early marks of Guerhard & Dihl. Later marks are their names in full, and MANUFACTURE DE MONS. LE DUC D'ANGOULÊME A PARIS, without name.

81.—Paris. *Nast,* manufacturer. Stenciled.

82.—LILLE. The early pieces have *à Lille.*

83, 84, 85, 86.—Paris. Factory established by Lamarre, 1784. 84, 85, 86 are initials of Louis Philippe Joseph, Duc d'Orleans, patron.

87, 88.—Paris. H. F. Chanou. Established 1784. The marks are penciled in red.

89, 90.—VALENCIENNES. Initials of Fauquez, Lamoninary and V. Early mark, *Valencien.*

91.—CHOISY LE ROY. Impressed.

92, 93, 94.—Vincennes. Factory of P. A. Hannong. Established 1786.

95.—Vincennes. Attributed to Hannong's, or another factory under the patronage of Louis Philippe.

96, 97.—Paris. Charles Potter. *Porcelaine du Prince de Galles.*

98.—Paris. Belleville. Jacob Pettit. The J has sometimes a dot above it.

99.—CAEN. Desmare et Cie. Established 1798.

100.—Paris. *Manufacture de S. M. l'Impératrice.* Also marked with full name of factory, and *P. L. Dagoty,* proprietor.

101–106.—STRASBOURG. 101, C. Hannong; 102, 103, Paul A. Hannong; 104, the same, with H in the paste; 105, J. A. Hannong, with numbers; 106, J. A. Hannong.

107.—BRANCAS LAURAGAIS.

108, 109.—ORLEANS. 108, of Gerault; 109, of LeBrun.

110.—Given by Jacquemart as the mark of Jacques Louis Broilliet on experimental porcelain, at *Gros Caillou* (Paris) 1765.

111, 112, 113.—MARSEILLES. Robert. 113 is doubtful.

114–121.—Niderviller. 114, Beyerle's period; 115, 116, 117, 120, Custine's period. These marks must not be confused with those of Ludwigsburg. 119 is Lanfray's cipher. NIDERVILLER in an open outlined letter is impressed on statues of Franklin and other biscuit pieces.

122, 123.—BORDEAUX. Marks of Verneuille.

124.—Unknown French. Resembles Limbach, in Germany.

125–131.—Unknown marks on French porcelain.

132.—Attributed by Baron Davillier to Marseilles.

MARKS ON PORCELAIN OF GERMANY AND OTHER EUROPEAN COUNTRIES

Note:—The MEISSEN Marks are listed as DRESDEN where the factory was located.

1–8.—DRESDEN. Marks stamped on Böttger red ware. Böttger's porcelain was never marked.

9, 10, 11.—Dresden. Initials of August Rex, in blue and in gold 1709–'26.

14, 15.—Dresden. King's period, from 1770; the mark with O about 1778.

16.—Dresden. Crossed swords, with star. Marcolini period, from 1796.

17, 18.—Dresden. Early marks for (17) *Königlicher* or (18) *Meissener Porzellan Manufactur*. Hannover says, "Not until about 1723 did a sparing use of a mark begin—in underglaze blue, with the cursive letters K.P.M. or K.P.F. (*Königliche Porzellan Fabrik*.)" He continues, stating that the mark or marks appeared usually on the sugar-basin and tea-pot of breakfast-sets and that it continued long after the crossed swords were adopted.

19, 20.—Dresden. First forms of the crossed swords, used from 1719. Here again there seems to be some difference of opinion for Hannover clearly states, "The crossed-swords mark occurs from about 1726 onwards; but even in 1730 the letters just mentioned are sometimes used—now and then in combination with the crossed swords." He also continues, "Until 1731, it was rather the exception than the rule for the Meissen factory to mark its porcelain."

21.—Dresden. Bruhl's time, 1750. Hannover says, "The sword mark, in its oldest form, consists of two swords with pommels, with the guard set at a right angle, and the blades crossing each other also at an approximate right angle. Towards the close of the 1730s the guards were set obliquely and the blades crossed at at an acute angle. From about 1750, the pommels disappear and the swords now become small and delicate. A few years later a comparatively long period begins, during which a dot was set in the rhombus formed by the swords and the cross-pieces; hence the name 'dot period' and *Saxe au point*. This is estimated by Berling as ranging from about 1756 till 1780. From about 1780 the well known star was placed under the swords. This is often taken to be the mark of Marcolini, though it was introduced a few years before his time, and remained in use a year or so after his death (in 1814), when it was succeeded by a Roman or Arabic numeral. All these marks were in blue under the glaze. Only on biscuit of the Marcolini period is the mark not painted, but incised, and at the same time enclosed in a triangle." We should add that he states earlier, "But when, in 1731, the mark began to appear on all new porcelain in underglaze blue, a quantity of old ware, originally unmarked, was at the same time furnished with the same mark" (the crossed swords) "in blue *over* the glaze."

22.—Dresden. Crossed swords; modern mark. The earliest form in Herold's period, sometimes closely resembles the modern form.

23.—Dresden. A modern mark.

24.—Dresden. On a service made for the Countess Cosel. (Kosel.) Hannover notes she fell into disgrace in 1718 and doubts it.

25.—Dresden. Used about 1730.

26.—Dresden. Dated 1739.

27.—Dresden. Early form of mark.

28, 29.—Dresden. Marks used 1718.

30, 31.—Dresden. Early marks.

32.—Dresden. Mark used 1718.

33.—Dresden. Date of use unknown; on statuettes, with or without crossed swords. (Chaffers) (doubtful?)

34, 35.—VIENNA, Austria.

36.—ELBOGEN.

37, 38.—SCHLAKENWALD, Austria. (See also #61.)

39–44.—HEREND, Hungary. 39 is impressed in the paste; 40, 41, usually printed in blue; 42, painted in black, with *Herend* impressed; 43, painted in red; 44, initials of M. Fischer.

45, 46.—ALTEN ROTHAU. *Nowotny*, maker.

47, 48.—PIRKENHAMMER. *Fischer & Reichembach*, and *Charles Fischer*.

49.—PRAGUE. *Kriegel & Co.*

50–53.—HÖCHST, Mayence. (See 15, 16, 17 in Marks on Pottery of Germany) 51 is the mark of Geltz; 52, of Zeschinger.

54.—Höchst. Mark of Dahl.

1.—FÜRSTENBERG. The F is made in various forms.

2.—HESSE CASSEL?

3.—HESSE DARMSTADT. (Jacquemart.)

4, 5.—FULDA.

6.—GERA? or GOTHA? See #25.

7, 8.—Gotha.

9.—WALLENDORF. (Also used at Berlin.)

10.—ARNSTADT.

11, 12, 13, 14.—LIMBACH.

15.—VOLKSTADT. Marryat says KLOSTER VEILSDORF. (See 24 below.)

16.—ANSPACH. So says Marryat. See 26, 46, 47, 48 below.

17.—RAUENSTEIN.

18, 19.—GROSBREITENBACH.

20.—Grosbreitenbach ?

21, 22, 23.—RUDOLSTADT. R was used in various forms.

24.—Volkstadt. See 15 above.

25.—GERA. Two forms of G.

26.—Attributed to both Gera and Anspach, Barber says probably the latter. Chaffers gives it with a D under a crown. The mark varies from a rude eagle (46) to this form. See 16.

27, 28.—BADEN-BADEN. The blade of an ax or of two axes, in gold or impressed.

29–35.—LUDWIGSBURG (KRONENBURG). The double C is the cipher of Charles Eugene, who died in 1793, but the mark was used till 1806. It must not be confounded with that of Niderviller, in Custine's time, which was sometimes accompanied by a coronet. The mark frequently appears without the crown, as in 31 and 32. The form 30 (L, with a crown) is also a mark of the time of Charles Eugene. The letters CC in mark 29 were changed in 1806 to T.R., the T.R. being sometimes in monogram; and in 1818 the letters W.R. were substituted. The stag's horns, singly, 35, or on a shield, as in 34, were also used.

36.—HILDSHEIM, Hannover. Sometimes the letter A only; from about 1760.

37, 38, 39.—NYMPHENBURG and NEUDECK. The first is the oldest mark. These are impressed, without color, and sometimes difficult to recognize. Found on pieces with marks of other factories, which bought and decorated them.

40–45.—FRANKENTHAL. 41, P. A. Hannong's mark; 42, Joseph A. Hannong; 43, initials of Carl Theodore, Elector; 44, supposed of Ringler; 45, supposed, of Bartolo.

46, 47, 48.—Anspach, Bavaria.

49.—BAIREUTH.
50.—REGENSBURG (RATISBON).
51.—WÜRTZBURG, Bavaria.
52–57.—BERLIN. The scepter is the general mark, made in several forms. 52, 53, 54 are the earliest marks of Wegely, 1750–1761; 56, globe and cross and K.P.M., for Königlicher Parzellan Manufactur, adopted about 1830; 57, modern mark, alone, and with K.P.M. The Wegely marks resemble Wallendorff and others, quite carelessly including Meissen, of course.
58.—CHARLOTTENBERG.
59.—PROSKAU.
60.—VIENNA. See also 34 and 35 preceding.
61.—SCHLAKENWALD, Austria. See 37 and 38 preceding.
62, 63, 64.—Unknown marks on German hard paste porcelain.
65–76.—Unknown marks on German hard paste porcelain.
77, 78.—Uncertain; possibly Frankenthal, *Hannong fecit.*
79.—WEESP, Holland.
80.—Weesp? Arnstadt? Saxe Gotha? Quite uncertain.
81.—LOOSDRECHT. Manufactur oude Loosdrecht.
82, 83.—AMSTEL (Amsterdam).
84.—AMSTERDAM. The lion frequently alone.
85.—THE HAGUE.
86, 87, 88.—BRUSSELS. 87 is the mark of L. Cretté.
89–92.—LUXEMBOURG. 92 is the modern mark.
93.—ZURICH, Switzerland.
94.—NYON, Switzerland.
95–98.—TOURNAY. 95 is Peterynck's mark from 1751; the tower is also assigned to Vincennes, and pieces thus marked are called "Porcelaine de la tour."
99, 100, 101.—MARIEBERG, Sweden.
102, 103.—COPENHAGEN. Three waving lines for the Sound and the Belts.
104–112.—ST. PETERSBURG. Royal factory; 104, time of Empress Elizabeth, 1741; 105, 106, Empress Catherine (Ekaterina), 1762; 107, Emperor Paul, 1796; 108, Emperor Alexander, 1801; 109, Emperor Nicholas, 1825; 110, 111, Emperor Alexander II, 1855; 112, shows system of dates by dots adopted 1871—one dot for 1871, two for 1872, etc.
113, 114.—St. Petersburg. Brothers Korniloff.
115–119.—MOSCOW. Gardners.
120–123.—Moscow. Popoff. Factory established 1830.
124.—KIEV, Russia, or near there at Mejxigorie. Pottery.
125.—BARANOWKA, Poland. Pottery.
126.—CHMELOFF, Poland. Pottery.
127.—Kiev, Russia. Pottery.
128.—KORZEC, Poland. Pottery.

MARKS ON POTTERY AND PORCELAIN OF ENGLAND

1–18.—Bow. Scratched marks, resembling 4, 11, and other unintelligible scratches occur. Other marks are in color; sometimes as in 14, 15, 16, 18 in two colors.
19.—Bow? Bristol? Impressed mark. Uncertain.
20, 21.—CHELSEA. The triangle impressed was formerly assigned to Bow till discovery of piece with mark 21. It is on an English pottery teapot in the T.-P. collection.
22.—CHELSEA. Anchor embossed. Early mark.

23, 24.—Chelsea. Forms of the anchor mark in colors or gold. The anchor was used by many other factories.

25, 26.—Uncertain. Bow?

27, 28.—DERBY. Chelsea-Derby period.

29, 30.—Derby. Crown-Derby period. 30 supposed to be mark on pieces made at Chelsea, after the purchase by Duesbury, and before closing the works.

31.—Derby. A mark of Duesbury's time, date unknown.

32, 33, 34, 35.—Marks used from about 1788. The earliest in puce or blue, later in red. 34 is of Duesbury & Kean.

36.—Derby. Bloor's mark.

37–41.—Derby. Bloor's marks.

42.—Derby. Modern mark of S. Hancock, present owner.

43, 44.—Derby? Uncertain marks on pieces resembling Derby.

45, 46.—Derby. Copies of Sèvres and Dresden marks on Derby porcelain.

47.—Derby. On a statuette.

48–52.—Derby. 48, 49, 50 are imitations of a Chinese symbol. 51 is uncertain, perhaps of Bloor's time. 52, a star, often impressed on figures.

53–57.—Bow? These marks occur in blue on figures.

58.—Bow? Supposed Monogram of Fry in blue.

59.—Bow? Impressed.

60.—DERBY. On service made for the Persian ambassador.

61.—Derby. On a plate.

62.—Derby. Used in 1842. Imitation of Sèvres.

63–76.—Derby. On various pieces. 71–75 are marks of Cocker, on figures, etc., made by him at Derby till 1840, and after that in London; 76 is an imitation of a Sèvres mark.

77–82.—WORCESTER. Workmen's marks on Worcester porcelain.

83.—CAUGHLEY. Forms of the crescent mark, and C in blue.

84.—Caughley. Forms of S, for Salopian, in blue or impressed.

85.—Caughley.

86, 87.—Caughley.

88–96.—Caughley. Numerals 1, 2, 3, etc., in fanciful style on printed wares.

97.—Caughley. Mark of Rose?

98.—COALPORT.

99–104.—COLEBROOKDALE. The first three are the older marks. 102, adopted 1851. 103 is a modern mark, being a monogram of S.C., for Salopian, Colebrook-Dale, and including C, for Caughley or Coalport; S, for Swansea; and N, for Nant-garrow, the combined factories.

105.—SHELTON. The *New Hall* factory. Modern marks of this factory are HACK-WOOD, or HACKWOOD & CO., from 1842 to 1856; then C & H, *late Hack-wood*, for Cockson & Harding; and since 1862 HARDING.

106–110.—PINXTON.

111–132.—WORCESTER. The early mark is the letter W, in various forms, as in 112. This stands for Worcester or Wall.

The crescent, also in different forms, as in 113, in blue, gold or impressed, was used prior to 1793. It must not be mistaken for the crescent of Caughley, which it so closely resembles that certain specimens can sometimes be identified only by the paste or decorations.

The marks numbered 111 are workmen's marks. These do not identify specimens with certainty, as of Worcester, for similar marks are found on other porcelains.

The square marks, 114, 115, 116, are early marks imitating Oriental.

Marks 117, 118, 119 are found on prints, and are the signatures of Robert Hancock, engraver. The anchor in 118 and 119 may be of Richard Holdship.

The 120–126 are early marks, fanciful imitations of Chinese. Other marks occur, resembling these in character.

127, 128, 129, 130 are imitations, of course, of the crossed sword mark of the Dresden factory.

131.—Is an imitation of the mark of Sèvres.

132.—Is an imitation of the mark of Chantilly.

133-146.—WORCESTER Flight purchased the works (1783), and used his name, impressed (mark 133), or painted (134), sometimes with the crescent mark in blue. 133 and 134 were used till 1792. After the king's visit, in 1788, mark 135 was sometimes used.

136.—Scratched mark of Barr after 1793.

137.—Flight & Barr, 1793–1807.

138-140.—Flight, Barr & Barr, 1807–1813. The F.B.B. impressed.

139.—Impressed mark, used 1813–1840.

141.—Printed mark, used 1813–1840.

142.—Chamberlain, 1788 to about 1804.

143.—Chamberlain, 1847–1850. Impressed or printed.

A Printed mark, *Chamberlain's Regent China, Worcester,* etc. under a crown, was used from 1811 to about 1820.

A written mark, *Chamberlains, Worcester, & 63 Piccadilly, London,* was used about 1814.

A printed mark, CHAMBERLAINS, WORCESTER, & 155 NEW BOND ST. LONDON under a crown, was used from 1820 to 1840. After the union of the two factories in 1840, the printed mark was CHAMBERLAIN & CO., 155 NEW BOND ST., & NO 1 COVENTRY ST. LONDON, under a crown.

In 1847 the mark was simply *Chamberlain & Co., Worcester.*

From 1847 to 1850 mark 143 was used.

144.—Was used 1850–1851.

145.—Mark adopted by Kerr & Binns, 1851, and since used.

146.—Kerr & Binns on special work.

147.—PLYMOUTH. In blue, red or gold.

148-164.—BRISTOL. The general mark is a cross (149), in slate color, blue, or in the paste, with or without numbers and other marks. Numbers from 1 to 24 are thought to be of decorators. B, with a number (marks 151–154), was frequently used. 155 shows Bristol and Plymouth combined; 157, John Britain, foreman in the factory. 159 shows an embossed T over the cross in blue. The Dresden mark was frequently used, as in 160, 161, 162, 163, in combination with numbers, etc. 164 is probably a workman's mark.

165-169.—STOKE. *Minton.* 165 is the earliest mark. 166, 167 are also early marks. 168 was used about 1850, and 169 later.

170-174.—Stoke. Marks of Josiah Spode, father and son. 170 is an old mark, neatly penciled in various colors.

175-183.—Stoke. Marks of the several successors of Spode since 1833.

175.—Copeland & Garret, 1833–1847.

176.—Used by Copeland & Garret.

177.—Copeland & Garret.

178, 179.—Copeland & Garret, 1833–1847.

180.—Copeland, 1847–1851.

181.—Copeland, after 1851.

182.—Copeland used, 1847–1867.

183.—W. T. Copeland & Sons, after 1867.

184.—ROCKINGHAM. Adopted about 1823. The mark of *Brameld* from 1807 was his name impressed, sometimes with a cross and four dots. Tea-pots have impressed marks; MORTLOCK, CADOGANS, MORTLOCK'S CADOGAN, ROCKINGHAM. Coffee-pots had sometimes the pattern name NORFOLK impressed.

185-187.—SWANSEA. The name SWANSEA, stenciled or impressed, was used about 1815; also SWANSEA, DILLWYN & CO., and DILLWYN'S ETRUSCAN WARE. Marks 185, 186 are impressed, date unknown. 187 is on an old pottery vase. *Cambrian Pottery* also appears.

188.—NANTGAR W. 1813–1820, painted, impressed or stenciled. *Mortlock,* in gilt, occurs on ware decorated in London, and also on Swansea ware.

189.—LONGPORT. *Davenport's* mark. The earliest mark was LONGPORT or DAVENPORT LONGPORT. The marks are impressed or printed and forms vary. After 1805, on ironstone wares the anchor was in a portico.

190.—LIVERPOOL. *Richard Chaffers.*
191.—Liverpool. *Pennington.* In gold or colors.
192.—Longport. *Rogers.* Pottery and ironstone.
193.—LANE DELPH. *C. J. Mason.* Various other marks, including the name. The
oldest marks include the name, MILES MASON; a mark is MASON'S CAM-
BRIAN ARGIL; and a late mark, FENTON STONE WORKS, C. J. M. & CO.
194.—TUNSTALL and BURSLEM. *Bridgwood & Clark,* 1857.
195.—LONGTON. *Hilditch & Son.*
196.—Tunstall. Bowers?
197.—Longton. *Mayer & Newbold.*
198, 199.—On Elers ware tea-pots.
200.—YARMOUTH. *Absolon.*
201, 202, 203.—LEEDS. 201 is *Charles Green.*
204.—LANE-END. *Turner.*
205.—EDINBURGH (Portobello) pottery.
206, 207, 208.—Liverpool. 206, 208 are Herculaneum pottery. Marks of this pottery
are found impressed, painted and printed on bottoms and sides of pieces. 207
is of *Case & Mort,* proprietors from 1833.
209–214.—BURSLEM and ETRURIA. Marks of *Wedgwood* and his factory. The
most common mark is the word WEDGWOOD, impressed.

MARKS OF AMERICAN POTTERS

MARKS OF PENNSYLVANIA POTTERIES

		Established
1.—Bonnin & Morris, Philadelphia, Pa.		1770
2.—Joseph Smith Pottery, Bucks County, Pa.		1767
3, 4.—Henry Roudebush, Montgomery County, Pa.		1811–1816
5.—Samuel Troxel, Montgomery County, Pa.		1823–1833
6.—George Hubener, Montgomery County, Pa.		1785–1798
7.—Jacob or Isaac Tany, Bucks County, Pa.		1794
8.—John Drey, Easton, Pa.		1809
9.—Andrew Headman, Rock Hill, Bucks County, Pa.		1808
10, 11.—Unidentified marks on German American pottery.		
12.—Jacob Schell, Tylers Port, Montgomery County, Pa.		1830
13.—Womelsdorf, Pa.		
John Menner		1784
Willoughby Smith		1864
14.—American China Manufactory, Philadelphia, Pa.		1825
15, 16.—Tucker & Hulme		1828
17.—Judge Joseph Hemphill		1832–1836
18–24.—Private marks of workmen.		
25.—Smith, Fife & Co., Philadelphia, Pa.		1830
26.—Ralph Bagnall Beach, Philadelphia, Pa.		1845
27.—Kurlbaum & Schwartz		1851
28.—Workman's mark.		
29.—The Phoenix Pottery, Kaolin and Fire Brick Co., Phoenixville, Pa.		1867
30.—Beerbower & Griffen, Phoenixville, Pa.		1877
31–34A.—Griffen, Smith & Hill, Phoenixville, Pa.		1879
35–37.—Chester Pottery Co. of Pennsylvania, Phoenixville, Pa.		1894
38.—The Philadelphia City Pottery, J. E. Jeffords & Co.		1868
39.—Galloway & Graff, Philadelphia, Pa.		1810
40–59.—The Mayer Pottery Co., Beaver Falls, Pa.		1881

Established

60.—Star Encaustic Tile Co., Pittsburg, Pa. 1882
61.—The Robertson Art Tile Co., Morrisville, Pa.
62.—The Shenango China Co., New Castle, Pa.
63, 64.—Moravian Pottery and Tile Works, Doylestown, Pa.
65.—The Wick China Co., Kittanning, Pa.
66–70.—The Ford China Co., Ford City, Pa.
71.—The New Castle Pottery Co., New Castle, Pa.
72.—The Derry China Co., Derry Station, Pa.
73.—Pennsylvania Museum and School of Industrial Art, Phila., Pa. 1903

MARKS OF NEW JERSEY POTTERIES

74–81.—The Jersey City Pottery, Jersey City, N. J. 1829
    D. & J. Henderson.
    American Pottery Manufacturing Co. 1833
82.—William Young & Sons, Trenton, N. J. 1853
83–90.—The Willits Manufacturing Co., Trenton, N. J. 1879
91.—The City Pottery Co., Trenton, N. J. 1859
92–98.—Greenwood Pottery Co., Trenton, N. J. 1861
99–101.—The East Trenton Pottery Co., Trenton, N. J. 1888
102, 103.—Millington, Astbury & Poulson, Trenton, N. J. 1853
104, 105.—Thomas Maddock & Sons, Trenton, N. J. 1859
105A.—Thomas Maddock's Sons Co., Trenton, N. J. 1902
106–108.—The Maddock Pottery Co., Trenton, N. J. 1893
109, 110.—John Maddock & Sons, Trenton, N. J. 1894
111–140.—The Glasgow Pottery, Trenton, N. J. 1863
141–155.—Ott & Brewer, Trenton, N. J. 1863
156–163.—The Cook Pottery Co., Trenton, N. J. 1894
164–166.—Isaac Broome, Trenton, N. J. 1880
167.—Coxon & Co., Trenton, N. J. 1863
168.—Trenton Pottery Co., Trenton, N. J. 1865
169–184.—Mercer Pottery Co., Trenton, N. J. 1868
185.—The New Jersey Pottery Co., Trenton, N. J. 1869
186–203.—International Pottery Co., Trenton, N. J. 1860
204–206.—American Crockery Co., Trenton, N. J. 1876
207–212.—Burroughs & Mountford Co., Trenton, N. J. 1879
213–217.—The Prospect Hill Pottery Co., Trenton, N. J. 1880
218–225.—Anchor Pottery Co., Trenton, N. J. 1894
226, 227.—Delaware Pottery, Trenton, N. J. 1884
228–240.—Crescent Pottery, Trenton, N. J. 1881
241–243.—Empire Pottery, Trenton, N. J. 1863
244.—Enterprise Pottery, Trenton, N. J. 1880
245–254.—Trenton Potteries Co., Trenton, N. J. Organized 1892
255.—The Bellmark Pottery Co., Trenton, N. J. 1893
256–258.—The Fell & Thropp Co., Trenton, N. J.
259, 260.—The Trenton Pottery Works, Trenton, N. J.
261.—Keystone Pottery Co., Trenton, N. J.
262.—Star Porcelain Co., Trenton, N. J.
263–267.—The Ceramic Art Co., Trenton, N. J. 1889
268.—The Trenton China Co., Trenton, N. J. 1859
269.—The American Art China Works, Trenton, N. J. 1891
270, 271.—Columbian Art Pottery, Trenton, N. J.
272.—American Porcelain Manufacturing Co., Gloucester, N. J. 1854
273, 274.—L. B. Beerbower & Co., Elizabeth, N. J. 1816
275.—Charles Wingender & Brother, Haddonfield, N. J.
276.—C. L. & H. A. Poillon, Woodbridge, N. J.

MARKS OF NEW YORK POTTERIES

	Established
277.—Salamander Works, New York, N. Y.	1848
278–286.—New York City Pottery, N. Y., N. Y.	1853
287–291.—Union Porcelain Works, Greenpoint, N. Y.	1876
292–298.—Onondaga Pottery Co., Syracuse, N. Y.	1871
299–302.—Volkmar Pottery, Greenpoint, N. Y.	1879
303.—East Morrison China Works, N. Y., N. Y.	
304–306.—The Faïence Manufacturing Co., Greenpoint, N. Y.	1880
307.—Charles Graham Chemical Pottery Works, Brooklyn, N. Y.	
308, 309.—Middle Lane Pottery, East Hampton, L. I. T. A. Brouwer, Jr.	
310, 310A, 310B.—The Chittenango Pottery Co., Chittenango, N. Y.	1897
311.—American Art Ceramic Co., Corona, N. Y.	1901

MARKS OF NEW ENGLAND POTTERIES

312–314.—Norton Pottery Co., Bennington, Vt.	1793
315–317.—United States Pottery Co., Bennington, Vt.	1849
318.—Nichols & Alford, Burlington, Vt.	1854
319–327.—New England Pottery Co., East Boston, Mass.	1854
328, 329.—Chelsea Keramic, Chelsea, Mass.	1866
330–332.—Dedham Pottery Co., Dedham, Mass.	
333–335.—Hampshire Pottery Co., Keene, N. H.	1871
336–342.—New Milford Pottery Co., New Milford, Conn.	1886
343–347.—The Grueby Faïence Co., Boston, Mass.	1897
348–360.—Artist's marks.	
361, 362.—Merrimac Ceramic Co., Newburyport, Mass.	1897
363.—The Low Art Tile Co., Chelsea, Mass.	1893

MARKS OF OHIO POTTERIES

364–367.—The Harker Pottery Co., East Liverpool, O.	1840
368–372.—The Goodwin Pottery Co., East Liverpool, O.	1844
373–377.—The Smith-Phillips China Co., East Liverpool, O.	
378–391.—The Vodrey Pottery Co., East Liverpool, O.	1848
392–401.—The William Brunt Pottery Co., East Liverpool, O.	1850
402–435.—The Knowles, Taylor & Knowles Co., East Liverpool, O.	1854
436.—D. E. McNicol Pottery Co., East Liverpool, O.	1863
437–443.—C. C. Thompson Pottery Co., East Liverpool, O.	1868
444–452.—The Homer Laughlin China Co., East Liverpool, O.	1874
453–463.—The Potter's Cooperative Co., East Liverpool, O.	1876
464–468.—Cartwright Brothers, East Liverpool, O.	
469–474.—The Globe Pottery Co., East Liverpool, O.	1881
475.—The Wallace and Chetwynd Pottery Co., East Liverpool, O.	
476–478.—The United States Pottery, East Liverpool, O.	
479–483.—The East Liverpool Pottery Co., East Liverpool, O.	1896
484–487.—The George C. Murphy Pottery Co., East Liverpool, O.	
488–493.—The East End Pottery Co., East Liverpool, O.	
494.—The East Liverpool Potteries Co., East Liverpool, O.	
495–498.—The Union Potteries Co., East Liverpool, O.	
499–510A.—The Burford Brothers Pottery Co., East Liverpool, O.	
511–514.—The Taylor, Smith & Taylor Co., East Liverpool, O.	1899
515, 516.—The West End Pottery Co., East Liverpool, O.	1893
517–521.—The Sèvres China Co., East Liverpool, O.	1900
522, 523.—The Ed. M. Knowles China Co., East Liverpool, O.	1901
524–526.—The Brockman Pottery Co., Cincinnati, O.	1862
527–540.—The Rookwood Pottery Co., Cincinnati, O.	1879

Established

541–543.—The Cincinnati Art Pottery Co., Cincinnati, O. 1879
544–546.—The Matt Morgan Art Pottery Co., Cincinnati, O. 1883
547.—Avon Pottery, Cincinnati, O. 1886
548, 549.—Miss M. Louise McLaughlin, Cincinnati, O. 1876
550–558.—The Wellsville China Co., Wellsville, O. 1879
559.—J. H. Baum, Wellsville, O. 1897
560.—The United States Pottery Co., Wellsville, O. 1899
561–574.—The Steubenville Pottery Co., Steubenville, O. 1879
575–578.—Lonhuda Pottery, Steubenville, O. 1892
579–584.—S. A. Weller, Zanesville, O.
585–587.—J. B. Owens Pottery Co., Zanesville, O.
588, 589.—The American Encaustic Tiling Co., Zanesville, O.
590.—The Mosaic Tile Co., Zanesville, O.
591–596A.—The French China Co., Sebring, O.
597–599.—The Sebring Pottery Co., Sebring, O. 1887
600, 601.—The Oliver China Co., Sebring, O. 1899
602–604.—The East Palestine Pottery Co., East Palestine, O.
605.—The Ohio China Co., East Palestine, O.
606.—The Crooksville China Co., Crooksville, O.
607–610.—The American China Co., Toronto, O. 1897
611–614.—The Cambridge Art Pottery Co., Cambridge, O.
615.—The Bradshaw China Co., Niles, O.
616, 617.—The Thomas China Co., Lisbon, O.
618, 619.—The Akron China Co., Akron, O.
620.—The Florentine Pottery Co., Chillicothe, O.
621–623.—The Bell Pottery Co., Findlay, O.
624.—Roseville Pottery, Zanesville, O.

MARKS OF SOUTHERN POTTERIES

625–647.—The Edwin Bennett Pottery Co., Baltimore, Md. 1846
648–655A.—The Maryland Pottery Co., Baltimore, Md. 1879
656–663.—Chesapeake Pottery Co., Baltimore, Md. 1880
664.—Morgantown, West Virginia 1785
665–680.—Wheeling Pottery Co., Wheeling, W. Va. 1879
681.—The Wheeling Potteries Co., Wheeling, W. Va. 1903
682–684.—Ohio Valley China Co., Wheeling, W. Va.
685–687.—The Warwick China Co., Wheeling, W. Va. 1887
688.—The Vance Faïence Co., Wheeling, W. Va.
689, 690.—The Chelsea China Co., New Cumberland, W. Va. 1888
691.—Edward Lycett, Atlanta, Ga. 1861
692, 693.—Geo. E. Ohr, Biloxi, Miss.
694.—Southern Porcelain Co., Kaolin, S. C. 1856
695–697.—Newcomb Pottery, Newcomb College, New Orleans, La. 1896

MARKS OF WESTERN POTTERIES

698–705.—The Peoria Pottery Co., Peoria, Ill. 1873
706.—The American Terra-Cotta Co., Chicago, Ill.
707.—The Monmouth Pottery Co., Monmouth, Ill.
708–721.—The Crown Pottery Co., Evansville, Ind. 1891
722.—The Pauline Pottery Co., Edgerton, Wis. 1883
723.—Mrs. S. S. Frackleton, Milwaukee, Wis.
724.—The Stockton Art Pottery Co., Stockton, Cal.
725–727.—The Geijsbeek Pottery Co., Golden, Colo. 1899
728, 729.—The Denver China and Pottery Co., Denver, Col.
730, 731—Mrs. Linna Irelan, San Francisco, Cal. 1899
732–734.—The Van Briggle Pottery Co., Colorado Springs, Col. 1901
735, 736.—Miss Mary Chase Perry, Detroit, Mich.

MARKS ON WARES OF ITALY, PERSIA, RHODES, ETC.

MARKS ON POTTERY OF FRANCE·

5 D2   6 D/14   7 lille

10 D.   Lille   11 FB / B   12   13 S.   14

15   16 R R   17 LV   18 Axc   19 ⚓   20 OP   21 SP

22 B.R.   23 St C / T   24 S.   25 S.pellevé   26 S.c.y.   27 J.A

28 AJ   29   30 R.v.   31 LR   32 RGM.   34 N   35   36

37   38   39 +   40 U&Cie   41 CH   42   43   44 H

45   46 H T9   47 H   48 H3   49 JSL   50 R   51 V   52

53 G   54 G.   55 G   56   57 A.L.   58

59   60 Jsc   61   62 A   63   64   65

66   67   68   69   70   71   72 ic.

73   74 Q.O.   75 J+L   76   77   78 ANf

79 AJ   80 RB.f   81 AB   82   83 F.   84 Si   85 Ef   86 Fe

87   88 Fd   89 Fd   90 G   91 M.C.   92 M.C.A.1756.J.A   93 P.F.

94 F.P   95 .oy.   96   97   98   99 R   100 R   101 R

102 R.X.   103 V.   104 V   105 B.   106 F.   107 R M   108   109 M

110 R   111   112 J.Boulard a Nevers 1622   113 D.F 1636   114

115 KB 1689   116 H.B 1689   117 S.   118 P.C   120 E.Borne 1689   119 di conrade A nevers

121 .F.R.1734   122 N   124 R.+Limoges   123

125   Le 18me may   J74J   di Conade antuers

126 avisseau atour 1855

127 A:C / Ae

128 ☼ (star/sunburst mark)

ΛN

129 A P.

130 A P

132 CD CABRI 1762

131 R

133 CB

134 ·C· ·S·

135 Ɔ

136 F

137 F.C̅- 1661

143 GDG 1780 2/2

138 ⧺FC⧺SC

139 FE.

140 f.f.

141 GAA

145 H'

142 "Fait par GDE, A⁰ 1761."

146 Ħ

144 H G i

147 J⸱Jamart 1696

148 H̊

149 S/H

150 ·II·

151 J

152 JB

153 (fleur-de-lis) •Leger•

154 Lejeune• •1730•

155 A.R. S

156 R

157 M

158 NICOLas H.V 1738

159 OIP, OP

160 OS

161 I·R·PAIVADEAVS 1643

162 PB

163 P

164 P+

165 P

166 GP

167 P

168 PO

169 P·R·

170 PV 3/2

171 R

172 R

173 R.B F

174 RL

175 R·M· f

176 S. G. h.

177 SE NE

178 T.C.E 1793 un 4t

179 .VM.

180 W/2

181 W

182 W H

183 (fleur-de-lis) ·P·

MARKS ON POTTERY OF BELGIUM AND HOLLAND

1 6✳

2 ✳B

3 ✳ G

4 CCC C·P,

5 ·IM

6 FP

7 B

8 B. L

9 (monogram)

10 GA

11

12 i

13 F 1677

14 F 1·6·8·0

15 R G

16 WD Sloot 1720

17 Jr G

UNKNOWN MARKS ON POTTERY OF HOLLAND

MARKS ON POTTERY OF GERMANY, SWEDEN,
DENMARK, SPAIN AND PORTUGAL

MARKS ON PORCELAIN OF ITALY, SPAIN AND
PORTUGAL

MARKS ON PORCELAIN OF SEVRES

MARKS USED BY PAINTERS, DECORATORS AND GILDERS AT SÈVRES

FIRST PERIOD. 1753–1799

Aloncle—birds, animals, emblems, etc.

Anteaume—landscape, animals.

Armand—birds, flowers, etc.

Asselin—portraits, miniatures, etc.

Aubert (senior)—flowers.

Bailly (son)—flowers.

Bardet—flowers.

Barre—detached bouquets.

Barrat—garlands, bouquets.

Baudoin — ornaments, friezes, etc.

Becquet—flowers, etc.

Bertrand — detached bouquets.

Bienfait—gilding.

Binet—detached bouquets.

Binet, Madame (née *Sophie Chanou*)—flowers.

Boucher—flowers, garlands, etc.

Bouchet—landscape, figures, ornaments.

Bouillat—flowers, landscapes.

Boulanger—detached bouquets.

Boulanger (son) — pastoral subjects, children.

Bulidon—detached bouquets.

Bunel, Madame (née *Manon Buteux*)—flowers.

Couturier—gilding.

Dieu — Chinese, Chinese flowers, gilding, etc.

Dodin—figure, various subjects, portraits.

Drand—Chinese, gilding.

Dubois—flowers, garlands, etc.

Dusolle—detached bouquets, etc.

Dutanda—detached bouquets, garlands.

Evans—birds, butterflies, landscapes.

Falot—arabesques, birds, butterflies.

Fontaine — emblems, miniatures, etc.

Fontelliau—gilding, etc.

Fouré — flowers, bouquets, etc.

Fritsch—figures, children.

Fumez—detached bouquets.

Fumez—another form.

Gauthier—landscape and animals.

Genest—figure and genre.

Genin—flowers, garlands, friezes, etc.

Bunel, Madame — another form.

Buteux (senior)—flowers, emblems, etc.

Buteux (elder son)—detached bouquets, etc.

Buteux (younger son)—pastoral subjects, children.

Capel—friezes.

Cardin — detached bouquets.

Carrier—flowers.

Castel — landscapes, hunts, birds.

Caton — pastoral subjects, children, birds.

Catrice — flowers, detached bouquets.

Chabry — miniatures, pastoral subjects.

Chanou, Madame (née *Julie Durosey*)—flowers.

Chapuis (elder) — flowers, birds, etc.

Chapuis (younger) — detached bouquets.

Chauvaux (father) — gilding.

Chauvaux (son)—detached bouquets, gilding.

Chevalier — flowers, bouquets, etc.

Choisy, De—flowers, arabesques.

Chulot—emblems, flowers, arabesques.

Commelin — detached bouquets, garlands.

Cornaille — flowers, detached bouquets.

Henrion—garlands, detached bouquets.

Héricourt — detached bouquets, garlands.

Hilken—figures, pastoral subjects, etc.

Houry—flowers, etc.

Huny — detached bouquets, flowers.

Joyau — detached bouquets, etc.

Jubin—gilding.

La Roche—flowers, garlands, emblems.

La Roche—another form.

Le Bel (elder)—figures and flowers.

Le Bel (younger)—garlands, bouquets, etc.

Léandre—pastoral subjects, miniatures.

Lecot—Chinese, etc.

Lecot—another form.

Ledoux—landscape and birds.

Le Guay—gilding.

Le Guay—another form.

Leguay—miniatures, children, Chinese.

Gerard—pastoral subjects, miniatures.

Gerard, Madame (née Vautrin)—flowers.

Girard—arabesques, Chinese, etc.

Gomery—flowers and birds.

Gremont—garlands, bouquets.

Grison—gilding.

Michel—detached bouquets.

Moiron—detached bouquets; also another form used by Michel.

Mongenot—flowers, detached bouquets.

Morin—marine, military subjects.

Mutel—landscape.

Niquet—detached bouquets, etc.

Noel—flowers, ornaments.

Nouailhier, Madame (née Sophie Durosy)—flowers.

Parpette—flowers, detached bouquets. .

Parpette, Dlle. Louison—flowers.

Pajou—figure.

Petit—flowers.

Pfeiffer—detached bouquets.

Pierre (elder)—flowers, bouquets.

Pierre (younger)—bouquets, garlands.

Philippine (elder)—pastoral subjects, children, etc.

Pithou (elder)—portraits, historical subjects.

Pithou (younger)—figures, flowers, ornaments.

Pouillot—detached bouquets.

Prevost—gilding.

Raux—detached bouquets.

Levé (father)—flowers, birds, arabesques.

Levé, Felix—flowers, Chinese.

Maqueret, Madame (née Bouillat)—flowers.

Massy—groups of flowers, garlands.

Merault (elder)—friezes.

Merault (younger)—garlands, bouquets.

Micaud—flowers, bouquets, medallions.

Rochet—figure, miniatures, etc.

Rosset—landscapes, etc.

Roussel—detached bouquets.

Schradre—birds, landscape, etc.

Sinsson—flowers, groups, garlands, etc.

Sioux (elder)—detached bouquets, garlands.

Sioux (younger)—flowers, garlands.

Tabary—birds, etc.

Taillandier—detached bouquets, garlands.

Tandart—groups of flowers, garlands.

Tardi—detached bouquets, etc.

Theodore—gilding.

Thevenet (father)—flowers, medallions, groups, etc.

Thevenet (son)—ornaments, friezes, etc.

Vandé—gilding, flowers.

Vavasseur—arabesques.

Vieillard—emblems, ornaments, etc.

Vincent—gilding.

Xrowet—arabesques, flowers, etc.

Yvernel—landscape, birds.

SECOND PERIOD. 1800–1874

André, Jules—landscape.

Apoil—figures, subjects, etc.

Apoil, Madame—figure.

Barré—flowers.

Barriat—figure.

Beranger—figure.

Blanchard—decorator.

Blanchard, Alex.—ornament worker.

Boitel—gilding.

Bonnuit—decorator.

Boullemier, Antoine—gilding.

Boullemier (elder)—gilding.

Boullemier (son)—gilding.

Archelais—ornament worker (pâtes sur pâtes).

Avisse—ornament worker.

Barbin—ornaments.

Drouet—flowers.

Ducluzeau, Madame—figure, subjects, portraits, etc.

Durosey—gilding.

Farraguet, Madame—figure, subjects, etc.

Ficquenet—flowers and ornaments (pâtes sur pâtes).

Fontaine—flowers.

Fragonard—figure, genre, etc.

Ganeau (son)—gilding.

Gély—ornament worker (pâtes sur pâtes).

Mark	Description
Bₓ.	Buteux—flowers.
	Cabau—flowers.
CP	Capronnier—gilding.
	Célos — ornament worker (pâtes sur pâtes).
LC	Charpentier—decorator.
F.C.	Charrin, Dlle. Fanny—subjects, figures, portraits.
C.C.	Constant—gilding.
C.Z.	Constantin—figure.
D	Dammouse—figure, ornament (pâtes sur pâtes).
D	David—decorator.
D.F.	Delafosse—figure.
D.F.	Davignon—landscape.
Dℓ.	Desperais—ornaments.
DC	Derichsweiller—decorator.
CD	Develly — landscape and genre.
Dh	Deutsch—ornaments.
D.I.	Didier—ornaments, etc.
D	Didier—another form.
A	Martinet—flowers.
E.deM	Maussion, Mdlle. de—figure.
M	Merigot—ornaments, etc.
AAR	Meyer, Alfred—figure, etc.
MC	Micaud—gilding.
M	Milet, Optat—decorator on faience and pastes.
MR	Moreau—gilding.
AM	Moriot—figure, etc.
PP	Parpette, Dlle.—flowers.
P.L.	Philippine — flowers and ornaments.
P	Pline—decorative gilding.
AR	Poupart—landscape.
R	Regnier, Ferd.—figure, various subjects.
RR	Regnier, Hyacinthe—figure.
R	Rejoux—decorator.
E 1000	Renard, Émile—decorator.
BMR	Richard, Émile—flowers.
ER	Richard, Eugène—flowers.
J.J.	Georget—figure, portraits, etc.
Gob.R	Gobert—figure on enamel and on pastes.
D.G.	Godin—gilding.
E.G.	Goupil—figure.
G	Guillemain—decorator.
H	Hallion, Eugène—landscape.
H	Hallion, François—decorator in gilding.
h.J.	Huard — ornaments, divers styles.
.C.h.	Humbert—figure.
E	Julienne — ornaments, style Renaissance, etc.
L	Lambert—flowers.
Lgᵉ	Langlacé—landscape.
L	Latache—gilding.
L.B.	Le Bel—landscape.
L	Legay — ornament worker (pâtes sur pâtes).
L.G.	Le Gay—figures, various subjects, portraits.
Lg	Legrand—gilding.
℮L	Leroy, Eugène—gilding.
R	Richard, François—decorator.
JhR	Richard, Joseph—decorator.
✳	Richard, Paul — decorative gilding.
R.	Riocreux, Isidore—landscape.
Rₓ	Riocreux, Désiré-Denis — flowers.
PR	Robert, Pierre—landscape.
CR	Robert Madame—flowers and landscape.
R	Robert, Jean-François—landscape.
PMR	Roussel—figure, etc.
P.S	Schilt, Louis-Pierre—flowers.
S.S.p	Sinsson (father)—flowers.
M	Solon—figures and ornaments (pâtes sur pâtes).
S.W.	Swebach — landscape and genre.
J.Z.	Trager—flowers, birds.
Z.	Troyon—ornaments.
W	Walter—flowers.

UNDETERMINED SIGNATURES, ETC.

W
Jg
CL
— Three marks on plate dated 1821, view of Moka, signed L. M., richly gilded. The first mark also on several plates dated 1812, lapis-lazuli borders, heavy gilding, antique cameo paintings.

'M̅'   On richly decorated and gilded plates, 1821.

Phim   On plate, time of Louis XVIII., richly gilded ; monochrome portrait of Racine : (probable mark of Philippine.)

DᵐᵉʳRogᵈ   On plate not dated, rich gilding, monochrome portrait of Bourdaloue.

BT   On fine plates and vases, 1812.

DˡˡᵉTᵛʳᵉ   On plate *temp* Louis XVIII., rich gilding, monochrome portrait of Bourdon (? Dlle. de Treverret).

R   Twice this size on plate, 1822, view of Sèvres factory ; possibly a *visa* of Riocreux.

Lp   In black on foot of ice vase, with river deities in superb gilding, dated 1831.

ARTISTS' SIGNATURES FOUND AT FULL LENGTH

Baldisseroni—figure.
Brunel—figure.
Bulot—flowers.
Cool, Madame de—figure.
Courcy, De—figure.
Froment—figure.
Gallois, Madame (née Durand)—figure.
Garneray—landscape.
De Gault—figure.
Goddé—decorator, enamels and relief.
Hamon—figure.
Jaccober—flowers and fruits.
Jacquotot, Madame Victoire—figure, subjects, portraits.
Jadelot, Madame—figure.

Lamarre—landscape.
Langlois, Polycles—landscape.
Laurent, Madame Pauline—figure, subjects, etc.
Lessore—figure, etc.
Meyer-Heine—figure and ornaments on enamel.
Parant—figure, etc.
Philip—decorator on enamel.
Schilt, Abel—figure, subjects, portraits.
Solon, Dlle.—figure, subjects.
Treverret, Dlle. de—figure.
Van Os—flowers and fruits.
Van Marck—landscape.

MARKS USED AT SÈVRES TO INDICATE DATES OF MANUFACTURE

A (Vincennes)	1753	N		1766
B "	1754	O		1767
C "	1755	P		1768
D	1756	Q		1769
E	1757	R		1770
F	1758	S		1771
G	1759	T		1772
H	1760	U		1773
I	1761	V		1774
J (see foot note)	1762	X		1775
K	1763	Y		1776
L	1764	Z		1777
M	1765			

AA	1778	JJ	1787
BB	1779	KK	1788
CC	1780	LL	1789
DD	1781	MM	1790
EE	1782	NN	1791
FF	1783	OO	1792
GG	1784	PP	1793
HH	1785	QQ	1794
II	1786	RR	1795

This mode of marking the date fell into disuse, and, from this period until 1800, it is found only on rare examples. In 1801, the custom of dating was resumed, and the letters replaced by the following signs:

T. 9 . . . . An IX. (1801)	9 . . . . 1809[1]
X. . . . . " X. (1802)	10 1810
11 . . . . " XI. (1803)	oz. (onze) 1811
–11– . . . . . . " XII. (1804)	d. z. (douze) 1812
⚡ . . . . . . " XIII. (1805)	t. z. (treize) 1813
⚡ . . . . . . " XIV. (1806)	q. z. (quatorze) 1814
7 1807	q. n. (quinze) 1815
8 1808	s. z. (seize) 1816
	d. s. (dix-sept) 1817

MARKS ON PORCELAIN OF FRANCE

MARKS ON PORCELAIN OF GERMANY, ETC.

113 ВРАТЬЕВЪ Корниловыхъ **114** **115** С **116** g **117** А **118** ГАРДНЕРЪ

119 ГАРДНЕРЪ **120** ПОПОВЫ **121** АП **122** АР **123** Р

124 ФГ Гуаина **125** Barandwka **126** Сmi **127** KIEBZ 13 II **128** Rorzec

MARKS ON POTTERY AND PORCELAIN OF
ENGLAND

MARKS OF PENNSYLVANIA POTTERIES

MARKS OF NEW JERSEY POTTERIES

MARKS OF NEW YORK POTTERIES

MARKS OF NEW ENGLAND POTTERIES

MARKS OF OHIO POTTERIES

MARKS OF SOUTHERN POTTERIES

667 668 669 670 672
671 LaBelle China.

673 674 675 676 677 678 679

680 681 682 683 685 686 687
684 O.V.

688 689 690 691 692 693 694

695 696 697
NEWCOMB COLLEGE

MARKS OF WESTERN POTTERIES

698 PEORIA ILLINOIS 699 700 701 702

703 HOTEL F P Co 704 705 706 707 708 JEWEL C.P.Co. 709 REGINA C.P. CO. 712

713 ALMA 714 HOBSON 710 C. P CO. ROYAL 711 C. P. CO. REX 719

715 HELEN. 716 CROWN HOTEL WARE. 717 718 Crown Porcelain. REX.

720 RENA. 721 722 723 724 STOCKTON CALIFORNIA REKSTON

725 726 727 728 729 DENVER

730 ROBLIN 731 ROBLIN 732 VAN BRIGGLE 1902 733 734

735 MCP 736 DEWABIC

PRIVATE MARKS OF ROOKWOOD DECORATORS

MARKS ON CHINESE WARES

The inscriptions sometimes occurring in the field of decoration on Chinese porcelains are poems or references to the subject of the painting rather than dates or place marks, though exceptions do occur as in the Wan Li blue and white vase and the small Sung period Tz'u Chou formerly in my own collection ir *which the six character reign mark is about the shoulder, and in the three beakers in the Metropolitan Museum on which the marks occur in small rectangular cartouches near the lip-rim. Generally speaking the stamped, incised or painted marks which throw light on the period of a piece are found on the bottom. Marks on Sung or Yuan pieces are exceedingly rare and Ming pieces which have marks usually have the characters in ordinary script (k'ai shu) rather than in seal characters (chuan shu) though the script characters are often enclosed by a square, rectangular or round frame of double lines, as though to suggest a seal. Chinese inscriptions are read right to left in perpendicular columns top to bottom. Sir Percival David has pointed out that Mongolian inscriptions read top to bottom, left to right and this has been a contributing factor in placing some pieces. (See Plate XXXVII, The Catalogue of Chinese Pottery and Porcelain in The Collection of Sir Percival David.)

Marks fall into five classifications:

1.—Reign or date marks.
2.—Hall marks.
3.—Factory marks and potter's names.
4.—Marks of praise, dedication, etc.
5.—Pictorial or symbol marks.

1.—DATE MARKS.—Usually the period is indicated by giving the honorific name assumed by the emperor on ascending the throne. This title (nien hao) is the name by which collectors are accustomed to know the reign; thus Chan Chi's reign is known as Hsüan Tê and Chien Shen's as Ch'êng Hua (See text). To quote Mr. Ralph M. Chait (Chinese Chronology), "He loses his personal name and does not assume any name or proper title as do European kings, but gives to the epoch of his reign a distinguished appellation, which designates at once his period. This, however, is not the name by which he is canonized after death. That is called the "Mia Hao". Therefore, in history the emperor is known by his Mia Hao, and in ceramic history he is called by his Nien Hao, because it is perfectly obvious that it would be impossible to do otherwise, as no one could tell what his canonized name would be." Most earlier wares are marked with six characters. The first two beginning at the upper right and reading downward refer to the dynasty, thus *ta ming* means Great Ming (dynasty). The next two, that is the bottom one on the right hand column and the top one on the left hand column are the *nien hao,* thus we might read Hsüan Tê and the last two are *nien chih* or "period made,"—the whole reading ta ming hsüan tê nien hao or literally Great Ming Hsüan Tê period made. Sometimes the last character is *tsao* but this also means "made."

Abbreviated marks sometimes leave off the first two characters, giving simply the *nien hao* and "period made." Abbreviated marks which read simply *ta ming nien chih* also occur on proper specimens but are to be mistrusted for the Japanese made use of such marks. Sometimes only the double ring is used without any characters in it and this occurs in Ming as well as Ch'ing times. It is explained by R. L. Hobson that one workman did the rings and another the characters so perhaps these were pieces which slipped through without the attention of the second workman. In any event such a mark seems to have no bearing on the quality whatsoever. A complete list of the Imperial *nien hao* will be found in the *Chinese Reader's Manual,* by Mayer, in Giles' *Dictionary,* and in *Handbook of Marks on Pottery and Porcelain* by Burton and Hobson.

Once again we must warn that Chinese marks were copied in later reigns, were freely placed on modern wares made for trade and were also counterfeited by the Japanese. In his very interesting book *Early Ming Wares of Chingtechen,* the late A. D. Brankston shows some most convincing comparisons in the calligraphy. Hobson states "The connoisseur will take little heed of the ordinary date marks unless they are supported by good collateral evidence."

Seal marks are usually arranged in three columns of two characters each instead of in two columns of three characters each. They are read the same way from upper right to lower left and the *nien hao* occurs in the two center characters.

Brankston adds a few notes on marks of the Hsüan Tê period, "Apart from calligraphy, there are several forms of writing the mark. On dishes and bowls with glazed bases the mark is usually underneath in six characters enclosed in a double, rarely a single circle. On dishes with unglazed bases the mark is sometimes written in a line under the rim on the outside. On stem-cups the mark is usually written inside the bowl in the center, on yellow glazed stem-cups the mark is incised inside." This last is not invariably the case in later examples as we know. He continues, "There is a scarce type of bowl in which the six character mark is written inside in a single column, enclosed in a double rectangle: Plate 12g. The example seen was decorated outside with the Eight Buddhistic Emblems supported on lotus scrolls. The Hsüan Tê mark in four characters is rarely seen on Imperial porcelain. Those jars and bowls marked *Hsüan Tê nien tsao* were apparently made for export, fragments have been found in many places on the trade route along the South China coast, and in the Philippines." Again he stresses the style of writing, "If, in the writing of the mark, any stroke which forms part of a character has been formed by two sweeps of the brush, the piece in question is with little doubt a later copy. This being so, the same fault should be found in the drawing, if in underglaze blue."

Rare specimens have a cyclical date as well as the *nien hao.* Thus in *The Wares of the Ming Dynasty,* R. L. Hobson shows a well known bowl from the S. D. Winkworth collection which is marked *ta ming hsüan tê kuei ch'ou nien tsao* or made in the *kuei ch'ou* year of the Hsüan Tê period, viz. 1433. This Chinese cycle consists of sixty years each of which has an individual name in two characters formed by combining one of the Ten Stems with one of Twelve Branches. The *Chinese Reader's Manual* gives

CHRONOLOGICAL TABLE

Mark	Transcription	Year of the Cycle	Mark	Transcription	Year of the Cycle	Mark	Transcription	Year of the Cycle
子甲	Chia-tzŭ	1	申甲	Chia-shên	21	辰甲	Chia-ch'ên	41
丑乙	I-ch'oŭ	2	酉乙	I-yu	22	巳乙	I-ssŭ	42
寅丙	Ping-yin	3	戌丙	Ping-hsü	23	午丙	Ping-wu	43
卯丁	Ting-mao	4	亥丁	Ting-hai	24	未丁	Ting-wei	44
辰戊	Mou-ch'ên	5	子戊	Mou-tzŭ	25	申戊	Mou-shên	45
巳己	Chi-ssŭ	6	丑己	Chi-ch'ou	26	酉己	Chi-yu	46
午庚	Kêng-wu	7	寅庚	Kêng-yin	27	戌庚	Kêng-hsü	47
未辛	Hsin-wei	8	卯辛	Hsin-mao	28	亥辛	Hsin-hai	48
申壬	Jên-shên	9	辰壬	Jên-ch'ên	29	子壬	Jên-tzŭ	49
酉癸	Kuei-yu	10	巳癸	Kuei-ssŭ	30	丑癸	Kuei-ch'ou	50
戌甲	Chia-hsü	11	午甲	Chia-wu	31	寅甲	Chia-yin	51
亥乙	I-hai	12	未乙	I-wei	32	卯乙	I-mao	52
子丙	Ping-tzŭ	13	申丙	Ping-shên	33	辰丙	Ping-ch'ên	53
丑丁	Ting-ch'ou	14	酉丁	Ting-yu	34	巳丁	Ting-ssŭ	54
寅戊	Mou-yin	15	戌戊	Mou-hsü	35	午戊	Mou-wu	55
卯己	Chi-mao	16	亥己	Chi-hai	36	未己	Chi-wei	56
辰庚	Kêng-ch'ên	17	子庚	Kêng tzŭ	37	申庚	Kêng-shên	57
巳辛	Hsin-ssŭ	18	丑辛	Hsin-ch'ou	38	酉辛	Hsin-yu	58
午壬	Jên-wu	19	寅壬	Jên-yin	39	戌壬	Jên-hsü	59
未癸	Kuei-wei	20	卯癸	Kuei-mao	40	亥癸	Kuei-hai	60

chronological tables with a full description of the system but the certainly ingenious table worked out by Hetherington is used by all collectors. It appears in his book, *The Early Ceramic Wares of China* (A. L. Hetherington) and also in *The Wares of the Ming Dynasty* (R. L. Hobson) from which our page was reproduced.

MARKS, INSCRIPTIONS AND CHINESE CHARACTERS

甲 chia	乙 i	丙 ping	丁 ting	戊 mou	己 chi	庚 kêng	辛 hsin	壬 jên	癸 kuei
子 [1] tzŭ	丑 [2] ch'ou	寅 [3] yin	卯 [4] mao	辰 [5] ch'ên	巳 [6] ssŭ	午 [7] wu	未 [8] wei	申 [9] shên	酉 [10] yu
戌 [11] hsü	亥 [12] hai	子 [13]	丑 [14]	寅 [15]	卯 [16]	辰 [17]	巳 [18]	午 [19]	未 [20]
申 [21]	酉 [22]	戌 [23]	亥 [24]	子 [25]	丑 [26]	寅 [27]	卯 [28]	辰 [29]	巳 [30]
午 [31]	未 [32]	申 [33]	酉 [34]	戌 [35]	亥 [36]	子 [37]	丑 [38]	寅 [39]	卯 [40]
辰 [41]	巳 [42]	午 [43]	未 [44]	申 [45]	酉 [46]	戌 [47]	亥 [48]	子 [49]	丑 [50]
寅 [51]	卯 [52]	辰 [53]	巳 [54]	午 [55]	未 [56]	申 [57]	酉 [58]	戌 [59]	亥 [60]

" The first horizontal line of characters represents the ten stems. One of these stems will be found in combination with one of the branches in every cyclical date mark. If the eye is carried vertically downwards from the stem which has been detected in the inscription until it recognises the branch character, the year can be read off at once." Take the inscription on Fig. 2 of Plate 15. The character 癸 (*kuei*) is detected and is found to be the tenth stem, reading the table from left to right. With it is the character 丑 (*ch'ou*), the second branch. By carrying the eye vertically down the column headed with 癸 the combination is found in the sixth horizontal line of the diagrams indicating the fiftieth year. In some inscriptions the cyclical date is all that is mentioned, and we are left to determine the particular cycle concerned as best we may from indications of style or other internal evidence. But here we have only to do with the cycle in which the Hsüan Tê period fell, and we have no difficulty in arriving at the date 1433.

The cyclical system is supposed to have been instituted in the year 2637 B.C.; but in the Ming period we are only concerned with the cycles which began in 1324, 1384, 1444, 1504, 1564 and 1624 A.D.

Simpler still, but very uncommon, are those convenient date marks in which the number of the year in the reign is specified. To read those one must know the Chinese numerals :—

1 = 一 i.	5 = 五 wu.	9 = 九 chiu.
2 = 二 êrh.	6 = 六 liu.	10 = 十 shih.
3 = 三 san.	7 = 七 ch'i.	
4 = 四 ssŭ.	8 = 八 pa.	

DYNASTIC PERIODS MENTIONED IN THIS BOOK

Han dynasty	206 B.C.– 220 A.D.
T'ang „	618 A.D.– 906 A.D.
Sung „	960 A.D.–1279 A.D.
Yüan „	1280 A.D.–1367 A.D.
Ming „	1368 A.D.–1644 A.D.
Ch'ing „	1644 A.D.–1912 A.D.

REIGNS OF THE MING DYNASTY

Hung Wu	洪	武	1368–1398.
Chien Wên	建	文	1399–1402.
Yung Lo	永	樂	1403–1424.
Hung Hsi	洪	熙	1425.
Hsüan Tê	宣	德	1426–1435.
Chêng T'ung	正	統	1436–1449.
Ching T'ai	景	泰	1450–1456.
T'ien Shun	天	順	1457–1464.
Ch'êng Hua	成	化	1465–1487.
Hung Chih	弘	治	1488–1505.
Chêng Tê	正	德	1506–1521.
Chia Ching	嘉	靖	1522–1566.
Lung Ch'ing	隆	慶	1567–1572.
Wan Li	萬	歷	1573–1619.
T'ai Ch'ang	泰	昌	1620.
T'ien Ch'i	天	啓	1621–1627.
Ch'ung Chêng	崇	禎	1628–1644.

CH'ING REIGNS MENTIONED IN THIS BOOK

K'ang Hsi	1662–1722.
Yung Chêng	1723–1735.
Ch'ien Lung	1736–1795.

Rarely there also occur marks in which the year in the reign is specified as on our Tz'u Chou example now in the Metropolitan Museum referred to above. Page 220 from *The Wares of the Ming Dynasty* gives the numerals 1 to 10 but I also find page 215 from *Chinesisches Kunstgewerbe* (Martin Feddersen) valuable as it shows how the higher numerals are arrived at and gives the seasons.

I also reproduce Feddersen's arrangement of the marks of the more important reigns of Ming and Ch'ing dynasties, as I think them most excellently arranged.

CHRONOLOGICAL GUIDE

一年　1. Year

元年　九年六月十日　9. Year　6. Month　10. Day

春夏秋冬　Spring　Summer　Autumn　Winter

五十六　56

1 2 3 4 5 6 7 8 9 10

百千萬　100　1000　10000

年歲月日　Year　Year　Month　Day

一二三四五六七八九十
1 2 3 4 5 6 7 8 9 10

十二　12
二十　20

NIEN-HAOS OF THE MING DYNASTY

年製 洪武
Hung-wu
(1368–1398)

年製 永樂
Yung-lo
(1403–1424)

大明宣德年製
Hsüan-tê (1426–1435)

化年製
大明成化年製
成化
Ch'êng-hua (1465–1487)

治年製
大明弘
Hung-chih
(1488–1505)

德 大
年 明
製 正

Chêng-tê
(1506–1521)

靖 大
年 明
製 嘉

Chia-ching
(1522–1566)

慶 大
年 明
製 隆

Lung-ch'ing
(1567–1572)

曆 大
年 明
製 萬

Wan-li
(1573–1619)

啟 大
年 明
製 天

T'ien-ch'i
(1621–1627)

年 崇
製 禎

Ch'ung-chêng
(1628–1643)

NIEN-HAOS OF THE CH'ING DYNASTY

治 大
年 清
製 順

Shun-chih (1644–1661)

熙 大
年 清
製 康

K'ang-hsi (1662–1722)

正 大
年 清
製 雍

Yung-chêng (1723–1735)

隆 大
年 清
製 乾

Ch'ien-lung (1736–1795)

年 嘉
製 慶

Chia-ch'ing (1796–1820)

光 大
年 清
製 道

Tao-kuang (1821–1850)

豐 大
年 清
製 咸

Hsien-fêng (1851–1861)

治 大
年 清
製 同

T'ung-chih (1862–1874)

緒 大
年 清
製 光

Kuang-hsü (1875–1908)

2.—HALL MARKS refer to certain halls or pavilions in the Imperial palace, to a studio of a shop for which the ware was ordered, and we can seldom determine which. They in which the piece was made, to the family hall name of the person for whom the vessel was made, some building such as a hall of justice and possibly to the name are very rare on Ming wares. We classify them as "Hall Marks" because they usually contain the word t'ang (hall) or an equivalent such as t'ing (pavilion), chai (study), etc. Hobson says, "The t'ang ming is the 'family hall name,' making reference to some outstanding event in family history, e.g. *wu tê t'ang chin*—Chin of the Military valour (wu tê) hall. It is inscribed in one of the chief rooms of the house, on graves, in deeds, etc."

Mr. Hobson says that one hall mark does occur more or less frequently on late Ming wares and that is *yü t'ang chia ch'i* or "Beautiful vessel of (or for) the Jade Hall." This may mean simply "Hall of pure worth," and may refer to a factory but the wares which bear it are considerably varied, so it may be simply a sort of mark of commendation.

He also gives another mark which occurs only on faked Ming wares. This is *shên tê t'ang* meaning simply Shên Tê Hall, a name the meaning of which we do not know.

Among Barber's marks which follow there are a number of hall marks with his translations which are entirely correct except that he renders the character yu or yuh, as he spells it, as *jewel* instead of as *jade* as we are accustomed to think of it. No doubt the wider meaning is also quite correct. It will also be noted that phonetic spellings are different from those in common use now. I do not agree with his calling the lichens "sesamum flowers" and I take with several grains of salt the statement that the "two fish mark" has appeared on a blue and white piece dating 969–1106 in the Sung period. Also the "standard table" is obviously a representation of a bronze ting or four-legged incense burner or sacrificial vessel (see discussion of the ting form in our first section). However, the marks are otherwise all right and I include them as many people have referred to them in years past.

3.—POTTER'S NAMES occur on potteries and wares from the smaller kilns but never on Imperial wares or those from the Imperial factories. No example has yet been found of the ware signed *Hu yin tao jên* by Hao Shih-chiu and of the Ming Yi-hsing potters we only know of examples which bear the seal-mark of Ming-yüan (see text) and a script mark of Hui Mêng-ch'ên one of which Hobson shows in *The Wares of the Ming Dynasty* a small simple tea-pot which is said to bear the inscription, *"ching ch'i hui mêng ch'ên chih"* translated as, "made by Hui Mêng-ch'ên of King-ki (another name of Yi-hsing).

Hetherington speaks of a curious mark resembling G to be seen on some K'ang Hsi blue and white wares and enameled wares of fine quality and says it may have been suggested by some European trader.

He also says the names Chiang Ming-kao and Ch'ên Kuo-chih are found on biscuit porcelain of the early 13th century, and that potter's names are also found on the white porcelain of Tê hua, Fukien province, on Yi-hsing wares and those called Fatshan from down near Canton. Little work has been done to trace these potters and, in fact, there is little data to go on.

4.—MARKS OF COMMENDATION, of praise or suggesting the use to which the vessel should be put sometimes accompany the date marks or those of the potters. Thus the altar cups of Hsüan Tê were inscribed *t'an* (altar); those of Chia Ching period *ch'a* (tea) or *chiu* (wine), etc. inside the cups while under the base, we are told by the *Po wu yao lan,* might appear *chin lu* (golden seal), *ta chiao* (great sacrifice) or as on one in the British Museum mentioned by Hobson, *han hsing* (to contain fragrance). Other legends such as the frequently found one *fu kuei chia ch'i* (fine vessel for the rich and honorable) and *ch'ang ming fu kuei* (long life, riches and honors) or *wan fu yu t'ung* (may infinite happiness embrace all your affairs) express good wishes or at times a moral precept as in *lu wei ch'ing kao* (rank and emolument without corruption).

5.—PICTORIAL OR SYMBOL MARKS also express longevity (the stork, peach or pine tree) or happiness (the bat). Most of these occur on later wares but Hobson speaks of the hare and stork used as marks under the base of some late Ming wares of Chia Ching or Wan Li reigns, of both blue and white and enamel type. In Chait's Chinese Chronology as well as in the Barber marks reproduced will be found the

MARKS AND SYMBOLS ON POTTERY OF CHINA

Marks, Symbols, etc.

Three forms of the two fish mark, found on old blue ware : one of the earliest known, from 969–1106.

The sesamum flower. Various flower marks are found, in ancient and modern periods

Hoa : a small flower inside a cup. Marks the Yung-lo period, 1403–1424.

Butterfly

Show : long life ; a wish for longevity, common in one or another of these and other forms on porcelain : some-

Fuh-che : happiness

Luh : wealth

Keih : good luck.

Yuh : a gem ; precious thing

Wan : literature.

Hing : flourishing.

Ke : a vessel ; vase ; ability.

Paou : precious.

Marks, Symbols, etc.

times repeated a hundred or more times. Such pieces are called "hundred show."

Circular show mark.

Oval show mark

Thin form of show

Fuh-che : happiness

Yuh-chin : precious gem.

Wan-yuh : beautiful gem.

Chin-wan : valuable rarity

Ta-keih : prosperity ; good luck.

Choo-foo : a polite expression in China. Mark used 1260–1367

Keang-tang : preserved ginger   Used 1522–1566

Tsaou-tang : preserves ; chow-chow. Used 1522–1566.

Tung-gan, a name.

Ting : perfect

Tsuen : perfect ; a name.

King : good wishes

A name.

Woo-fuh: the five blessings —long life, health, riches, love of virtue, a natural death.

Woo-chin: the five blessings.

Chin-yuh : precious gem.

Fung seen tang } Hall of ancestors

Tang Khe che yuh } Made for hall of wonderful beauty.

Tang Ching che ti } Made for hall of virtuous study.

Tang Pi che yuh } Made for hall of jeweled girdle.

Tang Tze che tze } Made for hall of violet embroidery.

Tang King che wei } Made for hall of worship.

Kea Yuh ke tang } Beautiful vase for hall of gems.

Chang Fuh chun kwei } Wealth, honor, long youth.

Chang Fuh ming kwei } Wealth, honor, long life.

Tze Teen fuh kwan } Heaven grant happiness.

Jou Khe woo chin } Wonderful as the five precious things.

Wan ming cheang (name) che (made).

Yung ching yu che; made for Yung ching.

Yung-ching, a name

Tsae Jun tang che } Made for the brilliant hall of the middle.

Wei foo ching } Made to add to the jasper.

Jin ho kwan } Hall of brotherhood.

Jou Khe yuh chin } Wonderful gem, resembling a jewel.

Jou Khe yuh wan } Same signification.

Ya Ching tsei yu } Remarkable meeting of philosophers and friends.

Chin Poo wan ku } Valuable curiosity for antiquaries.

Paou Wan ting yah } Elegant, perfect, precious ting; metal incense pot.

Shan Wan tow shang } Compliment; comparing to a mountain and the North star

Ya Mei che yuh } Made for one who knows gems.

Wan show woo keang : an unlimited long life

Wan show woo keang } Same. This is in the seal character.

Keang ming kaou (name); tsaou (maker)

Badge of authority; on pieces for mandarins.

Tablet of honor, including the swastika.

Another form of the same.

奇連成	Leen ching khe how (not translated).
后若深	
珍 藏	Jo shin chin tsang : precious property; Jo shin (name).
以歪淡	Same mark
甌	
珍乘莊菜	Same mark
鼎奇石寶	Ting Khe / che she / chin paou } Ting of very precious and costly stone.
之珍	
鼎奇玉宝	Ting Khe / che yuh / chin paou } Same meaning.
之珍	
玉忠 雅有美 製	Yuh Chung / ya yuh / che mei } For the true hearted, elegant gem made.
福壽比 如南山 東海	Long life as the south mountain. Happiness like the east sea

Another form.

A mandarin mark of honor.

The sounding stone.

Another sounding instrument.

Sacred ax.

Shell or helmet?

Shell?

Shell?

Standard table.

Leaves. Frequent marks.

Treasures of writing, stone for ink, brushes for writing, a roll of paper, etc. Found as a mark; and common, as are many of the previous designs, in the surface decorations of porcelains.

Beautiful vase for the wealthy and noble. Otherwise translated: wealth, honors and intellect.

Probably a name.

Valuable vase for divining

These three combinations or arrangements of lines, known as the eight diagrams of Fuh-hi, frequently occur on Chinese porcelain. They have reference to certain mystic ideas, utterly unintelligible to us, relating to the genders, the principles of creation, the origin of all things, etc., etc. Chinese philosophers profess to understand their meaning and suggestions, and the Chinese regard them as talismanic.

Bamboo leaves, used as a mark at King-te-chin, 1573-1619. We have also found the leaves used as an exterior decoration of porcelain dishes which we believe to be Persian.

Square marks, common on old specimens, in these and many other forms.

Paou : precious

"artemis leaf" or palm leaf with and without fillets, and called *chiao yeh*, the *ling chih* or fungus mistakenly called sesamum flower by Barber, the *lein hua* or lotus blossom, the *ting* or four legged incense burner called a "tripod" by Hetherington, the *pi ting ju i* or brush, ink-cake and jade sceptre reading according to Chait "May it be fixed as you wish," (a rebus), the head of a *ju-i* sceptre, the endless knot, the *fu shou shang* ch'üan another rebus meaning Happiness and longevity represented by the bat and peach combined, the "spider mark" actually a form of "show" or shou the longevity character similar to those shown at the bottom of the first column of Barber's marks, the mei hua or sprig of prunus (in a double ring) and, of course, the various forms of the swastika enclosed in squares or lozenges with and without fillets or with simple loops at the corners. None, not a single one, of these can be in any way depended upon to help date a given specimen as all are used freely on modern examples many of which do not even purport to be of any of the periods interesting to collectors. Added to these there are also the Buddhist emblems, Taoist emblems, etc. (See Ming section.) One very fancy mark is a circle or square with various writings in it and embraced on either side with dragons. This occurs only on modern pieces.

Chu shih chü (red rocks retreat).

Yu chai (quiet pavilion).

Ku yüeh hsüan chih (made by Ku Yueh Hsuan).

Lu i t'ang (hall of green ripples).

Shên tê t'ang chih (made for the hall of cultivation of virtue).

Ts'ai jun t'ang chih (made in the hall of brilliant colours).

Ching wei t'ang chih (made for the hall of respectful awe).

Ta ya chai (pavilion of grand culture).

Chiang ming kao tsao (made by Chiang Ming-kao).

Ch'ên kuo chih tsao (made by Ch'ên Kuo-chih).

Yü fêng yang lin (Yang-lin of Yu-fêng).

Pai-shih (white rock) and Ling nan hui chê (Canton picture).

Wang tso t'ing tso (made by Wang Tso-t'ing).

Wang ping jung tso (made by Wang Ping-jung).

Chao-chin.

Chung t'un shih (Chung-t'un family).

Li-chih.

Lai-kuan.

Chao tsung ho yin (seal of Ho Chao-tsung).

Chih (made to command).

Shop marks.

Ch'i yü pao ting chih chên (a gem among precious vessels of rare jade).

葛明祥製	Ko Ming hsiang chih (made by Ko Ming-hsiang).	珍玩玉雅玩全吉	Chên wan (precious trinket).
			Yü (jade).
葛源祥製	Ko yüan hsiang chih (made by Ko Yüan-hsiang).		Ya wan (elegant trinket).
宜興紫砂	Yi hsing tzŭ sha (brown earth of Yi-hsing).		Ch'üan (complete).
G	G mark.		Chi (good luck).
福	Fu (happiness).		Endless knot.
祿	Lu (rank).		
壽	Shou (longevity)		Ling chih furgus.
	Spider mark (a form of shou).		Head of a ju-i sceptre.
	A tripod.	卍	Fu (an embroidery ornament).

MARKS ON JAPANESE WARES

In the text I have explained the confusion which is met in the study of Japanese wares; many of the marks are of a character to add even to that confusion for, if an artist was known by many names so also did he use varied signatures of each or any of these names as, for instance the three writings of Kenzan's signature. I reproduce a few pages of the best known marks as listed by Barber and Hannover and for those who are further interested there are many books on the subject such as that of J. Bowes *Japanese Marks and Seals*, London, 1882, the catalogue by A. W. Franks and the Japanese Chronological Tables by W. Bramsen. Of course, these marks may be potter's names, the names of tea-ceremony masters, names of towns or sections along with poetic names of places and then all the various kinds similar to Chinese marks as listed above, and once again the student must be advised that all the important ones were freely copied as with Chinese marks.

MARKS ON JAPANESE POTTERY AND PORCELAIN

Marks of Periods		Marks of Periods		Marks of Periods.	
建德	Ken-tok, 1370.	永正	Yei-show, 1504	正德	Show-tok, 1711.
文中	Bun-tin, 1372.	大永	Dai-jei, 1521	享保	Kiyo-ho, 1717
天授	Ten-du, 1375	亨禄	Kiyo-rok, 1528	元文	Gen-bun, 1736.
弘和	Ko-wa, 1380	大永	Di-yei, 1532	寛保	Kwan-po, 1741.

中元 Gen-tin, 1380.	治弘 Ko-dsi, 1555.	享延 Yen-kiyo, 1744.
四德明 Mei-tok, 1393.	祿永元 Yei-rok, 1558.	延寛 Kwan-jen, 1748.
永應 O-yei, 1394.	龜元 Gen-ki, 1570.	曆寶 Ho-reki, 1751.
長正 Show-tiyo, 1428.	正天 Ten-show, 1573	和明 Mei-wa, 1764.
享永 Yei-kiyo, 1429.	祿文 Bun-rok, 1592.	永安 An-jei, 1772.
吉嘉 Ka-kitsu, 1441.	長慶 Kei-chiyo, 1596.	明天 Ten-mei, 1781.
安文宝 Bun-an, 1444.	和元 Gen-wa, 1615.	政寛 Kwan-sei, 1789.
德亨 Ho-tok, 1449.	永寛 Kwan-jei, 1624.	和亨 Kiyo-wa, 1801.
德 Kiyo-tok, 1452.	保正 Show-ho, 1644.	化文 Bun-kwa, 1804.
正康 Ko-show, 1455.	安慶 Kei-an, 1648.	政文 Bun-sei, 1818.
祿長 Chiyo-rok, 1457.	應承 Show-o, 1652.	保天 Ten-po, 1834.
正寛 Kwan-show, 1460.	曆明 Mei-reki, 1655.	化弘 Ko-kua, 1844.
正文 Bun-show, 1466.	治萬 Man-dsi, 1658.	永嘉 Ka-yei, 1848.
仁應 O-nin, 1467.	文寛 Kwan-bun, 1661.	久文 Bun-se, 1854.
明文 Bun-mei, 1469.	寳延 Yen-po, 1673.	治元 Man-yen, 1860.
亨長 Chiyo-kiyo, 1487.	和天 Ten-wa, 1681.	應慶 Bun-kin, 1861.
德延 En-tok, 1489	辛貞 Tei-kiyo, 1684.	治明 Gen-di, 1861.
應明 Mei-o, 1492.	祿元 Gen-rok, 1688.	政安 Kei-o, 1865.
龜文 Bun-ki, 1501	永寶 Ho-yei, 1704.	延萬 Mei-di, 1868.

Enamel Marks.

辰北 元勲津介製 — Enamel mark. Forgery? of Chinese date 1645.

大日本 — Di-Nipon: Great Japan.
Han-suki, maker. (Enamel.)

日本賴戶 瀨興六製 — Nipon: Japan. Next signs illegible.
Eurok, maker. (Enamel.)

Awata Potteries.

大日永 啃享製 — Great Japan.
Dioto, maker.

— Tokio, name of factory; and maker's names.

— Ae-rako, a name.

— Ki-yo, a name.

— Yu-ah-su-zan, a name.

和田 — Awata.

Banko Potteries.

萬古 — Banko.

— Banko.

Banko Potteries.

— Nipon, Japan.
Ari-nori, name.

— Banko.

— Shing-en, a name.

— Banko.

— Banko.

— Banko: eminent of flowers.

— Banko: an old mark.

— Guso, name.

— Maker's mark.

Bishu Porcelain.

尾州 — Bishu.

Hiradoson Porcelain.

— Hiradoson.
Shi-ae, maker.

— Hiradoson and maker's name.

Hezen Porcelain.

Mark	Description
肥前	Hezen, or Fisen.
肥州	He-shu.
田力三 肥前有	Hezen: Haritikami, maker.
信南造 肥前山	Hezen: Shinpo, maker.
肥璞山 川造	Hezen: Reksen, maker
西肥有田山 南里製	West Hezen: Nan-di, maker.
肥川有田	He-shu (Hezen): Tentai, maker.
百太造	Haridan, factory.

The following are Hezen factory villages:

Mark	Description
山内向大	Great mountain between rivers.
山内向三	Three mountains between rivers.
山泉和	Mountain of springs.
平禺攵	Beautiful upper plain.
平野本	Beautiful chief plain.
平野中	Middle plain.
平長	Long plain.

Hezen Porcelain.

Mark	Description
郎六	Great vase.
郎中	Medium vase.
川白	White stream.
町赤	Street of painters in red.
屋岩	The cave.
剝南	South bank.
尾囙	Outside tail.
田钅黒	Black field.
瀨廣	Firo-se.
瀨一	Itche-na-se.
右井	Imali.

Kaga Pottery and Porcelain.

Mark	Description
九谷	Kutani: the nine valleys.
九谷	Kutani.
九谷	Kutani.
九谷	Made at Kutani.
九谷	Made at Kutani.
九陽谷	Kagayo Kutani.
九加陽谷	The same.
加九谷	The same.

Kaga Pottery and Porcelain.

Mark	Description
九左朱谷	Kagayo Kutani.
大日本谷公製九	Great Japan, made at Kutani.
九谷不山	Kutani Bok-zan.
(mark)	Kutani: Touzan.
(mark)	Porcelain Mountain (Touzan).
(mark)	Rising-sun Mountain.
本山	Ponzan.
柳造	Dio, maker.

Kaga Pottery and Porcelain.

Mark	Description
壽	Long life.
福	Happiness.
祿	Riches.

Kioto Pottery.

Mark	Description
京都	Kioto.
錦光造 京都	Kioto, Japan; Kinkou-san, maker.
錦	Kinkousan, maker.

Satsuma Pottery.

Mark	Description
(mark)	Itsigaya, a place.
帶山	Tai-zan, maker.

Great Japan; Garden Mountain; strong pottery.

To-o.

Made at Kutani, long house.

Kutani.

Shiba (Tokei) Pottery.

Hikomakoro, maker at Sie-untei, in Shiba.

Unknown.

Awari Porcelain.

Awari.

Saeng-ets: beautiful moon; name of celebrated painter.

Ai-we, name.

Spring Mountain.

Painter's name (Yamamoto Sho-tan)

Symbols, Inscriptions, Names, etc.

Long life.

Long life.

Wealth, honors and long life.

Made at beautiful garden.

The same; maker's name (Gos-ki) added.

Tai-zan.

Tai-zan.

Tai-zan.

Den-ko, name.

Symbols, Inscriptions, Names, etc.

Happiness.

Wealth.

So-o.

Kami, maker.

Rakou-masa, maker.

Huzi-nori, name.

Imitation of Chinese marks: "Precious property of Joshin."

Shin-fo-se-seki, name.

Seven honorable societies.

Hall of increase of peace, harmony.

Wealth, honors and long youth.

Wealth, honors and long life.

Same factory name.

Sanfo, maker. These are on Nagasaki wares.

Sito in Japan, with maker's name; Nagasaki.

Factory-marks and signatures of artists on Japanese porcelain.

Place-marks on Japanese porcelain.

Signatures of artists on Japanese stoneware, etc.

Place-marks on Japanese stoneware.

INDEX

A

Abraham of Kutaia, 348
Abtsbessingen factory, 830
Achaemenid Empire, 269, 271, 289
Acier, 655
Adam, Lambert Sigisbert, 798
Adam and Eve plates, 884
Adams, William, 921
Africa, North, pottery, 342ff.
Agate, 813
Agate ware, 876, 919
Agate ware, English, 906, 907, 908
Alabastron, 46, 52
Alafia, 339
Alberello, 4, 331, 341, 354, 360, 380, 395
Albert, C. G., 669
Albrechtsburg, 644
Alcora, 717
Aldegraver, Heinrich, 411
Alders, John and Thomas, 908
Alders factory, 913
Aldersea, 913
Aldgate potteries, 880
Alexandria, 282, 391
Alfred University, School of Ceramics, 1067, 1073
Algeria, 342
Algiers, 993
Alhambra, 328, 332ff.
Alla Castellana ware, 348
Alla porcellana, 359, 370
Allegrain, 688
Allemande, 702
Almeria culture, 325
Alphen, Heinrich von, 819
Alsop, 995
Altamira, 9
Altar cups, 462
Altars of Friendship, 731
Altars of Love, 731
Alternating design, 29
Amateur potters, American, 1056ff.
Amberg factory, 824
Amoe, 296, 298
Amphora, 50, 51, 55, 57, 67, 69, 71, 102, 572
An Hua, 535
An-yang, 20ff., 85
Anam, 519
Andersson, J. G., 20, 22, 23, 24, 28
Andrae, Walter, 275, 284, 287, 288
Andreas, Johann, 637
Andreas, Wilhelm, 637
Andreoli, Giorgio, 357, 400
Andries, Guido, 878
Andries, Jasper, 879
Angivilliers, d', 690
Angoulême, 701, 703, 809
Anhwei, 122, 160, 423, 426, 437, 503, 504
Annam, 85, 87
Ansbach, 379, 638, 674, 823, 824
Antioch, 391
Antonibon, Giovanni Battista, 711
Antonibon, Pasquale, 711
Antonio, Maestro, 625
Apulia, 70, 71, 391, 669
Aquamaniles, 394, 865
Aragon, 328, 333, 338
Archers, frieze of, 283, 289
Ardus, 802, 809
Arezzo ware, 391
Argenteuil, 685
Arita, 256, 258
Arnheim, 788, 1017
Arras, 697
Arretine ware, 391
Artois, Comte d', 699
Artoisenet, Jacques, 791
Aryballos, 46, 48, 52, 58, 63, 967ff.
Ashikaga period, 232ff.
Ashur, 30, 275, 283, 285ff., 287, 345
Assyria, 18, 20, 47, 67, 268, 285, 286, 288, 289, 290, 341
Astbury, 616, 899, 900, 905–6, 909, 1007
Athens, 42ff., 48ff., 54ff., 59, 63, 67, 71

Augsburg, 823
Augustenburg, 829
Auliczek, Dominikus Jakob, 673
Ausschuss ware, 661
Austria, 13, 406, 838, 1016
Avelli, Xanto, 371
Avignon, 393, 394, 802
Ayliffe, 893
Aztec potteries, 942

B

Babylon, 42, 45, 282, 283, 288
Bachelier, 683, 686, 688
Bacon, John, 753, 760
Bagdad, 295
Bahram Gur, 269
Bailleul factory, 808
Bally, Johannes, 819
Baranovka, 721
Barber, Edwin Atlee, 640, 645, 979
Barbin, François, 632
Barbotine, 7, 392
Barnes, Zachariah, 775, 892
Barr, Flight and Barr, 764
Barr, Martin, 763
Barry, Du, 642
Bartman jug, 409, 412, 894
Basaltes, 916, 919
Basdorff factory, 633
Bastille 'faïence, 377
Basto, Pinto, 717
Bat hall mark, Chinese, 623
Batavian ware, 562
Battersea, 762
Bauer, Adam, 676
Bauer, Matthäus, 824
Bavaria, 418, 821, 1014
Baxter, Thomas, 767
Bayard, Charles, 805
Bayer, Johann Christoph, 733, 735
Bayreuth, 379, 645, 821, 823, 839
Bear jugs, English, 877
Beauvais, 393ff.
Behaghel, Daniel, 819
Belgium, 725, 791, 1017, 1027, 1035
Bell Krater, 50, 51, 55
Bell works, 913
Belleek, 739, 1050
Belleville, 587
Bellevue, 805
Belper, 898
Belvedere, 840
Benckengraff, Herr, 633
Benckgraff, Johann, 666, 667
Benckieser, Johann Adam, 826
Bennet, Edwin William, 1007
Bennet, James, 1006
Bennington, Vermont, 991
Benom, Ann, 875
Bentivoglio, 354
Bentley, Thomas, 914, 915
Berain, 628, 810
Berchem, Nicolas, 788
Berenvelt, Samuel P. van, 389
Berettino, 361
Bergdoll, Adam, 675, 678
Bergen factory, 859
Berington & Co., 772
Berlin, 379, 661ff., 828, 1015
Berling, 649
Bermondsey, 880
Bernard, François, 807
Bernard, Jacques Henri, 807
Berne, 836
Beromünster, 836
Berthevin, Pierre, 677, 736, 738, 827, 854ff.
Bessarabia, 13
Bettignies, 694, 697, 791
Beyer, Christian Wilhelm, 660, 679, 680
Beyerlé, Jean Louis, Baron, 698, 804
Bianchetto, 356
Bianco Sopra bianco, 359, 853, 857, 861
Billa I, etc., 15, 18

1151

Billingsley, William, 767, 770, 771
Bindenschild mark, 661
Bing & Gröndahl factory, 1022, 1041
Binney and Ronaldson, 1000
Birch, Niels, 726
Bird, Daniel, 908
Bird motifs, 853, 893
Birnkruge, 414
Birthday Plates, 578
Biscuit ware, 559, 633, 669, 680, 686, 943, 1052
Bishop bowls, 842, 861
Bisque figures, 689, 691
Bizen ware, 235, 239
Blaataarn, 726
Black Earth potteries, 12, 21, 24, 28, 29, 75
Black-figure ware, 46, 49, 51, 53, 58
Black gold ware, Chinese, 562, 563
Black Pottery People, 27
Blackburton wares, 878
Blanc de Chine, 444, 535ff., 614
Blankenburg, 788
Blauwerk, 415, 416, 417
Bleu Persan ware, 376, 796
Bleu-de-roi, 656, 684
Blondeau, 686
Bloomfield, John Caldwell, 739
Bloor, Robert, 753
Blue dragon pattern, 768
Blue jasper ware, 920
Blue leaf design, 853
Blue, Mazarine, 550
Blue, Mohammedan, 468
Blue, robin's egg, 594
Blue ware, Chinese, 579
Blue ware, Copenhagen, 1018, 1022
Blue ware, English, 885, 886
Boch brothers, The, 792
Boch, Pierre-Joseph, 792
Boch, William, 1005
Boeren-Delftsch ware, 787
Boileau, 686, 689
Boizot, Louis Simon, 689ff.
Bolomey, Benjamin, 724
Bonaveri, Carlo Antonio, 719
Bone, Henry, 773
Bone ash, 748
Bone China, 742, 991, 1003
Bonnefoy, Antoine, 810
Bonnet, 814
Bonnin, Gousse, 989, 990
Bonnin and Morris, 990
Bontemps, Valentin, 822
Boode, Peter, 141
Bordeaux, 699, 809
Borneo, 432, 510
Bornholm, 726, 1038
Borrmann, Johann Balthasar, 661
Bos, Cornelis, 411
Bosch, 856
Bossue, Jean, 807
Bottengruber, 659
Böttger, Johann Friedrich, 616, 633, 643ff., 682, 705, 824, 830, 900, 908
Bouchard, Noël, 802
Bouchardon, 689
Boucher, François, 642, 853, 857
Bouffioulx, 418
Boulé brothers, 814
Boulevard St. Garbin, 704
Boulle style, 796
Boumeester, Cornelis, 788
Bourdon des Planches, 700
Bourg-la-Reine factory, 632
Bourgoin, Jean-Baptiste-Alexis, 803
Boussemaert, François, 791, 807
Bouvignies, 418
Bow, 612, 742, 744, 757, 980, 989
Bowen, John, 887
Boxer vase, 38
Boyer, François, 805
Boyle, Samuel, 753
Braintree, Mass., 989, 990
Brampton, 898, 995
Brandenstein, 659, 662
Brankston, A. D., 101, 124, 421, 461, 467, 620
Braun, E. W., 666, 829
Brazil, 973
Brecheisen, Joseph, 726
Brehm, Johann Adam, 636
Breslau, 839

Briand, Thos., 773
Bricqueville, 809
Briot, François, 405
Brislington potteries, 806, 880, 882, 887
Bristol, 765, 772, 882ff.
Bromley, William, 739
Brongniart, 691ff.
Brooks, Hervey, 989, 990
Broome, Isaac, 979, 1005
Brouwer, Gerrit, 782
Brouwer, Hugo, 785
Brouwer, Huibrecht, 382
Brouwer, Justus, 387, 782, 784
Brühl, Count Heinrich, 652
Brüning, Heinrich Christian, 670
Brussels ware, 825
Bruyn, Abraham de, 411
Bry, Theodore de, 411
Buccaro ware, 49, 65ff., 239, 642, 643
Bucchero. See Buccaro
Budd, James, 979
Buddha, 231, 234, 455, 456
Buen Retiro, 714
Buglioni, Santi, 399
Bülow, Baron de, 791
Buontalenti, Bernardo, 625
Burlington, N. J., 979, 990, 998
Burslem, 876, 900, 913
Burton, William, 132, 170, 368, 400, 744
Busch, Christian Daniel, 659
Bushell, S. W., 534, 560, 581, 600, 612
Bustelli, Franz Anton, 639, 671, 679
Butler, A. J., 9, 282, 305ff., 332, 342
Bux, Johann Baptist, 828
Byzantium, 323

C

Cabaret, Antoine, 813
Caen, 699
Caffaggiolo, 354, 357, 360, 362, 367
Cafferi, 689
Caillat, 684
Calicut, 587
Callot figures, 646
Cambrette, Gabriel, 805
Cambrette, Jacques, 805
Cambrian pottery, 772, 921
Camellia green, 566, 594
Campania, 58, 69, 71, 391
Campaniform, 325
Camradi, 733
Canosa, 71, 391
Cantharus, 43
Canton, 520, 588, 608, 824
Capo di Monte, 372, 707, 714
Cappelen, Didrik von, 859
Capua, 50
Carl Theodor, Elector, 827
Carlsen, Emil, 464, 555
Carolsfeld, Schnorr von, 679
Carpentier, François, 791
Carthusian Monastery Mayence, 826
Cartlidge, Charles, & Co., 1005
Cartwright, 995
Casa Eccelma Vezzi, 705
Caselli, Giovanni, 707
Cassel factory, 640, 825
Castel Durante ware, 360ff.
Castelli, 366, 372, 838
Castilhon, 802
Castle Durante. See Castel Durante
Castleford pottery, 920
Catherine of Russia, 688, 720, 916
Caughley, 764, 768ff., 921
Cauldon potteries, 1025
Caussy, Pierre, 797
Caylus, Comte de, 914
Ceja de la Montaña, 944
Celadon, 147 et seq., 213, 436, 468, 502, 507, 560, 594, 1018, 1040, 1047, 1055
Cencio, Maestro, 357
Ceramic lamps, American, 1030ff.
Cerquate, 359
Chaffers, Richard, 775, 892
Chait, Ralph M., 142
Chamberlain, Robert and Son, 764
Chamberlain, Walter, 764
Chamberlans, 657
Champion, Richard, 772
Champlevé, Toltec, 942

Chang, 144, 197
Chang's ware, Younger, 148, 153
Chantilly, 628, 631, 696, 746, 815
Chapelle, Jacques, 696, 812
Chekiang, 27, 100, 120, 126, 423
Chelsea, 612, 742, 744, 751
Chêng Ho, 140, 459, 461
Ch'êng Hua, 467, 470, 474, 526, 535, 544
Chêng Tê, 477, 523
Cheng-tê Ching, 843
Chi Chou, 172, 422, 509
Chia Ching, 163, 343, 451, 461, 468, 474, 480, 486, 504, 517, 605ff., 623
Chicaneau, Pierre, 628
Chicken skin, 451, 463, 558
Ch'ien Lung, 444, 532, 565, 571, 589, 593, 598, 603, 612, 650, 853
Chien-yang, 425, 516
Chien yao, 169, 232, 428, 444
Chimu, 945ff.
China, La, factory, 714
Ching period, 436, 532ff., 559, 617
Ch'ing-ho Hsien, 174, 178, 180, 193
Ch'ing Pi Ts'ang, 131, 140, 147
Ching Tê, 132, 421
Ching-tê Chên, 124, 155, 168, 421, 422, 437, 442, 444, 458, 459, 461, 462, 476, 489, 742
Ching-tê Chêng, 131, 160, 344, 424, 441, 501, 502, 503, 511, 512, 517, 523, 533, 535, 560, 578, 582, 583, 588, 603, 607
Ch'ing Tz'u, 147
Chin-yen kiln, 100, 124, 125
Cho Keng Lu, 131, 141
Choisy, 814
Chosen, 215, 237
Chou Period, 23, 73, 75, 128, 619
Christian, Philip, 775
Ch'ü Chou, 125, 132, 144, 147, 151, 160, 423, 426, 502, 505ff., 560, 573, 591, 622
Chü-lü Hsien, 178, 193, 202
Chün, 42, 126, 129, 132, 141, 162ff., 204, 224, 421ff., 502, 517ff.
Cirou, Sicaire, 628
Cistercian ware, 870
Claesen, Dirck, 979
Clair, Adam, 674, 676
Clair de Lune, 559
Clark, Shaw & Cie, 815
Clarke, William, 807
Clarus, Johann Felician, 665, 825
Claw factory, 785
Clérissy family, 375, 798ff., 810
Clermont Ferrand, 802
Clews family, 1001, 1006
Cliff Bank factory, 908, 913
Clingnancourt, 701, 703
Clodion, 667, 689
Cloisonné technique, 587, 874
Coalbrookdale, 769
Coalport, 694, 769
Coblenz, 409, 411
Coburg factory, 829
Cognac factory, 809
Coke, John, 771
Colditz, 644
Cologne, 406ff., 879
Column Krater, 50, 51, 56
Combe, Joseph, 802
Commelin, 690
Commemoration wares, English, 1042
Commeraw's stoneware, 983
Conrade, Augustin, 376
Conrade brothers, 376
Constantinople, 295, 316, 323, 392
Contrada di San Giobbe, 712
Cooge, Abraham de, 386
Cookworthy, William, 772, 980
Copeland, 739, 753, 778, 1024
Copenhagen, 651, 669, 686, 822, 840ff., 1015ff., 1037ff.
Cordova, 332
Corinth, 45, 46, 47, 49, 67, 69
Cortona, 350
Cosijn, Avendt, 782
Cottage china, 777
Cotteau, 690
Courtille, La, 701
Cox, James, 744
Cox, Warren E., 1069
Coxe, Daniell, 979, 990
Cozzi factory, 705, 712

Crackle, 140, 145, 147, 450, 565ff., 909
Craft, Thomas, 759, 1001
Crailsheim factory, 828
Cranch, Richard, 989, 990
Crane, Walter, 1017, 1025
Crete, 11, 32ff., 41, 61, 65, 66, 290
Crolius family, 981ff.
Crouch ware, 900
Crown Derby ware, 1042. *See Derby*
Crowther, John, 759
Croxall family, 1006
Cuerda seca technique, 328, 484
Cushman's, Paul Stoneware Factory, 983
Custine, Comte de, 804, 827
Cyfflé, Paul Louis, 805, 913
Cyprus, 45, 269, 289
Czechoslovakia, 1027, 1043

D

Daibutsu-Den, 231
Damascus, 341, 344, 345, 347, 356
Damghan, 18, 313
Damm, 825
Danhofer, Joseph Philipp, 659, 821, 823
Danish ware, 841ff., 1036, 1017ff.
Dannecker, Johann Heinrich, 680
Danzig, 406
Darte, brothers, 703
Davenport, John, 777
David, Sir Percival, 101, 124, 135, 137, 210, 503, 504
De Cooge, Abraham, 386
Decoration, enamel, 325, 342, 625
De cuenca, 328
de Fulvy, Orry, 684
Delft, 380ff., 642, 726, 781, 785, 789, 825, 840, 853, 864, 878ff., 1035
Della Robbia family, 391, 395ff.
De Milde, Arij, 616, 645, 898
Demitoka, 348
Denmark, 11, 726, 841, 1017ff., 1036
D'Entrecolles, Père. *See Entrecolles, Père d'*
Derby, 694, 744, 751, 922, 1042
Derbyshire ware, 874, 995
Deruta, 358, 363ff., 368
Devil's work, 494, 501, 537, 920
Devonshire ware, 877
Dextra, 785, 788
Digne, factory, 798
Dijck, Cornelis Cornelisz van, **787**
Dillwyn, Lewis Weston, 772
Dipylon, 42, 43, 44, 45
di Savino, Guido, 878
Doccia, 707, 710
Does, Dirk van der, 782
Dommer and Co., 9, 723
Don pottery factory, 920
Dordrecht, 787
Dorez, Barthélemy, 628, **807**
Dorhalt factory, 859
Dorotheenthal factory, 829, 852
Dorset, Vermont, 993, 998
Dortie, Jacques, 719, 736, 737
Doulton, 995, 1023ff., 1042
Dragon design, 455, 481
Drammen factory, 859, 861
Dreihausen, 395
Dresden faïence, 379, 643, 680. *See Meissen*
Dubois, brothers, 682, 703, 808
Duccio, Agostino di, 397
Dudley Vases, 750, 755
Duesbury, William, 743, 744, 751, 753
Duijn, Johannes van, 781, 785
Duplessis, 683
Dupré, G., 405
Durante, Francesco, 367
Durell, Jonathan, 989, 990
Durlach factory, 826
Durot, Leperre, 698
Dutch East India Company, 384
Dutch ware, modern, 1035
Duvivier, Henri-Joseph, 696
Dwight, 616, 642, 894, 896, 900, 909, **913**

E

Earth spirits, 90, 91, 113
Earthworm marks, 164
East India Company, 816, 898
East Liberties kiln, 1001
East Liverpool, Ohio, 1006
Eberhardt, Johann, 380

Eberlein, Johann Freirich, 652
Eckert & Cie, 634
Edward Norton Co., 995
Eenhoorn, Lambertus van, 386, 388ff., 898
Eggebrecht, Peter, 643, 719, 830
Egypt, 9, 13, 30ff., 34, 41, 45, 47, 49, 51, 54, 65, 148, 275ff., 307
Ehrenreich, Johann, 736, 854, 855
Ehrenreigh, Ludwig, 380
Eigelstein, 413
Eight Immortals, 455, 481
Elers brothers, 616, 642, 894, 896ff.
Elizabeth, N. J., kiln, 1000
Embden, Rücker, 437
Emens, Jan, 414ff.
En grisaille, 656
Enamel, 342, 356, 467, 565ff., 625
Engobe, 289, 1012ff.
Ens, Karl, 634
Entrecolles, Père d', 495, 499, 534, 535, 541, 547, 550, 551, 556, 560, 564, 569, 571, 574, 576, 589, 610
Epigone Style, 961
Erfurt ware, 379, 830
Eskimo pottery, 927
Este, 714
Eterbeek, 725
Étiolles, 697
Etruria, 50, 65, 69
Etruria factory, 778, 915ff., 1005
Etruscan ware, 32, 49, 66ff., 656
Eumorfopoulos, George, 134, 160
Evans, Sir Arthur, 32
Ewer, The, factory, 785

F

Fabrique de ronsieur, 701, 703
Faenza, 350, 354, 358, 362, 369, 879, 882, 884
Faïence, 332, 354, 377ff., 813, 835ff.
Faience Pavilion, 316
Falcone, Antonio, 707
Falconet, 686, 688, 798
Falke, Otto von, 411, 417
Falkner, Frank, 885, 913
Fareham, 875
Farley, Malcolm, 430, 510
Farmer, Edward I., 1030
Fauchier, 810
Fauquez, 698, 791, 808
Feathered ware, 876
Feburier, Jacques, 807
Feilner, Simon, 666, 667, 675
Fên ch'ing, 140
Fên ting, 182
Fenton factory, 900ff.
Ferdinand, Anlers Nicolaus, 851, 852
Ferrara, 354, 365, 370
Ferretti, Domenico, 679
Ferris, Hugh, 1029
Ferro, Gian, 376
Ferrybridge pottery, 920
Fire-fly ware, 604
Fischer, Giovanni, 707
Fischer, Johann Sigmund, 659
Fischer, Sigismund, 712
Fishponds factory, 887
Five color ware, 452, 455, 483, 485, 497, 558, 571
Flambé ware, 555, 1023, 1027, 1054
Flight, 763
Flight and Barr, 763, 767
Flight, Barr and Barr, 764
Flint Enamel, 993ff.
Flintporslin, 813, 852, 857
Flora Danika Service, 733
Florida Indian potteries, 929, 930
Flörsheim factory, 826
Flötner, Peter, 413
Flower, 887, 889
Flux, 289
Flying Lion, 482
Fly's wing-enamel, 565
Fontainebleau, 685
Fontana, 371, 400
Fontebasso, 714
Forest factories, 634
Forsyth, Gordon, 1014, 1022, 1024
Fort de Eendragt, t', 788
Fouqué, Joseph, 799
Franconia wares, 816
Frankenthal, 640, 674ff.

Frankfort, 817, 821, 823, 836, 985, 987
Franklin Institute, 999, 1002
Frechen, 409, 411, 412, 879, 893
Freigang, Paul, 1066, 1071, 1076
Frothingham, Alice W., 308, 332
Frye, Thomas, 757, 980
Fukien, 423, 425, 430, 444, 535, 612, 628
Fulda factory, 635, 639, 825
Fulham factory, 894, 896
Fulper Pottery, 1049

G

Gabri ware, 289, 295ff., 348, 877
Gallipots, 452, 886
Gambini, Scipio, 376
Gambino, Giulio, 374ff.
Gamboa, Capitan Don Pedro Sarmiento de, 966
Ganaur, 295
Gardner Factory, 721
Gautier, Jacques, 809
Geijer, Bengt Reinhold, 852
Gekwaartel, 841
Gelder, H. E. van, 725
Gentile, Bernardo, et al., 372
Geometric period, 41ff., 71
Gera ware, 637
Gerault-Deranbert, 814
Germain, Nicholas, 838
German faïence, 378ff., 815ff.
German flowers, 655ff.
German soft paste, 633ff.
German tin-glazed ware, 374ff.
German ware, modern, 1014, 1015
Germantown, 983
Germany, 392ff.
Gerverot, 670
Gesarte, 338
Gessner, Salomon, 718, 836
Geyger, Johann Caspar, 639
Ghaznevid, 273
Gierlof, Christian, 841ff.
Gilbody, Samuel, 775
Gilze, Johann Christoph, 825
Ginori factory, 707ff.
Gioanetti, Vittorio Amadeo, 713
Giordano, Giuseppe, 710
Giorgio, Maestro, 369
Girard, Abel, 806
Glaisher, J. W. L., 870
Glaze, 75, 107, 132, 147, 231, 275ff., 325, 343, 395, 509, 530, 560ff., 626, 921, 1024, 1038, 1054ff.
Glost kiln, 1052
Glot, Julien Jacques Richard, 696, 812
Gobelins factory, 691
Göggingen, factory, 829
Gold, black, 562, 563
Gold, Norwegian, 861
Gold-Anchor period, 747
Gold lustre, English, 911
Göltz, Johann Christoph, 665, 666, 825
Goltzius, Konrad, 411
Gombroon, 318ff.
Goodale, Daniel, 997
Goshen, 991
Goss, W. H., 739
Gotha, 635
Goto Saijiro, 258
Gotskowsky, 637, 661ff., 683
Gräbner, Christian Zacharias, 637
Graesse, 645, 835
Graffito ware, 876ff.
Grain de riz ware, 318, 603
Granada, 332, 337
Granary urns, 81
Grand feu, 443
Grassi, Anton, 660
Gravant, François, 682ff.
Graz, 838
Greatbach, Daniel, 995, 1002
Great Lakes potteries, 931, 933
Greece, 11, 36ff., 48, 60ff., 65, 72, 106, 290ff.
Greek A, The, factory, 785
Green, cucumber, 565
Green, Guy, 892, 893
Green, John, 920
Green glazes, Wedgwood, 913
Green ware, 564, 571
Greiner, W., et al., 634ff.
Grenzau, 416

Grenzhausen, 409, 411, 416
Grès potters, French, 1011, 1013
Grey ware, 562
Gricci, Giuseppe, 707, 714
Grieninger, 661, 667
Grossbreitenbach, 637ff.
Grue, Carlo Antonio, et al., 372
Grünewald, 856
Gubbio, 357, 366
Guerhard & Dihl, 701
Guido da Castello Durante, 371
Guido da Marligno, 371
Guido di Savino, 380
Guido Durnatino, 371
Guido Fontana Vasaro, 371
Guillibaud, 795
Gulin and Popoff, 721

H

Haarlem, 380
Habaner wave, 838, 987
Hafner ware, 406, 408, 418, 867
Hagi-yaki ware, 235
Hague, The, 697, 724, 787, 1016
Haig, 1000
Hall marks, 392, 414, 416, 571, 621, 623, 635, 642,
    661, 794, 836, 838, 839, 840, 841, 843, 844, 852,
    854, 857, 859, 879, 882, 894, 919
Hallstadt culture, 13, 27, 32, 45, 65, 379
Hamadan, 295
Hamburg, 379, 818, 827, 829
Han period, 4, 73, 74, 75, 90, 107, 128, 131, 275,
    291, 409, 421, 432, 867, 1015
Hanau ware 379, 817, 819, 820, 823, 836
Hancock, John, 1001, 1006
Hang Chou, 120, 131, 140, 144
Hanley pottery, 921
Hannong, Charles, 675, 678, 689, 697, 700, 713, 802,
    839, 844, 857
Hannover, Emil, 71, 225, 275, 316, 334, 339, 341,
    357, 386, 402, 409, 413, 417, 461, 474, 498, 534,
    546, 549, 567, 686, 840, 842, 844, 852, 853, 857,
    864, 870, 874, 884, 896, 899, 900, 907, 910, 915,
    918, 919
Harker, 1006, 1007
Harrison, John, 994, 995
Hartford kiln, 998
Härtl, 670, 671
Hartley, Green & Co., 919
Hawthorn ware, 840
Heath, Thomas, 899, 900
Hellot, Jean, 683, 684
Henderson, David, 1002, 1005, 1006
Henry II ware, 400ff.
Hentschel, William E., 1055
Herculaneum factory, 775, 921
Herold, 635, 646, 650, 705
Herreboe factory, 843, 859, 861
Herring Fishery, The, 784
Hetherington, 170, 464, 519, 620
Hews, Abraham, 989, 990
Heylyn, Edward, 757, 980
Hideyoshi, 215, 234, 237
Himeji porcelain, 259
Hippisley, 588
Hirado, 256
Hirsvogel, 378, 406, 815
Hissar, 18, 29, 74
Hittites, 45
Hizen, 235, 237, 256, 578
Hjort pottery, 1023, 1038
Ho Chou, 178, 188, 202, 437, 508, 509
Hobby, Theodore, 540, 554
Hobson, R. L., 23, 75, 92, 93, 113, 124, 128, 133,
    135, 140, 141, 144, 147, 152, 160, 164, 169, 172,
    188, 198, 208, 225, 235, 308, 368, 423, 425, 426,
    428, 444, 449, 450, 459, 460, 461, 463, 464, 466,
    467, 485, 499, 502, 509, 517, 518, 519, 523, 529,
    534, 541, 546, 547, 554, 558, 562, 565, 566, 567,
    571, 572, 573, 578, 581, 591, 762, 865, 867, 893
Höchst, 633, 638, 665ff., 821, 825
Hochstadter, Walter, 126, 169, 174, 178, 185, 202, 203
Höhr, 409, 411, 414, 416
Holitsch, 825, 838, 839
Holm, 728, 733, 735
Homer Laughlin China Co., 1049
Honan, 24, 107, 126, 140, 155, 162
Honan Temmoku, 168, 169, 172, 235, 516, 592
Houzé de l'Aulnoit & Cie., 814
Howat, Walter, 555, 1062, 1068, 1070, 1075

Hsi-yin, 23, 24
Hsia, 73, 130
Hsia Tsung, 476
Hsiang-Lu, 421, 424
Hsiang-Shan, 187, 508
Hsieh Min, 145, 581, 583
Hsien Fêng ware, 605ff.
Hsien Lung, 448, 459, 461, 463, 483
Hsüan Tê, 163, 451, 461, 470, 485, 503, 517, 544
Hu, 26, 74, 75, 600
Hu-tien, 421ff., 444
Hua shih, clay, 147, 509, 546
Hugheson, 875
Hui hui wen, 343, 479
Hui Meng-ch'ên, 523, 623
Humble, Green & Co., 919
Hungarian ceramics, 808, 1033
Hunger, 646, 657, 705, 719, 726, 852

I

Ice crackle, 140, 142
Illinois pottery, 933
Imari, 228, 256ff., 578, 649, 767, 824, 843
Imitations, 585, 838ff., 851, 857, 861, 871, 879, 890,
    897ff., 902, 908ff., 919ff., 1017, 1024, 1030, 1047
Immortals, relief of the, 283
Imperial ware, 139
Imperial yellow ware, 564
Inca culture, 927, 944ff., 965, 967
India, 21, 30, 113
Indian design, 819, 835
Indian flowers, 632, 659, 683, 742, 820, 884, 975,
    984, 987
Indo-China, 521
Insets for furniture, porcelain for, 690
Ionians, 41, 49
Irak. See Mesopotamia
Iran, 18, 20. See also Persia
Ireland, 739, 1050
Iridescence, 291
Irish Belleek, 1050
Irminger, Johann Jakob, 643, 900
Iron glaze, 560, 561, 1038
Ironstone China, 1007
Isfahan, 313
Ishizara ware, 842
Ishtar, 283, 284
Isis, 277
Islam, 272
Isles of the Blest, 81
Ispahan, 318
Italian comedy groups, 640
Italy, 11, 32, 45ff., 48, 49, 60, 63, 65, 325, 332, 348ff.,
    354, 391, 395, 705, 879ff., 1027, 1043
Ivory ware, English, 894
Iwaki ware, 259
Iwami porcelain, 259
Iyo porcelain, 259
Izumi-yama, 256
Izumo porcelain, 259

J

Jackfield pottery, 769, 908, 921
Jacquemart, 608
Jade Hall, 622
Jakatsuguri glaze, 259
Janson, 878, 879
Japan, 24, 42, 88, 162, 240ff., 389, 432, 516, 646ff.,
    1046
Jasper ware, 779, 900, 916, 919, 996, 1024
Jaune jonquille, 685
Jayne, Horace H. F., 967
Jennewein, Carl Paul, 1049ff.
Jersey Porcelain and Earthenware Co., The, 995,
    1002, 1006
Jones, Quill, 816
Ju ware, 132, 135, 223
Ju Chou, 133, 135, 216
Ju Yao, 133, 216

K

K'ai-fêng, 140, 155, 437, 447, 458
Kakiemon, 256ff., 381, 578, 630, 648ff., 745, 760, 764
Kamares ware, 34, 36
Kändler, 638, 648, 651, 671, 743
K'ang Hsi period, 443ff., 480, 484ff., 533ff., 548,
    555ff., 591, 595, 668, 920
Kanne, 413ff.
Kansu Province, 27ff.
Kantharos, 42, 52, 63

Kaolin, 442, 644, 1004
Karatsu ware, 235, 237
Karlsruhe, 827, 1014
Kashan, 269, 316, 320, 321, 566, 1035, 1047
Kastrup, 825, 841ff.
Kelekian, K., 320
Keller, Guerin, et al., 805
Kelsterbach, 639, 674, 826
Kenton Hills procelains, 1055
Kenzan, 236, 238
Kerckhoff, Johan van, 788
Kerr and Binns, 764
Kertch ware, 60, 391
Kettle, Jonathan, 989, 990
Kevorkian, H., 315, 316
Keyser, Nicolas, 787
Kian Temmoku, 126, 429, 516, 620
Kiangnan Ting ware, 507ff.
Kiangsi, 122, 132, 421ff., 509ff., 535
Kiangsu, 423, 504, 508, 566
Kiel, 380
Kielland, Thor, 843, 860
King Stanislaus Augustus Poniatowski, 840
Kinuta, 142, 153ff., 1040
Kitchen Midden, 11
Kleffius, W., et al., 386, 389
Kloster Veilsdorf, 635, 637
Knossos, 32, 35, 36, 37, 40
Knowles, Taylor & Knowles, 1007
Knütgen, Anno, 414, 416
Ko ku yao lun, 128, 131, 139, 141, 160, 172, 182, 188, 216, 422, 424, 437, 458, 509
Ko Ming-hsiang, 520, 617
Ko ware, 132ff., 426, 501ff., 524, 594
Ko Yüan-hsing, 522, 617
Koch, Johann Heinrich, 825
Köln, 411ff.
Kongensgade Store, 841, 860
Koning, Hendrik de, 781
Korai period, 135, 174, 215ff., 235, 402, 460
Koran, 343, 479
Korean potteries, 24, 42, 88, 133, 147ff., 173, 214ff., 402, 460, 620, 1047
Kreussen, 379, 418ff., 816ff.
Kroeber, A. L., 925, 929, 964
Krug ware, 817
Ku Yüeh Hsüan, 600ff., 1047
Kuan, 132ff., 426ff., 522ff., 592
Kuang Hsü ware, 605ff.
Kuangtung ware, 168, 430, 500
Kubatcha, 320, 321, 345
Kuhnel, Ernst, 308, 310, 313, 316
Künersberg factory, 829
Kutaia, 348, 354
Kutanimura, 258
Kwaart, 389, 390, 819
Kwan Yin, 523, 535, 615
Kwangtung, 160, 213, 423ff., 436, 450, 452, 503, 519ff., 524, 570
Kylix, 39, 51, 52, 55, 56, 58

L

Lace-work ware, 604
Lambeth wares, 878ff.
Lambrequin design, 792ff., 1027
Lane End factory, 920
Lanfrey, François, 698, 804
Lang T'ing-tso, 533ff., 551
Lang yao, 447, 534
Large, Gunder, 859, 860, 861
Latvia, 1028
Laub and Bandelwerk, 644, 649, 852
Laufer, Berthold, 88, 93ff., 107, 113, 155, 430, 519
Leboeuf, André-Marie, 703
Leduc, Charles François, 838
Leeds pottery, 290
Leeuwenhock, Antoni Van, 598
Leigh, Jacob, et al., 814, 995, 1007
Lekythos, 39, 46, 52ff.
Leningrad, 334
Lenox ware, 1050
Lewis, Jacob, 1001
Li, 21, 23, 27, 84
Liège, 791
Lille, 628, 682, 698, 796, 807
Lilly, John, 764
Limbach, 637
Limekiln Lane pottery, 887
Limoges, 699ff., 802

Ling lung, 494, 920
Link, Konrad, 676, 677
Lisbon, 718
List, Johann Georg Friedrich, 827
Lister, Martin, 628
Litchfield, Conn., 990
Little Fenton pottery, 907, 908, 913
Littler, William, 775, 905
Liverpool, 775, 880, 889ff., 911
Loire factory, 815
Lokapala, 90, 113ff.
Lomax, C. J., 870, 873
London ware, 875, 880, 889
Longport, 777
Longton Hall, 753, 775, 905
Longwy factory, 814
Louisbourg, 681
Louvain, 791
Lowden factory, 765
Lowdin's China House, 763, 772
Löwenfinck, 665ff., 803, 825
Lowestoft, 608, 751, 774, 1047
Loyang, 73, 74
Lübeck, 406
Lück, Karl Gottlieb, et al., 640, 651, 659, 667, 675ff., 726, 750
Ludwigsburg, 638, 678, 827
Lunéville, 805
Lung-ch'üan ware, 125, 129, 132, 140ff., 216, 227, 422ff., 502ff., 560, 620
Luplau, Anton Carl, 669, 728, 730
Lustre, 305ff., 323ff., 357, 369, 625, 739, 911, 1014, 1017, 1023ff.
Lyman and Fenton, 992ff.
Lyons, 329, 374, 802

M

Majolica, 8, 332, 348ff., 838, 868, 879, 1014, 1064
Malaga, 332, 334, 337, 338
Malaysia, 430, 570
Malinowski, A., 1018, 1021
Manchuria, 24, 27
Mandarin porcelain, 604, 605
Mannheim, 639
Manor house, York, 897
Manship, Paul, 1071, 1074
Mantzius, Jacob Casper Leopold, 844
Maran factory, 809
Marble ware, 290, 499, 813, 854, 869, 894, 900, 987
Marcolini, Count Camillo, 656
Marieberg, 736, 840, 852, 853, 854, 856, 857
Marseilles, 699, 796, 799, 810, 838
Martabani, 148
Mayan pottery, 939, 942
Mecklenburg service, 751
Medici porcelain, 479, 625
Meissen, 611ff., 745, 746, 788, 838, 853, 861, 900
Melchior, J. P., 667, 674, 676
Mennecy, 630, 632, 696
Mesopotamia, 13, 14, 15, 29, 30, 32, 33, 34, 42, 45, 67, 275, 297, 345
Mexico, 934, 940, 975
Meyer, Friedrich Elias, 635, 648, 653, 655, 661, 664, 732, 822
Ming period, 139, 162, 239, 342, 397, 421, 436, 442, 500, 502, 503, 507, 516, 518, 523, 524, 532, 543, 544, 567, 569, 571, 573, 574, 591, 596, 612, 622, 920
Minoan culture, 32, 41
Minton, Thomas, 694, 777, 1025
Mishima, 191, 216, 226, 1047
Montauban factory, 809
Montpellier, 809, 838
Mortlake stoneware factory, 897
Moustiers, 375, 792, 796, 802, 838

N

Nagato, 235, 259
Nanking, 458, 564, 578, 882
Nantes ware, 376
Nantgarw plant, 770, 771
Naples, 707, 709
Nazca Pottery, 953ff.
Neale and Palmer, 921
Neolithic period, 9, 22, 23, 24, 34
Nevers, 376, 793, 796, 838, 885
New Canton, 759
Nicaragua pottery, 943
Niderviller, 677, 698, 804, 806, 838